INTRODUCTION TO
FLORICULTURE

CONTRIBUTORS

Christina Warren Auman

Seward T. Besemer

William H. Carlson

Charles A. Conover

G. Douglas Crater

August De Hertogh

P. Allen Hammer

Raymond F. Hasek

R. Kent Kimmins

Anton M. Kofranek

Roy A. Larson

Joseph W. Love

James K. Rathmell, Jr.

Marlin N. Rogers

Edward M. Rowley

James B. Shanks

Thomas J. Sheehan

T. C. Weiler

Richard E. Widmer

Gary J. Wilfret

H. F. Wilkins

ACADEMIC PRESS, INC.
111 Fifth Avenue, New York, New York 10003

United Kingdom Edition published by
ACADEMIC PRESS, INC. (LONDON) LTD.
24/28 Oval Road, London NW1 7DX

Library of Congress Cataloging in Publication Data

Main entry under title:

Introduction to floriculture.

Includes bibliographies and index.
1. Floriculture. I. Larson, Roy A.
SB405.I55   635.9   80–10769
ISBN 0–12–437650–9

PRINTED IN THE UNITED STATES OF AMERICA

81 82 83   9 8 7 6 5 4 3 2

INTRODUCTION TO
FLORICULTURE

Edited by

Roy A. Larson

Department of Horticultural Science
North Carolina State University
Raleigh, North Carolina

ACADEMIC PRESS
A SUBSIDIARY OF HARCOURT BRACE JOVANOVICH, PUBLISHERS
New York   London   Toronto   Sydney   San Francisco

Contents

I   CUT FLOWERS

1 Cut Chrysanthemums

Anton M. Kofranek

Carnations
Seward T. Besemer

Roses
Raymond F. Hasek

Snapdragons
Marlin N. Rogers

Orchids

Thomas J. Sheehan

Gladiolus

Gary J. Wilfret

Minor Cut Crops

Christina Warren Auman

II POTTED PLANTS

Bulbous Plants
August De Hertogh

Azaleas
Roy A. Larson

Pot Mums
G. Douglas Crater

11 Gloxinias, African Violets, and Other Gesneriads

R. Kent Kimmins

12 Poinsettias

James B. Shanks

13 Easter Lilies

H. F. Wilkins

14 Hydrangeas
T. C. Weiler

15 Cyclamen
Richard E. Widmer

16 Begonias
Roy A. Larson

Kalanchoe

Joseph W. Love

 Other Flowering Pot Plants

P. Allen Hammer

Bedding Plants

William H. Carlson and Edward M. Rowley

Hanging Baskets

James K. Rathmell, Jr.

Foliage Plants

Charles A. Conover

List of Contributors

Numbers in parentheses indicate the pages on which the authors' contributions begin.

Christina Warren Auman (183), Department of Horticultural Science, North Carolina State University, Raleigh, North Carolina 27650

Seward T. Besemer (47), Cooperative Agriculture Extension, University of California, San Diego County, San Diego, California 92123

William H. Carlson (477), Department of Horticulture, Michigan State University, East Lansing, Michigan 48824

Charles A. Conover (555), Agricultural Research Center, University of Florida, Apopka, Florida 32703

G. Douglas Crater (261), Cooperative Extension Service, College of Agriculture, University of Georgia, Athens, Georgia 30602

August De Hertogh (213), Department of Horticultural Science, North Carolina State University, Raleigh, North Carolina 27650

P. Allen Hammer (435), Department of Horticulture, Purdue University, West Lafayette, Indiana 47907

Raymond F. Hasek (81), Department of Environmental Horticulture, University of California, Davis, California 95616

R. Kent Kimmins* (287), Department of Horticultural Science, North Carolina State University, Raleigh, North Carolina 27607

*Present address: Department of Horticulture, Kansas State University, Manhattan, Kansas 66506

Anton M. Kofranek (3), Department of Environmental Horticulture, University of California, Davis, California 95616

Roy A. Larson (237, 395), Department of Horticultural Science, North Carolina State University, Raleigh, North Carolina 26707

Joseph W. Love (409), Department of Horticultural Science, North Carolina State University, Raleigh, North Carolina 27607

James K. Rathmell, Jr. (523), Floriculture Extension, The Pennsylvania State University, Norristown, Pennsylvania 19401

Marlin N. Rogers (107), Department of Horticulture, University of Missouri, Columbia, Missouri 65211

Edward M. Rowley (477), High Valley Nursery, Roosevelt, Utah 84066

James B. Shanks (301), Department of Horticulture, University of Maryland, College Park, Maryland 20742

Thomas J. Sheehan (133), Department of Ornamental Horticulture, University of Florida, Gainesville, Florida 32611

T. C. Weiler (353), Department of Horticulture, Purdue University, West Lafayette, Indiana 47907

Richard E. Widmer (373), Department of Horticultural Science and Landscape Architecture, University of Minnesota, St. Paul, Minnesota 55108

Gary J. Wilfret (165), Agricultural Research and Education Center, University of Florida, Bradenton, Florida 33505

H. F. Wilkins (327), Department of Horticultural Science, University of Minnesota, St. Paul, Minnesota 55101

Preface

Commercial floriculture is an intensified form of agriculture in which the most studious individuals are severely challenged to keep abreast of technological advances, impacts of imported flowers and the fuel crisis, and similar occurrences. No student, grower, researcher, teacher, or extension specialist in floriculture can know all that should be known about all the crops that are grown commercially. Potential authors, approached by publishers to write texts on flower crop production, justifiably have felt unequal to the task. Existing texts have been revised, excellent greenhouse management texts have been written, but no new book solely concerned with the production of floricultural crops has been published recently. This lack of a current textbook that contains information on major and minor greenhouse and field crops, and includes potted plants and cut flowers, has been readily acknowledged by teachers of commercial floriculture courses and by students in those courses.

"Introduction to Floriculture" overcomes the inadequacy of an individual to write a complete text on commercial floriculture by relegating the responsibility of writing to twenty authors, most of whom are internationally known for their knowledge of the crops they discuss. The chapters are well documented with meaningful tables, figures, and literature citations. This text, as stated in the title, is an introduction to commercial floriculture and the eager reader will make ample use of the cited references.

"Introduction to Floriculture" was written for students who have been exposed to a sufficient number of biology courses to acquaint them with many of the terms and plant processes discussed in the text. It would be beneficial if they have also taken a course in greenhouse management or are taking one concurrently with their floriculture course. The book can be used by commercial growers who constantly seek more information to enable them to realize maximum gain from the investments of labor, time, and capitol they have placed in this challenging field.

The rewards of most commercial enterprises are frequently expressed in terms of money or profit. It is hoped the reader will enjoy the benefits of financial success, but will also enjoy the satisfaction of growing floricultural crops that are of such high quality and in such demand that the environment is a better place because they have succeeded.

Appreciation is expressed to all who assisted in the publication of this book. Some names undoubtedly would be omitted if many individuals were recognized, so we would primarily acknowledge floriculturists, our predecessors and contemporaries, in academic and commercial fields, who brought floricultural knowledge to its present level. We also are grateful to the secretaries at various universities who typed the manuscripts, often more than once. Special thanks are due Emily Tate, a very competent secretary in the Department of Horticultural Science at North Carolina State University who typed so many chapters, the index, glossary, and countless letters to the publishers, authors, and other floriculturists throughout the nation. Appreciation also is extended to Gayle Steinbugler, artist in the Department of Agricultural Information at North Carolina State University, for her suggestions and expertise in helping to design the cover.

Roy A. Larson

INTRODUCTION TO
FLORICULTURE

I
CUT
FLOWERS

1
Cut
Chrysanthemums

Anton M. Kofranek

I. HISTORY

The florists' chrysanthemum is a complex hybrid which, if grown from seed, segregates into many diverse flower forms. Most of the species in the lineage of present day cultivars are from China. These include *Chrysanthemum indicum* (a yellow single), *C. morifolium* (lilac and rose colors), and the Chusan daisy (species unknown); the latter was brought to England in 1843 by Robert Fortune and is thought to be one of the parents of spray or pompon chrysanthemums. Even before this date the British and Dutch were hybridizing chrysanthemums. In the United States Elmer D. Smith began hybridizing for the florists' trade in 1889. He hybridized and named over 500 cultivars, some of which are presently being grown (Cathey, 1969; Langhans, 1964; Laurie *et al.*, 1979).

Commercial hybridization to improve cultivars continues today in America, Asia, and Europe. Selection is based not only on flower shape and color but also on suitability of seedlings for year-round flowering programs and for post-harvest qualities.

II. CLASSIFICATION

A. Inflorescence Forms

The florists' chrysanthemum is a composite inflorescence that has flowers borne on a receptacle or capitulum. The heads are borne on long peduncles in cymose clusters. The single inflorescences (daisy-like) have ray flowers (outside row) which are pistillate and disk flowers (the central ones or the "eye of the daisy") which are bisexual and usually fertile. The receptacle is flat or convex and is surrounded by an involucre of bracts.

Inflorescences are categorized on the basis of shape and form as suitable for garden or greenhouse culture (Ackerson, 1957). Some of the most common inflorescence forms grown commercially and in the garden are illustrated in Fig. 1 and described below:

1. Singles—daisy-like, composed of one or two rows of outer pistillate flowers (ray) and flat bisexual flowers (disk) borne centrally (Fig. 1B).

2. Anemones—similar to the single form except the disk flowers are elongated and tubular, forming a cushion. Disk flowers may be the same or a color different from the ray flowers (Fig. 1D).

3. Pompons—a globular head formed by short uniform ray flowers; the shape is considered formal; disk flowers are not apparent. The National Chrysanthemum Society (America) recognizes three distinct sizes: (a) small buttons, 4 cm or less in diameter; (b) intermediate, 4–6 cm in diameter (Fig. 1C); (c) large, 6–10 cm in diameter.

Fig. 1.   Typical chrysanthemum inflorescence forms: (A) spider, (B) single, (C) intermediate pompon, (D) anemone, (E) decorative, (F) large-flowered incurve (standard chrysanthemum). (Courtesy of Yoder Brothers.)

4. Decoratives—similar to pompons since they are composed mainly of ray flowers, but the outer rows are longer than the central flowers, giving the inflorescence a flat and informal shape. Sizes are mostly intermediate and large (Fig. 1E).

5. Large-flowered—blooms are greater than 10 cm and are classified in many shapes. Disk flowers are not apparent in most of these forms. (a) In-

curved double: globose and formal, with ray flowers similar in size to the disk flowers and that curve inward and toward the top (Fig. 1F). (b) Reflexed double: less formal and globose than the incurved double, with overlapping ray flowers curved downward, except for the ray flowers. (c) tubular ray flowers: (i) Spider—ray flowers tubular and elongated in the outer rows but short in the center. The drooping outer row ray flowers are sometimes hooked on the ends (Fig. 1A). (ii) Fuji—similar to the spider except the ray flowers may be shorter, droop less, and lack hooks on the ends. (iii) Quill—tubular ray flowers, long on the outside and short near the center, resembling feather quills. Ends of flowers are open and not flattened.

(iv) Spoon—similar to the quill except the outer row flowers are open and are flattened, resembling a spoon. (d) Miscellaneous—novelty types consisting of feathery, plume-like or "hairy" ray florets.

B. Commercial Use

Chrysanthemums are grown in two basic ways for cut flowers, depending on market demand.

1. Disbudded Inflorescences

All flower buds but the terminal one are removed to allow one inflorescence per stem to develop (Fig. 2). If the bloom is an incurved or reflexed form and is between 10 and 15 cm in diameter, it is usually referred to as a "standard." "Incurves" or "reflexes" smaller than 10 cm are known as "disbuds." Only cultivars which increase flower size markedly upon disbudding are used. These may include fuji, spider, quill, and even certain single mums as well as the more usual incurved or reflexed doubles.

2. Spray Inflorescences

The entire cyme is allowed to bloom but very often the central inflorescence (the oldest one) is removed about the time color begins to form in the ray flowers. Since this is the oldest bloom in the cyme (known as a spray), it will senesce before the lateral inflorescences if not removed. In addition, it also is larger than the surrounding blooms; therefore, it is removed to allow more even blooming of the laterals. These groups are usually known as pompons or spray chrysanthemums and may have any of the inflorescence forms described above, i.e., singles, anemones, formals, decoratives, and the class of tubular ray flowers.

C. Photoperiod Response

Hybrid cultivars used for year-round flowering are short-day plants. Natural flowering occurs during several months in the fall. In the Northern Hemisphere these cultivars have been classified as early (August to mid-October), midseason

Fig. 2. Top, the correct stage of development for lateral bud removal for disbudding a standard chrysanthemum (about the 28th short day). These laterals have peduncles that are long enough to "snap off" easily but that have not become too long and woody at this stage. Bottom, the disbudding is accomplished, i.e., lateral buds and the peduncles have been completely removed, leaving only the terminal bud. Waiting until lateral buds reach a morphological stage larger than this reduces the ultimate size of the terminal inflorescence at maturation.

(mid-October to mid-November), and late (after mid-November) flowering. They are now classified for natural or year-round flowering by response groups, i.e., 6- to 15-week cultivars. Cultivars in the 6-week response group require 6 weeks to reach harvest stage from the first inductive short day (SD). Other response groups require 7 or more weeks up to a maximum of 15 weeks to reach harvest stage from the first inductive short day.

III. PROPAGATION

Plants are propagated by rooting terminal cuttings. These vegetative cuttings are removed from stock plants maintained under long-day (LD) conditions to inhibit flower bud formation (see Section VI, Vegetative Growth of Stock Plants). Terminal cuttings 8–10 cm long that are removed from stock plants can be placed directly into the rooting medium or may be stored at 0°–3°C for several weeks in cartons lined with polyethylene to prevent desiccation. Some cultivars are not stored successfully in the winter. To enhance development of roots, basal ends of the cuttings are dipped in a talc containing 0.1 to 0.2% indolebutyric acid (IBA). The greenhouse temperature should be between 15° and 18°C, and the rooting medium temperature between 18° and 21°C. Between 500 and 600 cuttings per square meter are placed in the medium, depending on size of the lower leaf of the cultivar. Until rooting is accomplished mist nozzles should be set to spray a fine mist intermittently on the cuttings during the daylight hours. Some propagators increase the mist frequency from 10 A.M. to 3 P.M. when light intensity is the greatest. The mist is usually turned off a day or two before cuttings are removed to "harden" them prior to shipping or planting. Cuttings are well rooted in 10 to 20 days depending on cultivar and season. Cuttings with roots 1.5 to 2 cm long are desirable; longer roots make planting difficult.

Almost any porous mixture that is not toxic can be used as a rooting medium. Perlite plus sphagnum peat moss is perhaps the most common medium because it is easily obtained, produces consistent results, and does not separate from the roots during shipment. Vermiculite, sand, fine coal cinders, scoria, pumice, and a sandy soil mixture have also been used as rooting media. When cuttings are shipped by common carrier, a light-weight medium is always chosen.

Total salts below 15 milliequivalents per liter (mEq/liter) for the mist system does not affect rooting. However, magnesium should not exceed 70% (Paul, 1968). A high percentage of sodium (>67%) will cause "red root." Some calcium is necessary for good rooting. Applications of gypsum or ground limestone at rates of 20 to 30 kg/100 m² can be broadcast over the surface of the rooting medium prior to inserting cuttings. This treatment will supply adequate calcium and will reduce the proportions of sodium and magnesium if these cations are abundant in the irrigation water.

IV. SOIL PREPARATION

Chrysanthemums will grow in almost any soil if it is well managed. Plants are susceptible to several soil-borne pathogens (see Section XIII, Diseases); therefore, those organisms must be controlled to ensure maximum growth. Assuming the rooted cuttings are pathogen-free, it may be feasible to grow the crop in a soil that has never been used for chrysanthemums previously and is hence probably free of the soil-borne organisms that affect the crop. The same soil can be used with caution for several successive crops until soil pathogens reach epidemic proportions. If and when this occurs steam pasteurization or chemical treatment is necessary to control soil-borne pathogens.

Chemical treatments are fumigants that control most soil pathogens or specific pathogens such as *Verticillium albo-atrum*. A combination of 2 parts chloropicrin to 1 part methyl bromide can be used for *Verticillium*. However, a general chemical soil treatment (e.g., 98% methyl bromide and 2% chloropicrin) is useful. Where steam heat is available, the soil can be treated as described by Mastalerz (1977).

Before the soil is treated with chemicals or steam, plant stubble is removed or may be finely ground up and incorporated into the soil with a rototiller. Soil amendments such as sphagnum peat moss, wood shavings, fir bark, or other locally available organic material plus gypsum, limestone, and superphosphate can be incorporated into the growing medium (see Chapter 3, Roses, for details). Steaming clay soils can cause a temporary toxic condition to the roots because of an excessive buildup of ammonia and manganese. These excesses can be partially overcome by additions of gypsum or superphosphate after steaming or by allowing the soils to be inactive for several weeks until the microorganisms convert ammonia to nitrate (Mastalerz, 1977). Steaming sandy soils creates fewer problems. Soils that are chemically treated must be well aerated before cuttings are planted (usually a week).

After incorporation of amendments and fertilizers and after treatment of the soils for pathogens, the beds can be shaped into the desired width (usually 108 cm wide). Soil in the bed is usually marked for planting by scratching the soil with a pronged tool at a preset distance and planting the cuttings at those marks, or by planting cuttings in the middle of the squares of the support wires or string.

V. MINERAL NUTRITION

Chrysanthemums have large requirements for both nitrogen and potassium. Maintenance of high levels of nitrogen during the first 7 weeks of growth is especially important. If moderate deficiencies develop during this early period, later nitrogen applications will not recapture the flower quality that will have been lost. The findings of Lunt and Kofranek (1958) showed that the quality of plants and flowers produced was ideal when the plants were fertilized early in their growth cycle. No further fertilization was necessary after the inflorescences reached a diameter of 1 to 1.5 cm. Late fertilization is wasteful and too much nitrogen can cause brittle leaves in some cultivars. There should be adequate nitrogen (4.5–6%) in the leaves for use by the flowers. Figure 3 shows

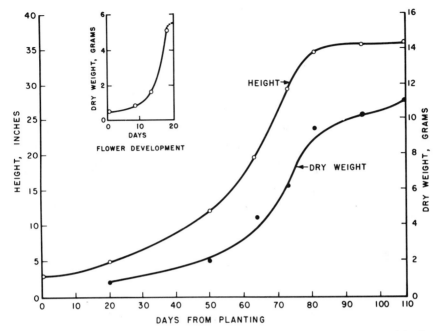

Fig. 3. The increase in height and dry weight of shoots and dry weight development of the flower (inflorescence) of the cultivar Albatross as a function of time. Flower development was timed from the day floret color was first detectable in the bud. [From Lunt and Kofranek (1958). Courtesy of the American Society for Horticultural Science.]

the growth curves of 'Albatross', a disbudded standard. During the first 80 days plants are growing rapidly and there is a large requirement for nitrogen. During the last 20 days only the inflorescence grows rapidly and mineral nutrients are translocated from the leaves.

Another way of envisioning the demand of cut chrysanthemums for nitrogen during the life of the plant is shown in Table I. During the first few weeks the root systems of individual plants are not extensive throughout the soil and there is low efficiency of nitrogen recovery. However, the efficiency increases with time and the greatest nitrogen requirement for all aboveground plant parts is between the 70th and 80th day. At maturity about 20 to 23% of the nitrogen of the aboveground plant portion of cultivars Albatross and Good News is located in the inflorescence.

Recommendations concerning chrysanthemum fertilization once stressed withholding fertilizers after planting rooted cuttings and until plants became established. These recommendations are no longer valid, as they were predicated on the assumption that the soil might have been high in salts from the previous crop. Soils with excessive salts should be leached before planting.

Before the soil is treated for pathogens, certain fertilizers of low solubility should be incorporated thoroughly. One possible recommendation is a moder-

Table I

Nitrogen Requirement of Chrysanthemum ('Albatross') for 10-Day Periods as a Function of Age[a]

Age of plant from planting (days)	Nitrogen requirement for 500 chrysanthemum stems for 10-day periods (gm)
1– 10	1.0
11– 20	2.5
21– 30	4.0
31– 40	6.0
41– 50	8.5
51– 60	20.0
61– 70	36.0
71– 80	60.0
81– 90	22.0
91–100	15.0
101–110	12.0
	187.0

[a]Flower buds were showing color on about the 90th day. Calculations of nitrogen needs are based on 500 stems from pinched plants which would normally be grown in an area of 100 ft² (10.76 m²). Adapted from Kofranek and Lunt (1966).

ate fertilizer application: 150 gm of single superphosphate, 250 gm of dolomitic limestone, and 250 gm of urea-formaldehyde per square meter. The urea-formaldehyde is a slow-release nitrogen that at warm temperatures mineralizes 25 to 35% in 3 weeks, 35 to 50% in 6 weeks, and 60 to 75% before 6 months. Only 6 to 10% nitrogen is immediately available. A majority of the nitrogen becomes available to the crop when it is required by the crop. After cuttings are planted they should be irrigated at once with a liquid fertilizer containing 200 ppm each of nitrogen and potassium. Liquid fertilizer should be applied at every irrigation. It is important, however, to analyze the soil at regular intervals for excess soluble salts and for a shift in pH. A pH between 5.5 and 6.5 is adequate and the (soluble salts) electrical conductivity of a saturated paste extract (EC_e) should not exceed 2.5 millimhos per centimeter (mmho/cm). An EC_e reading exceeding 2.5 mmho/cm indicates excess soluble salts and the soil should be leached with plain irrigation water to reduce them. If the pH exceeds 6.5, an acid fertilizer (e.g., ammonium nitrate) will lower the pH; an alkaline fertilizer (calcium nitrate) will raise the pH. With this system of fertilization, there is no need for soil analyses for the individual cations and anions except if troubles are suspected. A soil analysis can be used for "trouble shooting" but is not necessary as a routine operation.

The solubridge is an instrument to measure the EC_e of the soil and a pH meter is used routinely to measure shifts in pH from the norm. These two measurements are adequate tests for a short-term crop such as chrysanthemums.

Occasionally leaf disorders appear, indicating a problem in the soil. Leaf tissue analysis reflects the mineral status of the leaf more accurately than does a soil analysis. Tissue levels associated with the mineral status in the leaf appear in Table II. These levels may be useful as references in solving mineral deficiency disorders.

Usually the impurities in commercial grade fertilizer supply adequate microelements except for iron. Chelated iron is frequently added in liquid fertilizers to supply 3 to 5 ppm iron when fully diluted.

Table II

Leaf Tissue Levels Associated with Adequate or Deficient Levels of Selected Essential Elements in *Chrysanthemum* × *morifolium* 'Good News' [a]

Element	Adequate range	Critical level	Level found in moderate or severe deficiency	Plant part effectively reflecting mineral status
N (%)	4.5–6	4.0 Upper limit 4.5 Lower limit	1.5–3	Upper leaves
P (%)	0.26(?)–1.15	0.26 Upper limit (?) [b] 0.17 Lower limit(?) [b]	0.10–0.21	Upper or lower leaves
K (%)	3.5–10	2.75 Upper limit 2.15 Lower limit	0.2–2	Lower leaves
Ca (%)	0.5–4.6	0.40 Upper limit 0.46 Lower limit	0.22–0.28	Upper leaves
Mg (%)	0.14–1.5	0.11 (?)	0.034–0.064	Lower leaves
S (%)	0.3–0.75	0.25 (?)	0.07–0.19	Upper leaves
Fe (ppm)		— [c]	35	Upper leaves
Mn (ppm)	195–260	— [c]	3–4	Upper or lower leaves
B (ppm)	25–200 (240 is excessive)	20	18.1–19.5	Upper leaves
Cu (ppm)	10 ppm (?)	5	1.7–4.7	Middle leaves or leaves from lower axillary growth
Zn (ppm)	7.26 (?)	7	4.3–6.8	Lower leaves

[a] The adequate range for a given element extends from just above the critical level to the concentration at which toxic disorders develop. Except for boron, the upper limit of the adequate range is not well defined. Adapted from Lunt *et al.* (1964).

[b] Because *P* is redistributed within the plant at flowering, critical levels are estimates.

[c] Data are inadequate to estimate critical levels.

VI. VEGETATIVE GROWTH

A. Stock Plants

Two common spacings for stock plants are 10 × 13 and 13 × 13 cm. Long daylengths and liquid fertilizers are given from the day of planting to promote rapid vegetative growth. Plants are given a soft pinch (Fig. 4A) as soon as they are established to promote rapid development of shoots. It is not advisable to allow the new plant to grow to the size where the first "pinch" is large enough to be taken as the first cutting from that stock plant. This is tantamount to a hard pinch (Fig. 4B), which has the disadvantages of leaving too few nodes on the original plant and allowing the lower portion of the stem to become semiwoody before taking that cutting. Buds in the axils of leaves of semiwoody chrysan-

Fig. 4. (A) The "soft pinch" is most commonly used because buds which remain on the stem "break" (sprout) readily, since stem tissue is succulent and buds are reasonably large. As many as four to five breaks can be expected from a soft pinch during periods of high light intensity. (B) The "hard pinch" is made into semiwoody stem tissue. Note the bud just below the top thumbnail. These and lower buds are large but they do not "break" as rapidly as those buds that remain just below a "soft pinch" [see (A)]. A hard pinch is generally used to reduce plant size, especially in pots where some cuttings are taller than others. (C) The pencil point indicates where a "roll out" pinch is made. This pinch is only used on short plants or soon after cuttings are planted. The "breaking" (sprouting) of buds on the stem is less than satisfactory, i.e., not many shoots result from this type of pinch and bud growth is usually slower than from a soft pinch. (D) Left to right: portions of stem tips removed from a "roll out pinch" (c); a "soft pinch" (a); and a "hard pinch" (b). Note the degree of leaf removal with each pinching method.

themum stems do not grow as rapidly as do those of succulent stems. Of the three pinches shown in Fig. 4, the soft pinch is the best to promote rapid bud growth.

Cuttings should be taken as often as possible to keep the stock plant in a juvenile stage; premature flower buds are less apt to form on shoots that are actively growing. Usually stock plants produce flushes of growth (shoots) in the early stages because there is little light competition among shoots. Because of the lower light flux during the winter months fewer axillary buds sprout after a pinch than in the summer. Later, in the 10th to 15th week after planting, plants become so dense that cuttings or shoots long enough (8–10 cm) for harvesting are available only on an irregular basis and only on the periphery of the stock plant. This limited availability can be attributed to the denseness of the stock plants and limiting light that exists in the center of the plants.

When cuttings are taken at least two leaves should remain on the stock plant just below the point where the cutting is removed. The two leaves are the photosynthetic surface and those buds in axils of the remaining leaves become part of the next flush of cuttings. If too many leaves remain at each harvest, the stock plant becomes too large and competition for light becomes a serious problem. Removal of shoots, taken for cuttings, provides more light to the center and also removes shoot competition.

Stock plants are usually kept in beds for cutting production for 13 to 21 weeks. Leaving plants in beyond 13 weeks (about four to five flushes of cuttings) can result in premature budding of those cuttings removed for production, i.e., flower buds may form on those cuttings even under long-day conditions.

The longer a stock plant is grown the more apt it is to produce premature flower buds. Some cultivars are prone to initiating premature flowers (e.g., 'Festival,' 'Mandalay'). Stock plants of these cultivars must be replanted more frequently to avoid this problem. A young plant (juvenile) is less apt to initiate flower buds than an older one. One way to keep the plant vegetative is to remove (take) cuttings frequently even if there is no demand for them. Long (older) shoots on older stock plants (beyond 13 weeks) are very likely to have premature flower buds (partially induced) even if supplementary lighting and temperature are adequate.

Supplementary lighting for the inhibition of flower initiation is more critical for stock plants than it is for production of flowering plants. Cuttings taken with premature buds are almost worthless because the resultant plants flower on short stems. Even if the rooted cuttings are destined to be pinched after planting and the flower bud is thus removed, the resultant vegetative shoots are not as vigorous as those that sprout from a completely vegetative cutting. The only reason for pinching a plant with a premature flower bud is to promote (stimulate) vegetative shoots; however, pinching may result in weak shoots or may even be unsuccessful because the lateral shoots may also have flower buds. Lighting to promote vegetative growth and to inhibit flowering on stock plants must therefore be complete. A minimum light intensity of 10 fc (110 lx) from incandescent lamps for 4 to 5 hours in the middle of the night during the winter and 2 hours during the summer is adequate for even the cultivars most insensitive to supplementary lighting. 'Albatross' and 'Good News' are examples that require this high intensity with an adequate duration. Cyclic lighting with incandescent lamps *should be avoided* on stock plants since cyclic lighting is marginal illumination for insensitive cultivars (see Section VII, Flowering of Production Plants). As stock plants become older they are more apt to form flower buds if incandescent cyclic lighting is used. The use of fluorescent and low-pressure sodium vapor lamps is not well documented for stock plants.

B. Production Plants

Rooted cuttings in a vegetative state should be planted in a well-prepared moist soil, and then irrigated with a liquid fertilizer solution and illuminated at night to ensure a long-day effect from the first day. Spacing of cuttings in the bench or bed varies with season and cultivar and depends on whether plants are to be pinched or grown single-stem. Plants to be pinched are usually spaced 15 × 18 cm in summer and 18 × 20 or 18 × 22 cm in the winter. Interior-positioned plants are later pruned to two stems and outside plants are pruned to three stems per plant. Single-stem plants are usually planted 10 × 15 cm for summer and fall crops and 13 × 15 cm for winter crops. Some cultivars may require a wide spacing of 15 × 15 cm. These spacings are for beds that are approximately 1 m wide. An example of one type of spacing is shown in Fig. 5.

More cuttings are required per square meter for single-stemmed plants than for pinched plants, but this additional cost can be overcome because the time to grow a single-stemmed crop is less than for a pinched crop. Pinching temporarily delays the growth of any plant.

It is necessary to maintain production plants in a vegetative state both for rapid growth and to attain desired stem length before flower induction is desired. Vegetative growth in hybrid chrysanthemums grown for year-round flowering is promoted by long-day conditions and the proper night temperature. A daylength greater than 14.5 hours for plants grown at 15.5°C is required to maintain a vegetative state. Plants are most effectively illuminated with incandescent lamps in the middle of the dark period, which breaks up the night into two short periods; this supplementary lighting is known as "night break lighting." Duration of supplementary lighting varies with season and latitude because of the daylength. Recommendations given to growers for night break lighting is based solely on the daylength. Five hours may be recommended in northern latitudes (40° to 50° N) in the winter but only four hours are recommended between 25° and 40° N where the daylength is longer than at 40° to 50° N. Because daylengths in northern latitudes during the summer are so long, no night break lighting, or at the most two hours are recommended to ensure a

Fig. 5.   Field chrysanthemums about 10 days old from planting. The cuttings were planted within the wire mesh, which is raised for support as the plants grow. In this Stuart, Florida, planting no cuttings were placed in the center of the bed to allow for greater light penetration. The incandescent lamps with internal reflectors are 150 W and are spaced about 3 × 3 m apart and 2 m above the soil. Outdoor chrysanthemums such as these can be grown in frost-free southern Florida from November to April. If there is no protection from rain, pathogens spread by splashing water can reduce the commercial quality of the crop.

complete vegetative state. Near the equator illumination is recommended all year round for at least 3 hours per night. The light intensity for continuous lighting as a night break now recommended is between 7 and 10 fc (77 to 110 lx). However, recent experiments (Sachs and Kofranek, 1979) with Albatross, a cultivar generally requiring higher light intensity or duration for the night break than most cultivars, showed that considerably less light intensity for the night break (3 to 5 fc) was required during the winter than during the summer months (7 to 10 fc). The major difference between growing chrysanthemums in the greenhouse in the winter and summer is the daytime radiant energy (photosynthetically active radiation). Thus the higher the daytime radiant energy the *greater* the light energy required for an effective night break. This is the opposite of what has been generally understood or recommended. Moreover these findings underline the importance of photosynthetically active radiation, not merely daylength, for flower initiation and development (Cockshull, 1972).

Cyclic lighting during the night break, proposed by Cathey and Borthwick (1961), conserves energy since plants are illuminated only 20% of the time. Their work recommended that incandescent lamps be operational for a

Fig. 6. Plants of 'Florida Marble', a 9-week cultivar, were given various numbers of long days (LD) before starting short days (SD): (A) No LD (SD on day of planting); (B) 1 week of LD, (C) 2 weeks of LD, (D) 3 weeks of LD, and (E) 4 weeks of LD. After the LD period they were given continuous SD to promote flowering. Rooted cuttings were planted on November 9 and the photograph was taken 77 days later. These plants are typical of winter-grown chrysanthemums in a region of low light (Davis, California): The node number above the soil surface to the oldest inflorescence (indicated by the arrow) and the height above the soil surface are as follows:

	A	B	C	D	E
Weeks of long days	0	1	2	3	4
Average nodes per stem before short day induction	21	24	26	30	34
Final plant height (cm)	53	64	81	94	108

The morphological development of these sprays is typical for this cultivar for the time intervals shown. The inflorescence on the left has senesced, B is just beginning to senesce, C is ready for harvest (full bloom), and the D and E are not yet ready to harvest. Note that none of the oldest inflorescences indicated by the arrow was removed, as is commonly done in commercial practice for spray chrysanthemums (see text). The lateral flowering stems stretch above the oldest blooms.

6-minute interval every 30 minutes during a 4-hour night break with a minimum of 5 fc (55 lx). An interval of 1 minute of light in every 5 minutes, at 10 fc (110 x) or more, was found to be necessary for cultivars relatively insensitive to supplementary lighting, e.g., Albatross and Good News (Kofranek, 1963). A comprehensive review on cyclic lighting is offered by Mastalerz (1977). When long days are supplied by incandescent cyclic lighting, employed over a long period, e.g., 7 weeks, flower inhibition may be marginal or incomplete. Plants grown under a cyclic lighting regime reached full bloom as much as a week earlier, after short days began, than those given a continuous 5-hour night break for the same period (Kofranek, 1963). This result clearly demonstrates that the floral inhibition was not complete in the latter stages of the long-day period since the cyclically illuminated plants were also shorter than those grown with continuous light.

Fluorescent lamps are being used for some production plants and are more efficient than incandescent lamps at comparable wattages. The initial cost of fluorescent installation is high, but fixtures and lamps can be amortized with energy savings. Cool white fluorescent lamps were found to be more efficient than GroLux® and pink lamps for five cultivars tested (Acatti-Garibaldi *et al.*, 1977).

Low-pressure sodium lamps that have a narrow band of effective irradiation (589 nm) have been reported to be extremely efficient as a night break with four cultivars (Canham *et al.*, 1977).

When production plants are grown under long-day conditions, shoot apices continue to produce leaves and nodes at the rate of two to four per week (plastochron). Lower leaves mature first, and internodes in the region 10 cm below the apex elongate rapidly. Depending on cultivar and season, a shoot will reach the appropriate length (about 35–50 cm) in a set number of days. More time is required in the winter than in summer to produce the same number of leaves (nodes). Published chrysanthemum schedules list the time required from the pinch or planting time to the beginning of short days for floral induction. Figure 6 illustrates the need for the long-day cycle before the short-day cycles to obtain the final desired stem length; if 90 cm of stem were required for the cultivar, the plant should be grown vegetatively for 4 weeks in the winter to ensure that the minimum plant height is 1 m.

During cold weather when greenhouses are tightly closed, the carbon dioxide content of the air can become depleted; at these times, chrysanthemums respond favorably to carbon dioxide injections into the atmosphere. For details see Chapter 3, Roses.

VII. FLOWERING OF PRODUCTION PLANTS

When plants have reached the desired stem length (about 35–50 cm), they are given a short-day treatment. Lights which provided long days are turned off during a natural short-day period (winter) or the plants are covered with a blackout material during naturally occurring long days (summer). The blackout material can be either black sateen cloth with a minimum of 68 × 104 threads to the inch (2.54 cm) or black polyethylene. The blackout is best applied for a minimum of 12 hours, which is possible with an automatic blackout system (7 P.M. –7 A.M.). Manually applied blackout usually begins at 4:30 P.M., to conform to the usual work hours, and is removed beginning at 8:00 A.M. The sun is still high at 4:30 P.M. (especially with daylight savings time) and heat builds up under the black material. Excessive heat (above 30°C) can cause a "heat delay" of flower initiation during the early inductive short days, i.e., between the first and tenth short day. It is preferable to wait until 5:30 to 6 P.M. in mid-summer before covering plants to avoid heat problems under the black material.

The blackout must be applied for at least 21 to 28 consecutive short days if standard chrysanthemums are grown and for a longer period (42 days) if spray-type chrysanthemums are grown (see Section IX, Year-Round Flowering). After 14 consecutive short days the capitulum of the inflorescence is completely formed and the outer rows of florets are beginning to initiate. It is safe to skip the blackout one day a week after that stage of inflorescence development has been attained, i.e., after 14 short days. There may be 1 or 2 days' delay in flower maturity over those given the blackout every day, depending on temperature in the last days of development. High day and night temperatures which occur near maturity can advance harvesting up to 5 days but flower quality will diminish, compared to plants grown at optimum temperatures.

VIII. INFLORESCENCE INITIATION AND DEVELOPMENT

Hybrid chrysanthemums presently being grown for year-round flower production are short-day (long-night) plants when grown at minimum temperatures of 15.5°C. Post (1949) stated, based on work conducted at latitude 42°N, that a daylength of 14.5 hours (about August 15) was necessary for flower initiation, but that a shorter daylength of 13.5 hours (occurring about September 20) was required for flower bud development. Natural daylengths mentioned by Post include civil twilight.* He also noted that some cultivars initiated flower buds as late as the first week in September. Furuta (1954) found that late blooming cultivars required shorter daylengths to reach full bloom than did early flowering cultivars. Post and Kamemoto (1950) reported that an early cultivar, Gold Coast (9 weeks), initiated flower buds in about 4 days on a short photoperiod and that a late cultivar, Vibrant (14 weeks), initiated flower buds in 5 days. Doorenbos and Kofranek (1953) showed that after 24 continuous short days floral apices of 'Gold Coast' and 'Vibrant' were at the same morphological

---

*The light intensity when the sun is 6° below the horizon.

stage of inflorescence development. They concluded that early and late bloom-ing cultivars initiated floral receptacles and flowers (inflorescence) at about the same rate, but that the difference in the final flowering time (9 versus 14 weeks) was attributed to the different rate of development of inflorescences after the 24th short day.

Various response groups (see Section II, C) have different critical (maximum) daylengths for inflorescence initiation and development. Cathey (1957) re-ported the following maximum daylength requirements for selected cultivars in several response groups at minimum night temperatures of 15.5°C.

Cultivar	Response group	Critical daylength requirements (hours/day)	
		Flower initiation	Flower development
White Wonder	6-Week cultivar	16	13¾
Pristine	8-Week cultivar	15¼	13
Encore	10-Week cultivar	14½	13
Fortune	12-Week cultivar	13	12
Snow	15-Week cultivar	11	10

These data show that a shorter photoperiod is required for inflorescence development than is necessary for floral initiation for cultivars of different flower-ing periods. In this same study Cathey (1957) showed that the critical day-length for floral initiation and development of three cultivars was altered with a change in the minimum night temperature (Table III).

Extremely high night temperatures (an average of 30°C) will delay floral initiation (Furuta and Nelson, 1953). Low minimum temperatures (range: 13°–2°C) at the beginning of the photoperiod delay flower bud initiation from 1 to 49 days, depending on cultivar and duration (5 or 15 days) of low temperatures (Samman and Langhans, 1962). Lowering night temperatures to 10°C during the first 15 short days delayed flowering of temperature-sensitive 'Lemon Spider' but had little effect between the 16th and 30th short day (Carow and Zimmer, 1977).

Many chrysanthemum cultivars were classified by Cathey (1954) into tem-perature categories of flowering response:

1. Thermozero cultivars—those which show little inhibition for flowering be-tween 10° and 27°C. Flowering proceeds rapidly at 15.5°C. This category was suggested as the most likely category for year-round flowering.

2. Thermopositive cultivars—those in which flowering is inhibited below 15.5°C. Flower buds may initiate but do not develop beyond the capitulum stage at lower temperatures. These cultivars may be grown for year-round flowering if the temperature is properly maintained.

Table III

Interrelationships of Temperature and Critical Photoperiod for Flower Initiation and Development of Three Chrysanthemum Cultivars [a]

Cultivar	Period to flower (weeks)	Minimum night temperature		Maximum light period required for	
		°F	°C	Flower initiation (hours)	Flower development (hours)
White Wonder	6	50	10	13¾	13¾
		60	15.5	16	13¾
		80	27	16	12
Encore	10	50	10	13¾	13¾
		60	15.5	14½	13
		80	27	15¼	12
Snow	15	50	10	12	12
		60	15.5	11	10
		80	27	10	9

[a] Experimental range of photoperiods from 9 to 16 hours. Adapted from Cathey (1957).

3. Thermonegative cultivars—those in which flowering is inhibited above 15.5°C. Lower temperatures (10°C) may delay but do not inhibit initiation. These cultivars should only be grown when night temperatures can be controlled at 15.5°C or slightly lower. Summer culture should be avoided. This category includes the late season cultivars which are in the 13- to 15-week response groups ('Snow' in Table III, for example).

Cathey (1955) published an extensive list of cultivars in the above-mentioned three categories. Only a partial number from this list is offered (Table IV), based on those cultivars that are still being grown commercially. Some of these new cultivars may now be listed as 'Improved Mefo,' '#2 Shasta' or 'Yellow-Beauregard,' because improved mutations have been selected since the original list was published. It is assumed by the author that the temperature–photoperiod response of these recently selected mutants remained the same when they were selected for improved color, shape, and vigor.

The light flux in the first 2 weeks of short days can alter initiation of the capitulum and flowers. Low light intensities during this period will delay initiation by several days (Cockshull, 1972). Optimally the light intensity for growth and flowering should be above 3000 fc (32 klx) for a large portion of the daylight hours.

Additional information concerning the environmental control of chrysanthemum flowering can be found in several reviews (Cathey, 1969; Cockshull, 1972; Mastalerz, 1977; Searle and Machin, 1968).

Table IV

Temperature Categories of Selected Cultivars Available from Commercial Propagators, Showing Their Response to Different Night Temperature Regimes in Three Seasons[a,b]

Cultivar	Normal flowering date at 42°N	Minimum night temperatures for three seasons				
		Spring			Fall	Winter
		27°C	15.5°C	10°C	15.5°C	15.5°C
Thermozero cultivars (temperature insensitive) (days to flower)						
Bluechip	Nov. 1	70	67	84	61	62
Indianapolis White	Nov. 5	73	73	82	62	66
Indianapolis Yellow	Nov. 5	73	73	82	61	66
Shasta	Nov. 10	85	80	85	67	73
Thermonegative cultivars (low temperature to develop) (days to flower)						
Christmas Greeting	Dec. 15	A	102	B	97	87
Christmas Star	Dec. 12	A	92	C	89	87
Corsair	Dec. 10	A	92	C	90	85
Snowcap	Dec. 15	C	84	D	100	85
Snowcrest	Dec. 15	A	81	C	119	85
Vibrant	Dec. 20	C	92	D	100	102
Yuleflame	Dec. 25	A	92	D	97	104
Thermopositive cultivars (do well at high temperature) (days to flower)						
Albatross	Nov. 1	67	73	92	61	66
Beauregard	Nov. 5	73	77	102	69	71
Forty-Niner	Nov. 15	74	81	C	69	83
Gold Coast	Oct. 25	70	63	102	57	62
Goldsmith	Nov. 25	92	E	A	81	76
Good News	Nov. 1	80	80	102	67	71
Highbrow	Nov. 20	84	102	C	74	76
Horizon	Oct. 5	57	63	107	53	55
Mefo	Nov. 20	102	92	D	76	83
Mrs. Roy	Nov. 13	80	77	D	63	73
Paragon	Nov. 12	80	81	C	74	76
Pink Dot	Oct. 25	67	67	A	61	66
Pinochio	Oct. 25	57	63	B	55	59
Taffeta	Nov. 12	84	80	C	71	75
Thelma	Nov. 20	92	80	A	78	76
White Valencia	Nov. 28	102	84	C	78	83

[a]All figures represent the days required to reach maturity (days to flower). Where plants failed to bloom at the end of the experiment, reasons (indicated by letters) are provided. From Cathey (1955).

[b]Key to letters: A, crown bud followed by crown bud; B, terminal spray, but slow development of inflorescences; C, center inflorescences in spray developing slowly—crown buds followed by crown buds lower down on the stem; D, terminal spray, almost in bloom; E, delayed blooming.

IX. YEAR-ROUND FLOWERING

Year-round flowering of chrysanthemums was first suggested by Post (1947), although experiments on early flowering were first conducted by Professor Laurie using blackcloth. Research to perfect flowering of a number of cultivars was conducted over several years by different workers and then later by Yoder Brothers of Barberton, Ohio. Flowering schedules are available from several commercial companies that provide rooted or unrooted cuttings on a year-round basis.

Growers scheduling year-round production or even a single crop must follow certain principles in order to grow high-quality flowers. Briefly, the essentials are the following:

1. Rooted vegetative cuttings are planted in beds having a well-prepared soil and are provided with mineral nutrients in a liquid fertilizer solution from the first day. During bright weather plants should be shaded to minimize wilting.

2. Rooted cuttings are properly spaced based on whether the plants will be pinched or grown as a single stem (see Section VI, B).

3. After plants are established, they can be pinched to induce branching for multiple-stemmed plants and later pruned to a desired number of stems per plant. Some plants are not pinched; these are known as single-stemmed plants.

4. When the single stems or the branches of pinched plants reach a given height, they are given short days to induce flowering. Up to this point plants must be grown under long-day conditions to inhibit flower bud formation.

5. Plants are then given short-day conditions (a minimum of a 12-hour daylength) until induced flower buds develop to a stage no longer affected by daylength.

6. If the plant is grown for a single bloom, lateral flower buds should be removed beginning about the 28th short day or when it is possible to remove the buds physically (Fig. 2). Generally, disbudding is a two-step operation spaced about a week apart.

7. During periods of high light intensity the developing blooms that are beginning to show color should be shaded with cheesecloth or a light-shading material to prevent sun scald.

8. Flowers are harvested with the proper stem length and inflorescence development required by the wholesale market. Flower development within the bed is not uniform, and 5–10 days may be required for all flowers to reach the proper cutting stage. Less time is required in summer when high temperatures hasten flower maturity. More time is needed in winter when low daytime radiant energy delays flower development.

9. After flowers have been harvested, plant stubble and roots are removed from the soil or can be rototilled into the soil in preparation for the next crop. Soil must be prepared by a certain date to keep the year-round schedule intact.

Certain fundamental principles regarding the cultivar being grown must be understood before one can develop a year-round schedule. Some of this information is discussed in the preceding section on flowering. The most important points are listed below and will assist in understanding the sample schedules in Fig. 7.

1. Not all cultivars are suitable for year-round scheduling. Some may require night temperatures lower than those that can be attained during the summer months. These cultivars are typical of the 13- to 15-week response groups that

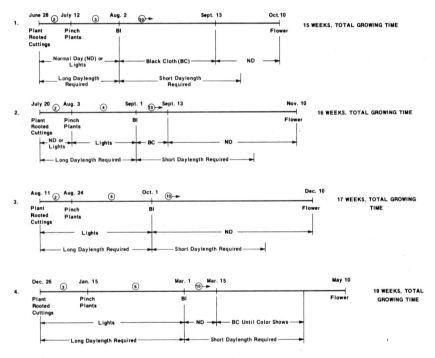

Fig. 7. Schedules for a 10-week cultivar during four periods having wide differences in light intensity. Definitions: Long daylength required—from planting date to bud initiation date. Short daylength required—from bud initiation date until the bud development is advanced enough to disregard the length of day. Lights—a night break with supplementary lighting to provide a long day length to maintain a vegetative condition. Black cloth (BC)—a blackout system to provide a short daylength to promote flowering. ND—natural daylength; a daylength of adequate length at a given time of year to promote vegetative growth or flowering as required. Plant rooted cuttings—planting date for crops. Pinch plants—the date for removal of growing points to induce branching. BI—bud initiation date; the day to change from a long daylength to a short daylength in order to promote flowering. Flower—a date to begin harvesting the blooms. Plants may bloom sooner if high temperatures prevail during short daylength cycle. The numerals 2,3,4,5,6, and 10 in circles refer to the number of weeks to complete a stage of plant growth or development.

require temperatures of 15.5°C or lower (Table IV) to develop quality flowers. These particular cultivars should only be used in greenhouses or outdoor growing locations where night temperatures will be cool during later stages of flower bud development. Cultivars should be grown that produce the best quality on a year-round basis. Cultivars in the 9-, 10-, or 11-week response groups usually are the ones which produce marketable quality during warm summer weather but also during low light intensity periods of winter. Although the 6- to 8-week cultivars reach the harvest stage more rapidly than the 10-week cultivars, their overall quality is not considered commercially adequate. Assuming that the greenhouse night temperature will be maintained at 15.5°C, the 9-, 10-, or 11-week cultivars produce the best quality in the most reasonable time from the beginning of short days until full bloom. Ten-week cultivars were chosen for scheduling samples (Figs. 7 and 8) and for the following discussion.

2. Rooted cuttings may require more time to become established in the soil after planting in winter than in summer, assuming plants are not allowed to wilt excessively during periods of high light and heat of summer. Those plants destined for pinching will be ready for tip removal in as little as 10 days in the summer or as much as in 21 days in late fall or winter. Plants are provided with long days during this period by supplying supplementary lighting or with natural long days during the summer, depending on the latitude.

3. Pinched plants should be pruned as soon as possible to a desired number of shoots for the spacing provided. Early removal of shoots encourages rapid growth of the remaining shoots by reducing shoot competition.

4. Plants grown as single stems are planted closer together than pinched plants because of less shoot competition. The growth of single-stemmed plants is unchecked and they reach the proper height for the cultivar [see point (4) on p. 24] earlier than pinched plants. A point worth repeating is that pinching always checks growth and that additional time is necessary for new shoots to develop after a pinch.

5. The time required from the pinching date to when shoots are long enough depends on available photosynthetic active radiation. As many as 6 weeks will be required for plants pinched in October, November, and December at latitudes 40°–50° N to attain the proper shoot length, but only 4 weeks may be necessary at latitudes 25° to 30° N during this same season. Daytime radiant energy at the northerly latitudes is more limiting for plant growth in winter than in the more southerly latitudes. During the late spring and early summer months of May, June, and July, as little as 3 weeks will be required to attain the proper shoot length at all the above-stated latitudes since light intensity for vegetative growth is not limiting during this season. Some cultivars grow so rapidly during natural long days that fewer than 21 days are required to obtain proper shoot length. Chrysanthemum catalogs or experience will reveal these rapid growing cultivars.

6. Once proper shoot length is attained (usually 35 to 50 cm), the plant is given the inductive short days for flower initiation and development. There are a

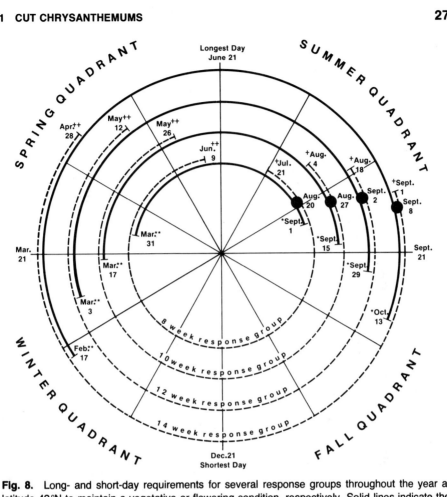

Fig. 8. Long- and short-day requirements for several response groups throughout the year at latitude 42°N to maintain a vegetative or flowering condition, respectively. Solid lines indicate the periods when black cloth must be used for flowering. Dotted lines indicate that supplementary lighting is necessary to maintain a vegetative condition. In the summer and fall quadrants: •, the approximate date of natural flower bud initiation; +, the date supplementary lighting should begin in late summer to maintain vegetative condition; *, the date when black cloth is no longer necessary because the daylength is naturally short. In the winter and spring quadrants: ++, dates when supplementary lighting can be eliminated to maintain vegetative growth. Some growers, however, light as much as 2 hours per night even during the longest days of the year (see text); **, the dates when black cloth must be applied to provide short-day conditions for flowering. Black cloth may be removed when many of the inflorescences in a spray show color (see text).

given number of leaf initials in various stages of morphological development within the zone of expansion (subapical meristem and the region of elongation). The zone of expansion of certain cultivars has as many as 18 to 20 leaves between the most recently expanded leaf and the apical meristem ('Albatross'); other cultivars have as few as 12 to 14 leaves (Fig. 9) in various devel-

Fig. 9. A shoot of 'Bright Golden Anne' with most of the large leaves removed to illustrate the size of a vegetative shoot above the most recently matured leaf. This shoot portion just above the leaf with the two white spots has 13 leaves which range in size from 2 cm long to primordial leaves at the apex. If this cultivar is given a soft pinch (Fig. 4A), that portion *above* the marked leaf, about 13 leaves, is removed. 'Albatross,' however, has about 18 leaves in a shoot of similar size. Much can be learned from marking recently expanded leaves with latex water paint (nonphytotoxic) and then observing subsequent vegetative or reproductive growth above the marked leaf.

opmental stages ('Princess Anne'). About 4 to 5 inductive short days are required to change the vegetative apex into a terminal flower bud (Post and Kamemoto, 1950). In that period, leaf initials (perhaps only two to three) are still in the process of being initiated before the apex becomes reproductive and the inflorescence receptacle is finally initiated. Although a shoot may only be 35 cm long on the first inductive short day, it is reasonable to assume that at full bloom that shoot may be between 70 and 100 cm long. The internodes within the zone of expansion (Fig. 9) as well as those just below the most recently matured leaf expand, which results in a doubling of shoot length at full bloom. Some cultivars are more efficient in internode expansion than others and this difference would indicate that the former require fewer long days from the pinch to the start of short days. The actual number of nodes in the zone of expansion at the time of the first inductive short day may or may not be of significance in the shoot reaching a marketable length. Environmental conditions (light intensity and temperature) surrounding the plant and the genetic makeup of the cultivar probably have more influence on ultimate shoot length by controlling the final internodal length than do the actual number of nodes within the zone of expansion when short days begin.

7. The minimum number of consecutive short days required to produce quality blooms depends on the cultivar and its culture. When a plant is grown for a single bloom as a standard, all buds except the terminal inflorescence are

removed; this disbudding procedure, if conducted early (starting about the 28th short day) creates a "source–sink relationship" within the plant. The source of sugars in the leaves is directed to the sink, i.e., the single inflorescence at the terminus. Under such conditions as few as 21 consecutive short days were required for 'Albatross' but 28 consecutive short days were required by 'Escapade' to develop a quality inflorescence. (Kofranek and Halevy, 1974). When plants are grown as sprays (not disbudded) one should assume that more consecutive short days would be required to promote full bloom of a majority of the inflorescences because the "sinks" are in many locations on the flowering branches and individual inflorescences vary in their morphological development. (Note: on a cyme the most mature inflorescence is the upper-most one and the inflorescences are progressively less mature on the lower branches; inflorescences are formed basipetally.) Most chrysanthemum scheduling catalogs suggest continuing short days until inflorescences show color. This could be as late as the 49th short day for a 10-week pompon chrysanthemum.

8. Sample schedules of a 10-week cultivar grown as a pinched crop during 4 periods at latitude 42° N are given in Fig. 7. The information for supplementary lighting to provide long days and for blackcloth for blackout periods to provide short days for flower induction was obtained from Fig. 8 in the 10-week response group circle.

X. FLOWERING DURING THE NATURAL SEASON

With the advent of year-round flowering, fewer chrysanthemums are being grown during their natural flowering season. For the year-round grower natural flowering may not be convenient to fit into the year-round schedule. In the future, when fossil fuels become extremely costly and year-round flowering may not be economically feasible, natural season chrysanthemums may again be grown for approximately 3 months per year out-of-doors in mild climates, or in greenhouses by supplying only limited heat.

Natural flowering is possible from early October until early January when the appropriate cultivars are chosen for their flowering succession. Rooted cuttings are planted every week starting in mid-June with the 7-week cultivars and ending in mid-August with the 15-week cultivars. As a general rule rooted cuttings of each response group are pinched 2 weeks after planting (Table V). Cuttings are easily established within 2 weeks of planting during these periods of high light intensity. Cultivars in the various response groups should be planted on the dates indicated in Table V in regions of latitude 42° N and 1 week earlier in more northerly latitudes and 1 week later in the southern latitudes. A soft pinch to induce branching is given 2 weeks later for the flowering periods indicated; this is known as the "time pinch." The purpose of the

Table V

Natural Flowering Dates of Various Response Groups Grown in Greenhouses in the Northern United States and Southern Canada[a]

Response group (weeks)	Approximate planting date	Approximate pinching date	Natural flowering dates
7	June 25	July 9	Sept. 22–Oct. 9
8	July 2	July 16	Oct. 12–Oct. 21
9	July 9	July 23	Oct. 22–Nov. 1
10	July 16	July 30	Nov. 2–Nov. 11
11	July 23	Aug. 6	Nov. 12–Nov. 21
12	July 30	Aug. 13	Nov. 22–Dec. 4
13	Aug. 6	Aug. 20	Dec. 2–Dec. 11
14	Aug. 13	Aug. 27	Dec. 12–Dec. 26
15	Aug. 20	Sept. 3	Dec. 27–Jan. 5

[a] Plants are generally pinched 2 weeks after planting for the flowering dates shown. Adapted from Yoder Brothers (1968).

time pinch is to improve the shape of the spray formation of pompon chrysanthemums (Fig. 10B). If the pinch is made too early, a premature crown bud (Fig. 10A) initiates and causes branching; if the pinch is made too late, a terminal bud initiates (Fig. 10C) surrounded by lateral buds on short peduncles. A time pinch made on the proper date for a particular response group results in a flower bud initiated in the center of the spray, which develops into an arrangement of inflorescences on peduncles of desirable length (Fig. 10B).

Although the rule is not rigid, the time pinch is made approximately 100 days before full bloom. The rationale is that the stem length from the resultant pinch attains the proper size for that cultivar, within a given response group, by the time it reaches its natural bud initiation date. The photoperiod (daylength) will then be short enough and floral buds will initiate on or about the date, and will continue to develop properly and bloom within the dates indicated (Table V). If planting and pinching are made earlier than indicated, such as 2 weeks earlier, the resultant shoots may initiate a crown bud (Fig. 11) before the natural bud initiation date. Because the daylength is not short enough to promote further flower bud development, the crown bud may not develop beyond the capitulum stage and will cause unwanted branching (Fig. 11). Thus a plant pinched too early (before the day indicated in Table V) will usually develop a spray formation as Fig. 10A with a crown bud low in the spray. Shoots below the crown bud elongate; later those shoots initiate a flower on or about the natural bud initiation date, thus forming an elongated spray. If plants are pinched at a later date than indicated, such as 2 weeks later, the resultant spray may resemble Fig. 10C. Those shoots reach maturity at a date later than the indicated natural bud initiation date; those buds therefore initiate and develop quickly to form a compressed spray. The peduncles below the inflorescence do not elongate adequately during the short days that follow the indicated bud initiation date and the spray develops a compressed appearance. When the plant is pinched approximately 100 days before the flowering date, the shoots have ample time to reach both maturity and the proper length to produce a marketable stem. The flower bud then initiates on or about the natural bud initiation date and develops lateral buds with peduncles of a desirable length (Fig. 10B). The pinching dates may vary slightly among cultivars, even within similar response groups, because of genetic variability of peduncle lengths. For instance, 'Iceberg' has naturally long peduncles; therefore, pinching this cultivar *late* may produce an even better quality spray formation than if it were time pinched 100 days before bloom.

Planting, pinching, and early shoot development occur during periods of high radiant energy and high temperatures of summer. Growth is rapid and should not be checked by creating water and nutrient stresses. Bud initiation also occurs during periods of high light intensities and high temperatures, but subsequent bud development of midseason and late cultivars occurs during periods of low radiant energy and low night temperatures. During this latter period, blooming may be greatly delayed by very low night temperatures (4°–

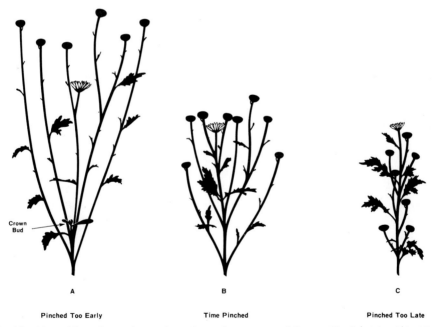

Crown
Bud

A   B   C

Pinched Too Early   Time Pinched   Pinched Too Late

Fig. 10.   Natural flowering and spray formations of pompons as influenced by the date of pinching prior to the natural bud initiation date in the fall.

Fig. 11.   A crown bud in the center of an inflorescence spray. The strap-shaped leaf growing below the bud and toward the right is typical of a crown bud. Buds such as these will never develop to anthesis because they lack true floral parts. Crown buds will cause branching when they form prematurely in shoots grown for their vegetative state.

8°C). Cultivars of the late response groups (13–15 weeks), however, often require cool temperatures (10°–12°C) for proper bud development. Earlier cultivars (9- to 11-week cultivars) require minimum temperatures of 12°C or greater for normal inflorescence development.

Standard chrysanthemums grown for the natural season should also be "time pinched," about 100 days prior to harvesting, to avoid the formation of premature crown buds that may not develop properly (Fig. 11). A crown bud, if selected (or "taken") as the one to become the marketable bloom, may be induced to develop by removing vegetative lateral buds below it. Crown buds, if selected or taken too early, are slightly larger, usually have paler colors, and develop on longer peduncles than those terminal buds selected at the proper time, i.e., after the natural bud initiation date. If buds are selected too early they may develop green centers because the daylength is marginal for development. Bud selection at a later date ensures that the days are amply short to promote proper bud development if the minimum temperatures are adequate.

XI. IMPROVING INFLORESCENCE QUALITY WITH PHOTOPERIOD

Some spray chrysanthemums develop cymes or sprays resembling those shown in Fig. 10C. The sprays can be made to open and be less compact as in Fig. 10B by manipulation of the daylength (Post, 1950). When the plants have attained the proper height, they are given 12 short-day cycles to initiate the inflorescences on the entire spray. Then the plants are given 10 consecutive long days (night break) and are later returned to short days to complete flower development. The long days elongate the peduncles below the inflorescences and improve the spray formation. Certain cultivars such as Iceberg and Polaris do not require any manipulation since their peduncles are naturally long.

The diameter of standards can be increased by subjecting disbudded chrysanthemums to long-day conditions after the 35th short day. This manipulation is called "after lighting" (Ben-Jaacov and Langhans, 1969). After lighting generally increases the length of ray flowers to increase the overall diameter of the inflorescence. All standards do not respond to this treatment, however.

XII. USE OF SELECTED GROWTH REGULATORS

A. Increasing Stem Length

Gibberellins can be used to increase the stem length of standard chrysanthemums. Concentrations as low as 1.5 to 6 ppm potassium gibberellate sprayed 1 to 3 days after planting and again 3 weeks later have resulted in significant increases of stem length without loss of stem quality under midwinter light conditions in California (Byrne and Pyeatt, 1976).

B. Reducing Peduncle Length of Standards

Succinic acid-2,2-dimethylhydrazide (B-Nine), SADH, is applied to standard chrysanthemums just after disbudding (Fig. 2) to shorten peduncles. One spray (2500 ppm) to the point of runoff is adequate for many cultivars. SADH reduces cell division and elongation in the region just below the inflorescence, where elongation occurs rapidly at the time the florets are actively developing.

C. Increasing Peduncle Length of Pompons

Some pompons develop short peduncles, and longer ones may be more desirable for floral arrangements. Peduncle elongation may be accomplished by spraying the tops of plants to runoff with 20 ppm gibberellic acid (GA) 4 weeks after the start of short days. This treatment is most effective during periods of high radiant energy and it varies with cultivars. High concentrations or applications of GA later than the 4-week period may result in weakened inflorescences.

D. Root Initiation

The most common rooting hormone used for chrysanthemums is 0.1 to 0.2% indolebutyric acid (IBA) mixed with talc (1–2 mg IBA to 1 gm talc). Although it is possible to apply IBA in an aqueous solution, it is generally not recommended because of the possible spread of bacterial diseases in the solution.

E. Floral Inhibition

As little as 3 to 4 ppm ethylene has been reported to inhibit floral initiation during inductive short days (Tjia *et al.,* 1969). Experiments by Cockshull and Horridge (1978) are being conducted using 2-chloroethylphosphonic acid (ethephon), to determine whether ethylene can be substituted for long days in chrysanthemum floral inhibition.

F. Chemical Disbudding of Standard Mums

Numerous experiments have been conducted to find a way of eliminating or retarding growth of lateral flower buds chemically without injuring the terminal inflorescence. Moderate success has been achieved with materials such as HAN, napthalenes, and 2,3-dihydro-5-6-diphenyl-1,4-oxanthin (UNI-P293) with selected cultivars (Zacharioudakis and Larson, 1976). The likelihood of any of these or related chemical compounds being used commercially is indeed far from reality. The reason is quite simple. Lateral buds must be *eliminated* or *retarded* at a very early morphological stage, i.e., between the 14th and 20th short day. During this active growth period, the immature terminal inflorescence is extremely vulnerable to injury from chemicals. Any miscalculation of chemical application can destroy or seriously injure the terminal inflorescence. Leaves adjacent to those lateral buds which are retarded or eliminated are usually seriously distorted. If the terminal bud is not injured there is a strong likelihood the lateral buds will also be unaffected. Use of chemical disbudding is too variable to be used by growers at this time.

G. Chemical Pinching

The methyl esters of fatty acids (Emgard 2077 and Off-Shoot-O) were studied experimentally for chemically pinching chrysanthemums. Results have been variable and not as successful as with azaleas. These materials used at low rates (2%) will drip down the stem and girdle it if not properly applied. Since the hazards of using these chemical pinching agents are so great, they are not recommended for commercial use.

XIII. DISEASES

Chrysanthemums are affected by fungi, bacteria, and viruses. Most of these are controlled by the commercial propagator who indexes the plants (Horst and Nelson, 1975) and renders them pathogen-free. Although cuttings may be free of pathogens, young plants are susceptible to infection from soil-borne pathogens if the soil is not treated properly prior to planting (see Section IV on soil preparation). Young plants may also be infected by knives, handling, or insects which transmit viruses. Precautions must be taken throughout the life of the plants to avoid or limit pathogen infestation (Horst and Nelson, 1977; Mc-Cain, 1977). The most common chrysanthemum diseases are briefly discussed below.

A. Fungus Diseases

1. Pythium Root Rot or Basal Stem Rot

a. Pathogen: Pythium spp.   *Phythium* is a soil-borne organism favored by excessive soil moisture; the spores are spread by contaminated soil or water. Infected plants are stunted because of a poor root system; blackish-brown lesions near the soil surface may cause girdling.

b. Control.   Treat the soil (see discussion of *Verticillium* below) or incorporate ethazol before planting. Drench bases of plants and soil with Diazoben when symptom(s) first appear.

2. Rhizoctonia Stem Rot

a. Pathogen: Rhizoctonia solani.   *Rhizoctonia* is a soil-borne organism favored by moist, warm conditions. Infected plants wilt during midday, growth is restricted, and stems rot at the soil surface.

b. Control.   Treat the soil with PCNB before planting or spray base of cuttings with benomyl or chlorothalonil after planting.

3. Verticillium Wilt

a. Pathogen: Verticillum dahliae or V. albo-atrum.   These pathogens are soil-borne organisms that may remain in the soil for many years (from chrysanthemums or other infected genera). One side of the plant wilts; leaves gradually become yellow and die beginning at the base of the plant. Dried leaves remain on the stem. The infection usually begins in cool weather and symptoms are obvious in warm weather.

b. Control. Steam the soil at 60°C for 30 minutes or fumigate with a 2:1 ratio of chloropicrin: methyl bromide under a gas-proof trap for 48 hours or more. Use cultivars resistant to the disease.

4. Gray Mold

a. Pathogen: Botrytis cinerea. Gray mold is favored by cool temperatures (10°–16°C) and high relative humidity and may sporulate on dead or dying plant tissue. Infected plants are brownish; water-soaked spots appear on florets and become a fuzzy mass of mycelia and spores under ideal conditions. Lower leaves can rot and the organism may enter the stem and girdle it.

b. Control. Clean up plant residue. Heat and ventilate greenhouse to keep humidity below 85%. Mist blooms and lower foliage with benomyl.

5. Cottony Rot

a. Pathogen: Sclerotinia sclerotiorum. Sclerotia may germinate in soil but airborne spores are forcibly spread from apothecia. Stems rot, appear similar to gray mold; a cottony mass appears on infected tissue; sclerotia (hard, black bodies) may form within stem.

b. Control. Remove plant residue to eliminate sclerotia; apply protective fungicide, PCNB, or benomyl.

6. Ascochyta Ray Blight

a. Pathogen: Mycosphaerella ligulicola (Ascochyta chrysanthemi). The conidia are spread by wind or splashing water from infected tissue; spread is favored by wet weather. Flower buds may rot before opening or florets become blackish. Infection can extend to the peduncle.

b. Control. Burn or remove plant debris; keep humidity low and avoid moisture on blooms and foliage. Spray with maneb, zineb, or chlorothalonil.

7. Septoria Leaf Spot

a. Pathogen: Septoria obesa (Most Common) or S. chrysanthemella. This organism may remain in plant debris for 2 years and is spread by splashing water, especially during wet weather when leaves remain moist for 12 or more hours. Leaf spots appear circular to irregular in shape, usually develop from base of plant upward, and may coalesce; spots are black, brown, or occasionally reddish.

b. Control. Keep relative humidity low, avoid wetting foliage, and protect it with a fungicide when disease appears.

8. Rust

a. Pathogen: Puccinia chrysanthemi.   Rust becomes serious when temperature (16°–21°C) and free moisture conditions are ideal for urediospore germination. Airborne spores are produced on living plants. Small reddish-brown pustules appear as flecks on the underside of leaves. The center of the pustule dies and turns blackish.

b. Control.   Avoid wetting foliage, keep relative humidity low, and cover leaves with zineb before likely infection begins.

9. White Rust

a. Pathogen: Puccinia horiana.   High humidity and temperatures between 15° and 21°c favor germination. The first symptoms are yellow spots on the upper side of the leaf; the center of the spot turns brown. The lower leaf surface has waxy pustules (2.5–5.0 mm) which are buff to pink but later turn white.

b. Control.   Follow the instructions for common rust (see above).

10. Powdery Mildew

a. Pathogen: Erysiphe cichoracearum.   Airborne spores of powdery mildew survive on living plants. This pathogen is favored by cool weather and high humidity and is often found in dense plant spacings. White to gray powdery growth is present on leaves and stems; leaves may become deformed.

b. Control.   Heat and ventilate to lower relative humidity. Spray regularly with benomyl or spray with dinocap plus a surfactant to eradicate infections.

11. Stemphylium–Alternaria Ray Blight

a. Pathogens: Stemphylium species and Alternaria species.   Infections occur at temperatures from 16° to 30°C but free water is necessary for about 12 hours. Small, pin-point necrotic lesions form on ray petals; lesions are reddish-brown on white florets, chocolate brown on yellow florets, and light brown on pink florets. Lesions do not enlarge.

b. Control.   Reduce the moisture for 10 hours or more. Clean up infected plants. Heat and ventilate the greenhouse.

B. Bacterial Diseases

1. Bacterial Blight

a. Pathogen: Erwinia chrysanthemi.   *Erwinia* is favored by high temperatures (27°–32°C) and high humidity and is spread by infested hands, tools, or other equipment. The first symptoms are the appearance of gray in leaves of certain branches; wilting follows on bright days. The stem is easily crushed or may split, and the pith becomes jelly-like; water-soaked lesions appear.

b. Control Break cuttings from stock plants (avoid using knives). Destroy plants as soon as symptoms appear. Do not dip cuttings in hormone solutions.

2. Crown Gall

a. Pathogen: Agrobacterium tumefaciens. Infections from soil or galls are favored by moist conditions. Round growths or galls appear on the stem just below the soil surface, but occasionally are found on leaves and stems.

b. Control. Remove infected plants as galls appear. Fumigate or heat-treat soils. Disinfest tools used for cuttings.

3. Bacterial Leaf Spot

a. Pathogen: Pseudomonas cichorii. Bacterial leaf spot is favored by high humidity and wet weather. Circular to elliptical spots appear, which may increase or coalesce to form lesions on lower leaves; with continued moisture lesions may develop in leaf margins; in serious cases the bacterium enters petiole and stems; infected flower buds die prematurely.

b. Control. Avoid susceptible cultivars. Spray foliage frequently during wet periods with tribasic copper sulfate.

C. Virus Diseases

1. Stunt

a. Pathogen: Chrysanthemum Stunt Viroid. Plants are studied; foliage may be pale; flowers are small and may bloom a week earlier than normal.

b. Control. Index program by propagator can ensure clean plants. Eliminate suspicious-looking plants. Avoid spreading virus with knives and other tools.

2. Spotted Wilt

a. Pathogen: Tomato Spotted Wilt Virus. This virus is spread by thrips from some weeds and cultivated plants. Ring patterns appear on the leaves of some cultivars; leaf necrosis and distortion are present and may be on only one side of the plant; necrotic streaks are also present on the stem.

b. Control.   Eliminate weeds in immediate vicinity of growing area and avoid specific plants which harbor virus. Reduce or eliminate local thrip populations.

3. Aspermy

a. Pathogen: Tomato Aspermy Virus.   Aspermy is spread by aphids, tools, and handling. There is inflorescence distortion and reduced size and color break in red, pink, and bronze florets.

b. Control.   Obtain disease-free plants and remove infected plants; control aphids.

4. Chlorotic Mottle

a. Pathogen: Chrysanthemum Chlorotic Mottle Virus.   This virus is spread by tools and handling. The first sign of chlorotic mottle is a mottle followed by a complete chlorosis (may be confused with a nutritional disorder).

b. Control.   Obtain disease-free (virus-indexed) plants.

5. Chrysanthemum Mosaic

a. Pathogen: Chrysanthemum Mosaic Virus.   This virus is spread by aphids. Symptoms include mottled and deformed leaves and vary with cultivar.

b. Control.   Use virus-indexed plants and control aphids.

XIV. PESTS

Pests include true insects, spider mites, slugs, and nematodes. No controls are offered since recommendations for insecticides change readily. One should make certain that pesticides have label clearance for application on chrysanthemums in the field or greenhouses.

A. Insects

1. Sucking Insects

These include numerous species of aphids, leaf hoppers, mealy bugs, tarnished-plant bugs, thrips, and white flies. They suck plant juice and may distort leaves and flowers.

2. Chewing Insects

These include beet armyworms, cabbage loopers, chrysanthemum gall midge, corn-ear worms, cutworms, garden millipedes, serpentine leaf miner, and spotted cucumber beetles.

B. Spider Mites

These mites suck plant juices and cause loss of leaf color.

C. Slugs and Snails

They are of various species that chew flowers and leaves during the night.

D. Nematodes

1. Leaf Nematodes

These are microscopic nonsegmented round worms; they are spread through stomates by splashing water and cause dark green to brownish angular lesions in leaves. The progression of the injury on the plant is upward.

2. Root Nematodes

Root nematodes suck juices from roots and cause root galls, thereby weakening plants. They are soil-borne or can be transmitted to uninfested soil on contaminated plants or soil.

XV. OTHER PROBLEMS

In growing chrysanthemums, problems arise other than those caused by diseases and the numerous pests mentioned above. Table VI gives the symptoms and various possible causes of some of these problems. However, one must assess the most probable cause on the basis of the past cultural practice. Written records of temperatures, application dates of fertilizer, and pesticides are invaluable to make these assessments.

XVI. POSTHARVEST HANDLING

Flowers should be cut about 10 cm above the soil line to avoid cutting into woody tissue that is less likely to absorb water. The lower one-third of stems are stripped of leaves at harvest and are placed as soon as possible in water containing a biocide to prevent plugging of the xylem with microorganisms. The most effective biocide for chrysanthemums is silver nitrate; effective concentrations are 25 ppm in the water or a brief immersion of stems for 10 seconds to 10 minutes in 1000 ppm silver nitrate followed by placement in water low in salts (deionized). Inflorescences *cut fully open* in the greenhouse or field require only a biocide in the water. Additions of sugar to increase longevity are of no value. Recent unpublished data have demonstrated that some well waters used for chrysanthemums should be filtered with a Millipore filter to

Table VI

Visual Symptoms and Possible Causes of Problems with Cut Chrysanthemums

Symptoms	Possible causes
Stunted growth with small leaves	Mineral deficiency, especially nitrogen
	Excess soluble salts in soil
	Overwatering (soil saturation)
	Underwatering (dry soil)
	Low temperature during vegetative period; plant develops slowly
	Low light intensity during vegetative period
	Soil-steaming injury
	Viruses (see Section XIII on diseases)
	Soil nematodes
Undesirable branching, i.e., interruption of vegetative growth including the initiation of a premature flower bud	Apical meristems of some cultivars are easily destroyed by emulsifiable concentrates used in certain insecticides
	Crown bud initiates but does not develop
	Calcium deficiency
	Boron deficiency
	Tarnished-plant bug injures the apical meristem
Occasional leaf wilting	An overlooked irrigation
	Sunny days following an overcast period—particularly on plants infected with Verticillium disease
	Cold soil temperature
Chronic wilting at a later stage of development	*Verticillium* in specific stems
	Recent injured root system from an excess fertilizer application
	Recent injured root system from an excessive irrigation (soil saturated for long durations)
Interveinal chlorosis of leaves	Soil pH too high
	Iron deficiency
	Manganese deficiency
	Poor root system (many possible causes)
	Spider mites *numerous* on leaves
	Soil nematodes
Light green leaves (general chlorosis)	Nitrogen deficiency
	Sulfur deficiency (rare)
	Viruses (see Section XIII on diseases)
	A combination of high light intensity and high summer temperatures
Marginal leaf burn (necrosis)	Potassium deficiency
	Excess soluble salts in soil
	Excess boron in irrigation water
	Poor root system causing water stress
	Verticillium causing water stress
	Insecticide damage
Bronze coloration in leaves	Phosphorus deficiency
	Low temperatures near maturity
Bronze coloration on lower leaf surface	Potassium deficiency

(*continued*)

Table VI (*continued*)

Symptoms	Possible causes
Brittle leaf	Nitrogen level too high near maturity
Leaf spots (other than those caused by pathogens)	Excessive daytime radiant radation ('Detroit News') Leaf hoppers, thrips, and red spiders feeding Insecticide damage
Death of lower leaves	Shading caused by dense planting Root diseases Leaf nematodes (typically between main veins)
Bleached inflorescences (especially bronzes and pinks)	Temperatures too high during floret development Stunt virus
Intense colors in bronze and pink inflorescences	Low night temperature during floret development
Pink coloration in white inflorescences (some cultivars)	Low night temperatures during floret development Florets beginning to senesce
Quilling of either central or outer florets	Lower-than-normal night temperatures Low light intensity during floret development Water stress conditions during later inflorescence development Lower storage temperatures, <3°C (immature inflorescences)
"Green centers" in standard inflorescences	Early selection of buds of normal season production (see p. 32) A long photoperiod interrupting the early stages of bud initiation
Distorted inflorescences	Crown bud initiates but does not develop normally because of marginal short days and/or inadequate temperatures Aster yellows (see Section XIII on diseases) Tarnished-plant bug injury after the 14th short day
Delayed or no inflorescence induction	Photoperiod unfavorably long, which can be caused by stray light at night or blackout system not being effective Night temperatures too low at the time of inflorescence induction Radiant energy too low during day at time of inflorescence induction Ethylene in atmosphere (3 to 4 ppm) at the time inflorescence induction is desired Tarnished-plant bug injury during the time of inflorescence induction

remove colloids and some gases to increase water absorption thereby increasing flower longevity.

After cut stems are hydrated, they are graded into units appropriate for the market. Pompons are graded into 250- to 340-gm bunches containing several stems. Floral sprays are overwrapped with a conelike plastic sleeve to prevent damage and to facilitate packing. Standards or disbuds of equal sizes are graded in groups of 10 or 12. Tissue paper is usually placed between flowers, especially for spider or Fuji mums, to prevent intertwining of ray flowers.

Mature chrysanthemum blooms can be wrapped in plastic and stored dry for 6 to 8 weeks at temperatures of −0.5°C. After storage, stems are cut and placed in tepid water (38°C) in a cool location (4°–8°C) to rehydrate the cut stems (Post and Fischer, 1952). Higher storage temperatures (2–3°C) may be used but should not exceed 2 weeks. Recommended temperatures for truck shipments across country (3–5 days) range between 2° and 4°C. Prior to shipment flowers should be air-cooled to these temperatures to attain the desired temperature rapidly before loading the fiberboard containers in the truck (Halevy *et al.,* 1978; Rij *et al.,* 1979).

Standard chrysanthemums can be harvested in an unopened stage, i.e., when the inflorescences are only 5 to 10 cm in diameter with only a few outer ray florets unfurled. Stems are placed in a solution of sugar and a biocide to develop into a high quality inflorescence. The biocide chosen may be either 200 ppm 8 hydroxyquinoline citrate (Marousky, 1971) or 25 ppm silver nitrate plus 75 ppm citric acid (Kofranek and Halevy, 1972); the sugar concentration ranges from 2 to 5% depending on cultivar. The opening room should be 21°C with 24 hours of light from fluorescent lamps (ca. 1100 lx or 100 fc). Quality

Fig. 12. Left to right, inflorescences matured in the greenhouse on an intact plant (GH), and detached buds opened with a 3% sucrose solution in a lighted room: buds were cut in stage 2 at 5–6 cm diameter or were cut in stage 3 at 7–10 cm diameter. Six days were required for complete opening of the cut buds of 'Albatross' in a sugar solution. This experiment was conducted in the winter when the light intensity in the greenhouse was poor. Note the flatness of the inflorescence allowed to develop in the greenhouse (left); the central flowers (florets) developed poorly under low light conditions. Those cut buds opened in the 3% sugar solution had well-developed central florets which resulted in a globular inflorescence; the sugar solution was the carbohydrate substrate necessary for growth of the immature florets. (From Kofranek *et al.,* 1972.) Photograph courtesy Florists' Publ. Co.

achieved is equal to or better than those allowed to develop in the greenhouse (Kofranek *et al.,* 1972) (Fig. 12).

REFERENCES

Accati-Garibaldi, E., Kofranek, A. M., and Sachs, R. M. (1977). Relative efficiency of fluorescent and incandescent lamps in inhibiting flower induction in *Chrysanthemum morifolium* 'Albatross.' *Acta Hortic.* **68,** 51-58.

Ackerson, C. (1957). "The Complete Book of Chrysanthemums." Amer. Garden Guild and Doubleday, Garden City, New York.

Ben-Jaacov, J., and Langhans, R. W. (1969). After-lighting of chrysanthemums. *N.Y. State Flower Grow. Bull.* **285,** 1-3.

Byrne, T. G., and Pyeatt, L. E. (1976). Gibberellin sprays to increase stem length of 'May Shoessmith' chrysanthemums. *Florists' Rev.* **157**(4077), 31-32, 75.

Canham, H. E., Cockshull, K. E., and Hand, D. W. (1977). Night-break lighting with low-pressure sodium lamps. *Acta Hortic.* **68,** 63-67.

Carow, B., and Zimmer, K. (1977). Effects of change in temperature during long nights on flowers in chrysanthemum. *Gartenbauwissenschaft* **42**(2), 53-55.

Cathey, H. M. (1954). Chrysanthemum temperature study. B. Thermal modifications of photoperiods previous to and after flower bud initiation. *Proc. Am. Soc. Hortic. Sci.* **64,** 492-498.

Cathey, H. M. (1955). Temperature guide to chrysanthemum varieties. *N.Y. State Flower Grow. Bull.* **119,** 1-4.

Cathey, H. M. (1957). Chrysanthemum temperature study. F. The effect of temperature upon the critical photoperiod necessary for the initiation and development of flowers of *Chrysanthemum morifolium. Proc. Am. Soc. Hortic. Sci.* **69,** 485-491.

Cathey, H. M. (1969). *In* "Induction of Flowering—Some Case Histories," (L. T. Evans, ed.), pp. 268-290. MacMillan, Australia.

Cathey, H. M., and Borthwick, H. M. (1961). Cyclic lighting for controlling flowering of chrysanthemums. *Proc. Am. Soc. Hortic. Sci.* **78,** 545-552.

Cockshull, K. E. (1972). Photoperiodic control of flowering in the chrysanthemum. *In* "Crop Processes in Controlling Environments" (A. R. Rees, K. E. Cockshull, D. W. Hand, and G. Hurd, eds.), pp. 235-250. Academic Press, New York.

Cockshull, K. E., and Horridge, J. S. (1978). 2-Chloroethylphosphonic acid and flower initiation by *Chrysanthemum morifolium Ramat.* in short days and long days. *J. Hortic. Sci.* **53,** 85-90.

Doorenbos, J., and Kofranek, A. M. (1953). Inflorescence initiation and development in an early and late chrysanthemum variety. *Proc. Am. Soc. Hortic. Sci.* **65,** 555-558.

Farnham, D. S., Thompson, J. F., Hasek, R. F., and Kofranek, A. M. (1977). Forced-air cooling for California flower crops. *Florists' Rev.* **161**(4162), 36-38.

Furuta, T. (1954). Photoperiod and flowering of *Chrysanthemum morifolium. Proc. Am. Soc. Hortic. Sci.* **63,** 457-461.

Furuta, T., and Nelson, K. S. (1953). The effect of high night temperature on development of chrysanthemum flower buds. *Proc. Am. Soc. Hortic. Sci.* **61,** 548-550.

Halevy, A. H., Byrne, T. G., Kofranek, A. M., Farnham, D. S., Thompson, J. F., and Hardenburg, R. E. (1978). Evaluation of postharvest handling methods for transcontinental truck shipments of cut carnations, chrysanthemums and roses. *J. Am. Soc. Hortic. Sci.* **103**(2), 151-155.

Horst, R. K., and Nelson, P. E. (1977). Diseases of chrysanthemum. *Cornell Univ., Inf. Bull. 85.,* Ithaca, New York.

Kofranek, A. M. (1963). Experiments continue on cyclic lighting for greenhouse mums. *Florists' Rev.* **133**(3434), 23-24, 55.

Kofranek, A. M., and Halevy, A. H. (1972). Conditions for opening cut chrysanthemum flower buds. *J. Am. Soc. Hortic. Sci.* **97**(5), 578-584.

Kofranek, A. M., and Halevy, A. H. (1974). Minimum number of short days for production of high quality standard chrysanthemums. *HortScience* **9,** 543–544.

Kofranek, A. M., and Lunt, O. R. (1966). Mineral nutrition programs for ornamentals. *Florists' Rev.* **138**(3577), 15–16, 63–67.

Kofranek, A. M., Shepard, P., and Kubota, J. (1972). Seasonal bud opening of 'Albatross' mums. *Florists' Rev.* **151**(3902), 22–23, 58–61.

Langhans, R. W., ed. (1964). "Chrysanthemums, A Manual of Culture, Insects and Economics of Chrysanthemums. N.Y. State College of Agriculture, Ithaca, New York.

Laurie, A., Kiplinger, D. C., and Nelson, K. C. (1979). "Commercial Flower Forcing." 8th ed. McGraw-Hill, New York.

Lunt, O. R., and Kofranek, A. M. (1958). Nitrogen and potassium nutrition of chrysanthemum. *Proc. Am. Soc. Hortic. Sci.* **72,** 487–497.

Lunt, O. R., Kofranek, A. M., and Oertli, J. J. (1964). Some critical levels in *Chrysanthemum morifolium* cv. Good News. *In* "Plant Analysis and Fertilizer Problems" (C. Bould, P. Prevot, J. R. Magness, eds.), Vol. IV, pp. 398–413. W. F. Humphrey, Geneva, New York.

McCain, A. H. (1979). Chrysanthemum disease control guide. *Leaflet 2861,* Univ. of California, Berkeley.

Marousky, F. J. (1971). Handling and opening bud-cut chrysanthemum flowers with 8-hydroxyquinoline citrate and sucrose. *U.S. Dep. Agric., Mark. Res. Rep.* No. 905.

Mastalerz, J. W. (1977). "The Greenhouse Environment." Wiley, New York.

Paul, J. L. (1968). Water quality and mist propagation. *Int. Plant Prop. Soc.* **18,** 183–186.

Post, K. (1947). Year round chrysanthemum production. *Proc. Am. Soc. Hortic. Sci.* **49,** 417–419.

Post, K. (1949). "Florist Crop Production and Marketing." Orange-Judd, New York.

Post, K. (1950). Controlled photoperiod and spray formation of chrysanthemums. *Proc. Am. Soc. Hortic. Soc.* **55,** 467–472.

Post, K., and Fischer, C. W., Jr. (1952). Commercial storage of cut flowers. *N.Y. State Ext. Bull.* **853,** 1–14.

Post, K., and Kamemoto, H. (1950). A study on the number of short photoperiods required for flower initiation and the effect of interrupted treatment on flower spray formation in two commercial varieties of chrysanthemum. *Proc. Am. Soc. Hortic. Sci.* **55,** 477–482.

Rij. E., Thompson, J. F., and Farnham, D. S. (1979). Handling, precooling and temperature management of cut flower crops for truck transportation. *U.S. Dep. Agric.,* ATT-W-5.

Sachs, R. M., and Kofranek, A. M. (1979). Radiant energy required for the night break inhibition of floral initiation is a function of daytime light input in *Chrysanthemum* × *morifolium* Ramat. *HortScience* (in press).

Samman, Y., and Langhans, R. W. (1962). Interaction of temperature and photoperiodism in *Chrysanthemum morifolium. Proc. 15th Int. Hortic. Cong., Nice, France, 1958* **2,** 400–411.

Searle, S. A., and Machin, B. J. (1968). "Chrysanthemums, The Year Round," 3rd ed. Blanford Press, London.

Tjia, B. O. S., Rogers, M. N., and Hartley, D. E. (1969). Effects of ethylene on morphology and flowering of *Chrysanthemum morifolium* Ramat. *J. Am. Soc. Hortic. Sci.* **94,** 35–39.

Wienke, John. (1968). Time to avoid crown buds. *Yoder's Grow. Circle News,* No. 69, Barberton, Ohio.

Zacharioudakis, J. N., and Larson, R. A. (1976). Chemical removal of lateral buds of *Chrysanthemum morifolium* Ramat. *HortScience* **11,** 36–37.

2
Carnations

Seward T. Besemer

Introduction to Floriculture
Copyright © 1980 by Academic Press, Inc.
All rights of reproduction in any form reserved.
ISBN 0-12-437650-9

I. INTRODUCTION

A. History and Development

The carnation (Caryophyllaceae; *Dianthus caryophyllus*) has been cultivated by man for over 2000 years. About 300 B.C. Theophrastus wrote about "Dianthus," which translated from Greek means "Divine Flower," because of its delightful fragrance. The species name, *caryophyllus,* was once used as the generic name for clove, the basic fragrance of the carnation. The common name, carnation, is likely derived from "coronation," as the Greeks wove Dianthus flowers into crowns for their athletes.

The carnation is indigenous to the Mediterranean area. The native species bloomed only in spring as a reaction to increasing photoperiods and temperature. Man's improvement of the native Dianthus began in the 16th century. The perpetual flowering race of carnation, leading to the American types, was developed in France in 1840 and introduced into America in 1852. Since then many firms and individuals have developed hundreds of cultivars for commercial flower production. Without doubt, the cultivar William Sim produced in 1938 or 1939 by William Sim of North Berwick, Maine, was the greatest contribution to the present carnation industry. From that one red flowering plant there have been mutations to white, pink, orange, and several variegated forms. Today, the Sim carnation strains are grown throughout the world.

Modern carnations have little resemblance to their ancestors for now they flower year-round, have long strong stems, much larger and fuller flowers, and a greater array of colors. For additional history and detail of carnation breeding students should refer to "Carnation Production" by W. D. Holley and Ralph Baker, and also to records of the American Carnation Society.

Years ago carnations were grown in local greenhouses near population centers. New England and Long Island, New York, were once major carnation producing areas serving the Northeast markets. In 1949, 67% of the nation's carnations were produced east of the Rocky Mountains, but by 1974 the western states were producing 88%.

What happened in the United States after 1949? Very simply, the capability of passenger airplanes to carry huge quantities of freight enabled western producers to sell carnations anywhere in the country. Increased production per unit of greenhouse area, along with high flower quality, could be achieved during winter months in the areas of high light intensity, namely, in Colorado and California. The advent of plastic film also made it possible for southern California growers to produce carnations in simple structures without winter heating (Fig. 1).

An economic study (Besemer, 1966) of the United States carnation industry showed the competitive positions of seven producing areas. The return to land, capital, and management after depreciation was 24% for southern California, 13% for nothern California, 11% for Colorado, and 10% or less for all eastern

Fig. 1. Typical southern California saw-tooth carnation greenhouses covered with polyethylene film. Vent openings face into the prevailing ocean breeze for natural ventilation. (Photo by Max Clover.)

areas of the United States. The trend toward most U.S. carnations being produced in the Western states was clearly due to more favorable climate and rapid air transportation. This western competition gradually forced many eastern producers to go out of business or convert to other crops.

B. World-Wide Carnation Competition

In the world, areas of "natural climates" for carnations generally occur near 30° N or S latitude and on the western edges of the continents. Examples are southern California, the Mediterranean area, near Perth, Australia, near Valparaiso, Chile, and in the Union of South Africa. These areas all produce large quantities of carnations except for Perth. Carnations are still produced in the eastern part of Australia, where most of the population is located.

Altitude can modify latitude for other suitable carnation areas. Examples are Bogota, Colombia, mountain areas of Mexico and Central America, and parts of Kenya in Africa. Bogota is only 4° north of the equator (more often tropical) but at an altitude of 2800 m the climate for carnation production is as near ideal as any place in the world. The temperature rarely goes above 18° or below 5°C. Photoperiods also are nearly a constant 12 hours year-round. This has a dramatic effect of causing more profuse branching of carnation plants as well as longer internodes to increase flower stem length. As in other "natural" carnation climatic areas, carnations near Bogota are produced under simple structures covered with plastic film and no winter heating is required. Labor costs are extremely low compared to most other carnation-producing countries.

World competition for carnation production is following a pattern similar to other agricultural and industrial products. Politically and economically, the developing countries are seeking the technologies of the developed nations to diversify their production of goods that can in turn be exported to the developed nations in exchange for stable currency and credit. For example, Colombia's economy was once largely dependent on the export of coffee. In the agricultural sector Colombia sought crops that would utilize large amounts of labor and produce a high income per unit. Flowers met these criteria, so in the late 1960s Colombia began to produce carnations for export.

The number of Colombian carnations exported to the United States in 1970 was 16.4 million blooms and this increased rapidly to 284.6 million stems by 1977 or about 55% of U.S.-produced carnations. Colorado and California producers then experienced the same kind of competition that they had exerted earlier against the eastern U.S. producers. Because southern California has the most favorable climatic situation in the United States, it can likely compete with Colombia for a longer period of time than either Colorado or northern California.

World competition for carnations has followed a similar pattern in Europe. Carnation production in the northern sector declined on account of imports from Israel, Italy, Spain, southern France, Kenya, and the Union of South Africa. Colombia also exports flowers to Europe. On an average day at the world's largest flower auction market at Aalsmeer, Holland one can see flowers flown to Europe from all over the world.

The Dutch, despite a decrease in local carnation production owing to imports from the "natural" climates, have been able to adjust their production to other items such as potted plants. The Dutch floral industry is so important to the nation's economy that much research and promotion are financed by the industry and matched by the government. These efforts even make it possible for Holland to export some specialty items! The European consumption of flowers and potted plants is much greater per capita than in the United States. Miniature carnations represent a much higher percentage of total carnations purchased in Europe, possibly 50%, whereas miniatures represented about 12% of the U.S. carnation production in 1977.

Israel's economy also depends a great deal on agricultural exports, including flowers. Miniature carnations and roses are the two leading flowers produced.

Thus, worldwide competition in the production of carnations and other flowers will continue in the future. It is a fascinating and intricate combination of political, economical, and environmental factors but is largely made possible by the airplane. Research is now oriented toward transporting perishable flowers and produce in environmentally controlled trucks and in ships with transit periods of 2 to 4 weeks.

For the student and potential grower of carnations, it might be most valuable first to gain an understanding of world competition and the basic concepts for low fossil energy production of carnations at a price that will compete in the world market. Then the multitude of available research details of growing the crop and the techniques of marketing can be utilized and combined with actual experience.

C. Characteristics of Commercial Carnations

A commercial carnation plant is capable of producing 10 to 20 flowers per year. Each flowering stem originates from a "break" or "shoot" that emerges from one side of a lower stem node. A typical flowering stem will develop 15 to 18 nodes with two opposite leaves at each node. The leaf pairs on the nodes alternate at 180° up the stem so that the leaves extend in two planes.

The first node at the base of a stem is the most vegetative with each succes-sive upward node becoming less vegetative. This characteristic explains why most cultivars are not pinched above the sixth node. Pinching forces lateral shoots, which will in turn be vegetative long enough to produce desirable length flower stems. The upper nodes produce small shoots with flower buds, in addition to the terminal flower. On the large standard flowering cultivars these shoots must be removed for appearance and to allow the terminal flower to reach maximum size. A long-time goal of carnation breeders is to develop cultivars of standard carnations which will not produce shoots at the upper nodes. Such cultivars would make it possible to eliminate "disbudding," the most costly labor operation in carnation culture.

Miniature or spray-type cultivars depend on three or four reproductive upper nodes to produce long laterals, each with a single flower. The terminal bud is removed so that the laterals can elongate and flower at about the same time.

A good commercial carnation flower has multiple petals surrounded at the base with a cuplike calyx. Cultivars with too many petals are susceptible to "calyx splitting." In the U.S. flower market "split" carnations command about one-quarter the price of flowers with perfect calyxes. Generally, calyx splitting is less of a problem with cultivars having broad calyxes and only a moderate number of petals.

The clove fragrance of carnations has been lost in many cultivars. Generally, cultivars with lavendar-colored flowers, such as 'Safari' and 'Orchid Beauty,' still have good fragrance. Most of the miniature cultivars also are fragrant.

Until very recently carnation hybridizers paid little attention to disease resis-tance, their main goals being flower size, form, color, and vigor or productivity. Fusarium wilt (*Fusarium oxysporum* f. *dianthi*) is considered to be the number one international problem of carnations. In the 1970s a few plant pathologists and hybridizers in Europe and the United States began selecting resistant seedlings and screening existing cultivars for tolerance to Fusarium wilt. There are at least two separate strains of this organism. Tolerances to another wilt disease, *Phialophora cinerescens,* and the carnation rusts are also being in-vestigated. Development of cultivars tolerant to several diseases, with less calyx splitting, and good flower characteristics and high productivity presents a supreme challenge to the carnation hybridizer.

Many carnation cultivars are relatively unstable chimeras subject to frequent mutation. Continuous selection plus test flowering and checking on productivity must be done to maintain superior commercial cultivars. Logically, hybridization, reselection, and production testing of cultivars should be conducted at the local level in each major climatic area of carnation production.

Finally, some carnation hybridizers are beginning to question the dependence on "Sim" carnations in the future. As stated earlier, the carnation industry owes much to the Sim strains for the production of carnations with long stems and large flowers. However, production of blooms per plant has not increased substantially in many years. The Sim strains have low disease tolerance and are basically not free branching. Some hybridizers believe that plants can be developed that are faster cycling and more productive. Stems might be somewhat shorter and flowers somewhat smaller, but these types could be more suitable for mass market bouquets.

II. PROPAGATION

The majority of American carnation growers purchase disease-free, high-quality rooted cuttings from professional propagation firms. This sytem enables the flower grower to specialize in flowers and the propagator to specialize in growing cuttings.

Years ago most small flower firms propagated their own plants from vegetative lateral shoots of the flowering plants. This system is no longer recommended since diseases are easily perpetuated and a gradual decline occurs in plant vigor, productivity, and true cultivar characteristics. A flower grower having financial difficulty often resorts to propagating from flowering plants to save the cost of purchased cuttings.

A medium-to-large size flower firm, during inflationary periods, may also be tempted to propagate its own cuttings. A very careful cost analysis should be conducted before such a decision is made. For example, the cost of a purchased carnation cutting in 1958 was about 10 cents. Twenty years later, in 1978, the average cost per cutting was about 14 cents, a 40% increase. During this same period total annual production costs increased about 250%, so reducing costs of cuttings may not be the best way to reduce general production costs. Furthermore, space for stock plants, labor, storage, and the ability to meet planting schedules are all considerations for the flower grower who must decide whether to produce his own cuttings.

Few flower growers would want to contend with the lengthy procedures for maintaining "disease-free" carnation cultivars. A flower grower who decides to propagate should buy quality cuttings, which in turn would be used to establish a stock plant area. Stock plants should be grown on raised benches in pasteurized media. These plants should be kept in a vigorous and vegetative condition and maintained by drip-type irrigation to keep foliage dry. Plants should be sprayed frequently to prevent foliage diseases and insect damage. Stock plants should be used only for one season of cutting production.

The commercial propagator follows a complicated system of continuously renewing a "certified nucleus block" of plants for each cultivar. The nucleus blocks are maintained as single plants in containers grown in an isolated greenhouse, which may have filtered air and positive pressure and may only be entered by persons with sterile clothing. Certified nucleus stock is developed or renewed by starting with a few cuttings from a new seedling, a mutation, or reselected cultivar (Fig. 2).

One to 2 years may be the actual time involved in renewing the "certified nucleus block." Test flowering of units from the nucleus block may be done simultaneously with checking of cuttings for diseases and viruses. Flowering of test units to check trueness of the cultivar characteristics, to record flower production during all seasons of the year, and to select the best individuals within a cultivar is particularly necessary in the whole process of developing uniform healthy stock plants for mass production of cuttings.

A typical carnation cutting, a sturdy vegetative stem tip, 10–15 cm long with four to five visible leaf pairs, weighs about 10 gm. Cuttings should be broken from the stock plant to avoid spreading disease through the wounded ends (as with a knife). Trimming of leaves is not necessary. Cuttings may be placed in plastic-lined cartons and stored at 0°C for several weeks before rooting, or cuttings may be stuck directly in a rooting bench. A rooting hormone is used by most propagators. A typical rooting medium is a combination of 1 part peat moss and 2 parts perlite plus sufficient calcium carbonate to bring the pH near 7.0. Cuttings normally are fully rooted in about 21 days at a rooting medium temperature of 15°C. Maintaining bottom heat at a constant 21°C can reduce rooting time to 15 days.

Cuttings are spaced 5 cm apart and intermittent mist is applied on bright warm days at an interval of about 10 seconds out of every 4 to 6 minutes. Misting schedules are modified for specific conditions depending on photoperiods and light intensity, temperature, and humidity. Full sunlight is preferred for carnation rooting with proper misting.

Sanitation is also important in propagation. The rooting medium should be steam-pasteurized for each successive group of cuttings. Dipping cuttings in fungicide solutions has been generally avoided, since bacterial wilt disease can be spread with dips. Fungicide drenches can be applied over the cuttings in the bench, however.

Supplying nutrients during the rooting period is not considered to be necessary if the stock plants are maintained at an adequate level of nutrition. Foliar fertilization of cuttings has been done, but drenching of cuttings with a mild nutrient solution after root initiation is another possibility.

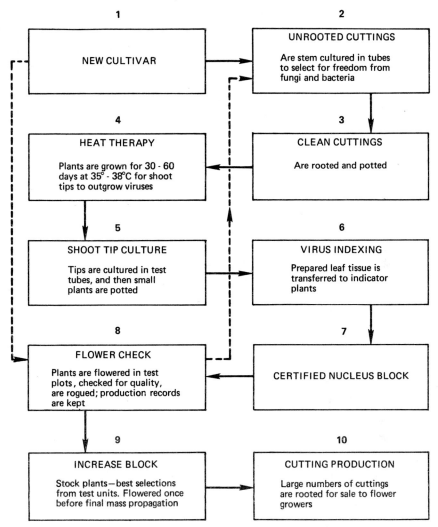

Fig. 2. A typical carnation propagation system.

III. VEGETATIVE STAGE

A. Culture of Young Plants

The goal of the carnation grower is to produce the maximum number of high quality flowers per unit area during periods of highest possible prices. A grower must begin with such decisions as soil preparation, the number of plants required, the ratio of flower colors for his projected market, plant spacing, the kind of pesticides needed and when to apply them, when to harvest, and how to prepare the flowers for market.

Years ago cuttings were planted out-of-doors in nurse beds during the summer and were pinched once or twice, and then the plants were lifted in the fall and planted in the greenhouse.

Another method was to grow young plants in peat pots. Both methods allowed the flowering crop to remain in the greenhouse 2 or 3 months longer while the young plants were being grown for replacement. These methods are seldom used today because of extra labor and space required and the increased possibility of disease and insect problems. Also, nurse bed plants and plants in peat pots are often too hard, causing a delay in growth after transplanting and cancelling out the advantage when compared to direct planting of rooted cuttings in the greenhouse.

Two-year culture is most common for standard carnations, with one-half of the greenhouse area being replanted each year. Miniature carnations are usually grown for only 1 year. Where carnations are planted directly in the ground and a high soil disease potential has developed, it often becomes necessary to replant each year.

A sandy loam or loamy sand soil is best for growing carnations. Soils with clay and silt are more difficult to manage and can be amended by incorporation of organic matter to improve aeration. Drainage of the top soil is important, ideally to a depth below 30 cm. If drainage is not adequate, drain tiles should be installed in the center of each ground bed, or box-type beds should be constructed above ground. Good soil aeration is most important to maximize carnation growth and also to provide an environment that is less conducive to diseases.

The ideal pH for carnations is between 6 and 7. The addition of calcium carbonate or dolomitic limestone corrects a too acid condition and also supplies calcium and magnesium for plant nutrition. The addition of sulfur or the regulated use of acid-forming fertilizers will help acidify soil if the pH is above 7. Based on preplant soil tests, superphosphate is generally incorporated in carnation soil prior to planting.

Three other considerations in soil preparation are the presence of nematodes, weed seed, or soil-borne disease pathogens which attack carnations. With ground-bed culture, a preplant chemical fumigation of the soil with methyl bromide. chloropicrin, combinations of these two, or products such as Vorlex and Vapam is necessary usually after the second or third year of production. For good fumigation results the soil should be moist, finely tilled as deeply as possible, and free of coarse plant debris. The fumigant must be uniformly applied at the recommended rate and covered immediately with plastic film. Chloropicrin–methyl bromide mixtures are usually injected through chisels on a tractor. Some fumigants can also be injected by hand "fumiguns." Methyl bromide can be injected through plastic tubing pulled underneath an installed plastic cover. Products such as Vapam and Vorlex can be injected, drenched, or sprinkler-applied in water before covering. The plastic cover is left in place for 48 hours or more.

Carnations have a specific susceptibility to bromide toxicity. Methyl bromide, therefore, is used only on sandy soils. Soil is aerated after removal of the plastic cover, followed by an application of 8 to 10 cm of water to leach away the bromide residue. Each of the chemical fumigants has its own characteristics; thus label instructions for use must be carefully followed and adequate time must be allowed after fumigation before carnation cuttings can be safely planted.

Steam pasteurization is the best method for treating soil in box-type benches above ground. Steam does not move deep enough in ground beds for good disease control, unless ground beds are lined with plastic and have steam-proof drainage lines. Drain lines will allow the air in the soil to be released so that steam can penetrate downward to control the deeper disease organisms or nematodes. Furthermore, aerated steam techniques of treating at temperatures of 60°–72°C have proved superior to normal steam temperatures of 100°C. When the soil is aerated, less steam is required, thus saving energy, and some beneficial soil organisms survive at the lower treatment temperatures.

B. Cultivars and Planting Schedules

For many years the leading carnation cultivars in the United States have been improved selections of 'White Sim,' 'Red Sim,' or 'Scania,' and 'Pink Sim.' New selections and new cultivars are constantly being developed. Growers also know that there are notable differences in productivity and flower quality among cultivars and within a cultivar grown in different climatic areas. Growers must rely on advice and experience of the propagation firms and other growers in the area for selecting the best cultivars available.

Years ago, a typical carnation grower planted about 30% each of red, pink, and white flowering cultivars, with the remaining 10% consisting of novelties such as yellow, orange, and variegated cultivars. As color tinting of carnations gained in popularity, the trend was to produce more white flowers. Today many growers produce at least 50% white, with red and pink making up most of the balance, except for about 5% novelties. Yellow flowering cultivars are seldom grown anymore, since yellow tints are very successful, and yellow cultivars also have never been too productive. The selection of cultivars is primarily a matter of what the market demands.

Planting schedules for carnations are the basic means of production planning for market demand. The timing of flowering from various planting dates is quite predictable under ideal environmental conditions. Planting schedules vary because of photoperiods, temperatures, and also light intensity. The shortest time between planting and peak flowering of carnations (with a single pinch) is about 110 days in southern California at latitude 33° N. This would be a planting made between April 15 and May 1. The longest time until flowering is about 150 days from a planting in late October or November. The planting dates for the earliest production will vary by 2 to 4 weeks in the United States, depending on location. Obviously, these planting dates for earliest flowering also will provide the maximum number of flowers per unit for a full year. All plantings are not made at this one time, however, because market demand does not always coincide with these peak flowering cycles.

Most carnation growers in the Northern Hemisphere make a few early plantings in April or May with the bulk of plantings made in June and July. With the use of supplemental lighting and carbon dioxide in heated greenhouses, some later plantings are possible in August or September. It has seldom been logical or economical to make carnation plantings between September and April.

The carnation grower who has good projections of his particular market demand by volume and flower colors for each day of the year has the best basis for planning the planting schedules for numbers of plants and cultivars. Despite good planning, the vagaries of weather can throw predicted production cycles off schedule by several weeks.

C. Plant Spacing

Carnations can be planted in several spacing patterns. Numerous plant density studies have compared total flower production and flower quality with spacings ranging from 25 to 180 plants/m². High-density plantings of 60 to 80 plants/m² have been used occasionally for single cropping or high yielding initial crops, but these densities seldom produce more flowers in a 2-year period than a less dense planting.

About 200 flower stems/m² of planted area is considered maximum production at any time, especially in midwinter. Since each plant will produce 4 to 6 flowering stems from a single pinch, the logical plant spacing is 35 to 45 plants/m² for 2-year culture. This is the best proved balance of plants costs, flower quality, and production.

Most carnation beds are about 1 m wide and 30 to 35 m long. Work aisles between the beds vary from 45 to 90 cm, with 60 cm being a good compromise. End aisles represent about 8% of the greenhouse area. Therefore, the actual planted area in most carnation greenhouses ranges from 50 to 65%, rarely approaching 70%.

Five carnation plant spacing patterns are shown in Fig. 3. Patterns C and D are used by most American growers. Patterns A, B, and C were developed to allow better air-flow between the plants, which in turn reduces the incidence of foliar diseases. Patterns A and C are identical arrangements of plants but the bed width and aisles differ; therefore, pattern A allows 3022 more plants/1000 m² of greenhouse. Pattern E is not common but was developed for using two plastic tubes for drip irrigation. There are many other possible plant spacings that can be adapted to different structures and equipment.

Pattern	Greenhouse width (cm)	Number of beds (width each bed, cm)	Number of aisles (width each aisle, cm)	Plants/m² of bed	Plants/1000 m² greenhouse
A	640	4 (115)	4 (45)	34.8	22,272
B	640	4 (100)	4 (60)	46.7	25,685
C	640	4 (100)	4 (60)	35.0	19,250
D	640	4 (100)	4 (60)	35.0	19,250
E	750	5 (90)	5 (60)	44.4	23,088

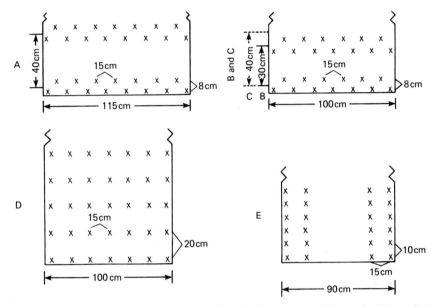

Fig. 3. Five carnation plant spacing patterns. The drawings represent the ends of long planted beds. (Drawing by Ramon Castillo.)

D. Depth of Planting and Plant Support

The depth that rooted carnation cuttings are planted can be a critical factor for success or failure. Carnations are sensitive to being planted too deep. Deep planting also increases the potential of stem rot caused by the fungus *Rhizoctonia solani*. Cuttings should be planted so that some rooting medium shows above the soil line. If the cuttings fall over, they can be straightened a few days after planting. To protect against *Rhizoctonia solani* the soil surface should be drenched at planting time with a specific fungicide for this organism.

Most modern carnation growers invest in welded wire mesh to support the carnation plants in an upright manner. Wire mesh lasts 10 to 15 years and will pay for itself in 1 or 2 years. Labor is reduced when compared to the old method of hand-stringing. Cuttings can be planted through three layers of mesh laid together on the soil surface. As the plants grow the layers are gradually raised so that the lower layer is about 15 cm above the soil, and the upper layers are spaced about 20 cm apart. Three layers of mesh will generally support a carnation crop through most of the first year. Plastic mesh is often used for the fourth and fifth support layers in the second year of culture. As plants grow the stems must be constantly "stalled" or "caged" within the respective mesh openings to maintain straight stems.

E. Pinching

Pinching is a standard practice in growing carnations. When the plants have been established 4 to 6 weeks and the lateral breaks from the lower leaf pairs are about 5 cm long, the top of the stem is snapped off by hand, usually just above the sixth node up from the bottom of the plant. Pinching should not be hurried. In early summer plantings a small bud can be visible on the main stem when plants are ready for pinching. Some carnation cultivars, particularly non-Sim types, do not require pinching for normal development of lateral shoots.

There are essentially four systems of pinching, each having an influence on timing of future flowering and on the production and quality of flowers produced. The systems are described below.

1. *Single pinch.* Only the original terminal stem is pinched. The resulting four to five vegetative shoots will elongate and flower at about the same time in the shortest possible time from planting. The plants will essentially be out of flower production until the second flower crop develops.

2. *Pinch-and-a-half.* This term is often confusing. It means a single pinch of the main stem, as above, and later when the resulting shoots are long enough, about one-half of the largest shoots on each plant are pinched. The "half pinch" actually is two or three pinches per plant at the later pinching time. This system reduces the amount of first crop flowers and provides a steady production of flowers without "peaks and valleys," at least in the first year of production.

3. *Double-pinch.* This term is also confusing. It means a single pinch of the main stem, plus a later pinch of all of the resulting shoots when they are long enough. Double pinching is seldom practiced because it tends to load the plants with too high a density of flowering stems at one time. A large first crop of flowers is produced. The numerous secondary shoots that result after the first harvest may produce many weak stems during the following crop.

4. *Single pinch plus pull pinches.* This is an unusual system, seldom practiced, but does serve a purpose. It starts with a regular single pinch. When resulting shoots are longer than for normal pinching, the growing tip is pulled out. This is in contrast to snapping off a larger part of the stem as with normal

pinching. Pull-pinching of large shoots is done frequently for as much as 2 months. This eliminates flowering of a large early crop, but provides constant production over a year or more. This system builds the plant up for rather heavy production, similar to double pinching. Probably the "single pinch plus pull-pinching" should be practiced only in high light climates.

Pinching affects flower timing and production. As mentioned earlier, future cultivars of non-Sim types may not require standard pinching. Some carnation cultivars respond to a method of just removing the flower bud on the original stem, leaving more leaf surface to encourage shoot growth.

F. Irrigation

When first planted, rooted cuttings wilt easily. Most growers sprinkle-irrigate for a few minutes several times per day if the weather is warm and bright. Roots elongate rapidly from the rooting medium and after 5 days the plants require less overhead wetting. Regular deep soil-type irrigations can usually be started 2 weeks after planting. Overhead irrigation can also be used until flower buds appear. At that time a soil-surface irrigation system should be used for the entire life of the plants, to avoid wetting flowers and foliage.

The frequency of irrigation of flowering carnation plants varies with soil texture, photoperiod, air temperature and humidity, air movement, and the mass of the plants relative to loss of water by transpiration. In general, soil should be kept moist at all times for good quality carnations. Irrigation frequency varies from about every 2 weeks in winter months to every 2 or 3 days in the summer period.

Tensiometers can be useful devices to assist the grower in evaluating the amount of water in the soil. Placement of the instruments is critical and generally such instruments should be used as irrigation guides rather than as absolute indicators of when to irrigate.

Inert media such as volanic scoria, fired clay aggregates, or gravel are suitable for carnations. Irrigation must be extremely uniform in these coarse media. Water is applied as often as three times per day and the balance of applied nutrients, including micronutrients, must be quite precise. Generally, coarse media culture is considered to be more expensive than soil culture and is a bit difficult for many growers to manage.

There are three basic methods for irrigating carnations. In southern California, where most carnations are grown directly in the ground, a furrow method is quite common. After the plants are established, furrows are made across the bed between each double row of plants. From a plastic pipe on one side of the bed water trickles from a small hole at each furrow. Another prominent irrigation system used for raised benches and ground beds is a plastic pipe around the entire perimeter of the bed. To equalize flow, water is fed by a flexible hose from an overhead line into the system at the center of the bed length. Along the perimeter pipe, spaced from 45 to 60 cm apart, are 180° flat-spray plastic

"Gates" nozzles which throw water toward the center of the bed. While also a very economical system, the Gates nozzles lack uniformity of water application, because of nozzle design and interference of the carnation plants. Adding a center line of nozzles helps to improve the water distribution. Drip-type irrigation systems are becoming more common for carnation irrigation. Drip systems offer the possibilities of more uniform water application for maintaining a more constant soil moisture level and irrigating a larger area at one time with less water, since drip systems operate at lower pressure and flow rates. There is no splashing of water and spreading of disease organisms. A well-aerated, well-drained soil and the maintenance of uniform soil moisture by irrigation are very important factors in carnation production.

G. Fertilization

Modern carnation growers fertilize young plants as soon as they are rooted in, which usually occurs a week or so after planting. Today, a regular supply of nutrients is applied at each irrigation. Research has shown that at least 200 ppm of nitrogen and potassium in solution will produce high-quality carnations. Calcium, magnesium, and phosphorus are usually supplied by the incorporation of these materials into the soil prior to planting. These three nutrients can also be supplied in the irrigation water if additional amounts are required, particularly in the second year. Some irrigation water contains adequate amounts of calcium and magnesium and has a high pH. Such water makes application of phosphorus fertilizers difficult because of chemical reactions causing precipitates, which in turn cause plugging of fine orifices in irrigation systems. Using 75% phosphoric acid will acidify irrigation water to reduce the formation of precipitates.

The nutrients for carnations are obtained from readily available soluble fertilizers combined in a concentrated solution. A fertilizer proportioner or injector dilutes the concentrate with the irrigation water to provide the proper amount of nutrients for delivery to the plants. Most injectors work on a dilution ratio of 1:100 or 1:200.

The most common materials used for supplying nitrogen and potassium are combinations of potassium nitrate with either calcium nitrate or ammonium nitrate. Charts are available from universities and propagation firm manuals for growers to make fertilizer concentrate solutions.

Some micronutrients may also be required, depending on the type of soil and the mineral content of the irrigation water. The most likely micronutrients to be added are iron, zinc, copper, manganese, molybdenum, and boron. Periodic laboratory analysis of plant tissue is advisable to determine whether micronutrients are needed, and also whether the major nutrients are adequate.

The soluble salt content of the soil also should be checked frequently. High salt levels can be very detrimental to plant growth and quality. Occasional leaching may be required to reduce salt levels in the soil.

Carnations are relatively slow growing plants. Descriptions of nutrient deficiency symptoms are available, but when these symptoms appear on a commercial crop it often takes a long time to correct the problem. Therefore, it is of utmost importance for the carnation grower to apply nutrients in the right amount and frequency and to have the nutrition monitored by a capable laboratory.

H. Young Plant Problems

More will be written about pest and disease problems of carnations later in this chapter, but young plants must be checked frequently for certain early problems. Under moist conditions, outbreaks of fungus diseases such as Alternaria branch rot or leaf spot and Fusarium stem rot are possible. With good air movement these diseases are seldom a problem. Growers should immediately apply specific foliar fungicides as soon as symptoms of these diseases occur.

Young plants can also be attacked by aphids, spider mites, thrips, several species of moth larvae, or slugs and snails. Suitable protective pesticides should be applied to control these pests. Thrips especially can cause insidious distortion of young shoots and protective sprays must be applied in advance of injury.

In certain soil conditions watermold fungi will cause delays in young plant growth. Fungicide drenches of the soil can be beneficial if these conditions exist. Proper irrigation schedules, nutrient application, and prevention of soluble salt accumulation in the soil are also important ways to prevent hardening of young plants, which in turn can delay their growth.

IV. THE FLOWERING STAGE

A. Environmental Factors

Light is the environmental factor that most influences the rate of growth and flowering of carnations during the year. Photoperiods and light intensity at different latitudes have much to do with the economic shifting of carnation production to the "natural" climates of the world.

Many areas do not have sufficient hours of winter light for quality carnation production. Possible exceptions to that statement are Colorado and northern California, but even those areas experience some weakness in stem quality during winter months. Since much of the traditional market demand for carnations is in the winter period, the amount and quality of winter light in the various production areas become an important competitive factor.

About 21.5 klx (2000 fc) as determined on a Weston photometer is considered to be the minimum natural light intensity for adequate photosynthesis of carnations. Light intensity in many areas of the world will go as high as 150 klx. These intensities can certainly exceed the photosynthetic capability of carnation plants, perhaps because of other limiting environmental factors. Large amounts of red light wavelengths, the main heat source of sunlight, will cause heat injuries to carnation flowers. Some shading of carnations has been practiced in summer months in areas of high light intensity.

The importance of light on carnation growth is best illustrated by removing a row of 1-year-old plants across a carnation bed. A production record per plant is readily determined by counting the stem stubs of harvested flowers. The "outside" plants receiving the most light and space along the walk aisles produce twice the number of flowers as the middle plant. The row across the bed produces a nearly perfect production curve based on the light received and relative space per plant.

Temperature is the second most important factor for carnations and is directly associated with light energy. Several studies have documented the effects of seasonal photoperiods and temperature on the growth rate and flower production of carnations. Figure 4 shows the annual growth rate in southern California for carnation buds 7 mm in diameter until they are harvested. This comparison was made in greenhouses heated to a minimum night temperature of 10°C in winter months versus unheated greenhouses. The overall effect of photoperiods and the effect of temperature are illustrated in Fig. 4.

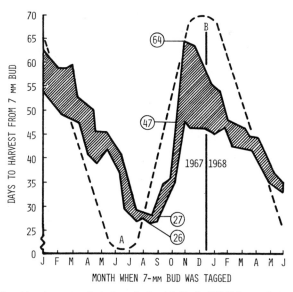

Fig. 4.   The relationship of seasonal photoperiods at latitude 32° N in southern California to the growth rate of 7-mm-diameter carnation buds in days to harvest. Seasonal photoperiods inversely plotted: A = 10 hours, B = 14+ hours. Shaded area equals difference in growth rate caused by temperature. (Drawing by Ramon Castillo.)

Cooling of greenhouses with evaporative pads and exhaust fans will increase production and flower quality in areas where summer temperatures exceed 20°C. As energy becomes less available and more costly the "natural" climates, where no heating or cooling are needed, become more attractive from an economic standpoint.

Carbon dioxide, also a very necessary ingredient of photosynthesis, can be depleted in a closed greenhouse environment. This is particularly so on cold winter days when no outside air is used for ventilation. In glass- and Fiberglas-covered greenhouses in more northern latitudes, it is common practice to inject carbon dioxide during daylight hours. Concentrations three to four times normal atmospheric levels of carbon dioxide are frequently used. Additional carbon dioxide under suitable conditions will increase flower production from 10 to 20%. Similar responses were demonstrated in southern California but the use of additional carbon dioxide was deemed impossible in a milder climate. Where day temperatures commonly reach 18°–20°C on winter days, greenhouse ventilation is necessary from about 9 A.M. to 4 P.M. This does not allow sufficient time for retaining increased carbon dioxide levels during the photoperiod. Furthermore, if carbon dioxide is injected at the expense of less ventilation, excess condensate in polyethylene greenhouses creates conditions that are ideal for fungus diseases. Thus, as with greenhouse cooling, the use of elevated carbon dioxide levels seems to be restricted to controlled environment in more extreme climatic areas.

B. Control of Flowering

As already mentioned, the control of flowering starts with planting schedules and time or method of pinching. The plants are then subject to light and temperature conditions, carbon dioxide concentration, and availability of water and nutrients. Several of these environmental factors can be manipulated to control time of flowering and the amount and quality of flower production.

A carnation shoot changes from a vegetative to a reproductive condition when it has about six pairs of leaves. When a flower bud is initiated the shoot begins to stretch more rapidly with increasing length of internodes. The photoperiod has a direct effect on the rate of flowering as well as on the characteristics of stems. Plants grown under 8-hour photoperiods have longer stems, slightly larger flowers, and produce more lateral shoots. Those grown under 16-hour photoperiods have shorter stems and fewer lateral shoots.

Artificial lighting of carnations is a useful practice for advancing the flowering time of peak crops for special markets. Lighting can be fitted into the whole schedule of planting and pinching. Some cultivars respond well to lighting whereas others do not. Lighting can also be used occasionally to force more flowers into the late spring market period, rather than in summer when the market is often weakest.

Lighting is a procedure that requires much study of the existing literature.

The carnation crop has the maximum number of shoots between 15 and 25 cm in length. The best time to begin lighting is when light is provided continuously from dusk to dawn by 150 W incandescent bulbs (General Electric PS 30/2) about 10.7 m apart and about 4 m above the plants in the center of four beds of carnations. About 0.02 klx (2 fc) is considered to be sufficient light at any location at plant level. Special fluorescent lamps can also be used. Cyclic lighting with incandescent lamps on a schedule of 30 seconds on and 30 seconds off has also been effective. A single 2- or 3-week lighting period is most often employed, although a second lighting period after a 2- or 3-week interval is also used. Too many weeks of lighting will delay or practically eliminate the formation of new lateral shoots for the next crop after the lighted crop. Lighting is not very effective unless minimum night temperatures of 10–12°C can also be maintained.

Another method for control of flower cropping is pruning or "hedging" of plants. This procedure is most often used on 1-year-old plants to eliminate production in midsummer when flower demand is poor. Hedging also renews the plants for the second year of production and is practiced on only a portion of a total planting. Plants should be hedged no later than the summer solstice. The resulting number of shoots is very dense and the first heavy crop of flowers is best harvested a few weeks before the winter solstice so that the young shoots of the following crop will have sufficient light during short winter photoperiods. Electric hedge shears are used to prune the 1-year-old plants in "green wood" about 25 to 30 cm above the soil level. Since most active foliage is removed, irrigation should be withheld about 1 week before hedging and the pruned plants should not be irrigated again until new shoots appear, a period of 3 to 4 weeks. Two-year-old plants are seldom hedged, but if so, they should be pruned about 45 to 50 cm above the soil level. All pruning debris should be removed from beds for sanitation purposes.

The manner of flower harvesting can also affect crop timing and the total number of flowers produced. The first flower crop from early summer plantings at 30° or greater latitude is normally short stemmed, owing to long photoperiods and warm temperatures. Growers often make the mistake of cutting this first crop too low so that many lower lateral shoots are lost. These are the shoots forming for the second flower crop. The short-stemmed flowers of the early crop are usually harvested in a summer marketing period when prices are lowest. It is better to sell short flowers and to retain two or three lower shoots below each cut, which will result in good quality flowers during a favorable winter market period.

Flower stems can be cut as long as desired in midwinter and early spring. Sacrificing lower shoots at this time will eliminate midsummer production and will provide extra-fancy stems during the spring market period. Just before the summer solstice lower shoots are again retained below the cut for late summer and fall flower production. If summer markets for carnations could be improved, the practice of eliminating lower shoots would not be necessary.

C. Disbudding and Calyx Banding

Standard carnation cultivars must be disbudded by removing lateral buds down to about six nodes below the terminal flower bud. The best time for disbudding is when the terminal bud is about 15 mm in diameter and the first bud below the terminal bud is large enough to be easily removed. Buds should be grasped with the finger tips and removed with a downward circular motion. If buds are pulled straight downward there is a danger of injuring the stem or a leaf, which may result in a bent neck below the flower. With miniature carnations, the terminal or center bud is removed to allow the lateral flowers to develop. Disbudding is a continuous procedure and is the single most costly labor operation in carnation culture.

Calyx splitting (Fig. 5) occurs in many carnation cultivars whenever the temperatures are too cool during the growth of the flower bud. A few warm days just before the flower is ready for harvest can cause a rash of calyx splitting. In the U.S. market, flowers with split calyxes are traditionally reduced in value. This is unfortunate since many consumers do not recognize split carnations as inferior. Nevertheless, the growers avoid producing splits by placing a band around each bud when the bud just barely shows a pinpoint opening at the tip. Although rubber bands and wire-paper "twistems" have been used in the past, the latest preferred method is banding with 6 mm wide clear plastic tape. Other types of bands must be removed at harvest but the tape is left in place. Banding must be done on all buds when conditions for calyx splitting exist. Banding should not be done when buds are too small, as an "hour-glass"-shaped bud will result. The band also must be placed around the largest diameter of the bud or about halfway from top to bottom.

Calyx splitting often occurs at the time when flower quality is best, since growth has proceeded with cool temperatures and bright days. When buds form during cool periods (temperatures less than 10°C) extra whorls of petals neu. These fat buds are called "bullheads" (Fig. 5) and are very suscep-

Fig 5. Er nie effects on carnation buds. Left to right: calyx splitting, normal, slabside, bullhead. (Photo by Mac Clover.)

tible to calyx splitting. Another flower malformation during cool periods is known as a "slabside" (Fig. 5). The bud does not open evenly so that petals protrude on one side only, giving a lopsided shape to the flower. This problem can often be avoided in heated greenhouses but not when temperatures are too cool.

D. Harvesting Flowers

Flowers are harvested by cutting with a sharp knife or with small pruning shears. Care must be used to pull the flower up through the support layers. Many growers still harvest by accumulating an armful of flowers as they move along the aisle. A better method is to use small frame carts with canvas liners (Fig. 6). The cart can be attached by a line to the worker's belt and dragged behind or pushed ahead of the worker. This allows both hands for cutting the flowers, which are placed one by one in the canvas liner. Several liners then

Fig. 6. Frame cart with canvas holder for gathering carnations in the greenhouse aisle. Larger cart in background for transporting several holders to the grading room. (Photo by Max Clover.)

can be hung on a larger cart at the main cross aisle for delivery to the grading area (Fig. 6). Two growers in southern California installed a simple cable and pulley overhead conveyor system in a rectangular pattern throughout the greenhouse range. The canvas liners of flowers could be attached to the cable by hanging spring clamps. Workers in the grading room could activate a push-button to the electric motor and bring the canvas liners of flowers on the conveyor to the grading room as needed. This complete system of using picking carts and the conveyor was calculated to reduce harvesting labor by 2½ persons per hectare of greenhouses. Several manual handlings of the flowers were also eliminated, thus reducing losses from breakage.

Standard carnation flowers have traditionally been harvested when the outer petals have unfolded nearly perpendicular to the stem. In recent years the trend has been to harvest flowers in a tighter condition. Advantages of bud harvest will be discussed later.

Spray-type carnations are cut when two flowers are open and the remaining buds are showing color. The partially developed buds will continue to open when exposed to room temperature and the stems are in a preservative solution.

V. PROBLEMS AND THEIR CONTROL

A whole chapter could be written just on diseases, pests, and all the environmental and physiological problems that can occur on carnations. Some mention has already been made about problems caused by temperature.

A. Invertebrate Pests

The four main groups of invertebrate pests requiring control in most carnation production areas are aphids, spider mites, thrips, and moth larvae. The latter include the looper, the carnation leaf roller, the orange tortrix, the tobacco budworm, and the beet armyworm.

Generally, aphids occur during cool conditions and cause distortion to carnation shoots or buds. A relatively low volume of insecticide spray applied over the tops of the plants will control aphids. Spider mites typically are a problem during dry, warm, summer conditions and feed on the undersides of the foliage as well as on the buds. A thorough high-volume spray application of a suitable miticide must be applied from the bottom of the plants. Because few chemicals control the egg stage, three miticide applications about 10 days apart are necessary for spider mite control. Some species of thrips feed on carnation foliage, whereas flower thrips cause a particular injury to flower petals. Since flower thrips are very slender the adults can enter the pin hole tip of a bud and lay their eggs inside, and the hatching young causes much rasping and discoloration of the petals long before the flowers are ready for harvest. Systemic insecticides, such as dimethoate, have been extremely useful in controlling flower thrips. Dimethoate can be applied in the irrigation water, about every 3 weeks, or spray applications can also be made. Dimethoate also controls aphids. The moth larvae are generally active during warm temperature conditions. Screening of controlled environment greenhouses keeps out most of the adult moths. Moth larvae are easiest to control when they are young. Thus sprays should be applied as soon as leaf damage first appears. Weekly sprays may be required during high populations of moths in natural environment carnation production.

Other insects that may affect carnations are the carnation leaf miner, the carnation bud or shoot mite, and even termites. Although ants are not a direct problem to carnations, ants encourage aphids and the spread of diseases. Ants are easily controlled with insecticide granules or sprays.

Snails and slugs are also common pests of carnations. They are readily controlled by baits, granules, sprays.

Nematodes are almost never a problem in pasteurized soil in raised beds. However, in sandy soils and in ground beds in a climate such as southern California, nematodes can cause severe plant losses. The root-knot nematode, *Meloidogyne* species, is usually the most troublesome. Nematode injury to carnation roots also encourages the spread of soil-borne wilt diseases. Nematodes are best controlled by soil pasteurization or chemical fumigation before planting. Some control is possible with postplant drenches of selective nematocides.

B. Diseases

The major carnation diseases, world-wide, are Fusarium wilt (*Fusarium oxysporum f. dianthi*) and Phialophora wilt (*Phialophora cinerescens*). These two diseases are systemic, usually invading the plant from contaminated soil, the fungi moving into the roots and upward in the vascular system. The plugging effect of the fungi in the water-conducting tissues results in a severe yellowing of the foliage and plant wilting. Bacterial wilt (*Pseudomonas caryophylli*) is also a systemic disease, but is generally less common. Fusarium and bacterial wilt are favored by warm temperatures, whereas Phialophora wilt is favored by cool soil temperatures. The best control for these diseases is soil pasteurization or cheical fumigation of the soil before planting, the sue of disease-free plants, and general sanitation in the greenhouse.

The stem rot carnation diseases are *Rhizoctonia solani, Fusarium roseum,* and another disease reported in southern Europe, *Phytophthora parasitica.* Rhizoctonia stem rot characteristically rots the stem of a young plant at the soil line. Fusarium stem rot also rots the stem at the soil line or higher on the plant. Despite soil pasteurization or fumigation, the soil surface should be dusted or sprayed, or the young basal stems should be sprayed with suitable fungicides immediately after planting. Plant propagators also have a responsibility to prevent stem rot infections by applying fungicides to stock plants on a regular basis.

The foliage diseases most common to carnations are Alternaria leaf spot or branch rot (*Alternaria dianthi* and *A. Dianthicola*), rust (*Uromyces caryophyllinus*), greasy blotch (*Zygophials jamaicensis*), and fairy-ring leaf spot (*Heterosporium echinulatum*). Three diseases that affect flower buds are gray mold (*Botrytis cinerea*), Fusarium bud rot (*Fusarium tricinctum*), and calyx rot (*Pleospora herbarum*). There are also other species of fungi that cause foliage and flower problems. These fungi are generally favored by high moisture conditions and discouraged by good air circulation. Fungicide sprays are necessary when prolonged environmental conditions are favorable to the progress of the diseases.

It would be fair to state that most commercial carnations in the world contain some virus. In fact, many carnations are infected by more than one virus, complexes that are difficult to identify. As stated early in this chapter, conscientious propagators use heat treatments, tip culture, and indexing on indicator plants in attempts to eliminate viruses from carnation stock. Despite attempts, viruses continue to escape the system, and some are rapidly regenerated by insect vectors, cutting tools, and handling in the flower production process. The effect of viruses on vigor and productivity of carnation plants is not well known, but most virologists believe that viruses can substantially reduce flower yield. The effect on quality is more obvious, since foliage injury caused by some viruses is so unattractive that the result is an unsaleable product.

The five main viruses of carnations are vein mottle, streak, mottle, ring spot, and etched ring. Vein mottle is spread by aphids, whereas ring spot and mottle are spread by cutting tools and handling. Streak and etched ring are not spread by tools or handling and vectors are unknown. There is no known control for viruses once flowering plants are infected.

C. Other Disorders

Weeds are seldom a problem in greenhouse carnation culture, as most weeds are killed by steam pasteurization or chemical fumigation. In nonscreened natural environment structures, even birds, ground squirrels, gophers, and domestic pets have been known to cause considerable crop damage. Poison baits, plastic fences on the greenhouse perimeters, noise makers, shiny objects, or traps are devices to handle one or more of these unusual pest problems.

Crop damage by people working in a carnation crop is seldom mentioned in most texts. One grower in southern California claims that one 15-minute worker training session per week would increase profit several thousand dollars per year by reducing losses from flower stem breakage. This profit increase also includes teaching workers exactly at what height to cut a flower stem so that future flowers from that stem are not sacrificed. Improper handling of carnation plants, poor harvesting procedures, and careless grading and packing of flowers cause more dollar losses than most growers are willing to admit. Workers should also be trained to understand the disease problems and how diseases are spread, to emphasize the importance of sanitation in the greenhouse.

There are numerous other disorders quite common to carnation culture. Examples are plant burn by hot water from leaking heat pipes; injury from improper applications of pesticides; over- and underwatering; salinity; fumigant toxicity; air pollution from imperfect combustion of gas heaters; herbicide injury from improper application; use of the wrong herbicide or fertilizer contaminated with herbicides; overfertilization; nutrient deficiency; incorrect pH of the soil; heat damage; cold damage; and many others.

VI. HANDLING OF THE FINISHED PRODUCT

A. Grading

Some carnation growers can produce a quality product but then ruin its saleability after harvest. It has been estimated that postharvest activities represent about 30% of the total cost before marketing. Good grading and bunching can enhance high-quality flowers and bring premium prices over flowers of equal quality that are poorly graded. Good grading cannot, however, improve a poor quality product. Unfortunately, since most carnations are sold unseen by the wholesale buyer, the "same grade" from two different producers may be sold at the same price, but in reality should be two grades and two prices. In this case, the high-quality producer is losing money at the expense of the poor quality producer or the poor quality producer is gaining more than is rightfully due. These are the inequities and problems of independent grading by each producer, and differences are quite common.

Central grading, where flowers from several producers are brought to one location and graded by trained and supervised impartial graders, can have the advantage of achieving more uniform grading whereby each producer profits according to his ability. Central grading theoretically should be slightly more economical and also allows the producer to concentrate on carnation culture, rather than on two major activities.

Various standardized grades have been proposed over the years, all based on a physical measurement (length of stem, diameter of flower, or even weight of stem and flower). Although these criteria have some relationship to quality, no method has yet been developed to replace human judgment. The factors requiring human decisions in flower grading are freedom from diseases and insects, other blemishes on flowers or foliage, sleepiness of flowers, stem crooks, slabsides and bullheads, split calyxes, and faded colors. Sorting machines are now available for grading by length of stem, but all other factors are still determined by human decision.

The most recent standard carnation grades developed by the Society of American Florists are given in the following tabulation:

Factors	1 Blue (fancy)	2 Red (standard)	3 Green (short)
Minimum flower diameter (mm)	Tight—50 Fairly tight—62 Open—75	Tight—44 Fairly tight—56 Open—69	Tight—none Fairly tight—none Open—none
Minimum length (cm) (overall)	55	43	30
Stem strength	Shall be determined by holding the stem horizontally at a point 25 mm above the minimum length for the grade, and the deviation of the flower head shall not be more than 30° below the horizontal plane with the natural curvature of the stem down		
Defects	Blue grade shall consist of full, symmetrical flowers reasonably free from defects such as slabsides, bullheads, blown heads, singles, sleepy appearance, splits, discoloration, insects, diseases, and other damage. Blue grade shall have an essentially straight stem free from disbuds, damage or discoloration by insects, disease, and other means. Red grade, other than diameter of flower and length of stem, shall have the same requirements as the blue grade with *moderate* variations		

Despite this specific classification system, no method has been devised to predict the postharvest life of carnations. Postharvest life varies widely depending on the environmental conditions and the method of handling flowers after harvest. In most climatic areas, summer and winter carnation flowers have about half the postharvest life as fall and spring flowers. The latter, grown under the most favorable light and temperature conditions, are firmer and contain more dry matter and more carbohydrates, the stems are heavier and thicker, and the flowers are larger with more intense color.

Most carnations are still hand-graded as soon as they are brought from the greenhouse. Since they are slightly flaccid, there is less breakage from handling. Usually the flowers are separated into piles of the three grades, plus a fourth lot of culls. Each grade is then bunched in units of 25 stems. Each bunch is firmly bound at the base with a "twistem," string, tape, or rubber band, and at least one other place below the flowers. Three basic arrangements of the flower heads have been used in the trade: (1) a flat fan design; (2) a round design with all flowers on the same plane; and (3) a shingle or tailored arrangement with five rows of five blooms each, two rows above and two rows just below (Fig. 7). The tailored bunch requires more labor, but packs well in cartons for shipping. A box device is often used to arrange the flowers in the bunch design. A patented box in Denver, Colorado, also includes an electronic "eye" so that the stems are automatically counted as they are laid in the box. A bunching ma-

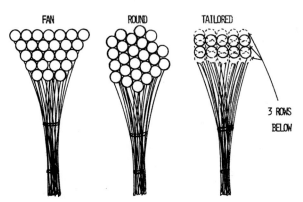

Fig. 7. Three types of carnation bunches for marketing 25 stems. (Drawing by Ramon Castillo.)

chine was also developed in the Denver area. The machine did not gain general industry acceptance because of its high cost and intricate mechanisms.

B. Conditioning of Flowers

Postharvest life of carnations can be substantially increased by conditioning the flowers after grading and bunching. The best carnation flower longevity can be achieved with the following procedure:

1 Trim the stem ends after bunching.

2. Immediately place the stem ends in plastic buckets of a preservative solution of warm (37°C) pure water, deionized or similar quality, containing the recommended amount of a preservative product formulated for carnations. Recipes are also available from several universities for making conditioning solutions. A good preservative solution for carnations should be acidic (pH 4.5) with 2 to 5% sucrose and a biocide not phytotoxic to carnations.

3. The flowers should be kept in the preservative solution at a room temperature of 21°C for 2 to 4 hours, then placed in a refrigerated room at 0°–2°C for 12 to 24 hours. The flowers are then properly conditioned and ready for market.

Hundreds of flower-keeping experiments have been conducted with various chemicals for carnation-conditioning solutions. Unfortunately all experiments did not compare standard treatments using deionized water and flowers harvested at the same time of year. Favorable responses have been reported with several kinds of biocides, kinetins, growth regulators, and metal ions. Increasing the amount of sugar, up to 12% in the solution, has produced incremental increases in carnation longevity when flowers are left in the solution. "Pulsing" flowers in 10% sugar solutions (with a biocide) for 12–18 hours before marketing is another technique of rapidly loading the stems to improve performance at the consumer level even when a preservative solution is not used again. Some carnation clones are damaged if left too long in a high sugar solution.

Other chemicals also can be injurious if concentrations of prepared preservatives are raised above the recommended solution content.

C. Tinting

Tinting of carnation flowers is a common practice. Many colors are possible, including green, blue, brown, and black, the colors absent in natural cultivars.

Carnations absorb dye solutions through the stems and into the flowers, leaving an attractive frosted edge on the petals. White cultivars are used for tinting, although light pink flowers can be used for some tints.

Special floral dyes are available for tinting. A concentrated liquid or powder is mixed in small amounts with warm (37°C) pure water. One must first experiment with various amounts of dye because recipes have been kept secret. Two or three basic dyes can be combined to create additional color tones. A wetting agent is also added to increase water movement in the stems.

Flowers for tinting are purposely left out of water for a few hours as slightly flaccid flowers more readily absorb the dye solution. Stems are recut before they are plunged into 8 to 10 cm of solution in a plastic bucket. Sufficient dye is absorbed by the flowers in 20 to 40 minutes. The degree of tint is controlled by the length of time the stems remain in the solution and concentration of the dye. After tinting the flowers can be kept in a regular preservative solution and refrigerated.

D. Storage

Open flowers of high quality harvested without exposure to extreme temperatures and without petal injury from botrytis or chemicals, can be stored for 2 to 4 weeks before marketing. Bud storage has even greater potential for several reasons. Buds are less likely to have been injured or infected by disease; buds are easier to handle, take less room in storage, and are considerably more tolerant of ethylene, which causes carnation sleepiness.

Storage allows some flexibility for accumulating a supply of flowers during a moderate market period and for having a greater supply during a strong demand period. With open flowers, 24 hours should be allowed after removal from storage for grading, bunching, and conditioning. "Tight" buds with little petal color showing may require 4 to 5 days to open and preparation for marketing. Buds with petals straight up from the calyx require about 2 days to open.

Buds or open blooms are harvested and placed directly into shipping cartons lined with polyethylene film. The full cartons should be precooled or placed a few at a time without lids in the storage room until cool. The plastic is then loosely folded on top of the stems and the lids closed. To ensure good air circulation in storage, the cartons should be stacked with slats between, and the stacks should be kept a short distance from the storage room walls.

The cold-storage room must be properly insulated with an outside vapor barrier, and should be designed to maintain a uniform 0°C with good air circulation and a constant relative humidity of 90 to 95%.

Carnations, especially buds, have been successfully stored for 8 to 10 weeks. No more than half this time is recommended. Some cultivars do not store well. After removal from storage, the stems of open flowers or buds are recut and then placed into warm conditioning solution. After several hours, open flowers are graded, bunched, and returned to the solution for refrigeration before marketing. Stored buds (or newly harvested buds) in their buckets of solution should be held in an opening room with constant light (minimum of 10.8 klx) and a temperature of about 21°C. After opening the buds are graded, bunched, retrimmed, and returned to the solutions for refrigeration before marketing.

Hypobaric, or low-pressure cold storage, is another method for holding carnations. Additional storage time over regular cold storage is somewhat questionable, as well as the question of cost. Ethylene scrubbers or absorbers in cold storage may be helpful although not absolutely necessary if flower and bud quality and storage conditions are properly maintained.

E. Shipping to Market

Carnations are most often sold at an agreed price at the production area with the wholesale buyer paying the additional cost of packing and transportation. Cartons of flowers are also sent on consignment to major markets. The shipper then pays the expenses and hopes for a fair return, not always knowing whether or not the flowers will be sold. Flowers are also sold locally to wholesalers or retailers, or at a terminal flower market.

About 800 carnations are packed in a standard size carton 30 cm high, 50 cm wide, and 122 cm long. The bunches are laid flat with the flower heads at each end of the carton. Two cross cleats in the center of the carton lock the bottom and top layers of stems to prevent shifting of the flower heads against the carton ends.

Although "precooling" of perishable produce has been a common practice for years, commercial precooling of flowers did not occur until 1978. Precooling cartons after packing reduces losses during transport and generally maintains original quality and potential consumer life of the flowers. Without precooling, flowers will generate sufficient heat from respiration to literally "cook" them during transit. Even refrigerated flowers warm up in the few minutes it takes to pack them in a carton at room temperature; thus all cartons should be precooled before shipping. Precooling also makes it possible to pack flowers directly in the field, remove the field heat rapidly, and have the flowers ready for market (Fig. 8).

Precooling chambers can be incorporated within a properly designed refrigerated room. Additional equipment capacity is required for rapid cooling. Cold

Fig. 8. Precooling system for packed cartons of flowers prior to shipment. Air at 0°C and 95 to 100% relative humidity is forced from cooling chamber through end vents of cartons. (Photo by Max Clover.)

air is forced through vent holes in the ends of flat cartons or the sides of upright cartons.

The vent holes, with flaps, should equal 5% of the end areas. The flaps are usually closed after cooling, and cartons should be well insulated when going by airfreight or other non-refrigerated transport. The flaps are removed if cartons are kept in refrigeration or transported in refrigerated vehicles.

Cartons should be precooled with air at 0°C and at least 95% relative humidity. Air velocity through the cartons should be in the range of 180–275 m/minute. Flowers must be packed so that paper or plastic material between the layers or near the flower heads does not restrict air flow. Dense flowers, such as carnations, may require 30–60 minutes to cool thoroughly.

Precooling flowers by growers and wholesale shippers, plus refrigerated transportation, has greatly improved the movement of flowers through the marketing system. Intermediate wholesalers and retailers should continue to keep flowers refrigerated and also to place them in solutions of pure water and preservatives. The consumer should be provided care information by the retailer and also a supply of preservative with each flower purchase. Experiments have clearly demonstrated that proper temperature conditions and the use of preservatives at each step from grower to consumer will ensure maximum consumer satisfaction. There is no reason why the consumer cannot expect and derive at least 7 to 10 days of enjoyment from fresh carnations.

VII. THE FUTURE

Many changes have taken place in the carnation industry, worldwide, since airplanes began to be used to transport flowers and since the introduction of plastics for greenhouse construction in the early 1950s. These influences were mentioned at the beginning of this chapter. The competition in the future certainly will intensify between traditional carnation production areas and the newer areas of "natural" carnation climates. Those areas with cheaper labor and government subsidies will prevail, unless more labor-saving systems and improved production can occur in the more traditional production areas.

Carnations should continue to be a major consumer item because of the large array of colors (all colors with tinting), a desirable fragrance, and excellent consumer life. Unfortunately, the labor requirement for carnation culture is greater than for most other flower crops. Large and level production units can certainly utilize more machinery in crop removal and soil preparation and replanting. Natural climate areas will continue to have the enormous advantages of no heating requirement and the use of cheap plastic film structures. The hand operations of disbudding, banding splits, placing plants in their support mesh, and harvesting may never be replaced by mechanization. Plastic irrigation systems have eliminated hand irrigation with a hose.

Plant breeders may yet produce standard carnation cultivars without lateral buds and with calyxes that do not split. Handling of flowers from the greenhouse and methods of grading, bunching, and packing for shipment can be further streamlined.

The market for standard carnations is likely to continue. However, the greatest potential in the future may be increased production of miniature carnations. Although more plants are used per unit of planting area, the labor requirement is substantially less. Disbudding is minimal, no calyx banding is required, the stems can be bunched as harvested, and the profit per unit area is greater, as compared to standard carnations. The American public is scarcely familiar with miniature carnations, whereas European consumers seem to prefer them. Miniature carnations are a natural bouquet type of flower and should be sold in high traffic locations for daily consumer purchases.

Again, plant breeders will likely develop cultivars of miniature carnations which are freer branching, more disease resistant, and more highly productive.

Improved display, better conditioning and temperature control from producer to consumer, improved containers for handling bouquets, and industry promotion could create additonal demand for carnations.

REFERENCES

Besemer, S. T. (1966). An economic analysis of the carnation industry in the United States. Masters Thesis, Colorado State Univ., Fort Collins, Colorado.

Besemer, S. T. (1974). Rate of carnation flower development for San Diego County. *Report #2. Cooperative Ext.,* Univ. of California, CP 261, 1–5.

Besemer, S. T. (1975). Carnation culture in San Diego County. *Cooperative Ext.,* Univ. of California, CP 195, 1–13.

Farnham, D. S., Thompson, J. F., Hasek, R. F., and Kofranek, A. M. (1977). Forced-air cooling for California flower crops. *Florists' Rev.* **161**(4162), 36–8.

Gloeckner, F. C., and Co., Inc. "Carnation Manual," 10th ed. pp. 1–45. Gloeckner, New York.

Guilfor, R. F., Jr., and Lundquist, A. L. (1971). Transport and handling of carnations cut in the bud stage—potential advantages. *Agric. Res. Serv., U.S.D.A. Report No. 899,* 1–10.

Holley, W. D., and Baker, R. (1963). "Carnation Production," pp. 1–142. W. C. Brown, Dubuque, Iowa.

Langhans, R. W., ed. (1961). "Carnations—A Manual of the Culture, Insects, Diseases and Economics of Carnations," pp. 1–107. Cornell Univ. Press, Ithaca, New York.

Maxie, E. C., Farnham, D. S., Mitchell, F. G., Sommer, N. F., Parsons, R. A., Snyder, R. G., and Rae, H. L. (1973). Temperature and ethylene effects on cut flowers of carnation (*Dianthus caryophyllus* L.). *J. Am. Soc. Hortic. Sci.* **98,** 568–572.

McCain, A. H. (1975). Carnation disease control guide. *Cooperative Ext.,* Univ. of California, CP 2723, 1–4.

Rij, R. E., Thompson, J. F., and Farnham, D. S. (1979). Handling, precooling, and temperature management of cut flower crops for truck transportation. *U.S. Dep. Agric., AAT-W-5.*

Robertson, J. L., and Sullivan, G. H. (1976). An analysis of interregional and foreign competition for carnations. *J. Am. Soc. Hortic. Sci.* **101,** 40–44.

Staby, G. L., Robertson, J. L., Kiplinger, D. C., and Conover, C. A. (1976). *Proc. Nat. Flor. Conf. Commod. Handl. Columbus, Ohio,* 1–71.

3

Roses

Raymond F. Hasek

Introduction to Floriculture
Copyright © 1980 by Academic Press, Inc.
All rights of reproduction in any form reserved.
ISBN 0-12-437650-9

here are many cultural practices, procedures, and methods used in the commercial production of roses as a cut flower. Local environmental conditions often dictate the best possible course that must be taken to ensure operating a greenhouse range at a profit. This chapter will be devoted to the more frequently used cultural and postharvest handling practices.

I. HISTORY

Present-day commercial rose cultivars are all hybrids of rose species several generations removed. Depending upon the taxonomic system followed, the hybrid tea rose of today traces its ancestory back to *Rosa gigantea* and *R. chinensis,* which were interbred in China before 1800 to produce Tea China or China roses. Rose production for cut flowers in the United States is reported to have occurred first around 1850 when the sale of a few buds of the cultivar Hermosa, described as a blush-pink fragrant China rose, was made. The famous 'American Beauty' cultivar was introduced about 1880 and for years remained one of the most popular cut flower roses forced for Christmas bloom. At the turn of the century cultivars such as 'Killarney,' 'Liberty,' 'Ophelia,' and 'Souv. de Claudius Pernet' were introduced. Intensive breeding was begun to produce cultivars that would bloom continuously year-round. The hybrid tea and floribunda types so prominent in the cut flower trade today are of relatively recent origin.

Both hybrid tea and floribunda roses are produced by most rose growers. More than 300 million blooms of hybrid tea and 120 million blooms of floribunda roses are sold in the United States annually with a wholesale value of $79 million. California growers produce approximately 40% of the total with producers in Colorado, Pennsylvania, Indiana, Illinois, and several other northeastern states accounting for the remainder.

II. BOTANICAL INFORMATION

Approximately 200 botanical species of roses are natives of the Northern Hemisphere. Owning to the occurrence of hybrid populations found in the wild, the actual number of true species is open to question. Roses have a determinant inflorescence that may assume corymbose, paniculate, or solitary form. When flowers are borne singly, as in many hybrid tea cultivars, there are still undeveloped flower buds in the axils of the leaves immediately below the terminal flower. These buds can develop into short flowering shoots under favorable environmental conditions. Flower colors range from red, white, pink, yellow, orange, to lavendar with many shades, hues, and tints between. Flowers are borne on upright, prickly stems. Fruit formed from fertilized flowers are called "hips." They are reputed to be high in vitamin C content and consequently are in demand by health food advocates.

III. CULTIVARS PAST AND PRESENT

Plant breeders have introduced hundreds of cultivars since the Depression days of the 1930s. In 1934 J. H. Hill Company introduced the cultivar appropriately named 'Better Times.' The firm proceeded to patent the cultivar as a red sport of 'Briarcliff.' It became the backbone of the rose industry for many years. Several other sports and selections of the cultivar were grown in later years but the original cultivar persisted as the mainstay until after World War II.

In the early 1950s the volume of air freight shipment of cut flower roses from the West Coast greatly increased. The cultivar Red Delight soon began to replace 'Better Times' because of its ability to withstand the rigors of long-distance shipment and retention of good red color during the hot summer months. In 1960 the cultivar Forever Yours was introduced and immediately replaced the other red cultivars with its free growing habit and excellent stem length. It continued to dominate the rose market until the 1970s. Other red cultivars appeared on the market during this time but they never reached the popularity of 'Forever Yours.' Several good red cultivars have been introduced within recent years and the names 'Cara Mia,' 'Samantha,' and 'Royalty' will replace past cultivars for some time to come.

One reason for consideration of red rose cultivars in the evolutionary sense of greenhouse rose production is that they make up approximately 60% of the total rose cut flower demand. A realistic distribution of rose colors that a wholesale house needs to satisfy the demands of its customers would be as follows: red hybrid teas, 62%; pink hybrid teas, 8%; yellow hybrid teas, 8%; novelties, 4%; white, 3%; and floribundas, all colors, 15%. Local demands may alter the above figures somewhat but in general the year-round needs will be satisfied. For given cultivars, the percentage of plants grown will differ from the foregoing color distribution figures since not all cultivars produce flowers equally as well. Demand for certain colors at specific holidays or during the popular wedding months of June and August make the color percentage of white, pink, yellow, and perhaps novelties appear to be insufficient. On the other hand, red roses are always in short supply for St. Valentine's Day. Production capacity must be based on a 365-day year instead of a few relatively short periods of cultivar imbalance.

IV. PROPAGATION

Roses can be propagated by seeds, cuttings, budding, and grafting. Seed propagation is used by rose breeders for the development of new cultivars or by amateurs who wish to experiment on their own. On a commercial basis budding is by far the most important method used to produce new plants for greenhouse cut flower production.

A. Seeds

Rose seeds do not germinate readily after harvest on account of the presence of an impervious seed coat. A period of "afterripening" is necessary before the seeds are ready to germinate. The steps needed to germinate rose seeds could be described briefly as follows. The fruits or "hips" should be harvested when the color changes from green to red, yellow or variations thereof. Seeds are removed from the "hips" and sown in flats containing moist shredded sphagnum moss or similar material and stored at 4°C for at least 3 to 4 weeks or until 5% of the seeds show germination. Seed flats are transferred to a temperature of 18°–21°C, where final germination takes place, usually within 2 to 3 weeks. Seedlings should be transplanted to a good growing medium for growth until first bloom.

"Hips" can be harvested while still green and have the seeds removed as described earlier. The seed embryos are extracted from the surrounding seed coats with a sharp instrument and sown on agar medium similar to that used for orchids. This procedure must be done under aseptic conditions to prevent fungal contamination.

B. Cuttings

Since all modern-day cultivars are patented it is necessary to obtain propagation rights and to pay lease fees for any plants used in greenhouse production should the propagator not be the holder of the patent. Not all cultivars grow as vigorously or produce as many flowers of comparable quality on their own roots as they do when budded or grafted on other rootstocks. Own-root plants are quite small when planted in the greenhouse bench. Considerable time is required to build the plant to sufficient size before harvest of the flowers begins. Time lost in this manner can be more expensive than the difference in cost between own-root and the higher priced budded plants.

Cuttings can be taken any time between October and March depending upon the intended planting date. Cutting wood should be selected from flowering shoots that have been allowed to develop to full bloom. In this way the propagator is certain the shoot producing flowers is true to type. Mature foliage so developed accumulates photosynthates that aid in producing better rooted cuttings. Blind shoots are less desirable since they are usually thinner and less vigorous by nature of their position on the plant. One-, two-, or three-eye cuttings can be made depending upon availability of propagative material. Three-eye cuttings are preferred since they are larger and have nodal tissue at the base, which could reduce loss due to disease. After the bases are dipped in a synthetic rooting compound, cuttings are stuck in a propagation bench containing vermiculite. Spacing is 2.5 to 4.0 cm between cuttings in rows 7.5 cm apart. Misting with conventional mist propagation systems maintains proper moisture conditions on the foliage and in the medium during the rooting period. Temperature of the medium should be maintained at 18°-21°C at all times. Drop curtains extending above the sides of the bench will prevent drafts drying out the foliage and distorting the spray pattern of the mist system. Rooting time is approximately 5 to 6 weeks depending upon time of year and cutting condition. After rooting, cuttings are planted in 7.5-cm rose pots or planted directly into the greenhouse bench.

C. Grafted Plants

Grafted plants are seldom used for commercial cut flower production. As with own-root plants a substantial amount of greenhouse time is required between planting and flower production. *Rosa manetti* understock used in the production of grafted plants is produced on the West Coast and in Europe. They are field-grown 1 year before they are dug in late fall, stripped of the growth made in the field the previous summer, and shipped to the greenhouse operator. Upon receipt the plants should be stored at 0°-1°C to prevent growth before use. After removal from the refrigerator, understocks are allowed to warm gradually. The roots are pruned slightly and the plants potted in 7.5-cm rose pots containing a steam-pasteurized, well-drained soil mixture. After being watered thoroughly they are placed in a 16°C greenhouse. In approximately 2 weeks the understocks are ready for grafting. One-eye named cultivar rose shoots are prepared by making a slanting cut approximately 2 to 3 cm long at the base. A similar slanting cut is made in the understock just above the soil line. The scion is placed on the understock at a slight angle so that the cambium surfaces make contact at as many points as possible. The grafts are tied with a "budding rubber" that is nothing more than a rubber strip approximately 13.0 cm long, 0.7 cm wide, and 0.5 cm thick. Grafted plants are placed in a Wardian case. The case temperature should be maintained at 24°C by supplying bottom heat. Care should be taken to prevent the grafts or foliage from drying out. If misting is necessary, a daily light mist over the tops of the plants should suffice.

After the graft unions knit in approximately 10 days, the case can be ventilated for a short period of time. Progressively longer periods of exposure are given in the days following until finally the case is left open at all times. The temperature is then dropped to 16°C.

In approximately 1 month the plants become acclimatized to their new environment and can be planted directly into a greenhouse bench or grown outdoors for a complete season before being dug as dormant plants and benched in the greenhouse the following winter.

D. Budded Plants

Budded plants are the most popular type used by commercial rose cut flower growers in the United States. Production of budded plants is a specialized business carried on by a dozen or so firms in California, Oregon, and Arizona.

The most common understock for budded plants is *R. manetti* with occasional use of *R. odorata*. Understocks are produced on especially maintained stock blocks normally segregated from regular growing areas. Wood used for planting of stock blocks is obtained from plants that have been heat-treated to free them from viruses and viruslike diseases. In late September, long shoots or whips produced by the stock plants during the growing season are cut, tied in bundles, and removed to the propagation shed. They are dethorned by rolling on a rough table and are given a 15-minute dip in sodium hypochlorite solution (⅓ of 1%) before they are cut into 20- to 21-cm lengths. A very sharp knife is used to de-eye the cuttings or sticks by removing all of the lower eyes and leaving three at the top end. The sticks are graded for size and turgidity before being dipped in a 200-ppm Agrimycin solution for crown gall control.

Some growers fumigate the rose fields with methyl bromide prior to planting. Others use nematicides or other treatments depending upon the problems they need to overcome. After the fields have been prepared, they are treated with preplant fertilizers previously determined from soil tests. Rows are marked 122 cm apart. In some instances the rows are covered with a strip of asphalt paper 31 cm wide. The paper contains prepunched holes spaced approximately 13 cm apart into which the stocks are subsequently inserted. As a standard practice the bases of the sticks are treated with Hormodin No. 2 rooting hormone powder prior to sticking. Planting of the understocks begins in mid-November and is completed by mid-December. The fields are irrigated as soon as the sticks are in place to settle the soil around the base. By the first of May rooting has taken place and the top growth is 15 to 25 cm long. Budding can start if the bark "slips" or can be peeled away freely at the cambium layer.

The budding procedure consists of making a vertical and horizontal cut in the understock to form a "T." The T is placed well below the shoots that arise from the understock. Cuts are made only to the depth of the cambium layer. An eye is removed from a previously prepared shoot of a named cultivar by making a shallow slicing cut to form a shieldlike piece as backing for the bud. It is inserted between the flaps formed by the bark on either side of the T. A budding rubber is wrapped around the shank of the understock above and below the eye to hold it in place. Budding operations are completed by June 15.

Three to 4 weeks after budding, *R. manetti* understock is cut approximately one-third of the way through directly above the inserted bud and the top is broken over. This places the bud in an apical position on the shank of the understock, where it begins to grow. Three weeks after the tops are broken over they are removed entirely from the plant. Top removal is done in two stages to prevent complete defoliation at any time.

Plants budded after June 15 are grown as dormant eyes. The top of the *R. manetti* understock is allowed to remain on the plant until just before digging time. The presence of these shoots surpresses growth of the named cultivar eye, thereby giving the plant its name of "dormant" eye.

Digging of budded plants is begun in mid-December and is completed by the end of January. The plants are hauled to a shipping shed where they are washed, pruned to remove injured shoots and roots, and finally graded. The Triple X grade is the best and most desired by greenhouse operators. These plants have good fibrous root systems and two to three heavy top canes. Double X plants are of lesser caliper top growth and have a smaller root system. Plants not suitable for either grade are culls.

After the plants have been graded they are packed in corrugated cardboard cartons lined with waterproof material and taped shut. Depending upon the grade, 250 to 350 plants are packed per box. The plants are then stored at 0°–2°C until shipped to the grower sometime between January and June.

V. PLANT CULTURE

A. Preplant Preparation and Planting

In California most roses are planted directly in ground beds. In a few special locations benches containing 25 cm of soil are used because of poorly drained on-site soils or hardpans. Elsewhere in the country, concrete V-bottom benches, either raised or on the ground, are in common use. Wooden benches containing 15 cm of soil are still used by some eastern growers. Where roses are grown in V-bottom benches, drain tile is placed at the bottom of the V and pea gravel is used to cover the tile to the top of the V. Soil is added to the desired depth on top of the gravel.

Regardless of bench construction, soils in which roses are grown should have reasonably good structure and be well aerated and well drained, to prevent waterlogging. Soils can be maintained at a high moisture content to reduce water stress in the plants provided there is sufficient air pore space to supply the roots with ample oxygen.

Preplant preparation of the soil is extremely important. Amendments such as fir or redwood bark, redwood sawdust, rice hulls, and many other organic materials have been used. Rose soils should not be overamended. Most inexpensive materials used for this purpose are relatively low in water-holding and cation exchange capacity. In a shallow bench containing highly amended soil it is possible that plants could be growing in a medium having low water and nutrient retention characteristics, thereby requiring compensatory cultural practices such as frequent watering and fertilization to ensure satisfactory growth. A rule of thumb for use of amendments is to incorporate approximately 20% by volume to the soil at first planting and lesser amounts thereafter. In a ground bed the amendment is frequently worked into the top 15 to 20 cm of soil. This amendment can act as a thick mulch that retains more water than desired in the soil immediately below the amended region. In winter, roots which penetrate the lower soil profile may be subjected to long periods when the soil is saturated. Such a condition is not conducive to good plant growth.

Addition of preplant fertilizers should be based on soil tests. The tests are not infallible; therefore, they should be used merely as a guide for preplant additions. In most situations, phosphorus and some form of liming material such as oyster shells, dolomitic limestone, or hydrated lime are incorporated in the soil, especially if the use of acid residue fertilizers is contemplated.

Steam pasteurization is probably the most widely used method for weed, soil pest, and disease control. Methyl bromide fumigation has been used effectively in West Coast greenhouses, where severe nematode infestations are found in ground bed plantings. Care must be taken to ensure adequate phosphorus and zinc levels since deficiencies of these elements have been reported in methyl bromide-fumigated soils. Tools used in working the soil after pasteurization should be pasteurized also to prevent spread of diseases and other soil pests.

Planting in new houses or replanting in older ones is usually done from January to June. Timing and scheduling of the planting operation require consideration of many factors. Plants that have been growing poorly can be removed after Christmas and the area can be replanted in time for a heavy Mother's Day crop. Under these circumstances the plants are cropped heavily for Christmas since flowers cut at that time have high unit value and are the last to be produced by the plants. Some growers prefer to replant after St. Valentine's Day, Easter, or Mother's Day so that the summer months when prices are low can be used for building the plants.

The most common planting distance is 30.5 × 30.5 cm in beds or benches. Some cultivars are planted 30.5 cm apart in the row across the bed and 38.0 cm between rows. Only heavy growing cultivars such as 'Red Garnette' are so treated. Despite research several years ago that showed that the two center rows in a four-row bench produce substantially fewer flowers than either of the outside rows, growers persist in continuing the four-row practice. It is much easier to spray and cut flowers, and generally maintain plants in three-row benches. Houses planted to three-row benches usually contain only one less row of plants. Such plantings result in several more outside rows of plants thereby more than compensating for the fewer total plants.

Roses should be planted at the same depth as in the field. The roots should be covered with 5 to 8 cm of soil or just enough to maintain the plants in an upright position. Roots should be well distributed in the soil and not twisted into a tight ball for convenience in planting. Planting too deep often results in roots striking from the named cultivar. Under these circumstances the plants become virtually own-root plants.

Watering-in of the plants is done by hand to ensure that the soil is settled and in good contact with the roots. Many eastern growers "spot" water. This is the application of water to a limited area around each plant. West Coast growers water the bench thoroughly immediately after planting and at least once more the following day.

At planting time, plants are removed from storage and allowed to warm slowly in the greenhouse. If the plants appear desiccated as they are taken from the packing cases it is best to soak the roots in water for 24 to 48 hours before planting. This practice ensures planting a turgid plant that has a better chance for survival and growth. After planting, plants can be covered with clear polyethylene sheets to maintain high humidity around the tops. Such environmental conditions are conducive to faster growth of buds. Night temperatures should be 16°C from the time of planting. After 1 week or 10 days when the shoots have begun to develop the plastic covering should be removed. This prevents burning of the shoot tips coming in contact with the cover under high light conditions.

As the plants develop they need support. Heavy No. 9 wire stakes can be stuck at the site of each plant and the tops of the stakes clipped to wires running the length of the bench. Rose shoots are tied individually to the stakes with string as the plants grow. Another method of support is to run wires at each side of the bench. Bamboo canes are laid across the bench and the ends are clipped to the wire. The rose canes are thus divided into slots or cages. The bamboo cane system is more adaptable to cultivars that grow vigorously.

B. Watering

On account of high labor costs hand watering is a thing of the past in an efficiently run rose range. The Gates system of watering is employed extensively. In this system water is applied to the bed or bench from nylon flat spray nozzles inserted in plastic pipes on the perimeter of the bed or bench. Some West Coast growers are applying water by twin wall or Viaflo slow delivery systems, wherein the tubes are laid on the soil surface between rows of plants running the length of the bench. The tubes are supplied with water from a header at either end or branched from a water source at the center of the bench. In both irrigation methods little or no compaction of the soil occurs, such as that which takes place when hand watering is practiced. The absence of compaction has made the use of mulches less necessary; consequently, many growers use no mulch at all during the entire life of the plant.

Soils that tend to compact and form excessive cracks on drying can benefit by the use of mulches. An effective method of watering these soils is to apply a light watering first. This is followed by a heavy watering after a time lapse of ½ hour or more. The soil swells as a result of the first watering. This seals the cracks and forces the water from the second irrigation to percolate through the soil mass. Single heavy waterings often run through the soil and out the bottom of the bench in a virtual torrent. Such water flow could be misinterpreted to mean the soil is saturated when in reality it is barely moistened in the area of the cracks.

C. Fertilization

If phosphorus and calcium in the form of lime have been incorporated in the preplant preparation of the soil the primary nutrients needed on a more or less regular basis are nitrogen, potassium, magnesium, and perhaps iron. Magnesium is easily applied in a liquid fertilizer program as magnesium sulfate or Epsom salts. Iron also can be applied in chelated form in the liquid fertilizer. If the pH of the soil tends to rise, iron sulfate as a surface application is a good means of control. Potassium is most often applied as muriate of potash or potassium nitrate. The former is an acid residue type whereas the latter has alkaline residue characteristics. Of the nitrogen sources, ammonia forms such as ammonium nitrate and ammonium sulfate are highly acidic types. Calcium nitrate and potassium nitrate are both alkaline residue materials. To some extent the soil pH can be regulated through judicious fertilizer selections. Liquid fertilization is now the most common method of supplying nutrients to greenhouse rose plants. Delivery is made through accurate proportioning of stock solution dispensed by Gates- or Viaflo-type systems. The amounts of the various elements used in the stock solutions can be varied using soil tests or foliar analysis guides, so the plants are exposed to a relatively constant level of nutrients in the soil at all times. Failure to maintain proportioners in good working order can lead to underfeeding with loss of flower production or overfeeding, also with loss of production or loss of plants. Liquid fertilizers containing 200 ppm of nitrogen and 150 ppm of potassium, plus iron and magnesium as needed, can be applied with good results in a wide range of soil conditions.

D. Temperature

For most modern rose cultivars a greenhouse night temperature of approximately 16°C is optimum for growth. Under certain cropping conditions slightly higher or lower temperatures might be maintained for relatively short periods of time without serious ill effects. Day temperatures are generally maintained at 20° or 21°C on cloudy days and 24°–28°C on sunny days. During the fuel crisis of the mid-1970s many growers attempted to reduce greenhouse night temperatures by as much as 6°C with serious consequences. The growth rate was drastically reduced, which meant less flower production for a given time period. Return crops required excessive time to bloom or completely failed to do so. Flowers of some cultivars developed excessive numbers of petals under low temperature conditions. These flowers had poor color and poor shape (formed cabbage heads) and often had poor keeping qualities even if they opened. In greenhouses where temperatures are maintained too high, flower size is small, petal count is low, and keeping quality is poor owing to soft growth of flowers and stems. Soft growth in this instance is probably a good indicator of low photosynthate content.

E. Ventilation

Air exchange in a greenhouse is of the utmost importance, especially during daylight hours. At sunrise, outdoor temperatures are usually too low to allow for ventilation without severe loss of heat from the greenhouse. Carbon dioxide levels have been measured during this period and found to be limiting for plant growth. Additions of carbon dioxide in the greenhouse atmosphere through the use of generators or direct piping from carbon dioxide reservoirs have proved beneficial. Ordinarily, ventilators are opened when the house temperature reaches 20°–21°C. Research has shown that it is possible to allow the greenhouse temperature to rise a few degrees higher before ventilators are opened provided 500 to 1200 ppm carbon dioxide is maintained in the air. Normal levels of 300 parts per million are rapidly depleted if no new supply is forthcoming through ventilation. During midday hours, additions of carbon dioxide appear to be of little or no benefit for roses grown in regions where heating is not needed and ventilators must be open for temperature control. Under winter conditions or in colder climates where daytime ventilation is not economical additions of carbon dioxide are necessary for optimum plant growth. A secondary period when carbon dioxide additions have proven beneficial is the interim period between closing of the ventilators in late afternoon and sunset. Ventilation reduction starts at approximately 20°C. Progressively less air exchange is allowed as the temperature drops to 17°C, when the ventilators are closed entirely. If complete closing occurs several hours before sunset, carbon dioxide levels in the greenhouse atmosphere continue to be reduced by the photosynthetic process in plants. Unless replenished, carbon dioxide can reach growth-limiting levels.

Closing ventilators at higher temperatures to conserve heat can also lead to fungal disease problems. Air of higher temperatures can retain more water vapor at a given relative humidity than air at a lower temperature. Trapping air of high temperature and high moisture content in the greenhouse by early closing of the ventilators can result in condensate forming on the plants as the temperature drops and approaches the dew point. Fungal diseases thrive under these conditions. Spraying for disease control can be futile unless the practices which provide excellent environmental conditions for the growth and spread of diseases are corrected. Supplying heat to the greenhouse before closing ventilators is very effective if coupled with closing ventilators at lower temperatures.

Ordinarily, increased production or improved flower quality can be expected if carbon dioxide deficiencies are corrected during the periods mentioned; however, the cost–benefit ratio must be calculated before the economic value of carbon dioxide additions can be determined. It must be remembered that carbon dioxide is not a substitute for other factors affecting plant growth, such as light.

F. Light and Lighting

Growth rates for most rose cultivars follow the total light curve throughout the year. Flower production is potentially high in summer when high light intensities and long total daylight hours prevail. Conversely, the opposite is true in winter when light intensities are low and total daylight hours few. It is ironic that greenhouses must be covered with a shading compound during the summer when total light is abundant. Intense heat which accompanies high light intensities make such practices necessary. In most parts of the country light intensity in summer approaches 129 klx or slightly more. Shading of the greenhouse reduces the level to half of this potential. As the weather becomes warmer in spring, shading becomes necessary as early as March in some areas and a month or two later in others. The first application of shading compound should be light so that the plants are not subjected to a drastic change in light intensity in a short period of time. Additional applications can be made as the season becomes warmer. In most rose growing areas dust begins to accumulate on the greenhouse roof as summer wears on. Where possible the dust layer should be washed off and shading reapplied if the light intensity drops below 54 klx. Shade removal can begin around Labor Day. It is usually delayed well beyond that date in California where weather conditions are still hot, bright, and clear during September and early October.

For many years it was believed that the rose did not respond to supplementary light. Research in this area within the last decade has shown this assumption to be false. Using an array of light sources from the high-intensity discharge types to combinations of fluorescent and incandescent lamps, researchers have shown that in the northeastern portion of the United States rose production can be improved significantly through the use of the supplementary lighting. Reports of as much as 50 to 240% increase in production are in the literature. However, a good portion of the increase has been found in the shorter-stemmed flowers. The distribution of dates when the increased flowers were produced make a decided difference in whether or not supplementary lighting is profitable. With such great increases in production during the winter supplementary lighting would appear feasible in northeastern states. Installation of lighting equipment must be amortized over a short period of time to make lighting pay from a tax standpoint. Lighting trials were run along the coast in northern California. In spite of sunny winter weather the cultivar Tropicana produced more flowers when lighted with sodium vapor lamps at intensities of

4.3 klx in the cutting zone from dusk to dawn. Unfortunately, the cost to produce the additional blooms varied between 14 and 17 cents per bloom just for
the electricity. Flowers from the lighted plants were insignificantly different on a
fresh weight basis from the unlighted check flowers. Whether lighting of rose
plants pays dividends is closely tied to weather conditions in the region in
which the roses are grown. Where winter involves frequent overcast and snow
conditions lighting could be very profitable. In regions having bright sunny
winters the economics of supplementary lighting is questionable.

G. Cutting and Pinching Practices

There is a saying among rose growers that "the man who cuts the flowers is
the man who either makes or loses a profit for you." To a great extent this is
true. Examination of the rose stem will show there are pointed buds at the base
of the strap-shaped leaf, three-leaflet leaf, and first five-leaflet leaf below the

Fig. 1. Distribution of bud types on a rose flowering shoot.

Fig. 2. Fully mature flowering shoot on the right, showing secondary bud development. Inflorescence on the left is still in immature bud stage.

flower bud (Fig. 1). At the bottom of the shoot the eyes are quite flat at the base of the strap-shaped leaves. If forced into flower the pointed buds would produce short-stemmed flowers (Fig. 2). When a shoot is pinched it is necessary to remove the entire top portion to a point below the first five-leaflet leaf. This procedure ensures a reasonably long stem on the subsequent flower.

Pinching is nothing more than removing the flower bud at some stage before bloom. As soon as the bud is visible it may be removed along with the stem and leaves to the second five-leaflet leaf. This is referred to as a soft pinch. Pinches are considered to be soft until the bud develops to the size of a pea or slightly larger. Thereafter it is a hard pinch. There is generally little difference in the subsequent flowering shoot produced from either of these pinches; however, a soft pinch usually requires a few days more time to bloom.

When cutting above the point of origin of a flowering shoot it is imperative that at least one five-leaflet leaf be left on the plant. Flowering shoots on free breaking cultivars such as 'Forever Yours' are generally cut above the hook, a commercial growers' term, leaving a single five-leaflet leaf. Flowers on less vigorous cultivars are usually cut, leaving two five-leaflet leaves to ensure better breaks. From mid-February in California, and a month later in other parts of the country, a system of cutting might well follow the suggestion as shown in Fig. 3. When a thin-stemmed flowering shoot arises from a thin shoot below, the flower should be cut below the hook. If a thin-stemmed flower arises from a fairly heavy cane below, the flower should be cut within a one-quarter inch above the hook. Such cuts are sometimes also referred to as knuckle cuts. If a flower with a long stem arises from a cane of substantial caliper below, the flower should be cut above the hook, leaving one or two five-leaflet leaves dependent upon the vigor of the cultivar.

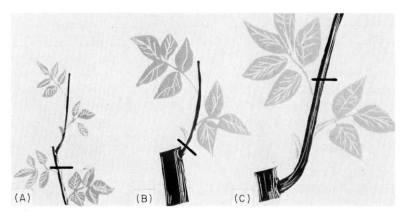

Fig. 3. System of cutting for various caliper shoots. (A) Thin shoot from thin shoot; cut under the hook. (B) Thin shoot from thick shoot; cut at the knuckle. (C) Thick shoot from thick shoot; cut above hook, leaving one good five-leaflet leaf.

H. Pruning

Pruning is the practice of removing the tops of the plants to a point where cutting and pinching can once again manage plant growth. Most rose plants need some pruning during the second year and each year thereafter. The first pruning after planting should be done to remove the tops to a point 60 to 90 cm above the soil line (Fig. 4). Cutting back should be accomplished by cutting above a good eye situated on wood having green bark. Through proper pinching and cutting practices the second pruning can be made at a point slightly above that of the previous year.

Pruning can be done gradually on the plants by cutting the canes individually as flowering shoots are removed. This is called "green pruning" since the plants do not become dormant before pruning and are cut while they are "green." This procedure is begun after Mother's Day and is completed by July 15. Another form of green pruning is the practice of using pruning shears or hedge clippers to prune all canes to a predetermined height at one time. It is a more drastic process and is usually done on flowering shoots that have been allowed to bloom out as the Mother's Day comeback crop flowers in June. No reference is made to cutting above a good eye with this method. It is used by some growers who wish to take houses out of production during the July and early August period so that vacations can be scheduled during a period of light work load.

Israeli workers have suggested pruning plants from August to October but in most parts of the United States such late pruning results in a poor canopy of shoot growth going into the winter. Production suffers as a consequence.

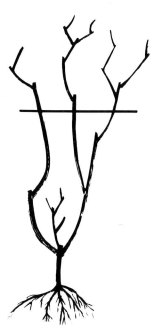

Fig. 4. First-year pruning method 60–90 cm above the soil line.

I. Cropping

Growers who plan a comprehensive cropping schedule for their plants can assure themselves a reasonable profit for their efforts. Just as a grower should consult his wholesaler, sales force, or customers for the distribution of colors and cultivars mentioned earlier, he also needs to be aware of his day-to-day market demands. With such knowledge he should be able to formulate a plan for year-round production. Many California growers have followed this procedure for years.

In any cropping schedule target dates for peak holiday production or other periods of high demand must first be determined. Calculating backward on the calendar, the grower must determine pinching and cutting dates to produce flowers when needed. He must further calculate backward to determine earlier pinching and cutting schedules that will supply him with the required pinchable material when needed. The yearly cycle is best begun at the time of pruning. Timing of the comeback crops through pinching and cutting will allow the grower to predict reasonably well when shoots or flowers of a certain stage will be available. In any year-round schedule replanting must be considered. Many growers use young replants to supply a good portion of the Easter and Mother's Day crops.

Variability in cycling time for individual cultivars can be determined by close observation of production records and some judicious tagging of shoots. In addition to all of the foregoing factors some adjustment in pinching dates is usually necessary, owing to the difference in temperatures encountered from one end of the greenhouse to the other. Within a given greenhouse or range three zones most often exist: the cold end, the middle portion, and the hot end. Pinching dates differ in all three areas if flowering on a definite target date is desired. Regardless of how well a cropping schedule is thought out it is still of little use unless written down.

VI. INSECTS, DISEASES, AND PHYSIOLOGICAL DISORDERS

There are many plant pests and physiological disorders reported on greenhouse roses but in any specific locality the major problems may be relatively few. Since 1972 when the Environmental Protection Act was passed many of the pesticides formerly available to rose growers have been removed from the market, declared illegal for their use or placed under tight restrictions by federal, state, or local agencies. Any suggested control measures are subject to local restrictions. It is the obligation of the greenhouse grower to ascertain the rules and regulations regarding the use of pesticides in his locale and operate within the framework of the law. Label recommendations must be followed at all times when using registered materials.

A. Insects

Two-spotted spider mite (*Tetranychus urticae*) is the most serious insect pest of greenhouse roses. Though often referred to as red spiders, those found on greenhouse roses are green with two distinct black dots on the backs of the adults. The life cycle under greenhouse conditions is approximately 12–14 days. Leaves infested with this pest exhibit a stippled spotting. Eventually the leaf becomes yellowish-bronze. Severe infestation results in premature leaf drop. Pentac sprays applied twice 7 to 10 days apart are very effective in controlling this pest.

1. Aphids

At least three species of aphids attack indoor roses. They are green in color and measure 4 to 5 mm in length. They feed on young shoots, young leaves, and flower buds. Damage is in the form of distorted leaves and outer petals on flowers. Orthene sprays will successfully control aphids.

2. Thrips

The migrating thrips (*Frankliniella tritici*) are extremely abundant in the eastern United States. They enter the greenhouse through side and top ventilators of the greenhouse. Adults enter flower buds in the tight stage and feed on the edges of the petals, causing browning and some distortion of the petals as the flowers develop. Screens can be placed over the side ventilators to reduce the number of thrips entering the greenhouse. Orthene sprays provide good control.

3. Leaf Rollers

Several species of insects have been described as "worm" pests of greenhouse roses. Only one or two are presently of concern. The larvae crawl into tender leaf crevices and begin feeding. The leaf is curled around them in the later stages, making it difficult to control them, but Orthene sprays can be effective.

4. Cane Borers

Occasionally several young shoots on rose plants in an area of a greenhouse wilt and die. Close examination of the stem shows a slight puncture immediately below the wilted top. This is the point at which a female sawfly has deposited an egg in the stem. After the egg hatches the larva bores a tunnel in the center of the stem up toward the growing tip. Infestations occur in late spring. Wilted shoots should be removed by cutting a few inches below the affected area. The affected areas should be destroyed or burned.

B. Diseases

Many of the fungal diseases attacking the foliage and stems of roses can be inhibited or prevented by maintaining proper greenhouse environment. Spray programs can help reduce losses from some of the diseases, but unless the conditions in the greenhouse conducive to the growth of the disease organism are corrected eradication is difficult.

1. Powdery Mildew (Spaerotheca pannosa)

Powdery mildew is the most important disease of flowers, foliage, and stems with which rose growers must contend. When the standard method of controlling spider mites was syringing, powdery mildew was of very little concern to the growers. With the development of effective acaricidal sprays syringing became unnecessary but there was an increase in mildew infestations. The disease covers young tissue of buds, leaves, stems, and even thorns with white mycelium. Growth is distorted and the unsightly appearance makes the flowers unsalable. Conditions found to be conducive for the growth and spread of this organism are low greenhouse temperatures and high humidity at night coupled with high temperatures and low humidity during the day. Avoidance of these temperature and humidity cycles contributes immensely to control. Pipron or Benomyl sprays can be used. Vaporization of sulfur from steam pipes or electrically heated sulfur pots also are effective.

2. Gray Mold or Botrytis (Botrytis cinerea)

A problem in greenhouses on the West Coast, this disease attacks flowers and stems. It appears as a gray mass when the spores appear in spots on the flowers or stems. Often stems are completely girdled and die. Benomyl sprays can be used for nonresistant strains, and Zineb sprays for others.

3. Rust (Phragmidium disciflorum)

Rust is another disease more important to rose growers on the West Coast. Under winter conditions high humidity favors its growth and spread. The fungus appears as orange rust spots or pustules on leaves and other plant parts. Proper ventilation late in the day as discussed previously helps prevent growth and spread of the organism. Plants should not be syringed. Zineb sprays will control rust. Plantvax sprays can be used where the fungicide is registered.

4. Black Spot (Diplocarpon rosae)

Water-borne spores of black spot can be spread by splashing water or syringing. Black spots appear on the upper surface of the leaves and young stems. Severe infection of the leaf causes defoliation. Infected leaves should be removed and burned, and relative humidity should be kept low. Daconil 2787 sprays are somewhat effective.

5. Canker Diseases

Several organisms cause cankerlike diseases. General symptoms are brown cankers, with gray or dark centers that appear on stems, often in older wood. As the tissue dies black spore-bearing structures appear on the dead tissue. Infection can occur through wounds and is more prevalent on weakened plants. Diseased tissue should be removed by cutting to a node. Plant vigor should be maintained.

6. Downy Mildew (Peronospora sparsa)

Dark purplish spots appear on leaves of current growth. Fruiting bodies can be seen on the underside of the leaf. Leaves abscise either as leaflets or entire leaves. High humidity or moisture favors growth. Closing ventilators and not heating during cloudy highly humid weather also favor occurrence of the disease. Relative humidity should be below 85% in the greenhouse. Zineb sprays are effective.

7. Crown Gall (Agrobacterium tumefaciens)

Galls form on the stems within 50 cm of the soil line or on the roots. The disease enters through wounds when grown in infested soil. Soil should be steamed before planting, and galls painted with Gallex if the disease occurs.

8. Viruses

There are several viruses that cause pattern designs on the leaves and distort foliar growth as well as stem development. Once the disease is in the plant there is no cure. Most often the viruses are transmitted through infected root stock or budwood; however, there is evidence that at least two of these diseases may be transmitted by an aerial vector. Virus-free plants should be purchased.

9. Nematodes

Several types of nematodes are known to be associated with reduction in growth of rose plantings. The root-knot nematode is the most noticeable but others might cause as much or more damage. Until a substitute for Nemagon is available little can be done to eliminate the pest once the plants are growing in the greenhouse. Preplant fumigation with methyl bromide or thorough pasteurization with steam is presently the best control.

C. Physiological Disorders

1. Bullheads

This condition is a result of flower petals not developing normally. Sometimes petals are shortened and produced in excessive amounts. Although only one pistil is present the flower occasionally appears to be made up of two buds joined together. Thrips are blamed for producing the condition but often bullhead flowers appear on very vigorous shoots when thrips are not present. No definite cause has been determined experimentally.

2. Leaf Drop

Any drastic change in the growth rate of the rose plant can produce some degree of leaf drop. This is especially true when vigorous shoots are produced after a pinch. The area around the petiole base expands rapidly, increasing the diameter of the shoot at that point. Petiole bases not having meristematic tissue cannot expand; consequently, rupture of the petiole tissue occurs with ensuing leaf drop. What appears to be a severe leaf drop may be a natural growth process. Some diseases such as black spot and downy mildew produce ethylene, which can result in leaf drop if the disease becomes prevalent. Insecticides of various types are known to cause leaf drop within 5 to 7 days after application. Gases such as sulfur dioxide and ammonium are also known to cause leaf drop.

3. Distorted Leaves and Stems

Phenoxy-type weed killers can produce severely twisted and distorted symptoms on the young growth of rose shoots. The sources of the weed killers are many. Drift from sprayers used in controlling weeds outside of greenhouses can cause symptoms. Using weed killers in spray equipment normally reserved for pest control in the greenhouse is deadly. Some weed killers are virtually impossible to eliminate from spray equipment once it is contaminated. Another source is the mulch used on rose soils. Piling mulch in areas sprayed with weed killers before applying it to greenhouse benches is hazardous. At least one case is on record of alfalfa straw used as a mulch causing problems. The alfalfa from which the straw came was used for seed. Weed control regulations permit more drastic chemicals to be used on fields of seed alfalfa than those destined for livestock feed. In this instance the actual weed killer used was undetermined but the injury was quite evident. Phenoxy weed killer symptoms appeared in the greenhouse at random points wherever a bale of contaminated straw was used. Removal of contaminated straw was the only control.

4. Mercury Injury

Much has been written about the dangers of using mercury or mercury-bearing materials in rose greenhouses. Paints containing mercury for wood preservation have been known to cause irreparable damage when used in rose greenhouses. The slight degree of vaporization of mercury from the wood causes the shoot tips to wither and die. A broken thermometer containing mercury is another source. Should such an accident occur the soil must be removed to rid the area of as much mercury as possible. Fine iron filings should be spread over the soil to neutralize the mercury. If the mercury falls inside a bench the cleanup might be more difficult or impossible.

VII. POSTHARVEST HANDLING

The stage of development at which a rose is cut has an important bearing on the longevity of the flower and customer satisfaction. Harvesting the flower too early in its development can result in bent necks. This occurs when a stem does not transmit enough water to keep the flower and stem immediately below in a turgid condition. Flowers of cultivar Cara Mia frequently have this trouble unless they are handled properly. Flowers allowed to mature excessively before harvest reduce vase life for the consumer. As a rule of thumb, most red and pink cultivars are cut as the calyx reflexes below a horizontal position and the first two petals begin to unfold. Yellow cultivars are better harvested slightly earlier in development. White cultivars are usually harvested at a more open stage than other cultivars.

After harvest, flowers should be removed from the warm greenhouse to the grading room refrigerator as soon as possible. Field heat can be removed rapidly by dipping the stems in cold water or exposing the flowers and stems to refrigerator temperatures by spreading them out on shelves while still dry. For extended storage before shipment the cooled flowers are placed in airtight containers and held at 1°C up to 2 weeks or until needed.

A. Grading

There are no standard grades for roses in the United States. On the West Coast the stem length differential between grades is in approximately 5-cm increments. The shortest hybrid tea flowers graded are those having stems 25.0 to 30.5 cm long. Subsequently better grades are 30.5 to 35.5 cm, 35.5 to 40.5 cm, and so forth. Eastern growers have used the 7.5-cm increment. Their grades begin at 23.0 to 30.5 cm and progress to 30.5 to 38.5 cm and each 7.5 cm thereafter. Some experimentation with 10-cm increments has not been accepted in general. Grading is done by placing the flowers against a pre-marked color-coded board or by placement on an endless belt grading machine. Grading machines carry the flowers over bins with trigger trips at the appropriate grade to drop the flower off the belt. In either method the base of the stem is recut. Twenty-five flowers from an individual grade are bunched with the heads on an even plane. Stems are tied together with string and a parchment or waxed paper wrapped around the heads for protection. Some growers prefer to use clear plastic film for this purpose. A few eastern markets demand the flat pack in which 25 flowers are laid on a sheet of waxed paper and stacked until packed for shipping.

After grading, the flowers are returned to the refrigerator, where the stems are immersed in a preservative solution. The solution usually contains 1 to 3% sugar and 100 to 200 ppm 8-quinolinol citrate plus aluminum sulfate, citric acid, or silver nitrate. The composition depends upon personal preference. Flowers should be held in the preservative solutions at least 3 to 4 hours, preferably longer. Flowers that have been stored dry for any length of time should have the stems recut and should be placed in preservative for 4 to 6 hours before shipping. Clean containers should be used at all times.

B. Shipment to Market

As with the grading of rose flowers, there is no standard carton or number of flowers packed in the unit. A typical shipping container would have the approximate dimensions 100 cm long × 51 cm wide × 30.5 cm deep. It could contain 500 hybrid tea roses of various lengths plus 100 blooms of floribundas. Insulated cartons are used by West Coast growers and wholesalers shipping to eastern markets by air freight and eastern wholesalers shipping short distances during the winter. Properly handled insulated cartons can keep excessive cold out to prevent freezing as well as maintaining a cool interior. Insulation is in the form of styrofoam or Fiberglas liners or polyurethane sprayed directly on the corrugated carton interior. Roses are laid in five-bunch rows, alternating heads toward one end of the box and then the other. They are held in place with wooden cleats and flake ice is spread over the stems of each layer for cooling. Packing should be done in a cool atmosphere. During warm weather the topless packed cartons should be refrigerated to ensure a cold interior before putting on the lids.

Transcontinental truck shipments are handled differently. The roses are packed as usual but in special boxes that have holes cut in each end. Cold air is drawn through the cartons inside a refrigerator until the temperature inside reaches 2°C. Cartons are moved directly into refrigerated trucks, where the cold temperature is maintained until delivery.

C. Care of Roses

Careful handling at all stages after harvest will ensure long vase life for roses. Procedures at each step of the way are as follows:

1. Growers
    a. Harvest at the proper stage of maturity.
    b. Keep flowers as cool as possible after harvest.
    c. Pulse in preservative solution 4 to 6 hours before shipping.
    d. Use deionized or low conductivity water in preparing solutions.
    e. Use clean containers.
    f. Precool packed containers before shipment.
2. Wholesalers
    a. Recut stems when unsure of previous handling.
    b. Place stems in preservative.
    c. Use deionized water for making perservative solutions.
    d. Use clean containers.
3. Retailers
    a. Place stems in preservative solution.
    b. Recut stems and immerse in 40°C water if wilted.
    c. Use preservatives in arrangement containers and so indicate to the customer.
    d. Include packet of powder preservatives with each cut flower order.
4. Consumer
    a. When receiving arrangements, keep vases filled with warm water daily.
    b. Use preservatives in vase water when making own arrangements.
    c. Recut stems and immerse them in 40°C water at the first sign of wilting.
    d. Use clean containers.

REFERENCES

Carpenter, W. J. (1975). Rose plant renewal with growth regulating chemicals. *Roses, Inc. Ann. Rep.*, Haslett, Michigan.

Carpenter, W. J., and Anderson, G. A. (1972). High intensity supplementary lighting of greenhouse roses. Presented at 1972 Roses, Inc. Ann. Meet.

Carpenter, W. J., and Rodreguez, R. C. (1971). Supplemental lighting effects on newly planted and cut-back greenhouse roses. *Hortic Sci.* **6,** 207–208.

Gamble, J. A. (1950). "Roses Unlimited." Amer. Rose Soc., Columbus, Ohio.

Hartmann, H. T., and Kester, D. E. 1975. "Plant Propagation Principles and Practices." Prentice-Hall, Englewood Cliffs, New Jersey.

Hasek, R. F., Sciaroni, R. H., and Enomoto, R. (1976). Unpublished data.

Hubbell, D. S. (1934). A morphological study of blind and flowering rose shoots with reference to flower bud differentiation. *J. Agric. Res.* **48,** 91–95.

Johnson, D. E., Lear, B., Miyagawa, S. T., and Sciaroni, R. H. (1969). Increased rose cut production results from the control of plant parasitic nematodes. *Florists' Rev.* **144**(3713), 22–23, 51–52.

Kofranek, A. M. (1976). Pulsing or loading solutions for cut flowers. (Unpublished report).

Langhans, R. W. (1976). Supplementary lighting of greenhouse roses. *Roses, Inc. Bull., March 1976,* 73–76.

Laurie, A., Kiplinger, D. C., and Nelson, K. S. (1968). "Commercial Flower Forcing." McGraw-Hill, New York.

Mastalerz, J. W., and Langhans, R. W. (1969). "Roses." Pennsylvania Flower Growers, Penn. State Univ., State College, Pennsylvania.

McCain, A. H. (1977). Greenhouse rose disease guide. *Leaflet 2726, Div. of Agr. Sci.,* Univ. of California, Berkeley.

Paz, U. (1973). Studies in growing roses in hothouses in Israel. State of Israel Ext. Service, Div. of Floriculture.

Post, K. (1959). "Florist Crop Production and Marketing." Orange-Judd, New York.

Secor, G. A., Kong, M., and Nyland, G. (1977). Rose virus and virus-like diseases. *Calif. Agric.* **31,** 4–7.

Smith, D. E., and Kohl, H. C. (1970). Effect of height of cut-back on subsequent stimulation of rose renewal canes. *J. H. Hill Mem. Found. Rep.,* Haslett, Michigan.

Staby, G. L., Robertson, J. L., and Kiplinger, D. C. (1978). "Chain of Life." Ohio Florists' Association, Columbus, Ohio.

4

Snapdragons

Marlin N. Rogers

I. INTRODUCTION

Ancestors of the greenhouse snapdragon (*Antirrhinum majus* L.) originally were native to the Mediterranean region, where they grew as tender, summer-flowering perennials. Cultivars were first grown in the United States as open-pollinated, inbred lines for flowering during long-day periods in the field or greenhouse, but about 1926 Mr. Frank Volz of Chevoit, Ohio, introduced a cultivar, Chevoit Maid, that flowered during winter (Lindstrom, 1966).

The first F_1 hybrid greenhouse-forcing snapdragon, 'Christmas Cheer,' was introduced by Fred and Helen Windmiller in Columbus, Ohio, in 1938 (Ball, 1952). This was quickly followed by many other F_1 types such as 'Maryland Pink' (Fred Winkler), and 'Mary Ellen' and 'Dorcas Jane' (J. S. Yoder). These hybrid types combined the early flowering characteristics of the winter greenhouse-forcing types with the strong vegetative growth characteristic of F_1 hybrid plants. George J. Ball, Inc., and Yoder Brothers, Inc., have been the principal introducers of new F_1 hybrid cultivars for greenhouse forcing since about 1950.

A. Classification of Greenhouse-Forcing Cultivars

Greenhouse-forcing types are classified into four response groups based upon growth and flowering responses in relation to temperature and daylength. Group I cultivars (winter and early spring group) are highly reproductive and flower quickly at 10°C night temperatures during the short, dark days of mid-winter in northern growing areas. Group II (late winter and spring group) cultivars have resulted from crosses of more vegetative inbreds, and flower with good quality at 10°C night temperatures, but require more crop time than group

Table I

Recommended Times for Flowering and Approximate Time to Flower of Different Snapdragon Response Groups for Northern and Southern Growing Areas in the United States

Response group	Northern United States		Southern United States	
	Best flowering period	Seed to flower (days)	Best flowering period	Seed to flower (days)
I	December 1–February 15	130	Not recommended for southern United States	
II	February 15–May 1	155	December 15–April 1	130
	November 1–December 1	100	—	—
III	May 1–July 1	110	April 1–June 1	95
	September 15–November 1	85	November 1–December 15	85
IV	July 1–September 15	85	June 1–November 1	85

I cultivars. Group III (late spring and fall group) cultivars are extremely slow to flower at 10°C, but perform much better at 15.5°C night temperatures under longer days and higher light intensities. Cultivars in group IV (summer group) are reproductive only at high night temperatures (15.5°C or higher), and at 10°C are blind (nonflowering). They are used for midsummer flowering. (Duffett, 1960). A summary of recommended flowering periods for cultivars from each of the response groups in both northern and southern growing areas is shown in Table I. The dividing line between northern and southern areas would be about latitude 38° N—roughly a line from Washington, D.C., through Cincinnati and Kansas City.

B. Timing in Different Areas

As can be seen from the summary timing information given above, there is considerable variation in the time required to produce a crop at different seasons and in different growing areas. Detailed studies have been completed on the timing required in most of the major producing areas: Florida (Raulston, 1972a,b), Alabama (Sanderson and Martin, 1975), Oklahoma (Payne, 1970), Colorado (Holley, 1966), Pennsylvania (White, 1961), and Michigan (Haney, 1951). Timing representative of growing conditions in Missouri is shown in Fig. 1.

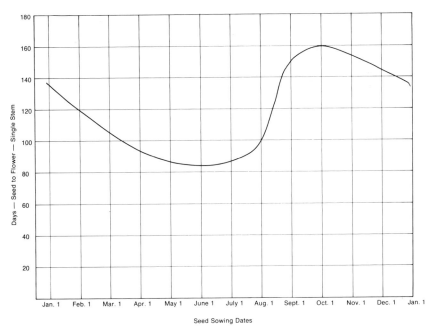

Fig. 1. Snapdragon timing for Missouri conditions. The number of days from seed to flower (harvestable maturity) for single-stem snapdragons planted at different times during the year.

The point of practical importance is that beginning about August 1 in mid-America plantings made 1 week apart will stretch out for flowering to 2 to 3 weeks apart. If one is attempting to time plantings so that one can cut a crop every other week, plantings will have to be made much closer together than every other week when light levels are consistently decreasing. During the spring, as light levels are increasing, plantings made about 3 weeks apart will mature about 2 weeks apart.

C. Economic Importance

Snapdragons were included as an individual flower crop for the first time in the 1959 Agricultural Census of Horticultural Specialty Crops, and at that time they were ranked as the seventh most valuable cut flower crop produced—eclipsed by roses, carnations, pompon chrysanthemums, standard chrysanthemums, gladiolus, and *Cattleya* orchids. At that time snapdragons comprised 3.2% of the total wholesale value of flowers produced in the United States—about $4.5 million out of a total of $142.5 million. The most important states involved in the production of snapdragons were Pennsylvania, New York, Ohio, Massachusetts, Michigan, New Jersey, Indiana, Illinois, Minnesota, and Maryland.

In 1977 snapdragons were included in the annual report for "Production of Flowers and Foliage Plants" for the first time, and were reported as having a gross wholesale value of $2.8 million, which represents a decrease in total value from 20 years earlier. Since the value of all other flowers produced has increased greatly in that same period of time, snapdragon now represents an even smaller percentage of the total value of such crops grown. Principal states now involved in their production are Massachusetts, North Carolina, New York, Pennsylvania, Florida, Ohio, and Maryland, indicating a southern movement of the production area.

II. CROP PRODUCTION

A. Propagation

Although snapdragons were propagated almost exclusively by the use of cuttings in the early part of this century, they are now completely seed propagated. Seedlings can be grown fairly easily by the producer, or purchased from specialist propagators. A number of factors are important in securing high germination percentages.

Seeds can be infected internally with several fungi, e.g., *Alternaria alternata, Phyllosticta antirrhini,* and *Stemphyllium botryosum,* all of which are pathogenic to snapdragons and can result in poor germination percentages. Infection is more common when seed is produced under high humidity conditions outdoors than when it is grown in a well-ventilated greenhouse. Treatment with seed fungicides such as thiram is not effective in overcoming the problem and appears even to be detrimental to germination of healthy seed (Harman *et al.,* 1973). Most greenhouse-forcing snapdragon seed is greenhouse-grown today but garden cultivars would more frequently be field grown.

Snapdragon seedlings are highly susceptible to *Pythium* and *Rhizoctonia,* so the seed should be sown in pathogen-free media. It is worthwhile to prepare the germinating medium in the flat, and then to pasteurize the flats and medium simultaneously. Seed can be sown as soon as the medium is cool. A loose, open, well-aerated medium is necessary for good root development and ease of transplanting.

Seeds germinate well under a mist propagation system during the summer when medium temperatures can be maintained at 20–21°C. At other seasons, when the mist might cool the medium to lower temperatures, better germination will probably be obtained by covering flats with a polyethylene sleeve to retain moisture. Optimum germination of snapdragon seed occurs at temperatures of 18–21°C, and is also enhanced by light (Cathey, 1969).

Seedlings should not be too crowded in the seed flat. A spacing of about 3000 seedlings/m^2 was recommended by Delworth (1946). After germination is complete, cooler, drier conditions result in stocky growth. High light intensitites are desirable. Supplemental lighting hastens growth of the seedlings to transplanting size (Petersen, 1955) (see Section II,F).

Snapdragon seedlings are one of the easiest kinds of plants to store, should this become necessary. They can be held for up to 6 weeks at 2–4°C if provided with fluorescent light at 2.7 klx for 14 hours daily. The flat should be wrapped in a polyethylene sleeve to prevent excessive drying of the medium during the storage period (Kumpf *et al.,* 1966).

B. Plant Culture

"Unchecked growth" results if seedlings are transplanted when the first set of true leaves have developed and the seedlings are 1 to 3 cm tall. At this stage in their development, transpirational water losses are small and roots readily absorb the moisture requirements of the plants.

In earlier times seedlings were either potted into small pots or peat strips or transplanted into flats at a spacing of about 5 × 5 cm before being planted in the final growing location (Delworth, 1946). It was important that final transplanting not be delayed; if plants were permitted to grow taller than 10 cm before final benching, stunting and loss of quality in the final crop resulted (Fig. 2) (Rogers, 1959, 1960). By the mid-1950s most experts were recommending direct benching of seedlings from seed flat to flowering bench for maximum growth response (Ball, 1957).

A spacing of 115 to 125 cm^2 per stem has been recommended for winter crops (7.5 × 15 cm or 10 × 12.5 cm), and 75 to 100 cm^2 (7.5 × 10 cm or 7.5 ×

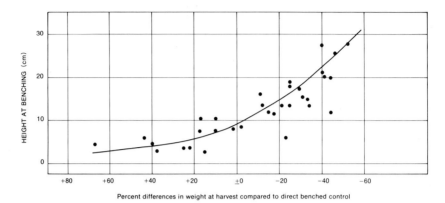

Fig. 2. The effects of height of potted snapdragon seedlings at the time of benching on the fresh weight of cut flower stems at harvest. When plants were more than 10 cm tall at time of benching, flower stems at harvest were lighter in weight than control plants directly benched using seedlings from the seed flat. (From Rogers, 1959.)

12.5 cm) for summer crops (Fries, 1962; Delworth, 1946; Sanderson, 1975b). Should a pinched crop be planned, individual plants would be planted farther apart, and the number of branches to be retained would be calculated to give about the same amount of space per flowering stem.

If only a single crop of flowers is desired from a given planting, two tiers of support that can be moved upward as the crop grows will be adequate. Years ago when second and third crops of flowers were harvested from the same planting, it was necessary to have four to six tiers of support 15 to 20 cm apart to keep stems of new crops coming up from ground level from becoming crooked. Welded wire mesh or nylon mesh is used almost exclusively today. Support fabrics with mesh sizes of 10 × 15 cm, 15 × 15 cm, or 15 × 20 cm are all suitable for this purpose.

Snapdragons grow best in open, porous, well-drained, and well-aerated media. Because snapdragons need good soil aeration, proper preparation of the growing medium prior to planting is important (Miller, 1957). Unamended field soil does not result in as good plant growth as soil to which leaf mold, peat moss, or other sources of organic matter have been added (Willis, 1954).

Severe soil compaction also causes stunted plant growth, weak root systems, and delayed flowering. When plants were grown in a uniform, screened soil compacted by tamping to bulk densities varying from 1.08 gm/cm^3 (untamped) to 1.47 gm/cm^3 (severely packed), a 30% reduction in growth of both roots and tops occurred in the severely packed plots compared to the untamped control plots (Carpenter, 1963). Excellent quality plants have been grown in media ranging from a completely soilless medium of a 1 : 1 mixture of peat : perlite, to a 1 : 1 : 1 mixture of peat : soil : perlite or sand, to a 3 : 1

soil : sand mix (Hanan and Langhans, 1962), provided soil watering, aeration, and nutritional control were properly maintained.

C. Nutrition

Traditionally, snapdragons have been considered to have relatively low nutritional requirements compared to some other crops such as chrysanthemums, roses, or poinsettias. Howland (1946) noted that relatively large differences in nitrogen, potassium, or pH levels caused no significant differences in average stem length or number of flowers produced per plant. No statistically significant differences in plant growth resulted between plants grown in soils at Spurway soil test values over the range of 1 to 10 ppm phosphorus, or 5 to 30 ppm potassium; there were differences, however, between 2 to 5 ppm and 25 to 50 ppm nitrate levels (Rogers, 1951), with stronger growth occurring at the higher nitrogen levels.

Flint and Asen (1953) grew snapdragons in sand culture with a median nutrient solution containing 160 ppm nitrogen, 32 ppm phosphorus, 240 ppm potassium, 176 ppm calcium, and 64 ppm magnesium plus minor elements, and other solutions at ¼, ½, 2, and 4 times the median concentration. No signficant plant growth differences occurred between the plants grown at the median level or lower. Nutrient concentrations higher than the median caused leaf chlorosis, fading of flower color, fewer flowers, decreased dry matter production, and shorter, weaker stems, which were attributed to the high levels of soluble salts present.

If nitrogen levels are on the low side at time of benching seedlings, liquid fertilization with nitrogen should begin promptly to ensure development of thick, heavy stems (Boodley, 1962). Overfertilization with nitrogen, on the other hand, can lead to excessive grassiness and should be avoided. Sanderson (1975c) recommends using about one-half the normally recommended 200 ppm nitrogen and potassium levels if snapdragons are to be given constant liquid fertilization. Young plants respond better to nitrate than to ammonium forms of nitrogen, so the actual nitrogen source should be selected with this response in mind (Haney, 1961).

Haney (1961) reported excellent snapdragon growth by using a formula mixture of soluble fertilizer materials (Table II) for regular liquid fertilization of snapdragons established in a 1 : 1 : 1 soil : peat : sand mixture to which had been added basic applications of dolomitic limestone and 20% superphosphate. Since phosphorus had been supplied in the basic growing medium and to the young seedlings as a complete soluble fertilizer shortly after benching, no additional soluble phosphorus was included in the fertilizer mixture used to finish the crop.

Amounts of chemicals listed in the Table II were dissolved in 20 liters of water in a glass container, and 335-ml aliquots of this concentrated solution were put

Table II

A Soluble Fertilizer Mixture Formulated to Meet Special Nutritional Needs of Snapdragon[a]

Ingredients	Formula	Quantity [b] (kg)
Potassium nitrate	KNO_3	2.2
Calcium nitrate	$CA(NO_3)_2$	4.8
Ammonium nitrate	NH_4NO_3	3.0
Magnesium nitrate	$Mg(NO_3)_2$	2.0
Borax	$Na_2B_4O_7$	0.0058
Chelated iron		0.0275

[a]From Haney (1961).
[b]This amount of each chemical was dissolved in a 20-liter container of stock solution, which was subsequently diluted for application to the plants with a Hozon proportioner (1 : 15 ratio).

into 8 liters of water, which was applied through a Hozon proportioner to 10 m² of bench area at weekly intervals. This mixture provides approximately 300 ppm nitrogen and 150 ppm potassium, and when applied once weekly approaches the recommendations given by Sanderson (1975c).

Two detailed studies to observe nutritional deficiency symptoms have been published (Laurie and Wagner, 1940, and Oertli, 1970a–h); the observations are summarized below.

Nitrogen deficiency causes stunted plant growth and an overall yellow-green color of the foliage. Few side branches are produced and stems tend to be thin, hard, and wiry.

Phosphorus deficiency also causes stunted plant growth and young leaves become very dark green in color. In some cases, purpling, especially of the undersides of older leaves, is noted. Young leaves may have the tips recurved downward and inward toward the central stem. If too much phosphate is applied to prevent phosphorus deficiency, however, there is a possibility of its reacting with calcium and magnesium ions in the soil to form insoluble calcium and magnesium phosphate salts, with calcium and magnesium deficiency problems arising later (Haney, 1961).

Potassium deficiency causes symptoms in snapdragons somewhat different from those in most plants. Both Laurie and Wagner (1940) and Oertli (1970c) reported an interveinal chlorosis of the young leaves similar to the classic iron deficiency as the initial response of snapdragons to deficient potassium. This was followed later by the development of the symptoms normally associated with potassium deficiency, such as necrosis of tips and margins of older leaves on the plant.

Calcium deficiency in snapdragons first affects the developing root system, since calcium is an element essential for the formation of primary cell walls in meristematic areas. Seedlings placed in calcium-deficient nutrient solutions died very quickly and had thin, poorly branched, and poorly developed root systems. Older, more developed plants placed under calcium-deficient conditions began to wilt after 1 or 2 weeks and died shortly thereafter. Symptoms similar to the iron chlorosis noted previously for potassium deficiency were also seen by Oertli (1970d).

The symptoms of magnesium deficiency in snapdragons are more typical of the classic pattern. Interveinal chlorosis and necrosis appear first on older leaves of the plant while young, newly developing leaves remain relatively healthy in appearance. The tips of the older leaves have been reported to curl downward and the tips of younger leaves to curl upward. High levels of ammonium nitrogen antagonize magnesium uptake (Haney, 1961), so growers should consider this antagonism as one possible cause of a magnesium deficiency problem. Since snapdragons appear to have a higher than normal magnesium requirement (Dunham *et al.,* 1956) and since magnesium uptake is also antagonized by high levels of calcium and potassium, low to medium levels of these latter cations in the growing medium should also be important for balanced nutrition of the plant.

Sulfur deficiency causes pale, yellow-green, upper leaves in which the main veins are lighter than the rest of the leaf blade. As the deficiency continues, the symptom pattern progresses downward. A fine, interveinal chlorosis may be seen on the older leaves, whereas the young leaves are more uniformly yellow-green.

Iron chlorosis of snapdragon appears first as interveinal yellowing of the youngest, most recently developed leaves and progresses to nearly complete loss of all green color from these leaves. Small axillary shoots that develop on the main stem may be almost completely white. Such symptoms may appear even in the presence of adequate supplies of iron in the growing medium if any interference with root growth or function occurs, such as might be caused by excessive levels of soluble salts, improper pH levels, calcium deficiency, root rot problems, overwatering, or inadequate soil aeration. Iron in most plants cannot be accumulated for future use but must be taken up daily to meet the plant's daily needs. Any interruption in the plant's ability to do this can result in the appearance of iron deficiency symptoms in the young leaves.

Boron deficiency has also been reported as a problem in snapdragon culture (Mastalerz, 1957; Furuta, 1960). Lack of boron inhibits meristematic activity and a common symptom will be death or abortion of the terminal growing point (in snapdragons, the terminal flower spike) followed by the growth and development of bypassing shoots from axillary buds further down the stem (Fig. 3). Boron deficiency symptoms can be precipitated by overapplication of calcium-containing fertilizers or lime, on account of an antagonistic interaction

SNAPDRAGON

0.0 PPM BORON

CALCIUM 200 PPM   1000 PPM

Fig. 3. Boron deficiency symptoms in snapdragons, right, are made more severe by the antagonistic effects of high levels of calcium in the nutrient solution. (From Carmichael, 1968.)

between the two ions in the soil (Carmichael, 1968). Since boron is a trace element, only small quantities are needed. Normal recommendations for application to snapdragons would be a maximum of 3 gm of household-grade Borax/m² of bench area per year, which may be broken up into two or three applications at lower concentrations (Mastalerz, 1957).

Other nutrient deficiency symptoms have occurred so rarely in normal snapdragon production that they can usually be disregarded.

D. Moisture and Aeration

Since the pore spaces in the growing medium are filled with either air or water, these two environmental factors need to be considered together. Many growers have noted that if snapdragons are grown at relatively high moisture levels they often succumb to root rot and wilt as plants near maturity. Because of this problem, it has often been recommended that the crop should be grown on the "dry side" to prevent such problems.

Short-term waterlogging of the medium when snapdragon plants are in the seedling stage can cause damage that will show up as decreased growth and quality of flower spikes produced at maturity (Miller, 1957). When potted seedlings were completely submerged in water for a period as short as 3 days, significant reductions in grade of the flowering stems occurred. This response was probably caused by damage to the existing root system and by the necessity of generating a new functional root system after the period of flooding.

A major complicating factor in attempting to study effects of relative air–moisture balances in the growing medium in which snapdragons are produced is the almost universal presence of *Pythium* root rot pathogens in most growing situations. Although severity of root rot problems caused by this pathogen may be reduced in some other kinds of plants by reducing soil moisture levels, degree of control of the disease achieved in snapdragon from reducing frequency of watering was not sufficient to overcome the simultaneous decrease in total plant growth resulting from moisture stress (Hanan et al., 1962, 1963).

Further exhaustive studies in this area (Hanan and Langhans, 1963, 1964) showed that if *Pythium* is rigorously excluded from the growing medium snapdragons can be grown to perfection in a wide variety of media over a range of soil moisture contents (24–34% by volume, or from 2.5–25 cm of Hg tension on a tensiometer), and when air fills between 45 and 55% of the total pore space in the root zone. Moisture contents in excess of 40% by volume reduced final product quality. When moisture levels became that high in some growing media, oxygen diffusion rates began to approach levels (18 to 23 $\times$ 10^{-8} gm/cm²/minute), which had been shown previously (Stolzy et al., 1961) to limit initiation of new roots in snapdragon. These oxygen diffusion rates were somewhat lower than the critical rate for tomatoes (30 to 40 $\times$ 10^{-8} gm/cm²/minute), which suggests that snapdragons are somewhat more tolerant of low soil aeration than some other crops.

Although growing snapdragons at high moisture levels and with minimum moisture stress maximizes total growth and flower grade, it does cause a reduction in percentage dry weight and a probable reduction in keeping quality of the product. At the same time, efficiency of water usage is reduced (Hanan, 1965). Conversely, with coarse-textured soils, lateral movement of water by capillarity is slow, which can result in high water stress in plants grown in them unless they are watered frequently. This means that the commercial grower has to maintain fairly critical balances in this area for optimum results. If *Pythium* is eliminated, and if growing media are deep enough (15 cm or greater) and porous enough to offset deleterious effects of the perched water table at the bottom of the bench, plants can be watered daily during periods of high solar radiation when moisture stress is maximum (Rutland, 1972) for optimum growth and quality. Today's commercial snapdragon producer should probably adopt this system to ensure consistent success with the crop.

E. Temperature

Seeley (1965) indicated only small differences in growth and development of snapdragons between growing medium temperatures of 11°–14°C and 20°–23°C. A more recent study, however, was carried out under more rigidly controlled environmental conditions in a growth chamber rather than in a greenhouse (Rutland and Pallas, 1972). This showed that soil or root temperatures of 10°C, when compared to those of 25°C, greatly reduced the plant's ability to maintain high levels of transpiration and resulted in increased plant moisture stress, stomatal closure, and probably reduced photosynthetic rates. Marked resistance to passage of water through roots is known to occur at temperatures lower than 25°C (Kramer, 1940). This is undoubtedly a major reason for midmorning wilting of snapdragon foliage on healthy, well-watered plants on clear winter mornings when light levels are high enough to encourage high transpiration rates before soil temperatures warm up in a greenhouse with a night temperature of 10°C. Cultivars that maintained higher leaf hydration values because of earlier stomatal closure under moisture stress produced higher quality cut flowers (McDaniel and Miller, 1976) under southern summer greenhouse conditions than cultivars that had less control of moisture loss. Cut flower quality would probably be improved by use of soil warming treatments if soil temperatures were low enough to cause any appreciable plant wilting.

Although many plants probably have different optimum temperatures for growth at different stages in their overall development, this relationship has been studied more intensively for snapdragons than for most other plants (Miller, 1958a,b, 1959, 1962a,b; Tayama and Miller, 1965). They have shown that optimum growing temperatures for snapdragons, based on dry weight accumulation of the top of the plant, decreased from a high of about 27°C for young seedlings held at constant day and night temperatures to a low of about 15°C for plants approaching flowering. A series of plants grown at a constant day temperature of 15°C but at various night temperatures showed optimum night temperatures varying from 20°C for young plants to night temperatures of 13°C for plants near flowering (Table III).

The causes for these differences were later shown to be changes in the ratio of leaf dry weight to total plant dry weight as plants aged. Young plants had high leaf dry weight (tissue capable of carrying on photosynthesis) in relation to total dry weight (tissue capable of carrying on respiration). In young plants photosynthesis is the dominant process; in older plants respiration dominates. High temperatures, then, would increase the rate of photosynthesis in young plants to a greater extent than respiration, and this would result in increased rates of dry matter accumulation. In older plants, with a lower ratio of leaf area

Table III

Optimum Temperatures for Dry Weight Production by Snapdragons, Cultivar Brokers Tip, of Various Sizes[a]

Age when treated (weeks)	Constant day–night temperature (°C)	Night temperature (°C)
20	15	13
18	16	—[b]
16	17	16
12	18	17
10	22	—
8	27	17
5	31[c]	—
4	24	20

[a]Held during 4 weeks at constant day–night temperatures, or at approximately 15°C during the day with various night temperatures. Data obtained from regression equations. From Miller (1962).

[b]Dash indicates that plants of this age were not included in this series of night temperature treatments.

[c]The highest temperature used experimentally was 26.7°C. It seems likely that this value is abnormally high, perhaps because of the difficulty of calculating a maximum for a regression line with as little curvature as the one for plants at 5 weeks of age.

to total bulk, lower temperatures would tend to retard respiration (the dominant process in such plants) more than they would photosynthesis, and thus would result in maximum rates of dry matter accumulation (Tayama and Miller, 1965).

Some authors have suggested that reducing night temperatures after dark, cloudy days and increasing them after bright, sunny days might increase growth rates and quality of some flower crops. Miller (1960) attempted this procedure with snapdragons. He found that reducing night temperatures after cloudy days had no measurable effect on size or quality of flower spikes but that increasing night temperatures from the "normal" 10°C to 15°C after bright days resulted in slightly earlier flowering but slightly smaller flower spikes. Differences were probably not great enough to be commercially important.

Snapdragons have long been grown as a cool greenhouse crop with a night temperature of 10°–11°C being considered optimum. Group I or group II cultivars should be selected for growth under such conditions in the northern greenhouse during midwinter months. Another alternative has also been suggested (Duffett, 1961): to grow group III cultivars at 15°C night temperatures in the same greenhouse with year-round chrysanthemums. Quality was good and timing of the crop was similar to that required for a single-stem chrysanthemum crop grown during the same season. Many group I or II cultivars grown at these warm night temperatures in Missouri, however, were found to have soft, short stems and poor overall quality, and were considered unsalable (Rogers, 1961).

F. Light

Snapdragons were long-day, summer-flowering plants until 1926 when 'Chevoit Maid,' the first winter flowering cultivar, was introduced (Lindstrom, 1966). Since that time many cultivars have been introduced, some which flower better in winter and others which are more satisfactory for summer flowering.

Early work by Laurie and Poesch (1932), Roberts and Struckmeyer (1939), and Post (1942) indicated that snapdragons responded to daylength, flowering earlier under long days. Haney (1953) suggested giving young snapdragon plants short days by pulling black cloth during September and October to prevent premature flowering of late fall and early winter crops caused by unusually bright, warm fall weather. Increased stem length also resulted from this practice. These findings were confirmed by Rogers (1958), who used other cultivars developed at a later date.

The response of snapdragons to daylength differs from the daylength response of chrysanthemums or poinsettias (Maginnes and Langhans, 1967a). Instead of inhibiting or promoting flowering as was true for the latter two crops, daylength treatments exerted quantitative effects on snapdragons, and plants have now been classified as quantitative long-day plants in their response to daylength (Hedley, 1974). Long days hasten flowering in most cultivars; short days retard flowering, but do not completely prevent it in most cases, with the possible exception of some of the group IV cultivars.

It also became evident that snapdragons reacted most markedly to daylength treatments when plants were between 5 and 20 cm high (Haney, 1953), when they had 10 to 12 leaves (Maginnes and Langhans, 1967a), or 5 to 7 weeks after seeding (Rogers, 1958; Maginnes and Langhans, 1967a). Long-day treatments applied prior to the beginning of and during this light-sensitive stage reduced the number of leaves produced by the plant, hastened flower bud initiation, shortened stems, and also hastened flower development to salable maturity. Short-day treatments applied at the same stage of development caused opposite effects. Although temperature modified responses of some cultivars, it was judged to have a rather minor influence in the plant's response, except as it affected overall growth rates (Maginnes and Langhans, 1967a).

Cultivars from the different response groups responded in the same general way to daylength treatments with some differences in degree (Sanderson and Link, 1967). In recent studies in England, (Hedley, 1974: Hedley and Harvey, 1975), it was found that cultivars from groups I or II become increasingly more responsive to brief long-day flower induction treatments with increasing plant age, whereas cultivars in Group IV did not. It appears that the latter cultivars require a considerably greater flower inducing stimulus than do Group I or II cultivars. The exact reason for this difference in response is still under study.

Four-hour exposures from 10 P.M. to 2 A.M. to flashing light from incandescent lamps at 100 to 270 lx intensities were shown to be as effective in providing long-day treatment for snapdragons as a continuous 4-hour light break during the same period, if the light was on at least 10 or more seconds each minute. At 5 seconds per minute, plant response was not quite as marked as at longer exposures (Maginnes and Langhans, 1967b).

In addition to responding to length of day as a facultative long-day plant, snapdragons have also been shown to respond photosynthetically to supplementary lighting at intensities and durations higher than needed to elicit photoperiodic responses. Petersen (1955) showed marked increases in dry weight of young snapdragon plants following all-night supplementary lighting with fluorescent lamps at 86 to 108 lamp W/m² with the tubes 20 to 25 cm above the plants (Fig. 4).

Application of supplementary lighting at the same intensity level during the daytime had little or no beneficial effect upon growth of the plants. It was concluded that extending the number of hours each day during which photosynthetic activity could occur was of more benefit than attempting to increase light intensity levels during daylight hours. Flint (1960) also demonstrated that given amounts of supplementary light applied over long periods daily produced longer stems, greater leaf area, and greater dry weight than the same amount of light applied over a shorter time span.

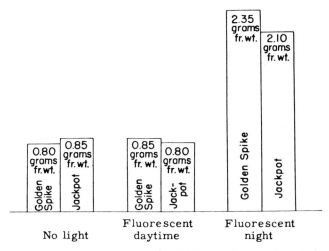

Fig. 4. The effects of supplementary fluorescent lighting at 86 to 104 lamp W/m² on growth of snapdragon (Golden Spike or Jackpot) seedlings. Significantly better growth resulted from lighting at night than from lighting in the daytime. fr. wt., Fresh weight. Growing conditions: temperature, 50°F; duration, 30 days. (From Petersen, 1955.)

Snapdragons have also been shown to benefit from higher midwinter light levels achieved by reflecting additional natural sunlight onto greenhouse benches using bright aluminum foil reflectors placed on the north side of benches oriented east-west (Carpenter, 1964).

Since high-intensity supplemental lighting is relatively expensive to apply, it is recommended that such treatments be carried out only during the small plant stage, before plants have been transplanted at final spacing to the cut-flower benches (Flint, 1958). However, if young seedlings are kept in small pots before benching to make it possible to apply economical supplementary light-ing treatments, the plants soon benefit more from transplanting to the final bench than from continued lighting (Rogers, 1960). This pivotal point appears to be when plant height reaches approximately 10 cm (see Section II, B) (Rogers, 1959). Apparently plants suffer from either moisture or nutritional stress if held for too long in small containers.

In still another study, Rogers (1961) found that providing snapdragons with 1100 to 3300 lx of supplementary lighting, using mercury vapor lamps for 3 weeks after benching in a 10°C night temperature greenhouse, gave final plant quality and timing results comparable to growing the plants at approximately 15°C night temperature without supplementary lighting. Plant growth was has-tened about equally by either warmer growing temperatures or added light.

G. Carbon Dioxide Enrichment

Although roses and chrysanthemums have been shown to respond dramati-cally to carbon dioxide enrichment of the greenhouse atmosphere, especially at slightly elevated day temperatures (Shaw and Rogers, 1964a-d), snap-dragons were found to be much less responsive in midwinter in Missouri. Little difference in stem length, stem weight, or flower spike length resulted from carbon dioxide enrichment at either 10° or 15°C night temperatures and higher day temperatures. Flowering was accelerated about 10 days, however, com-pared to control plants that did not receive additional carbon dioxide.

Koths (1964) also reported only slight benefits from carbon dioxide enrich-ment at 400 to 500 ppm when both treated and untreated plants were grown in Connecticut at 10°C night temperature. Lindstrom (1966) grew cultivars rep-resenting groups I, II, III, and IV at approximately 15°C night temperatures and at carbon dioxide levels of 1500 and 4000 ppm in Michigan. Under such growing conditions, cultivars from groups I or II were not considered salable, either with or without additional carbon dioxide. Groups III or IV cultivars, however, flowered sooner and were of higher grade when grown under condi-tions of carbon dioxide enrichment, and were considered to be of excellent quality. There were not enough additional benefits, however, from 4000 ppm CO_2 over 1500 ppm to justify the additional cost of adding it.

Duffett (1968) recommended the use of 15°C night temperatures and carbon dioxide enrichment to 800 ppm for routine winter culture of this crop under the low light conditions of northern Ohio. Since the cost of carbon dioxide enrichment came to only $0.40–0.50/m²/yr, the 2 to 6 weeks' saving in bench time for each crop made its use a highly profitable innovation. Carbon dioxide levels higher than 800 ppm were conducive to excessively heavy stems and grassy growth in that area.

Under the milder winter conditions of North Carolina, where the time that greenhouse ventilation could be restricted enough to make carbon dioxide injection feasible was very limited, carbon dioxide enrichment at either 750 or 1500 ppm was found to have only slightly beneficial effects for snapdragon production (Nelson and Larson, 1969). It would seem then, that carbon dioxide enrichment to about 800 ppm and warmer than normal temperatures are commercially desirable practices only when the later flowering response groups are used, and predominantly in the low-light, colder growing areas of northern United States.

III. PLANT PROTECTION AND PEST CONTROL

A. Air Pollution Problems

Of the various air pollutant gases that can affect plants injuriously, ethylene (Fischer, 1950) probably is the most damaging to snapdragons. This gas causes shattering or premature dropping of florets. Haney (1953) conclusively demonstrated that this problem is controlled by a single gene dominant for shattering. In the development of new hybrid cultivars, one test given routinely by some breeders is an ethylene test to separate shattering from nonshattering cultivars (Anonymous, 1961).

B. Diseases

Several reviews, some well illustrated, on the subject of diseases have been published in recent years (Judd, 1975; Williamson, 1962; Nelson, 1962; Dimock, 1958; Forsberg, 1958). The most common and serious diseases of greenhouse snapdragons vary from one growing area to another. Botrytis blight, for example, is a very serious disease in the cool, moist, low winter light area of northeastern United States, but is rarely seen in many other areas. Powdery mildew and downy mildew are likewise much more troublesome in some areas than others.

Two of the newer systemic fungicides have been shown to be useful for snapdragon growers. Benomyl has been shown to give effective control of powdery mildew when applied either as a soil drench or foliar spray at proper concentrations (Raabe et al., 1970a). Plantvax, a new oxycarboxin fungicide, used as a postplanting soil drench, gave effective protection against snapdragon rust (Raabe et al., 1970b).

Several diseases, previously unreported as occurring on snapdragons, have recently been noted. *Alternaria* species and *Helminthosporium* species have been found infecting snapdragon flowers in Florida, producing symptoms very similar to *Botrytis* flower infection. Instead of producing masses of gray mold mycelium and spores on the surface of rotted tissue typical of *Botrytis,* however, *Alternaria* produced abundant masses of black spores on tissue, and *Helminthosporium* sporulated on the infected tissue, but did not develop dense spore masses characteristic of the other two fungi (Engelhard, 1971).

Snapdragon leafspot, caused by *Cercospora antirrhina,* has been a serious problem for many North Carolina growers for the past 10 to 15 years (Porter and Aycock, 1967). All greenhouse cultivars tested were about equally susceptible. The fungus may survive in dried infected leaves for over 14 months and in leaves in or on the soil for over 3 months. For these reasons, careful sanitation to remove potential inoculum sources is recommended as a primary control measure. Use of fungicidal sprays as protectants prior to inoculation would also seem prudent for growers who have experienced this problem in the greenhouse.

C. Insects

In general, the snapdragon is relatively free of insect pests, but several species may invade plantings. Aphids, spider mites, and looper larvae are the most common (Poe, 1971). Since it is illegal according to the Federal Environmental Pesticide Control Act of 1972 to use any pesticide in any way inconsistent with the product label, only materials labeled for the crop and for the pest concerned should be used. The materials listed in Table IV are currently registered for use on snapdragons for control of the pests mentioned.

Table IV

Chemical Pesticides Effective for Control of Principal Insect and Mite Pests of Snapdragons

Pest	Pesticide registered for use	
Aphids	Aldicarb (Temik)	Granules
	Endosulfan (Thiodan)	Foliar spray
	Nicotine	Vapors, smoke generator
	Oxydemetonmethyl (Meta-Systox-R) and others	Foliar spray
Spider mites	Dicofol (Kelthane)	Fog
	Pentac	Foliar spray
Looper larvae	*Bacillus thuringensis* (Thuricide, Dipel, Biotrol)	Foliar spray
	Trichlorfon (Dylox)	Foliar spray

Snapdragons have been reported sensitive to the following chemicals used for pest control, and these normally should be avoided, or plant injury may occur: malathion, nicotine, tetraethyl pyrophosphate (TEPP), sulfur, and chlorobenside (Poe, 1971).

There is also some potential for satisfactory biological control of some snapdragon pests. Harbaugh and Mattson (1973) reported effective control, at a commercially acceptable level, of aphids on greenhouse snapdragons from the predatory activities of lacewing (*Chrysopa carnea*) larvae released twice during the growth of a crop. It must be noted, however, that these experiments were carried out during the summer when greenhouse temperatures ranged from 13° to 29°C (21° ± 8°C), and also that predator activities were much greater at the warmer end of the temperature scale. It is unlikely that this predator could operate effectively during winter in snapdragon greenhouses at 10°–15°C night temperatures.

IV. CARE AND HANDLING OF THE FINISHED PRODUCT

A. Harvesting and Grading

Traditionally, snapdragons have been harvested when the florets on the lower third of the spike are open. Since the cut flowers are subject to tip curvature if stems are placed other than vertically (Teas and Sheehan, 1957), they must always be held in an upright position. In recent years cut flowers have been shipped in upright containers such as gladiolus hampers to prevent crooked tips (Sanderson, 1975).

Several papers have reported the possible use of chemical growth regulators to overcome geotropic bending (Bennett and Smith, 1955; Teas and Sheehan, 1957; Joiner et al., 1974). Experimental Alanap (n-1-napthylphthalamic acid) treatments appeared to reduce greatly or prevent tip bending, but the treatment has not yet been widely used commercially.

The Society of American Florists has established standard grades for snapdragons based on stem length, stem weight, and number of open florets per stem (Table V). Material to be marketed under these grade standards must have reasonably straight stems, and clean, uniform foliage free of insect or disease injury. Foliage on the lower third of the stem should be removed.

B. Long-Term Storage

The earliest work on long-term holding of snapdragons was done by Mastalerz (1953). This involved the use of −1°C temperature and dry-pack storage. Under these conditions some snapdragon cultivars could be held for up to 3 weeks without appreciable loss of quality or vase life (compared to that of freshly harvested flowers). It was necessary to cut spikes before the oldest

Table V

Minimum Specifications for S.A.F. Standard Grades of Snapdragons [a]

Grade name	Label color	Weight per spike (gm)		Minimum open flowers per stem (number)	Minimum stem length (cm)	Stems per bunch (number)
		Minimum	Maximum			
Special	Blue	71	113	15	91	12
Fancy	Red	43	70	12	76	12
Extra	Green	29	42	9	61	12
First	Yellow	14	28	6	46	12

[a]The term *utility* is not a grade within the meaning of these standards. Material that does not grade because of crooked stems, foliage injury, or abnormal growth may be marketed under the designation *utility* (white label). The term *unclassified* is not a grade within the meaning of these standards but is provided as a designation to show that no definite grade has been applied to the lot.

floret was more than 1 week old, since florets that opened following storage were often faded in color.

Snapdragons that are cut when only one or two florets are open can now be opened successfully in floral preservative solutions containing 8-HQC (8-hydroxyquinoline citrate) and sucrose (Raulston and Marousky, 1971). Chrysanthemums, gladiolus, *Strelitzia,* and carnation buds react similarly, and these can open successfully even after prolonged holding of cut buds in low-temperature dry-pack storage conditions (Kofranek, 1976). It should not take too much longer to perfect the same techniques for snapdragons.

Another development that may have future potential in this area is the use of hypobaric storage. Burg (1973) found that snapdragons could be held at 40 mm Hg pressure for up to 6 weeks in good condition, compared to the 3-week maximum for the best methods used previously.

C. Snapdragon Tip Breakage

Breakage of the tips of snapdragon spikes during harvesting and grading is a common problem with certain cultivars, particularly during months of low light intensity. The break is usually clean, without any appreciable tearing of stem tissues. The point of breakage has been shown to be at the top end of the lignified xylem column, which was close to the apex in red and rose cultivars, and much lower in bronze and yellow cultivars. This is logical since pigments present in bronze and yellow cultivars and xylem lignification are both dependent upon phenyl propanoid precursors. In cultivars where there is a strong demand on these precursors for flower pigment formation, xylem lignification will follow at a greater distance below the apex and the break point will be lower when stems are handled (Adams and Urdahl, 1972). Since this is a genetically controlled plant characteristic there is a good chance that improvements in cultivars could be made by plant breeders who choose to work on the problem.

D. Postharvest Physiology

Few cut flower crops are more responsive to good postharvest treatment than snapdragons. Freshly cut flower spikes of most cultivars will have a vase life of about 1 week in tap water or distilled water. When the best combination of flower preservatives is used, vase life can be increased two or three times.

Larsen and Scholes (1966) and Raulston and Marousky (1970) found that longest vase life, greatest number of florets opening, and greatest increase in spike length after cutting occurred when flowers were held in a solution containing 300 ppm of 8-hydroxyquinoline citrate (8-HQC) + 1.5% sucrose. The former researchers also found the addition of 25 ppm alar (n-dimethylamino-succinamic acid) to be beneficial. Johnson (1972) got best results from a solution of 300 ppm 8-HQC + 0.5% sucrose.

Both light and floral preservatives are crucial for proper development of floret color in florets that open after harvest (Marousky and Raulston, 1970). Regardless of the solution used, spikes held in darkness produced little anthocyanin and were poorly colored. In the light, those spikes held in 8-HQC + sucrose produced much more intensely colored florets than those held in tap water. Light (2150 lx) incident on the developing floret at the time of opening was critical for anthocyanin production.

Self-generated ethylene gas can be a prime cause of early senescence in cut snapdragons. One of the reasons for excellent results with hypobaric storage is the constant removal of trace quantities of ethylene from the storage atmosphere. Another approach to control of ethylene problems has involved use of chemicals to suppress ethylene formation (Wang, et al., 1977). In this study, two analogs of rhizobitoxine and sodium benzoate were tested to determine the relationships between their effects on ethylene production by flowers, and keeping quality. Both ethoxy and methoxy analogs of rhizobitoxine significantly reduced ethylene production and increased vase life. Perhaps this new family of chemicals will be beneficial in enhancing snapdragon keeping quality on an applied basis.

REFERENCES

Adams, D. G., and Urdahl, W. A. (1972). Snapdragon stem tip breakage as related to stem lignification and flower color. *J. Am. Soc. Hortic. Sci.* **97,** 474–477.
Anonymous (1961). How Yoder checks snaps for shattering. *Yoder Grower Circle News* **7,** 10.
Ball, V., ed. (1952). "The Ball Red Book," 8th. ed., Geo. J. Ball, Inc., West Chicago, Illinois.
Ball, V., ed. (1957). "The Ball Red Book," 9th ed., Geo. J. Ball, Inc., West Chicago, Illinois.
Bennett, J. L., and Smith, J. E., Jr. (1955). A geotropic response of snapdragons to treatment with trichlorophenoxypropionic acid. *Natl. Snapdragon Soc. Bull.* **4,** 2.

Boodley, J. W. (1962). Fertilization. *In* "Snapdragons" (R. W. Langhans, ed.), pp. 28–34. N.Y. State Flower Grow. Assoc., Inc., Ithaca, New York.

Burg, S. P. (1973). Hypobaric storage of cut flowers. *HortScience* **8,** 202–205.

Carmichael, O. E. (1968). "Boron Toxicity of Flowering Plants." Masters Thesis, University of Missouri, Columbia.

Carpenter, W. J. (1963). Soil compaction studies. *Florists' Rev.* **132**(3408), 26.

Carpenter, W. J. (1964). Response of snapdragons and chrysanthemums to supplemental reflective sunlight. *Proc. Am. Soc. Hortic. Sci.* **84,** 624–629.

Cathey, H. M. (1969). Guidelines for the germination of annual, pot plant and ornamental herb seeds-3. *Florists' Rev.* **144**(3744), 26–29, 75–77.

Delworth, C. I. (1946). Fundamentals and details in producing quality snapdragons. *Florists' Rev.* **99**(2559), 35–36.

Dimock, A. W. (1958). Snapdragon diseases common in New York. *N.Y. State Flower Grow. Bull.* **145,** 2–3.

Duffett, W. E. (1960). Response groups and varieties for year-round snapdragons. *Ohio Florists' Assoc., Bull.* **371,** 4–5.

Duffett, W. E. (1961). Grow these snaps in 60° greenhouses along with mums. *Yoder Grower Circle News* **7,** 3.

Duffett, W. E. (1968). Culture of greenhouse snapdragons. *Ohio Florists' Assoc., Bull.* **466,** 5–7.

Dunham, C. W., Hamner, C. L., and Asen, S. (1956). Cation exchange properties of the roots of some ornamental plant species. *Proc. Am. Soc. Hortic. Sci.* **68,** 556–563.

Engelhard, A. W. (1971). Botrytis-like diseases of rose, chrysanthemum, carnation, snapdragon, and King aster caused by *Alternaria* and *Helminthosporium*. *Proc. Fla. State Hortic. Soc.* **83,** 455–457.

Fischer, C. W., Jr. (1950). Production of a toxic volatile by flowering stems of common snapdragon and calceolaria. *Proc. Am. Soc. Hortic. Sci.* **55,** 447–454.

Flint, H. L. (1958). Snapdragon lighting. *N.Y. State Flower Grow. Bull.* **145,** 1, 3–5.

Flint, H. L. (1960). Relative effects of light duration and intensity on growth and flowering of winter snapdragon (*Antirrhinum majus* L.). *Proc. Am. Soc. Hortic. Sci.* **75,** 769–773.

Flint, H. L., and Asen, S. (1953). The effects of various nutrient intensities on growth and development of snapdragons (*Antirrhinum majus* L.). *Proc. Am. Soc. Hortic. Sci.* **62,** 481–486.

Fries, H. (1962). Planting, pinching, spacing, and supporting. *In* "Snapdragons" (R. W. Langhans, ed.), pp. 24–27. N.Y. State Flower Grow. Assoc., Inc., Ithaca, New York.

Forsberg, J. L. (1958). Snapdragon diseases. *Ill. State Flor. Assoc. Bull.* **186,** 5–8.

Furuta, T. (1960). Test boron deficiency in snapdragons at Auburn. *Florists' Rev.* **126**(3244), 25

Hanan, J. J. (1965). Efficiency and effect of irrigation regimes on growth and flowering of snapdragons. *Proc. Am. Soc. Hortic. Sci.* **86,** 681–692.

Hanan, J. J., and Langhans, R. W. (1962). Soil aeration-progress report. *N.Y. State Flower Grow. Bull.* **198,** 1–2, 6.

Hanan, J. J., and Langhans, R. W. (1963). Soil aeration and moisture controls snapdragon quality. *N.Y. State Flower Grow. Bull.* **210,** 3–6.

Hanan, J. J., and Langhans, R. W. (1964). Soil water content and the growth and flowering of snapdragons. *Proc. Am. Soc. Hortic. Sci.* **84,** 613–623.

Hanan, J. J., Langhans, R. W., and Dimock, A. W. (1962). Soil aeration and the *Pythium* root rot disease of snapdragon. *N.Y. State Flower Grow. Bull.* **195,** 1–6.

Hanan, J. J., Langhans, R. W., and Dimock, A. W. (1963). *Pythium* and soil aeration. *Proc. Am. Soc. Hortic. Sci.* **82,** 574–582.

Haney, W. J. (1951). Timing of single stem snaps. *Mich. Florist* **244,** 13.

Haney, W. J. (1952). Snapdragon shattering. *Mich. Florist* **258,** 24.

Haney, W. J. (1953). Daylength manipulation to time snapdragons. *Natl. Snapdragon Soc. Bull.* **2,** 1–3, 12.

Haney, W. J. (1961). Snapdragon culture. *Mich. Florist.* **366,** 25–26, 29.

Harbaugh, B. K., and Mattson, R. H. (1973). Lacewing larvae control aphids on greenhouse snapdragons. *J. Am. Soc. Hortic. Sci.* **98,** 306–309.

Harman, G. E., Heit, C. E., Pfleger, F. L., and Braverman, S. W. (1973). Snapdragon blight—a serious problem caused by seedborne fungi. *Plant Dis. Rep.* **57,** 592–595.

Hedley, C. L. (1974). Response to light intensity and day-length of two contrasting flower varieties of *Antirrhinum majus* L. *J. Hortic. Sci.* **49,** 105–112.

Hedley, C. L. and Harvey, D. M. (1975). Variation in the photoperiodic control of flowering of two cultivars of *Antirrhinum majus* L., *Ann. Bot.* (*London*) **39,** 257–263.

Holley W. D., Jr. (1966). Year around culture of snapdragon in Colorado. *Colo. Flower Grow. Assoc. Bull.* **200,** 1–4.

Howland, J. E. (1946). Foliar dieback of the greenhouse snapdragon *Antirrhinum majus* and a study of the influence of certain environmental factors upon flower production and quality. *Proc. Am. Soc. Hortic. Sci.* **47,** 485–497.

Johnson, C. R. (1972). Effectiveness of floral preservatives on increasing the vase-life of snapdragons. *Florists' Rev.* **149**(3868), 47, 95–97.

Joiner, J. N., Sheehan, T. J., and Mitchell, K. F. (1974). Control of ageotropic response in snapdragon flower spikes. *Proc. Fla. State Hortic. Soc.* **86,** 374–376.

Judd, R. W., Jr. (1975). Snapdragon diseases. *Conn. Greenhouse Newslett.* **65,** 6–12.

Kofranek, A. M. (1976). Opening flower buds after storage. *Acta Hortic.* **64,** 231–237.

Koths, J. S. (1964). The effects of CO_2 enriched greenhouse atmosphere on growth of snapdragons. *Mich. Flor.* **399,** 15.

Kramer, P. J. (1940). Root resistance as a cause of decreased water absorption by plants at low temperatures. *Plant Physiol.* **15,** 63–67.

Kumpf, J., Horton, F., and Langhans, R. W. (1966). Seedling storage. *N.Y. State Flower Grow. Bull.* **244,** 1–3.

Larsen, F. E., and Scholes, J. F. (1966). Effects of 8-hydroxyquinoline citrate, *N*-dimethyl amino succinamic acid, and sucrose on vase-life and spike characteristics of cut snapdragons. *Proc. Am. Soc. Hortic. Sci.* **89,** 694–701.

Laurie, A., and Poesch G. H. (1932). Photoperiodism—the value of supplementary illumination and reduction of light on flowering plants in the greenhouse. *Ohio, Agric. Exp. Stn. Res. Bull.* **512,** 8, 31, 35.

Laurie, A., and Wagner, A. (1940). Deficiency symptoms of greenhouse flowering crops. *Ohio, Agric. Exp. Stn. Res. Bull.* **611,** 19–21.

Lindstom, R. S. (1966). Snapdragons—60°F and CO_2. *Florists' Rev.* **139**(3591), 18–19, 51–54.

Maginnes, E. A., and Langhans, R. W. (1967a). Photoperiod and flowering of snapdragon. *N.Y. State Flower Grow. Bull.* **260,** 1–3.

Maginnes, E. A., and Langhans, R. W. (1967b). Flashing light affects the flowering of snapdragons. *N.Y. State Flower Grow. Bull.* **261,** 1–3.

Marousky, F. J., and Raulston, J. C. (1970). Enhancement of snapdragon floret color with light and floral preservatives. *HortScience* **5,** 355 (Abs.).

Mastalerz, J. W. (1953). Low-temperature conditioning of snaps. *Natl. Snapdragon Soc. Bull.* **3,** 1, 3.

Mastalerz, J. W. (1957). Boron deficiency of snapdragons. *Penn. Flower Grow. Bull.* **75,** 3–6.

McDaniel, G. L., and Miller, M. G. (1976). Transpiration of snapdragon under southern summer greenhouse conditions. *HortScience* **11,** 366–368.

Miller, R. O. (1957). Snaps need good drainage. *N.Y. State Flower Grow. Bull.* **140,** 1–3.

Miller, R. O. (1958a). "A Study of the Vegetative Growth and Flowering of Snapdragons (*Antirrhinum majus*) as Affected by the Interrelationship of Light Intensity and Night Temperature." Ph.D. Thesis, Cornell University, Ithaca, New York.

Miller, R. O. (1958b). 50° for snapdragons? *N.Y. State Flower Grow. Bull.* **145,** 1, 8.

Miller, R. O. (1959). What temperature for greenhouse snapdragons? *Natl. Snapdragon Soc. Bull.* **10,** 3.

Miller, R. O. (1960). Growth and flowering of snapdragons as affected by night temperatures adjusted in relation to light intensity. *Proc. Am. Soc. Hortic. Sci.* **75**, 761–768.

Miller, R. O. (1962a). Snapdragon temperature studies. *Ohio Florists' Assoc. Bull.* **395**, 2–3.

Miller, R. O. (1962b). Variations in optimum temperatures of snapdragons depending on plant size. *Proc. Am. Soc. Hortic. Sci.* **81**, 535–543.

Nelson, P. (1962). Diseases. *In* "Snapdragons" (R. W. Langhans, ed.), pp. 70–80. N.Y. State Flower Grow. Assoc., Ithaca, New York.

Nelson, P. V., and Larson, R. A. (1969). The effects of increased CO_2 concentrations on chrysanthemum (*C. morifolium*) and snapdragon (*Antirrhinum majus*). *N.C. Agric. Exp. Stn., Tech. Bull.* **194**, 1–15.

Oertli, J. J. (1970a). Nutrient disorders in snapdragons. *Florists' Rev.* **146**(3773), 20–21.

Oertli, J. J. (1970b). Phosphorus deficiency. *Florists'. Rev.* **146**(3774), 28–29.

Oertli, J. J. (1970c). Potassium deficiency. *Florists'. Rev.* **146**(3775), 29.

Oertli, J. J. (1970d). Calcium deficiency. *Florists'. Rev.* **146**(3776), 51.

Oertli, J. J. (1970e). Magnesium deficiency. *Florists'. Rev.* **146**(3777), 23.

Oertli, J. J. (1970f). Sulfur deficiency. *Florists'. Rev.* **146**(3778), 28.

Oertli, J. J. (1970g). Boron deficiency. *Florists' Rev.* **146**(3779), 65.

Oertli, J. J. (1970h). Iron deficiency. *Florists' Rev.* **146**(3780), 24.

Payne, R. N. (1970). Timing of snapdragons under fiberglass in Oklahoma. *Okla. Greenhouse Grow. Newslett.* **7**, 4–6.

Petersen, H. (1955). Artificial light for seedlings and cuttings. *N.Y. State Flower Grow. Bull.* **122**, 2–3.

Poe, S. (1971). Major pests of snapdragon. *Fla. Flower Grow.* **8**(2), 1–3.

Porter, D. M., and Aycock, R. (1967). Snapdragon leafspot caused by *Cercospora antirrhina*. *N. C. Agric. Exp. Stn. Tech. Bull.* **179**, 1–31.

Post, K. (1942). Effects of daylength and temperature on growth and flowering of some florist crops. *N.Y. (Cornell) Agric. Exp. Stn. Bull.* **787**, 56.

Raabe, R. D., Hurlimann, J. H., and Sciaroni, R. H. (1970a). Powdery mildew control with benomyl for greenhouse-grown snapdragons. *Florist Nursery Exch.* **153**(17), 4.

Raabe, R. D., Hurlimann, J. H., McCain, A. H., and Sciaroni, R. H. (1970b). Snapdragon rust control with Plantvax—a progress report. *Florists' Rev.* **147**(3812), 19, 45.

Raulston, J. C. (1972a). 1970–1971 evaluation of snapdragon cultivars for Florida field (saranhouse) production. *Fla. Flower Grow.* **9**(1), 2–8.

Raulston, J. C. (1972b). Cultivar selection and crop timing for production of snapdragons in Florida field culture. *Fla. Flower Grow.* **9**(2), 1–9.

Raulston, J. C. and Marousky, F. J. (1970). Enhancement of snapdragon floret color with light and floral preservatives. *HortScience* **5**, 355 (Abs.).

Raulston, J. C., and Marousky, F. J. (1971). Effects of 8–10 day 5°C storage and floral preservatives on snapdragon cut flowers. *Fla. Flower Grow.* **8**(2), 4–10.

Roberts, R. H., and Struckmeyer, B. E. (1939). Further studies on the effects of temperature and other environmental factors upon the photoperiodic response of plants. *J. Agric. Res.* **59**, 699–709.

Rogers, M. N. (1951). "Greenhouse Soil Fertility Analysis and Interpretation," Masters Thesis, University of Missouri, Columbia, Missouri.

Rogers, M. N. (1958). Year around snapdragon culture. 1. Effects of lighting and shading snaps seeded during the summer months. *Mo. State Florists News* **18**(3), 3–7.

Rogers, M. N. (1959). Year around snapdragon culture. 2. Summer snapdragons. *Mo. State Florist News* **20**(6), 3–6.

Rogers, M. N. (1960). Direct benching vs. potting snapdragon seedlings. *Penn. Flower Grow. Bull.* **118**, 3–5.

Rogers, M. N. (1961). The reactions of varieties of different response groups grown during the winter months at night temperatures of 60°F, 50°F, and 50°F with supplementary lighting. *Natl. Snapdragon Soc. Bull.* **13**, 1–6.

Rutland, R. F. (1972). Transpiration of *Antirrhinum majus L.* in relation to radiant energy in the greenhouse. *HortScience* **7,** 39–40.

Rutland, R. B., and Pallas, J. E., Jr. (1972). Transpiration of *Antirrhinum majus* L. 'Panama' as influenced by soil temperature. *J. Am. Sco. Hortic. Sci.* **97,** 34–37.

Sanderson, K. C., and Link, C. B. (1967). The influence of temperature and photoperiod on the growth and quality of a winter and summer cultivar of snapdragon, *Antirrhinum majus L., Proc. Am. Soc. Hortic. Sci.* **91,** 598–611.

Sanderson K. C. (1975a). A crop to meet the energy crisis—snapdragons. Introduction, scheduled production and cultivar selection. *Florists' Rev.* **156**(4036), 23–24.

Sanderson, K. C. (1975b). Propagation, transplanting, crop support. *Florists' Rev.* **156**(4037), 58, 110–111.

Sanderson, K. C. (1975c). Fertilization, watering, temperature, light and photoperiod. *Florists' Rev.* **156**(4038), 17, 59–61.

Sanderson, K. C. (1975d). Shattering, diseases, insects. *Florists' Rev.* **156**(4039), 31.

Sanderson, K. C. (1975e). Harvesting, grading and quality, packing and shipping. *Florists' Rev.* **156**(4040), 81, 136–139.

Sanderson, K. C. and Martin, W. C. (1975). Evaluation and scheduling of snapdragon cultivars. *Ala. (Auburn) Agric. Exp. Stn., Bull.* **468,** 1–21.

Seeley, J. G. (1965). Soil temperature and the growth of greenhouse snapdragons. *Proc. Am. Soc. Hortic. Sci.* **86,** 693–694.

Shaw, R. J., and Rogers, M. N. (1964a). Interactions between elevated carbon dioxide levels and greenhouse temperatures on the growth of roses, chrysanthemums, carnations, geraniums, snapdragons, and African violets. *Florists' Rev.* **135**(3486), 23–24, 88–89.

Shaw, R. J., and Rogers, M. N. (1964b). Roses—heat + CO_2. *Florists' Rev.* **135**(3487), 21–22, 82.

Shaw, R. J., and Rogers, M. N. (1964c). Chrysanthemums. *Florists' Rev.* **135**(3488), 73–74, 95–96.

Shaw, R. J., and Rogers, M. N. (1964d). Various flowers. *Florists' Rev.* **135**(3941), 19, 37–39.

Stolzy, L. H., Letey, J., Szuszkiewicz, T. E., and Lunt, O. R. (1961). Root growth and diffusion rates as functions of oxygen concentration. *Soil Sci. Soc. Am., Proc.* **25,** 463–467.

Tayama, H. K., and Miller, R. O. (1965). Relationship of plant age and net assimilation rate to optimum growing temperature of the snapdragon. *Proc. Am. Soc. Hortic. Sci.* **86,** 672–680.

Teas, H. J., and Sheehan, T. J. (1957). Chemical modifications of geotropic bending in the snapdragon. *Proc. Fla. State Hortic. Soc.* **70,** 391–398.

Wang, C. Y., Baker, J. E., Hardenburg, R. E., and Lieberman, M. (1977). Effects of two analogs of rhizobitoxine and sodium benzoate on senescence of snapdragons. *J. Am. Soc. Hortic. Sci.* **102,** 517–520.

White, J. W. (1961). Timing snapdragons. *Penn. Flower Grow., Bull.* **125,** 5–7.

Williamson, C. E. (1962). Root diseases and soil sterlilization. *In* "Snapdragons" (R. W. Langhans, ed.) pp. 62–69. N.Y. State Flower Grow. Assoc., Ithaca, New York.

Willis, W. W. (1954). Plant response to soil conditions. *Kan. State Coll. Florists' Bull.* **5,** 2–3.

5
Orchids

Thomas J. Sheehan

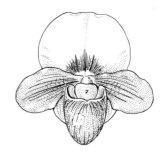

133

I. INTRODUCTION

The cultivation of orchids is not new. Confucius (551–479 B.C.) mentioned orchids in his writings. He speaks of the fragrance of lan (orchids) in the home, indicating that the Chinese were using orchid flowers to decorate their homes (Withner 1959). However, the evolution of orchid culture from the hobbyist to commercial production was very slow. The early Greeks and Romans looked to the orchids more for their medicinal than for their esthetic qualities. It was not until the 1700s that interest in orchids really began to develop. During the early 1700s, sea captains, missionaries, and botanists began introducing orchids into Great Britain from all parts of the world. Plants were often brought back as gifts for their sponsors or benefactors. As these exotic plants bloomed they helped stimulate additional interest in dispatching collectors to distant corners of the globe. Yet it was not until 1821, when Conrad Loddiges and Sons started growing orchid plants commercially at their nursery in Hackney, near London, that the orchid industry was born. Conrad Loddiges started producing flowering orchid plants for sale to the landed gentry, who could afford the glass houses needed to grow them.

Almost another century passed before commercial production of orchids for cut flower sales came into vogue. In 1913 the Sun Kee Nursery opened in Singapore to produce spray-type orchids for cut flower sales. This nursery is still in production and has 13.3 ha devoted to *Arachnis, Aranda,* and *Aranthera* orchids. Most of the flowers are exported to Europe. Some of the earlier growers in the United States were Pitcher and Manda, in South Orange, New Jersey; Lager and Harrell, in Summit, New Jersey; Baldwin, in Mamaroneck, New York; and Linden in New York City.

Cut flowers are still widely grown in many areas of the world. *Cymbidium* flowers, for example, are produced mainly in California, New York, and Australia. Individual *Cymbidium* ranges in California may cover over 9 ha with most plants flowering during late winter and early spring. However, flowers are available on a year-round basis with production from the Southern Hemisphere supplementing California and New York production.

Dendrobium hybrids are being grown mainly in Hawaii, Thailand and Singapore. Thailand presently is the largest exporter of *Dendrobium* sprays, having sold over $10 million in 1977.

Singapore, Malaysia, and Thailand also export large quantities of other cut orchid sprays, with most of the production being exported to Europe, especially West Germany.

Although there are many major cut flower production areas around the world, in the United States growers are again producing plants. The demand for plants by the hobbyist has made plants sales more profitable than growing orchids for cut flowers.

The lastest census figures indicate that the value of all orchid sales in the United States was $12,773,754 (1973).

II. BOTANICAL INFORMATION

Taxonomically, orchids are a unique group of plants. They are vastly different vegetatively, yet all species can be tied together by their floral characteristics as members of this huge family. The Orchidaceae contain over 800 genera and over 25,000 known species of monocotyledonous herbaceous perennial plants. Plants may be erect growers (monopodial) or prostrate (sympodial) (Fig. 1) with a few tree climbers (*Vanilla*). Although the majority of orchids are so-called green plants, there are a few saprophytes and leafless plants in the family. The stems may have one or more swollen internodes (pseudobulb) and have one to many leaves.

The parallel-veined leaves, either thick and leathery or thin, soft, and often pleated, come in a variety of shapes from linear to oval to orbicular. They are arranged alternatively along the stem.

The flowers are very distinctive and range in size from a few millimeters to 45 cm in diameter. They come in every color and include many bicolor and tricolor flowers (*Cattleya bicolor* and *Vanda tricolor*). Some orchids have no odor whereas others may have a wide variety of fragrances. Two highly fragrant orchids are *Maxillaria tennuifolia* and *Aerides odorata*.

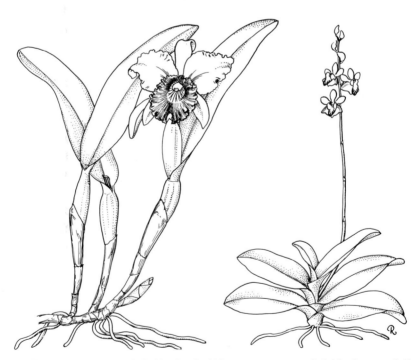

Fig. 1. The two major growth habits in *Orchidaceae* are sympodial (*Cattleya* on left) and monopodial (*Doritis* on right).

Fig. 2.   The *Cattleya* flower is a typical zygomorphic flower. It can be cut in only one plane, to produce two equal halves.

There are five distinguishing characteristics that separate orchid flowers from all others in the plant kingdom. These floral characteristics are

1. Zygomorphic flowers—The orchid flower is a special type of irregular flower in that it has bilateral symmetry (*zygomorphic*). It can be cut only in one plane and will divide into two equal halves. Cutting the flower in any other plane would result in two unequal pieces (Fig. 2).

2. Pollen—the pollen of orchid flowers is agglutinated into small packets called *pollinia* (Fig. 3) that are removed by insects in the act of pollination. The number of pollinia per flower varies in different genera from 2 to 8 with one species, *Brassavola cucullata,* having 12. The number of pollinia, and their arrangement within the flower, can often be used in identification of the flower, e.g., *Cattleya* has 4 whereas *Laelia* has 8.

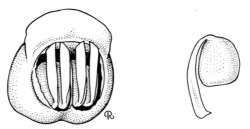

Fig. 3.   The pollen of orchids is agglutinated into packets called pollinia. The figure on the left shows four pollinia within the anther cap. A single pollinium is on the right.

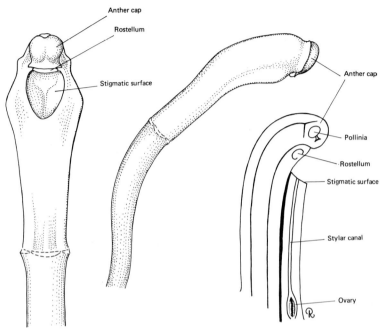

Fig. 4. The reproductive structures of the orchid flower are fused to form the column. Left, column in ventral view showing anther cap at the apex and stigmatic surface. Center, column side view. Right, a diagrammatic sketch of the column.

3. Column—The reproductive structures of the orchid flower (anther and pistil) have been fused together in a waxy unit called the *column* (gynandrium). Within the column there is a canal leading from the stigmatic surface to the ovary. The column may bear one fertile stamen, represented by an anther terminal on the column (*Cattleya*) or by two lateral anthers situated midway along the sides of the column (*Paphiopedilum*). The stigmatic surface is on the under side of the column (Fig. 4).

4. *Rostellum*—On the underside of the column between the anther cap and the stigmatic surface lies the *rostellum.* The rostellum is a gland formed at the apex of the style and often appears as a beaklike projection between the stigma and anther cap (Fig. 4).

The rostellum performs two unique functions. First, it acts like a dam separating male and female portions of the flower, thus preventing self-pollination. The second function is that of a gland, wherein it disperses a viscid substance on the back of any insect that comes in contact with it. As an insect forces its way toward the base of a flower to partake of the nectar its back rubs the rostellum and a bead of gluey material is applied. As the insect backs out the glue comes in contact with the stipe (caudicle) of the pollinia and the insect takes the pollinia to the next flower it visits, thus ensuring cross-pollination.

Fig. 5. Typical orchid seeds.

5. *Seeds*—Orchid flowers produce copious amounts of seed. A single orchid seed pod may contain between 500,000 and one million minute seeds (Fig. 5). These seeds, unlike corn or peas, contain no endosperm and are often called *"naked seed."* Since the seeds contain no endosperm they cannot germinate in the wild without the aid of a fungus, whereas under laboratory conditions they have to be germinated aseptically with all the necessary chemicals supplied via the germination medium.

Any plant that has four or more of the aforementioned characteristics in the flower would belong to the orchid family. Once one becomes familiar with the basic characteristics of orchid flowers it becomes easy to identify unknown flowers as orchids.

III. PROMINENT GENERA GROWN AS CUT FLOWERS

A wide variety of orchid genera are grown as cut flowers. The number will vary from country to country and in some cases area to area within a country, depending on climatic conditions. Listed below are some of the better known genera.

A. *Cattleya*

A genus native to Central and South American tropics, *Cattleya* has over 50 species and thousands of hybrids. Plants, species, and hybrids can be selected to provide a grower with flowers every month of the year. Some species and their hybrids are photoperiodic responders and can be flowered twice in 1 year (Hager, 1957). The colors range from white through various shades of lavender, yellow, and red. Bicolors, white with purple lips and yellow with purple lips, are available. Flower size ranges from 6 to 15 cm (Fig. 6).

B. *Cymbidium*

Cymbidium is native to Asia and the Phillippines. The species and hybrids grown are the cool types requiring 10°C night temperatures for flowering. Flow-

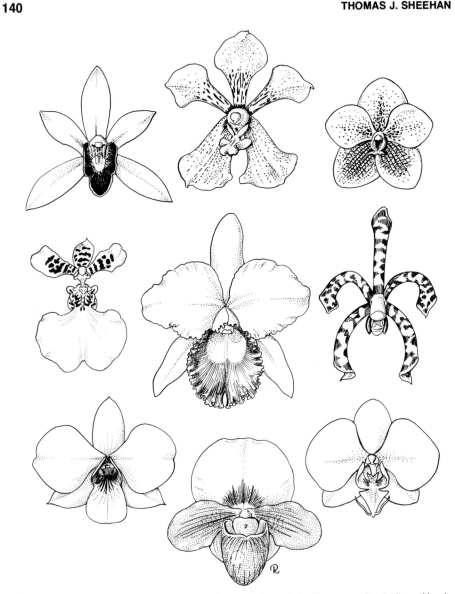

Fig. 6. Orchid genera grown as cut flowers from left to right. Top row: *Cymbidium, Vanda, Ascocenda.* Middle row: *Oncidium, Cattleya, Arachnis.* Lower row: *Dendrobium, Paphiopedilum, Phalaenopsis.*

ers (7.5–12.5 cm) are grown basically for spring trade (Easter and Mother's Day), when their pastel shades are most fitting. However, flowers are available year-round since growers in Australia supply the northern markets during the Australian spring when plants in the United States are vegetative (Fig. 6).

C. *Phalaenopsis*

These orchids, native to Asia, the Phillippines, and Indonesia, are very popular for use in wedding bouquets. White flowers, hybrids of *Phalaenopsis amabilis,* are available year-round as these plants can be maintained in flower continually. Pink and other colors are available in fall and spring (Fig. 6).

D. *Dendrobium*

These natives of the Western Pacific basin are widely grown for their long-lasting sprays of cut flowers. Thailand, Singapore, and Hawaii are the largest producers of *Dendrobium* sprays. A typical Thailand spray is cut with seven flowers and seven buds. Most of the production in Thailand and Singapore is shipped to West Germany. This large genus, with a wide variety of flower colors, sizes, and shapes, has great untapped potential for cut flower production and new hybrids being developed at the University of Hawaii look very promising for year-round flowering (Fig. 6).

E. *Vanda*

These natives of southeast Asia have long been popular plants. Probably the best known is *Vanda* Miss Joaquim, which has been used in Hawaiian leis for many years. It also has been widely used as a promotional flower. *Vanda* flower sprays are now being grown in Singapore, Thailand, and Hawaii. The latter are available throughout the year in a variety of sizes and colors (Fig. 6).

F. *Ascocenda*

These hybrids of *Vanda* and *Ascocentrum* resemble miniature vandas and have an excellent shelf life. Presently, most of the cut flower production is in Thailand and all of the flowers are shipped to West Germany. Yields as high as 150 spikes m²/year have been reported (Fig. 6).

G. *Arachnis* and Its Hybrids [*Aranthera (Arachnis* × *Renanthera)* and *Aranda (Arachnis* × *Vanda)*]

These southeastern Asia natives are widely grown as cut flowers in Singapore and Malaysia. They are grown in open fields with minimal care and produce up to 12 spikes per plant per year. One hectare is capable of producing between 660,000 and 799,000 spikes per year depending on the number of plants per hectare (Fig. 6). A variety of colors is available.

H. *Oncidium* Golden Showers

A hybrid of Central and South American plants, this *Oncidium* is a very popular cut flower used in West Germany. Most of the production is in Singapore where the plants flower all year. The sprays of dainty bright yellow flowers are excellent for use in flower arrangements (Fig. 6).

I. *Paphiopedilum*

The lady slipper orchids, natives of southeast Asia, have long been popular cut flowers in Europe and the northern parts of the United States. Most of those cultivars grown are hybrids of species, such as *Paphiopedilum insigne* and require cool nights (10°C) for best flowering, so production is limited to the more temperate climates. However, recent interest in the warm types, such as *P. nivium* and *P. callosum,* should lead to the introduction of more warm-growing types, which could be produced commercially as far south as Florida (Fig. 6).

Other genera are cut and sold on a limited basis in tropical and subtropical areas. These may be native plants such as the *Eulophia* sold in the markets in Nairobi, Kenya. *Phaius* spikes have also been sold as cut flowers by nurseries growing these plants for landscape use in central and southern Florida. Undoubtedly, many other genera, especially native plants, are cut and sold elsewhere in the world. Most of these, however, are not grown commercially for the flowers.

Today these and many more genera, especially small-flowered species, of little importance as cut flowers, are grown as pot plants for sale to hobbyists. Many orchid nurseries are predominantly in business to supply plants, from seedlings in flasks all the way up to large flowering-sized plants in pots or baskets.

IV. PROPAGATION

Orchids, like most floricultural crops, may be propagated either sexually or asexually. Since most orchids do not come true from seed, once a hybrid or a clonal selection has been made, then all further propagation must be by asexual means to be sure offspring will be true to type. Orchids are asexually propagated by several means not commonly used to increase other floricultural crops. Some unique characteristics of the orchids themselves make this possible.

A. *Seed Germination Technique*

Orchid seeds are very small, usually 80–130 μm wide and 470–560 μm long. If put end to end it would take 50 seeds to make a line 2.5 cm long. The seeds are not only small but also lack endosperm and hence are difficult to germinate. In their native habitats, germination takes place only when certain fungi are present which supply sugars to germinating seed until such time as the seedling has sufficient chlorophyll to produce its own sugars and sustain itself.

As early as 1903 scientists, such as Bernard (1903) at the Paris Botanic Garden, were trying to germinate orchid seed. Both he and Burgeff (1909) concluded that the fungus was necessary to germinate orchid seeds in the laboratory. In the early 1920s, Knudson showed that the fungus was converting starch in the medium to sugar, and that the seeds used the sugar for germination. Knudson substituted sugar for starch and got excellent growth without the fungus (1922). Just to prove his point, Dr. Knudson grew an orchid plant from seed to flower in a 12-liter flask without any fungus. This research was the basis for the development of the industry as we know it today. Orchid seeds now are as easy to germinate and grow as any other floricultural crop, but they do require some special handling.

Knudson's work led to the development of Knudson's "C" Solution for orchid seed germination (1923). This formula has been the basis for most of the solutions used to germinate orchid seed today (Table I).

A grower may either make up his own medium or buy a prepared medium. The latter is simply mixed with water and autoclaved and is ready to use as soon as it cools.

A variety of containers may be used. Old square milk bottles or new orange juice bottles are very popular but any size of glass container can be used. Erlenmeyer flasks are also very popular.

When the medium is prepared each chemical is weighed out and dissolved separately in a liter of water. Sugar is dissolved and agar is added at the end. The solution should be heated until the agar is dissolved. The pH is adjusted to 5.0 to 5.2, and the medium is poured into containers and autoclaved at 10,546.5 kg/m² for 15 minutes. Sufficient medium should be poured into the container to provide a layer of medium approximately 1 cm deep.

Table I

Knudson's "C" Solution

Component	Amount
$Ca(NO_3)_2 \cdot 4H_2O$	1 gm
KH_2PO_4	0.25 gm
$MgSO_4 \cdot 7H_2O$	0.25 gm
$(NH_4)_2SO_4$	0.50 gm
$FeSO_4 \cdot 7H_2O$	0.25 gm
$MnSO_4 \cdot 4H_2O$	0.0075 gm
Agar	15 gm
Sucrose	20 gm
H_2O (distilled)	1 liter

After autoclaving and cooling, containers are ready for seed sowing. Sowing should be done in a clean area. All surfaces should be cleaned and the room free of dust. Before sowing, the seed must be cleaned. Seed should be placed in a vial and then covered with a 10% solution of calcium hypochlorite (10% Clorox). The container is closed and shaken vigorously. The seed should be treated for 5 to 10 minutes to be sure it is clean. A good rule of thumb is to sow the seeds when they turn yellow. If one waits too long seeds will turn white and will have lost most of their viability.

Before the seed is sown in a container, gather all materials and light a Bunsen burner or alcohol lamp. Open the container, flame the neck, pick up the wire loop, heat it, and then pick up a loop full of seed and transfer the seed to the flask; flame the neck and replace the stopper. Gently shake the flask to distribute the seeds evenly over the surface of the medium.

Depending on the genus sown, the seeds will turn green after only a few days or after a few months. Flasks should be checked for contamination as it is most apt to occur within 3 to 5 days after sowing. Little contamination should occur after the first week. Seedling cultures should be maintained at a minimum of 21°–22°C (Post, 1949) with a maximum light intensity of 1.6 klx in a greenhouse. In the laboratory 16 hours at 1.0 klx of light at 21°C will be sufficient for good growth.

Seedlings will remain in the flask for possibly a year before they are transplanted to community pots. Some growers, depending on the genus being grown, may reflask the seedlings after several months and then at the second transplanting use community flats.

B. *Vegetative Propagation*

1. *Cuttings*

Most monopodial orchids (*Vanda, Arachnis*) can be propagated by tip cuttings. Usually orchid cuttings are much larger than the 7.5 to 10-cm cuttings used for many floricultural crops. *Vanda* tip cuttings (Fig. 7A) are usually 30 to 37 cm tall and bear up to 12 leaves and usually a few aerial roots. Cuttings can be potted and will grow without being put in a propagation bed. *Arachnis* cuttings are usually 45 to 60 cm in length (Fig. 7B). They, too, will have aerial roots and can be lined out directly in the field or potted up.

Some monopodial and sympodial orchids produce offsets. Those genera such as *Dendrobium* and *Epidendrum* produce offsets in an axil of a leaf. The offsets root while still attached to the plant (Fig. 7C). Once four or more roots have formed the offset can be snapped off, potted up, and grown as any transplant with little retardation of growth. Many offsets on reed-type *Epidendrum* plants are often in flower when snapped off and if properly handled will not lose any flowers after they are potted up.

Two genera, *Phalaenopsis* and *Phaius,* can be increased by using flower

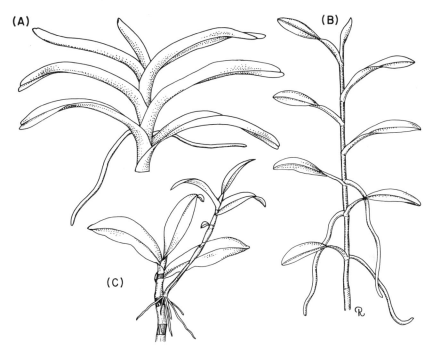

Fig. 7. Vegetative cuttings. (A) *Vanda* tip cutting. (B) *Arachnis* tip cutting. (C) *Dendrobium* offset.

stalk cuttings. Although both are increased by this method, the techniques used are entirely different. A typical *Phauis* flower stalk will have seven or more nodes between the lowest flower and the base of the stem (Watkins). Each of these nodes is covered with a leafy bract that protects a small bud. After the last flower is gone the spike is ready to harvest. The spike is removed as close to the pseudobulb as possible. The top portion is then cut off just below where the first flower was, leaving a cane 37 to 45 cm long. The canes are laid on their sides in a flat of moist sphagnum moss, with the ends of the canes covered with the moss to prevent drying out. After 2 to 3 months a small plant will arise at each node. Once the plant has three or four roots it can be snapped off and potted up and in 2 to 3 years will be a flowering-sized plant.

Phalaenopsis flower spikes must be propagated aseptically (Rotor 1949), as are seeds. The spike is ready to propagate as soon as the last flower is gone. Like *Phaius* it will have about seven nodes, each containing a bud. In most cases, however, the top node, just below where the first flower opened, will contain a flower bud and the bottom node frequently will not have a viable bud. Thus, only the center nodes should be used. The spike is cut 2 cm above and below the node. The bract is carefully dissected to remove all rough edges that could harbor fungus spores. The trimmed stem segments are placed in 10%

Clorox for 10 to 12 minutes. The segments are removed and the ends are recut with a sterile knife. Each segment is placed in a test tube containing Knudson's "C" solution. After 3 months a plant will start forming at the node. When it has formed two to three roots the plant can be removed from the agar and potted up.

2. Division

Cattleya and other sympodial orchids are propagated by division of the parent clump. This is usually accomplished on plants that have six or more pseudobulbs. The rhizome is cut between the third and fourth pseudobulbs and both sections are potted up as individual plants. Since most *Cattleya* plants produce only one new leaf per year, most plants are divided every 3 years. Genera such as *Paphiopedilum* and *Cymbidium* can be divided more frequently, as a division containing only one fan of leaves or one pseudobulb is all that is necessary to increase these plants.

3. Mericloning

Mericloning is a relatively new technique whereby, under aseptic conditions, one can have within 1 year one million plants identical to the parent plant. Like seedlings, they will take several years to flower.

This technique, first discovered by Morel in 1960 and later modified and refined by others, was first used to free plants of viruses. Now it can be used, however, to increase plants rapidly (Arditti, 1977).

The technique is similar for most orchids and should be done in an aseptic room or area in a laboratory. A rapidly growing shoot is selected. In the case of *Cattleya* or *Cymbidium* the shoot is usually 3 to 5 cm long. The shoot is severed from the plant with a sharp knife. The shoot is cut as close to the base as possible. The severed shoot is placed into 10% Clorox for 10 to 15 minutes to sterilize it. Three or four of the outer leaves are removed after sterilizing. The shoots are sterilized in 5% Clorox for 8 to 10 minutes. The remaining two to three leaves are then removed to expose the growing point and leaf primordia. The shoots are again sterilized in 3% Clorox for 3 to 5 minutes. The leaf primordia is removed, and a small cube of tissue (2 mm^3) is cut out and dipped in 1% Clorox and plated out on a multiplication medium such as that of Murashige-Skoog. This tissue can then be divided, flasked, and reflasked until the desired number of explants are available. As previously mentioned, a single meristem can be increased to one million in less than 1 year.

Once the required number of plants have been obtained the explants can be treated as normal orchid seedlings and carried through to flowering as with any seedling population. The mericloned plants will all be identical to the parent plant, whereas the seedlings differ at time of flowering.

This brief description just outlines the process. A much more comprehensive review has been prepared by Arditti (1977) and the reader should refer to that article for additional details.

V. PLANT CULTURE

There is no difference in the culture of orchid plants, whether they are grown for pot plant sales or for cut flowers. In general orchids being grown for cut flower sales will be repotted every 2 to 3 years. At this time they may be divided or tip cuttings taken. The divisions, if in excess of the cut flower grower's needs, are then sold as flowering plants.

A. Greenhouse Production

1. Media

The type of medium used for growing orchids will vary depending on whether the orchid is an epiphyte or a terrestrial orchid. Epiphytic orchids (e.g., *Cattleya*) are found growing on trees in their native habitats. Hence the medium should be similar to that on which they grow in their native habitat. Most epiphytic orchids (*Cattleya, Phalaenopsis, Dendrobium, Vanda*) can be grown in *Osmunda* fiber, tree fern fiber, tree fern–redwood chips, fir bark, and even cinderlike materials such as Solite and Holite.

a. Osmunda Fiber. This fiber is the root of the *Osmunda* ferns native to eastern United States. There are two types, the soft light brown fiber and the dark brown wiry form. Osmunda decomposes slowly and will last 2 to 4 years before decay sets in. It contains 2 to 3% nitrogen, which is released slowly as the fiber decomposes. Plants growing in *Osmunda* should be fertilized with a 1:1:1 ratio fertilizer.

b. Tree Fern (Tree Fern–Redwood Chips). This fiber comes from the stems of tree ferns. They are shredded or sawed into plaques. The stiff wiry fibers are very long lasting; some last 5 to 7 years before decay occurs. A 1:1:1 ratio fertilizer should be used for plants growing in tree fern.

c. Barks (Mainly Fir Barks). These barks are by-products of the lumber industry. The chips are graded as large, medium, or fine. Large chips are used in 20-cm or larger pots. Medium is the most widely used grade for 3.5 to 17.5-cm pots, and fine chips are used for thumb and community pots. Fir barks contain little or no nitrogen, and although slow to decay (3–4 years), they are broken down by a myriad of microorganisms. These microflora are capable of obtaining nitrogen at the expense of the plant and a grower must compensate for this loss. Plants grown in bark are fertilized with a 3:1:1 ratio fertilizer.

d. Aggregrated Materials (e.g., Solite, Holite). Materials that are inert and capable of holding moisture can also be used for epiphytic orchids. Most aggregates are about the same size as medium grade bark and are ideal for

7.5 to 15-cm pots. Since the aggregate does not decompose it will last for years. It can be used over and over again, but should be cleaned and sterilized before being reused. This procedure prevents the transfer of disease organisms from one plant to another. A 1:1:1 fertilizer should be used on plants grown in aggregates. Actually, these materials are very similar to volcanic rock.

Terrestrial orchids (*Cymbidium, Phaius*) are found growing in rich organic soils in their native habitats. Any well-drained potting mixture containing 50% or more organic matter can be used. Peat, shavings, and sand (1:1:1, v/v) and even 100% peat moss have been recommended.

Recent studies by Poole (1977) have indicated that both terrestrial and epiphytic orchids can be grown in a mixture of peat and perlite (1:1, v/v) with excellent results. The use of this medium for growing orchids in the future looks very promising. Growers who have tried this medium say adjustment of watering to prevent overwatering is the most critical phase at this time.

B. Environmental Controls

1. Watering

It has often been said that more orchids are killed by overwatering than by any other factor. Watering and the quality of water used on orchids are the most important environmental factors involved in orchid culture.

Like any floricultural crop, orchids should be watered thoroughly and then not watered again until the surface of the potting mixture begins to become dry. The number of days it takes for the surface of the potting mixture to become dry will be governed by climatic conditions, types of container and medium, age of the medium, and size of the plant in the pot. The best practice is to group orchids by pot size, type, and medium, thus ensuring that all plants are properly watered.

Quality of water is as important as the quantity of water applied. Fortunately, *Cattleya* orchids can be watered with water having a pH range of 4 to 9 (Northern, 1970), and hard or soft water appears to have little effect on growth of orchids. Hard water, however, should not be used in an overhead sprinkler system because the orchid leaves will soon be covered with a thin film of calcium crystals, resembling white salt, on the leaves.

The most important factor to consider is the level of soluble salts in the water. Water having soluble salts of less than 125 ppm is excellent to use, 125 to 500 ppm is good, 500 to 800 ppm should be used with caution, and water with salts above 800 ppm should not be used. Most city water would fall within the good to excellent range and can be used. Well water should be analyzed to be sure it is safe to use on orchids.

2. Temperature

Temperature regimes used will be governed by the genera grown. *Cymbidium* orchids require 10°C night temperatures to produce flowers. Thus, a range of 10°C night temperature and 21°–24°C day temperature would be ideal. During the summer plants can survive 32°C temperatures but should not be exposed to them for long periods of time. *Cattleya* species and hybrids thrive best at night temperatures between 15° and 18°C. *Phalaenopsis,* especially the white-flowered cultivars, grow best with 18°C night temperatures and up to 27°C during the day. Pink *Phalaenopsis* cultivars flower better when the night temperatures are 13°–15°C. When several orchid species are grown in one house, a compromise of temperature has to be reached and that usually means 15°C night temperature and up to 27°C during the day. If *Cymbidium* is included in a mixed group then the night temperature will have to be dropped to 10°C to ensure flowering on *Cymibidium;* however, it will delay flowering of *Cattleya* and *Phalaenopsis.*

3. Fertilization

Orchids should be fertilized every 2 weeks for maximum growth. This, of course, assumes they are being provided the proper light, temperature and water. The ratio of fertilizer used will vary with the medium. *Osmunda,* tree-fern, terrestrial mixtures, Holite and Solite should be fertilized with a 1:1:1 ratio fertilizer such as 10:10:10 at the rates of 453 gm/393 liters of water applied to 43.3 m² of growing area. Fir barks or other barks should be fertilized with a 3:1:1 fertilizer, 30:10:10 at the rate of 453 gm/393 liters of water. Bark media require additional nitrogen to offset that required by the myriad of microorganisms breaking down the bark in the containers. However, since bark decomposes very slowly there is no danger of a rapid release of nitrogen tied up by microorganisms during the time the medium is in the pot.

Slow-release fertilizers have been successfully used on orchids. If they are used, the same fertilizer ratios will apply and the same amounts should be used. Some growers prefer a combination of slow release and liquid fertilizer, which provides a more uniform supply of nutrients over a longer period of time.

Slow-release fertilizers are safe to use and are less apt to be damaging if an accidental overdose is applied. However, this does not mean that care should not be taken to be sure the proper amounts of any given fertilizer are applied. The old adage, "If a pound is good, two pounds is better," does not hold true.

4. Light

Light, like many other cultural factors, will vary depending on the orchid genus under cultivation. *Phalaenopsis* plants thrive at 1.6 to 1.9 klx, and *Cattleya* at 2.6 to 3.9 klx; *Cymbidium* will grow under full sun. Therefore, it becomes necessary to shade some orchid greenhouses to ensure that the proper amount of light will be available for good orchid growth. Any greenhouse shading compound can be used. The compound should be applied in late spring as the days are becoming brighter. In the fall in northern climates the shading compound should be allowed to wear off as the low light intensities encountered in the winter months will reduce plant growth. In the

South or in Florida, California, and Hawaii, however, shade will be required all year as winter radiation in these areas will often be four times that of the northern United States.

Some cultivars or orchids, notably *Cattleya trianaei* and *Cattleya labiata* and their hybrids, can be manipulated photoperiodically (Rotor, 1952) and the same plant can be flowered twice in 1 year. As an example of how it is done, the following schedule was developed by Hagar (1957).

Cattleya labiata

Light: June 5–October 12; temperature, 18°C (NT) (standard chrysanthemum lighting)
Normal days: October 12–December 15
Harvest flowers: December 15–20
Light: December 15–April 1
Shade: use standard chrysanthemum blackcloth April 1–June 5; Temperature, 18°C (NT)
Harvest flowers: June 5–10

Many *Cattleya labiata* and *C. trianaei* hybrids can be manipulated in the same manner, doubling flower production without increasing the number of plants.

The time to flowering of *Cattleya* can also be shortened by temperature manipulation in case the crop is running late. If bud size is known and the numbers of days left are counted, then the proper night temperature can be selected (Table II) (Hager, 1957).

5. Flowering

There are so many species, cultivars, and hybrids of orchids available that it is possible to have flowers the year round just by the selection of cultivars. *Cattleya* and *Vanda* flowers are relatively easy to obtain year-round and a grower needs to select only a few species and their hybrids to have flowers all year (Table III).

Some orchid plants, such as *Phalaenopsis amabilis* and its white hybrids, can be kept in flower all year. It is possible to harvest three or more crops of flowers from an individual plant. The primary flower spike is produced in the fall and will flower for a long period of time. Some spikes have been known to produce flowers for over 2 months. Once the last flower has been harvested,

Table II

Number of Days to Flower

Bud size (cm)	Night temperature (°C)		
	13	16	21
2.0	67	50	36
2.5–5.0	53	38	28
5.0–7.5	42	24	18
7.5–10.0	30	20	12

Table III

A Selection of Some *Cattleya* and *Vanda* Species to Provide Year-Round Flower Production

Genus and species	Months in flower											
	Jan.	Feb.	Mar.	Apr.	May	June	July	Aug.	Sept.	Oct.	Nov.	Dec.
Cattleya												
gigas					X	X	X	X				
labiata									X	X		
Mossiae				X	X							
Trianaei	X	X	X									X
Luddenmanniana			X	X	X							
Vanda												
coerulea	X	X						X			X	X
dearei						X	X	X				
Sanderana							X	X	X	X	X	
Merrillii			X	X	X	X	X					
Miss Joaquim	X	X	X	X	X	X	X	X	X	X	X	X

the top of the spike is removed just below the point of attachment of the first flower bud. A secondary flower spike will be produced in approximately 8 weeks and when it has finished, it too can be cut off, just below the first flower and a tertiary spike will form. Frequently, the tertiary spike will still be in flower when the next primary spike is being produced in the fall.

Cymbidium orchids require cool nights for flower production. These plants then primarily flower in the spring. Selection of hybrids is very important as the range of flowering can be spread from December to May, or even longer. Most growers prefer mid spring and late spring flowering cultivars because they are very popular corsage flowers for Easter and Mother's Day.

Dendrobium, especially *Dendrobium phalaenopsis* and its hybrids, are excellent plants to produce sprays of flowers for late fall, winter, and early spring. The flowers are very suitable for corsages and two or three flowers make an outstanding corsage. These plants will flower all year in the tropics.

A grower, by carefully selecting orchids, can have a wide variety of sizes, shapes, and colors, not to mention some very fragrant orchid flowers available year-round. Orchid flowers come in many colors of the rainbow and many have two or even three colors on an individual flower.

VI. FIELD PRODUCTION IN THE TROPICS

Today in tropical countries there is a rapidly increasing interest in growing flowers and many of these countries are growing spray-type orchids for export. At present the major production area is in southeast Asia and is centered around Thailand and Singapore. Hawaii and Sri Lanka are also developing production areas.

The majority of spray orchids are field grown with little or no protection and with minimal maintenance. In Singapore field-grown orchids are called "ground orchids" although they are epiphytes. The base of the stem is in the ground when they are set out in the field.

The size of the farms varies from small units of 0.8 to 1.2 ha to over 44 ha. During a visit to Malaysia in 1971, the author saw one field of *Aranthera* James Storie that covered almost 30 ha on the side of a hill. As an illustration of the size of this industry, in 1978 Thailand exported over $10 million (U.S.) of cut orchids and the majority were *Dendrobium* Mme. Pompadour.

Actually, there are two distinctly different methods used for orchid production in the tropics. Most *Arachnis, Aranthera, Aranda, Vanda,* and *Renanthera* species and hybrids are grown in full sun in the field on trellises. *Dendrobium,* some *Arandas* (Wendy Scott, Christine #1), *Ascocenda,* and *Oncidium* cultivars are grown in pots, often under 40 to 50% lath shade.

The culture of *Arachnis* Maggie Oei can serve as a good example of the typical "ground orchid" grown in the tropics. Native woods are used to build trellises in the fields prior to planting. Uprights (about 5 × 5 cm) are spaced in rows, approximately 2.4 m apart with rows usually 1 m apart. Cross bars are spaced about 60 cm apart (Fig. 8). Spacing the trellises in this manner will allow the grower to plant between 25,000 and 30,000 cuttings per 0.4 ha.

After trellises are in place, tip cuttings 60 to 75 cm long are planted. Cuttings will have aerial roots and may even have flower spikes developing. A trench, usually 10 to 15 cm deep, is dug along the row. Individual cuttings are spaced 15 to 20 cm apart along the row. The base of the cutting is placed in the trench and the top is tied to the first cross arm. After the row of cuttings is tied in place, the trench is filled with native soil, covering the lower 7.5 to 10 cm. In 4 to 6 months, the cuttings are considered flowering-size plants (although some flowers may have been cut all during this growth period) and spikes will be harvested from these plants for 18 months. At that time (2 years from cuttings) plants are 2.4 m tall and sprays are difficult to harvest. The grower will then take tip cuttings from these plants and replant the field or expand his production. If a grower is interested in expanding production, he can leave the old plants in the field after taking cuttings and in 6 months he will be able to remove another set of cuttings. This time the harvest may be two to 2.5 times the original harvest as each of the plants cut the first time will produce two to three secondary growths.

Arachnis plants and their hybrids are fast growing, producing a new leaf every 2 weeks and up to 12 flower spikes per stem per year in tropical areas. Hence, 0.4 ha of *Arachnis* Maggie Oei is capable of producing 300,000 to

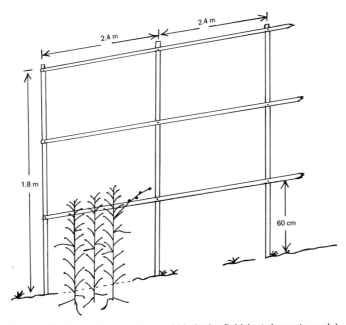

Fig. 8. Trellis used for growing orchids in the field (not drawn to scale).

360,000 spikes per year. This, of course, is ideal production, but the plants have to be replanted every 2 years, which will reduce production, because they produce only 18 months out of every 2 years. Thus, actual production per year is reduced to 225,000 to 275,000 spikes per 0.4 ha per year. Even if only half of these spikes were salable (112,000–137,000) and sold for 10 cents per spray, the return would still be $11,200–13,700 per 0.4 ha per year.

Aranda hybrids, such as Wendy Scott and Christine, *Ascocenda* hybrids, *Oncidium* Golden Showers and *Dendrodium* hybrids, are all grown in pots and are generally grown under approximately 50% lath shade in the tropics.

Although these orchids are all grown in pots, culture varies from genus to genus. *Aranda* Wendy Scott or Christine are handled very similarly to *Arachnes* Maggie Oei. Tip cuttings 37 to 45 cm tall, with aerial roots, are taken. Two cuttings are usually tied to a 2.5 × 2.5 × 45-cm stake. The cuttings and their stakes are then placed upright into a 15 to 20-cm clay pot. A few rocks are placed in the bottom of the pot to hold plants in place. As soon as roots adhere to the sides of the pot plants will support themselves. Growers are also using various media, such as coconut husks, and are adding chemical fertilizers, such as 10-10-10 at the rate of 453 gm/393 liters of water and applying it as a normal watering every 2 weeks.

Like *Arachnis,* these cuttings are considered flowering-size plants after 4 to 6 months and flowers are harvested for 18 months. At this time *Aranda* plants

Fig. 9. *Aranda* Wendy Scott growing on raised benches in clay pots in Singapore.

Fig. 10. Tying *Aranthera* cuttings to the first crossbar in a trellised field planting.

are becoming too tall for the pots; tip cuttings are taken and the cycle is started all over again.

Dendrobium plants in southeast Asia are often grown in cut-up coconut husks. Husks are fitted into the pot like a jigsaw puzzle and hold the rhizome in place. Plants can remain in the pot for 3 or 4 years before they need to be divided and repotted.

Potted dendrobiums are usually grown on raised benches. Camp and Philipp (1976) suggest using benches 1.2 × 28.6 m long. A 60 × 63-m shade house would have 58 benches and could house 21,244 or more plants (1976). The two most widely grown *Dendrobium* cultivars in Hawaii are 'Louis Bleriot,' which produces 5 to 15 spikes per year depending on the age of the plant, and UH 44, with 6 to 24 spikes. The lower figure is for the first year and the last figure for the fourth year. If the 60 × 63-m house were half in 'Louis Bleriot' and half 'Jacqueline Thomas' (UH-44), a yield of 18,553 dozen could be expected; if they sold for $2.53 per dozen the gross sales would be $46,939.09, leaving a net return of almost $10,000.

A small farm in Singapore, consisting of 1.2 ha of which 0.8 were planted in *Arachnis* Maggie Oei and 0.2 ha in *Aranda* Christine or Wendy Scott and 0.2 ha of *Aranthera* James Storie, the farmer could have a return of over $33,755.27 (Jamison *et al.,* 1971). On the other hand, 1.2 ha of *Aranthera* James Storie or Wendy Scott would have a gross sales potential of between $92,563.29 and

Fig. 11. A typical orchid nursery being established in Singapore.

$113,132.91 per year. These figures are based on 70% of the cut being exported and 30% being available for local sales at a reduced price compared to export.

Since the aforementioned plants flower all year in tropical parts of the world, flowering is not a problem as there is always a constant supply with some genera (*Dendrobium*) having a peak of flowering in August.

Although the majority of the spray type orchids produced today are sold in Europe, they have great potential for sale in other parts of the world, because there are few spike flowers readily available except gladiolus and snapdragons.

VII. INSECTS, DISEASES, AND PHYSIOLOGICAL DISORDERS

The numbers of pests that attack orchids in cultivation are relatively few compared to those that attack orchids in the wild. In general, with proper care and sanitation there is little potential for pests to build up. However, environmental conditions that are conducive to good orchid growth are also favorable for development of orchid pests. The grower should constantly monitor his plants for any signs of disease and insect problems.

A grower should be especially watchful when new plants are introduced into his range. All new plants should be isolated for at least 1 month. Careful checking and application of preventative sprays will provide the protection needed to prevent introduction of unwanted organisms.

A. Insects and Related Pests

A variety of insects commonly attack orchids. However, scales, spider mites, slugs, and roaches are some of the most troublesome pests. Scales, both armored and soft, will attack orchids. The scales attach themselves to leaves and suck the juices from the cells.

1. Armored Scales

Boisduval scale (*Diaspis boisduvalii*) is the most common armored scale found on orchids. The first indication of a Boisduval scale attack is often a yellow spot on the upper surface of the leaf. The small circular scales are frequently attached to the underside of leaves, in tight cracks, or under pseudobulb sheaths and often go undetected until large colonies have built up. Males gather in great numbers and look like cotton on the leaf surface.

Orchid scale (*Furcaspis biformis*) is also almost circular. The waxy covering is a dark red with usually a little lighter color near the perimeter. Males and females are alike in color and shape, but males are the smaller of the two. Like Boisduval, this scale attacks both leaves and pseudobulbs.

Vanda orchid scale (*Genaparlatoria pseudaspidiotus*) has an oval, waxy, dark brown covering, with a light-colored halo around the margins. Both sexes are similar but the male is smaller.

According to Dekle (1968), "thirty-one species of armored scale have been reported on orchids in Florida. Only Boisduval, and proteus scale are considered economically important."

2. Soft Scales

Brown soft scales (*Coccus hesperidum*) are small oval scales, usually greenish-brown in color. They usually attack leaves, but in severe infestations may be found on stems. There have been reports of ants introducing brown soft scale into greenhouses, where they will pasture them on plants to obtain honeydew.

3. Mealybugs (Pseudococcus and Ferrisia)

Mealybugs move about more than scales and their white appearance is due to a secretion that covers their bodies. Underneath the covering they may look pink or yellow. These, too, secret honeydew and attract ants. When there are large infestations, sooty mold may develop on the leaves.

4. Mites

The two most common mites on orchids are the *Phalaenopsis* mite (*Teniupalpus pacificus*) and the two-spotted mite (*Tetranychus urticae*). These minute, sucking insects are hard to detect, but the telltale signs of their feeding give them away. As they suck the juices from the cells, empty cells reflect light and soon little silver dots show up all over the leaves. In heavy infestations webbing will appear on the plants. These are very prolific pests and in dry, hot weather will build up enormous populations in a very short period of time.

5. Cockroaches (Periplanta)

These pests can be very harmful to orchids. They will eat the tips off young roots and also buds and newly opened flowers. Since they are active only at night they often go undetected. Although the damage they cause is very similar to that of snails and slugs, they should be immediately suspected when no slime trails are evident.

6. Snails and Slugs (Slytommatophora)

Snails and slugs are also nocturnal feeders, often hiding in slits in the bottom of orchid pots during the day. They will eat root tips, young leaves, flower buds, and even open flowers. If slime trails are detected in the early morning hours it is evident that snails and slugs are present and need to be brought under control.

B. Disease Pests

Diseases, like insects, can be a serious problem with orchids, sometimes just marking the foliage and making the plants unsalable, or sometimes destroying plants completely. Probably the most serious at present are the viruses which attack orchids, since they are often hard to detect and no reliable control measures are available.

According to Burnett (1965), "For the orchid grower it is better to prevent diseases from developing in the first place. This is often possible if a grower will use good cultural practices unfavorable for the entrance of disease organisms."

There are a number of cultural practices that can be used to help prevent disease organisms from building up. Water should be kept off plants as much as possible. Plants should be watered in the morning. All tools used in cutting orchid flowers and in propagating should be disinfested. Insects should be avoided as much as possible and all new plants should be isolated for up to 3 months just in case they harbor a disease organism. All of these practices will help reduce the incidence of disease in any greenhouse range.

The most commonly encountered diseases are petal-blight, black rots, bacterial rots, viruses, and a wide variety of minor leaf spots. The latter, although disfiguring, do not usually destroy plants.

1. Petal-Blight (Botrytis cinerea)

As the name denotes, petal-blight attacks flowers of a variety of orchids (Cattleya, Phalaenopsis, Dendrobium, Oncidium, Vanda). This disease is most prevalent during cool, moist weather. It is typified by small, brown, circular spots on the petals and sepals of flowers. In advanced stages the entire flower may be covered with spore masses. All infected flowers should be cut off and destroyed. Keeping water off flowers and having good air movement help control this disease.

2. Black Rots (Pythium ultimum and Phytophthora cactorum)

Black rots are widespread throughout the world and since one fungus is prevalent in cool weather (*Phytophthora*) and the other in warm humid weather (*Pythium*), they can occur at anytime during the year. *Pythium* is the most dangerous, as it spreads throughout the plant at a very rapid rate. The symptoms of both fungi are similar with infected parts turning black, sometimes with a yellow margin. These fungi usually attack leaves, but may attack pseudobulbs and stems as well. They attack a wide variety of orchids. Care should be taken to keep foliage dry when these fungi are present.

3. Viruses (Cymbidium Mosaic Virus and Odontoglossum Ringspot Virus)

Viruses are potentially the worst enemies of orchids. First, there are no known control measures and, second, they are easily transmitted on cutting tools during propagating and cutting of the flowers. Whether dividing plants or cutting flowers, one should sterilize all tools between use on each plant to prevent spread of viruses.

Some viruses (*Cymbidium* mosaic virus, CMV) will develop chlorotic streaks in leaves, which eventually become pitted dark areas. These are easy to detect. However, color-break virus is visible only when plants are in bloom and color break can be detected in the flowers. The rest of the time the plant looks healthy. This virus may be spread during propagation since virus symptoms are not evident. Because the plant appears clean, tools may not be sterilized and the virus is thus spread. Again, it is important that all tools be sterilized between use on plants. A saturated solution of trisodium phosphate or lime water with a pH of 12 or higher should be used. Dipping tools in either of these solutions will help keep viruses from spreading.

When a plant is suspected of having a virus it should be isolated and checked by the local agricultural experiment station. If the results indicate presence of a virus the plant should be isolated or destroyed.

4. Leaf Spots (Colletotrichum, Cercospora, Gloeosporium, Phyllostictina)

Leaf spots are often found on orchids. Some cause tip dieback on leaves whereas others cause a variety of spots, yellow to black sunken areas, on leaves. Most leaf spot organisms will not kill the leaves, but once the spots form they will be present as long as the leaves remain on the plants, making the leaves unsightly.

C. Control of Insect Pests and Diseases

The rapidly changing picture in the pest control field makes it very difficult to give recommendations for control of most pests. Regulations vary from country to country and even between states within a country. Therefore, it is best to contact the local agricultural authorities to obtain the best control method available in an area, because some pesticides are not cleared for orchids.

D. Physiological Disorders

There are two physiological disorders occurring in orchids that are often confused with diseases. These disorders are difficult to identify and may require expert assistance to detect.

Calcium deficiency (Poole and Sheehan, 1970) occurs in a variety of orchids, especially during warm weather when plants are actively growing. Young leaves or new leads of *Cattleya* will turn black, usually commencing near the tip and progressing toward the stem. Immature leaves may turn completely black and drop off, or in severe cases the young pseudobulb will turn black. As the black area moves down the leaf it is preceded by a thin yellow halo. Applications of calcium will prevent this.

Mesophyll cell collapse occurs most frequently in *Phalaenopsis* plants in winter months (Sheehan and McConnell, 1978). The surface of one or more leaves on the plant will become pitted and the pitted areas turn yellow to tan to black, finally looking like a virus infection. The next leaf, however, will develop normally, indicating it is not a virus. This disorder occurs on cold nights (temperatures below 7°C) or when cold water is applied to leaves that are near maturity. The malady can be prevented by using water that is at the same temperature as the greenhouse atmosphere or by keeping the greenhouse above 15°C at night.

VIII. HARVESTING AND HANDLING CUT FLOWERS

A. Grading

As with many other floricultural crops, there are not standardized grades for orchid flowers. Prices will often be governed by size. For example, a box of *Cymbidium* orchid flowers may contain 6, 8, or 12 flowers and is often sold at a flat price per box. Assuming $12.00 per box the cost of the individual flower will run from $1 to $2 between the smaller and larger flowers. The same flower may be even cheaper if it is sold by the spray and may only be 50 to 75 cents per flower.

In the case of *Cattleya* flowers both size and color are considered in pricing. A white flower will cost more than a purple flower or a white flower with a purple lip, when flowers are of equal size.

Attempts have been made to standardize some flowers. In Thailand a No. 1 *Dendrobium* Mme. Pompadour flower spike has seven open flowers and seven buds. *Aranthera* James Storie is graded as a single spray or a branched spray, but no limits are put on size of the spray. *Arachnis* Maggie Oei sprays usually have one to three flowers open and four or more buds.

Grading is left primarily to the grower and will often vary from country to country. In general, grading is done mainly on length of the flower spike, flower number, and size and arrangement of flowers on the spike. In some cases the number of lateral branches on the inflorescence is also taken into consideration.

B. Cutting Flowers

Unlike many of our floricultural crops, orchid plants are kept for many years, so harvesting flowers is one cultural activity that is extremely important to growers. Actually, it is much more important than most growers will admit. Perhaps more viruses are spread when orchid flowers are cut than in any other way. Consequently, it is essential that all orchid flowers be harvested to avoid the spread of viruses. Harvesting can be done in a number of ways. One recommendation is for the grower to use disposable surgical blades. A person harvesting can carry a pocketful of blades and, after harvesting the flowers from an individual plant, change knife blades and go on to the next plant. These blades can be sterilized and reused.

Cutting tools (e.g., knives) should be dipped between the cutting of each plant. A solution of trisodium phosphate or a saturated lime solution (pH 12) is good for disinfecting knives.

In general, orchid flowers do not mature until 3 to 4 days after they open, so it is important to know how old blooms are before harvesting. Flowers cut before they mature will not hold up and may wilt before they reach the wholesaler.

Spray-type orchids present no problem. Each flower opens 1½ to 2 days apart. If three or more flowers are open on the spike, the lower flower is mature and can be harvested. Some growers allow the entire spike to open before they harvest, to ensure that the flowers are mature.

Cattleya flowers are a little more difficult to handle as it is very difficult, when there are large numbers of plants in flower, to determine when any one flower opened. Frequently more than one flower will open on the same spike in one day. One of the easiest ways to keep track is to have the grower go through the house each morning and insert a colored golf tee, colored plastic label, or other such label in each pot where there is a flower opening. By using a different color each day the grower knows exactly when each flower opened. This system makes it easy to send any person into the house to cut flowers; for example, telling him/her to cut flowers from the pots with red markers.

When individual *Cattleya* and *Cymbidium* flowers for market are cut, the peduncle should be immediately inserted into a tube of water (orchid tubes with rubber or plastic covers). The tubes are generally filled from a pan of water that has been standing in the greenhouse overnight and has reached ambient temperature.

Spray-type orchids are cut and often shipped dry to the market. In Hawaii and Singapore some *Dendrobium* and Aranda growers immerse the entire spray of flowers in water for 15 minutes before packing and shipping. Still other growers will wrap a little moist cotton around the base of stems before shipping and place 12 stems in a clear plastic bag.

C. Packaging

There are as many ways to package orchid flowers as there are cultivars grown. As previously mentioned, *Cymbidium* flowers in small tubes are packed 6, 8, or 12 in glassine-fronted boxes, ready to be made into corsages. Spikes of *Cymbidium* flowers are often packaged 100 flowers to a box. *Cattleya* flowers are packaged in standard florist boxes. Tubes are taped to the bottom of the box and shredded wax paper is placed around flowers to protect sepals and petals in transit.

Hawaiian *Dendrobium* is packaged four dozen sprays per box. The standard box is 75 × 25 × 17.5 cm. In Singapore, growers will pack up to 12 dozen stems of *Arachnis* Maggie Oei in almost the same size box. The sprays actually have to be compressed in order to put the lid on the box. Nevertheless, when the box is opened in the market the sprays spring back to their uncompressed state.

D. Storage

Orchids, unlike many cut flowers, do not store for any length of time at −1°C. Flowers start turning brown in 3 days at this temperature and lose their salability very rapidly.

Since most orchid flowers are long-lived on the plants, up to 3 or 4 weeks, growers will often leave them on the plants until they are needed. If they must be cut and stored they should be stored at 5–7°C. At this temperature most orchids can be safely stored for a 10- to 14-day period. If orchids are not at their peak then storage time will be less.

E. Shipping

Since orchids are very durable flowers they can be safely shipped long distances. It is not uncommon to ship orchid flowers halfway around the world. Orchids are shipped almost daily from Singapore and Bangkok to many cities in western Europe and arrive in excellent condition. If they are properly handled, as mentioned under harvesting and packaging, they should be very salable upon arrival.

There are reports of some shipments of orchids arriving with flowers in a very bleached condition. Flowers such as lavender *Vanda* Miss Joaquim appear to be a dirty white. This can occur when the pollinia have accidentally been removed from the flower and flowers have been shipped in a sealed plastic bag. If one pollinium has been removed, that flower begins to produce ethylene, which soon builds up in the container and bleaches the flowers. Punching a few holes in the bag, as for apple bags, will eliminate most of this problem.

F. Consumer Care

Orchid flowers, although long-lived, should be handled as other cut flowers to ensure maximum shelf life. Immediately upon arrival, individual flowers are removed from the tubes. Tubes may even be empty when the flowers arrive, depending on the length of time they have been in transit. The lower 0.75 cm of the peduncle is cut off, and the flower is inserted into a fresh tube of water with preservative added. If the flower is made up in a corsage, the corsage is placed in the refrigerator at night and will last for many days, as it can be worn evening after evening.

Spray-type orchids should be handled in the same manner as gladiolus or chrysanthemums. The basal 2.5 cm of the stem is cut upon arrival, placed in warm water at 38°C with a floral preservative, and hardened off at 5°C. When used in an arrangement, a preservative is placed in the water to prolong shelf life.

REFERENCES

Arditti, J. (1977). In "Orchid Biology," pp. 203–293. Cornell Univ. Press, Ithaca, New York.

Bernard, N. (1903). La Germination des Orchidees. *G. R. Acad. Sci. Paris* **137,** 483–485.

Burgeff, H. (1909). "Die Wurzelpilae der Orchideen, ihre Kulture und ihr Leben in der Pflanze." Fischer, Jena.

Burnett, H. (1965). Orchid diseases. *Fla. Dept. of Agric.* **1**(3), 1–57.

Camp, S. G., and Philipp, P. F. (1976). The economics of growing Dendrobium on Oahu for mainland export. *Hawaii Agric. Exp. Stn. Dept. Paper 37*, pp. 1–12.

Davidson, O. W. (1960). *Proc. World Orchid Conf., 3rd, 1960*, pp. 224–233.

Dekle, G. W. and Kuitert, L. C. (1968). Orchid insects, related pests and control. *Fla. Dept. of Agric. Bull. No. 8*, pp. 1–28.

Hager, H. (1957). *Proc. World Orchid Conf., 2nd, 1957*, pp. 130–132.

Jamison, F. S., Schwartz, M., Link, D., and Sheehan, T. J. (1971). Production and marketing of vegetables, orchids and other flowers, including hydroponics. *FAO No. TA 2997*, pp. 1–47.

Knudson, L. (1922). Non-symbiotic germination of orchid seeds. *Bot. Gaz. (Chicago)* **73,** 1–25.

Northern, R. T. (1970). "Home Orchid Growing." Litton, New York.

Poole, H. A., and Sheehan, T. J. (1970). Effects of levels of phosphorus and potassium on growth, composition and incidence of leaf-tip die-back in *Cattleya* orchids. *Proc. Fla. State Hortic. Soc.* **82,** 465–469.

Poole, H. A., and Sheehan, T. J. (1973). Leaf-tip die-back of cattleys—what's the real cause? *Am. Orchid Soc. Bull.* **42,**(3), 227–230.

Poole, H. A., and Sheehan, T. J. (1977). Effects of media and supplementary micro element fertilization on growth and chemical composition of *Cattleya*. *Am. Orchid Soc. Bull.* **46**(2), 155–160.

Post, K. (1949). "Florist Crop Production and Marketing," pp. 663–717. Orange-Judd, New York.

Rotor, G. B. (1949). A method of vegetative propagation of *Phalaenopsis* species and hybrids. *Am. Orchid. Soc. Bull.* **18**(8); 738–739.

Rotor, G. B. (1952). Daylength and termperature in relation to growth and flowering of orchids. *Cornell Exp. Stn. Bull. 885.,* Ithaca, New York.

Sheehan, T. J. (1966). *Proc. World Orchid Conf., 5th, 1966,* pp. 95–97.

Sheehan, T. J. (1975). Floricultural potential in Kenya, Part I & II. *FAO KEN/528,* pp. 1–47 and 1–39.

Sheehan, T. J., and McConnell, D. B. (1978). *Proc. World Orchid Conf.,* 9th, 1978, in press.

Watkins, J. V. (1956). "ABC of Orchid Growing," 3rd ed., pp. 25–26. Prentice-Hall, Englewood Cliffs, New Jersey.

Withner, C. L. (1959). "The Orchids," pp. 1–648. Ronald Press, New York.

6
Gladiolus

Gary J. Wilfret

Introduction to Floriculture
Copyright © 1980 by Academic Press, Inc.
All rights of reproduction in any form reserved.
ISBN 0-12-437650-9

I. INTRODUCTION: HISTORICAL BACKGROUND

The modern gladiolus (family, Iridaceae; genus, *gladiolus*) cultivars (Fig. 1) offer a diversity of colors, shapes, and sizes available in few other flowering plants. They are used as landscape plants in the home garden, as specimens for exhibition, and as cut flowers. Gladiolus flowers can be all colors except true blue, although some of the violet shades appear to be very near to blue in subdued light. Floret shapes can be round, triangular, flat, hooded, or orchid-like, and petals can be plain, ruffled, laciniated, recurved, needle-pointed, or deeply crinkled. Florets range from miniatures about 2 cm across and widely spaced on thin, single, or multi-branched stems to the towering 2-m giants with florets 18 or more cm in diameter in a two-rowed formal display. A grower can choose any combination of these characteristics and can be almost sure of finding a matching cultivar.

Very few flowers match the complex ancestry of *Gladiolus* and a recent revision of the South African species (Lewis *et al.,* 1972) has further compli-

Fig. 1. A modern exhibition and cut-flower gladiolus cultivar, T-210. Note symmetry, floret arrangement, and placement.

cated the understanding of its development. *Gladiolus* species were recognized over 2000 years ago growing in the fields of Asia Minor and were called "corn lilies." The European species were cultivated at least 500 years ago. Prior to 1730 the major garden species in England were *Gladiolus communis, G. segetum,* and *G. byzantius,* the latter being introduced in 1629 from Constantinople. With the establishment of trade routes from England to India via the Cape of Good Hope, several South African species were sent to England, starting in 1737. The species *communis, carneus (blandus),* and *cardinalis* were the prominent types grown prior to 1880 and, since they are sexually compatible, many natural hybrids were cultivated (Buch, 1972). The first gladiolus was hybridized by W. Herbert, Dean of Manchester, who crossed *G. cardinalis* and *G. carneus (blandus),* whose progeny were fertile, and *G. tristis* and *G. recurvus,* whose offspring were sterile. The first important gladiolus hybrid was made in 1823 at Colville's Nursery in Chelsea, England, where *G. tristis* var. *concolor* was pollinated by *G. cardinalis* to produce the Colvillei hybrids, which soon became the most important types for growing under glass for spring flowering. *Gladiolus carneus (blandus)* was then crossed with *G. cardinalis* to produce *G. insignis,* a small, early-flowering type. In 1833 Schneevogt in Holland pollinated *G. insignis* with *G. oppositiflorus (floribundus)* to produce the Ramosus hybrids. The cross that led to the development of present Gladiolus was made in 1837 by H. Bedinghaus of Belgium, who pollinated the parrot gladiolus *G. natalensis (psittacinus)* with *G. oppositiflorus* to give the summer flowering Gandavenesis hybrids. Much controversy has arisen over whether the pollen parent was *G. cardinalis* or *G. oppositiflorus,* but the latter species is more likely (Lewis *et al.,* 1972). In 1846 W. Hooker of England produced the Brenchleyensis hybrids by crossing *G. natalensis (psittacinus)* with *G. carneus (blandus).* In 1848 Carolus crossed the Ramosus hybrids with *G. carneus (blandus)* to produce the Leopoldi hybrids, and Cole made a similar hybrid with Gandavensis and *G. carneus,* which he called Willmorecanus hybrids. Up to this time many progeny were available from hybridization among Gandavenesis and Ramosus and, in 1852, E. Souchet of France added *G. carneus (blandus)* to this complex. These were the first hybrid gladiolus imported to the United States and were the major cultivars grown for the next 30 years. These cultivars were tall and showy but needed moist, cool climates for optimum growth. Further development of the small-flowering Nanus hybrids continued in the Channel Islands with the use of *G. insignis* and *G. scullyi (venustus)* and probably *G. tristis* and *G. carneus (trimaculatus).* These, like the Colvillei hybrids, required fall planting for spring bloom.

In the mid-1860s the scarlet-flowering *G. cruentus* was introduced from Natal and was used by J. Standish of England in crosses with the Brenchleyensis hybrids to produce over 100 named cultivars. In 1877 M. Leichtlin crossed *G. cruentus (saundersii)* with Gandavenesis hybrids; the resultant progeny he called Leichtlin hybrids. These were then sold to J. Childs of Long Island in 1891 and became known as Childsi hybrids, which are the basis of many of our modern cultivars. In the 1870s a yellow-flowered form of *G. papilio (purpureo-auratus)* was introduced into France and it was not only hardy but also produced multiple daughter corms and numerous cormels from a single corm. V. Lemoine of France crossed *G. papilio* on the Gandavenesis hybrids and named 152 Lemoine hybrids. In 1885 he crossed the Lemoine hybrids with the Childsi hybrids to produce the Nancianus hybrids, of which 75 cultivars were available. One of these was 'Emile Aubrun,' considered the grandmother of the "grandiflorus" gladiolus. The Nancianus hybrids were crossed with Souchets hybrids to produce many outstanding cultivars, one of which was 'Golden Measure,' which is the ancestor of many of the modern yellow gladiolus available today. Lemoine also crossed the dull-purple flowered form of *G. papilio* to the Lemoine hybrids to produce the small-flowered blue "butterfly" gladiolus. At about the same time M. Froebel of Zurich crossed Gandavenesis with *G. saundersii*, and J. Sander of England crossed Gandavenesis with the maroon and green *G. dracocephalus*. J. Kelway of England made numerous hybrids among the Gandavenesis and Lemoine hybrids and called the progeny Kelwayi hybrids, which were known for their size and hardiness. In 1900 Lemoine added *G. aurantiacus* to the gene pool in crosses with the Leichtlin hybrids. The progeny, which he called Precoces, were early flowering.

A whole new race of garden gladiolus originated when a yellow form of *G. natalensis (primulinus)* was collected at Victoria Falls and introduced in 1902. Crossed with the larger hybrids, the progeny have become the so-called primulinus hybrids, which are an important ancestor of modern cultivars, and the basis of many of the small-flowered "prims." Use of these hybrids in breeding programs continued in Europe following World War II. Most of the European gladiolus breeding has continued in Holland and England.

The use of gladiolus as cut flowers in North America developed from Souchet's hybrids and in 1870 up to 10,000 spikes per day were shipped to New York from local fields. Luther Burbank soon developed cultivars that had greater substance and could withstand the bright sun and dry atmosphere of California. After the introduction of the Childsi hybrids in 1893, H. Groff of Canada incorporated the best qualities of Burbank's, Souchet's, and Child's hybrids to produce the Groff hybrids, known for their strong stems and good cut-flower characteristics. These could be grown in fields and then cut with the basal floret open and shipped to local markets. A. Kunderd of Indiana soon developed the ruffled and laciniatus types of gladiolus, which were unlike the plain-petaled European types. When Dr. E. F. Palmer of Canada introduced 'Picardy' in 1932, the gladiolus cut-flower industry of the South and West was born. This cultivar was a blend of the Gandavenesis and Primulinus types and was the first that could be cut in the bud stage and shipped to distant markets where the florets would open. Field production of 'Picardy' and its progeny soon eliminated greenhouse production of gladiolus. Soon after World War II L. Butt of Canada introduced his 'Rufmins,' which were small-flowered non-prim types, the most famous of which was 'Crinklette.' These are now commercially known as "Pixiola" types. A few of the modern hybridizers of gladiolus cut flowers in the United States are C. Fischer of Minnesota, H. Turk of Oregon, E. Frazee of California, and G. Wilfret of Florida.

The gladiolus cut-flower industry in the United States peaked in the 1950s and demand for the flowers has steadily declined. Several reasons have been given for this decline, such as the flower's association with funerals, limited use for small arrangements, or emergence of other favored flowers, such as snapdragons. For whatever reason, the industry in 1977 was concentrated in six states (United States Department of Agriculture, 1978), where over 166 million spikes grown on 3153 ha were sold. The wholesale value of these spikes was 16.5 million dollars. Year-round production continued in California on more than 365 ha that produced almost 30 million spikes. Most flower production was in Florida, where 2147 ha yielded 102.5 million spikes from October through May. Summer production was primarily in Alabama, Illinois, Michigan, New Jersey, and North Carolina. Another separate industry is corm production and sales, where at least 40 million are sold each year for cut-flower and landscape use, with a wholesale value close to 5 million dollars.

II. TAXONOMY

The genus *Gladiolus* of the Iridaceae is represented by 180 species (Lewis *et al.,* 1972). It is found throughout Africa and the Mediterranean area, with the greatest concentration in southern Africa. Two species are endemic to Madagascar and 15 are found in countries bordering the Mediterranean. The Cape species are primarily diploids ($2n = 30$) whereas the European species are polyploids ($2n = 60$–130), indicating a southern origin of the genus. Modern hybrids, designated as *G. grandiflorus,* are a complex of at least 11 species, several of which are represented by different color forms or botanical varieties. *Gladiolus* is a herbaceous plant that develops from axillary buds on a corm. The leaves overlap at the base and may number from 1 to 12. The inflorescence is a spike and originates as a terminal axis. Florets number up to 30 or more and are tubular with flower parts in threes. Individual florets are enclosed in two green spathe valves. The pistil consists of a three-lobed stigma, a simple unbranched style, and an inferior ovary. The capsule contains between 50 and 100 ovules which mature within 30 days after fertilization. Florets are either bilateral or radially symmetric.

Gladiolus cultivars are classified by use of a three-digit number. The first digit indicates floret size, the second digit basic color, and the third digit depth of color. An odd-third digit indicates the presence of a conspicuous mark (CM) in the lip or throat. The diameter of the lowest floret, without spreading or flattening of the petals, determines the size.

The second digits from 0 to 8 correspond to a progression from yellow-green through orange, red, purple, and violet. White is given a value of 0. In addition,

Table I

Size and Color Classifications of *Gladiolus* as Designated by The North American Gladiolus Council

Class [a]	Designation	Floret size (cm)
100	Miniature	<6.4
200	Small or miniature	≥6.4 to <8.9
300	Decorative	≥8.9 to < 11.4
400	Standard or large	≥11.4 to −14.0
500	Giant	>14.0

Color [b]	Pale	Light	Medium	Deep	Other
White	00				
Green		02	04		
Yellow	10 [c]	12	14	16	
Orange	20	22	24	26	
Salmon	30	32	34	36	
Pink	40	42	44	46	
Red	50	52	54	56	58 Black red
Rose	60	62	64	66	68 Black rose
Lavender	70	72	74	76	78 Purple
Violet	80	82	84	86	
Smokies		92	94	96	
Tan	90				98 Brown

[a]The first digit indicates floret size in the five classes.
[b]The last two digits in the classification indicate floret color and shade. An odd last digit indicates a conspicuous mark or blotch.
[c]Includes cream.

many gladiolus cultivars have a smoky hue, and have been assigned a number of 9, depending upon the base color. The classification as adopted by The North American Gladiolus Council is seen in Table I.

III. PROMINENT CULTIVARS

With the ease of hybridization of *Gladiolus* (Wilfret, 1974), over 10,000 cultivars have been recorded. Any extensive listing of cultivars would soon be obsolete but several have persisted over the years as cut flowers and need to be mentioned (Jenkins, 1963b; Wilfret, 1970). In the winter-growing areas of Florida, major cultivars grown are 'White Friendship,' 'T-210' (white); 'Friendship,' 'Pink Parade' (pink); 'Traveler' (rose); 'Valeria,' 'Intrepid,' 'Red Majesty' (scarlet or red); 'Jacksonville Gold,' 'Jester,' 'T-590,' 'Goldfield' (yellow); 'Beverly Ann,' 'T-704' (lavender); 'Spic & Span,' 'Flamingo' (salmon); and 'Peter Pears' (orange). These cultivars are grown because they can be harvested in the tight bud stage and will open at the retail shop. They also are less day-length sensitive and less temperature responsive than most cultivars and produce long spikes with at least 16 florets regardless of season. In the northern growing areas, the number of cultivars used is extensive, some of which are 'Impala,' 'King's Ransom' (red); 'Spring Song,' 'True Love' (pink); 'White Prosperity,' 'Morning Bride' (white); and 'Lemon Lime,' 'Golden Scepter,' 'Golden Harvest' (yellow). In addition, several growers have invested in their own breeding programs and have developed cultivars for their exclusive use.

IV. PROPAGATION

A. Cormel Production

Gladiolus corms (Table II) are propagated from cormels which grow in clusters on outgrowths (stolons) between mother and daughter corms. Cormels are usually graded into three sizes: large, ⩾1.0-cm diameter; medium, ⩾0.6 and <1.0 cm; and small, <0.6 cm. Number of cormels per 100 liters ranges from 71,000 for the large to 425,000 for the small. One hundred liters of cormels weighs approximately 52.5 kg. Most commercial growers use only large cormels for planting stock production. Cormel stocks should be chosen carefully to prevent spread of disease into developing corms and preferably should only be saved from "mother" blocks of corms that have been grown in fumigated soil and carefully rogued. In addition, cormels should be treated in a hot water solution to eradicate latent fungus, insects, and nematodes. Within the last few years use of tissue culture has been demonstrated to be feasible with gladiolus to provide a source of clean stock for future propagation (Simonson and Hildebrandt, 1971; Wilfret, 1971; Ziv *et al.,* 1970).

Table II

Grades of Gladiolus Corms Developed by The North American Gladiolus Council

Description		Size (diameter, cm)
Large		
Jumbo		>5.1
No. 1	Flowering stock	>3.8 to ⩽5.1
Medium		
No. 2		>3.2 to ⩽3.8
No. 3		>2.5 to ⩽3.2
Small		
No. 4		>1.9 to ⩽2.5
No. 5	Planting stock	>1.3 to ⩽1.9
No. 6		>1.0 to ⩽1.3

The so-called hot-water treatment of cormels (Forsberg, 1961; Milholland and Aycock, 1965) has been modified to include the addition of fungicides in the solutions to complement the action of the hot water (Magie, 1971, 1975). Basically, this treatment consists of a 30-minute immersion of pretreated cormels in a suspension of benomyl (0.1 kg/100 liters water) plus an additional fungicide, such as captan (0.18 kg/100 liters) or thiram (0.18 kg/100 liters) held at 53°–55°C. Cormels used should have been dug during the warm months and stored at 24°–32°C for 8 weeks prior to treatment. Two days prior to treatment, cormels should be covered with warm water (32°C) to soften the husks. Any cormels that float should be discarded. Cormels enclosed in mesh sacks should be submerged in the hot suspension for 30 minutes and then plunged for 10 minutes in cool running water. Treated cormels should be air-dried in thin layers in sterilized trays and then placed in cold storage (2°–4°C) until planted. Dormancy of larger cormels is usually broken within 4 months of treatment. Root bud swellings indicate that cormels are ready to be planted. It is a good practice to soak cormels in water for 2 days just prior to planting to ensure uniform sprouting.

Land preparation consists of soil fumigation, maintenance of a soil pH of 5.8 to 6.5, and incorporation of approximately 280 kg/ha of a 10–4.4–8.3 (N,P,K) or equivalent dry fertilizer. Gladioli require full sun and a well-drained soil for optimum growth. Moist cormels are planted in single rows in 10- to 13-cm-wide furrows spaced 60 to 75 cm apart. Cormels should be covered with about 8 cm of soil, which is then leveled and compressed. A suitable herbicide is applied, based upon soil type and cultural conditions. About 130 large cormels are planted per meter of row or 1.5 million liters per hectare (Magie *et al.*, 1966). The soil must be kept moist initially to obtain good germination, and then soil moisture should be reduced gradually to obtain optimum growth. Monthly applications of a dry or liquid fertilizer are necessary to obtain maximum yield within 5 to 6 months after planting (Waters, 1965). Small corms are dug with a modified potato digger. Yields of about 100 corms larger than 1.3 cm diameter can be dug per meter of row in a good operation when large cormels are used. Corms from 1.3 to 2.5 cm diameter are called "planting stock" and are used for the production of flowering-size corms.

B. Planting Stock Production

Planting stock treatment is similar to that of cormels except the temperature of the fungicide suspension is decreased to about 46°C and the time the corms are submerged is limited to 15 minutes (Magie, 1975). Small corms <2.5 cm diameter are planted in one or two rows per bed at a depth of 6 to 8 cm. Number of corms planted per meter of row ranges from 50 to 80, depending upon corm size. The soil should provide adequate moisture and nutrition for good growth but should not be allowed to be saturated with water. Irrigation should cease 2 to 3 weeks prior to harvest to prevent rotting of corms in the field and to facilitate cleaning of the new corms. Removal of flower spikes improves corm size but many growers allow the first floret to open to observe purity of the stock and allow roguing of odd plants. Yields of 430,000 flowering size corms (≥2.5 cm diameter) or more can be expected per hectare (Magie *et al.,* 1966). Corms should be cleaned and dipped in a fungicide solution within 2 days of digging to obtain maximum effect of the fungicide. Corms dug in the warm part of the year are dormant and require 3 to 4 months of cold storage (2°–4°C) to break this dormancy. An alternative method to break dormancy is to expose the corms to ethylene chlorohydrin (Denny, 1938; Jenkins *et al.,* 1970). Corms and cormels, following at least 1 week of cold storage, are sealed in 1-liter container that contains 4 ml of 40% ethylene chlorohydrin solution and are then held for 3 to 4 days at room temperature (23°C). Another method is to soak cormels in a 3% solution of ethylene chlorohydrin for 3 to 4 minutes and then to seal them in a tight glass container for 24 hours at 23°C. Corms and cormels planted immediately after treatment will sprout within 3 to 4 weeks. The major endogenous growth inhibitor controlling cormel germination has been identified as abscisic acid and can be regulated by cold storage plus 6-benzyladenine or by prolonged cold storage alone (Ginzburg, 1973).

V. FLOWERING STOCK CULTURE

A. Field Production

Gladiolus produce the best flower spikes when grown in deep, well-drained sandy loam soils, but they can be grown in sandy soils having less than 1% organic matter if proper cultural conditions are practiced. A heavy clay soil with poor drainage should be avoided whenever possible, as the gladiolus root system is easily damaged by excessive soil moisture. Soil fumigation with Vorlex (327 liters/ha) or methyl bromide–chloropicrin (400 kg/ha) is used for maximum flower production but many growers rely on a 3- to 4-year crop rotation system to reduce buildup of soilborne diseases. Size of corms used for flower production is dependent upon the planting season. Many northern growers are able to produce marketable spikes in the summer from No. 2 and No. 3 corms. While under short-day, cool-night winter conditions, southern growers plant No. 1 or Jumbo corms. Corms are spaced in furrows at 13 to 17 per meter of row, with row spacing dependent upon soil type and irrigation method. Single rows spaced 0.76 m apart are adequate in heavier soils whereas sandy soils require wider spacing. In Florida, growers use either single rows on 1.4-m centers or two rows per bed spaced 0.4 m apart with beds on 1.8-m centers. Corm density for single rows on 0.76- and 1.4-m centers is 173,000 and 96,000/ha, respectively. Double rows in beds on 1.8-m centers can hold approximately 136,000 corms/ha. Large corms are planted 15 to 23 cm deep while medium corms are covered with only 13 to 16 cm of soil. Irrigation methods used are primarily open ditches or subtiles in Florida and overhead in other areas of the country. The latter method is used for three purposes: (1) to provide adequate moisture; (2) to prevent freezing of very early and very late crops; and (3) to reduce sunburning of florets. Floret count per spike can be greatly reduced when plants are grown excessively dry, especially from time of emergence to the second-leaf stage (Halevy, 1965). High temperature and high light intensities are well tolerated by gladiolus (Beijer, 1962), but blind plants or reduced floral bud count occur during short-days, low light intensity, and cool night temperatures (Shilo and Halevy, 1966). Plants are especially sensitive at the two-leaf stage, which is approximately the time of floral bud initiation. Various chemicals have been applied to stimulate rooting and flower formation (Halevy and Shilo, 1970; Zimmerman, 1938), but none have been shown to be advantageous.

B. Nutritional Requirements

Fertilizer requirements for rapidly growing plants vary with climatic conditions, irrigation method, and soil type. In sandy soils, it is necessary to provide fertilizer frequently, especially during the rainy season. In some heavier loam soils, little or no fertilizer is required for flower production (Stuart and McClellan, 1951; Van Diest and Flannery, 1963; Woltz, 1955a), as the large supply of inorganic and organic nutrients present in large corms is sufficient. In fact, the benefit of fertilizer is often seen only during the second season.

Nitrogen deficiency can be manifest as a reduction in number of spikes and number of florets per spike as well as the typical pale green foliage. Symptoms of phosphorus deficiency are dark green upper leaves and a purple coloration in the lower leaves. A lack of potassium causes reduced floral bud count, shortening of the flower stem, delay in flowering, general yellowing of older leaves, and interveinal yellowing of younger leaves. Several symptoms of minor element deficiency have been reported for gladiolus (Woltz, 1957, 1965, 1976). Calcium deficiency can cause cracking of the spike generally below the second or third floret and more severe cases are evident as bud blasting or bud rot. Magnesium deficiency causes interveinal chlorosis of older leaves whereas iron deficiency is manifested by interveinal chlorosis of new leaves. Deficiencies of boron cause cracking of leaf margins, deformed leaves, and stunted inflorescenses. Brown tip of leaves and spathes has been associated with fluoride toxicity (Brewer et al., 1966; Jenkins, 1963a; Woltz, 1957), but similar symptoms may result from anything that injures the root system, such as close cultivation, disease, nematodes, and waterlogging of soil.

The nutritional requirements of gladiolus vary depending upon prior fertilization of the mother corm, but in general a gladiolus crop grown on sandy soils should have 90 to 135 kg nitrogen (supplied partly as nitrate and partly as ammonium), 90 to 180 kg phosphate (as P_2O_5), and 110 to 180 kg potash (as K_2O) per hectare (Woltz, 1955b, 1965, 1976). Secondary nutrients, such as calcium, magnesium, iron, and boron, may be applied as fritted trace elements during land preparation. At least four applications of fertlizers are advisable: (1) preplant incorporated; (2) side-dressed at the two- to three-leaf stage; (3) side-dressed at the "slipping" stage when the inflorescence emerges from leaves; and (4) side-dressed about 2 weeks after flowering to develop the new corm and cormels (Wilfret, 1970). Corms are dug 6 to 8 weeks after flowering and are given postharvest handling similar to planting stock.

VI. PEST CONTROL

A. Insects, Mites, and Nematodes

Gladiolus are excellent host plants for many insect pests (Kelsheimer, 1956; Magie and Cowperthwaite, 1954; Magie and Poe, 1972; Short, 1976). Several species of aphids attack gladiolus, including green peach aphid (*Myzus persicae*), potato aphid (*Macrosiphum solanifolii*), and melon aphid (*Macrosiphum gossypii*). These sucking insects damage developing foliage and flowers and transmit many virus pathogens. Aphids are controlled effectively with organic pesticides such as dimethoate, malathion, or endosulfan. Use of disulfoton or aldicarb granules in the furrow at planting has been beneficial. Unsightly scars on florets are often caused by both the gladiolus thrips (*Taeniothrips simplex*) and common flower thrips (*Frankliniella* species). Use of diazinon, monocrotophos, or acephate in conjunction with good weed management will keep these under control. Loopers (*Trichoplusia ni* and *Pseudoplusia includens*), armyworms (*Spodoptera frugiperda, S. eridania,* and *S. exigua*), cutworms (*Feltia subterranea* and *Prodenia dolichos*), and corn earworms (*Heliothis zea*) feed on gladiolus foliage and flowers. There are three stages in the crop cycle when these larvae are more damaging: (1) at plant emergence to the two-leaf stage; (2) at the slipping stage; and (3) just prior to opening of the lowest floret. Regular spray programs of *Bacillus thuringiensis* (a bacterial pathogen), monocrotophos, and trichlorfon will control these organisms. Two species of mites (*Tetranychus urticae* and *T. bimaculatus*) have been identified in gladiolus but generally do not create a major problem in commercial plantings (Engelhard, 1969). Nematodes, particularly those causing root-knot (*Meloidogyne* spp.), are controlled by hot-water treatment of corms and cormels and by soil fumigation (Overman, 1962, 1969).

B. Diseases

Diseases of gladiolus can be divided into those of the neck, leaf, and flower, and those of the corm and roots (Jenkins *et al.,* 1970; Magie and Cowperthwaite, 1954; Magie, 1957, 1967; Magie and Poe, 1972). Botrytis blight (*Botrytis gladiolorum*) can damage both leaves and flowers. It develops primarily in cool, wet weather and is evident as small brown or gray spots on one side of the leaf but may progress to both sides when advanced. Flower symptoms are small to large water-soaked spots on petals that may develop into a gray mold. Control is by sprays of maneb (with zinc) and benomyl. Curvularia blight (*Curvularia trifolii* f. sp. *gladioli*) attacks young leaves during warm, humid weather and may develop in flowers. It is particularly destructive on young cormels, where it destroys the plant at the soil line. Sprays with maneb and chlorothalonil are effective in its control. Bacterial leaf and neck rots (*Pseudomonas marginata* and *Xanthamonas gummisudans*) are especially destructive in warm, rainy seasons. No effective bactericides have been found to control these rots, but sanitation is helpful in reducing their spread. Stromatinia dry rot (*Stromatinia gladioli*) occurs in cool, moist weather and is evident as yellow-brown tissue above the corm with a sharp, moldy odor. Small black sclerotia are usually visible between the leaf bases. Hot-water treatment of corms and cormels, soil fumigation, and incorporation of dichloran in the planting bed help to keep this disease under control. Infested soils should be avoided during cool seasons.

Fusarium corm rot (*Fusarium oxysporum* f. sp. *gladioli*) is the most destructive disease of gladiolus (Forsberg, 1955, Magie, 1971). The fungus can exist as latent infections in the corm and cause storage rot, deformed and blind plants, and floret disfigurement. This fungus is a worldwide problem and no host resistance has been found. Control measures include hot water treatment of cormels, fungicide dips of corms, and soil fumigation. Other corm rots can be caused by *Curvularia, Stromatinia,* and *Botrytis* (soft rot). Postharvest fungicide dips of corms will generally keep these under control. Other fungi and bacteria have been reported on gladiolus but they normally are not a serious problem in commercial operations (Magie and Poe, 1972).

In addition to the fungus and bacterial diseases, gladiolus can be infested by a number of viruses. Cucumber mosaic, tomato ringspot, tobacco ringspot, and bean yellow mosaic viruses have been reported on gladiolus (Bing, 1972; Beute *et al.,* 1970). Symptoms of these include leaf and spathe chlorosis, flower mottling, spike distortion, and plant stunting. Control is only by propagation of disease-free stock, roguing of infested plants, and proper insect control.

C. Weeds

Chemical weed control is essential for commercial operations and herbicides are applied both pre- and postemergence of the crop. Since most herbicides are specific for soil types and prevalent weed populations, no one chemical can be used universally. Several herbicides have been reported as safe on gladiolus corms, such as alachlor, trifluralin, 2, 3, 5, 6-tetrachloro-1,4-benzene dicarboxylic acid dimethyl ester (DCPA), and diuron (Bing, 1977,

1978; Jenkins *et al.*, 1968; Raulston and Waters, 1971; Waters, 1967; Waters and Raulston, 1972). Small corms and cormels are more sensitive to these chemicals and due care should be exercised in the use of any herbicide.

VII. HARVESTING AND HANDLING FLOWERS

A. Harvest

Gladiolus spikes can be harvested from 60 to 100 days after planting, depending upon cultivar and time of year (Jenkins, 1963, Jenkins *et al.*, 1970; Wilfret, 1970). Spikes are cut in the tight-bud stage with two to three leaves remaining on the stem and from one to five floral buds showing color. Care is taken to not damage leaves remaining on the plant as these are needed for development of the new corm and cormels (Compton, 1960; Hussein *et al.*, 1962; Wilfret and Raulston, 1974). Spikes are bundled in groups of 100 and sent to the packing house for grading. They are transported in an upright position to prevent curving or crooking of stems. Some growers stand the cut spikes in water or a floral preservative and transport them in refrigerated trucks from the field to the packing house.

B. Grading

Spikes are sorted into five grades based on overall quality, spike length, and floret number (Table III). When graded, they are bunched in units of 10 and held together by rubber bands. They are then held upright in cold storage (4°–6°C) until packed. Many growers stand the spikes in a floral preservative to prevent desiccation prior to and after grading. Recent studies have shown that sucrose pulsing of stems prior to storage of 7 or 10 days resulted in greater floret opening (Bravdo *et al.*, 1974; Kofranek and Halevy, 1976; Mayak *et al.*, 1973).

Table III

**Grades of Cut Flowers Used in Florida by
Commercial Gladiolus Growers**

Grade	Spike length (cm)	Number florets (minimum)
Fancy	>107	16
Special	>96 to ≤107	14
Standard	>81 to ≤96	12
Utility	≤81	10

C. Packing, Storing, and Shipping

Graded spikes are usually stored less than 24 hours before they are packed and shipped to the markets. They are held at a minimum temperature of 4°C, as many cultivars will not open well when stored at a lower temperature. The 10-spike bunches are packed without water in hampers made of fiberboard or wood which measure 33 cm wide and deep and from 107 to 130 cm tall. Fifteen to 24 bunches per hamper are wrapped in Kraft paper or polyethylene for protection from sudden temperature fluctuations, bruising, and moisture loss. The hampers are then stored at 4°C until shipped. Spikes may remain in these hampers from 3 to 7 days prior to use by the retailer, with quality decreasing with increased number of days of storage. Most gladiolus flowers are shipped in refrigerated trucks or by air to wholesalers or directly to retailers. They may be in transit from 1 to 3 days, depending upon distance to market. Spikes must be held in an upright position to prevent distortion of the stems because of the expression of negative geotropism.

D. Consumer Care of Flowers

Spikes should be removed immediately from the hamper upon arrival. The basal 2.5 cm of each stem should be cut off and stems placed in a floral preservative that contains at least a carbohydrate source and a bactericide. Flower life can be extended by 3 to 5 days by using the floral preservative instead of water (Kofranek and Paul, 1974; Marousky, 1968, 1969, 1971). Water quality is important also and should be low in soluble salts (Waters, 1966, 1968) and free of dissolved fluorides (Marousky and Woltz, 1971; Spierings, 1970; Waters, 1968). As little as 0.25 ppm fluoride has been shown to damage some gladiolus cultivars (Marousky and Woltz, 1971). Flowers should be opened at a moderate temperature (21°–23°C) with some light but not in direct sunlight. Once flowers have opened or are in the desired arrangement, they should be stored at 4°–6°C until displayed. Vase life of these flowers varies from 5 to 10 days, depending upon cultivar and room temperature.

REFERENCES

Beijer, J. J. (1962). The forcing of Gladioli in the hothouse. *Ann. Br. Gladiolus Soc. 1962,* pp. 22–25.
Beute, M. K., Milholland, R. D., and Gooding, G. V. (1970). A survey of viruses in field-grown gladiolus in North Carolina. *Plant Dis. Rep.* **54,** 125–127.
Bing, A. (1972). Virus. *In* "The World of the Gladiolus" (N. Koenig and W. Crowley, eds.), pp. 182–191. Edgewood Press, Maryland.
Bing, A. (1977). Preemergence weed control in gladiolus cormels, 1976. *North Am. Gladiolus Coun. Bull.* **130,** 62–65.
Bing, A. (1978). Preemergence weed control in gladiolus cormels, 1977. *North Am. Gladiolus Coun. Bull.* **133,** 55–56.

Bravdo, B., Mayak, S., and Gravieli, Y. (1974). Sucrose and water uptake from concentrated sucrose solutions by gladiolus shoots and the effect of these treatments on floret life. *Can. J. Bot.* **52,** 1271–1281.

Brewer, R. F., Guillemet, F. B., and Sutherland, F. H. (1966). Effects of atmospheric fluorides on gladiolus growth, flowering, and corm production. *Proc. Am. Soc. Hortic. Sci.* **88,** 631–634.

Buch, P. O. (1972). The Species. *In* "The World of the Gladiolus" (N. Koenig and W. Crowley, eds.), pp. 2–7. Edgewood Press, Maryland.

Compton, O. C. (1960). Effects of leaf clipping upon the size of gladiolus corms. *Proc. Am. Soc. Hortic. Sci.* **75,** 688–692.

Denny, F. E. (1938). Prolonging, then breaking, the rest period of Gladiolus corms. *Contrib. Boyce Thompson Inst.* **9,** 403–408.

Engelhard, A. W. (1969). Bulb mites associated with diseases of gladioli and other crops in Florida. *Phytopathol.* **59,** 1025. (Abs.).

Forsberg, J. L. (1955). Fusarium disease of gladiolus: Its causal agent. *Ill. Nat. Hist. Surv., Bull.* **16,** 447–503.

Forsberg, J. L. (1961). Hot water and chemical treatment of Illinois-grown gladiolus cormels. *Ill. Nat. Hist. Surv., Biol. Notes* **43,** 1–12.

Ginzburg, C. (1973). Hormonal regulation of cormel dormancy in *Gladiolus grandiflorus. J. Exp. Bot.* **24,** 558–566.

Halevy, A. (1965). Irrigation experiments on Gladiolus. *In* "The Gladiolus" (P. C. Vasaturo, ed.), pp. 129–136. Maxfield Press, New Hampshire.

Halevy, A. H., and Shilo, R. (1970). Promotion of growth and flowering and increase in content of endogenous gibberellins in *Gladiolus* plants treated with the growth retardant CCC. *Physiol. Plant.* **23,** 820–828.

Hussein, M. F., El-Gamassy, A. M., and Serry, G. A. (1962). Effects of number of leaves at flower cutting on the yield of Snow Princess and Bloemfontein gladiolus corms and cormels. *Agric. Res. Rev. Cairo* **40,** 1–9.

Jenkins, J. M. (1963a). Influence of different plant nutrients upon brown tip of gladiolus. *Plant Dis. Rep.* **47,** 976–977.

Jenkins, J. M. (1963b). Some characteristics of commercial gladiolus varieties. *North Am. Gladiolus Coun. Bull.* **75,** 37–38.

Jenkins, J. M., Chambers, E. E., and McGee, F. G. (1968). Chemical weed control in Gladiolus. *Weed Sci.* **16,** 86–88.

Jenkins, J. M., Milholland, R. D., Lilly, J. P., and Beute, M. K. (1970). Commercial gladiolus production in North Carolina. *N. C. Agric. Ext. Circ.* **44B,** 1–34.

Kelsheimer, E. G. (1956). Insects and other pests of gladiolus and their control. *Fla. Agric. Exp. Stn. Circ. S-91.*

Kofranek, A. M., and Halevy, A. H. (1976). Sucrose pulsing of gladiolus stems before storage to increase spike quality. *HortScience* **11,** 572–573.

Kofranek, A. M., and Paul, J. L. (1974). The value of impregnating cut stems with high concentrations of silver nitrate. *Acta Hortic.* **41,** 199–206.

Lewis, G. J., Obermeyer, A. A., and Barnard, T. T. (1972). Gladiolus—A revision of the South African species. *J. S. Afr. Bot.* **10**(Suppl.).

Magie, R. O. (1957). Soil fumigation in controlling gladiolus Stromatinia disease. *Proc. Fla. State Hortic. Soc.* **70,** 373–379.

Magie, R. O. (1967). Bacterial neck rot of gladiolus in Florida. *NAGC Bull.* **89,** 99–100.

Magie, R. O. (1971). Effectiveness of treatments with hot water plus benzemidazoles and ethephon in controlling fusarium disease of gladiolus. *Plant Dis Rep.* **55,** 82–85.

Magie, R. O. (1975). The hot water treatment for gladiolus propagation. *GladioGrams* **17,** 4–6.

Magie, R. O., and Cowperthwaite, W. G. (1954). Commercial gladiolus production in Florida. *Fla. Agric. Exp. Stn., Bull.* **535.**

Magie, R. O., and Poe, S. L. (1972). Disease and pest associates of bulb and plant. *In* "The World of the Gladiolus" (N. Koenig and W. Crowley, eds.), pp. 155–181. Edgewood Press, Maryland.

Magie, R. O., Overman, A. J., and Waters, W. E. (1966). Gladiolus corm production in Florida. *Fla. Agric. Exp. Stn. Bull.* **664A.**

Marousky, F. J. (1968). Influence of 8-hydroxyquinoline citrate and sucrose on vase-life and quality of cut gladiolus. *Proc. Fla. State Hortic. Soc.* **81,** 415–419.

Marousky, F. J. (1969). Conditioning gladiolus spikes to maintenance of fresh weight with pretreatments of 8-hydroxyquinoline citrate plus sucrose. *Proc. Fla. State Hortic. Soc.* **82,** 411–414.

Marousky, F. J. (1971). Effects of temperature, container venting, and spike wrap during simulated shipping and use of floral preservative on subsequent floret opening and quality of gladiolus. *Proc. Trop. Reg. Am. Soc. Hortic. Sci.* **15,** 216–222.

Marousky, F. J., and Woltz, S. S. (1971). Effect of fluoride and a floral preservative on quality of cut gladiolus. *Proc. Fla. State Hortic. Soc.* **84,** 375–380.

Mayak, S., Bravdo, B., Guilli, A., and Halevy, A. H. (1973). Improvement of opening of cut gladioli flowers by pretreatment with high sugar concentrations. *Scientia Hortic.* **1,** 357–365.

Milholland, R. D., and Aycock, R. (1965). Propagation of disease-free gladiolus from hot-water treated cormels in southeastern North Carolina. *N. C., Agric. Exp. Stn., Tech. Bull. No. 168.*

Overman, A. J. (1962). Effective use of soil nematicides for gladiolus. *Proc. Fla. State Hortic. Soc.* **74,** 382–385.

Overman, A. J. (1969). Gladiolus corm dips for root-knot nematode control. *Proc. Fla. State Hortic. Soc.* **82,** 362–366.

Raulston, J. C., and Waters, W. E. 1971. Use of herbicides in ornamental flower production under sub-tropical conditions. *Proc. Trop. Reg. Amer. Soc. Hortic. Sci.* **15,** 229–238.

Shilo, R., and Halevy, A. H. (1966). The effect of low temperature on the flowering of Gladioli. *In* "The Gladiolus" (P. C. Vasaturo, ed.), pp. 239–245. Maxfield Press, New Hampshire.

Short, D. E. (1976). Pest control guide for commercial flower crops in Florida. *Univ. of Fla. Ext. Entomol. Rep.* **50.**

Simonson, J., and Hildebrandt, A. C. (1971). *In vitro* growth and differentiation of *Gladiolus* plants from callus cultures. *Can. J. Bot.* **49,** 1817–1819.

Spierings, F. (1970). Injury to gladiolus by fluoridated water. *Fluoride Q. Rep.* **3,** 66–71.

Stuart, N. W., and McClellan, W. D. 1951. Effect of nutrient supply and fertilizer practices on Gladiolus growth in the greenhouse and field. *Gladiolus Mag.* **15,** 2.

United States Department of Agriculture (1978). Floriculture crops—production area and sales, 1976 and 1977; intentions for 1978. *U.S. Dep. Agric. Crop Reporting Board SpCr* **6**-1(78).

Van Diest, A., and Flannery, R. L. (1963). The nutritive requirements of gladiolus in New Jersey soils. *Proc. Am. Soc. Hortic. Sci.* **82,** 495–503.

Waters, W. E. (1965). Nutrient requirements of gladiolus cormels on sandy soils of Florida. *Proc. Soil and Crop Sci. Soc. of Fla.* **25,** 59–63.

Waters, W. E. (1966). The influence of post-harvest handling techniques on vase-life of gladiolus flowers. *Proc. Fla. State Hortic. Soc.* **79,** 452–456.

Waters, W. E. (1967). Influence of herbicides on gladiolus flower and corm production in Florida. *Proc. South Weed Conf.* **20,** 171–178.

Waters, W. E. (1968). Relationship of water salinity and fluoride to keeping quality of chrysanthemums and gladiolus cut flowers. *Proc. Am. Soc. Hortic. Sci.* **92,** 633–640.

Waters, W. E., and Raulston, J. C. (1972). Weed Control. *In* "The World of the Gladiolus" (N. Koenig, and W. Crowley, eds.), pp. 150–154. Edgewood Press, Maryland.

Wilfret, G. J. (1970). A critical evaluation of the commercial gladiolus cultivars grown in Florida. *Proc. Fla. State Hortic. Soc.* **83,** 423–427.

Wilfret, G. J. (1971). Shoot-tip culture of gladiolus: An evaluation of nutrient media for callus tissue development. *Proc. Fla. State Hortic. Soc.* **84,** 389–393.

Wilfret, G. J. 1974. Gladiolus Breeding. *In* "Breeding Plants for Home and Garden—A Handbook" (F. McGourty, Jr., ed.). *Brooklyn Bot. Gard. Rec.* **30,** 35–38.

Wilfret, G. J., and Raulston, J. C. (1974). Influence of shearing height at flowering on Gladiolus corm and cormel production. *J. Amer. Soc. Hort. Sci.* **99,** 38–40.

Woltz, S. S. (1955a). Effect of differential supplies of nitrogen, potassium, and calcium on quality and yield of gladiolus flowers and corms. *Proc. Am. Soc. Hortic. Sci.* **65,** 427–435.

Woltz, S. S. 1955b. Studies on nutritional requirements of gladiolus. *Proc. Fla. State Hortic. Soc.* **67,** 330–334.

Woltz, S. S. (1957). Nutritional disorder symptoms of gladiolus. *Florists Exch.* **129,** 17–20.

Woltz, S. S. (1965). Fertilizing gladiolus. *Fla. Flower Grow.* **2,** 1–5.

Woltz, S. S. (1976). Fertilization of gladiolus. *GladioGrams* **21,** 1–5.

Zimmerman, P. W. (1938). Adventitious roots with B-indolebutyric acid. *Contrib. Boyce Thompson Inst.* **10,** 5–14.

Ziv, M., Halevy, A., and Shilo, R. 1970. Organs and plantlets regeneration of Gladiolus through tissue culture. *Ann. Bot.* **34,** 671–676.

7
Minor Cut Crops

Christina Warren Auman

Introduction to Floriculture
Copyright © 1980 by Academic Press, Inc.
All rights of reproduction in any form reserved.
ISBN 0-12-437650-9

I. INTRODUCTION

There are over 70 plant species used as commercial cut flower crops in the floriculture industry. Over 80% of the wholesale gross value was obtained from the sale of chrysanthemums, roses, carnations, and gladioli in 1970 in the United States, whereas orchids accounted for 4% and snapdragons for 3%. The remaining crops, referred to as "minor perishables," obviously comprise a minor portion of the floriculture industry but in some instances they are the only crops grown by individuals or firms, and are of great value to those individuals. These minor cut flower crops and florists' greens add variety and beauty to floral arrangements. Their absence on the market would be strongly felt by florists and their customers.

Innovations in cultural technology, transportation, and changes in consumer preferences have resulted in drastic changes in minor cut flower production. Sweet peas and calendulas, once popular, now are seldom seen in floral pieces, whereas the once-exotic anthuriums and birds-of-paradise have gained in popularity. A wide assortment of minor cut flower crops, such as bachelor's button, gypsophila, and statice, once were produced in fields in eastern North Carolina and shipped by truck to many of the eastern states. Very few of the companies still exist, and now statice and similar crops are being flown in to the United States from Israel. Greenhouse production of some crops has been replaced by field production in milder climates, and the shortage of fuel could make the trend even more prevalent. In some instances, however, field production with all its risks has been replaced by protected cultivation.

Some of the minor cut flower crops grown in the United States are shown in Table I. States leading in the production of those crops are also listed. None of these crops individually account for a significant percentage of the total wholesale value of cut flower crops in the United States.

It would be difficult to describe in detail the culture of all minor cut flower crops and florists' greens as there are so many. The reader should be aware, however, that a multitude of minor cut flowers exists and that they are important in the floriculture industry. Some crops are discussed in some detail in this chapter and the culture of some are listed in Tables II and III. Prominent cut florists' greens are shown in Table IV.

Disease and insect control have been discussed in several other chapters. Similar approaches to pest control should be followed for the minor cut flower crops. Optimum postharvest handling methods are not too well known for some of these crops but most of them will benefit from low-temperature storage (0°–4°C) and the use of floral preservatives. None of the crops has a universal system of grading, and the criteria of quality might be stem length, flower size, and stem weight.

References listed at the conclusion of this chapter should be of value to the reader who wishes to acquire additional knowledge on specific crops.

Table I

Minor Cut Crops of Relative Importance in the United States [a,b]

Cut flower	Major production areas (ranked in order of volume produced)
Daisies	California, Florida, Michigan
Iris	California, Florida, Washington
Daffodils	Washington, California, Oregon
Stock	California, Arizona
Anthurium	Hawaii, Wisconsin
Gypsophila	Florida, California, North Carolina
Tulips	Washington, New Jersey, New York, California
Asters	California, Florida, Arizona
Gardenias	California, Pennsylvania, Hawaii
Easter lilies	Florida
Peonies	North Carolina, Pennsylvania, Illinois
Statice	Florida, California
Stephanotis	California, Oregon, Minnesota
Anemone	New York, California, Massachusetts
Calla lily	California, Florida, Michigan, Ohio
Heather	California, Oregon, Minnesota
Freesia	California, New York, Pennsylvania
Strelitzia	California, Hawaii, Florida
Delphinium	Michigan, California, Florida
Camellia	California, New York, Alabama
Violets	New York
Cornflower	California, New York, Michigan
Zinnia	Michigan, New York, California
Gerbera	New York, California, Ohio
Ranunculus	California, New Jersey, New York
Hyacinth	Pennsylvania, New York, Ohio
Dahlia	California, New York, New Jersey
Ginger	Hawaii
Larkspur	Ohio, Virginia, North Carolina
Eucharis	Pacific Coast
Lily of the valley	Pennsylvania, New York
Waxflower	California
Acacia	California
All others	California, Hawaii, Michigan

[a]Crops are ranked in decreasing order of economic value.
[b]Data compiled from U.S. Census Bureau: Census of Agriculture Special Reports on Horticultural Specialties 1970.

Table II

Minor Cut Flower Crops, Propagated Primarily Vegetatively

Common name	Scientific name	Area of origin	Description	Primary propagation method	Spacing	Stem length	Harvest stage
Allium, ornamental onion	*Allium* species	Himalayas and North America	Large number of very small flowers in an umbel usually in shades of blue to lavender, yellow, white	Bulbs, offset	15–45 cm	100–120 cm	One-third to one-half florets open
Alstroemeria, Peruvian lily	*Alstroemeria aurantiaca*	Chile, Brazil	Whorl composed of cymes; up to eight flower stalks per stem. Shades of yellow, rose-pink, lilac, also white; some with yellow throats, all with black markings	Division of fibrous roots	45 × 52 cm 52 × 52 cm	100–105 cm	Cut when four to five flowers are open in the cluster
Yarrow	*Achillea filipendulina*	Europe, Asia	Flowers showy, yellow-orange in flat topped clusters; pungent foliage	Division	30–60 cm	6J–90 cm	—
Agapanthus, Blue African lily, lily of the Nile	*Agapanthus africanus* also called *A. umbellatus*	South Africa	Flowers in cluster (umbel) 2.5–10 cm across. Corolla funnel shaped; white and shades of blue	Division of fleshy roots	1 m	60–90 cm	When one-fourth of florets open in the umbel
Bouvardia	*Bouvardia humboldtii* and *B. ternifolia*	American tropics	Showy, fragrant, white or red tubular flowers in flattish cymes	Terminal cuttings	25 × 30 cm		—
Feverfew	*Chrysanthemum parthenium*; also sold as *Matricaria capensis*	Europe and Asia	Small, daisylike flowers; rays white, 2 cm wide, with yellow disk flowers	Formerly grown from cuttings, more often grown from seed	25 × 25 cm	30–60 cm	Cut when only a few of the flowers on stem have fully opened

(continued)

Table II (*continued*)

Common name	Scientific name	Area of origin	Description	Primary propagation method	Spacing	Stem length	Harvest stage
Clivia, Kafir lily	*Clivia miniata* and hybrids	South Africa	Flowers in terminal umbel with funnel-shaped corolla, 12 to 20 flowers per cluster, orange to scarlet with yellow throats; some hybrids in shades of yellow, salmon, scarlet, also white	Bulbs	45–60 cm	30–38 cm	—
Eremurus, foxtail lily, desert candle	*Eremurus* hybrids	Asia	Thirty–100-cm-long spike bears star-shaped flowers in a cluster (raceme); white, yellow, cream, pink, orange	Division of fibrous roots	45–100 cm	1–2.5 m	Cut when bottom florets are beginning to open
Euphorbia, scarlet plume	*Euphorbia fulgens*; also known as *E. jac-quinaeflora*	Mexico	Showy red-orange to scarlet bracts on wiry, slender drooping branches	Four-5-inch terminal cuttings; mist and rooting hormone recommended	10 × 15 cm; 15 × 20 cm after pinching	60–90 cm	Cut when showing enough color to be saleable
Forsythia, golden bell	*Forsythia* × *intermedia*, a cross between *F. suspensa* and *F. viridissima*	China	Numerous clusters of yellow flowers (several in a cluster) 3 cm long	Hardwood cuttings in spring	—	30–60 cm	—
Ixia, African corn lily	*Ixia* hybrids	South Africa	Pendulous, bell-shaped flowers 5 cm across on wiry stems; red, pink, orange, yellow, cream with dark centers	Corms, cormels	5 × 5 to 5 × 10 cm	25–38 cm	—

Common name	Botanical name	Origin	Description	Propagation			Harvest
Tritoma, red-hot poker, torch lily	*Kniphofia uvaria*; also called *K. aloides*, *K. pfitzerii*, *Tritoma uvaria*	Africa	Flowers in tall spikes (racemes) red or yellow	Division	—	—	Cut when a majority of florets are open or showing color
Ornithogalum, star of Bethlehem, chincherinchee	*Ornithogalum thyrsoides*, *Ornithogalum* species	South Africa	Star-shaped white flowers in clusters (racemes) very fragrant	Bulbs	15–20 cm	15–45 cm	—
Tuberose	*Polianthes tuberosa*	Mexico	Waxy, white, very fragrant flowers 5 cm across in terminal racemes	Bulbs, offset	15–20 cm	60 cm	Cut when majority of the florets open
Protea, pink mink	*Protea* species	Cape Region of South Africa	Dense clusters lacking petals, many colors, also black; 8–15 cm across	Recently matured terminal cutting 6-8-inch long	—	25–45 cm	—
Scilla, squill	Mainly *scilla sibirica*	Temperate areas of Europe and Asia	One-to-2-cm flowers, pendulous bells in clusters—up to 100 flowers/stem; usually blue but also pink, purple, white	Bulbs, bulblets	30–45 cm	15–30 cm	

Table III

Minor Cut Flower Crops, Propagated Primarily from Seed

Common name [a]	Scientific name	Area of origin	Number of seeds/28 gm	Optimum germination temperature (°C)	Time required for germination	Spacing
English daisy, true daisy (P,A)	*Bellis perennis*	Europe	135,000	Alternating 21 night, 29 day	8 Days	10 × 10 cm to 22 × 22 cm
Calendula, pot marigold (A)	*Calendula officinalis*	Southern Europe	3,000	21	10 Days	30 × 30 cm
Pyrethrum, painted daisy (P)	*Chrysanthemum coccineum;* usually sold as *Pyrethrum roseum*	Caucasus Mountains, Persia	18,000	16–21	2–3 Weeks	15 × 20 cm
Cosmos (A)	*Cosmos bipinnatus* and *Cosmos sulfureus*	Mexico	4,000–5,000	20–30	1–2 Weeks	30 × 80 cm
Sweet William (A,B)	*Dianthus barbatus*	Russia, China, south to the Pyrennes	27,500 (biennial) 25,000 (annual)	21	1–2 Weeks	15–20 cm
Gaillardia, blanket flower (P)	*Gaillardia aristata;* also known as *G. grandiflora*	Western United States	10,000	21–24	2–3 Weeks	45 × 80 cm
Godetia, farewell to spring, satin flower (A)	*Godetia amoena* and *Godetia grandiflora*	Western United States, particularly California	14,000	21	20 Days	15 × 20 cm
Sunflower (A,P)	*Helianthus* species	North America	700	18–24	2–3 Weeks	30 × 100 cm (annual); 1 × 1.6 m (perennial)
Strawflower, everlastings (A)	*Helichrysum bracteatum*	Australia	36,000	21	7 Days	20 cm
Hyacinth, flowered or rock candytuft (A)	*Iberis amara coronaria* also known as *I. coronaria*	England, Central and southern Europe	9,500	21	8–10 Days	15 × 15 cm
Globe or annual candytuft (A)	*Iberis umbellata*	Italy, Crete, Spain	9,500	16	14 Days	20 × 25 cm
Sweet pea (A)	*Lathyrus odoratus*	Sicily	350	13	15 Days	8 × 17 cm

Common name	Scientific name	Origin	Seeds per gram	Germination temperature (°C)	Germination time	Spacing
Liatris, gayfeather (P)	Liatris pycnostachya and L. spicata	Illinois to Texas	Variable	18–24	3–4 Weeks	
Lupine (A)	Hybrids derived from Lupinus luteus, L. hartwegii, L. hirsutus, L. pubescens	Mexico	1,300	16–18	21 Days	20 × 30 cm (greenhouse); 30 × 37 cm (field)
Lupine (P)	Lupinus polyphyllus "Russell hybrids"	Western North America	1,000	21 night, 29 day	30 Days	20 × 30 cm (greenhouse); 30 × 60 cm (field)
Bells of Ireland, shell flowers (A)	Molucella laevis	Western Asia	4,200	10 night, 29 day	21 Days	7 × 14 cm
Forget-me-not (A,P)	Myosotis sylvatica, also called M. oblongata	Europe and Asia	44,000	13	2–3 Weeks	25 × 25 cm
Iceland poppy (A)	Papaver nudicanle	Arctic regions of both hemispheres	275,000	12 night, 21 day	12–14 Days	25 cm
Annual phlox (A)	Phlox drummondii	Texas	14,000	18	10–14 Days	20 × 20 cm
Mignonette (A), peaches and cream	Reseda odorata	North Africa	Data not available	12	2–3 Weeks	17 × 22 cm (pinched); 5 × 15 cm (single-stem)
Salpiglossis, painted tongue (A)	Salpiglossis sinuata	Chile	125,000	21–24	10–14 Days	20 × 20 cm (greenhouse); 30 × 60 gm (field)
Sweet Scabious, mourning bride, pincushion flower (A)	Scabiosa atropurpurea	Southern Europe	4,500	21	12–14 Days	20 × 20 cm (greenhouse); 30 × 60 cm (field)
Scabious, pincushion flower (P)	Scabiosa caucasica	Caucasus Mnts.	2,400	16	2–3 Weeks	30 × 60 cm
Marigold (A)	Tagetes erecta T. patula Tagetes hybrids	Mexico	9,000–10,000	21–24	7 Days	10 × 10 cm (greenhouse); 30 × 30 cm (field)
Blue laceflower (A)	Trachymene caerulea also known as Didiscus caerulea	Australia	10,000	21	21 Days	15 × 25 or 20 × 30 cm

[a]A, annual; P, perennial; B, biennial.

Table IV

Prominent Cut Florists' Greens

Common name	Scientific name	Area of origin	Leaf description	Major areas of production	Propagation	Lasting quality (vase life)	Storage requirements
Smilax	*Asparagus asparagoides*	South Africa	Branching, leafless vine; branches oval, 2 cm long	Missouri	Division	1–2 Weeks	Short storage life; store 2–4°C; guard against excessive drying
Asparagus, plumosa fern	*Asparagus setaceous, formerly A. plumosus*	South Africa	Leathery, fernlike vine; leaves needlelike, 1 cm long; wiry stems	Florida	Division	1–2 Weeks	Same as above
Boxwood	*Buxus sempervirens*	Southern Europe, Northern Africa, Western Asia	Leaves opposite, 2–3 cm long	Florida	Softwood or semihardwood cuttings	1–2 Weeks	40°C in a preservative solution
Camellia	*Camellia japonica*	China and Japan	Oval leaves, 7–10 cm long	California	Terminal or leaf bud cuttings	1–4 Weeks	40°C in a preservative solution
Croton	*Codiaeum variegatum*	Java, Australia, South Pacific Islands	Smooth, oval-like, or oblong often narrow leaves in variegated colors	Florida	Cuttings	1–3 Weeks	2–4°C in a preservative solution
Ti, Hawaiian Ti, Dracaena	*Cordyline terminalis* also known as *Dracaena terminalis*	Eastern Asia	Leaves clustered at end of stem blade lance-shaped, 30–100 cm long	Hawaii	Seeds, cuttings, root layerings	1–2 Weeks	2–3 Weeks at 4°C in a preservative solution
Scotch broom	*Cytisus scoparius*	Europe	Needle-like leafets 1 cm long on long stems		Terminal cuttings	1–3 Weeks	40°C; use a preservative solution

Common name	Scientific name	Origin	Description		Propagation	Storage life	Storage conditions
Baker fern, leatherleaf	*Dryopteris erythrosora*	Eastern North America	Fronds 20-40 cm	Florida	Division	1-2 Weeks	2°-4°C for 2-3 weeks in a preservative solution
Eucalyptus, euc	*Eucalyptus pulverulenta*	Australia	Alternate rounded leaves 6 cm across, bluish-gray green on flexible stem		Seeds	1-4 Weeks	2°-4°C in a preservative solution
Salal, lemon-leaf	*Gaultheria shallon*	Alaska to California	Leaves round to oval, shaped, 7-12 cm long, evergreen shrub	California	Seeds, division, cuttings	1-3 Weeks	0°C in moisture-retaining packs
Variegated California ivy, ghost tree ivy	*Hedera canariensis arborescens* "variegated"	Madeira and Canary Islands, North Africa	Round or heart-shaped, 5-7-lobed leaves 5-15 cm long; variegated reddish stems	California	Cuttings	1-2 Weeks	2°-4°C for 2-3 weeks in a preservative solution
English holly and variegated English holly Christmas holly	*Ilex aquifolium* and *I. aquifolium* "Albo-marginata"	Europe, Asia, North Africa	Evergreen tree; silvery margined, 3-6 cm long oval or oblong leaves, dark green type, also much prized for their berries	Oregon	Seeds, cuttings, grafting, budding, air-layering	Up to 2 months	0°C for 1-3 weeks; must be enclosed in moisture-retaining packs
Pittosporum, mock orange and variegated mock orange	*Pittosporum tobira* and *P. tobira variegatum*	China and Japan	Thick, leathery leaves, dark green and variegated 7-10 cm long, oval with blunt tip	Florida	Seeds or cuttings	1-2 Weeks	4°C in preservative solution
Podocarpus	*Podocarpus macrophyllus*	Japan	Lance-shaped needles 7-10 cm long		Stem cuttings	1-3 Weeks	4°-7°C; use a preservative solution

Some crops that have been now relegated to this chapter because of their relatively minor economic importance might warrant individual attention in future editions of the textbook as technology and consumer preferences alter production patterns in the future. Although, some of the more prominent crops are listed below, space does not permit a lengthy discussion of each crop.

II. PRINCIPAL CROPS

A. *Acacia baileyana, A. armata,* and *A. pubescens* (Acacia, Golden Mimosa, Cootamundia Wattle)
    1. *Area of origin*—Australia.
    2. *Description*—Acacias are fast-growing shrubs of the pea family. The flowers are very small (1 cm across), sometimes fragrant, and are borne in dense globular clusters. All species grown for cut flower use are yellow.

Stem cuttings of recently matured wood are taken in the summer or fall. Cuttings root easily but have a pronounced taproot, which makes them very difficult to transplant. They can also be grown from seed. Plants take 2 to 3 years to reach the flowering stage when started from seed. Seeds must be soaked prior to planting, either in concentrated sulfuric acid for 20 to 120 minutes or in warm water for 12 to 48 hours.

    3. *Culture*—Acacias are grown outdoors in the summer but brought into a cool greenhouse before the first frost. A forcing temperature of 4°–10°C is adequate.

The woody stems seldom take up water so prolonged storage is not recommended. Stems will last 3 to 4 days at 4°C. The flowers will last 4 to 5 days after removal from storage.

Mealybugs, scale, thrips, and aphids are the major pests of acacia.
B. *Anemone coronaria* (Anemone, Poppy Anemone, Lily of the Field)
    1. *Area of origin*—Southern Europe.
    2. *Description*—These flowers are perennials of the buttercup family and have solitary flowers without petals but with petal-like sepals on stalks 25 to 45 cm long. Single, double, and semidouble forms come in shades of red, blue, pink, lavender, and white. The flowers can be as much as 7 cm in diameter.

The primary method of propagation is by seeds (35,000 seeds/28 gm). Germination temperature is critical (16°C) as the seeds are adversely affected by higher temperatures. It requires 5 to 6 weeks for germination to occur. Light is not a factor in germination. Plants grown from seeds are favored since they tend to be more disease-free than those grown from tubers.

    3. *Culture*—Seedlings are spaced 10 by 25 cm with the crown level with the soil surface and are planted in April and May. High temperatures can cause short stems and small flowers. Temperatures of 4°–7°C are satisfactory. Plants grown from seed in early spring will flower the following March and April.

Flowers are cut just when the buds begin to open, can be stored for 1 to 2 days at 4°–7°C, and then will last 3 to 5 days after removal from storage.

The major insect pests are thrips, aphids, spider mites, mealybugs, and leaf rollers.

C. *Anthurium andraeanum* and *A. scherzerianum* (Anthurium, Flamingo Flower, Painted Tongue)

   1. *Area of origin*—Tropical America.

   2. *Description*—*Anthurium andraeanum* has a yellowish-white flower spadix (columnar structure that bears the true flowers). The spathe is leathery, heart-shaped, brilliant orange to red and 8 to 15 cm across.

   Anthurium scherzerianum has a coiled, yellow spadix. The spathe is red, yellow, pink, or white, 5 to 7 cm across, and more or less oval.

   Propagation of anthuriums is with offshoots with aerial roots from the main stem or two to three-leaved terminal cuttings rooted under intermittent mist. They can also be grown from seeds. Plants will flower in 3 years.

   3. *Culture*—*Anthurium* is field grown in Hawaii and in warm greenhouses elsewhere. A minimum night temperature of 18°C and a relatively low light intensity are recommended. Anthuriums should not be refrigerated, as temperatures of less than 7°C result in blackened flowers. They can be stored at 13°C for 2 to 3 weeks, and will last 2 to 4 weeks in an arrangement. Anthuriums are cut when the spadix is almost fully developed. The stems are placed in lukewarm water (38°C) and allowed to stand overnight prior to shipment.

   The most damaging disease in Hawaii is anthracnose, known as black nose or spadix rot. It is especially a problem in high rainfall areas. Thrips and spider mites are the major pests.

D. *Callistephus chinensis* (China Asters, Asters)

   1. *Area of origin*—China and Japan.

   2. *Description*—China aster is an annual not closely related to the genus *Aster*. The solitary flowers, 5 to 10 cm in diameter, are somewhat similar to chrysanthemums. Blue, lavender, rose, and white are the prominent colors. Asters are propagated by seed (12,000 seeds/28 gm), and will germinate in 8 to 10 days at 21°C.

   3. *Culture*—Asters can be grown in greenhouses or fields but are most commonly grown in a clothhouse. Seeds are started in April and the seedlings are transplanted to beds in mid-May or when danger of frost is over. Seedlings are spaced 30 × 30 cm. An earlier crop can be produced by starting seeds in Jiffy Pots in mid-March and lighting for 4 hours a night from emergence until seedlings are transplanted to the clothhouse. Flowering time should be 1 month earlier with this method. Asters can be flowered year-round in areas where the night temperature can be kept at 10°C. Supplemental lighting must be supplied from the seedling stage until they reach a height of 50 to 60 cm. No lights are necessary from May 15 to August 1. Spacing is 20 × 20 cm in the greenhouse. Pinching is not necessary but the lateral shoots should be dis-

budded of side shoots or "suckers" to obtain the best-quality flowers. Production time is 5 to 6 months from sowing to flowering.

A major drawback to aster production in the past has been the great susceptibility to a number of diseases and pests. Stem rot (Fusarium wilt) can be very serious. There are some resistant cultivars on the market but steam sterilization of soil and all equipment used is essential. Aster yellows can be virtually eliminated in the clothhouse, if the leafhopper is excluded by using cloth with at least 22 threads/2.5 cm. Rust and Botrytis blight can also be troublesome. Leafhopper, aphids, spider mite, cyclamen mites, thrip, whitefly, mealybugs, and caterpillars are also pests on asters.

E. *Camellia japonica* (Camellia)

   1. *Area of origin*—China and Japan.

   2. *Description*—Camellias are evergreen shrubs with waxy, long-lasting flowers that are 5 to 17 cm in diameter, white, multicolored, and shades of pink and red; the yellow stamens are in a dense cluster in the center. Both single and double forms exist. Camellias can be propagated by seeds, cuttings, grafting, and air-layering. Most commercial propagation is by cuttings which are not difficult to root. Recently matured tip cuttings are taken in midsummer to early fall. The cuttings should be 7 to 15 cm long with two to three leaves. Stem ends are wounded and treated with 20 ppm indolebutyric acid (IBA) for 24 hours. Leaf-bud cuttings may also be taken.

   3. *Culture*—Most camellias for cut flower use are greenhouse-grown, as flower injury too frequently occurs with outdoor production. The growing medium should have a pH of 5.0 to 5.5. A night temperature of 4°–10°C is satisfactory. Vegetative growth will be most vigorous at 10°C. The light intensity must be reduced in the summer. Long days promote bud formation, but after buds have formed short days are required. Plants will bloom from fall through spring. Only one flower is allowed to develop per stem, to obtain maximum flower size. The flowers are cut when fully open. No leaves are removed with the flowers. The flowers are "fashioned" or "dressed," in the same way as gardenias. Camellia or gardenia leaves (usually gardenia leaves since they are easily manipulated) are attached to a paper collar and fastened to the flower. Individual flowers are packaged in airtight boxes, and sprinkled with water to maintain humidity. They are never stored in water. Prolonged storage is not recommended but the flowers can be held at 7°C for 3 to 6 days.

F. *Centaurea cyanus* (Cornflower, Bachelor's Button)

   1. *Area of origin*—Southern Europe.

   2. *Description*—The flowers are borne in heads and the petals are only tubular (no rays as usually found in the Compositae). The marginal flowers are expanded and raylike. The typical color is blue but can also be red, maroon, pink, purple, or white. The stem length is 30 to 90 cm. Cornflowers are propagated from seed (7000 seeds/28 gm). The seed germinate in 10 days at 16°C.

   3. *Culture*—Cornflowers are grown in both field and greenhouses and, therefore, are available throughout the year. The seeds are usually sown from

November to January and flower 5 to 6 months later. Seedlings are spaced 30 × 30 cm and grown at 10°–13°C. Centaurea flowers ship well but prolonged storage is not recommended. Flowers can be stored at 4°C, for up to 3 days, and will last 4 to 5 days in an arrangement.

Botrytis blight on flowers, aster yellows, rust, and powdery mildew are major diseases, and insect problems are aphids, thrips, spider mites, leaf rollers, and leafhoppers.

G. *Chrysanthemum maximum* (Shasta Daisy, Majestic Daisy)

　1. *Area of origin*—Pyrenees Mountains.

　2. *Description*—Shasta daisy is a herbaceous perennial that is most often treated as a biennial. The flowers are both single and double with sizes ranging from 5 to 7 cm single and 10 to 15 cm double. They are almost always white tinged with yellow, blue, or pink with yellow centers. Stem length is 25 to 40 cm. Propagation of shasta daisy is from seed (18,000–25,000 seeds/28 gm), which germinate in 12 to 14 days at 16°–18°C. For best germination seeds require light; only a sparse crop of flowers is produced the first year with maximum production the second year. In areas other than the West Coast plants do not survive after the second season. Sowing is in early February.

　3. *Culture*—This daisy is almost exclusively a field-grown crop. Spacing is 45 × 75 cm; shasta daisies will grow in any moderately well-aerated soil.

H. *Chrysanthemum frutescens* (Marguerite, Boston, or Paris Daisy)

　1. *Area of Origin*—Canary Islands.

　2. *Description*—This plant is a perennial and often has a woody base. The flowers are 5 to 12 cm across, with yellow centers with petals of white, yellow, or pink often tinted with pink, blue, or orange. The stem length is 25 to 40 cm. Marguerite daisies are vegetatively propagated by stem cuttings.

　3. *Culture*—Requirements for *C. frutescens* are almost identical to those of *C. morifolium.*

Both shasta and Marguerite daisies are cut when the flowers are fully open. The optimum storage temperature for both species is 4°C. Shasta daisies can be stored for as long as 8 days but Marguerite daisies will be acceptable for up to 3 days of storage only.

Disease problems of daisies are rust, mildew, aster yellows, and Botrytis blight, while insect pests are aphids, leaf miners, thrips, and mites.

I. *Consolida ambigua* (Hybrids)* (Larkspur, Annual Delphinium)

　1. *Area of origin*—Southern Europe.

　2. *Description*—Larkspur is a hardy annual. The flowers are borne in long spikes in shades of blue, salmon, rose, lilac, purple, or white. Total stem length is 1 to 2 m. There are branching types with several flower spikes on each plant; the hyacinth-flowered type has only one flower spike. Larkspur is propagated by seed (8000 seeds/28 gm) that germinate in 3 weeks at 13°C. The germination temperature is critical.

---

*Formerly *Delphinium* ajacis changed to the genus Consolida.

3. *Culture*—The crop can be grown commercially in fields or greenhouse. Seeds are sown both in early spring and late fall for field production. Fall sowing is done 6 to 7 weeks before the ground freezes. Plants will survive over the winter without protection except in parts of the country where winters are extremely severe. A fall planting will flower several weeks to a month earlier than those started in the spring. Irrigation is necessary during dry periods. Seed should be sown directly in fertile well-drained soil. Seedlings are spaced 20 to 30 cm apart. The blooming period is mid-spring to early fall if two sowings are made 2 to 3 weeks apart in the spring. Sanitation is necessary to produce a profitable greenhouse crop. Night temperature should not exceed 10°C for the first 2 months, and then should be raised to 13°–18°C. Plants in the greenhouse are spaced at 25 × 30 or 30 × 30 cm. Plants started from seed in September and October will bloom in late April through June. Stems are cut when two to five of the first florets have opened. The florets fall under almost any conditions. The stems must be shipped upright and in water. They can be stored at 4°C but not for longer than 1 to 2 days.

Plants are subject to the same disease problems as perennial delphiniums. *Rhizoctonia* (seedling damping-off) can be a severe problem with larkspur.

J. *Convallaria majalis* (Lily of the Valley)

1. *Area of origin*—Europe and Asia. Similar races are found wild in the Appalachian mountains from Virginia to South Carolina.

2. *Description*—Lily of the Valley is hardy perennial with white bell-shaped, and nodding flowers, that are lightly fragrant which are borne in loose, often one-sided clusters (racemes). The tips of the corolla are recurved. The rhizome of *Convallaria* produces a large underground bud with its own roots called a pip. The pip is removed with its attached roots and used as the planting stock. Pips are separated and replanted each year until they reach flowering size (3 years). These pips are stored and can be forced into bloom any time. Pips should be stored at −4° to −2°C for at least 2 months. They can be stored up to 1 year if kept moist. Plants should be grown in highly organic acid soil (pH 4.5–6.0) and kept moist at all times. The pips are planted in rows 0.3 m apart and 1 or 2 cm apart in the row. Lily of the valley will bloom in approximately 1 month at 18°C. Some reduction in light intensity is required at all times of the year but especially in the summer. The stems should be cut when the bells are well developed on the stem (when the terminal bell has lost its deep green color). The flowers can be stored dry for 2 to 3 weeks at −1°–0°C, or for 1 week at 2°C if placed in water. They are shipped in bunches of 25, with foliage attached. They are usually loosely wrapped in waxed paper which is open at both ends.

Botrytis blight can be a problem unless air is kept circulating.

K. *Costus* species (Ginger)

1. *Area of origin*—Tropical regions.

2. *Description*—Yellow, red, or white flowers with three-lobed tubular calyx.

3. *Culture*—Ginger is propagated either by cuttings, when the stalks are cut into 0.5-cm lengths and rooted in a sand, peat moss medium, or from rhizome

divisions. The plants are almost exclusively field grown in areas with high temperatures, high humidity, and rich organic soil. Flowers can be stored at 13°C for 3 to 4 days.

L. *Dahlia pinnata* (Dahlia)

1. *Area of origin*—Mexico.

2. *Description*—Dahlias are tender perennials treated as bulbous annuals, consisting of hundreds of cultivars. The American Dahlia Society recognizes 14 different flower groups. The decorative, large cactus and pompon types are some of the important ones for cutting. There are many flower colors, except blue. Sizes range from less than 0.5 cm to almost 30 cm across. Many types are grown from seeds (2800 seeds/28 gm) but the prominent cultivars are propagated by stem cuttings or division of the tuberous roots. Ten- to 15-cm cuttings are taken in late winter and rooted under mist at 18°C. Clumps are dug in the fall, stored at −1° to 10°C, and covered with soil or vermiculite to prevent drying over the winter. In spring the clumps are divided so that each tuber has one or more sprouts or eyes.

3. *Culture*—Dahlias for cut flower production are mostly field grown. Seedlings are spaced 30 × 30 cm, whereas vegetatively propagated plants are planted 37 to 75 cm apart. Primary flower production occurs in the fall, as bud formation occurs under short days. Maximum quality and production are achieved in areas with warm days and cool nights. The plants require staking or some type of support. Dahlias require an abundance of water but the site needs to be well drained. They also require high amounts of available phosphorous and potassium. After establishment plants can be side- or top-dressed with a complete fertilizer such as 5-10-5. The flowers are cut when they are almost fully opened. The stems must be immersed in boiling water for 30 seconds or seared with a flame to permit water uptake. Stem length varies from 30 cm to 1 m, depending on the type of dahlia. Flowers can be stored at 4°C for 4 to 5 days.

M. *Delphinium* Hybrids (Delphinium)

1. *Area of origin*—Europe and Asia.

2. *Description*—Delphinium is a herbaceous hardy perennial (Fig. 1). The flowers are arranged in a long terminal cluster (raceme or spike). Each floret is 0.5 to 1 cm in diameter. Flowers are available in shades of blue, purple, pink, and white. Total stem length is 0.5 to 1.5 m. Delphiniums are propagated by seeds (10,000 seeds/28 gm) which germinate in 18 days at 10°–13°C. They can also be propagated by softwood cuttings in the spring, or by division.

3. *Culture*—Delphiniums can be grown commercially in the field or greenhouse. For field production the seeds are sown September 1, transplanted 7 cm apart into flats, and hardened off. Plants are given winter protection and will bloom the following summer. For greenhouse production seed are sown August 1 and transplanted into flats in a cold frame. Plants are moved into a cool greenhouse in November. Spacing is 12 × 20 cm. On February 1 plants are grown at 4°–7°C. The temperature is increased to 10°C nights in late

Fig. 1.   Delphinium flowers, a hardy herbaceous perennial.

March. Flower production occurs in May through July. Plants in the field are supported with stakes, whereas wire mesh is used in the greenhouse. The florets shed easily under any conditions, and the spikes do not ship well. The spikes can be stored at 4°C for 1 to 2 days.

   Major disease problems are powdery mildew, bacterial leaf spot, and crown rot. Aphids, mites, and caterpillars are major insect pests.

N. *Erica* species (Heather, Heath)

   1. *Area of origin*—South Africa and Mediterranean region.

   2. *Description*—*Erica* is often sold as heather although true heather belongs to the genus *Calluna*. Heather occurs as small shrubs with needlelike leaves in clusters of three to six. The flowers are arranged in clusters (umbels or spikes). The corolla is very small and bell-shaped. Colors are rose and lavender, or sometimes white or red. Branches are 22 to 30 cm total length. The propagation of heather is most often accomplished by terminal cuttings of partially matured growth, which occurs at different times for different species. A

rooting hormone is usually used and temperature should be kept above 16°C. Bottom heat is recommended. Two years are required to reach flowering size.

3. *Culture*—Cut heather is most often grown in the field but can also be produced in the greenhouse. Soil high in organic matter with a pH of 5.5 should be used. An acid fertilizer is used twice during the growing season, once in early spring and then a month later. The plants grow best at night temperatures of 4°–10°C, with a maximum day temperature of 18°C. Reduction in light intensity is needed during the summer months. Pruning is necessary to limit size and to encourage branching. Heather cut stems can be stored at 4°C for up to 1 week. The flowers will remain attractive for 7 to 10 days when arranged and placed in water. Dried heather will be attractive for 1 year or more.

O. *Eucharis grandiflora* (Also *E. amazonica*) (Eucharis, Amazon Lily)

1. *Area of origin*—South America, primarily Colombia.

2. *Description*—*Eucharis* has daffodil-like flowers that are very fragrant, white, and 5 cm in diameter. They are borne in a terminal umbel of three to six blooms. The plants have shiny leaves 20 to 30 cm long and are propagated by bulb divisions.

3. *Culture*—The culture of the Amazon lily is very similar to *Amaryllis* culture. Plants seem to bloom best when their roots are confined in pots but will flower at any time, with alternate growth and rest periods. The optimum temperature conditions are 18°–21°C at night and 24°C or higher during the day. Three to four bulbs are planted in a 20-cm pot, with the tips even with the soil line. Flowers are cut individually and handled in the same manner as gardenias and camellias. The flowers, which can be stored at 7°–10°C for 7 to 10 days, are popular in wedding bouquets.

P. *Freesia refracta* (Freesia)*

1. *Area of origin*—South Africa.

2. *Description*—These plants are tender perennials grown from corms. The flowers are borne in a spike which is at a 90° angle to the rest of the stem. There are four to eight florets per spike in shades of yellow, pink, red, blue, or white. Each floret is up to 5 cm in diameter. Freesias were traditionally grown from corms, but the disadvantage in using corms is that they often contain viruses that limit production. Although propagation from seed takes 2 to 3 months longer for production it is becoming popular as a suitable means for avoiding serious disease problems.

3. *Culture*—Freesias, second only to carnations in Europe in the quantity of stems produced, require 5 months to bloom if started from corms. The corm should be planted with the apex just above the soil line. A minimum temperature of 16°C should be maintained until three to four leaves are visible and then the temperature should be lowered to 13°. After the foliage dries up corms can be dug up and stored for production the next year. Seedlings can be transplanted 4 to 5 weeks after sowing and grown at 15°–18° until at least seven

*The primary species from which hybrids and cultivars grown today are derived.

leaves are visible. The temperature then is lowered to 13°C. It requires 7 to 8 months from seed to flower. Seedlings are spaced 7 × 7 cm whereas plants obtained from corms are spaced 5 to 10 cm apart in rows 15 cm apart. Flowers can be stored for 7 to 10 days at 0°–1°C. Once removed from cold storage the flowers will last for 5 to 10 days.

Freesias are subject to the same diseases that attack gladioli, such as Botrytis leaf blight, Fusarium yellows and corm rot, bacterial scab, Stromatinia rot, white break, and other viruses. Spider mites and thrips are the major insect pests.

Q. *Gardenia jasminoides* (Gardenias, Cape Jasmine)

1. *Area of origin*—China. But originally gardenias were considered to have originated at the Cape of Good Hope—hence its name of Cape Jasmine.

2. *Description*—Gardenias occur as a tropical shrub, with very fragrant, white or cream, solitary flowers 7 to 12 cm in diameter that are produced in the leaf axils. The calyx is tubular, the corolla is short and tubular and has 5 to 11 waxy, petal-like lobes. Terminal cuttings are rooted under intermittent mist with bottom heat (24°C) in a 1:1 sand:peat moss medium. Cuttings are shaded from direct light. They are usually taken in the winter. One to 2 years are required for the plants to reach flowering maturity.

3. *Culture*—The plants should be grown in a well-aerated soil high in organic matter and with a pH of 5.0 to 5.5. Night temperature of 16°–18°C is critical for flower bud formation, with a day temperature of 21°C. One-year-old plants are spaced 30 × 30 cm and 2-year-old plants are spaced 46 × 45 cm. Gardenias are cut when almost fully open, but the outer petals should be no more than at a 90° angle to the stem. They are usually harvested without foliage attached. The individual flowers are wired—attached to a paper collar with leaves attached to the collar. Flowers are placed in trays, sprinkled with water, and sealed to keep humidity high. They can be stored at 0°–2°C for up to 2 weeks, without water and will last about 2 days at room temperature. Gardenias should be handled as little as possible, as any contact with the petals causes browning.

Gardenias are particularly susceptible to canker caused by *Phomopsis gardeniae,* bacterial leaf spot, and root-knot nematode. Mealybugs, scale, spider mites, and whiteflies are insect problems in gardenia production.

R. *Gerbera jamesonii* (Gerbera, Transvaal Daisy)

1. *Area of origin*—Transvaal (South Africa).

2. *Description*—Gerbera is a tender perennial (Fig. 2). The flowers are solitary and occur on hairy stalks. The rays are very showy: yellow, salmon, pink, orange, red, or white. The flowers are 5 to 12 cm across. Stem length ranges from 25 to 40 cm. Both single and double forms are found. Gerberas are propagated from divisions with two or more growing points in June. Single divisions or rhizome divisions may also be made. Gerberas can also be started from seeds but the quality of seedlings is not uniform. Many gerbera plants grown from seed close at night and this is a detrimental quality for use as cut flowers.

Fig. 2. Greenhouse production of gerbera.

3. Culture—Gerberas are planted with the crowns slightly above the soil level, to avoid crown rot. The plants apparently do not respond to daylength, but they flower best under high light intensity. Some shading will result in longer, more desirable stems. A night temperature of 16°C is satisfactory. Plants produced from divisions can be planted 30 by 30 cm, whereas those propagated from single or rhizome divisions can be spaced 20 × 20 cm. Plants from divisions made in June will flower in late fall and winter, although 1 year will be required for plants produced from seed. The harvest stage is critical, as the flowers should not be cut before the outer row of flowers show pollen, or the flowers will wilt and close at night. Flowers can be stored at 4°C for up to 8 days. The vase life is 3 to 8 days. Gerberas exhibit positive phototropism and must be wired to retain their position in an arrangement.

Diseases can be a major factor in limiting gerbera production. The major problem is with the soil-borne pathogens such as *Pythium, Phytophthora*, and *Rhizoctonia*. Other diseases are powdery mildew, *Botrytis, Alternaria, Fusarium,* and *Verticillium*. Whiteflies perhaps are the worst insect pest but aphids, leafhoppers, leaf miners, caterpillars, spider mites, and thrips can be troublesome.

S. *Gypsophila paniculata* (Gypsophila, Gyp, Baby's Breath)

1. *Area of origin*—Europe and Asia.
2. *Description*—The flowers are numerous and usually occur in profusely

branched clusters (panicles). Most commonly they are white but also may be pink or red. Vegetative cuttings have replaced the traditional method of grafting. Cuttings are handled in the same manner as are carnation cuttings. Shoots which are elongated and thin (have initiated flowers) should not be used for propagation. Plants can also be grown from seed but this method is rarely used by commercial growers.

3. *Culture*—Gypsophila are mostly field-grown, especially in Florida and can be produced in any area where chrysanthemums can be grown. They are grown in dry, calcareous, gravel type soils. Good drainage is essential. A soil pH of 6.5 to 7.5 is essential, as indicated by the generic name. The plants are spaced 0.7×1.3 or 1×1.7 m in the field, because they will be quite large at time of harvest. The flowering season is from February to October. Gypsophila is harvested when the flowers are open but not overly mature. Flowers on the plant do not open simultaneously, as the tip of the spray opens first and is harvested separately. The flowers are very susceptible to drying after harvest, and must be placed in water and refrigerated immediately. A floral preservative is strongly recommended throughout the post harvest process. Flowers can be stored for 1 to 2 days at 4°C. Dried flowers will last at least for 1 year. The vase life of gypsophila is 5 to 7 days.

Crown gall is a major disease problem, and red spider mites, leaf miners, and armyworms are troublesome insect pests.

T. *Leptospermum scoparium* "Keatleyi" (Waxflower, Pink Tea Tree)

1. *Area of origin*—Australia.

2. *Description*—Waxflower occurs as a shrub or small tree. The white and pink flowers are 1 cm wide, single or double, and are borne in the leaf axils.

3. *Culture*—The plants can be grown outdoors or grown in the cool greenhouse at 4°–10°C until February or March when the temperature is raised to 13°–16°C for forcing. Flowers are available from late December through early May. Flowers can be stored at 4°C for 1 to 2 days, and will last 3 to 10 days under room conditions.

U. *Limonium* species (Statice, Sea Lavenders)

1. *Area of origin*—Mediterranean region and the Canary Islands.

2. *Description*—These plants (Fig. 3) once belonged to the thrift genus (*Armeria*), but there was much confusion over the names and the sea lavenders were changed to the genus *Limonium*. The name statice was entirely rejected botanically but is still in common usage. Numerous, small flowers occur in loose clusters (panicles). *Limonium sinuatum* (Notchleaf statice) is purple, lavender, rose-pink, blue, red, white and yellow. The perennial *L. latifolium* (German statice) is light mauve. There are both annual and perennial forms but primarily the annuals are grown commercially.

3. *Culture*—*Limonium* is mostly field grown in Florida and California. The best method of propagation is from seeds that have been cleaned from the dried flower heads. There are 10,000 seeds/28 gm (decorticated), and they

Fig. 3. *Limonium* flowers (better known in the floriculture industry as statice).

germinate in 5 to 9 days at 18°–21°. The seed is sown from July to October and planted into individual pots when the first true leaves appear. A commercial potting mix satisfactory for bedding plants is recommended. Seedlings should be well fertilized, by using a slow-release fertilizer or a liquid fertilizer that supplies 200 ppm nitrogen in the irrigation water. Plants are moved to raised beds in the field 4 to 5 weeks later. Production time is 90 to 150 days, depending on the cultivar. Statice will flower under a wide range of temperatures but consistent and early flowering is best under cool conditions, such as 10°–13°C night and 16°–18°C day combination. Flowers are harvested when individual inflorescences have most of the calyxes open and are showing color. The flowers are sold in bound bunches usually containing seven to ten stems. Flowers can be stored for 2 to 3 weeks at 2°C. The flowers will last 1 to 2 weeks in arrangements, and 1 year or more when used as dried flowers.

Disease problems are anthracnose, Cercospora leaf spot, Colletotrichum crown rot, Southern blight, and seedling blights. Cutworms, armyworms, aphids, mealybugs, thrips, and spider mites are insect problems.

V. *Mathiola incana* (Also *Matthiola*) (Stock, Gilliflower)

1. *Area of origin*—Southern Europe.

2. *Description*—This annual has flowers (Fig. 4) in terminal clusters (racemes), 2 to 5 cm in diameter, in white or shades of rose, red, purple, and

Fig. 4. Field production of stock (*Matthiola incana*).

yellow. Both single and double forms exist. Stem length is 30 to 45 cm. Florists' stock is columnar and nonbranching. Stock are propagated from seed (16,000 to 20,000/28 gm) and germinate in 2 weeks at 18°–24°C.

3. *Culture*—Stock once was a very popular greenhouse-grown crop. Florist demand is now supplied from field-grown plants in California and Arizona. Greenhouse-grown stock is available from January to early June. Field production extends the season through summer. A major problem is that only double flowers are desired but approximately 50% of the flowers are often single. Stock is subject to potassium deficiency, which is seen as burning on the older leaf margins. The crop is grown at 16°C nights until at least ten fully developed leaves are produced, and this treatment is followed by at least 3 weeks at 10°C. The temperature can then be raised again to 16°C. Stock will not flower if it receives more than 6 hours per day at 18°C. For maximum flower quality the best night temperature is 2°–4°C. Buds should be present 9 weeks before the expected cutting date. Seedlings are planted 7 × 15 cm apart. Spikes are cut when one-half to two-thirds of the florets have opened. Flowers are stored at 4°C for up to 3 days, and the flowers will last 3 to 4 days when moved to room temperatures.

Stem rot (*Rhizoctonia*) is a major disease problem. Steam sterilization of soil is required with biweekly applications of a protective fungicide. *Botrytis* rot is also common. Aphids and thrips are major insect pests.

W. *Paeonia lactiflora,* Also *P. albiflora* (Chinese Peony), *Paeonia officinalis* (Common Peony)

1. *Area of origin*—China, Siberia, Southern Europe (Common Peony), Japan.

2. *Description*—This hardy perennial has a thickened root system and large, solitary flowers with numerous petals. The Chinese peony is classified as single, Japanese (anemone), or double up to 25 cm across in pure white to pale yellow and shades of pink to dark red. Stems are 0.7 to 1.3 m tall. The common peony is up to 12 cm across; the single form is dark crimson. Double forms are white, pink, or red. Stem length is 0.7 to 1 m. Peonies are propagated from divisions of clumps, with three to five eyes. Three to 5 years are required for plants to reach flowering maturity.

3. *Culture*—Peonies are grown outdoors in cool or cold climates. Divisions are planted 2 to 5 cm deep and at least 0.7 m apart in the early fall. Plants are grown in full sun and fertilized twice a year in the spring and late summer after cutting. Peonies are cut in the bud stage but they should be showing some flower color. Flowers can be stored in the dry bud stage for 4 to 6 weeks at 0°–2°C but only for 2 to 3 weeks at the same temperature if the flowers are open.

Root knot nematode, Phytophthora blight, and stem rot are disease problems. There are no major insect pests, though ants will frequently be seen on the buds.

X. *Ranunculus asiaticus* (Ranunculus, Turban, or Persian Buttercup)

1. *Area of origin*—Europe and Asia.

2. *Description*—This tender perennial has flowers 2 to 10 cm in diameter. There are one to four flowers per stem in white and shades of yellow, orange, red, or pink. The flowers are usually double. The stems range from 25 to 50 cm long. Ranunculus is propagated from seeds or divisions of tuberous roots but most often grown from the roots.

3. *Culture*—The culture of this crop is almost identical to the production of anemones. Both crops are field and greenhouse grown, but field production has become most common in the United States. Flowers are available in January and through the spring months. The production time for ranunculus propagated from tubers is 4 to 6 months, whereas 1 year is required if the crop is propagated from seed. Temperatures of 7°–10°C at night and maximum day temperatures of 20°C are suggested. Flowers are stored at 4°C for 2 to 3 days, and the vase life is 3 to 5 days.

Disease and insect pests are the same as those listed for anemones.

Y. *Stephanotis floribunda* (Stephanotis, Madagascar Jasmine)

1. *Area of origin*—Madagascar and the Malay Archipelago.

2. *Description*—Stephanotis occurs as a woody vine. The fragrant flowers, in umbel-like clusters are white, waxy, and up to 5 cm across. The calyx has five

sepals; the corolla is tubular-shaped with a crown at the opening of the tube. Stephanotis are propagated as cuttings of partially matured shoots taken in the spring.

3. *Culture*—Trellis support is necessary, as the plant is a vine. Plants grow best in full direct light. Plants are spaced 1 m apart. A minimum temperature of 18°C is required for flower bud initiation. Flowers are picked when fully open, and are not placed in water. They can be stored for 1 week in a moist atmosphere at 4°C. The flowers will remain attractive for 3 to 4 days if kept moist and refrigerated.

Stem canker and root knot nematode can be disease problems and mealybugs and scales are troublesome insect pests.

Z. *Strelitzia reginae* (Bird of Paradise)

1. *Area of origin*—South Africa.

2. *Description*—These tender perennials have flowers enclosed in boat-shaped green-purplish 10- to 15-cm bracts. The outer petals are reddish-orange and the inner petals are deep blue. Petals are pointed, 7 to 10 cm long. The stem length is 0.7 to 1 m. Divisions of rhizomes are the means of producing new plants. Two to 3 years are required for plants to reach flowering maturity.

3. *Culture*—The physiology of the flowering of bird of paradise is still poorly understood. Temperatures of 10°–13°C at night, and 20°–22°C during the day are suggested. Direct sunlight, with partial shade during the summer, is required. Flowers are usually cut after the first floret opens. Recent research (Halevy *et al.,* 1978) has opened the possibility of cutting flowers in the tight bud stage and increasing the storage period up to 1 month. This is done by what is known as "pulsing," a pretreatment (prior to shipment) of sucrose, 8-hydroxyquinoline citrate, and citric acid. The tight flowers are kept in this solution for 2 days at 22°C. Presently prolonged storage of these flowers is not recommended and they are normally held for up to 4 days at 10°C. The vase life is 7 to 10 days. Strelitzia have very heavy stems and special precaution needs to be taken to provide proper support in an arrangement.

Root rot can be a disease problem, and mealybugs and scale are important insect pests.

AA. *Viola odorata* (Violets)

1. *Area of origin*—Europe, Africa, Asia.

2. *Description*—Violets, a hardy perennial have white or deep violet, solitary, often nodding fragrant flowers. Single and double forms are 2 cm across. Division of the rhizome-like stems, which are separated from the crown and treated as a cutting, is a popular propagation method.

3. *Culture*—Flowers are not produced at high temperatures, so 4°–10°C is recommended. Shading is required in the summer months. Plants are spaced 20 × 20 cm. Violets are sold 100 to a bunch with violet or *Galax* leaves. The flowers are not placed in water. The bunches are wrapped in waxed paper and stored at 1°–4°C for up to 2 weeks. The flowers lose their fragrance after several days.

Leafspot and root rot are disease problems, while insect pests are violet gallfly, violet sawfly, slugs, spider mites, aphids, mealybugs, and leaf rollers. BB. *Zantedeschia aethiopica* (White Calla); *Zantedeschia elliottiana* (Golden Calla or Yellow Calla); *Zantedeschia rehmannii* (Pink Calla) (Collectively known as Calla Lily).

1. *Area of origin*—South Africa.

2. *Description*—This tropical perennial has a solitary, showy spathe. *Zantedeschia aethiopica* has a fragrant white spathe 15 to 22 cm long that tapers to a point; *Z. elliottiana* has a trumpet-shaped, yellow spathe 12 cm long; and *Z. rehmanii* has a rose or pink spathe and is a dwarf. It is not often used for cutting. Propagation methods vary, depending upon the species. Rhizome divisions are most common.

3. *Culture*—Year-round production of calla lily can be achieved. Plants are spaced 0.7 m apart, in benches. Some plants are grown in pots to reduce spreading root and rhizome rots to which callas are very susceptible. Plants are grown under full light except during the summer when partial shade is required. White-flowered calla lilies are grown at 13°C night temperatures whereas yellow and pink-flowered cultivars are grown at 16°C. Day temperatures of 16°–21°C are used for all cultivars. Strict attention to proper watering is needed, and well-drained, porous soil helps to minimize the root rot problem. Calla stems are pulled, not cut, to avoid stem curling. The flowers are harvested just before the spathe begins to turn downward. Flowers are stored for 7 days at 4°C.

Rhizomes should be treated with a fungicide prior to planting and those with soft, rotted areas should be discarded. Insect pests are mealybugs, aphids, and red spider mites.

CC. *Zinnia elegans* (Zinnia, Youth-and-Old-Age)

1. *Area of origin*—Mexico.

2. *Description*—Zinnia is an annual and has flowers up to 10 cm in diameter across in solitary heads. The disk florets are yellow-orange or purplish-brown. The ray florets are every flower color except blue. Stem length is up to 1 m. Dahlia and cactus-flowered classes are most popular for cut flowers. Zinnias are seed-propagated (2500 to 10,000 seeds/28 gm). The seed germinates in 1 week at 21°C.

3. *Culture*—Flowers are available from May to October. They can be forced in greenhouses or grown in the field. Spacing in the greenhouse is 10 × 10 cm whereas plants in the field are spaced 30 × 30 cm. The plants will grow vigorously in hot weather if they are irrigated regularly. Long days delay bud development, whereas bud development is hastened under short days. Flowers can be stored at 4°C for up to 5 days and will last 4 to 5 days after removal from storage.

Diseases affecting Zinnias include damping off, powdery mildew, and Alternaria leaf spot. Common Insect pests found on zinnias are thrips and aphids.

REFERENCES

Bailey, L. H. (1976). "Hortus Third." Macmillan, New York.

"Ball '79 Seed Catalog." Geo. J. Ball, Inc., West Chicago, Illinois.

Ball, V. ed. (1975). Ball Red Book, 13th ed. Geo. J. Ball, Inc., West Chicago, Illinois.

Conover, C. A., and Sheehan, T. J. (1965). Anemone flower production in Florida. *Fl. Flower Grow.* **2** (5), 1.

Conover, C. A. (1970). Gerbera production. *Fl. Flower Grow.* **7**(4), 2.

Consumer Guide (1976). "Cut Flower Selection and Care." Publications International, Skokie, Illinois.

Cornell recommendations for commercial floriculture crops. Parts I & II. Cornell Floriculture Staff, Ithaca, New York. (1974). Cornell University, Ithaca, New York.

Criley, R. (ed.). (1976). Cut flower or potted plant—*Euphorbia fulgens. Hortic. Dig., Co-op. Ext. Ser. Univ. of Hawaii No. 34,* Manoa.

Criley, R. (ed.). (1977). Flowering of *Gardenia radicans. Hortic. Dig. Co-op. Ext. Ser. Univ. of Hawaii No. 40.*

Crockett, J. U. (1971). "Annuals." Time-Life Books, Alexandria, Virginia.

Crockett, J. U. (1972). "Flowering Shrubs." Time-Life Books, Alexandria, Virginia.

Crockett, J. U. (1972). "Perennials." Time-Life Books, Alexandria, Virginia.

Crockett, J. U. (1977). "Greenhouse Gardening." Time-Life Books, Alexandria, Virginia.

Gilbertson, T. L., and Wilkins, H. F. (1977). Fragrant, vividly colored freesias answer what's new and economical. *Florists' Rev.* **160**(4140) 22–23, 72–73.

Gilbertson-Feriss, T., and Wilkins, H. F. (1978). A brief introduction to freesia growing. *Florists' Rev.* **161**(4183), 59–61.

Halevy, A. H., Kofranek, A. M., and Besemer, S. L. (1978). Post-harvest handling methods for bird-of-paradise flowers (*Strelitzia reginae* Ait.). *J. Am. Soc. Hortic. Sci.* **103**(2) 165–169.

Hartmann, H. T., and Kester, D. E. 1975. "Plant Propagation Principles and Practices." Prentice-Hall, Englewood Cliffs, New Jersey.

Jenkins, J. M. (1965). Larkspur culture. *Florists' Rev.* **137**(3546), 62–64.

Jenkins, J. M., and Aycock, R. (1958). Growing larkspur in North Carolina. *N.C. Agric. Ext. Serv.* Raleigh, North Carolina.

Laurie, A., Kiplinger, D. C., and Nelson, K. S. (1968) "Commercial Flower Forcing." McGraw-Hill, New York.

McDonald, E. (ed.). (1966). "Handbook for Greenhouse Gardeners." Lord and Burnham, New York.

Marousky, F. J. (1977). Control of bacteria in cut flower vase water. *Proc. Fla. State Hortic. Soc.* **90,** 294–296.

Mastalerz, J. W. (ed.). (1976). "Bedding Plants. A Penn State Manual." Pennsylvania Flower Growers, University Park, Pennsylvania.

Northern, H. T., and Northern, R. (1973). "Greenhouse Gardening." Ronald Press, New York.

Proc. 4th Ann. Protea Workship, 1976, Co-op. Ext. Ser., Misc. Pub. No. 139, Univ. of Hawaii, Manoa.

Proc. 5th Ann. Protea Workshop, 1977, Co-op. Ext. Ser., Misc. Pub. No. 157. Univ. of Hawaii, Manoa.

Proc. of Nat. Floric. Con. Commod. Hand., 1976, Ohio Florists' Assoc., Columbus, Ohio.

Post, K. (1950). "Florist Crop Production and Marketing." Orange-Judd, New York.

Rathmell, J. K. "Crop Alternatives," Pennsylvania State Univ., University Park, Pennsylvania.

Raulston, J. C., Poe, S. L., and Marousky, F. J. (1972). Cultural concepts of *Gypsophila paniculata* L. production in Florida. *Fla. State Hortic. Soc.* **85,** 423–428.

Smith, C. N. (1975). Shifting comparative advantage for floricultural products in the Americas. *Acta Hortic.* **55,** 121–126.

Society of American Florists. "Care and Handling of Flowers and Plants " (1976). Alexandria, Virginia.

Taylor, N. (1957). "Taylor's Encyclopedia of Gardening." The American Garden Guild, Inc., and Houghton, Boston.

White, E. A. (1933). "The Florist Business." Macmillan, New York.

Wilfret, G. I., Raulston, J. C., Poe, S. L., and Engelhard, A. W. (1973). Cultural techniques for the commercial production of annual statice (*Limonium* spp. Mill.) in Florida. *Fla. State Hortic. Soc.* **86,** 399–404.

Wilkins, H. F. (1976). Post harvest physiology of cut flowers. *Minn. State Florists' Bull. Agric. Ext. Ser.,* Univ. of Minnesota, June 1 pp. 4–5.

Wilkins, H. F., and Heins, R. D. (1976). Alstroemeria—general culture. *Minn. State Florists' Bull. Agric. Ext. Ser.,* Univ. of Minnesota, October 9, pp. 10–13.

United States Bureau of the Census, Census of Agriculture Special Reports (1970). "Horticultural Specialties 1970." Vol. 5, Pt. 10. Washington, D. C.

United States Department of Agriculture (1968). The commercial storage of fruits, vegetables, and florist and nursery stock. *Agric. Handbook No. 66,* Washington, D. C.

United States Department of Agriculture (1973). Selected terminal wholesale markets for flowers. *Mar. Res. Rep. No. 1005,* Washington, D. C.

II
POTTED
PLANTS

8
Bulbous Plants

August De Hertogh

Introduction to Floriculture
Copyright © 1980 by Academic Press, Inc.
All rights of reproduction in any form reserved.
ISBN 0-12-437650-9

215

I. INTRODUCTION

A. Diversity of Bulbous Plants

Bulbous plants are normally forced for use as cut flowers and flowering pot plants. They can also be fully programmed and sold as pot plants for consumer forcing (growing pot plants). The spring-flowering species described in this chapter (Table I) can be utilized for one or more of these purposes.

Bulbous species are classified as bulbs, corms, tubers, tuberous-roots, and rhizomes (Hartmann and Kester, 1975); collectively, they are referred to as "bulbs." With the exception of *Crocus,* all the species discussed are true bulbs. The main storage organs of bulbs and corms are scales and leaf bases, and stem tissue, respectively. Each species described in Table I has a protective tunic, but they differ greatly in their rooting and flowering characteristics as well as in their precise cultural conditions. Because of this diversity, only general cultural information will be presented. For specific forcing information and cultivars for North American conditions consult the Holland Bulb Forcers Guide (De Hertogh, 1977) and the Ball Red Book (Ball, 1975). For those interested in research aspects of bulb forcing, several references are available (Bergman *et al.,* 1971; De Hertogh, 1974; Hartsema, 1961; Rees, 1972; and Rees and van der Borg, 1975).

B. Basic Growth Habits and Cultural Requirements

Because of the origins of these species (Table I), they have a requirement for an annual warm–cool–warm thermoperiodic cycle for growth and development (Hartsema, 1961). Light, moisture, nutrients, plant growth regulators, and ventilation also are important and their effects will be covered later.

To place the handling of the bulbs for forcing into a logical sequence, a four-phase forcing system has been devised (De Hertogh, 1977). The phases are (1) production, all practices which go into producing marketable bulbs; (2) programming, all handling procedures from bulb harvest until they are placed under greenhouse conditions; (3) greenhouse; and (4) marketing, the development of the plants until the optimal marketing stage has been reached. For cut flowers or flowering pot plants, all four phases are used. When they are sold as growing pot plants, however, the greenhouse phase is not used. In view of the low energy requirement, this latter product should become very important to the floriculture industry.

Prior to a description of the production and forcing procedures, mention must be made regarding "dormancy" in bulbs. These species have evolved the bulbous or tuberous storage organs as a means of survival under adverse climatic conditions, Thus, from an exterior examination, many species appear to be at rest during certain developmental periods, but morphologically and

Table I

Description of Spring-Flowering Bulbs Commonly Forced in Commercial Greenhouses

Taxonomic classification	Common name(s)	Origin of species	Storage organ	Root system	Flowering habits
Amaryllidaceae					
Narcissus species	Daffodils, jonquils	Central Europe to Mediterranean	Bulb	Nonbranched, contractile	Single- and multiflowered inflorescences
Iridaceae					
Crocus species	Crocus	Southern Europe to southwest Asia	Corm	Nonbranched, contractile	Large corm produces two to three flowers
Iris hollandica	Dutch iris	A hybrid	Bulb	Branched, contractile	Usually single-flowered inflorescence
Iris reticulata	Dwarf iris, specie iris	Caucasus	Bulb	Branched, contractile	Singled-flowered inflorescence
Liliaceae					
Hyacinthus orientalis	Hyacinths	Greece to Asia Minor	Bulb	Nonbranched, contractile	Multiflowered inflorescence
Muscari armeniacum	Grape hyacinths	Mediterranean to southwest Asia	Bulb	Branched, contractile	Multiflowered inflorescence
Tulipa species	Tulips	Mediterranean to China	Bulb	Nonbranched, noncontractile	Single- and multiflowered inflorescences

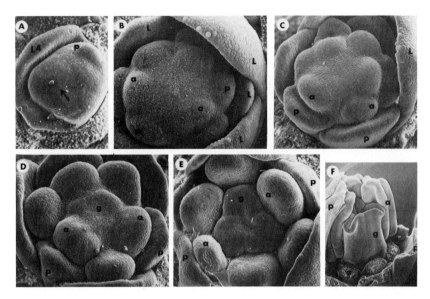

Fig. 1. Scanning electron micrographs of the floral developmental stages of a tulip. Artifacts (see arrow) on apical surfaces are contaminants from carbon dioxide utlized in critical point preparation system. (A) Stage P_1. First set of perianth (p) and last leaf primordium (L4) are visible. (B) Early stage A_1. Leaf primordia (L), two sets of perianth (p), and first set of androecium (a) are visible. (C) Late stage A_2. Leaf primordium (L) as well as double sets of perianth (p) and androecium (a) are visible. (D) Very early stage G. Double sets of perianth (p) and androecium (a) are visible as well as gynoecium (g) being initiated in center of apex. (E) Stage G. (F) A maturing floral bud. (From Shoub and De Hertogh, 1975b.)

physiologically, this is not the case. For example, many developmental changes occur in the tulip from July (Fig. 1A) to September (Fig. 1F). During this period, no external changes occur. Floral development is regulated by temperature but it can be modified by factors such as poor ventilation and ethylene. Therefore, it is imperative that bulbs be handled with care at all times. Although losses of 1 to 5% can occur under normal circumstances, improper handling can lead to severe economic losses.

II. BULB PRODUCTION PHASE

A. Basic Procedures

The bulb production phase consists of five steps: (1) harvesting, grading of the bulbs into planting stock and marketable bulbs, and preplanting storage; (2) planting, rooting, and low temperature mobilization for flowering and/or bulbing; (3) leaf and flower stalk growth; (4) flowering; and (5) increases in bulb size and/or numbers. There are two basic systems of reproduction, natural or artificial, which are integrated into this cycle. In addition, many bulbous species have been tissue cultured either for rapid multiplication and/or to obtain specific pathogen-free clones. Detailed production practices for bulbs can be found in Bulbs and Corm Production (1964), Gould (1957), and Rees (1972). Basic procedures are summarized below.

B. Commercial Bulb Production Practices

1. Crocus species

The two main species used for forcing are *Crocus vernus* and *C. flavus* (large yellow). The primary source of corms is The Netherlands.

The corms propagate naturally by annual replacement and are harvested in late June to early July and graded as soon as possible. The planting stock is stored at 20°– 23°C until October 1, and then at 17°C until it is planted in October through early November. Plants normally flower in March and then the foliage is allowed to senesce until harvest time. Flowers are not removed.

2. Hyacinthus orientalis

Hyacinth bulbs are produced mainly in The Netherlands and are harvested in the following order: (1) prepared bulbs for early forcing; (2) propagation bulbs for scooping or scoring; (3) early-flowering cultivars; and (4) late-flowering cultivars. Harvesting begins in mid-June and ends in mid-July.

Since hyacinths are perennial bulbs and the natural method of offset bulblet reproduction is slow, hyacinth growers use two techniques for rapid multiplication (Hartmann and Kester, 1975). When bulbs are scooped, the entire basal plate is carefully removed, leaving only the scales. When bulbs are scored, the basal plate is cut three times in a pie-shaped pattern. In both instances, adventitious buds are formed on the cut scale surfaces. The basic differences between the two techniques are that scooping produces more bulbs, but takes 3 years to produce bulbs of commercial size. Scoring produces fewer but larger bulbs in the first year and the cycle takes only 2 years.

The propagation bulbs and larger size of planting stock are held at 25.5°C. Small (1-year) bulbs are given special heat treatment to control the bacterium *Xanthomonas hyacinthi*, which is known as "yellow disease." Temperatures used are 30°C to September 1, 2 weeks at 38°C, 3 days at 44°C, followed by 30°C until planting.

The bulbs are planted in mid-October to mid-November. Hyacinths normally flower in April and florets are left on the flower stalks.

3. Iris hollandica

Dutch iris were developed from crosses between *Iris xiphium preacox*, *I. tingitana*, and *I. lusitanica*. The most widely used cultivars are 'Wedgwood,' 'Ideal' (a sport of 'Wedgwood'), and 'Prof. Blaauw' (also known as 'Blue Ribbon').

Dutch iris are primarily produced in the United States, The Netherlands, and France (Rees, 1972). In the United States, bulbs produced in the coastal valleys of western Washington are widely used by U.S. and Canadian forcers. Thus, only the production of these irises will be discussed (Gould, 1957).

Dutch iris naturally reproduce by annual replacement. They are harvested and graded in mid-July to early August. The small sizes for replanting are stored at 16°–18°C to aid in preventing flower formation. To produce large, round bulbs for marketing, it is important to prevent flowering of the planting stock. Plants that flower in the field produce flat bulbs which are generally considered nonmarketable. They are planted from September to November and, if properly handled, there should be little or no flowering of the plants in the spring.

4. Iris reticulata

These dwarf *iris* reproduce by natural annual replacement and are primarily produced in The Netherlands. The bulbs are harvested in early June and then graded. After storage at 23°–25°C, planting stock is planted in early November and the plants flower in March. Flowers are not removed.

5. Muscari armeniacum

The major source of bulbs for this species is The Netherlands. It reproduces by natural offset bulblets and the parent bulb persists. Harvest is in July and, after grading, planting stock is stored at 20°–23°C until it is planted in September or October. The plants flower in mid-March to mid-April.

6. Narcissus species

Narcissus (daffodils) are widely produced but there are three major areas of production: United States, The Netherlands, and England. Forcers in the United States and Canada use bulbs from The Netherlands as well as the United States. Daffodils increase by natural offset bulblet production; the mother bulb is perennial. Twin-scaling to obtain virus-free stocks is also being selectively practiced.

Bulbs are harvested in July and August, with the earliest flowering cultivars being dug first. Graded planting stock is stored in well-ventilated areas at 17°–20°C. During July or August, bulbs are normally given a hot water (44°C) dip using formalin and/or other pesticides for 4 hours to control nematodes and *Fusarium.* Planting takes place in September and flowering occurs in April. In the past, flower heads were removed to encourage bulb growth. Nowadays, in order to increase income, most daffodil growers cut and sell the field-grown flowers. Because of the labor problem, flowers that are not cut are left in the field.

7. Tulipa species

Like daffodils, tulips are widely grown. However, the major source of bulbs for forcers in the United States is The Netherlands. Production in the United

States is limited to only a few cultivars, some of which are used for forcing. The tulip reproduces by natural annual replacement.

The harvest season starts in mid-June and continues through July. Bulbs are graded shortly after harvest and planting stock is divided into two groups, depending on their ability to increase bulb size and number. Normal bulbing cultivars are stored for 3 to 4 weeks at 25°–27°C, at 20°C until November 1, and thereafter at 17°C. Difficult bulbing cultivars are given 23°C until September 1, 25°–27°C until October 1, followed by 20°C until November 1, and thereafter at 17°C.

Tulips are planted from mid-October through November. The controlling factor is soil temperature. It must be lower than 17°C so that growth of *Fusarium* is not stimulated. Tulips flower, depending on cultivar, from late March to May. After the lots are checked for trueness-to-type and viruses, the plants are deflowered to direct the translocation of photosynthates to the developing bulbs. After deflowering, the foliage is allowed to senesce naturally since it is during this period that maximum growth of the daughter bulbs occurs.

III. MARKETABLE BULBS

A. Factors Affecting Flower Development

There are four basic factors influencing flower formation and development in bulbous plants. These are (1) bulb size, (2) leaf formation, (3) environment, particularly temperature and light, and (4) relationship of flower formation to harvest and low temperature requirements. These factors have been reviewed in detail by Hartsema (1961) and will be discussed only briefly.

With the exception of *Narcissus* bulbs, which are sold on the basis of the number of readily observable noses (Double-Nose I and II), tulips, hyacinths, and others are measured and marketed by bulb circumference. The normal sizes (in centimeters) used for forcing are tulips 11–14; hyacinths, 15–19; *Crocus* 9–11; *Muscari,* 9–11; Dutch iris, 8–12; and *Iris reticulata,* 6–7. If bulbs of these sizes are used, the minimum bulb size requirement is avoided and flower size and/or the number of flowers produced by the bulb is increased.

Closely related to bulb size is the requirement for leaf formation. For the tulip, when a bulb is too small to flower it forms only one leaf. When the tulip is a flowering-sized bulb, however, it must form the entire compliment of leaves, three to five, depending on the cultivar. In contrast, the number of leaves of the flowering-sized hyacinth can be variable and it was this characteristic that permitted the development of the "prepared" hyacinth. Dutch *iris* must form more than three leaves before forming a flower. If the bulb forms only three leaves, the plant will not produce a flower. Minimum leaf numbers have not been reported for other species covered in this chapter.

The most important factor regulating flower initiation and development in bulbous species is temperature. Although light is not a controlling factor in tulips, hyacinths, and other bulbous species, it does influence the forcing of high-quality flowers and pot plants. A minimum of 2500 lx is preferred. For Dutch *iris,* however, light intensity is very important (Fortanier and Zevenbergen, 1973). Flower abortion could occur if sufficient light (10,000 lx) is not provided.

A final factor to consider is stage of development of the apical meristem when bulbs are harvested. Prior to cooling, all bulbs (except for Dutch *iris,* which does not form a flower until after it has been cooled) must have a full complement of flower parts. The control of this development will be covered in subsequent sections.

B. Transportation of Bulbs

Since the majority of bulbs are produced in The Netherlands or must be transported considerable distances from the West Coast, there are some special considerations related to bulb transport. The species discussed in this chapter do best if they are stored in well-ventilated areas. Consequently, they should be shipped in well-ventilated packing materials, such as wooden or plastic tray cases. In addition, the shipping period should be as short as possible and at the proper temperatures. In some cases, air freight is desirable. For bulbs shipped from The Netherlands by boat, well-ventilated controlled-temperature containers are available. When bulbs are shipped in large units or when the transport period is in excess of 5 days, automatic temperature recorders should be used to monitor temperatures en route.

On arrival, forcers should perform three steps. (1) Ventilate the bulbs. If they were in tray cases, this is easily done; however, if cardboard boxes were used for transport, they must be opened. (2) Inspect the bulbs. Check all cultivars for obvious physical damage and for serious diseases (see Section V). Take a few bulbs of each cultivar and cut them longitudinally to be certain that all the organs and, especially the shoot, are normal. If tulips are included and they are to be precooled, be certain that the cultivar has reached stage G (Fig. 1E). Consult the Holland Bulb Forcers Guide (De Hertogh, 1977) for details on this procedure. (3) Store bulbs prior to planting at the proper temperature (De Hertogh, 1977).

IV. PROGRAMMING AND GREENHOUSE PHASES

A. Basic Concepts of Bulb Forcing

The objective of bulb forcing is to produce high-quality potted plants or cut flowers. Depending on the species, pot plants should be 15 to 30 cm tall and cut flowers a minimum of 35 cm and preferably 40 to 50 cm tall. Depending on

Table II

Concept of Standard Forcing of Spring-Flowering Bulbous Crops

Forcing phase	Natural seasons	Important forcing processes
Programming	Summer	Harvesting of bulbs; postharvest storage at warm temperatures to control flower development
Programming	Fall	Planting, rooting under cool–moist conditions
Programming	Winter	Low temperature mobilization
Greenhouse	Spring	Leaf growth, flower stalk elongation, and flowering

the technique used (Tables II and III), the greenhouse phase should be less than 25 and 50 days for standard forcing and special precooling, respectively. In addition, the plants should have strong stems and large flowers. Last, the percentage of aborted flowers should be less than 5%.

Two basic techniques (Tables II and III) have been developed to force spring-flowering bulbs. Each has specific limitations and uses. Standard forcing is adaptable to all the bulbs in Table I except Dutch iris and it is the most widely employed in the United States and Canada. This technique follows the natural production cycles outlined earlier. To utilize this technique, a forcer must have a controlled-temperature rooting room and utilize suitable forcing cultivars. In contrast, special precooling is utilized only for specific periods of cut tulip forcing and for Dutch iris. The principal differences between this technique and standard forcing are that the entire low-temperature treatment is applied to unplanted bulbs and that rooting takes place in the greenhouse rather than during programming.

For specific details on cultivar utilization and commercial applications of these techniques, consult the Holland Bulb Forcers Guide (De Hertogh, 1977), Forcing Flower Bulbs (de Pagter, 1972), the Ball Red Book (Ball, 1975), and Cornell University Extension Bulletin 1221 (Bing, 1971).

Table III

Concept of Special Precooling of Spring-Flowering Bulbous Crops

Forcing phase	Natural season	Important forcing processes
Programming	Summer	Harvesting of bulbs; postharvest storage at warm temperatures to control flower development
Programming	Winter	Low temperature mobilization
Greenhouse	Fall and Spring	Planting and rooting; leaf growth, flower stalk elongation, and flowering

B. Standard Forcing

For all bulbs there are a number of considerations used in forcing. Normally, the planting media consist of various proportions of soil, sand, peat, perlite, vermiculite, bark, or other amendments. Regardless of the exact mixture, there are five criteria that must be observed. (1) The medium must be well drained but should hold sufficient moisture for bulb growth. (2) It must be sterile. (3) The pH should be 6 to 7. (4) The soluble salts level must be low. (5) At planting time, the medium must be cool and moist. The size and type of container used for pot plant forcing depend primarily on the market and the bulb species. For example, it is possible to force 1 hyacinth or 3 tulips in a 10-cm pot or to use 12 tulips or 6 hyacinths in a 20-cm bulb pan. Cut tulips or daffodils are normally planted in $35 \times 40 \times 10$-cm flats. They can also be planted in forcing pallets, if this system is used.

When tulips are planted in pots, the flat side of the bulb should always be placed against the inside of the pot. It is advisable to wet down hyacinths before planting. This procedure aids in reducing the skin itch which can occur because of dry tunics. When large-sized bulbs, e.g., tulips, hyacinths, and daffodils, are planted, only the nose of the bulb should be out of the medium. The small-sized bulbs should be covered with 1 to 2 cm of the planting medium.

Since temperature control is paramount, modern forcers utilize controlled-temperature ($\pm 1°C$) rooting rooms (De Hertogh, 1977). This facility is as essential to bulb forcing as lights and blackcloth are to photoperiodic plants like chrysanthemums. This facility must be capable of not only permitting the rooting of the bulbs but also satisfying the cold-week requirement of the bulbs. The rooting room should be compartmentalized and capable of exchanging air every 24 hours. To reduce labor costs, many forcers have palletized their rooting rooms.

The basic operation of the rooting room is to place the bulbs initially at 9°C until the roots of the bulbs protrude out of the holes of planting containers. Then, the termperature is lowered to 5°C until the shoots of the most advanced bulbs are 5 cm above the nose. Subsequently, 0°–2°C is used to retard the growth of the shoots until the remainder of the cold requirement is satisfied. As long as the bulbs are in the rooting room, it is essential that they be kept moist at all times. In addition, it is advisable to use preventative fungicidal sprays to control leaf diseases.

In the greenhouse phase, day and night temperatures, watering, light, fertilization, ventilation, sanitation, and pests must be controlled. Many of these factors are interrelated, e.g., watering, sanitation, and ventilation all affect pest control. In the following sections, the greenhouse factors important for each bulb type will be discussed. Only night temperatures are given. Day temperatures should be only 2°C above night temperatures.

1. Forcing Tulips

Standard forced tulips can be utilized either as pot plants or as cut flowers (De Hertogh, 1977). The basic differences depend on either the cultivars used or the length of the low-temperature treatment. The flowering season extends from late December to early May.

When tulips are harvested, the apical meristem is vegetative, and to force the bulbs requires that they be given a sequence of warm–cool–warm temperatures (Hartsema, 1961). Flower initiation and organogenesis are controlled by the postharvest warm temperatures. The precise temperatures used depend on whether the bulbs are forced early, in the middle of, or late in the season.

For early forcing, bulbs are harvested in mid-June to late June and treated for 1 week at 34°C. They are then placed at 17°–20°C to accelerate flower initiation and organogenesis (Fig. 1). When the flower bud reaches stage G (Fig. 1E) in mid-August to late August, the bulbs are placed at 7°–9°C for 6 weeks of regular precooling prior to planting. This treatment is given to permit further development of the flower as well as the roots (Shoub and De Hertogh, 1975b). After planting, the bulbs are rooted at 9°C and then the remainder of the low-temperature treatment is given at 5°C. When the cumulative cold treatment equals 15 weeks, bulbs of suitable cultivars can be moved to an 18°C greenhouse. For early forcing, plants may be stretched in the dark until the lowest internode becomes visible. The plants then must be exposed to light. In the greenhouse, cut and pot tulips should be fertilized once a week with $Ca(NO_3)_2$ at 908 gm/liter (2 pounds/100 gallons). On an alternate 3-day basis, cut tulips should also receive 200 ppm nitrogen in 20-20-20.

For midseason forcing, e.g., Valentine's Day, bulbs are harvested in late June to early July and are placed at 17°–20°C to develop the flower. For cut flower usage some cultivars may have to be precooled at 9°C starting in the first week of September; the others can be planted in mid-September. For pot plants, only nonprecooled bulbs are needed and they are planted in early October. The conditions in the rooting room are the same as those described for early forcing. After 16 to 20 cold weeks for cut tulips and 14 to 16 cold weeks for pot tulips, they are placed in a 17°C greenhouse. Again, they should be fertilized but stretching in the dark is not required.

For late forcing, e.g., Easter, bulbs are harvested in July and stored at 23°C until September 1, at 20°C until October 1, and then at 17°C. Cut tulips are planted in late October or early November and pot tulips in early to mid-November. The exact planting date is dependent on cultivar, use, and desired flowering date. Rooting room and greenhouse procedures are the same as those described for medium forcing.

2. Forcing Hyacinths

Hyacinths are primarily used as pot plants (De Hertogh, 1977). However, the flowers can be cut and, if desired, the individual florets can be used in corsages. In addition, the bulbs can be forced on water using special forcing glasses.

The apical meristem of hyacinths is vegetative when the bulbs are harvested and to force them requires a sequence of warm–cool–warm temperatures (Hartsema, 1961). The specific temperature requirements are 5°–7°C higher than for tulips. The flowering season extends from mid-December to April, and to control the development throughout the period, two types of bulbs are available, prepared and regular.

Prepared bulbs, which are used for December and January flowering, are harvested in mid-June and placed at 30°C for 2 weeks, at 25.5°C for 3 weeks, and then at 23°C until the uppermost floret reaches stage A_2 (identical to tulip in Fig. 1C). The bulbs are then held at 17°C until they are planted in September. In contrast to tulips and other bulbs, hyacinths are not precooled. After planting, prepared bulbs need only 10 to 12 weeks of rooting and cooling at 9°C before being placed in a 23°C greenhouse. When the florets begin to show color, the temperature should be dropped to 20°C. If desired, some stretching in the dark can be used for 4 to 5 days immediately after the plants are placed in the greenhouse. There are no data to indicate the hyacinths should be fertilized in the greenhouse.

For midseason and late forcings, regular bulbs are harvested in late June and early July and stored at 25.5°C until planted. Planting will be in late September to mid-November depending on the desired flowering date and cultivar. For late forcings, e.g., Easter, it is critical that shoot length not exceed 10 cm in the rooting room. Therefore, as soon as the plants are rooted at 9°C, the temperature should be lowered to 5°C. When the first shoots reach 5 cm, the temperature should be lowered to 0°–2°C. The minimum cold-week requirement is 13 weeks and up to 23 cold weeks can be used. These plants can be forced in 15°–17°C greenhouses and do not require dark conditions for stem elongation.

3. Forcing Narcissus

Standard forced *Narcissus* are utilized either as pot plants or as cut flowers (De Hertogh, 1977). The season extends from mid-December to April. As with tulips, the major differences are cultivars and temperatures used in the rooting room and the greenhouse.

At harvest, *Narcissus* have an almost completely formed flower (Hartsema, 1961), the flower being initiated in May shortly after the mother bulb flowers. To force the bulbs, a warm–cool–warm temperature sequence is required.

For early forcing, bulbs are harvested in July and given 1 week at 34°C. They are then held at 17°–20°C until precooled in August at 9°C. The handling of cut and pot daffodils after planting in early October is different. Cut daffodils are rooted and cooled continuously at 9°C, which is the optimal temperature for shoot elongation. When a total of 15 to 16 cold weeks has been accumulated, forcing takes place in a 13°–15°C greenhouse. If desired, stretching in the dark can be used. In contrast, pot daffodils are rooted at 9°C but as soon as they are rooted the temperature is lowered to 5°C. Then, after 15 cold weeks, they are forced in the greenhouse at 16°–18°C. These variations in temperature either promote increased length or inhibit growth, depending on the product desired. There are no data to indicate that daffodils benefit from fertilization in the greenhouse.

For midseason and late forcings, bulbs are harvested in late July or August and stored at 17°–20°C until planted. Since time is no longer a major factor, bulbs are planted to provide 17 to 18 cold weeks for cut daffoldils and 14 to 16 cold weeks for pot daffodils. They are rooted at 9°C and then cooled at either 5° or 2°C, depending on shoot growth. Shoot growth should not exceed 10 cm in the rooting room. Pot and cut daffodils are forced in the greenhouse at 16°–17°C or 13°–15°C, respectively.

4. Forcing Crocus, Iris reticulata, and Muscari

Collectively, these "bulbs" are referred to as "miscellaneous bulbs" (De Hertogh, 1977). Their normal flowering season is from January to mid-March; exceptions would be *Iris danfordiae,* which can be forced for Christmas, and *Muscari,* which can be forced as late as April. These plants are primarily used as pot plants, but *Muscari* flowers can be cut and used in designs. *Crocus* can also be forced on water, if special forcing glasses are used.

When these bulbs are harvested in June or July their apical meristems are vegetative. They require a warm–cool–warm temperature sequence.

For early forcing, *Crocus* and *Muscari* are given 1 week at 34°C followed by 17°–20°C until they are precooled at 9°C. *Iris reticulata* bulbs are stored at 23°C to July 1, and then at 17°–20°C until precooling in late August. Bulbs are planted at 9°C in early October. As soon as they are fully rooted, the temperature must be dropped to 5°C and later to 0°–2°C. They require 15 to 16 cold weeks. It is important to keep shoots of these species as short as possible. These plants can flower in the rooting room without light if not handled properly. The plants should be forced in a 15°–16°C greenhouse without fertilization.

For midseason forcing, *Crocus* and *Muscari* are stored at 17°–20°C until planting. *Iris reticulata* bulbs are again stored at 23°C to August 1, and then at 17°–20°C. After planting, they are rooted at 9°C and then the temperatures held at 5°C followed by 0°–2°C; 15 to 16 cold weeks are optimal. For these forcings, a 13°–15°C greenhouse is preferred.

C. Special Precooling

As previously described, special precooling (Table III) of tulips and Dutch iris for cut flower use is not a natural growing sequence. If the bulbs are not programmed at the greenhouse location, transport of precooled bulbs must be as short as possible, preferably fewer than 5 days, and the bulbs must be kept cool (<15°C).

Since these bulbs are handled like seeds, it is most important to use a well-drained, sterilized planting medium and to protect the bulbs against root rot diseases. Thus, dipping bulbs in approved fungicides and using fungicidal drenches after planting are advised. Also, for the first 14 days, planting medium temperatures should be measured. This is because root growth takes place during this period, and roots are a key to successful forcing of special precooled bulbs.

1. Tulips

The initial postharvest temperatures for tulips are the same as those described for standard forcing. If Dutch-grown bulbs are used, transportation of bulbs before precooling is very important. Experience has demonstrated that bulbs used for this technique should be shipped in open tray cases and in controlled-temperature (17°–20°C), ventilated containers. There are specific limitations on the cultivars which can be subjected to this technique (Bing, 1971; De Hertogh, 1977).

There are three basic steps to follow for special precooling tulips. They are the following: (1) before precooling, the flower bud must have reached at least stage G (Fig. 1E); in fact, development beyond this stage is preferred; (2) the bulbs must be precooled at 5°C (±0.5°) for 12 to 13 weeks; and (3) the bulbs must be planted in the greenhouse directly into 20-cm-deep raised benches or full ground beds for forcing. Steps 1 and 2 comprise the programming phase for this technique and Step 3 is the greenhouse phase (Table III).

After arrival of the bulbs, they should be examined and then, prior to precooling, should be stored at 13°C. On the appropriate dates, bulbs must be transferred to 5°C for a 12-13 week special precooling treatment. During this period, the rooms should be well ventilated and the humidity kept to 80 to 90%. Periodic checks should be made for the development of any diseases.

Immediately prior to planting, the tunic (skin) of the bulb should be carefully removed from the basal plate. Failure to remove the tunic can lead to 5 to 15% losses. Because each bulb will be handled individually, it is an excellent opportunity to eliminate any diseased bulbs. Either just prior to or on the day of planting, the bulbs should be dipped in approved fungicides for at least 30 minutes.

The bulbs should be planted with the nose approximately 2.5 cm below the level of the planting medium. Then the bulbs should be watered and kept moist. Use soil thermometers to assist in maintaining the temperature at 13°C. Air temperatures should not exceed 16°C. Some greenhouses have hydroponic arrangements using pea gravel for a support medium, and special precooling tulips can be forced under such conditions. The same procedures are used, but the plants need to be fertilized daily with 200 ppm nitrogen in 20-20-20 starting 10 to 14 days after planting. For tulips forced in a soil-based medium, they should be fertilized once a week with 20-20-20, starting 10 to 14 days after planting. In addition, an alternate fertilization with $Ca(NO_3)_2$ is advised (see Section IV, B on standard forcing).

2. Dutch Iris

The bulbs of Dutch iris are only used as cut flowers (Ball, 1975; Gould, 1957). In the United States and Canada, the flowering season extends from December to May. The principal source of bulbs for forcing in the United States and Canada is the state of Washington. Under normal circumstances, bulb suppliers carry out the programming of Dutch iris and the forcer plants them immediately on arrival.

When the bulb is harvested, the apical meristem is vegetative. To flower, this species requires a sequence of high–cool–warm temperatures (Stuart et al., 1955). 'Wedgwood' or 'Ideal,' the cultivars commonly used for early flowering, are given 10 days at 32°C followed by 17°C for 2 to 4 weeks and then 6 weeks at 9°–10°C. After this treatment, they are planted in a 13°C greenhouse. The greenhouse must provide high light intensities and the planting medium must be kept moist. In the greenhouse, bulbs should be fertilized with 200 ppm nitrogen in 20-20-20 and $Ca(NO_3)_2$ on a 3- to 4-day alternating basis. This should start about 2 weeks after planting to allow roots to develop.

For later forcing, bulbs are held at 30°C (retarding) until 8 weeks prior to the desired planting date. At this time, they receive 2 weeks of 17°C followed by 6 weeks of 2°–9°C. It is not desirable to have sprouts emerge from the bulbs and if this is observed, the lower temperatures are used. Greenhouse conditions are the same as described above for early forcing.

D. Plant Growth Regulators for Bulbs

1. Ancymidol (A-Rest)

Ancymidol is effective for height control of pot tulips. It does not affect timing of the plants, flower size, or percentage of plants flowering. It is officially cleared for industry use. For details on application techniques and cultivar requirement, consult the Holland Bulb Forcers Guide (De Hertogh, 1977).

2. Ethephon (Florel)

Recent studies (unpublished) have shown that ethephon can be used to prevent stem topple of hyacinths (Shoub and De Hertogh, 1975a). Also, Briggs (1975) has shown that it can be effective for controlling the height of daffodils. Ethephon, however, is not officially cleared for use on these species.

V. DISEASES, INSECTS, AND PHYSIOLOGICAL DISORDERS

A. General Aspects

There are many diseases, insects, and physiological disorders of bulbous plants (Gould, 1957; Schenk, 1971; Moore, 1949). If proper precautions are taken, very few are encountered during forcing (De Hertogh, 1977). Only the most prevalent ones will be mentioned. Some of these originate in the production fields and carry over to forcing. Others occur as a result of improper programming and/or greenhouse practices.

B. Diseases

1. Tulips

The most serious disease is *Fusarium* and infected bulbs have a characteristic sour smell. Because *Fusarium*-infected bulbs produce ethylene (see below), they must be eliminated. A second disease is *Penicillium* or blue mold. Unless the bulbs have been mechanically damaged, this is not a serious disease and it can be controlled by suitable fungicides. There are several soilborne diseases, e.g., *Rhizoctonia* and *Pythium,* which can infect bulbs. These can be eliminated by proper sterilization and handling of the planting medium. *Botrytis* can be a problem in the rooting room and greenhouse, but there are several effective fungicides that can control this disease.

2. Hyacinths

Penicillium is the most prevalent disease encountered during forcing of hyacinths. It can become a problem when the relative humidities are high and if it attacks the basal plate. Keeping the bulbs well ventilated or dipping them in a fungicide prior to planting will normally control the disease.

3. Narcissus

The major disease of daffodils is *Fusarium* basal rot. This disease originates in the production fields and infected bulbs must be discarded.

4. Miscellaneous Bulbs

There are no serious diseases of *Crocus* or *Muscari* during forcing. For *Iris reticulata,* the only disease of consequence is ink spot disease (*Mystrosporium adustum*), which can be identified by black fungal spots on the scales. Infected bulbs should be discarded.

5. Dutch Iris

The two most serious diseases are *Fusarium* and *Penicillium.* Both of these attack the basal plate of the bulbs. The best control procedure is to dip the bulbs in an approved fungicide prior to planting.

C. Insects

The most prevalent insect encountered during forcing is the aphid. It can be readily controlled by a number of approved insecticides.

D. Physiological Disorders

There are a few serious physiological disorders of bulbs that occur during forcing (De Hertogh, 1977). Most of these can be avoided or minimized by using procedures outlined in earlier sections of this chapter.

1. Tulips

The most prevalent disorder is flower blasting (abortion). This is the failure of a bulb to produce a plant with a marketable flower after the flower parts have been initiated. The disorder is complex and is not completely understood. There are, however, several known causes. Among them are abnormally high temperatures, failure to maintain a proper moisture balance, and poor ventilation. In addition, ethylene is a primary factor in promoting abortion (Kamerbeek and De Munk, 1976). This is why it is important to remove *Fusarium*-infected bulbs. Also, it is for this reason that bulbs should never be stored in the presence of ethylene-producing fruits and vegetables.

A second disorder is "stem topple." This is characterized by a collapse of the internode just beneath the flower. It is a symptom of calcium deficiency and can be prevented by the use of $Ca(NO_3)_2$ during the greenhouse phase of forcing.

2. Hyacinths

The main disorder is known as "spitting." This is the release of the entire floral stalk from the basal plate. It can be caused by freezing of the bulbs. When proper rooting room temperatures are used it normally does not occur.

3. Narcissus

One disorder is "bull-nosing." This is a late form of flower abortion characterized by the bud failing to develop beyond the "goose-neck" stage of development (Fig. 2). It appears to be related to excessively high greenhouse temperatures.

4. Miscellaneous Bulbs

The only disorder which is encountered is flower abortion. This could be due to high temperatures, insufficient number of cold weeks, or forcing a cultivar too early.

5. Dutch Iris

Two physiological problems in Dutch iris can be encountered. "Blindness" is the failure of the plant to form a flower. Blindness, only three leaves are produced, can be due to the use of small-sized bulbs that were forced too early or by improper programming temperatures. Dutch iris are also prone to flower blasting. As with tulips, this is very complex. The known causes are low light intensities and high temperatures, insufficient watering, and lack of fertilization in the greenhouse.

VI. HANDLING OF MARKETABLE PRODUCTS

A. General Aspects

Specifics on handling procedures for species discussed in this chapter have been described by De Hertogh and Springer (1977). In addition, the Holland Bulb Forcers Guide (De Hertogh, 1977) contains information.

B. Growing Pot Plants

These plants should be marketed directly out of the rooting room; however, it is essential that bulbs have been given a proper programming treatment. Before leaving the greenhouse, tulips should be treated with ancymidol. Consumers only need to place these plants in a well-lighted area and to water them daily.

C. Flowering Pot Plants

The optimal flower "bud" stages for the sale of pot plants are as follows: tulips—first sign of color; hyacinths—as soon as the floral bud is visible in the leaves; daffodils—pencil to "goose-neck" stage; *Crocus* and *Iris reticulata*—as soon as leaves expand, but before the bud has color; *Muscari*—first sign of color. If these plants have to be stored prior to marketing, they should be placed at 0°–2°C before any flower color is visible. Prior to storage, the planting medium should be moistened, the foliage allowed to dry, and the plant treated with a protective fungicide. Again, consumers only need to place these plants in a well-lighted area and to water them daily.

D. Cut Flowers

Tulips should be harvested when the flower bud is 50% colored. There are three cold (0°–2°C) storage techniques available: (1) for short periods followed by immediate usage—grade, bunch, and wrap the tulips and place them in water; (2) for 1 to 5 days—place wrapped tulips in dry storage in a horizontal position; and (3) for storage up to 14 days—store the flower with the bulb attached in a dry, upright position; bulb removed, grading, and wrapping should take place after storage. Daffodils should be cut when they are in the "goose-neck" stage of development (Fig. 2). If storage (0°–2°C) is needed, hold them dry in an upright position. Dutch iris should be harvested when the flower petals just begin to open. Storage (0°–2°C) of flowers should always be upright and in water.

To condition these flowers prior to use, the retailer or consumer should recut the stems, leave the flowers wrapped (especially tulips), and condition them for 2 to 4 hours in 15 to 20 cm of warm (32°–42°C), preferably distilled, water at

Fig. 2. The "goose-neck" stage of flower development of the daffodil. This is the proper stage to cut this bulb flower.

room temperature. Cut tulips and daffodils must not be conditioned or stored in the same water since the sap of daffodils can injure tulips. Flower preservatives have not proved to be highly beneficial for cut bulb flowers. Users are urged to test materials under their conditions before using them extensively.

REFERENCES

Anonymous (1964). "Bulb and Corm Production." Her Majesty's Stationery Office, London.
Ball, V., ed. (1975). "The Ball Red Book." Geo. J. Ball, Inc., West Chicago, Illinois.
Bergman, B. H. H., Eijkman, A. J., van Slogteren, D. H. M., and Timmer, M. J. G., eds. (1971). First international symposium on flowerbulbs. *Acta Hortic.* **23,** 1–440.
Bing, A. (1971). Cut Tulips for Commercial Growers from Dry-Stored Bulbs. *Cornell Univ. Ext. Bull. 1221,* Ithaca, New York.

Briggs, J. B. (1975). The effects on growth and flowering of the chemical growth regulators ethephon on *Narcissus* and ancymidol on tulip. *Acta Hortic.* **47,** 287–296.

De Hertogh, A. A. (1974). Principles for forcing tulips, hyacinths, daffodils, Easter lilies and irises. *Scientia Hortic.* **2,** 313–355.

De Hertogh, A. A. (1977). "Holland Bulb Forcers Guide." Netherlands Flower–Bulb Institute, New York.

De Hertogh, A. A., and Springer, G. (1977). "Care and Handling of Spring Bulb Flowers and Plants and Suggestions on the Use and Marketing of Bulb Flowers and Plants." Holland Flower–Bulb Tech. Serv. Bull., No. 4. Netherlands Flower–Bulb Institute, Hillegom, the Netherlands.

de Pagter, J. W. A. (1972). "Forcing Flower Bulbs." Netherlands Flower–Bulb Institute, Hillegom, the Netherlands.

Fortanier, E. J., and Zevenbergen, A. (1973). Analysis of the effects of temperature and light after planting on bud blasting in *Iris hollandica. Neth. J. Agric. Sci.* **21,** 145–162.

Gould, C. J., ed. (1957). "Handbook on Bulb Growing and Forcing." Northwest Bulb Growers Assoc., Mt. Vernon, Washington.

Hartmann, H. T., and Kester, D. E. (1975). "Plant Propagation, Principles and Practices." Prentice-Hall, Englewood Cliffs, New Jersey.

Hartsema, A. M. (1961). Influence of temperatures on flower formation and flowering of bulbous and tuberous plants. *In* "Handbuch der Pflanzenphysiologie" (W. Ruhland, ed.), Vol. XVI, pp. 123–167. Springer-Verlag, Berlin, and New York.

Kamerbeek, G. A., and De Munk, W. J. (1976). A review of ethylene effects in bulbous plants. *Scientia Hortic.* **4,** 101–115.

Moore, W. C. (1949). "Diseases of Bulbs." Her Majesty's Stationery Office, London.

Rees, A. R. (1972). "The Growth of Bulbs." Academic Press, New York.

Rees, A. R., and van der Borg, H. H., ed. (1975) Second international symposium on flowerbulbs. *Acta Hortic.* **47,** 1–446.

Schenk, P. K., Chairman. (1971). "Ziekten en Afwijkingen bij Bolgewassen. Deel I: Liliaceae." Nauta and Co., Zutphen, the Netherlands.

Shoub, J., and De Hertogh, A. A. (1975a). Floral Stalk Topple: A disorder of *Hyancithus orientalis L.* and its control. *HortScience* **10,** 26–28.

Shoub, J., and De Hertogh, A. A. (1975b). Growth and development of the shoot, roots, and central bulblet of *Tulipa gesneriana* L. cv. Paul Richter during standard forcing. *J. Am. Soc. Hortic. Sci.* **100,** 32–37.

Stuart, N. W., Gould, C. J., and Gill, D. L. (1955). Effect of temperature and other storage conditions on forcing behavior of Easter lilies, bulbous iris and tulips. *Rep. 14th Int. Hortic. Cong.* **1,** 173–187.

9

Azaleas

Roy A. Larson

Introduction to Floriculture
Copyright © 1980 by Academic Press, Inc.
All rights of reproduction in any form reserved.
ISBN 0-12-437650-9

Azaleas have been grown as flowering potted plants in American green-houses for over a century but the popularity of the crop has fluctuated from one decade to the next. At the present time the high production costs of this long-term crop have resulted in prices that seem excessive to many customers, and many growers have curtailed production. Census figures have shown continuous increases in wholesale value of potted azaleas and in numbers of plants produced, but there were almost 200 fewer commercial azalea growers in 1970 than in 1950 (Fossum, 1973). Growers who have plants of good quality, however, seem to sell most of the plants they produce.

Scott (1899) stated that azalea culture in Europe had been perfected to such a state that it was doubtful if American growers would ever seek a different source of plants. Later, White (1923) blamed Plant Quarantine No. 37 for a drastic reduction in the number of Belgian azaleas that were being imported, and American production costs were so high that few retail stores were selling azaleas. He still considered the azalea crop to be a very important one in retail shops, and reported that the demand for azaleas at Christmas and Easter exceeded the supply.

These apparent inconsistencies seem to be as valid now as they were 100 or 50 years ago.

I. TAXONOMY

The azalea is one of 43 series in the genus *Rhododendron* (Leiser, 1975). There are six azalea subseries but the most important subseries containing azaleas for forcing is *Rhododendron obtusum.* Primarily nine species of this subseries have been used in the development of cultivars that are most promi-nent today; *R. obtusum* and *R. simsii* perhaps have been used more exten-sively in breeding programs than any other species. Currently, azalea taxonomy is in a rather confused state and it is not easy to determine the ancestry of some cultivars currently used in the industry. The hybrid groups to which the cultivars belong have been reported by Stadtherr (1975) and are shown in Table I. It is helpful if one can distinguish between Kurume or Indica cultivars since the dormancy-breaking requirements, flower size, and number do differ.

Azaleas also can be classified by flower types. There are single, single hose-in-hose, semidouble, semidouble hose-in-hose, double, and double hose-in-hose, as described and illustrated by Lee (1958). There are different flower shapes and sizes and a wide array of color choices, although red, pink, and white flowers are most popular. Some cultivars have relatively fragrant flowers but the most prominent ones seem to be almost odorless. Foliage shape, size, and color also can vary.

The characteristics that are most desirable for an azalea cultivar that is to be used for forcing are (1) ease of propagation, (2) rapid attainment of flowering size, (3) relative resistance to diseases and insects, (4) ready and uniform

Table I

Prominent Azalea Cultivars in Commercial Production in the United States [a]

Cultivar	Hybrid group/originator	Flower type [b]	Color	Season [c]
Alaska	Rutherford/Bobbink and Atkins	S, H, SD	White with chartreuse blotch	E–M
Ambrosieur	Indian/?	D	Dark scarlet red	M–L
Coral Bells	Kurume/E. H. Wilson	S, H	Light silver to coral pink	E
Dogwood	Kurume/Oregon State University	S	Pure white with red penciling	E
Gloria	Rutherford/?	H	Salmon and white, red spots in throat	E–M
Hershey's Red	Kurume/?	D	Bright red	L
Hexe	Indian/Otto Forster	H	Carmine red with pale purple reflex	M–L
Red Wing	Indian/Brooks	S, H	Orange red	E–M
Roadrunner	Whitewater/Motzkau	S, H	Deep pink to red	M–L
Snow	Kurume/Domoto Bros.	S, H	White	E–M
Sweetheart Supreme	Pericat/Pericat	H, SD	Red, camellia rose	M–L
Whitewater	Whitewater/Motzkau	H, SD	White	E–M

[a] Excerpts from a table compiled by Stadtherr (1975).
[b] Flower types: S, single; H, hose-in-hose; D, double; SD, semidouble.
[c] Season: E, early; M, midseason; L, late flowering.

Table II

Prominent Azalea Cultivars in Commercial Production in Europe [a]

Cultivar	Hybrid group/originator	Flower type [b]	Color	Season [c]
Ambrosiana	Indian/R. Ambrosius	D	Crimson red	E
Doberlug	Indian/E. Herrmann	D	Red with white edge	E–M
Friedhelm Scherrer	Indian/O. Stahnke	SD	Red	M
Hellmut Vogel	Indian/O. Stahnke	D	Crimson	E
Inga	Indian/O. Stahnke	D	Crimson	E
Knut Erwen	Indian/De Meyer	SD	Red	L
Leopod-Astrid	Indian/J. Haerens	SD	White with red edge	M–L
Madame Petrick	Indian/S. Mardner	D	Red	E–M
Mevrouw	Indian/R. DeLoose	SD	Red	L
Perle De Noisy	Indian/Bullens	D	Pink	E–M
Reinhold Ambrosius	Indian/R. Ambrosius	D	Crimson	E–M

[a] List supplied by J. Heursel, Institute of Plant Growing, Melle, Belgium in January, 1978.
[b] Flower types: D, double; SD, semidouble.
[c] Season: E, early; M, midseason; L, late flowering.

initiation and development of flower buds, (5) attractiveness when in the flower bud stage, (6) popular flower color, and (7) long-lasting flowers. Perhaps no one cultivar has all these characteristics to the extent desired but some cultivars achieve most of these requirements. Cultivars differ in popularity from region to region but there are some that are popular throughout the United States (Table I). Few of the prominent American cultivars are widely grown in Europe (Table II).

II. PROPAGATION

Azaleas can be propagated sexually (by seed) and asexually (vegetative propagation by grafting, budding, layering, or terminal cuttings). Seed propagation of evergreen azaleas used in potted plant production is confined to plant breeders. Information on azalea seed propagation is available in general azalea references, such as those of Lee (1958) and Galle (1974). Grafting, budding, and layering are now rarely used in vegetative propagation, particularly in the United States, but are discussed in references such as those already cited. The vast majority of azaleas produced in the United States are started as rooted cuttings.

The first requirement for a successful propagation program is an adequate supply of healthy, vigorous stock plants. These plants can be grown in the field, under lath or shadecloth, or in greenhouses. The extent of protection provided to the stock plants is determined by temperatures to which plants will be exposed, but growers often provide shelter to plants grown in mild climates. An occasional exposure to very cool temperatures can cause enough plant injury and losses to offset any financial savings that might have been realized by growing plants as cheaply and unprotected as possible. Also, disease and insect controls are easier to achieve with protected cultivation. Some of the most serious disease organisms are spread by splashing water, or the disease is accentuated if the growing medium is kept excessively moist, as might occur during prolonged rainy weather.

Stock plants can be grown in pots or planted in beds, and cuttings can be removed when the shoots are sufficiently well developed. The healthy condition of the shoots can be ensured with a preventive spray program, while an adequate fertilization program can promote vigorous growth.

Most growers propagate cuttings in June and July but the propagation season does not have to be restricted to these months. Cuttings can be taken from stock plants grown in protective shelters during any period of the year, if proper environmental conditions are maintained. It is not easy for the novice to know if the shoot is at the proper stage of development for removal as a terminal cutting, but Galle (1974) suggests using the brittleness of the shoot as a guide: shoots that "break with a snap" are best. Shoots that are very succulent and limber do not root as readily as those that are more mature and seem to be more susceptible to disease infection in the propagation bench.

Cuttings approximately 7 to 10 cm long are removed from the stock plants and frequently dusted with a rooting hormone to promote or accelerate rooting. Some growers dip basal ends of the cuttings in a hormone solution, but disease problems, such as those caused by *Cylindrocladium scoparium,* can be intensified with this practice. Hoitink and Schmitthenner (1972) developed a hormone–fungicide dip that promoted rooting of disease-free rhododendron cuttings.

Mist systems are ideal for azalea propagation, particularly when bottom heat of approximately 25°C is supplied to the propagation bench. Several mist propagation systems are available, but major considerations in selecting a mist system are relative freedom from mechanical failures and flexibility of misting cycles. Enough moisture, as a fine mist, should be applied to the cuttings so wilting is avoided, but leaching of nutrients from foliage will occur if the mist comes on too frequently or for extended periods of time. Some shading on the glass or directly over the mist bench would be desirable but an advantage of mist propagation is that cuttings can be rooted under higher light intensities than would be possible without mist.

Cuttings can be placed in individual propagation blocks, such as Kys Kubes, peat pots, and similar products but most growers propagate azalea cuttings in flats or trays filled with a medium such as peat : perlite or sand. Basal leaves are often removed, so cuttings can be spaced closely together in rows across the flat. Excessive crowding should be avoided.

Cultivars differ in ease of rooting, but an average range for rooting might be 6 to 8 weeks from the date of removal from stock plants. Perhaps the most frequent error made by some propagators is leaving unpinched cuttings in the flat for as long as 1 year before transplanting. Cuttings should be transplanted as soon as adequate root systems have been established. Plants usually are transplanted into plastic or clay pots. It would be preferable if the rooted cuttings were placed in pots approximately 10 cm in diameter, because overwatering often will occur if larger pots are used for the small plants. Some growers do plant immediately into larger-sized pots, however, to avoid later handling. The cuttings also could be planted in beds rather than in pots, but later transplanting is more difficult when this procedure is followed.

Tissue culture now is used in the vegetative propagation of several floricultural crops such as orchids, carnations, and gerberas. The procedure is not well established for azaleas and this sophisticated method of plant propagation has not yet made any impact in azalea production.

III. PLANT CULTURE

The propagation period of 6 to 8 weeks is a relatively small fraction of the time the azalea crop might be on the grower's premises. It is not unusual for azalea plants to be at least 2 years old before they are sold as flowering plants.

This period can be divided into vegetative and reproductive stages of plant culture.

A. Vegetative Development

The size of the plant when it is sold as a flowering pot plant is one of the main factors influencing the price of that plant. Higher prices can be expected for larger plants with numerous flowers compared to smaller plants with fewer flowers. Consequently, the grower should try to produce large plants as quickly as possible, so much attention should be focused on this phase of azalea production. This perhaps is the phase most neglected by the average grower, however.

Temperature, light intensity and duration, and water are very important environmental factors to consider. Knowledge of proper fertilization and of timely pinching practices are necessary so plants can be growing continuously.

1. Temperature

Growers should attempt to maintain optimum temperatures to promote growth. Rapid, vigorous growth can be expected when the day temperatures are 25°–30°, with night temperatures of approximately 20°C. These conditions occur naturally during portions of the year in areas such as Florida, where azaleas are produced outdoors. In cooler climates such temperatures can be provided only under protected cultivation for much of the year, and such high temperatures are costly to maintain. Fuel rationing has been established by some fuel suppliers, so the desirable warm temperatures can be difficult to achieve. Adequate vegetative growth can be realized at night temperatures of 16°–18°C, with day temperatures of 22°C (Larson and Biamonte, 1972). Some northern growers have used temperatures as low as 13°C but the plants grew slowly and it might have been a more economically sound practice for these growers to purchase large plants grown in southern areas. Florida, Alabama, South Carolina, California, and Oregon have become centers for the production of vegetative azaleas because of the temperature advantages associated with those areas.

Most temperature studies have been concerned primarily with air temperatures, but the temperature of the growing medium and the water can be equally or perhaps even more important. Pettersen (1968) is one of the few researchers who used soil temperature as one of the variables in his studies, but he altered the day temperatures as well as the soil temperatures so the direct effects of soil temperature are hard to evaluate. He did find that azaleas grown at 20°C air, 23°C soil temperatures had fewer but larger shoots than plants grown at 15°C air and 18°C soil temperatures. The energy crisis has prompted increased interest in media temperature and more information can be expected in the future.

Water temperature also can play a significant role in azalea growth. Plants at

North Carolina State University were irrigated with water that would get as cold as 4°C before all the azaleas had been watered. Chlorosis and slow growth were evident on all cultivars. The problem was easily corrected with a hot water heater that maintained a water temperature of 24°C. Cold water and, consequently, cold potting medium apparently affected absorption and translocation of nutrients, and the warmer water corrected these deficiencies with no alteration in the fertilization program.

2. Light

Intensity and daily duration of light both affect azalea growth. Undoubtedly light quality also influences growth but very little information is available.

The effects of light intensity cannot be separated completely from the effects of temperature because leaf temperatures do increase as light intensity increases. Transpiration is increased as the light intensity and temperatures increase, so water supply, relative humidity, and light intensity must be considered simultaneously. The stage of development of the plant also influences the effects of the light intensity to which the plants are exposed. Newly transplanted cuttings cannot be subjected to the same high light intensities as can plants that are better acclimated to such conditions. Leaves actually can be "sunburned" on newly pinched plants, whereas the same leaves on unpinched plants would not be adversely affected at that same light intensity.

Azaleas usually are protected from full sunlight by placing shadecloth or lath over the plants outdoors, or by placing a shading material on the greenhouse glass or plastic covering. The shading material might be Saran cloth or tobacco cloth, or it could be a chemical compound sprayed on the covering material. A suggested light intensity range is 21 klx (approximately 2000 fc) as a minimum and 42 klx (approximately 4000 fc) as a maximum intensity. Higher light intensity can be used if relative humidity is high than if the atmosphere is dry.

Azaleas have been considered as day-neutral with regard to photoperiodic effects on flowering. Kiplinger (1952) reported that 'Coral Bells' plants initiated flower buds at the same time under 9-hour or 16- to 17-hour photoperiods. Skinner (1939), however, noted that vegetative growth was promoted by long days. Love (1975) reported that extending the daylength to at least 16 hours does cause some cultivars to remain vegetative longer than if the plants are subjected to the short days that occur in the fall and winter months. In year-round flowering schedules, such as those suggested by Larson and McIntyre (1967b) and Skou (1969), 16-hour days or interrupted dark periods were recommended immediately after the plants were pinched, particularly if the pinch occurred in fall and winter months. Vegetative growth was stimulated under long-day conditions. The same lighting systems utilized in chrysanthemum production are used for lighting azalea crops, to keep the plants vegetative. A light intensity of 0.1 to 0.2 klx (10–20 fc) is adequate. Incandescent lights are most often used, primarily because of the relatively low cost of installation. Most commercial azalea growers, however, do not use supplementary lighting. The vegetative stage of azalea culture perhaps could be reduced by approximately 30% if growers used lights on most cultivars.

3. Water

Water is an extremely important factor in azalea culture. Vegetative growth is retarded, and flower bud initiation actually can be promoted, if the potting medium is allowed to become excessively dry. Overwatering also must be avoided, as azalea roots are readily damaged or killed if the medium remains too wet for a prolonged period of time. Syringing of foliage, either by hose, water stakes, or sprinkler systems, is practiced by some growers but foliar disease problems can be very serious with overhead watering. Careful applications of water by hose, tubes, or even capillary mats reduce the possibilities of serious disease troubles.

Proper selection of growing medium can do much to simplify the task of watering azaleas. The major ingredient in an azalea potting medium usually is peat moss because of its acidic pH (a pH of approximately 5.0 could be considered as almost ideal for azaleas), high organic matter content, and water-holding capacity. Materials such as perlite, peanut hulls, or bark often will be added to facilitate drainage and reduce costs. The proportion of peat moss to other ingredients frequently will be approximately 3 : 1 on a volume basis. There are several types of peat moss, and European peat moss traditionally has been used with greater success than domestic peat moss. One grower, in an effort to economize by using local peat moss in Florida, encountered difficulty in getting plants to grow, compared to plants grown in imported peat moss (Fig. 1). Dickey (1965) observed chlorotic, small leaves on azalea plants grown in Florida peat moss, primarily because of a copper deficiency.

Approximately 10% more water should be applied to the medium than the medium can hold, so excess water will leach away accumulated salts. Failure to do so can be very damaging to azalea root systems. Water quality is taken for granted in many areas but growers should be knowledgeable about the water quality. In some areas the water is too alkaline for good growth. Kofranek and Lunt (1975) list levels of tolerance of azaleas with regard to bicarbonate (no greater than 2 to 3 mEq/liter), electrical conductivity (no greater than 0.5 mmho/cm), boron (not to exceed 0.3 ppm), and sodium absorption ratio (no greater than 4). Such water analysis can be conducted by some state agencies or private analyses laboratories.

Relative humidity has an important though perhaps indirect influence on growth. Day temperatures and light intensity can be higher if relative humidity is high. No optimum relative humidity really has been determined but growth is most rapid in areas or greenhouses, where a relative humidity of at least 60% is maintained. The high humidity is not without its disadvantages, as diseases such as petal blight, Cylindrocladium disease, powdery mildew, and Botrytis are favored by high humidity, particularly if the high humidity persists. Humidity

Fig. 1. 'Gloria' azalea plants treated identically except the plant on the left was grown in Florida peat moss and the plant on the right was grown in imported peat moss.

also has an impact on the effectiveness of Off-Shoot-O, a chemical pruning agent. The chemical evaporates so quickly at low relative humidities that the shoot apexes are not damaged and a pinching effect is not achieved. At high humidities the chemical remains on the foliage for so long that leaf burn can occur.

Carbon dioxide levels have not been evaluated extensively in azalea production but Skou (1969) used levels of 1200 to 1500 ppm in the production schedule at Yoder Brothers in Barberton, Ohio. Most azaleas are grown at the ambient levels of approximately 300 ppm.

4. Nutrition

The nutrition of floricultural crops is discussed very thoroughly by Mastalerz (1977). Some highlights of azalea nutrition will be presented here.

Optimum environmental conditions will not ensure the successful growing of azaleas if the fertilization program is improper. The importance of pH of the growing medium already has been stressed. Availabilities of certain elements are much affected by pH. Iron is readily available in an acid medium but chlorosis will be readily apparent when iron becomes unavailable to plants growing in neutral or alkaline media. Manganese also is more available in an acid medium. Application of the deficient elements will correct the problem temporarily but the proper corrective measure would be to lower the pH of the medium. Additions of sulfur to the medium prior to potting, or application of acid fertilizers once plants are growing, can assist in this corrective procedure.

Deficiency symptoms are well described by Twigg and Link (1951) and Oertli (1964a,b,c), and azalea nutrition has been thoroughly discussed by Kofranek and Lunt (1975). Only a few key comments on azalea nutrition will be made here. Deficiency symptoms are summarized in Table III, and critical levels of elements in the foliage are listed in Table IV, as presented by Mastalerz (1977).

Nitrogen frequently is the nutrient that most limits vigorous growth as it is required in greater quantities than the other nutrients and is readily leached from the growing medium. Ammoniacal forms of nitrogen are preferred to nitrate sources and there are several such fertilizers commercially available such as ammonium sulfate, diammonium phosphate, and ammonium nitrate. Calcium nitrate or potassium nitrate can be included occasionally in the fertilization program. In 1967 George J. Ball, Inc., personnel devised fertilization programs for different pH conditions. These programs are the following:

Fertilizer "A"—23-10-12
   315 gm ammonium nitrate/378 liters
   180 gm diammonium phosphate
   180 gm potassium nitrate
This program is used when the medium is in the pH range of 4.9 to 5.4, and the fertilizer is applied weekly.
Fertilizer "B"—21-0-0
   720 gm ammonium sulfate/378 liters
   480 gm iron sulfate
This fertilizer treatment is used when the pH of the medium becomes higher than 5.5. They state that this treatment should not be used immediately following pinching, as leaf drop will occur.
Fertilizer "C"—15-3-3
   1260 gm calcium nitrate/378 liters
    90 gm monocalcium phosphate
   120 gm potassium nitrate
This treatment is recommended when the pH of the medium drops below 4.8. It is suggested that water alone should be applied between applications of the "C" fertilizer.

At North Carolina State University vigorously growing plants have been produced which received applications of 21-7-7 (neutral) at a rate of 600 gm/378 liters of water at weekly intervals in the summer months and every 10 to 14 days in the darker months. Urea formaldehyde, such as Borden's 38, is added as a top-dressing to the medium after the plants are well established, at a rate of about 2 gm per 12.5-cm pot.

Periodic applications of a soluble trace element mix also are made to avoid minor element deficiencies. Iron occasionally will be applied alone, as Sequestrene Fe 330, if chlorosis because of iron deficiency becomes apparent.

Table III

Some Nutrient Deficiency Symptoms on Azaleas[a]

Nutrient	Reference	Deficiency symptoms
Nitrogen	Oertli (1964a)	Older leaves turn yellow, chlorosis is uniform over entire leaf
Phosphorus	Oertli (1964a); Twigg and Link (1951)	Reddish-purple blotches in the middle area of the leaf; blotches eventually turn brown; leaf drop occurs first at bottom of shoot
Potassium	Twigg and Link (1951)	Interveinal chlorosis of young leaves; lesions eventually develop, particularly near leaf tips
Calcium	Oertli (1964b)	Cessation of growth; young leaves are very small; leaf tips become burned or distorted
Magnesium	Oertli (1964b); Twigg and Link (1951)	Older leaves become chlorotic, beginning at the tips of the leaves; leaf drop can be severe
Iron	Oertli (1964c); Twigg and Link (1951)	Interveinal chlorosis in young leaves; midrib and side veins remain green while remainder of leaf can be almost white
Copper	Dickey (1965); Twigg and Link (1951)	Browning of shoot tip; chlorosis, dwarfing, and cupping of young leaves; shortened internodes
Boron	Twigg and Link (1951); Oertli (1964c)	Cessation of growth, distorted new foliage, death of shoot tips
Sulfur	Oertli (1964b)	Chlorosis of young foliage; small area at leaf tip can remain green

[a] Twigg and Link (1951) used the cultivar Coral Bells and Oertli (1964a,b,c) used the cultivar Sweetheart Supreme.

Table IV

Critical Leaf Analysis Values for Azaleas[a]

Element	Deficiency range	Normal range	Excess range
Nitrogen (N)	<1.8%[b]	2.0–3.0%[b]	3.0 or greater
Phosphorus (P)	<0.20%	0.29–0.50%	0.65 or greater
Potassium (K)	<0.75%	0.80–1.60%	
Calcium (Ca)	<0.20%	0.22–1.60%	
Magnesium (Mg)	<0.16%	0.17–0.50%	
Manganese(Mn)	<30 ppm	30–300 ppm	400 ppm or greater
Iron (Fe)	<50 ppm	50–150 ppm	
Copper (Cu)	<5 ppm	6–15 ppm	
Boron (B)	<16 ppm	17–100 ppm	200 ppm or greater
Aluminum (Al)			Very tolerant
Zinc (Zn)	<15 ppm	5–60 ppm	
Sodium (Na)		<1500 ppm	1500 ppm or greater

[a] From Mastalerz (1977).
[b] Percent of dry weight.

Some growers alter their fertilization programs immediately before and after pinching, supposedly because not as much fertilizer or nutrients would be required immediately following the removal of foliage when several centimeters of top growth are removed. This practice becomes difficult to follow when plants at several stages of development are located in the same greenhouse or field. At North Carolina State University the fertilizer schedule has remained the same regardless of pinch date, with no apparent deleterious effects.

5. Pinching

A very important but often neglected procedure in azalea culture is removal of shoot tips (pinching) to overcome apical dominance and to stimulate lateral shoot initiation and development with the subsequent increase in plant size and floriferousness (Fig. 2). The plants might be pinched five times from the date of propagation until the plants initiate and develop flower buds. Plants will attain flowering size most rapidly if no time is wasted between pinches, but usually growers delay pinching and prolong the duration of the crop. Plants grown indoors where temperature control can be maintained can be pinched more often and sooner than plants in the field, where only one pinch might be done in a growing season. When grown in the greenhouse plants could be pinched at approximately 6- to 8-week intervals, depending on temperature and daylength to which plants are exposed following the pinch.

The pinch, which refers to the amount of the shoot tip that is removed, can be

Fig. 2. Proper pinching should result in uniform flowering on a multibranched plant.

"soft," "medium," or "hard." A soft pinch is one in which very little of the shoot tip is removed and is in the succulent portion of the shoot. The length of the removed section might be as little as 1 cm. Five to 6 cm might constitute a medium pinch, whereas a hard pinch would exceed that length and the pinch would occur in hardwood. Often plants are sheared to shape at the time of pinching so some pinches will be hard, but more lateral shoots will develop from medium or soft pinches, as more leaf axils remain from which lateral shoots can emerge.

Pinching usually is done manually with pruning shears or mechanically with electrical clippers. Manual pruning is laborious and time-consuming but discretion can be used in pinching plants. Mechanical pruning is more efficient and rapidly accomplished but many shoots can be missed and shoot development will not be uniform.

In the early 1960s researchers showed that certain chemicals effectively overcame apical dominance in plants. Cathey et al. (1966) were the first to describe effects of chemical pruning agents on ornamental plants, and research by Stuart (1967) set guidelines for using the chemical, Off-Shoot-O, on azaleas. This methyl ester of a fatty acid (methyl decanoate) stimulates lateral shoot development by physically damaging shoot apices, primarily by desiccation. The chemical is not translocated within the plant so Off-Shoot-O must be applied to shoot tips. The influence of environmental factors on the effectiveness of Off-Shoot-O already has been mentioned. Cultivars also differ in response to the chemical. 'Coral Bells' responds readily to relatively low rates of Off-Shoot-O because of morphological features of the shoot tip, as reported by Sill and Nelson (1970), whereas 'White Gish' does not respond as dramatically. Larson and McIntyre (1967a) showed that very low rates of Off-Shoot-O could break apical dominance if the chemical was applied directly to the growing point but that higher concentrations were needed to achieve the same results when the entire plant was sprayed until the solution ran off the foliage.

Off-Shoot-O now is used commercially, often at concentrations of approximately 4% active ingredient, or a dilution ratio of 1 part Off-Shoot-O to 10 parts of water. Growers are advised by the manufacturer to mix the chemical slowly with warm water until the desired concentration is attained. Only a few plants should be treated with the desired concentration in the morning, and the remainder of the crop can be treated the following day if preliminary results look satisfactory and if weather conditions remain the same.

Atrinal is another chemical pinching agent with a much different mode of action. Bocion et al. (1975) and de Silva et al. (1976) reported that Atrinal is translocated through the phloem to the shoot apexes and inhibits DNA synthesis. Shoot tip dormancy can be observed within 1 hour when Off-Shoot-O is used. Evidence of Atrinal effects is delayed for about 2 weeks after application, although Arzee et al. (1977) detected Atrinal in the shoot apexes within hours after foliage application. Larson (1978) worked with several azalea cultivars and noted chlorosis, narrow young leaves, and delayed shoot emergence when Atrinal was used at concentrations of 2 to 3%. There were more new shoots on the plants treated with Atrinal, compared to plants treated with Off-Shoot-O or manually pinched. A common practice now used with Atrinal is to pinch the plants manually to break apical dominance, but to apply Atrinal 2 days later to stimulate lateral shoot development. This practice does not eliminate manual pruning but does increase shoot number and final plant size. Atrinal is used commercially in this manner in Belgium and Switzerland. A 2% solution is used in the cool months of the year and 3% is used in the summer.

B. Flower Initiation and Early Development

After the final or "timed" pinch, flower buds will be initiated at the shoot tips. The time required for flower bud initiation to occur is dependent on the cultivar, daylength, and temperature, and whether or not a growth regulator such as B-Nine SP (SADH) is used. Short days, night temperatures of approximately 18°C, and a B-Nine SP or Cycocel spray application applied 5 weeks after the pinch date all promote flower bud initiation. Eventually flower bud initiation will occur under less desirable conditions, but initiation and development will not be as uniform or rapid on all shoots.

Stuart (1964, 1965) is largely responsible for implementing control of flower bud initiation and development with environmental and chemical control. The national cooperative trials he coordinated in 1963 (Stuart, 1964) promoted much interest in azaleas and prompted numerous studies throughout the United States. These studies have been reviewed by Criley (1975).

Flower initiation seems to occur in azaleas because of negative effects of various factors on continued vegetative development. Azaleas that are injured, diseased, or lacking in nutrients frequently will initiate and develop flower buds while adjacent plants that are not adversely affected will continue growing vegetatively. Altering environmental conditions also can stop vegetative growth and promote flowering. Knowledge of these effects has made control of flower initiation possible, with positive methods, as shown by Larson (1975).

1. Temperature

A minimum night temperature of approximately 18°C long has been regarded as optimum for flower bud initiation for most cultivars. This temperature should be maintained for at least 8 weeks. The greenhouse operator is simulating temperatures that azaleas receive outdoors in natural plantings during summer months. Plants will remain vegetative or flower initiation will be sporadic if temperatures are 15°C or less. Initiation will occur if temperatures exceed 18°C, which is fortunate for growers in southern areas, but fuel would be wasted if unnecessarily high night temperatures were maintained in the greenhouse. Flower buds will continue to develop at 18°C or higher until a stage is reached where the buds become dormant and lower temperatures are required to break this dormancy.

2. Light

Daylength and light intensity both affect initiation. Long days favor vegetative growth for many cultivars, so it could be assumed that short days promote flower bud initiation. With many cultivars, flower bud initiation will occur more readily under a 9-hour daylength than under a 16-hour daylength, and under natural conditions flower bud initiation does occur as the daylengths become shorter. The effect of photoperiod on azalea flowering is not as definite for azaleas as it is for crops such as poinsettias and chrysanthemums. Night temperature has a bearing on the importance of daylength in flower bud initiation. Pettersen (1972) has reported that azaleas do not respond to daylength changes when the night temperature is 16°C. Larson and Biamonte (1972) did obtain flowering on 'Red Wing' plants when the night temperature was 14°C, but that was not the optimum temperature for flower bud initiation.

As for photoperiod, influences of light intensity on flower bud initiation and development are not clear-cut. Full light intensity in the summer, combined with very high leaf temperatures and perhaps inadequate moisture, can be damaging. Criley (1975) recommended a light intensity of approximately 28 to 30 klx during the initiation period, with later decreases in intensity to accelerate development. More shoots will form multiple flower buds under relatively high intensities. This response can be noted when azaleas are crowded on the bench or in the field, and shoots on the sides of plants remain vegetative while the uppermost shoots initiate flower buds.

3. Growth Retardants

Growth retardants were first used to control excessive height of potted crops such as chrysanthemums and poinsettias. Stuart (1965, 1975) showed that these same chemicals could cause a cessation of growth in azaleas, with subsequent flower bud initiation and development. Cycocel is used successfully as a foliar application, applied 5 weeks after the final pinch date, at a concentration of 60 to 90 ml/3.8 liters of water. B-Nine SP can be applied once as a foliar spray at 2500 ppm, or twice, at 1500 ppm each time. Applications are made 1 week apart, with the first application occurring 5 weeks after the final pinch. Cycocel has caused a delay in flowering, especially with the Christmas crop of the cultivar 'Chimes.' Plants treated with B-Nine SP can be smaller than untreated plants. The advantages of uniform bud initiation and controlled growth and shape of the plants have offset these disadvantages, however.

The azalea flower bud goes through several stages of development, as reported by Kohl and Sciaroni (1956), and eventually a stage will be reached where the flower buds become dormant. Flowering will not occur unless dormancy is overcome.

C. Flower Bud Dormancy

The most commonly used method of breaking azalea flower bud dormancy is exposing plants to temperatures of 2°–10°C. This treatment occurs naturally when plants are grown outdoors and are subjected to winter conditions in mild climates. Most potted azaleas used in forcing are grown under protected cultivation, however, and low temperature exposure occurs in cold frames, unheated greenhouses or refrigerated storage. Growers in some areas of the country can utilize natural cooling with greater chances for success than growers in milder climates. It is more difficult to schedule azalea flowering precisely when natural cool temperatures are used, but is less expensive than using refrigerated storage. Growers who break dormancy with natural cool temperatures but under protected cultivation such as in a plastic greenhouse will usually cover the plastic film with a shading material such as Saran cloth that will exclude approximately 50% of full sunlight (Fig. 3). Reduced light intensity reduces radiant energy in the greenhouse, affecting both air and leaf temperatures. Only enough heat is added to the greenhouse to keep the plants from freezing, or to prevent injury to flower buds that are near side walls. Plants with well-developed flower buds will be placed in these houses in the fall months and then will be transferred to warmer greenhouses for forcing approximately 6 weeks prior to the desired date of flowering.

The schedule for using refrigerated storage is much more precise than it is

Fig. 3.   Azaleas being given "natural" cool temperatures in a shaded greenhouse, to break flower bud dormancy.

for natural cooling. Storage requirements are not too complex. Incandescent lights are needed if the temperature exceeds 4°C, or excessive leaf drop will occur. A light intensity of only 0.2 klx is required for 12 hours daily for the 4- or 6-week period. Lights are not needed if the temperature ranges from 2° to 4°C. Access to water is required in either the lighted or the unlighted cooler, as plants will need occasional watering. The plants can be watered on a regular schedule because the "climate" in the storage unit remains constant. A relative humidity of at least 60% also helps prevent defoliation. No fertilizer applications are needed while the plants are in refrigerated storage but fungicide applications might be needed if some foliar diseases should occur.

Kurume azalea cultivars only require 4 weeks of cool temperatures, whereas the Indica cultivars require 6 weeks. Severe defoliation or plant injury will occur if Kurume cultivars are kept in storage for 6 weeks.

After storage, azaleas are moved to a greenhouse maintained at temperatures of at least 16°C. Most cultivars will bloom in 4 to 6 weeks, depending on time of year, amount of sunshine, and day and night temperatures. Flowering can be accelerated by increasing temperature or delayed by subjecting plants to lower temperatures.

In some areas temperatures are not consistently cool enough for "natural cooling," and some growers consider refrigerated storage to be too expensive. Perhaps the ideal solution for breaking azalea flower bud dormancy would be to use a chemical that could be applied in the greenhouse or field where plants are grown. Gibberellic acid (GA_3) does have the attributes of such a chemical. Boodley and Mastalerz (1959) were among the first to show the possibilities of using GA_3 as a complete substitute for the cold treatment, and since then several other researchers (Larson, 1975) have modified the original procedure. A relatively simple and effective method is to make five applications of GA_3 or $GA_{4\&7}$ at 1000 ppm, at weekly intervals after the flower buds are well developed [at least stage 7 as described by Kohl and Sciaroni (1956)]. Plants treated in this manner will bloom earlier than plants placed in refrigerated storage on the same date as the first gibberellin application is made. The difference in flowering time could be as much as 5 weeks. Flower diameter, particularly on a cultivar such as 'Red Wing,' can be increased by 2 to 3 cm. Flower color will not be as intense if excessive GA_3 is used, and keeping quality can be adversely affected. There is some merit in combining both methods of breaking dormancy, by subjecting the plants to 3 weeks of cool temperatures and then making three applications of GA_3 at 250 ppm.

IV. CONTROL OF PESTS

Observance of the latest cultural practices and use of the most recently introduced cultivars will be of little value to growers if inadequate attention is given to pests that can damage or destroy azalea plants.

A. Insects, Mites, and Nematodes

Azaleas perhaps are not plagued by as many pests as are some other floricultural crops, but there are some prominent pests that must be considered. It would be difficult to choose a most serious pest, as whichever trouble a grower encounters will be the most serious problem at that time.

A very conspicuous insect affecting azaleas is the azalea lace bug, *Stephanitis pyrioides*. Upper surfaces of leaves will become mottled, and the underside of the foliage will be bronze in color. This insect pest is particularly troublesome in field culture, especially in dry weather. Repeated spray applications of an appropriate insecticide are required to control azalea lace bugs.

Leaf miner or leaf roller (*Gracillaria azaleella*) is another pest that can cause noticeable damage. The grower probably will not be aware of an insect problem until he sees tips of new leaves that have been rolled back and turned brown. Infestation can be severe in the greenhouse and moderately troublesome in the field. Eggs of this insect are laid on the underside of the foliage and the immature insect is protected from spray applications. One control procedure is to eliminate the moths, or to use repeated applications of appropriate insecticides to control the larval stage.

Aphids, thrips, and whiteflies can be troublesome pests on azaleas but they usually are not as devastating as the insects mentioned above. A very serious pest that is not truly an insect is the spider mite. There are several different types of mites but the one most commonly found on field-grown azaleas throughout the United States is the Southern red mite (*Oligonychus ilicis*). The two-spotted mite (*Tetranychus urticae*) will be often found on greenhouse-grown azaleas (Streu, 1975). Mites feed on the underside of the foliage. Mottling and bronzing of the foliage occur. Webs, dust, and other debris will be very noticeable on the undersides of leaves, but mites are so minute that a hand lens usually will be required to detect the pests. Mite infestations can be particularly severe if azalea beds or greenhouses are surrounded by vegetation that is not subjected to any control measures. Mites are difficult to control chemically because they do develop resistance to some pesticides to which they are frequently exposed. Diligent spray programs, application of systemic pesticides, and weed control in adjacent areas will be required for adequate control.

Some areas of the country once had poor reputations as sources of azalea plants because of nematodes that were shipped out with plants. The stylet nematode (*Tylenchorhynchus claytoni*), stunt nematode (*Trichodorus christiei*), and root knot nematode (*Meloidogyne incognita*) perhaps are the most common nematode species affecting azaleas. There does seem to be a relationship between nematode infestation and the disease, azalea decline, so nematode control is especially important. Nematodes severely affect roots of azaleas; infested plants will be smaller than noninfested plants, and the foliage will be bronze or reddish in color. Badly infested plants should be removed from the field and destroyed. Nematocides and soil sterilization, either with steam or chemicals, have reduced nematode infestations but continued vigilance is needed.

B. Diseases

There are some very serious diseases that have discouraged growers from continuing in azalea production. Plants are subject to disease infection from the propagation stage through anthesis. Some of the disease troubles are accentuated because of the cultural practices followed by azalea growers.

A very common and damaging disease is Phytophthora root rot, also referred to as azalea decline or littleleaf disease (Aycock and Daughtry, 1975). The latter names are descriptive of the symptoms of the disease. Plants infected with this pathogen (*Phytophthora cinnamomi*) do not die immediately but gradually decline from one season to the next. Foliage on infected plants also will be smaller than foliage on healthy plants. The disease will be especially severe if the growing medium is poorly drained, as the disease organism is a water mold. Azaleas are grown in media high in organic matter with water retention properties, aggravating the problem. Plants that have been planted too deep in the field or pot also will be vulnerable to the disease organism. Fungicide drenches can be effective but improvements in cultural techniques will be very beneficial in disease control.

A disease that causes a much faster plant response is cylindrocladium disease, caused by the pathogen, *Cylindrocladium scoparium.* Azaleas infected with this organism can be blighted or wilted. Brown to black leaves will be evident if the plants are blighted, and these leaves will drop within a few days. Girdling of the stem also can occur, the plants will lean over in the field or pot and will wilt (Fig. 4). This disease can affect stock plants, cuttings in the propa-

Fig. 4.   Azalea plant infected with *Cylindrocladium scoparium,* causing a wilted appearance.

gation bench, or at any other stage of growth. Some cultivars such as 'Road-runner,' 'Hershey Red,' and 'Chimes' are more susceptible to the disease than cultivars such as 'Coral Bells' and 'Snow.' Plants unprotected from rain, watered overhead, or syringed frequently are particularly vulnerable because spores are spread by splashing water, and disease development is enhanced under humid conditions.

Disease-free stock plants, fungicide applications to plants at all stages of development except those in full flower, selection of tolerant cultivars, sanitary field or greenhouse practices, and protection from splashing water can reduce the prevalence of Cylindrocladium disease.

Botrytis can be a problem when azaleas are placed in unlighted or poorly ventilated storage areas to break flower bud dormancy. Powdery mildew also can be troublesome under humid conditions, particularly on a cultivar such as 'Roadrunner.' Petal blight, leaf gall, and septoria leaf spot can affect azaleas but usually are not as damaging or as frequent as the diseases that have been mentioned in greater detail.

Pesticide lists are changing constantly, so one should keep abreast of the latest releases of chemicals for insect and disease control, as well as the curtailment of pesticides presently available.

V. PHYSIOLOGICAL DISORDERS

Not all azalea problems are caused by pests but can occur because of inappropriate environmental or cultural conditions. Nutritional problems already have been discussed and will not be mentioned here, although deficiencies or excesses of nutrients do cause physiological disorders.

Occasionally azaleas will not flower uniformly or flowering will be delayed for a specific holiday. Late pinching with inadequate warm temperature for flower bud initiation and early development can cause irregular flowering. Excessively early pinching can result in early flower bud initiation and development, but if dormancy-breaking treatments are delayed numerous vegetative bypass shoots will develop and surround the flower bud. These undesirable shoots must be removed so flowers will be noticeable, and to avoid flower bud abortion if too many shoots develop.

Defoliation of azaleas in refrigerated storage has occurred because of ethylene pollution. Azaleas should not be stored in rooms containing fruits, vegetables, or other sources of ethylene.

There have been instances of herbicide damage to azaleas in the field and greenhouse. Only appropriate herbicides should be used to control weeds in azalea beds, and at this time there are no herbicides cleared for use on any greenhouse crops.

Hasek and Kofranek (1975) have tabulated the most common visual symptoms and possible causes of azalea problems. Space limitations prevent publication of the table in this chapter but the reader should consult the original article for more information.

VI. MARKETING OF PLANTS

A major problem confronting the azalea grower is determining the costs of the plants he has grown and the price he must charge to realize a profit. Plant size often determines the price, no matter how long the grower has had the plants on the premises, so grading of plants is an important part of azalea production. It also is a very difficult task. Azalea cultivars differ in growth habit and shape, so plant diameter does not necessarily have a close relationship to shoot or flower number. Azalea plants similar in size can differ greatly in stage of floral development. There also are regional preferences for plant shape that can affect grading by plant size.

A. Grading

Azaleas sold to growers for forcing are most commonly graded by plant crown diameter. A plant 20 × 25 cm (8 × 10 inches) is one which is 25 cm across at the widest portion of the plant and 20 cm at midpoint at right angles to the 25-cm measurement. Sizes might range from 15 × 15 cm to as large as 30 × 30 cm. Yoder Brothers of Barberton, Ohio, grade their plants by diameter and average number of flower buds (Lindstrom, 1975). For example, a plant 22 cm in diameter would have approximately 25 flower buds while a plant 32 cm in diameter would average 45 flower buds. Such a grading system gives the customer more definite information about the plant than size alone can do. Another azalea producer sells plants as 2-pinch or 3-pinch liners (Anonymous, 1967), which also indicates shoot number differences, although not as precisely as the diameter–shoot number grade.

Plant size is largely determined by age of the plant and number of pinches, so the largest plants should bring the highest prices, as the plants have occupied space and labor for the longest period of time. Some growers use pot size as a grading measurement. There can be some correlation between plant and pot size but they are not criteria of plant quality.

B. Packing and Handling

Azalea liners or dormant plants generally are removed from their containers, individually wrapped in paper, packed in cardboard boxes and shipped to the flower grower who will force the plants. Shipments must be protected from excessive heat or cold but the grower does not have to worry about flower bruising. Growers who sell flowering plants must be concerned about damage to the blossoms, although only 25 to 30% of the flowers will be fully open at the time of sale. Azaleas frequently are placed in pot sleeves that protect the flowering plants and also enable the grower to get more plants in the delivery vehicle. Azaleas sometimes are boxed if the distance to market is long and the grower is trying to get a maximum number of plants in the truck. Plants should be removed from sleeves or boxes as soon as possible when they are received by florists or other retail outlets. The potting medium should be examined immediately for moisture content. Some of the plants will be placed on display for sale while the remainder can be stored briefly. In most instances retailers will not have adequate refrigerated storage for a large number of plants but keeping quality will be enhanced if the surplus plants are kept at 4°–10°C.

As mentioned previously, plants will not be in full flower at time of sale. The customer will realize much longer beauty from a plant which has only one-fourth to one-third of the flower buds fully expanded when the plant is purchased. Cultivars do differ greatly in keeping quality. Flowers drop very easily and quickly on 'Red Wing' plants whereas flowers on a cultivar such as 'Gloria' will be much more persistent. Flower quality also is affected by water stress. Petal burn will occur on 'Red Wing' plants if the medium becomes too dry, whereas wilted petals of cultivars such as 'Dogwood' or 'Gloria' will retain turgidity after watering with no conspicuous damage unless water deficiency is prolonged.

C. Retailing

A key to the successful and rapid sale of azalea plants is the proper display of the plants in the retail shop. Usually pot foil and ribbon will attract the customer but major selling points will be plant and flower quality. Many of the red-flowered cultivars do not show to the greatest advantage under fluorescent lighting. A combination of fluorescent and incandescent lights would be helpful.

Care tags should accompany plants that are sold, as most customers will not realize the full beauty of the plants without some instructions on the care of the plants in the home or office. Instructions should be brief and simple. Important points to include in the instructions would be daily checking of the medium for moisture content, placement of the plant in a well-lighted place in the home or office, away from hot or cold drafts.

Customers in the southern and western regions of the country might successfully plant azaleas in the home landscape when flowering is over and there is no danger of frost. Planting instructions would be helpful.

REFERENCES

Anonymous (1967). "Schedule and Growing Procedure for Year Around Azalea Production." Geo. J. Ball, Inc., West Chicago, Illinois.

Arzee, T., Langenaver, H., and Gressel, J. (1977). Effects of dikegulac, a new growth regulator, on apical growth and development of three compositae. *Bot. Gaz. (Chicago)* **138**(1) 18–28.

Aycock, R., and Daughtry, B. (1975). Major diseases. *In* "Growing Azaleas Commercially" (A. M. Kofranek and R. A. Larson, eds.), Sale Publ. No. 4058, pp. 78–88. Univ. of California, Berkeley.

Bocion, P. F., Huppi, G. A., de Silva, W. H., and Szkrybalo, W. (1975). A group of new chemicals with plant growth regulatory activity. *Nature (London),* 258, 142–144.

Boodley, J. W., and Mastalerz, J. W. (1959). The use of gibberellic acid to force azaleas without a cold temperature treatment. *Proc. Am. Soc. Hortic. Sci.* **74,** 68–85.

Cathey, H. M., Steffens, G. L., Stuart, N. W., and Zimmerman, R. H. (1966). Chemical pruning of plants. *Science* **156**(3742, 1382–1383.

Criley, R. L. (1975). Effects of light and temperature on flower initiation and development. *In* "Growing Azaleas Commercially" (A. M. Kofranek and R. A. Larson, eds.), Sale Publ. No. 4058, pp. 52–61. Univ. of California, Berkeley.

de Silva, W. H., Bocion, P. F., and Walther, H. R. (1976). Chemical pinching of azalea with Dikegulac. *HortScience* **11**(6), 569–570.

Dickey, R. D. (1965). Copper deficiency of some container grown woody ornamental plants. *Proc. Fla. State Hortic. Soc.* **78**, 386–392.

Fossum, M. T. (1973). "Trends in Commercial Floriculture Crop Production and Distribution. A Statistical Compendium for the United States 1945–1970." Marketing Facts for Floriculture, under the auspices of SAFE, Alexandria, Virginia.

Galle, F. C. (1974). "Azaleas." Oxmoor House, Birmingham, Alabama.

Hasek, R. F., and Kofranek, A. M. (1975). Problems of evergreen azaleas. *In* "Growing Azaleas Commercially" (A. M. Kofranek and R. A. Larson, eds.), Sale Publ. No. 4058, pp. 97–99. Univ. of California, Berkeley.

Hoitink, H. A., and Schmitthenner, A. F. (1972). Control of *Phytophthora* root rot (wilt) of *Rhododendron. Am. Hortic.* **51,**42–45.

Kiplinger, D. C. (1952). Studies on the effect of photoperiod and night temperature on flower bud initiation in the azalea Coral Bell (*Rhododendron obtusum japonicum*). Ph.D. Thesis, Ohio State Univ., Columbus.

Kofranek, A. M., and Lunt, O. R. (1975). Mineral nutrition. *In* "Growing Azaleas Commercially" (A. M. Kofranek and R. A. Larson, eds.), Sale Publ. No. 4058, pp. 36–46. Univ. of California, Berkeley.

Kohl, H. C., and Sciaroni, R. H. (1956). Bud initiation of azaleas. *Calif. Agric.* **10**(5), 15.

Larson, R. A. (1975). Continuous production of flowering azaleas. *In* "Growing Azaleas Commercially" (A. M. Kofranek and R. A. Larson, eds.), Sale Publ. No. 4058, pp. 72–77. Univ. of California, Berkeley.

Larson, R. A. (1978). Stimulation of lateral branching of azaleas with dikegulac sodium (Atrinal). *J. Hortic. Sci.* **53**(1), 57–62.

Larson, R. A., and Biamonte, R. L. (1972). Response of azaleas to precisely controlled temperatures. *J. Am. Soc. Hortic. Sci.* **97**(4), 491–493.

Larson, R. A., and McIntyre, M. L. (1967a). N. C. State studies on chemical pinching of azaleas. *Florists' Rev.* **141**(3653), 21, 22, 82.

Larson, R. A., and McIntyre, M. L. (1967b). "Out-of-season" flowering of quality azaleas. *Am. Rhododendron Soc. Q.t. Bull.* **21**(2), 67–70.

Lee, F. P. (1958). "The Azalea Book." Van Nostrand, Princeton, New Jersey.

Leiser, A. T. (1975). Taxonomy and origin of azaleas used for forcing. *In* "Growing Azaleas Commercially" (A. M. Kofranek and R. A. Larson, eds.), Sale Publ. No. 4058, pp. 9–14. Univ. of California, Berkeley.

Lindstrom, R. S. (1975). Grades and standards. *In* "Growing Azaleas Commercially" (A. M. Kofranek and R. A. Larson, eds.), Sale Publ. No. 4058, pp. 100–102. Univ. of California, Berkeley.

Love, J. W. (1975). Vegetative growth. *In* "Growing Azaleas Commercially" (A. M. Kofranek and R. A. Larson, eds.), Sale Publ. No. 4058, pp. 47–51. Univ. of California, Berkeley.

Mastalerz, J. W. (1977). "The Greenhouse Environment. The Effect of Environmental Factors on Flower Crops." Wiley, New York.

Oertli, J. J. (1964a). Azalea nutrition disorders. 1. Nitrogen, phosphorus and potassium deficiencies. *Florists' Rev.* **134**(3482), 20, 62.

Oertli, J. J. (1964b). Azalea nutrition disorders. 2. Calcium, magnesium and sulphur deficiencies. *Florists' Rev.* **134**(3483), 21, 62.

Oertli, J. J. (1964c). Azalea nutrition disorders. 3. Chlorisis, tipburn, result of iron and boron deficiencies. *Florists' Rev.* **134**(3484), 31, 80.

Pettersen, H. (1968). Effect of light and temperature on the number of shoots after pinching of azalea and on the subsequent growth of the shoots. *Meld. Nor. Landbrukshoegsk.* No. 134, 18–20.

Pettersen, H. (1972). The effect of temperature and daylength on shoot growth and bud formation in azaleas. *J. Am. Soc. Hortic. Sci.* **97,** 17–24.

Scott, W. (1899). "The Florists' Manual." Florists' Publ. Co., Chicago, Illinois.

Sill, L. Z., and Nelson, P. V. (1970). Relation between bud morphology and effectiveness of methyl decanoate as a chemical pinching agent. *J. Am. Soc. Hortic. Sci.* **95,** 270–273.

Skinner, H. T. (1939). Factors affecting shoot growth and flower bud formation in rhododendrons and azaleas. *Proc. Am. Soc. Hortic. Sci.* **37,** 1007–1011.

Skou, W. (1969). Year-around production of azaleas for wholesale growers. *Florists' Rev.* **145**(3757), 25, 62–63, 73–74.

Stadtherr, R. J. (1975). Commercial cultivars. *In* "Growing Azaleas Commercially" (A. M. Kofranek and R. A. Larson, eds.), Sale Publ. No. 4058, pp. 17–29. Univ. of California, Berkeley.

Streu, H. T. (1975). Insect, mite and nematode control on azaleas. *In* "Growing Azaleas Commercially" (A. M. Kofranek and R. A. Larson, eds.), Sale Publ. No. 4958, pp. 89–96. Univ. of California, Berkeley.

Stuart, N. W. (1964). Report of co-operative trial on controlling flowering of greenhouse azaleas with growth retardants. *Florists' Rev.* **133**(3477), 37–39, 74–76.

Stuart, N. W. (1965). Controlling the flowering of greenhouse azaleas. *Florist Nursery Exch.* **144**(11), 22–23.

Stuart, N. W. (1967). Chemical pruning of greenhouse azaleas with fatty acid esters. *Florists' Rev.* **140**(3631), 26–27, 68.

Stuart, N. W. (1975). Chemical control of growth and flowering. *In* "Growing Azaleas Commercially" (A. M. Kofranek and R. A. Larson, eds.), Sale Publ. No. 4058, pp. 62–72. Univ. of California, Berkeley.

Twigg, M. C., and Link, C. B. (1951). Nutrient deficiency symptoms and leaf analysis of azaleas grown in sand culture. *Proc. Am. Soc. Hortic. Sci.* **57,** 369–375.

White, E. A. (1923). "The Principles of Floriculture." Macmillan, New York.

10
Pot Mums

G. Douglas Crater

Introduction to Floriculture
Copyright © 1980 by Academic Press, Inc.
All rights of reproduction in any form reserved.
ISBN 0-12-437650-9

I. INTRODUCTION

A. History

Year-round pot mums continue to be the undisputed number one pot plant among major pot crops. Numerous cultivars of chrysanthemums were grown in Europe prior to 1800 as garden flowers. Since that time the chrysanthemum has been refined and developed to the point where it is now a year-round crop and the primary pot plant grown in much of the world. The real growth in the pot mum industry has occurred since the 1940s and new innovations are being developed every day.

B. Botanical Information

The chrysanthemum is a member of the Composite or Aster family. There are between 100 and 200 species of this aromatic annual or perennial herb. It is native to the Northern Hemisphere, chiefly Europe and Asia, with a few from other areas. Many authorities claim that the chrysanthemum originated in China. Chrysanthemums are primarily grown as ornamentals, but certain species are cultivated as a source of the important insecticide, pyrethrum. The cultivated chrysanthemum that is used for pot culture is a hardy or semihardy aromatic plant with flowers that exhibit a wide range of colors. The chrysanthemum has been developed into several groups such as single, cascade, anemone (with center cushion), pompon (globular), decorative (asterlike), spider, incurved, and large exhibition.

The species of chrysanthemums that is used for pot or cut flower culture is the *Chrysanthemum morifolium* Ram. Today there are hundreds of chrysanthemum cultivars which vary greatly in characteristics that are available to the grower. Chrysanthemum cultivars that are suitable for pot mum culture must exhibit the following characteristics: form a well-shaped plant, branch easily, produce flowers quickly on relatively short stems, and have flowers of the desired color, shape, and size.

Chrysanthemums bloom under short days and long nights; therefore, they are termed photoperiodic. Cultivars are classified according to their response group. Response groups are determined by the time from the initiation of short days to flowering (length of time required to bloom). Cultivars used in most areas are classified as 8- to 12-week response groups. For example, a 10-week response group takes 10 weeks from initiation of short days to flowering. The time from planting until short days are provided is, however, not included in the response time. To grow a crop of pot mums takes about 2 to 3 weeks longer than the response group that is used. From potting to flowering the pot mum is about a 3-month crop.

C. Prominent Cultivars

With regard to specific cultivars that should be used or are recommended, every supplier or propagator has many good cultivars that are on the market. As plant breeders and hybridizers develop new cultivars, many of the older ones are replaced. In selecting specific pot mum cultivators it is best to check several growers in the area to see what grows best locally. Usually sales personnel from supply firms and propagators can recommend good cultivars with which to begin production. Each grower will find that certain cultivars will do better than others.

The types or cultivars of potted chrysanthemums that are most widely sold are shown in the following tabulation:

Spider	Narrow and lacy-petaled flowers
Daisy	Wider petals, resembling the ordinary daisy
Spoon	Flat-petaled flowers that are spoon-shaped
Feathered	Quilled or feathery petals
Incurved	Exhibition type with petals that curve inward; disbudded, single flower
Decorative	Disbudded, single flower with flat, as opposed to incurved, petals

All of these cultivars come in many colors, with most emphasis on whites, yellows, lavenders, pinks, and bronzes.

II. PROPAGATION

A good quality cutting is the start toward success in pot mum production. Quality cuttings are disease- and insect-free and uniform in size. Most propagators who supply cuttings do an excellent job of providing the grower quality cuttings. Some growers propagate their own cuttings, but it is difficult for such a grower to supply his greenhouse regularly with uniform, disease-free cuttings. Stock plants and propagation benches also utilize bench space that might be used more profitably for growing flowering plants.

A. Stock Plant Culture

Maintaining and growing stock plants may be risky. Disease and insect problems can affect crop quality and completely ruin a crop. If a large number of cuttings is going to be used, however, then producing one's own cuttings could help reduce the overall cost of production for the crop. If a grower is going to produce cuttings, then he/she should purchase new cuttings from a reputable propagator each time stock plants are replanted. Before the stock bed is replanted the area should be fumigated or sterilized to reduce or prevent diseases, insects, nematodes, and grass problems.

Rooted cuttings are usually spaced 15 × 20 cm in beds similar to cut flower beds. Watering, fertilization, and insect and disease control should be similar to any crop of chrysanthemums. Stock plants should be grown under full sun (especially during late fall, winter, and early spring). Daylength should always be long and it should be supplemented with an additional 4 hours of light per night of 10 fc between 10:00 or 11:00 P.M. and 2:00 or 3:00 A.M.

When should stock plants be replaced? Too many growers try to get one more crop of cuttings from their stock plants and wait too long. Usually after five or six flushes of cuttings plants should be removed and new plants should be put in their place. After the fifth or sixth flush, new cuttings that form are on tips of old breaks and are more likely to set crown buds. Chances of maintaining disease-free stock also diminish with each succeeding month in the greenhouse.

B. Propagation of Plants

Cuttings should be taken from disease-free stock and should be removed from stock plants by breaking or snapping them just above a node. It is best not to use a knife or a cutting instrument because they transmit disease organisms readily. The cutting should be approximately 4 to 5 cm long, depending on cultivar and time of year. Unrooted cuttings can be stored at −1°C for up to 4 weeks. This is sometimes done so cuttings can be accumulated for a specific planting date. Cuttings are usually stored in polyethylene bags with cool air circulating around them.

In many cases unrooted cuttings are stuck directly into the pot, where they will be finished. This procedure will save time and labor but can also result in a pot where one or more cuttings do not root, thereby creating an uneven mature plant.

Propagators of chrysanthemums sell two or three types of cuttings. Unrooted, calloused, or rooted cuttings can be obtained. When rooting a cutting most propagators use a rooting hormone to increase the number of roots, ensure more uniform rooting, and hasten rooting. If a rooting hormone is applied, the basal end of the cutting should not be dipped into powder or liquid because this is an easy way to spread diseases. The best method of applying the rooting hormone is to dust it over the basal end of the stems with a small duster.

Many different media can be used in propagation. A well-drained medium is desired. Cuttings root best when the rooting medium stays between 21° and 27°C. Bottom heat to maintain this temperature accelerates rooting. Misting the foliage of cuttings 5 seconds every 10 minutes is also beneficial. Mist schedules will vary for each propagator because of specific conditions.

Cuttings should be spaced approximately 2.5 cm in rows, and the rows should be 2.5 to 5 cm apart. Some propagators apply a light feeding of nutrients through the mist to enhance plant growth. Cuttings should be removed from the propagation bed when new roots are between 0.6 and 1.2 cm long. These rooted cuttings can also be stored at 0°C for 1 or 2 weeks if necessary.

Growth and development of young plants will be best if the night temperature is kept at 18°C and the atmosphere is kept moist. Cuttings should be prevented from wilting after they are planted. One of the best methods is to place cuttings under intermittent mist. The mist should keep cuttings turgid but not overly wet and should be turned on 1 hour after sunrise and turned off 1 hour before sunset. On clear, sunny days the mist should run 6 seconds every 15 minutes in the summer and 6 seconds every 30 minutes during the winter. This cycle should be adjusted according to local conditions.

If a mist system is not used, then a polyethylene tent over the cuttings will help maintain a high humidity. Usually cuttings are kept under the polyethylene tent for 5 to 10 days or until some growth can be seen.

Many growers have a separate area where the mist system is located. This area has bottom heat under the benches and the temperature is usually run 2°–6°C higher than the rest of the greenhouse area. In this area they also might add lights to provide long days and short nights for vegetative growth. Thus they do not have to shade all of the greenhouse during the late fall, winter, and early spring when there is a natural long night, but only have to shade the area where they are lighting.

III. PLANT CULTURE

A. Vegetative Stage

The vegetative stage in pot mum production is the time when long days and short nights are provided to give the plant time to get established and to get enough growth before flower buds are initiated. This vegetative stage gives the plant its start and indirectly influences its height.

1. Growing Medium

a. Natural Mixes. It is hard to suggest a growing medium that will be acceptable to every grower or for every condition. Water, nutrients, and soil become interrelated and there is no one absolute mix that will fit every grower's situation. A good growing medium will be loose and well drained. Most topsoils do not have the qualities required to produce optimum root and plant growth. Without good root growth the plant cannot absorb an adequate amount of water and fertilizer; thus a weak plant develops that will not be as vigorous or produce as many breaks as will a well-rooted plant.

Where soil will be used in the growing medium, one should determine whether the soil is high in clay or high in sand. Where clay predominates, the soil should be diluted with organic matter and inert materials. Where sand predominates, the soil should be diluted primarily with organic matter, such as sphagnum peat moss, pine bark, peanut hulls, or other similar items. Inert materials such as coarse sand, perlite, vermiculite, or calcined clay can be used.

For areas where topsoils are high in clay, the following proportions are suggested on a volume basis: 1 part soil: 1 part organic matter: 1 part inert material.

If the soil is a loam or does not have an extremely high clay content, then 2 parts of soil should be used. Organic matter and inert material could be any of the ones previously mentioned.

For areas where topsoils are high in sand the following proportions are suggested on a volume basis: 1 part sandy soil: 1 part organic matter.

If the soil is very loamy or has some clay, then some inert material should be added to loosen up the mix. A mix composed of 2 parts sandy soil, 2 parts organic matter, and 1 part inert material should be used in this type of situation. If the soil has a very fine sand, then the mix should be 1 part sandy soil: 1 part organic matter: 1 part inert material.

Many growers forget about soil pH, but this should be adjusted and corrected before cuttings are planted. Optimum soil pH for pot mums is between 6.2 and 6.7. A soil test should be run to determine adjustments to be made to the growing medium. To raise the pH 0.1 unit, 354 gm of dolomitic agricultural limestone per cubic meter of potting soil mix should be incorporated. To reduce the pH 0.2 unit, 354 gm of aluminum or iron sulfate per cubic meter is needed. Elemental wettable sulfur at 354 gm per cubic meter will lower the pH 1 full unit.

Many growers feel that they are using a good soil mix but neglect adequate preparation. No mixture is good unless it is mixed properly. The most important step is having a soil mix that will provide optimum growing conditions for pot mums.

Many growers carry mixing too far and run the soil and peat through a soil shredder. This procedure shreds coarse peat moss into a powder form, or pulverizes a soil with good structure into powder form. The end result of using a soil shredder is a fine soil mix that will provide very poor aeration for plant growth. A concrete mixer is a much better tool for mixing soil. Five minutes is usually long enough to do a thorough job of blending components.

b. Artificial Mixes.   Many growers are using "artificial" media that they mix themselves or buy premixed. There are several reasons for using artificial mixes. First, it is increasingly difficult to find good topsoil that is uniform in physical and chemical properties. Second, handling and mixing soil require time and labor, and labor costs are constantly increasing. Third, an artificial mix is usually free of disease organisms, insects, and weed seed.

Some growers have found that an artificial mix is actually more economical. When they compared costs of obtaining, mixing, sterilizing, and handling soil to costs of buying an artificial mix already prepared and ready to use, they found that the artificial mix was not "that expensive." There are several excellent prepared artificial mixes available and growers have found them very satisfactory. New, inexperienced, or small growers often find it best to start with a prepared artificial mix.

2. Potting

It is advisable to grade cuttings according to size before potting. A grower who plants both tall and short cuttings in the same pot will get an uneven product at flowering. Even if the grower tries to correct the problem by pinching tall cuttings hard and short cuttings soft, this approach will still result in an unbalanced plant since more breaks will develop from the soft pinch. Before planting the cuttings should be grouped according to height: tall, medium, or short.

Cuttings should be planted shallow and the roots should just barely be covered by the mix. Cuttings planted too deeply are more likely to become affected by root or stem rot. If cuttings are planted at a 45° angle, so they lean out over the rim of the pot instead of straight up, a better-shaped plant will result. Usually more breaks and better flowers will be obtained because more light can get to the center of the plant, where light is usually shaded out.

Immediately after cuttings have been planted they should be watered-in thoroughly. They should be watered-in twice, and the second watering should contain a soluble fertilizer. With a 20% nitrogen fertilizer, a rate of 28 gm of fertilizer to 11.4 liters of water is recommended. Research has shown that the most critical period of pot mum fertilization is during the first half of the growing time. Therefore, the fertility level of the soil mix should be in the optimum range as soon after planting as possible. Early application of fertilizer will get nutrient levels to the optimum range.

3. Spacing

Many growers believe that the amount of the space given to a pot mum is almost directly proportional to the final quality. Space management must go hand in hand, however, with what price a pot mum will bring. Spacing too close during early stages of growth must, however, be avoided to ensure maximum development of breaks.

When cuttings are first planted the pots are not spaced, but are placed pot to pot. Usually, after plants are removed from the mist area or from under the polyethylene tent, they are placed at their final spacing. Spacing pots at final distance immediately after pinching is very important to ensure that plants are not shaded by each other and, therefore, receive the maximum amount of sunlight. Spacing of 15-cm pots at 40 × 40 cm to provide 0.5 m² per pot is ideal.

The following are some spacings that are used successfully by many pot mum growers:

> 7.6 cm—pot to pot or 12 × 12 cm, one plant per pot
> 10 cm—18 × 18 cm, one plant per pot
> 15 cm—30 × 30 cm, three to five plants per pot
> 18 cm—36 × 36 cm, five plants per pot

It is possible to space the pots several times, gradually giving them more space as the plants grow. Gradual spacing may conserve some space, but it requires more labor. Closely spaced plants cast shade on adjacent plants and do not develop as well as plants spaced more generously.

In some cases one may want to grow pot mums at a close spacing because of market demands and economics. However, a better-quality plant will be grown when more spacing is provided.

4. Number of Cuttings per Pot

Pot mums in 15-cm pots should average 20 to 30 flowering shoots per pot. Four or five cuttings should be used during the spring, summer, and fall months, and five cuttings should be used per pot for the winter months. Only one cutting is required for a 7.5- to 10-cm pot.

5. Photoperiod

Lighting of cuttings is done to prevent flower buds from forming too early because of the natural bud-promoting effects of long nights. To prevent plants from setting flower buds, the dark period must not be any longer than 7 continuous hours of darkness. The following recommendations should be observed to supply correct lighting for the cuttings:

1. For benches 1 to 1.2 m wide, a 60-W bulb with reflectors should be placed 1 m apart and 0.6 to 0.9 m above the tops of the plants.
2. Approximately 1¼ W of light/0.3 m² of bench area should be provided.
3. Lights should not be turned on before 10:00 P.M. and should be left on for 3 to 4 hours.

With increased electric rates many growers are changing to intermittent lighting. Compared with continuous lighting systems, only a fraction of the normal electrical input is necessary with intermittent lighting (approximately 20%). These recommendations should be followed:

1. Make sure plants are getting a minimum of 10 fc at the top of the plants.
2. Run intermittent lighting for the same 4 hours one would normally use for continuous lighting.
3. With intermittent lighting the lights will need to be on 6 minutes out of every 30 minutes (on 6 minutes, off 24, on 6 minutes, off 24, etc.) until 4 hours are completed.

Chrysanthemums are lighted because they form leaves and increase in stem length under long days whereas they form flower buds and the stems terminate with flowers under short days. The chrysanthemums should have approximately 12 hours of darkness to set flower buds.

When sticking unrooted cuttings, it usually takes approximately 5 more days of lighting than when rooted cuttings are planted. Research has shown that plants must have some root initials before they are responsive to photoperiods.

6. Temperature

For rooting cuttings, temperature plays a very important role in the success of root formation. Plants must have warm temperatures of at least 21°C during the day, and bottom heat is best. A rooting medium should never get below 21°C until after roots are formed.

The most favorable temperature for growth of young pot mum plants is higher than for older plants. For this reason, it is suggested that pot mums be grown at a minimum night temperature of 18°C for the first 4 weeks after potting. The minimum night temperature for the next 4 to 5 weeks should be 16°–17°C.

The maximum temperature should be 32°C. Above this level flowering can be delayed and flower pigments do not develop properly. The minimum temperature for growing pot mums is 10°C, and this is only after flowers are developed. The cooler temperature intensifies color in several cultivars, but it can also cause pink coloration in white petals, an undesirable trait.

For many southern growers cooling is more important than heating. A fan and pad cooling system is imperative to supply ideal growing conditions for pot mums in high temperature areas.

7. Light Intensity

Pot mum growers have found that it is usually best to grow pot mums under full sunlight. Vegetative growth, quality, and production of pot mums will be improved under high light. Sometimes in midsummer growers (especially in the southern United States) apply a light shade to their greenhouses to reduce heat and to prevent sunburn on newly opened flowers. This shading is usually 20 to 35% shade and never over 50%. Shading helps cool the greenhouse and reduces watering. Excessive shade has been shown to reduce production on certain cultivars over 55%, as measured by quality and number of blooms.

8. Fertilization

A proper fertilization program is essential in the production of a pot mum crop. It will improve flower keeping quality or vase life, reduce disease problems, and produce higher yields. There are many kinds of fertilizers that can be used, such as soluble inorganic, organic, and slow-release fertilizers. The soluble inorganic sources of fertilizers are usually recommended.

Pot mums use large quantities of nitrogen and potassium during the vegetative growth stage. During the last third of the growing cycle the nitrogen rate should be cut in half.

It is very important that a pot mum be fertilized immediately after planting. Research has shown that a pot mum's requirements for fertilizer are more critical during the first half of the growing time. They should be fertilized when the cuttings are first watered-in.

After the initial fertilization of 28 gm to 11.4 liters of water, fertilize, using an injector, with 200 ppm nitrogen and 200 ppm potassium every time plants are watered. A higher rate can be used if fertilizer is applied weekly.

Improved growth has been observed where a slow-release fertilizer has been used in addition to constant liquid fertilization. Slow-release fertilizer is applied immediately after planting and prior to watering-in at the rate of 1 level teaspoon per 15-cm pot. This rate could vary with different types of slow-release fertilizers, so recommendations on the bag should be noted. Best results with slow-release fertilizers occur by applying the fertilizer as a top-dressing. When it is mixed in the soil it will continue to release nutrients as long as the medium is moist, and most growers have a tendency to keep their plants too wet, thus resulting in soluble salts problems when a slow-release fertilizer is mixed with the soil.

Soluble salts in the growing medium primarily come from the applied fertilizer. Soluble salts in the growing medium are composed primarily of ammonium nitrate, calcium, magnesium, potassium, sodium, bicarbonate, chloride, and sulfate ions. When the soluble salts level becomes too high roots are damaged, which reduces their ability to absorb nutrients and water. Many times plants with soluble salts injury show the same deficiency symptoms as plants that are not getting enough fertilizer or water. Actually, plants that are burned by high soluble salts levels may be deficient in some nutrients, not because these nutrients are not in the medium, but because plants cannot absorb the nutrients on account of root damage from the toxic high soluble salts levels. Some other symptoms that may be observed from high soluble salts levels are marginal leaf burn, leaf chlorosis, stunting, yellowing of new growth, excessive wilting, small flowers, and, in some cases, a reduction in growth.

How can one control soluble salts? Some growers water very lightly and do not apply enough water for it to run out the bottom of the container; this procedure results in a buildup of salts in the medium. If the medium then becomes dry, soluble salts become more concentrated because of evaporation of water. All pot mum crops should be watered heavily at least every 2 weeks so that water will leach excess salts out the bottom of the container and prevent a buildup of a high level of soluble salts.

One should be alert for soluble salts problem. It is a good idea to have a soil analysis run periodically so one can observe the salts and nutrient levels. A foliar test is also good because this will supply more information on exactly what the plant has been able to obtain. Many growers buy a Solubridge so they can do their own monitoring of soluble salts.

9. Watering

Hand watering is still the most common practice for small production areas. Many large growers even use hand watering because they feel they can more closely supply the correct amount of water at the proper time. This practice, however, is time-consuming and more growers are switching to some automated type of watering. Some growers feel that automatic watering is a must. There are many advantages to watering crops automatically, such as the following: (1) saves labor; (2) results in more thorough watering; (3) almost eliminates soil compaction; and (4) keeps foliage dry, reducing disease problems.

Good results have been obtained with the automated watering system that uses small plastic tubes running to each pot. Frequency of watering may be controlled by either a weight scale or an electric timer. Regardless of the method used, 0.5 liter of water should be applied each time pots are irrigated. With automatic watering, excellent drainage of the soil is imperative.

Always apply enough water when irrigating pot mums. Applying an insufficient amount of irrigation water may lead to two problems: (1) excessive soluble salts and (2) water stress. Both problems, of course, result in poorer crop quality. One-half liter should be applied per 15-cm pot at every irrigation.

Mat watering is also being used very successfully with pot mums. Many types of mats are available and all work successfully. Water is applied to mat and is soaked up through the bottom of the pot. Algae are sometimes a problem but can be controlled chemically. Leaching is very important when mats are used.

10. Pinching

Pot mums are pinched to produce multistemmed plants. "Pinching" is the removal of the central growing point (bud) so that lateral shoots, and, therefore, the maximum number of shoots, will develop. Before the plant is pinched it should have made enough growth so the pinch can be made in new growth. A "soft" pinch is when a small amount of the stem tip is removed (rolled out). When a plant has had a soft pinch and was grown properly, it should have approximately 10 leaves below the pinch.

"Hard" pinching is when the stem is pinched back to allow fewer than 6 leaves to remain on the stem, but usually severely limits the number of breaks that may develop. One reason hard pinching is used is to even up the height of pot mums at pinching time: short cuttings in a pot are pinched soft, whereas the taller ones are pinched hard.

Pinching is usually done between 10 and 14 days after planting. Plants should be actively growing with 10 to 14 leaves (counting those just unfolding around the bud) on the stem. It should be noted that the pinch date does not affect time of flowering.

11. Growth Regulators

An ideal pot mum is approximately 2 to 2½ times as high as its pot. Therefore, height control is of utmost importance to the pot mum grower. Under long-day conditions chrysanthemums form leaves and increase in stem length; under short-day conditions flower buds form and the stem terminates. Therefore, daylength, and especially the number of long days, can be used to influence the final height of the plant. Short-growing varieties are provided with more long days to increase stem length than are tall-growing varieties.

Height control can be achieved to a certain extent by controlling the number of long days, but additional control of height is sometimes needed and can be done with some chemicals. Chemical growth retardants not only retard stem elongation but also help increase the color depth of foliage and stiffen stems, thus making them stronger.

There are three major growth regulators used on pot mums: B-Nine, A-REST (Ancymidol), and Phosfon. B-Nine is most widely used because it is easy to apply and plant response is predictable. It is applied as a foliar spray to newly emerging shoots or to visibly budded plants to control overall plant height. Plants should be sprayed with a 0.25% solution (18 ml/3.8 liter of water) when the breaks are 4 to 5 cm long. Pot mums are usually sprayed about 2 weeks after pinching, and in some instances a second spraying may be used 1 or 2 weeks later or at time of disbudding. This second spraying is especially recommended for tall cultivars. With some fast-growing cultivars and especially during summer months a rate of 0.50% (36 ml/3.8 liters) may be necessary. The following tabulation should help simplify mixing B-Nine (however, mixing recommendations by the manufacturer should be followed):

Solution (%)	Amount of B-Nine to be mixed in 3.8 liters of water (ml)	ppm
0.25	190	2500
0.40	304	4000
0.50	380	5000

When B-Nine is applied too close to disbudding, pink flowers have a tendency to fade. Some white-flowered cultivars become cream-colored.

A-Rest is a relatively new plant growth regulator that is very effective in reducing internode elongation of pot mums. It is usually applied when new shoots are 2 to 3 weeks old and not over 15 cm long. It is effective either as a spray or a soil drench. Where bark is used as a soil amendment the effectiveness of A-Rest tends to be reduced when applied as a drench.

Phosfon is still being used by some growers, particularly in Europe. It can be used as a soil or pot treatment, but it is not commonly used because of the uncertainty of results. Phosfon is a persistent chemical and soil or pots once treated have been noted to retain retarding characteristics on succeeding crops that are planted in them. This is not a problem to a commercial grower who sells the container with the plant.

It is impossible to give a blanket statement on use of any growth retardant. There are several things that can affect effectiveness of growth regulators. The growing schedule, vigor of plants, time of year, and reaction of the cultivar are factors. Each grower will have to observe growing conditions and utilize growth retardants to their best advantage for his/her operation.

B. Flowering Stage

1. Photoperiod

Chrysanthemum morifolium is classified as a short-day plant, although flowering is controlled by length of the dark period. The plant remains vegetative and continues to grow without producing flowers under long days (daylength is 14.5 hours or longer). When days are less than 14.5 hours flower buds are initiated, but flower buds do not develop until the daylength is less than 13.5 hours. Some cultivars will vary slightly from this critical photoperiod, but these times will work for most commercial cultivars.

A grower can have complete control over flowering by manipulating the hours of darkness a plant receives. This can be done by using normal daylengths, by lighting, by shading, or by a combination of these. Lighting is used to keep plants vegetative when natural daylengths are short and shading with blackcloth is used to get plants to flower when daylengths are too long.

a. Lighting.   Lighting is done between September 1 and March 31 to keep plants vegetative and is usually applied to stock plants year-round, primarily as insurance. The number of weeks that pot mums are lighted is usually determined by how fast the plants grow and whether they are tall, medium, or short growing plants. Lighting, shading, and planting schedules are usually furnished by major chrysanthemum propagators or suppliers. Before scheduling a pot mum crop this type of scheduling guide listing the specific cultivar being grown should be consulted.

There are two types of lighting used, continuous lighting or cyclic lighting. With continuous lighting, at least 7 to 10 fc of light intensity is required to prevent premature budding. For a bench 1 to 1.2 m wide, use 60-W incandescent lights spaced 4 feet apart and 2 to 3 feet above the plants or use 100-W bulbs spaced 6 feet apart and 2 to 3 feet above the plants. When lighting, precaution must be taken to prevent light drift to those plants in a flowering program.

Many growers use flash or cyclic lighting to prevent premature flower initiation of the potted chrysanthemum. Artificial light may be supplied for 20% of the normal lighting period or 6 minutes for each 30 minutes using a minimum of 7 fc of light. Instead of lighting consecutively for 4 hours, a total of 48 minutes of light spread over a 4-hour time period will provide comparable results.

b. Shading.   During spring and summer months days are longer than the critical photoperiod of 13.5 hours. To develop flower buds on pot mums, at least 12 hours of darkness is required for each 24-hour period. A good grade of black sateen cloth or black polypropylene is required to prevent penetration of more than 2 fc of light. Shading should be practiced daily until flower color develops. Failure to shade each day results in delayed flowering and taller plants, but some growers do skip pulling black cloth on Saturday nights.

The no-light or dark period should be 12.5 hours long for best results, but this creates two problems in greenhouse operations. The first is a time problem for getting the covering and uncovering done by employees, whose normal working hours are from 8:00 A.M. to 4:30 or 5:00 P.M. The second is a problem of heat buildup under black cloth or plastic, particularly in the summer. The first problem can be worked out by either extending the dark period or having someone to do the shading at the proper times. The second problem, heat buildup, can be avoided by covering after the potential solar load has decreased a significant amount. This would mean delaying shading until after 6:00 P.M. standard time (7:00 P.M. daylight saving time). An alternative would be to provide positive air movement (fan and pad cooling) through the plant area under the shade material. It is not very easy to do this alternative and still maintain the desired level of darkness, but it can be done and is strongly recommended for southern growers.

Plants can be shaded by manually pulling shade cloth over the plants or by mechanizing the procedure. A time clock can activate the drive mechanism to open or close the shade at preset times. During the hot summer the mechanized shading is ideal because shade cloth can be pulled at 6:00 or 6:30 P.M. and reopened after dark to reduce plant temperature. The automated system can recover the plants around 5:00 A.M. and then reopen at 8:00 A.M. This helps to prevent a heat buildup and eliminates heat delay and damage to plants.

c. After Lighting.   Some recent research indicates that many cultivars flower successfully when shaded for 35 days, followed by long days. Since many cultivars do not respond to such treatment, growers are cautioned to try "after lighting" only on a trial basis.

2. Scheduling

Scheduling or timing can be modified by changing temperature and fertilizer practices as well as lighting. There are various schedules designed to grow plants of a certain height. Height desired will depend on the market. The standard height is for the plant to be 2 to 2½ times as high as the pot. Propagators and distributors have suggested schedules that growers can follow but these schedules are for average conditions. Each grower will have to adapt this schedule to his/her particular growing conditions.

C. Response Groups

Commercial varieties are divided into response groups that refer to the number of weeks from start of short days until flowering. A 9-week cultivar takes 9 weeks from start of short days, whereas an 11-week cultivar takes 11 weeks from start of short days to flowering. The most common response groups are the 9-, 10- and 11-week cultivars for use in a year-round schedule. In the South some response groups will flower in less time than in northern areas.

D. Temperature Effects

Temperature can really affect the growing schedule of a pot mum crop. When night temperature exceeds 27°–29°C, many cultivars do not flower in the allotted time. There are at least three possible ways to combat heat delay. The first method is to grow cultivars that have less tendency for heat delay. The second is to cover plants later in the evening and uncover later in the morning. During the hottest months it would be well to cover at 9:00 P.M. and uncover at 9:00 A.M. In addition, it would be advisable to use cloth instead of plastic, since cloth will allow for some air exchange. The third is to air-condition the greenhouse, using a method similar to the fan and pad system of cooling.

A minimum night temperature of 17°C should be maintained to ensure proper flower development. Lower temperatures will result in uneven flowering, if flower initiation and development do occur.

A low night temperature of 13°–15°C provided during the final 2 to 3 weeks results in pink shades for many white-flowered cultivars. A low temperature finish for cultivars, however, intensifies flower color.

E. Cropping Tips

In scheduling, enough time should be allowed before pinching so that enough new growth will be made to result in about 10 leaves below the pinch. Short-growing cultivars usually require at least 1 week of long days after the pinch in order to provide for the additional stem length. Short days for the tall-growing varieties are started about a week before the pinch to reduce height at which the plants are finished. This is called a "delayed" pinch, as it occurs after the start of short days. It must be remembered that chrysanthemums do not grow as rapidly in cool, dark weather as in sunny, warm weather. Therefore, it usually takes more long days during the cool, dark winter months.

F. Garden Mums

Certain cultivars can be flowered as spring pot plants without shade or lights. Garden cultivars make good Easter and Mother's Day items because the plants can be cut back and planted outside as the flowers deteriorate. These plants will usually flower again in the fall and for several years thereafter.

For growing spring flowering garden mums, rooted cuttings should be potted around the first of March. A soft pinch is made about 2 weeks after potting. The plants will not require any supplemental lights or shade. The temperature must be kept at 16°C until flower buds are set. Then the temperature can be dropped to 10°C for the remainder of the growing season. Some cultivars require pinching of center buds although others do not. They can be grown in 7.5- to 15-cm containers, but are usually grown in the smaller containers with a close bench spacing. Better-quality plants will result if some space is provided between containers.

G. Single-Stem Pot Mums

Some growers are planting large-flowered mum varieties and growing them single-stem in 15-cm or larger pots. These plants are not pinched. This type of pot mum produces fewer but much larger flowers and makes an entirely different quality plant for special sales. Market demand will vary, but these plants usually sell best during winter and spring holidays. Some growers even grow cut mums in this manner.

H. Year-Round Program

In a year-round program, a specified quantity of pots is produced throughout the year. The potential production is about four pots per $\frac{1}{3}$ m² of bench area per year. Space required for a year-round program will vary according to the number of pots produced. A medium-size grower will produce approximately 1000 15-cm pots each week. When plants are first potted, under mist and light, they can be spaced pot to pot. This spacing would require about 183 m² of bench area. When the plants are moved to their final spacing of 40 cm² per pot, this will require approximately 4270 m² of bench space for short days until the plants flower.

A small grower may want to produce 50 pot mums every other week. He will need about 130 m² of bench space, a good minimum program for a small retail grower.

I. Disbudding

Disbudding is the process of removing immature flower buds, which are not desired on the chrysanthemum stem, to provide for either a small number of large flowers or a larger number of smaller flowers. Most pot mums are disbudded to remove lateral flower buds so the plants will be more attractive and uniform and have larger flowers. Usually with the daisy types and some others the terminal bud is removed so the lateral buds will develop and provide for numerous, small flowers. With certain cultivars that are grown as pot plants, no disbudding is required.

Disbudding should be done as soon as the buds can be easily rolled out between the thumb and forefinger. If disbudding is done too early the terminal buds or stem may be damaged. If done too late, however, it will result in later flowering, smaller flowers, and longer stems. The bud and pedicel should be completely removed, with no stubs remaining on the stem.

IV. CONTROL OF INSECTS, DISEASES, AND PHYSIOLOGICAL DISORDERS

A. Insects

Control of insect pests on pot mums is a major problem. In addition to using insecticides and miticides, growers should control weeds around their greenhouses. These weeds may harbor insects that will then move into the growing area. Pesticides should be applied, before enormous insect populations infest the crop. A grower should inspect his crop daily so that insects will not become a problem. Most insects feed on the lower sides of the leaves, so the grower should especially examine these areas and be certain the undersides of leaves get sprayed with the pesticide.

Pesticides to control certain insects are constantly changing. For recommended pesticides against a specific insect on a certain crop, the local county extension agent or the Agricultural Cooperative Extension Service should be contacted.

The following are insect pests on pot mums.

Aphids are sucking insects less than 3.2 mm long. There are various kinds and colors. Aphids disfigure young growth and can be difficult to eliminate. Corn Earworms feed on the flower bud and petals of the open flower and also consume large amounts of young, tender foliage.

Cutworms are usually associated with cutting off plants at the soil line; however, some species eat the foliage or flowers.

Cyclamen mites are usually found at the very tip of the stem, but they are too small to be seen with the naked eye. These pests are generally recognized by the damage they do. They cause malformation of new growth and sometimes cause a bronzing color on young foliage.

Foliar nematode is a microscopic eelworm that must have a film of moisture on the leaf to move from one plant to another. It enters the leaf through damaged areas and stomata. After it enters the leaf the foliage dies, leaving a wedge-shaped brown area between leaf veins. Keeping foliage dry prevents foliar nematode from spreading.

Grasshoppers eat leaves, stems, and flowers and do much damage in a short time period.

Larvae of leaf miners tunnel through the foliage between the upper and lower epidermis, making irregular, light-colored patterns in the leaf. Injury to foliage causes it to be unsightly and decreases market value. With a serious infestation, some leaf drop can occur.

Leaf rollers are small caterpillars that chew the underside of the foliage and leave the upper epidermis, which dries, causing a parchment-like appearance. They cause leaves to roll, then form a web, and later emerge as moths.

Loopers, commonly known as cabbage loopers, damage pot mums by eating holes in young leaves and by injuring the tender growing point.

Mealybugs are soft-bodied, sucking insects with white cottony masses that cover the gray pests. They are usually found in leaf axils and feed on sap in leaves and stem.

The chrysanthemum midge makes galls on foliage and stems. Inside the galls are larvae that feed for about 28 days before they emerge to mate and repeat the cycle.

Slugs and snails eat foliage, leaving ragged holes, and occasionally attack the flowers. They feed at night but their slime trails will often reveal their presence.

Sowbugs are common greenhouse pests that usually feed on decaying organic matter. They often become so plentiful that they eat the bases of stems on newly planted cuttings.

Spider mites are a serious pest to pot mums because they suck the juices from the leaves and cause a light mottling of the leaves. Mites are very small and usually can not be seen with the naked eye. Reproduction is rapid, and a single female can have over one million descendants in a month at a temperature above 21°C. They also acquire resistance to organic phosphate insecticides.

Spittle bugs are rarely a pest on pot mums, but they may sting the young growth and cause minor disfiguration. A frothy white mass reveals that this pest is around.

Symphylids tend to stunt plant growth when they injure root systems.

Tarnished plant bug damages the plant by puncturing the stem. This can cause excessive branching and sometimes blindness in a stem. It also feeds on foliage, causing small, grayish dead areas in the leaf and often wilting of leaf tips. It is, however, usually not difficult to control.

Termites can sometimes be a problem in wooden benches with wooden legs. They sometimes bore into stems of plants, causing wilting.

Thrips are slender sucking insects, just visible to the eye, and infest foliage, developing buds, and open flowers, primarily during the spring and sometimes in mid-fall. They rasp the foliage and flowers and cause light-colored streaks on foliage and brown or light streaks on flowers.

Whitefly can be a pest on pot mums. The nymphs suck the juices of the leaves and in large quantities can damage the plant.

B. Diseases

There are two basic ways that diseases can be controlled. First is prevention, and it is the most effective and most economical. By knowing what factors cause or contribute to the disease, one can remove or prevent them. The second is use of an eradicant, usually in the form of a chemical to control, kill, or prevent the disease organism from reoccuring or attacking a healthy plant.

There are several procedures that can prevent or control diseases besides use of chemicals:

1. Keep foliage dry, because most fungi and bacteria require several hours of free moisture for spores to germinate.
2. Provide good air circulation. This will reduce free moisture on foliage.
3. Remove weeds growing around the greenhouse.
4. Remove and destroy severely affected plants, or at least move them to an area where they will not infest other plants.
5. Select cultivars that have more resistance to disease problems, although presently there is not much difference among cultivars.
6. Provide for good drainage and do not keep the growing medium too wet.
7. Make sure the growing medium has been properly pasteurized.
8. Prevent recontamination by cleaning all equipment, containers, and supplies that are taken into the growing area. Disinfectants such as sodium hypochlorite or LF 10 can be used.
9. Avoid overwatering. Wait until the medium is dry before rewatering.
10. Thoroughly clean the growing area when a crop is removed and before another crop is brought into this area.
11. Purchase disease-free cuttings from cultured stock.

Chrysanthemum diseases can be divided into three general groups according to causal agents: fungi, bacteria, or viruses. The following are some diseases found on pot mums.

Ascochyta blight or ray blight is derived from the fact that symptoms most often appear on ray florets of a developing flower, causing the flower to be malformed. In severe cases this disease may progress down the flower stem and onto the leaves. The leaf symptom may resemble septoria leaf spot and stem injury will be similar to that caused by tarnished plant bug. This organism germinates only if free water is on the plant.

The first symptom of bacterial wilt is wilting of young plants or new vegetation. When stems are cut open they are filled with a soft, jellylike, usually red, mass. In most cases the plants will wilt as the disease progresses and will eventually die. Sometimes symptoms do not appear until the flower begins opening. Plants with this disease should be removed and burned.

Botrytis is sometimes called gray mold because of its appearance. It causes flower petals to turn brown and appear water-soaked. It is also found on foliage. It is most troublesome when the air is very moist. Dry air, adequate spacing, and removal of infected plant parts can reduce severity of botrytis.

Fusarium is generally more prevalent under warm temperature conditions, and affects stems, which are usually decayed, with brown streaks extending upward. The plants wilt at time of flowering.

Powdery mildew is prevalent under high humidity conditions, especially in dark weather. The white powdery fungus on leaves is unsightly and in severe cases can also affect the stem.

Pythium is a root and stem rot that affects some cultivars more than others. It can be distinguished in that rotting usually starts at root tips. In severe cases it will destroy the root system, causing a retardation in growth and eventually killing the plant. Good drainage in a pasteurized medium can reduce losses.

Rhizoctonia stem rot usually occurs when cuttings are planted too deep or overwatered. It is distinguished from pythium rot in that decay originates near the soil surface and may rot plants upward from this infection at the soil line.

Root-knot nematodes cause gall-like knots on roots and usually stunt the plant severely. Clean stock and pasteurized media are the best preventative measures for root-knot nematodes.

Rust appears as small blisters that erupt, exposing the chocolate-brown spores on lower leaf surfaces.

Sclerotia is easily recognized by the dense, white, wet-appearing, cottony, masslike growth in which are found hard, black seedlike objects. This disease is rarely found on pot mums unless it is cool and very moist inside the greenhouse. Usually proper ventilation prevents this organism from being a problem.

Septoria leaf spot is sometimes known as black spot, and is caused by a fungus that causes irregular black blotches on the foliage. These blotches usually become brittle in the center and sometimes fall out. Affected leaves may turn yellow and die. Some cultivars are more susceptible than others.

Stunt is a slow-moving virus disease that severely dwarfs plants and causes fading of pink, red, and bronze flower cultivars.

Verticillium wilt, sometimes known as Siedeivitz disease, is a vascular fungus that affects most cultivars. Leaf margins turn yellow and eventually wilt or dry up. This yellowing and wilting begin at the base of the plant and work up the stem. The wilt may affect one side of the plant more than the other. Verticillium seldom kills plants. Cuttings taken from stock plants that have verticillium generally have the fungus within them.

Yellows is a virus that affects the flower. A portion of the flower is yellow-green rather than its normal color and flowers are usually much smaller than normal. This virus is spread by aphids and leafhoppers that feed on infected plants and transfer it to healthy plants.

C. Physiological Disorders

Pot mums can have a lot of problems that are related to cultural practices and that are not disease- or insect-related. Physiological disorders can be divided into a number of categories.

1. Plants Too Short

Plants too short can be caused by several factors, such as poor root growth, insufficient nitrogen in the early growing stages, failure to provide enough long days, or excessive use of growth retardants.

2. Plants Too Tall

Plants too tall can be caused by too many long days, crowded conditions, growth in a shaded location, and temperatures that are too high.

3. Uneven Flowering

Uneven flowering may be a problem, especially in winter, because of cool nights, as flower buds fail to form at night temperatures below 16°C. Stray lights striking plants during the long dark periods can also cause this problem.

4. Not Enough Shoots

The development of too few shoots usually occurs during the first 2 weeks after cuttings are potted. Some problems that may develop during this time that could cause fewer shoots to develop are poor root growth, cool night temperatures, very dry air, too hard a pinch, and insufficient nitrogen.

5. Malformed Flowers

Malformed flowers can be caused by diseases or insects, by poor control of daylength or fluctuation of short days and long days, or by poor-quality shade cloth or light leaks around the shadecloth.

6. Poor Growth

Poor growth can be caused by not enough sunlight in very dark weather, too much fertilizer, too low a pH, poor drainage, overwatering, and lack of fertilizer. Growers need to keep records of their cultural practices and also some notes on extreme weather conditions. These records will help determine the causes of poor growth.

7. Crown Buds

The major distinction between crown buds and terminal buds is that leaves beneath a crown bud are strap-shaped, while leaves beneath a normal terminal bud are lobed. Vegetative shoots can emerge around a crown bud if the causative factor is not corrected. Crown bud formation results from failure to apply blackcloth consistently, time clock failure, insufficient light intensity during the lighting period, or application of blackcloth too late after pinching.

8. Bract Buds

During the warm summer months it is not unusual to find overdeveloped individual floret bracts on some cultivars. Bract buds may develop when day and/or night temperatures exceed 27°C, blackcloth is removed too soon, blackcloth is worn or leaks light, or incandescent lighting is not uniform over the plants.

9. Sun Scald

Sun scald develops when high temperatures and high light intensities cause rapid evaporation of moisture from flower petals and is often confused with botrytis blight. Sun scald and botrytis blight are easy to distinguish because the former occurs on younger petals at the center of the flower and the latter infests the tips of older petals. Botrytis will often affect petals damaged by sun scald. Sun scald can be prevented by supplying a light shade over the plants as color starts to show on the flower buds, and by proper selection of cultivars for certain areas or time of the year.

V. HANDLING OF FINISHED PRODUCT

A. Harvesting

Pot mums are ready to go to market when flowers are about one-half to fully open. Many growers send pot mums to market as soon as flower petals begin to unfold but before flowers are fully open. These earlier harvested plants do not usually obtain as large flower size as those that are allowed to mature before shipping. For local sales, mature flowers are much more desirable.

There are no standard grades for pot mums. It is usually thought that the plant should be 2 to 2½ times as tall as its pot, bushy with dark green foliage, and free of insects and diseases, with a full, white, actively growing root system. There should be a minimum of 15 flowers, and a plant with 20 to 25 flowers of good size would be much more desirable.

B. Packing

Pot mums are packaged by inserting them in paper or polyethylene sleeves to protect them during shipment. Pots are then placed upright in cardboard boxes in groups of six. Plants are sold individually and the grower does not have to do any special packaging or wrapping. For retail sales, pots are sometimes wrapped in aluminum foil to improve their appearance.

C. Storage

Pot mums can be stored up to 2 weeks without reducing quality. The cooler the storage temperature, the longer the pot mums will keep. When storing pot mums for 2 weeks, the temperature should be approximately 4°C. Pot mums will not store very long if the temperature is above 13°C.

If pot mums are stored in light they will retain their quality longer than when stored in the dark. A minimum of 50 fc should be provided. Beneficial effects of light can be achieved by raising the light intensity up to 400 fc. Light prevents foliage from becoming depleted of its food materials.

D. Shipping

Pot mums are usually grown within 100 miles of the market because of weight of the pot and growing medium. This weight almost prohibits greater distances because of shipping costs. This is the reason pot mums are a good local crop. A grower usually does not have to worry about some grower a long distance away shipping pot mums into his area. Pot mums will hold up well in shipment, if handled properly.

E. Keeping Quality

The most important factor in ensuring long life for the pot mum is related to maintenance of an active growing root system during the latter part of the growing season. Major causes of root losses are overwatering, high soluble salts, and root-rot organisms. All of these can be controlled and will provide pot mums that will last much longer and better satisfy the consumer.

Nutrition also affects keeping quality of pot mums. Too much nitrogen fertilization at the end of the growing season will decrease the keeping life. Many growers withdraw complete fertilization during the last 2 weeks of growth. If a nitrogen fertilizer must be applied late in the growing season, research has shown that nitrate nitrogen does not lower the keeping life as much as an ammonium nitrogen fertilizer. Therefore, for optimum keeping life, nitrogen fertilization must be controlled carefully.

F. Consumer Care of Product

A pot mum can be held at the retail outlet for up to 2 weeks and still be attractive and salable if it is cared for properly. The retailer should do the following to ensure a long life for the pot mum:

1. Remove the pot mum from the shipping box as soon as it arrives, and water it thoroughly. Most plants are shipped on the dry side to prevent crushing and excessive weight.
2. Remove broken or bruised blossoms and leaves.
3. Display the plant to show off the bright flowers to the fullest.
4. Do not overcrowd pot mums in the display or storage area.
5. Water plants as they need it. Do not let them wilt, but also do not keep the medium too wet. Let the medium dry out between waterings.

6. Keep plants out of direct sunlight.
7. Do not set plants in front of an air conditioner or heat ventilator.

To increase sales of pot mums, the customer should be taught how to take care of the plant. Proper watering procedures must be explained. The plant should be placed in a bright location in the home, but not in direct sunlight, and should be kept out of drafts. Broken or crushed leaves or flowers should be removed. Most pot mums will not require fertilizing in the home.

REFERENCES

Anonymous (1971). *Proc.—Pot Chrysanthemum Sch., Hortic. Ser., Ohio Agric. Res. Dev. Cent.* No. 378, pp. 1–28.
Ball, V., ed. (1975). *In* "Ball Red Book " (V. Ball, ed.), 13th Ed., pp. 275–290. Geo. J. Ball, Inc., West Chicago, Illinois.
Gloeckner, F. C., and Company, Inc. (1977). "Gloeckner, 1977 Chrysanthemum Manual," pp. 74–83. New York.
Laurie, A., Kiplinger, D. C., and Nelson, K. S. (1969). "Commercial Flower Forcing," 7th Ed., pp. 392–399. McGraw-Hill, New York.
Staff of The Liberty Hyde Bailey Hortorium (1976). "Hortus Third," pp. 266–269. Macmillan, New York.
Tayama, H. K., and D. Kiplinger, D. C. (1968). "Pot Chrysanthemum Culture," Leafl. No. 142. Coop. Ext. Serv., Ohio State Univ., Columbus.
Waters, W. E., and Conover, C. A. (1967). "Chrysanthemum Production in Florida," Bull. No. 730, pp. 3, 5, 6, 11–15, 19–64. Agric. Exp. St., Univ. of Florida, Gainesville.

11

Gloxinias, African Violets, and Other Gesneriads

R. Kent Kimmins

I. INTRODUCTION

There are approximately 125 genera and over 2000 species in the Gesneriaceae. Of this number about 300 species have been cultivated. These species have a worldwide distribution, including tropical America, Spain, Asia, and Africa. They are found on limestone cliffs, in rain forests, on the forest floor, and on mountains over 15,000 feet high (Burtt, 1967).

Individual species range in size from plants less than 5 cm tall (*Sinningia pusilla*) to small trees (*Cytrandras* species). The flowers range from only slightly bell-shaped to those with a long tubular or cylindrical shape.

For the commercial grower the two most important members of the Gesneriaceae are *Sinningia speciosa* (florist's gloxinia) and *Saintpaulia ionantha* (African violet). Other gesneriads that are increasing in popularity are the *Episcia* hybrids, miniature *Sinningia,* and hybrid *Streptocarpus.*

Specific details pertaining to the culture of several gesneriad genera are mentioned in the text, and are summarized in Table I.

II. *SINNINGIA SPECIOSA*—FLORIST'S GLOXINIA

Sinningia speciosa was first named *Gloxinia speciosa* in 1817 by Conrad Loddiges, an English nurseryman, after he had studied the new plant from Brazil. Although incorrect, the name gloxinia has remained in use.

Sinningia speciosa has one or more stems with paired leaves. The blade of the leaf is large and very pubescent. The nodding flowers are approximately 6 cm wide and usually pale lavender. The flowers are produced on plants 10 to 15 cm tall, although the size may be variable. The type species came from Brazil. Most florists' gloxinias are of the convariety *fyfiana,* the name originating

Table I

Environmental Conditions Suitable for Growth and Flowering of Major Commercial Gesneriads

		Cultural conditions		
	Water	Temperature (°C)	Light (klx)	Humidity (%)
Gloxinia	Moist	21	25.8	50–70
African violet	Moist	21	10.7–11.8	70
Episcia	Moist	18	11.8	75
Miniature Sinningia	Moist	21	10.7–11.8	70
Streptocarpus	Dry slightly between waterings	16	12.9	70

Fig. 1. *Gloxinia.*

from *Gloxinia* × *fyfiana* (Moore, 1957). The red cultivars are commercially most popular (Fig. 1).

Through hybridization and selection, gloxinias may be single-or double-flowered with colors ranging from pure white through pink, lavender, and red, to dark purple. Popular single cultivars include 'Improved Red Velvet,' with large ruffled cardinal red flowers; 'White Velvet,' pure white; 'Pink Velvet,' a soft pink with a more deeply colored center; and 'Royal Velvet,' a deep purple. Popular double-flowered cultivars are 'Royal Red,' a deep red; 'Royal Frosted Red,' a deep red with white edge; 'Royal Pink,' a pure light pink; and 'Royal Frosted White,' a pure white.

For commercial production, plants are grown from seed. A plant with a large single head of flowers can be produced using this method in approximately 6 to 7 months in a 12.5-cm pot. There are some specialists who produce and sell seedlings. The seeds are sown on a soilless medium and placed under intermittent mist in a shaded house with 21°C night temperature for rapid germination. When the seedlings are large enough to handle, they are transplanted into 6-cm pots. Plastic or clay pots may be used successfully. A soilless medium or a mixture including peat moss, sand, perlite, and vermiculite can be used. When the seedlings are approximately 3 months old, they are shipped to the grower, where they are transferred into the final pot (Ball, 1975).

The seedling production procedure can also be used by the retail or wholesale grower if warm greenhouse conditions are available and space is not limited. When the seedlings are transplanted by the grower, it may be easier to transplant the seedlings into flats as soon as they can be handled.

The plants should be spaced 2 to 4 cm apart. When the foliage of the plants begins to touch, the plants should be transferred to either a 12.5- or 15-cm azalea pot. Plastic or clay pots may be used with success.

The media for growing the transplanted seedlings can be soilless mix or a soil mixture such as a 1 : 1 : 1 (light organic soil, peat moss, and coarse sand or perlite, on a volume basis). A pH of 6.0 should be obtained by adding dolomitic limestone to the medium. Plants may be potted slightly lower in the pot for a more compact finished plant, should be spaced on 30- to 40-cm centers, and watered immediately. It is very important that water not be allowed to remain on the foliage. A fungicide can be added with the water to prevent disease from injuring roots or leaves, especially if the plants are to be shipped.

The production of gloxinia is best achieved in a greenhouse with a 21°C night temperature. Optimum growth can be obtained with a radiant flux of 25.8 klx, as noted by Mastalerz (1977). The growing medium should never be allowed to become dry. Tube watering and mat watering methods have been used with excellent results. The fertilization program should begin immediately after transfer to the finishing pot. A complete fertilizer (15–15–15 or 20–20–20) should be used for vigorous growth. Small (1976) recommended 1.1 kg of a 15–15–15 analysis fertilizer per 378 liters of water. With sufficient natural light and temperature, additional lighting should not be necessary. If, however, the night temperature is 16°C additional lighting may be beneficial to reduce the chance of flower delay. Good results are obtained with 100-W incandescent bulbs spaced 120 cm above the plants and turned on 4 to 5 hours each night. The additional lighting seems most effective immediately after the seeds have germinated. When plants are well budded, a more uniform plant may be obtained by removing the first two flower buds as soon as color is evident.

The use of chemicals to control plant height might be necessary, particularly in the summer when heavy shade to reduce temperature causes stretching of the internodes. Small (1976) noted that B-Nine, at a diluted strength of 0.10% solution, worked well when applied 1 to 2 weeks after transfer into the finished pot. He noted that late application would not shorten the plant enough to be a quality plant. Sydnor *et al.* (1972) found that B-Nine applications resulted in compact plants and that flower color was intensified on pink cultivars used in the study.

Fortunately there are few pests or diseases that are problems on gloxinias. Red spider mites, cyclamen mites, and loopers or army worms are the main pests. Crown rot (*Pythium* species) and stem rot (*Phytophthora* species) are the primary diseases affecting gloxinias. The best controls are adequate spacing and ventilation and proper watering.

Since certain cultivars of gloxinias have large brittle leaves, they are not easily shipped. Most growers either sell their plants locally, or only ship cultivars that are small enough to place in sleeves.

When the florist or retailer receives the plants, they should be unpacked immediately and watered. Damaged leaves should be removed. The plants should then be placed in bright light, but not in direct sunlight. If they are not placed in the proper light conditions, many of the buds will turn brown and fall from the plant. The soil should be kept moist, but the plant should not be overwatered. The consumer should provide light and water requirements similar to those noted for the retailer.

III. *SAINTPAULIA IONANTHA*—AFRICAN VIOLET

The African violet is currently considered one of the most popular hobby plants in the United States (Fig. 2). Hybridizers have greatly improved the selection of cultivars that are available to the consumer.

The African violet was discovered in 1892 in Tanga, East Africa, by Baron Watler Von Saint Paul, governor of German East Africa. Hermann Wendlan, a prominent German botanist, named the genus *Saintpaulia* in honor of its discoverer.

The African violet was first introduced into the United States about 1894. George Stumpp, a New York florist, purchased two plants in Germany and brought them to the United States. In 1927 Walter L. Armacost of the Armacost and Royston Nursery in Los Angeles imported the first seed into the country from England and Germany, thus starting the first commercial production of the African violet in the United States. The first plants named and offered for sale in this country were grown by Armacost and Royston in 1936. Several of the original cultivars are still available today.

African violet plants have very short stems with leaves arranged in a rosette. The blades of the leaves vary from ovate-elliptic to round and are usually hairy.

Fig. 2. *Saintpaulia.*

The margins may be entire or may be undulate. The flowers are produced in a cyme with five to ten flowers per cyme. The calyx is five-lobed. The corollas are usually blue, blue violet, bicolored, or nearly white.

Currently, most of the hybrid African violets developed in the United States are progeny of the original ten named cultivars introduced in 1936. Some of the original cultivars are still available, such as 'Blue Boy' and 'Neptune.' New cultivars are now being introduced, including the 'Ballet,' 'Rhapsody,' and 'Optimara' series. These cultivars have been bred to continually produce large, long-lasting flowers that stand well above the foliage.

New forms of African violets are causing increased interest among some breeders. The miniature African violets and the trailing African violets, both standard- and miniature-sized, are becoming popular. There are not too many cultivars at this time, but with additional breeding color variation will probably equal that of the standard types.

African violets can be grown from seed, but only a few cultivars will come true from seed. A flowering plant can be produced from seed in about 10 months. The seed should be sown on a screened soilless medium or milled sphagnum moss (Laurie et al., 1968). A 21°C night temperature with high relative humidity should be maintained. When the seedlings are large enough to handle they should be transplanted to 10-cm plastic or clay pots, and filled with a highly organic well-drained medium. Many of the soilless media provide excellent conditions for active growth. If a soil medium is used it should be steam-pasteurized. The seedlings should be grown under 10.7 to 11.8 klx of light.

The principal commercial method for propagating African violets is by leaf petiole cuttings. Mature leaves that are firm and a good green color are selected. The petiole is cut at a slant to about 2 to 3 cm long. A rooting hormone may be used to promote more rapid root formation. Flats are filled with a pasteurized rooting medium. Many different materials are used by growers. A few of the media include peat moss and sand; peat moss, sand, and vermiculite; and vermiculite alone. The leaves are stuck into the prepared flats so that leaves do not touch each other. The flats are then placed in a shaded 21°C greenhouse. In approximately 8 to 12 weeks the plantlets will be ready to be transplanted. They are separated from the leaf when they are about 2 cm tall and are potted into a 6-cm pot and then later shifted to a 10-cm pot. From a cutting to a finished 10-cm pot takes 8 to 10 months (Fisher, 1971).

Many media are used for finishing seedlings or rooted plantlets. Soil mixtures that are loose, well-drained, and high in organic matter are often suggested for African violets. Soil mixtures should be pasteurized before use. Many new soilless mixtures are now available for growing violets, and excellent results may be obtained if the mixture does not stay too moist (Wilson, 1970).

The plants should be potted at the same depth they were growing in the propagation medium. Clay or plastic azalea pots may be used for African violets. Plastic pots are preferred by some growers because the pots are clean and lightweight for shipping.

African violets grow most rapidly at a night temperature of 21°C. Unlike other plants, African violets seem to grow best with a warmer night temperature and a cooler day temperature. Went (1957) noted that night temperatures of 20°–23°C and a day temperature of 14°C produced excellent growth.

The light intensity for good growth and flowering is 10.8 to 11.8 klx (Stinson and Laurie, 1954). If the irradiance is above 13.9 klx chlorophyll destruction will occur, causing the leaves to turn yellow. African violets can be grown very satisfactorily under artificial lights. Kiplinger (1953) noted that better growth and flowering occurred under artificial light compared to natural light. Stinson and Laurie (1954) found that excellent plants were grown under daylight fluorescent lamps at 6.5 klx for 12 to 18 hours daily. Hanchey (1955) noted that plants can be irradiated continuously if the radiant flux is reduced to 4.3 klx. It was also found that the time to produce a 10-cm pot of African violets could be reduced using artificial light (Kiplinger, 1953).

Media in which violets are grown should be kept moist, but not soaked, at all times. If the plants dry to the wilting stage there can be root damage. This is one reason that most media contain large amounts of organic matter. The method of watering is very important in preventing damage to the foliage. Elliot (1946) and Poesch (1940) noted that a leaf and water temperature differential of 8°C could cause foliage damage, called ring spot (Fig. 3). The damage can

Fig. 3.   Cold water damage to African violet foliage.

be prevented if water temperature is similar to leaf temperature. In the production of 10-cm pots some growers are now using the tube or mat watering systems to avoid foliage damage.

Most growers use water-soluble fertilizers for African violets. Shanks (1960) noted that African violets are very sensitive to high soluble salt levels. He suggested that a solution with only 75 ppm each of nitrogen and potassium was sufficient for good growth. A fertilizer with higher phosphorus (15-30-15) is recommended by some growers. Small (1976) recommended a 15-15-15 fertilizer at a rate of 1.1 kg/378 liters of water.

In areas where greenhouses cannot be ventilated in cold weather, carbon dioxide injection can be beneficial. Shaw and Rogers (1964) noted that plants grown in greenhouses with 1000 ppm CO_2 produced greater dry weight and were of a salable size sooner than plants grown in an environment where additional carbon dioxide was not injected.

Cyclamen mite and mealybugs are two of the most common pests on African violets. Cyclamen mites cause a distortion in the leaves in the center of the crown. Leaves appear curled and dwarfed. Mealy bugs can become a problem if not treated before they multiply and are most noticeable in the axils of the leaves and on the undersides of the leaves. Both of these insects can be treated with chemical sprays. Directions on the labels of recommended chemicals should be followed.

Another pest which can attack African violets is nematodes, both root-knot and foliar. The best practice is to use steam-pasteurized growing media, pots, and benches. Infected plants should be discarded.

Botrytis blight can be a problem if there is a lack of good air circulation. The best control is adequate spacing of the plants, no syringing of the foliage, and good sanitation practices in the greenhouse.

Crown rot and root rot (*Pythium* species) can also be problems. Again, pasteurization of growing media, pots, benches, and other equipment are the primary methods of control.

African violets are usually shipped in 6- or 10-cm pots. The plants may be put in plastic or cellophane sleeves and then packed in boxes with cardboard divisions with one plant per opening. Plants also may be wrapped with cylinders of corrugated cardboard and packed side by side in the shipping carton. In either case, plants should be watered prior to packing. Care must be taken not to break the foliage while packing the plants. Plants may be shipped by air or motor freight, often depending on the size of the order and shipping distance.

On arrival the plants should be unpacked immediately and watered, and then should be placed under artificial lights to keep the flowers in good condition until the plants are sold.

The consumer should provide adequate natural light or use artificial light to keep the plants growing and blooming. The soil should be kept moist without getting water on the foliage. A complete fertilizer should be applied at one-half the recommended rate monthly. Old flowers should be removed to prevent disease problems.

IV. *EPISCIA* SPECIES—FLAMING VIOLET

Episcias are native to Central and South America and the West Indies. There are ten species of *Episcia* in cultivation. Three of the species, *Episcia cupreata, Episcia lilacina,* and *Episcia reptans,* have been hybridized and many of these hybrids are now commercially grown (Fig. 4).

The bulk of the hybrids originated from *Episcia cupreata,* a native of Colombia and Venezuela. It has copper-colored leaves 8 to 10 cm long and 6 to 8 cm wide. Hybrids of *E. cupreata* have foliage ranging from 3 to 20 cm long. Flowers of all the *E. cupreata* hybrids are orange red with a yellow throat, and are sometimes spotted (Dekking, 1974).

Episcia lilacina is another of the other major species used in hybridizing. Originating from Costa Rica, Nicaragua, and Panama, this species has large lilac/blue flowers, often with a lemon yellow throat. Foliage is a very dark bronze with a lighter green venation, and is approximately the same size as that of *Episcia cupreata.*

Fig. 4. *Episcia.*

The third *Episcia* species used in hybrization is *Episcia reptans,* which originated from Colombia, Brazil, and French and British Guiana. Foliage is dark green with pale green and silver markings. Flowers are deep red with a pink throat.

Some of the most colorful and popular cultivars available are 'Chocolate Soldier,' 'Painted Warrior,' 'Tri-Color,' 'Pinkiscia,' 'Chocolate and Cherries,' 'Mrs. Fanna Haaga,' and 'Filigree.' Another hybrid from two different species is *Episcia Cygnet (E. dianthiflora × E. puntata).*

For most *Episcia* hybrids, propagation is by stolons. The most desirable plants are obtained when young, medium-sized, 5- to 7.5-cm stolons are used for cuttings. All but the top four leaves should be removed. If the leaves remaining are too large, the bottom two leaves may be reduced in size. The stem should be cut about 1 cm below the node. Rooting powder should be applied. Cuttings can be stuck in pots or rooting flats, filled with any well-drained medium which has been pasteurized. Various media have been used successfully, including sphagnum peat moss, perlite, vermiculite (1 : 1 : 1, v/v/v); sphagnum peat moss, charcoal, and vermiculite (1 : 1 : 1, v/v/v); or only coarse vermiculite. Cuttings should be maintained at a relative humidity as near 80 to 90% as possible or under intermittent mist. Cuttings should be shaded until they are rooted, which should occur in 2 to 3 weeks. After rooting, fertilization should begin, using a dilute solution of a complete fertilizer. If the cuttings were grown in flats, they should be potted into 6- to 7.5-cm pots after rooting. Other methods of propagation, such as leaf petiole cuttings as described for African violets, have the disadvantage of not producing plants true to the parent leaf variegation.

As the plants grow they should be shifted into larger pots, depending on the final use of the plants. Some growers make hanging baskets and others sell the plants in small pots or just shift them to 10-cm pots for later sale. Regardless of the final use, the plants should be spaced so the leaves do not touch each other.

Hybrid *Episcia* plants produce the best growth at temperatures above 18°C. Some hybrids will die if the temperature is below 16°C. The optimum temperature in the greenhouse is 18°C at night and up to 32°C during the day, with a 75% relative humidity. At higher temperatures, a higher humidity is required to prevent plant injury. At the higher temperatures and higher humidity it is very important to have good air circulation to prevent mildew.

The light intensity for most episcias should be about 11.8 klx. Dekking (1974) reports that light green and silvery-leafed forms will bloom in light intensities less than those needed to produce flowers in African violets. The darker-leaved forms need higher light intensities to produce flowers.

The growing medium should be kept moist and no cold water should be allowed to touch the foliage. The use of tube or mat watering system would be of great value in growing these plants. Fertilization at rates for African violets have been suggested by Small (1976).

Episcias are not very susceptible to diseases and pests. Cleanliness is still the best preventative for disease control. With a high growing temperature and high humidity mildew can be a problem without adequate air circulation. Disease can also become a problem if the plants are crowded.

Mealybug can be troublesome, especially if plants are crowded. Mites can be difficult to control if they get started on several plants. Chemical sprays should be used to control these two pests. Root-knot nematodes can cause damage, but if the benches, pots, and media are pasteurized there should be no problem.

Crown rot can also affect episcias. Control recommendations are the same as for other diseases and nematodes.

Most episcias are grown in 6- to 7.5-cm pots and shipped to retailers. Packing and shipping procedures are similar to those used for African violets. Care of plants on arrival at the florist shop or other retail outlets is important. They should be unpacked, watered immediately, and placed in a warm well-lighted location. Consumer care should be similar to that for African violet.

V. *SINNINGIA PUSILLA* AND THE MINIATURE HYBRIDS

Sinningia pusilla is the smallest of all the gesneriads. It was introduced into the United States in the late 1950s, although it was collected and described in the early nineteenth century (Shalit, 1976). The leaves are about 1.5 cm long. Stems are very short and almost not apparent. The 2-cm tubular lavender-to

Fig. 5.   Miniature *Sinningia* in 10-cm pot.

lilac flowers are displayed above the crown of the foliage. *Sinningia pusilla* has contributed its small size to many of the miniature hybrids, none exceeding 12.5 cm in height (Fig. 5). Some of the most popular cultivars are *S. pusilla, S.* 'Dollbaby,' *S.* 'Little Imp,' *S.* 'Bright Eyes,' *S.* 'Snow Flake,' and *S.* 'Coral Baby' (Stewart, 1975).

Propagation of these plants can be by seed or tubers. The species can be obtained from seed but the hybrids must be started by tubers to obtain the true cultivars. A well-drained medium similar to that used for African violets can be used. Plants should be spaced so leaves do not touch each other on adjacent plants. The plants can be grown to blooming size in 6- to 7.5-cm pots and should not be crowded in too small a pot (Katzenberger, 1975).

The miniature plants grow well if the night temperature is not over 21°C. A light intensity of 10.8 klx is adequate for good foliage and flower production. These plants produce excellent flowers under fluorescent lights for 12 to 16 hours daily.

Most of the miniature hybrids should be grown at a relative humidity of approximately 80%. The growing medium should remain moist (Progebin, 1975). If the plants dry out, they will become dormant. With many of the hybrids the dormant period may only be for a few weeks or for several months. The plants should be fertilized at the recommended rate for African violets every 7 to 10 days.

The same pests and diseases affecting African violets can be found on miniature sinningias. Similar control measures should be followed.

Most of these plants are grown and shipped in 6-cm pots, ready for immediate resale. When the plants are received they should be unpacked, watered, and then placed under artificial lights.

When the plants are sold, the consumer should provide conditions similar to those suggested for African violets.

VI. STEMLESS *STREPTOCARPUS* HYBRIDS

Most of the *Streptocarpus* plants available to growers and consumers today are hybrids of many different species. In England in 1947 the cultivar Merton Blue was crossed with *Streptocarpus johannis*. The result was a cultivar with excellent characteristics called 'Constant Nymph.' In 1952 the Weismoore hybrids were introduced in Germany. Radiation treatment was applied to obtain additional 'Nymphs' in the 1960s. Additional work has provided a broader color range of *Streptocarpus* plants by breeding within the two groups.

Most of the hybrids produce leaves to 30 cm long in an asymmetric clump, similar to a rosette. The flower stalks carrying many flowers arise from the center of the clump, producing a well-balanced potted plant (Fig. 6).

Some of the best known hybrids are the 'Nymph' series, including *S.* 'Constant Nymph,' *S.* 'Netta Nymph,' *S.* 'Mina Nymph,' *S.* 'Purple Nymph,' and a sport called *S.* 'Maasen's White.' Other popular individual cultivars are 'Diana,'

Fig. 6. *Strepocarpus.*

'Fiona,' 'Karen,' 'Marie,' 'Paula,' 'Tina,' and 'Helen.' Also becoming available is the 'Ultra Nymph,' with larger flowers similar to the Weismoore hybrids.

Most commercial propagation is by leaf sections to maintain the cultivars. A blooming plant can be obtained in about 6 months. A mature leaf with the midvein removed is one of the methods recommended (Murphy and Southall, 1976). The two pieces are placed lengthwise in propagation media (vermiculite, or a 1:1:1 sphagnum peat moss, perlite, vermiculite by volume with 7.01 gm dolomitic limestone per liter of mixture). As many as 20 plants may be obtained in this manner from one original leaf. The medium should be kept moist and at 21°C. Plantlets appear in about 2 months and are large enough to transplant in about 3 months.

Streptocarpus plants can be grown in a well-drained medium. Unlike the medium for the African violet, this medium should not be acidic. Some growers suggest no peat moss at all, but others use a mixture such as (1 : 1 : 1) peat moss, vermiculite, and perlite or (1 : 1 : 1) peat moss, soil and perlite. Azalea pots should be used because of the shallow root systems of these plants. Plastic pots 6.0 or 10 cm in size are usually used to grow *Streptocarpus*. Pots should be spaced so the leaves on adjacent plants will not touch as the plants grow.

Temperature is extremely important in *Streptocarpus* culture. Most of the hybrids will do poorly if the day temperature exceeds 27°C. Night temperatures of 16°C produce satisfactory results. A very high humidity is not necessary, and 50% humidity is sufficient.

Streptocarpus plants will produce flowers if they have a light intensity of about 12.9 klx, slightly higher than that for African violets. With sufficient light, hybrids bloom throughout the year.

The growing medium for these plants should be allowed to dry slightly between waterings. These plants are easily overwatered and thereby injured. The plant roots can be easily damaged by overfertilization. Balanced fertilizer should be used at one-half the recommended rate every 2 weeks for vigorous blooming plants.

Crown rot (*Pythium* species) can be a problem on *Streptocarpus* if the plants are overwatered. Mealybugs can become a problem if they get started. Since Malathion can damage the foliage, other pesticides should be used.

These plants are handled and shipped like African violets. The consumer should be advised about overwatering the plants and about the temperature requirements of the plants.

REFERENCES

Ball, Geo. J., Inc. (1975). "The Ball Red Book," 13th Ed. Geo. J. Ball, Inc., West Chicago, Illinois.

Burtt, B. L. (1967). Gesneriads as a family. *Plants Gard.* **23,** 54–57.

Dekking, M. (1974). Episcias: The peacocks of the gesneriad family. *Gesneriad Saintpaulia News* **11,** 26–34.

Elliot, F. H. (1946). Saintpaulia leaf spot and temperature differential. *Proc. Am. Soc. Hortic. Sci.* **47,** 511–514.

Fisher, E. (1971). Violet culture in depth. *Gesneriad Saintpaulia News* **8,** 22–35.

Hanchey, R. H. (1955). Effects of fluorescent and natural light on vegetative and reproductive growth in *Saintpaulia. Proc. Am. Soc. Hortic. Sci.* **66,** 378–382.

Katzenberger, R. (1975). Miniatures in a greenhouse. *Gloxinian* **25,** 21.

Kiplinger, D. C. (1953). Fluorescent lights and saintpaulias. *Ohio Florists' Assoc. Bull.* **290,** 2.

Laurie, A., Kiplinger, D. C., and Nelson, K. S. (1968). "Commercial Flower Forcing," 7th Ed. McGraw-Hill, New York.

Mastalerz, J. W. (1977). "The Greenhouse Environment," pp. 165, 175. Wiley, New York.

Moore, H. E., Jr. (1957). "African Violets, Gloxinias, and Their Relatives." Macmillan, New York.

Murphy, H. T., and Southall, R. M. (1976). How to get gesneriads started the lazy way. *Gesneriad Saintpaulia News* **13,** 19–21.

Poesch, G. W. (1940). Tests show *Saintpaulia* ring spot caused by cold water. *Florists' Rev.* **87,** 21.

Progebin, L. (1975). Miniatures—Culture of miniature *Sinningias. Gloxinian* **25,** 23–26.

Shalit, P. (1976). *Sinningia pusilla. Gloxinian* **26,** 12.

Shanks, J. B. (1960). Some suggestions on planning a fertilizer program. *Md. Florists* **68,** 4–8.

Shaw, R. J., and Rogers, M. N. (1964). Interactions between elevated carbon dioxide levels and greenhouse temperatures on the growth of roses, chrysanthemums, carnations, geraniums, snapdragons, and African violets. *Florists' Rev.* **135**(3491), 19, 37–39.

Small, E. J. (1976). "Hybrid Gloxinia Seedlings." Earl J. Small Growers, Inc., Pinellas Park, Florida.

Stewart, M. (1975). Specialize with miniatures. *Gesneriad Saintpaulia News* **12,** 27.

Stinson, R. F., and Laurie, A. (1954). The effect of light intensity on the initiation and development of flower buds in *Saintpaulia ionantha. Proc. Am. Soc. Hortic. Sci.* **75,** 730–738.

Sydnor, T. D., Kimmins, R. K., and Larson, R. A. (1972). The effects of light intensity and growth regulators on gloxinias. *HortScience* **7,** 407.

Went, F. W. (1957). "The Experimental Control of Plant Growth. Chronica Botanica, Waltham, Massachusetts.

Wilson, H. Von P. (1970). "Helen Von Pelt Wilson's African Violet Book." Hawthorn Books, New York.

12
Poinsettias

James B. Shanks

I. INTRODUCTION

A. History

The common name poinsettia given to *Euphorbia pulcherrima* [(Willd. ex. Klotzsch) Euphorbiaceae] is a result of its introduction into the United States by Joel Robert Poinsett who, finding these plants growing on the hillsides near Taxco, Mexico, sent plants to his home in Greenville, South Carolina, shortly after assuming the office of first U.S. ambassador to Mexico in 1825. Ecke and Matkin (1976) indicated that poinsettias had been cultivated by the Aztecs and were used by Franciscan priests who had settled in the area around Taxco, Mexico, during the seventeenth century in a nativity procession known as the Fiesta of Santa Pesebra. Other common names ascribed to this plant include descriptive terms such as Christmas flower, Christmas star, painted leaf, and Mexican flameleaf. Poinsettias were grown commercially for Christmas sales in the latter part of the nineteenth century, and both propagation stock and young plants were offered for sale in the trade magazines of the early twentieth century.

The Ecke firm in Encinitas, California, became intimately associated with the commercial production of poinsettias through their shipments of field-grown, dormant stock throughout the United States and elsewhere in the world. This firm began when Albert Ecke, newly arrived from Switzerland, began the field production of cut flowers (including the poinsettia) for local sales. By 1910 the Eckes were specializing in poinsettias, having collected the available varieties from local sources where they were being grown as outdoor ornamental plants. Paul Ecke assumed management of the firm in 1919, at which time they listed for sale to the trade "best early and late outdoor grown, strong 1- and 2-year-old poinsettia plants" for propagation purposes. The extensive use of these field-grown stock plants began in 1927 when the Ecke firm made its first carload lot shipments to eastern greenhouses.

B. Current Status

The commercial production of poinsettias has steadily increased in the United States and Canada in recent years. Over 20 million pots were produced in the United States in 1977 with a wholesale value of $47 million, of which the leading states were California, Ohio, Texas, Illinois, and Michigan. Canadian production, centered mainly in Ontario, was approximately 2.5 million pots in 1977.

Poinsettias have become an important flowering pot plant elsewhere in the world, particularly in Western European countries, where they are also produced for the Christmas season. In Norway alone there is an estimated production of two million pots of poinsettias for 1978 or one plant for every two persons. In areas where the poinsettia is not intimately associated with this holiday it may be produced at other times of the year and there is a limited production in Eastern European countries. South of the equator, the natural flowering period is during the short days of June rather than December.

C. Flowering Habit

The flowers in the genus *Euphorbia* are borne in a small cuplike structure known as a cyathium, from which a single pistillate flower emerges as a three-parted pistil on a short pedicel followed by many staminate flowers, each consisting of but a single pollen-bearing anther. In *E. pulcherrima* the first few cyathia form only staminate flowers. The cyathia themselves may bear appendages that in the poinsettia appear as yellow-edged nectaries. In other species the appendages may be petaloid, giving each cyathium the appearance of a single flower as in the "two-petaled" cyathium of *E. milii* (crown of thorns) or the "five-petaled" cyathium of *E. fulgens* (scarlet plume), the popular cut flower euphorbia of some years ago.

The showy structures of the poinsettia are the petaloid leaves (bracts), which form in conjunction with the formation of the cyathia. Under long-night conditions the vegetative apex begins the formation of a cyathium and stem growth is terminated. The last two internodes do not elongate and the upper three leaves typically become bractlike. The buds in the axils of the upper three leaves begin to grow but immediately form another cyathium subtended by a bract. Another axillary bud begins to grow, forms another cyathium and bract, and the process is repeated with the resulting flower display consisting of three main branches bearing bracts and bractlike leaves around a central cluster of cyathia. Poinsettia bracts may be red, pink, white, or variegated but, since they are leaflike rather than being true petals, these showy parts have a long life span, producing a very satisfactory and long-lasting indoor decorative plant.

D. Development of Cultivars

Cultivars such as 'Early Red' used in pot plant production early in this century were mostly selections from those found growing outdoors in southern California by the Ecke firm and were essentially wild types having the characteristic tendency to abscise leaves under stress conditions.

One of the first cultivars to retain leaves until sale at Christmas was 'Oak Leaf' which, with its slightly improved mutation 'Ruth Ecke,' further mutated to a series of partial and complete tetraploids with variations in height, branching, and bract color. This group, developed and named by the Eckes, became the basis of greenhouse poinsettia production from approximately 1930 through 1965. The bracts of tetraploid cultivars were thicker and had the advantage of extending in a horizontal plane instead of drooping as did diploid bracts. 'Ecke White,' a seedling introduced in 1945, was the first cultivar to retain leaves and bracts really well under home conditions, and a sport to a partial tetraploid known as 'New Ecke White' was introduced in 1958. A number of breeding programs were begun in the United States in the 1950s in an effort to improve poinsettia cultivars, particularly in their ability to retain leaves and bracts. 'Ecke White' was frequently used as a parent.

A red seedling from Mikkelsen's, Inc., having stiff stems and the ability to retain both leaves and bracts under adverse conditions, was first tested in 1961 and made available to the trade in 1964 as 'Paul Mikkelsen.' This cultivar underwent successive mutations to pink-bracted, variegated, and white-bracted forms as well as to the tetraploid 'Mikkel Swiss' and together became the most important group of poinsettias by 1967. Another type of mutation from 'Paul Mikkelsen' was found in 1968 by the Rochford firm in England. This self-branching cultivar designated 'Mikkel Rochford' again mutated to pink-bracted, variegated, and white-bracted forms and to several degrees of tetraploidy.

In 1967 a red seedling known as 'Eckespoint C-1,' having very strong stems and large horizontal bracts, was introduced by Paul Ecke, Inc. This and its pink-bracted, variegated, and white-bracted forms became the important "premium" cultivars of 1970. A more recent mutation of 'C-1,' found in the Baltimore greenhouses of Fantom & Gahs and known as 'Jingle Bells,' had red bracts with pink blotches (Fig. 1).

The Norwegian firm of Thormod Hegg and Sonn introduced a poinsettia with self-branching and long-lasting characteristics at the Sarpsborg Exhibition in 1967 as 'Hegg 67,' later renamed after Thormod's first grandchild, Annette. 'Annette Hegg' was introduced into the United States in 1968 by Paul Ecke, Inc., which has also distributed the many pink, variegated, white, tetraploid, and other mutations of the original plant developed by the Hegg firm. Gregor Gutbier of West Germany has also released seedling selections with the self-branching characteristic which were first distributed in the United States by Paul Ecke, Inc., in 1977.

Stewart and Arisumi (1966) studied the steps in mutation of bract color in 'Paul Mikkelsen.' The red pigments were principally the anthocyanins chrysanthemin and antirrhinin and were found concentrated in the epidermal cells with much lesser amounts in the internal parenchyma cells. The pink sport 'Mikkel pink' resulted from a periclinal chimera in which the bract epidermis (arising from the L-I histogen layer) contained no anthocyanin. The variegated bract (pink with white margin) resulted when the nonpigmented cells of L-I origin replaced normal L-II cells leaving only the lightly pigmented cells of L-III origin to produce the pink area in the center of the bract. The lack of any pigment-producing cells from any histogen layer of the white-bracted form resulted in plants that bred genetically true for white. Pink-bracted mutants may breed as homozygous red, whereas adventitious buds from root or stem produce red bracts.

Stewart found genetically pink plants, in which all cells of the bract contained anthocyanins in lesser amounts, to have a uniform or smooth pink appearance rather than the uneven color of some of the previously studied chimeral pink

Fig. 1. Multiflowering plant of 'Jingle Bells,' a mutation of 'Eckespoint C-1.' (Courtesy of Paul Ecke Poinsettias, Encinitas, California.)

bracts in which the color appears more intense at the veins of the bract. More recently, the cultivars 'Mikkel Pink Rochford,' 'Eckespoint C-1,' and 'Annette Hegg Dark Red' have produced mutants with uniformly pink bracts not having the darker veins of their earlier counterparts.

E. Changing Cultural Practices

Changes in the characteristics of the cultivars have had a tremendous impact upon the production techniques and the popularity and sales of poinsettias for indoor decoration. Increased leaf retention dictated a change in the production of cuttings from dormant, field-grown stock plants to the use of young vegetative plants for stock plant purposes. These are produced throughout the year by the specialists. Most cultivars are patented and propagation rights are granted for propagation for self-use and for the sale of young material to others. Many producers of blooming plants no longer propagate their own plants but buy young plants from the propagating firms or from the poinsettia specialists disseminating the cultivars. Royalties are paid on plants used for propagation purposes and on plants to be sold for decorative use.

The older cultivars were precisely timed to be ready for sale just before Christmas so as to be satisfactory for home decoration through the Christmas season. Many growers delayed flower initiation for up to 2 weeks by photoperiod adjustment. Long-lasting cultivars need not be delayed in flowering, and sales of poinsettias have been earlier each year as consumers realized their long-lasting qualities. The common practice of placing a fern in the center of each pot has disappeared, because the fern is no longer needed to hide leafless poinsettia stems. Cultivars with strong stems do not need to be staked and tied, as was common with older types. The more flexible bracts of newer cultivars no longer need the special wrapping formerly done to protect tetraploid bracts from bruising. Such plants are more adaptable to packing and shipping long distances.

Self-branching cultivars have ushered in a new era in which "multiflowering plants," resulting from the planned pinching of a single plant, have supplanted to a great extent the use of many individual unbranched (standard) plants in a single container. Simplified cultural techniques, improved leaf retention, and earlier flowering have also made possible the production of poinsettias under cloth protection in frost-free areas.

The production of poinsettias for commercial decoration and for sales promotions in shopping malls, stores, and other businesses has created a demand for plants in late November or early December. These plants must be started earlier and flowered sooner by the use of black cloth. The pink-bracted, variegated, and white-bracted forms are extremely satisfactory decorative plants for any time of year. Attempts to popularize the poinsettia as a spring flowering plant or as an outdoor summer bedding plant have so far failed in North America, where the plant has been so intimately associated with the Christmas season.

II. GROWTH REQUIREMENTS AND PLANT RESPONSES

A. Flowering

Flowers are initiated in poinsettias whenever there is an uninterrupted dark period of approximately 12 hours or longer and other conditions are suitable. A 12-hour dark period occurs under natural conditions from about October 5 until March 10 throughout the Northern Hemisphere, where poinsettias are produced (Hawaiian Islands and Mexico City at latitude 20° N to Northern Europe at latitude 60° N). The actual date of flower initiation in the fall is modified by the age of the shoot undergoing initiation. Older shoot tips apparently have more natural flowering stimulus and may initiate flowers as much as 10 days earlier (September 25) whereas plants recently propagated or pinched will be equally delayed in initiation.

The optimum temperature for flower initiation will vary with cultivar but most present-day cultivars initiate flowers readily at 15°–20°C. Flower initiation will be delayed at a warmer temperature under the natural photoperiods of the fall. Satisfactory flower initiation will take place at night temperatures up to 28°C provided the dark period is also longer, as would be provided by blackcloth shading from 1700 to 0800 hours daily to produce a 15-hour dark period.

Poinsettias are quite sensitive to red radiation although of short duration or of low intensity, and any such radiation received during the dark period may delay flower initiation and development. Light pollution from sources containing relatively small amounts of red light, such as high- or low-pressure sodium lamps or certain fluorescent lamps, is not as detrimental to flowering as from incandescent lamps, although any light source should be considered danger-ous. Light pollution from street lights, buildings, or passing vehicles must be eliminated by black shades for successful poinsettia production. Moonlight, containing little red radiation, does not interfere with flowering.

Lengthening the dark period for early flower initiation in the fall need not be continued after October 10, and where spring poinsettias are being produced the practice is resumed by March 1. The optimum dark period for flower de-velopment is considered to be longer than for flower initiation. Development will be retarded and chlorophyll may form, giving the bract a greenish color, if long nights are not continued until bract maturity.

It may be desirable to retain poinsettias in a vegetative state for propagation or for continued growth in fall and winter months. The interruption of the dark period from September 15 to March 25 by 2 hours of 100 lx of incandescent light should ensure a vegetative condition in all cultivars.

Adequate mineral nutrition and sunlight are essential for flowering and bract development. Conditions of reduced sunlight, such as might occur with plants on gutter benches, under hanging baskets, or by the failure to remove light reducing materials by the end of summer, may delay flower initiation and the rate of development. Any nutrient deficiency, particularly one of nitrogen or phosphorus, will delay initiation and the proper development of the bract dis-play. Adequate fertilization just prior to and during the flower initiation period is beneficial.

B. Light

Poinsettias are high light intensity plants and maximum sunlight should be provided at all times unless some reduction is dictated by the necessity to reduce summer heat. Light reduction during the summer may produce unde-sirably long stems and large leaves. If used, any light-reducing material should be removed by September 1 in northern greenhouses or by October 1 in southern areas.

Successful crops of poinsettias are produced only in those greenhouses with good light transmission qualities, although they are grown under cloth protection in frost-free areas. High light conditions produce the best bract development and lower greenhouse temperatures can be maintained under conditions of good sunlight. Growth of poinsettias is slow under the low light of winter in northern greenhouses, but excellent quality plants may be finished in the high light conditions of spring. Other growing procedures must be regulated in accordance with the amount of light available for photosynthesis, especially temperature and the fertilization and watering practices.

C. Temperature

The poinsettia is a warm-temperature plant and when provided with adequate sunlight grows vigorously in the range of 20°–30°C with the lower limit for growth close to 12°C. Greenhouse temperature may become considerably higher than 30°C during the summer unless an efficient ventilation system, evaporative cooling, or some light reduction is used. Temperatures above 35°C may result in reduced growth, thin stems, small leaves, slower rooting of cuttings, and malformed growth. Poinsettia stock plants may be taken outdoors in midsummer to recover sooner than waiting for the cooler night temperatures of late summer.

The optimum growing temperature decreases with the reduction in available light in mid-fall, and during the heating season best plant growth is at 14°–18°C. The optimum greenhouse forcing temperature for the production of poinsettias has been considered to be close to 17°C with daytime temperatures being permitted to rise to 22°–25°C. Present energy costs dictate that this be reduced as much as is consistent with finishing a quality crop in time for Christmas sales. Several approaches to reduced temperatures have been suggested:

1. Elevated day temperature to make possible a lower night temperature and still maintain growth. This approach has not been as effective as anticipated and has resulted in lowered plant quality in current trials.

2. The use of a lower night temperature (10°–12°C) for most of the night but raising the temperature to a growing temperature (17°C) for the most critical period of the night. Present trials have indicated that this approach is feasible and that the most efficient use of the higher night temperature would be in the 5-hour period of 1700 to 2200 hours.

3. Initiate early flowering to permit bract development under the more favorable light and naturally warmer temperatures of early fall, after which plants are held at the lowest acceptable temperature until sale. Starting short-day treatment on September 10 with a minimum greenhouse temperature of 10°C and a

natural daytime rise to 23°C has produced high-quality plants in Maryland (latitude 39° N).

It is desirable to reduce the night temperature for many red-bracted cultivars as they approach maturity to enhance bract color. Early flowering plants may be held in the greenhouse at a minimum night temperature as low as 10°C until they are sold without reduction in quality, provided a low relative humidity can be maintained.

D. Soils and Watering

Poinsettias may be produced in a wide range of potting media provided minor adjustments are made in watering and fertilizing practices. An ideal medium would have some permanence, substance, and weight for plant stability as well as water and fertilizer retention to simplify care in the greenhouse and in the home. Drainage and aeration are essential to permit heavy watering and to ensure a healthy root system and vigorous top growth. Three-component mixes are common, and standard media contain equal parts by volume of soil, peat moss, and perlite or peat moss, perlite, and vermiculite. Composted barks and leaves may be freely substituted for any of these materials while other satisfactory ingredients may be locally available.

Poinsettias grow freely in slightly acid soil (pH, 5.5–6.5). Ground limestone is added to adjust acidity and to supply calcium and magnesium. The medium should contain enough additional limestone to neutralize the acid residue of the fertilizer to be used. Many premixed fertilizers have their potential acidity given in terms of the amount of limestone required to neutralize a given amount of applied fertilizer. Soilless media should contain 4.5-7 kg limestone/m^3 of medium.

Complete fertilizer formulations may contain expressed or implied amounts of minor elements, but it is frequently advisable to add a slowly available source of minor elements to the medium. This is most important in a soilless medium or if native soil is low in certain minor elements. Fritted trace elements are frequently used at 100 gm/m^3 of medium. Thorough mixing is essential. The major nutrient elements can be conveniently supplied in a soluble or slow release form to the soil surface after planting. Soluble trace element mixtures are available but must be used with caution to avoid overdosage.

The final requirement is the elimination of all weeds and potential pathogens by heat or appropriate chemical treatment followed by protection of the prepared medium from recontamination.

Poinsettias are grown in many styles of containers made of clay, plastic, or wood. Three-quarter depth pots are used to reduce plant height and provide a wide base. Plastic containers are satisfactory for use with any well-drained medium, but styles with both bottom and lower side drainage openings are preferred.

Different growth patterns may develop from different methods of watering. Overhead sprinkler systems have been used in the summer production of cuttings but are wasteful of water and the cuttings produced may be soft. Poinsettia foliage should be kept dry except during rooting, when cuttings are commonly kept turgid by intermittent mist.

The use of a hose and breaker may add greatly to labor cost, but excellent growth is possible with an experienced person applying the water. The most common method of applying water is by a trickle tube to each pot. Automation of tube watering is possible either with timers adjusted to water for 5 to 15 minutes once or twice each day, depending upon the judgment of the grower, or by the use of a plant set upon a weight activated switch ("Moist-Scale") to sense the change in soil moisture from moist to dry.

Poinsettias watered by capillarity, such as placing pots on a wet mat, are never subjected to moisture changes or moisture stress. Such watering produces lush growth with a bright leaf and bract color, but the plants will require more space, and more attention must be given to height control. Periodic applications of liquid fertilizers may be made as with hand-watered plants.

E. Soil Fertility

Poinsettias require high levels of the major elements, particularly nitrogen, but are intolerant of high soluble salts in the soil solution, so soil fertility levels must be carefully controlled. Some cultivars show nutrient disorders more frequently than others.

The basic requirement of high nitrogen with moderate phosphorus and potassium can be met by the application of all-soluble, complete fertilizers in liquid form either on a scheduled basis or by constant injection into the water supply. Adjustments to a predetermined program may be dictated by changing environmental conditions and the stage of plant growth, as indicated by soil or tissue analysis, or based upon plant appearance and grower judgment.

Plant appearance can be a valuable guide to determining adjustments in the fertilizer program and in correcting nutritional problems:

1. Light or yellow green mature leaves denote a need for more nitrogen whereas the interveinal yellowing of mature leaves may indicate lack of magnesium. Both deficiencies may be corrected with additional applications of nitrogen containing fertilizer as more nitrogen permits the uptake of more magnesium.

2. Dark green stunted growth may be the initial result of phosphorus deficiency followed later by leaf yellowing. Low phosphorus nutrition of stock plants has been associated with slower rooting of cuttings, particularly at higher temperatures. Use of a complete fertilizer at all times is recommended.

3. Pinpoint necrotic areas or marginal yellowing and browning of lower leaves usually indicate a deficiency of potassium and frequently are seen at the

conclusion of the propagation period where growth has taken place under mist without fertilization or without roots to absorb fertilizer. Use only a complete fertilizer and continue applications during propagation.

4. Marginal or tip dieback of lower and middle leaves is associated with fertilizer accumulation and soluble salt injury to roots. Plants may wilt on sunny days even though the soil remains moist. Soluble salts may result from premixing slow-release fertilizers with potting media. More thorough watering will avoid accumulation after initial flushing to remove excessive soluble materials.

5. Yellowing of leaf margins followed by marginal browning and yellowing of lower leaves may indicate ammonium toxicity (Boodley, 1970). The ammonium ion may accumulate if soilless medium becomes more acid than a pH of 5.5 and a high proportion of nitrogen has been applied in the ammonium form. Use adequate lime and change to a low ammonium formulation in late fall.

6. Necrotic, pinpoint speckling of upper leaves and misshapen young leaves indicate a deficiency of zinc usually attributed to overliming or alkaline soil. Marginal yellowing followed by a more general yellowing and marginal browning of upper mature leaves indicates molybdenum deficiency, which may occur in acid soils deficient in this element or in soilless media that have become more acid (Jungk et al., 1970). Proper liming, the inclusion of a slowly available source of minor elements, care in the addition of slow-release fertilizers to the potting medium, sound watering practices, and the development of a practical fertilizer program should ensure the avoidance of nutritional problems.

The periodic fertilizer program is based upon weekly applications of a complete fertilizer in liquid form having a nitrogen concentration up to 750 ppm. Common formulations suitable for poinsettias are 20-20-20 (20-8.8-16.6 as N-P-K) and 25-10-10 (25-4.4-8.3 as N-P-K). Maximum concentrations containing approximately 750 ppm nitrogen would be 3.6 kg of 20-20-20/kl or 3 kg of 25-10-10/kl. Young plants should receive an application of 20-20-20 shortly after rooting or potting with weekly applications to begin as active growth is resumed, usually within 2 weeks. A young stock plant is usually potted in a larger volume of soil than a flowering plant and the second application should be delayed another week. For most of the growing period a 25-10-10 formulation will provide adequate phosphorus and potassium.

A resin-coated type of slow-release fertilizer may be used in supplementing the soluble fertilizer program to supply special needs. It is convenient to make a surface application of a 3-month release 14-14-14 formulation to poinsettia stock plants (1 tablespoon per plant) 2 weeks before the first cuttings are removed to increase the general fertility and available phosphorus instead of making additional applications of 20-20-20. It may also be advantageous to apply 1 teaspoon of 3-month release 14-14-14 to each 15-cm pot of poinsettias by September 15 (2 weeks before flower initiation) instead of additional 20-20-20 at this time.

Periodic fertilization must be reduced to one-half the former concentration by the onset of low light conditions (usually mid-November) until plants are sold. A change to a formulation containing predominantly nitrate nitrogen may also be made during the late forcing period.

Fewer changes are required in a fertilizer program utilizing soluble fertilizer in the irrigation system since the water requirement of a container-grown plant closely parallels the fertilizer requirement of the same plant. The water at each irrigation should contain approximately 200 ppm nitrogen from the same fertilizer formulations as for weekly application. This would be provided by 1 kg of 20-20-20/kl or 0.8 kg of 25-10-10/kl of irrigation water.

F. Greenhouse Aeration

Substantial growth in greenhouse poinsettias has been observed under conditions of increased carbon dioxide; the plants are frequently taller, which may not be desirable. It is not clear how much of the increased growth is due to the higher temperature and humidity resulting from the lack of ventilation while retaining the carbon dioxide within the greenhouse, rather than to more carbon dioxide.

High humidity leads to an increase in disease problems, promotes excessive stem elongation, and is associated with the physiological disorder known as "crud" resulting from exuding sap. Ventilation of poinsettia houses is essential at all times to maintain a low humidity and normal ambient carbon dioxide concentration as well as for greenhouse cooling on sunny days.

Poinsettias are very susceptible to the volatiles from herbicides and phenolic wood preservatives. Products considered safe for other plants in and around the greenhouse have injured poinsettias. Trifluralin applied under the greenhouse bench, or even outside the greenhouse, has resulted in severe injury to poinsettias growing in the greenhouse. Actual damage from the common air pollutants such as sulfur dioxide or the smog from internal combustion engines is suspected but not well documented. Damage has been demonstrated in controlled fumigation experiments.

G. Growth Regulation

Poinsettias are naturally very vigorous and some control of growth is essential to keep plant height and number of flowering stems appropriate to the size of container. Fortunately, the restriction of root growth in a container is itself a growth control process through the limited root growth, water supply, and nutrition.

The length of the growing period before flower initiation is the basic control over stem length. Early propagated plants will be taller than plants from later propagations, and early floral initiation by blackcloth procedure will produce a shorter plant than plants permitted to flower naturally.

There are normally six to seven unexpanded internodes within the stem tip at the time of flower initiation, and even a late propagated cutting can become too tall if all of these internodes expand to their maximum potential. It is important to provide maximum light intensity, maintain low humidity, avoid high temperatures, and provide adequate growing space at all times to avoid excessive internode elongation.

Guidelines have been developed for the production of the different sizes of poinsettias, although these must be modified for different cultivars, local growing conditions, and market demands. The latest dates for satisfactory production of plants for the Christmas market in the middle latitudes is approximately September 20 for standard and August 25 for multiflowering plants in 15-cm or smaller pots. Additional height for plants in larger containers is obtained by propagation 5 to 10 days earlier for each additional 2.5-cm increase in container diameter (Fig. 2).

The number of flowering stems in a container is determined by the number of individual plants placed in the container for the production of standard plants and by the pinching procedure in multiflowering poinsettias. In the efficient

Fig. 2. Container sizes for multiflowering poinsettias. Upper: 25-cm hanging basket. Lower: 10-, 15-, and 30-cm pots of appropriate height plants. (Courtesy of Paul Ecke Poinsettias, Encinitas, California.)

production of multiflowering plants, self-branching cultivars are permitted to become well established in the final container and to produce the number of leaves equivalent to the number of flowering branches to be produced. The stem tip is removed (pinched) to induce the bud in the axil of each remaining leaf to begin growth if they have not already begun to develop. Thus, for a 10-cm pot only three to four leaves are permitted; up to six leaves remain on a plant in a 15-cm pot; three to four individual plants are placed in a 30-cm container with each pinched to permit six to eight flowering branches. For standard production a 30-cm container should contain up to 15 individual plants.

H. Chemical Growth Regulation

Chemical growth regulators are available that can benefit rooting, promote general growth or branching, or reduce stem length. Some of these may not be presently labeled for commercial use.

Aids in rooting usually are preparations of naphthaleneacetic acid or indolebutyric acid, to be used either as a powder or liquid for the treatment of the basal portion of cuttings. They may be used routinely but are particularly recommended for use in very hot weather or for late season propagation. Preparations of 0.1 to 0.3% in talc or 200 to 500 ppm in water are satisfactory.

There is a potential use for growth-promoting chemicals to overcome the dwarfing effect of cool temperature forcing, to increase the height of short cultivars or to produce taller plants for a special situation, and to delay abscission of leaves, bracts, and cyathia. Trials have demonstrated desirable promotive effects from a foliar spray in mid-October of a gibberellin (GA_3 at 20 ppm or $GA_{4,7}$ at 40 ppm) or the combination of $GA_{4,7}$ with a cytokinin (BA) known as Promalin, at 50 ppm. Abscission in the greenhouse and under home conditions has also been delayed by a spray of BA or of Promalin at 50 ppm in the early bract-forming period.

Although BA has been shown to promote branching in poinsettias, this can be more effectively accomplished by a foliar spray of Atrinal at 2500 ppm 7 to 10 days prior to pinching. The chemical may also be used on stock plants but in any case it must be applied to young vigorous plants before natural branching has begun and while still under long day conditions. The concentration should not exceed 2000 ppm for the cultivar Amy. Atrinal applied to self-branching cultivars without the removal of the stem tip will produce a natural arrangement of flowering branches including the main stem.

A number of situations dictate the use of one of the growth-retarding chemicals registered for use on poinsettias: (1) propagation sooner than desirable; (2) a vigorously growing cultivar being grown in a small pot; (3) growth conditions conducive to stem elongation such as low light intensity, crowding, or delayed flowering by the use of incandescent light for photoperiod manipulation.

The need for one of the growth-retarding chemicals should be anticipated, and plants are treated as soon as the young plants become established and growth commences. The main effect of retarding chemicals is the production of shorter internodes following treatment, although bracts may be slightly shorter. Undesirably small bracts and delayed bract development may result from the use of a retarding chemical on plants of low vigor, application late in the season, or of overtreatment with the chemical.

Cycocel (chlormequat) is registered for application to the soil and provides uniform internode shortening when applied in this way. The use of Cycocel as a foliar spray may lead to temporary leaf yellowing or more severe leaf injury. A-Rest (ancymidol) is registered to be applied either to the soil or as a foliar spray. B-Nine SP (daminozide) is registered for use as a foliar spray but two applications may be required for adequate dwarfing.

Research has shown that ethephon (Ethrel or Florel) was effective in retarding stem elongation in poinsettia and that the best results were obtained by applying 200 ml of a 200-ppm solution to the soil in a 15-cm pot. Other trials have demonstrated that combinations of the retarding chemicals were additive in their effect and that two chemicals could be applied together for greater effectiveness. An example would be combining Cycocel and B-Nine in an effective foliar spray, although such use does not have label clearance.

III. COMMERCIAL PRODUCTION

A. Stock Plants

The commercial production of blooming poinsettias may begin with the receipt of young plants for stock plant purposes from April through June, with cuttings or young plants received in August and September, or with prefinished pots in October and November. All are available from specialists or their licensed propagator–distributors.

Young plants in 5-cm pots or rooting cubes can be obtained in early June, planted in containers of approximately 8-liter capacity, and spaced on 30-cm centers. An alternative is to plant in cut-flower beds on 30-cm centers or four plants across the usual width bed. Young plants obtained sooner must be grown in larger containers and provided with more space. Standard cultivars may be pinched when 20 to 30 cm tall and again at 4-week intervals, with the last pinch being made 5 weeks before cuttings are wanted. A second crop of cuttings can then be obtained in another 4 to 5 weeks. Two leaves are permitted to remain on the plant when the cutting is removed if another crop of cuttings is desired.

Stock plants of self-branching cultivars may be pinched when 30 cm tall or pinching may be delayed until 3 weeks before the last cuttings are to be harvested. A second crop of cuttings or cuttings taken from self-branching plants given a second pinch may have stems of small caliper. These small cuttings may be avoided when self-branching stock is not pinched until late in the season, but slightly fewer cuttings are produced. Cuttings from late-pinched stock are in constant supply through the season and the tip may be rooted as a prepinched cutting as late as September 20.

Stock plants of standard cultivars started in early June should produce up to 50 cuttings per plant, and twice this number can be obtained from a self-branching plant.

B. Rooting Cuttings

Easiest rooting is done by sticking cuttings directly in the regular growing medium in the pots in which they are to be sold and placing them under intermittent mist. Forced air movement will shift the mist pattern, so it is best to have adequate natural ventilation. Low-pressure, moderately fine mist to cover all cuttings should be used at frequencies (usually once each minute) which will prevent any wilting of cuttings. There is little danger of over-misting of cuttings stuck in a loose growing medium except when excessive mist might reduce the temperature below the 21°C optimum for rooting. This seldom occurs until late in the season when bottom heat may be an advantage. Roots form on most cultivars in 14 to 18 days. Rooting can be noted by the horizontal position of leaves. The duration and frequency of misting are gradually reduced until normal watering can supply moisture requirements.

Larger containers call for more than one plant (or cutting) and care in the selection of uniform cuttings to go into each container is important. Another means of gaining plant uniformity within a container is to root cuttings individually in propagation blocks that are then planted in the final container as soon as the cuttings are acclimated. The selection for uniformity is thus delayed about 3 weeks with a savings of space in the propagation area.

C. Scheduling Production

Multiflowering plants of the self-branching cultivars have become the basis for production in many areas. The most popular size has been the 15-cm pot with an increasing use of even smaller sizes. Suggestions for the timing and scheduling of operations are based upon trial and experience in the middle latitudes and may be modified to suit local market demands and growing conditions. Tables I and II may be used as a basis for planning propagation and other operations essential to producing a satisfactory crop. Young plants from a propagator–distributor should be obtained 2 weeks later than the propagation date.

If a standard cultivar is to be pinched it must be done by removing approximately 1 cm of the tip. Pots of 15 cm are pinched at 10 days, 20-cm pots at 20 days, and 25-cm pots at 25 days before the flower initiation date. A well-grown,

Table I

Suggested Schedule for Production of Standard Poinsettias

Pot size (cm)	Number of cuttings per pot	Dates of propagation		Average space requirement [b] (cm²)
		Early flowering [a]	Natural flowering	
10	1	August 25	September 25	400 (20 × 20)
12.5	1–3	August 25	September 25	750 (25 × 30)
15	3–4	August 20	September 20	1200 (30 × 40)
17.5	5–6	August 15	September 12	1600 (40 × 40)
20	8–10	August 10	September 5	2250 (45 × 50)
25	12	August 5	August 25	3000 (50 × 60)

[a]Plants to be given long nights from September 10 to October 5 by covering with blackcloth from 1700 to 0800 hours.
[b]Spacing is indicated in parentheses.

self-branching plant initiates branches autonomously and may be pinched when it reaches the right stage of development, although the same schedule will apply. Cuttings are started earlier to produce a greater number of flowering branches.

Hanging baskets of poinsettias have attained considerable demand because they provide a spectacular display when either suspended or used as a centerpiece. They contain nine to ten individual, pinched plants per 25-cm basket, and although expensive to produce they presumably utilize free space

Table II

Suggested Schedule for Production of Multiflowering Poinsettias

Pot size (cm)	Number of cuttings	Pinch (leaf number)	Dates of propagation		
			Early flowering [a]	Natural flowering	Spring flowering [b]
10	1	4	August 10	September 1	December 20
12.5	1	5	August 5	August 25	December 10
15	1	6	July 31	August 20	December 1
17.5	1–2	8–6	July 25	August 12	—
20	3	6	July 20	August 5	—
25	4	7	July 15	August 1	—

[a]Plants to be given long night from September 10 to October 5 by covering with black sateen cloth from 1700 to 0800 hours.
[b]Cuttings are taken from vegetative stock and kept vegetative by incandescent light until January 20. Natural long nights after that date must be supplemented with blackcloth beginning March 1 for plants to mature in mid-April.

Fig. 3(A-C). Illustration of the construction of a three piece 25-cm hanging basket. (Courtesy of Paul Ecke Poinsettias, Encinitas, California.)

Fig. 3. *Continued*

within the greenhouse as long as they do not reduce the quality of plants on the benches. Cuttings of self-branching cultivars are propagated by August 20, rooted individually in 8-cm pots, pinched to five leaves on September 25, and planted to baskets 3 to 6 weeks later. The three-piece basket, which accommodates six plants in the slots provided around the outside, is most widely used. The upper half of the pot is snapped in place after placing plants through the side slots and three or four additional prepinched plants are planted on the top (Fig. 3).

D. Avoiding Troubles

1. Cultural and Physiological Problems

Most cultural problems are avoided by carefully following the principles already established. Improved poinsettia cultivars are no longer subject to early leaf abscission but are very subject to the many other problems encountered through environment and management irregularities. The grower must always be alert to herbicide or other chemical injury, unbalanced fertility or high salt levels, excessively hot temperature, unnecessary light reduction, and extraneous light pollution during the flowering period.

2. Diseases

Pathogenic diseases of poinsettia occur on the roots, stems, leaves, and bracts. Losses from soilborne pathogens have been significantly reduced by the recognition by growers of the extreme susceptibility of the poinsettia plant and the importance of clean media, containers, and benches. As an additional precaution, the use of a chemical deterrent (fungicide) is recommended to reduce the disease potential should the growing medium become recontaminated.

a. Root and Stem Pathogens.

The most common root and stem pathogens (Fig.4) are listed below:

Rhizoctonia solani results in a shreddy-rot of the basal portion of the stem as well as the roots. It is more serious under conditions of hot weather and moderately high moisture. Soil applied deterrents are benomyl and PCNB.

Pythium ultimum becomes most serious at high moisture levels and, in severe cases, results in the sudden collapse of the entire plant owing to the destruction of the root system. This water mold is deterred by diazoben and ethazol.

Thielaviopsis basicola is a relatively slow-growing fungus that produces the typical late season, black root rot and basal stem lesions accompanied by a lack of growth and plant wilting. A strain of the fungus adapted to the poinsettia formerly caused severe losses but it has become relatively unimportant with the clean growing practices of recent years. Benomyl is a deterrent.

b. Leaf- and Stem-Infecting Organisms.

Under proper cultural conditions there should be little problem with leaf- and stem-infecting organisms. However, infection by the following must be guarded against:

Botrytis cinerea, the gray mold fungus, may be serious under mist or where high-humidity conditions persist, as in some plastic houses, the cool greenhouse, or during mild but rainy fall weather. The edge or tip of a leaf may deteriorate and turn brown while red bracts develop purple margins or necrotic spots. Scheduled foliar applications of benomyl to stock or pre-flowering plants have increased resistance. Highly susceptible cultivars should not be grown.

Erwinia carotovora, if present in the propagation medium, can result in the rapid soft rot of cuttings under mist, particularly in hot weather. Sanitation procedures must be relied upon for prevention.

Rhizopus species are common fungi, and may infect poinsettia plants under conditions of crowding, poor light, high temperature, and moisture on the foliage from overhead sprinkling. More precise environmental control is suggested.

3. Insects

Poinsettias in the greenhouse are most frequently infested by the greenhouse whitefly (*Trialeurodes vaporarium*) or by spider mites (*Tetranychus urticae*). Infestations by aphids, soft scales, or mealybugs may also occur but are not frequently serious because of the controls in use for whitefly and mites. The most successful control has been by scheduled applications to the soil of the systemic material aldicarb, which is registered for use on poinset-

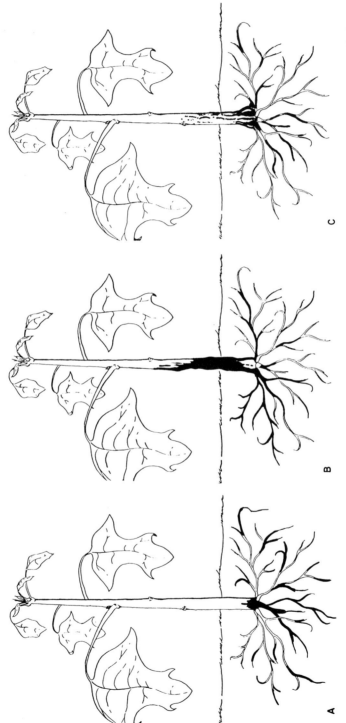

Fig. 4. Principal soilborne pathogens of poinsettia. (A) *Pythium*—water mold root rot. (B) *Rhizoctonia*—stem and root rot. (C) *Thielaviopsis*—black rot. (Courtesy of Paul Ecke Poinsettias, Encinitas, California.)

tias in the greenhouse as Temik. Temik must not be applied to flowering plants within 4 weeks of sale. Resmethrin is an insecticide of low toxicity useful in the late season control of whitefly.

E. Notes on Cultivars

1. 'Eckespoint C-1'

This cultivar has a large, horizontal, bright red bract display on medium-to-tall, very strong stems. Bracts are long lasting but leaves abscise sooner. Cutting production is limited but roots form readily. It is best grown as a standard plant but will average three flowering branches when pinched. It is late maturing, requiring 75–80 days, and short days should be provided by September 20 to flower with other cultivars. [Also: 'Eckespoint C-1 New Pink' (not veined), 'Eckespoint C-1 White,' and 'Jingle Bells' (pink blotches on red bracts).]

2. 'Annette Hegg Dark Red'

Medium red bracts of this cultivar may droop at maturity on medium height thin but stiff stems. This cultivar has exceptional leaf and bract retention but cyathia tend to abscise early; early maturation (65-70 days); a self-branching habit with six to eight flowering branches from a programmed pinch and excellent cutting production. These cultivars may be grown as standard or multiflowering plants. [Also: 'Annette Hegg Brilliant' (bright orange-red bracts), 'Annette Hegg Diva' (brick-red bracts), 'Annette Hegg Top Star' (vigorous, bright red bracts), 'Annette Hegg New Pink' (not veined), 'Annette Hegg Marble' (pink-variegated white bracts), 'Annette Hegg White'.]

3. 'Mikkel Improved Rochford'

This cultivar has bright red bracts which may droop at maturity on medium height, thin but stiff stems; a self-branching habit with excellent cutting production and producing six to eight flowering stems from a programmed pinch; exceptional leaf and branch retention but the cyanthia tend to abscise early; and early maturity (66–71 days). These cultivars may be grown as standard or multiflowering plants. [Also: 'Mikkel Super Rochford' (vigorous partial tetraploid with thicker, bright red bracts), 'Mikkel Vivid Rochford' (tetraploid with bright, orange-red, stiff bracts), 'Mikkel Fantastic' (bright, clear pink bracts), 'Mikkel White Rochford'.]

4. 'Gutbier V-14 Glory'

Bright red, horizontal bracts with few cyathia are borne on moderately short, very strong stems. This cultivar has exceptional leaf and bract retention; a self-branching habit producing abundant cuttings which root readily with the potential for six to eight flowering stems from a programmed pinch; and moderately late maturity (70–75 days). These cultivars can be grown as standard or multiflowering plants. [Also: 'Gutbier V-10 Amy' (The light red, medium-sized bract display with a free-branching, short growth habit make 'Amy' most suitable for the production of small pots. This cultivar is self branching, producing abundant cuttings with many flowering stems when pinched and basal flowering shoots when grown as a standard plant; has moderate but satisfactory leaf and bract retention and very early maturity (63-68 days). A relatively cool night temperature is recommended for a more intense bract color).]

IV. CONSUMER SATISFACTION AND MARKETING

A. Holding in the Greenhouse

Poinsettias should not leave the growing environment before they are fully mature, and plants for early sales should be specifically grown for that purpose because immature bracts will continue growth but will not be fully pigmented unless under full light. Plants produced for early sales can be held for late sale with no reduction in lasting ability provided they are kept in the greenhouse under proper conditions of spacing, light, temperature, and humidity. Plants held in a cool greenhouse will have a more intense bract color.

Cyathia are an important part of the floral display and their premature loss detracts from plant appearance. Present-day, self-branching cultivars do not retain cyathia well and may have few or no cyathia present at the time of sale. Retention has been better under good growing conditions, particularly high light and cooler temperatures, and on standard (unbranched) plants.

B. Shipping

Plant deterioration starts as the poinsettia leaves the greenhouse. Shipping containers, storage rooms, and display areas can all detract from the life of the plant and consumer satisfaction. Poinsettias, like orchids, do not withstand cold storage temperatures, but they deteriorate less when shipped at 10°–12°C than when warmer. A reduced night temperature and provision for continuous light could well be used in display and sales areas. Incandescent light is recommended for the display of red poinsettias.

Poinsettias are commonly "sleeved" in tapered tubes of paper or plastic for protection in handling before leaving the growing area. Plants are also boxed to permit stacking for long distance shipping. Some cultivars are particularly susceptible to epinasty (downward bending of leaves and bracts) following sleeving for 24 hours or longer. Such plants gradually return to normal leaf and bract orientation in the greenhouse or a well-lit room but the process may take up to 5 days. Recent work (Sacalis, 1978; Saltveit et al., 1979) has indicated that the distortion was caused by the production of ethylene in the bent petioles of sleeved plants and in petioles subsequently released from pressure upon removal of the plant sleeve. 'Eckespoint C-1' and 'Gutbier V-14 Glory' were shown to be less susceptible to epinasty following sleeving than several 'Annette Hegg' cultivars. Chemical blocking of the ethylene production is possible but more research is needed to establish the practicality of such a procedure. Poinsettias should be sleeved no longer than necessary and inspected following shipment. Malformed plants should be permitted to resume their normal habit under uncrowded, well-lighted conditions before being sold.

C. Consumer Education

The life of a poinsettia plant at room temperature in complete darkness may be limited to 3 weeks, but the long life of this plant in the home should be emphasized in all sales promotions. It need only be adequately watered and otherwise placed for best display and enjoyment in the home. Early purchase can be promoted with the assurance that it will last through the holiday season. Where 9 or more hours of either artificial light or low-level, natural light reach the plant it may retain leaves and bracts for several months. Growth in the home is not desirable and should not be encouraged by fertilization. .

The consumer can plant the poinsettia plant in the garden for the summer and bring it indoors again in the fall but should be told of the necessity for both sunshine and uninterrupted long nights if repeated flowering is to be expected. This should create additional interest and encourage, rather than prevent, a repeat sale. References to the possibility of human poisoning resulting from the ingestion of poinsettia leaves may be vigorously refuted as controlled feeding studies have not indicated that such a toxin exists. Further information is available from the Society of American Florists (Walker, 1972) and from the American Association of Nurserymen (Lederer, 1972).

D. Cultivar Improvement

Extensive poinsettia breeding and selection programs for the improvement of poinsettias have been developed in North America and in Europe by both commercial specialists and research institutions. Crosses are most successful on older plants growing at a 22°C minimum temperature. Naturally flowering plants may be pollinated in late December; seed is harvested by April and sown in July; and seedlings flower in December. The self-branching characteristic is desirable for ease of culture and propagation. Retention of leaves and bracts is essential; bright and deep red bracts are most in demand; and some degree of disease resistance (particularly to *Botrytis*) is required. Large, horizontal, distinctive bracts on sturdy stems, early maturity, the capability of development at a cool temperature, and the retention of cyathia in a tight center of the bract display are all desired qualities to be gained by such programs.

REFERENCES

Boodley, J. W. (1970). Nitrogen fertilizers and their influence on growth of poinsettias. *Florists' Rev.* **147**(3800), 26–27, 69–73.

Ecke, P. Jr., and Matkin, O. A. (1976). "The Poinsettia Manual." Paul Ecke Poinsettias, Encinitas, California.

Jungk, A., Malsheb, B., and Wehrmann, J. (1970). Molybdänmangel an Poinsettien eine Ursache von Blattschäden. *Gartenwelt* **17**(2), 31–35.

Lederer, R. F. (1972). "Poisonous Plants." The American Association of Nurserymen, Washington, D.C.

Sacalis, J. N. (1978). Ethylene evolution by petioles of sleeved poinsettia plants. *HortScience* **13**(5), 594–596.

Saltveit, M. E., Pharr, D. M., and Larson, R. A. (1979). Mechanical stress induces ethylene production and epinasty in poinsettia cultivars. *J. Am. Soc. Hortic. Sci.* **104**(4), 452–455.

Stewart, R. N., and Arisumi, T. (1966). Genetic and histogenic determination of pink bract color in poinsettia. *J. Hered.* **57**(6), 217–220.

Walker, J. H. (1972). "Poinsettia and Mistletoe Toxicity—A Witch Hunt." Society of American Florists, Alexandria, Virginia.

13
Easter Lilies

H. F. Wilkins

I. ORIGIN AND NATIVE HABITAT

The Easter lily (*Lilium longiflorum* Thunb.—Liliaceae family) is a native of Japan and its center of origin is apparently Japan's three small southernmost islands. Although this white or trumpet lily was found under cultivation on the mainland of China and Formosa by early Western explorers, it is only endemic to the Liu-chiu (Ryukus) Islands and is unknown in the wild state elsewhere (Wilson, 1925).

The native *Lilium longiflorum* grows on the Japanese islands of Amami, Erabu (Okino-erabu), and Okinawa, in pockets filled with soil in the coral rock (limestone) next to the sea. Furthermore, this species is a tropical plant. Bamboo, sugar cane, cycads, palms, and other tropical plants grow on the islands. The average annual temperature is near 21°C. The latitude of Erabu Island is 27°N, which is approximately the same latitude as Cairo, Egypt, Delhi, India, and Miami, Florida (Wilkins, 1973).

II. HISTORY

"*Lilium*" is derived from the Celtic word "*li*," meaning whiteness. This refers, no doubt, to *Lilium candidum,* the Madonna lily. However, *L. longiflorum* has become much better known and indeed is the most valuable species of the genus *Lilium* (Bailey, 1916). As this chapter will illustrate, it is obvious that no other lily species, or indeed few other plants, have had their cultural requirements worked out to the most minute details as have the cultivars of *L. longiflorum.*

The Japanese name, Riukie-yuri (lily of the Liu-chiu Islands) is referred to in one of Japan's oldest gardening books, the "Kadan Komoju," published in 1681. Lilies have also been used in religious ceremonies for over 2000 years. In Japan the Easter lily is commonly called "blunderbuss" or "gun lily" because of the long trumpetlike flower (Ogilvie, 1957). In Western literature, "blunderbuss" was first mentioned in 1794 by Carl Thunberg, a physician for the Dutch East India Company's compound in Japan (Pfeiffer, 1966). At this period, Japan was closed to the Western world and his travels were limited. Plants were probably brought to him in his compound. His description is recognized as the first, and hence "Thunb." follows *Lilium longiflorum* in the latin binomial system (Stearn, 1947).

Lilium longiflorum Thunb. was introduced to England about 1819, and almost immediately became one of the most popular plants in commercial floriculture when it gained general acceptance as the Easter plant.

Japan was exporting *L. longiflorum* bulbs to Europe and the United States as early as 1876. By the late 1800s and early 1900s millions of bulbs were imported annually from Japan, Formosa, and Bermuda to England and the United

States. Bermuda lily production peaked in 1896 and, because of virus infections, was gone by 1925. After the demise of the Bermuda industry, the
Japanese began to export large quantities of bulbs to be forced in
greenhouses as potted plants (Ogilvie, 1957). Cultivars imported from Japan
are now grown in northern greenhouses mainly as cut flowers or in the South-
west and South as potted plants. Japanese cultivars frequently grow into excessively tall potted plants in northern greenhouses. Because of disease problems, the Second World War, and the introduction of new cultivars in the United
States, use of Japanese bulbs declined in northern greenhouses.

The main production of bulbs to be forced for potted plant production in
northern greenhouses is now concentrated along the West Coast of the United
States, in the northern part of California, and the southern part of Oregon.
About ten million bulbs are produced annually between Smith River, California,
and Brookings, Oregon. 'Nellie White' and 'Ace' are the two leading cultivars
grown in the Pacific Northwest for forcing in the United States and Canada.
Some "southern" cultivars are grown in the southern United States for field
forcing for potted plants or as cut flowers in northern greenhouses.

III. MORPHOLOGY

A. Bulb Parts

A lily forcer receives a harvested lily bulb in October. This bulb is composed
of scales, a basal plate, an apical meristem, and roots. The scales are modified
leaves that function as storage organs. Two sets of scales are present, an outer
and an inner group. Outer scales are the previous year's inner scales. Outer
scales surround the current year's inner scales. Inner scales are formed from a
new active meristem near the old flowering stem and at the base of an inner-
most inner scale. This lateral meristem becomes dominant (apical) and forms
scales that enlarge to become next year's inner scales (Fig. 1). All scales are
attached to the basal plate, which is a compressed modified stem (De Hertogh
et al., 1971). The apical meristem is located on top of the basal plate and is
surrounded by the new scales until the shoot starts elongating. In production
fields the apical meristem lays down scales until around July, at which time
leaves begin to form. In the greenhouse, the apical meristem continues to form
leaves until late January, when flower buds form (Blaney and Roberts, 1967;
Hartley, 1968). Roots are present and are attached to the basal plate when the
greenhouse forcer receives the bulbs. These roots should not be removed or
allowed to dry out.

Annually, in the axis of an inner scale, a lateral bud becomes apically dominant about the time plants flower (July) in the field and a new apical meristem is
formed. At first the new meristem forms new inner scales, which enlarge to
increase bulb size. Next the meristem shifts into forming leaves (vegetative

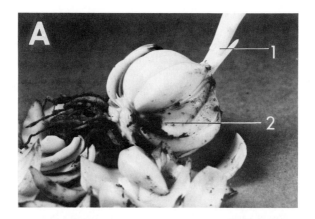

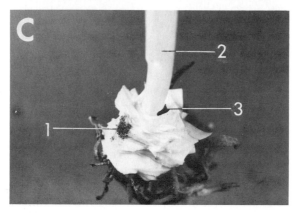

Fig. 1. Morphological parts of a *Lilium longiflorum* bulb. (A) A young shoot (1) from a bulb with a portion of the older or outer scales removed to show the scar (2) where the old flowering stem was attached. (B) All the outer scales have been removed showing the basal plate (1), the site where the old flowering stem was attached (2) and the inner scale complement (3). (C) All the outer and inner scales have been removed showing the scar (1) where the old flowering stem was attached, the present flowering stem (2), and early stages of the new apical meristem (3) that will flower after it follows the prescribed rotation of anatomical events.

growth period), and a floral apex forms (reproductive growth period); then the cycle is repeated when the shoot ultimately flowers (Blaney and Roberts, 1967). The apical meristem is producing leaves during harvesting, packing, shipping, cold-storage programming, planting, emergence, and up to when floral buds form in January. Thus, the Easter lily bulb does not have a distinct dormancy period; the lily bulb and plant are continually monitoring their environment and could be called a "biocomputer" (De Hertogh and Wilkins, 1971a,b).

B. Promotors and Inhibitors: Location and Presence

Inner scales contain inhibitors that apparently control rapid shoot elongation and flowering. If the inner scales are surgically removed from noncooled bulbs, rapid shoot elongation and flowering occur without exposing bulbs to low temperatures or shoots to long days (Lin and Roberts, 1970). Exposing the bulbs to a moist, cold treatment or the newly emerged shoots from noncooled bulbs to long days overcomes this inhibition, which results in rapid shoot elongation and flowering (Wang and Roberts, 1970; Waters and Wilkins, 1967; Wilkins *et al.,* 1968a).

Tsukamoto (1971) in Japan has shown that with the cultivar Tonoshita No. 1, growth promotors increase and inhibitors decrease in the outer scales of bulbs given a low temperature treatment. At room temperature, however, the inhibitor level decreased, but the promotor did not increase. He postulated that promotors were in the outer scales, because when the outer scales were removed, shoot emergence was inhibited. Lin *et al.,* (1975), in Minnesota, working with 'Nellie White,' found no increase in gibberellins (GA) in inner scales during 40 days at 4.5°C; GA increased only when bulbs were placed in the forcing greenhouse at 15.5°–21°C. This increase was related to actual shoot emergence (Fig. 2). Abscisic acid (ABA) activity patterns were similar to the GA levels and GA activity was greater in the inner scales whereas ABA activity was greater in the outer scales. This work generally agrees with that of Lin and Roberts (1970), when 'Nellie White' inner scales were removed and shoot emergence was rapid. Roh and Wilkins (1974a, b) found that red or far-red light treatments of the inner scales, depending on time of lighting or prior light treatment, accelerated shoot emergence and that the phytochrome pigment was present and reversible in the inner scales.

With lilies, exogenous GA was found to induce dormancy-breaking (Lin and Wilkins, 1975b; Wang and Roberts, 1970), to replace partially the cold treatment influence (Laiche and Box, 1970), and to reduce flower number (De Hertogh and Blakely, 1972; Kays *et al.,* 1971). Exogenous ABA partially negated the cold treatment, and inhibited emergence and flowering (Lin and Wilkins, 1975b). At present there is little practical application or use of GA or ABA on Easter lilies.

Roots on many other bulb species play an important role in changes of endogenous growth hormones and lily roots also may be a site of synthesis.

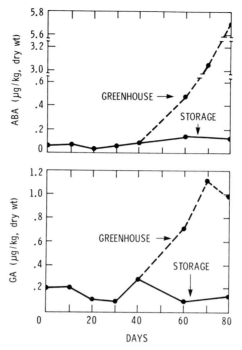

Fig. 2. GA and ABA levels in bulbs harvested September 18 and stored at 4.5°C for 40 days and moved to a greenhouse (21°C/15.5°C, day/night) for forcing or continued at 4.5°C for 40 more days (Lin *et al.*, 1975a).

Presence of roots has been postulated to be the reason why more lily flower buds are formed on shoots from bulbs which were rooted prior to the cold treatment (De Hertogh *et al.*, 1969).

IV. INFLUENCE OF TEMPERATURE AND PHOTOPERIOD TREATMENTS ON FLOWER INDUCTION

The purpose of forcing the lily bulb is to have a potted flowering plant at Easter (Table I). The final plant at Easter time is a direct function of the production, programming, and various greenhouse forcing stages. These stages encompass a period of many months and it is essential that bulbs and subsequent developing plants are handled with care. Historically, bulb programming has been accomplished by subjecting bulbs to a moist cold or a "vernalization" treatment (Stuart, 1954). This bulb treatment is given in moist peat or soil surrounding the bulbs for 1000 hours or 6 weeks. In 1967 Waters and Wilkins realized that a 6-week light treatment to a shoot from a noncooled bulb also programmed the plant to flower and could substitute for a bulb cold treatment.

Table I

General Grouping of Easter Dates[a]

Class	Group	Time span
Early	1	March 26–31
	2	April 1–5
Medium	1	April 6–9
	2	April 10–13
Late	1	April 14–18
	2	April 19–22

[a]From De Hertogh and Wilkins (1971a,b).

The ultimate growth responses are essentially identical since the flowering plants are similar (Roh and Wilkins, 1973a). Another similarity between programming a plant to flower rapidly by a bulb cold treatment or a shoot light treatment of which all forcers should be aware is that temperatures over 21° can result in devernalization immediately after bulbs are removed from cold storage (Miller and Kiplinger, 1966) and that at temperatures over 21°C the long photoperiod treatment cannot be perceived by the shoot (Lin and Wilkins, 1973).

A. Photoperiod and Low Temperature

Historically, photoperiodic lighting was stated to have little or no effect on rate of flowering, but instead increased height and decreased bud count (Smith and Langhans, 1962). These data were taken from plants from vernalized bulbs and shoot lighting was given late in the forcing sequence. Lighting, however, can act as a total programming agent only if given to shoots from nonvernalized or partially vernalized shoots upon emergence. Long photoperiods and cold treatments are equally substituted on a week-for-week basis, i.e., shoots from bulbs given 6 weeks of cold treatment will flower at the same time as those shoots, which upon emergence have been given long photoperiods for 6 weeks when forced under equal greenhouse conditions. There is little difference between plants whose bulbs were programmed by cold or whose shoots were programmed by light. It is felt that there are two independent pathways or methods by which a lily can be programmed to flower rapidly, either by a bulb cold treatment or by a shoot long photoperiod treatment (Roh and Wilkins, 1973a). In its natural environment, the plant is probably induced to flower by photoperiod because the average temperature in Erabu is near 21°C (Wilkins, 1973).

Lighting of plants is most effective when given as a night interruption for 4 hours from 2200 to 0200 hours (378 lx). Lighting from 0400 to 0800 hours is somewhat less effective, whereas lighting from 1600 to 2000 hours is not satisfactory (Wilkins and Roh, 1970). Photoperiod treatments must be given at temperatures below 21°C (Wilkins, 1973). Incandescent and fluorescent (cool white) light sources are satisfactory. Both red and far-red light appears to be effective for rapid floral induction (Roh and Wilkins, 1977d). If one desires to conserve electricity, a cycle of 15 minutes off, 15 minutes on is acceptable (Roh and Wilkins, 1977c). Lighting at emergence is not effective on shoots from bulbs which are cold-saturated, or totally vernalized. Lighting at emergence is not destructive or deleterious to flower bud potential or future plant height, and can be used to ensure a crop that has been totally programmed to rapidly flower.

A practical application can be made to use the knowledge of the substitution of long photoperiods for the cold treatments by lighting lily shoots in a routine manner at emergence for 1 or 2 weeks. This procedure will ensure that the plant is totally programmed to rapidly flower and has been termed an "insurance policy" (Wilkins et al., 1968b). Because of annual dormancy and maturity variations or human error, we can never be sure that all bulbs are adequately programmed by cold. Lighting also appears to even up the crop, particularly when the slow-emerging population is lighted. Lighting should be a standard practice regardless if Easter Sunday is early or late.

B. Temperature

Classically, lily bulbs have been cooled for 6 weeks at a temperature of 1.5°–7°C (Stuart, 1954). If bulbs are harvested, never cooled, and always exposed to temperatures of 21°C or above when forcing, they will never flower, regardless of photoperiod (Lin and Wilkins, 1973). A "pseudobulb" forms on the apex of these plants after 9 to 12 months when grown at 21°C or above (Fig. 3). If, however, these plants with a terminal "pseudobulb" are shifted to temperatures of 18°C, flowering is accomplished within 65 days: 30 days are required for formation of a visible bud and 35 days for its development and opening. This means that the bulb or growing point is acquiring a vernalization-like treatment at temperatures below 21°C. Nevertheless, the recommended bulb temperature treatment of 1.5°–7°C is most rapid and efficient for commercial use.

Another interesting point in reference to temperature responses is that these plants with a terminal "psuedobulb" and which have been grown at 21°C for many months have a curious phenomenon of going through a normal new apical shoot rotation sequence. The new sprout for the next growth cycle will emerge from the bulb and immediately flower with a stem having only a few leaves (Wilkins, unpublished). This means that natural field conditions on the West Coast of the United States must be programming into a bulb an inhibitor/dormancy system that must be overcome by cold temperatures or long days. Recent work (Stimart, unpublished) with lily tissue culture of scales has shown that regenerated bulblets grown in the dark at 30°C have no dormancy and will form an expanded shoot axis. However, if cultures are grown at 25°C, dormancy exists and bulblets require a cold treatment for shoot elongation.

Fig. 3 A longitudinal section of a "pseudobulb" formed on the apex of a plant grown from a nonvernalized bulb at temperatures above 21°C for 9 months; when the bulb was moved to 18°C, flowering occurred within 65 days. Note the two floral pedicels on the left (Lin and Wilkins, 1973).

V. COMMERCIAL BULB PRODUCTION, PROGRAMMING, AND FORCING

A. Production Phase

It is not practical to go into a detailed description of practices used in producing a commercial bulb (Blaney and Roberts, 1967). There are, however, certain aspects that directly relate to forcing. The principal means of propagating is by scale bulblets. Mother bulbs are carefully selected and mother block propagation stock is developed from their scales. This is conducive to producing a uniform bulb for forcing. Two years are required to produce a commercial-size bulb.

The annual lily bulb harvest in Oregon and California starts in September and ends by early October, the warmest and driest part of the year. Replanting stock (yearlings) is separated from commercial bulb sizes and replanted as soon as possible. Commercial bulbs are graded according to bulb circumference. Commercially, grades in the United States are presently known as "6 to 7, 7 to 8, 8 to 9, or 9 to 10-inch" size, and bulbs are packed in moist peat for shipment.

At this point of the production phase, two aspects are important to consider in forcing bulbs. First, there will always be some yearly variation in bulb size of the crop (Table II) and in rate of shoot emergence (dormancy) and response to cold temperature programming (maturity) (Lin and Wilkins, 1975a). For example, in 3 consecutive years, shoots from noncooled bulbs harvested the 15th of August emerged in 104, 100, or 139 days from potting. When given 6 weeks of 4.5°C they emerged in 38, 37, or 39 days from potting. When harvested the first of September noncooled bulbs emerged in 101, 79, or 135 days; when cooled at 4.5°C they emerged in 35, 38, or 32 days; when harvested the 15th of September, noncooled bulbs emerged in 64, 85, or 120 days; when cooled they emerged in 17, 36, or 35 days. Similar trends and differences exist among the number of days to flower, number of flowers, and leaves.

The forcer should realize that the bulbs are under the influences of seasonal variations when forced in a greenhouse; the interaction between maturity (the capacity to perceive cold and sprout), and dormancy (the capacity to emerge). These seasonal variations appear to be inescapable and they are not totally understood. Therefore, one must assume that differences will exist each year

Table II

Variations over a 3-Year Period of Growth Responses for 'Nellie White' "8-to 9-Inch U.S.A. Grade" (20- to 22.5-cm) Bulbs Which Were Control Temperature-Forced[a]

	Year		
	1 (92 gm)	2 (111 gm)	3 (114 gm)
Circumference (cm)	19.9	20.2	21.1
Days to emerge	17	38	32
Days to visible bud	104	89	117
Days to flower	141	138	147

[a]From Lin and Wilkins (1975a).

and that no two lily crops will respond or force alike. Thus, the ability of the crop to be programmed and the floral bud potential will vary each year.

The second point, which is extremely important, is moisture in the peat moss. It has been demonstrated that peat should be moist at the time of packing of the bulbs (Stuart, 1954). This moisture is necessary for two reasons. First, moisture will maintain existing basal roots of the bulbs. Second, if bulbs are to be properly vernalized, moisture content (30–50%) must be optimal if bulbs are to perceive the cold treatment properly and to respond properly during greenhouse forcing.

After packing, bulbs are held for a minimal time in common storage until they are shipped. All bulbs are shipped by refrigerated trucks so that the arrival time at either the greenhouse or the commercial precooling facility will be approximately no later than October 15. The bulb grower's and jobber's responsibilities should end here as far as providing a healthy and insect-free bulb, i.e., a sound basal plate, roots, and a meristem on which flower buds can be formed. It is well known, however, that 100% of the bulbs do not emerge. There can be small losses (up to 5%); and these must be expected as a normal part of the forcing process and should be figured into the overall cost of production.

Approximately half of the future total leaf count is present in October (Blaney and Roberts, 1967). Thus, cultural events beginning with the programming phase are critical for the future quality of the plants that will be produced.

B. Programming Phase

Programming a lily plant to flower for the Easter holiday has historically been accomplished by giving bulbs a cold treatment. Six weeks of vernalization results in rapid and uniform shoot emergence and subsequent rapid and uniform flowering. Cooling, however, reduces the number of potential flowers the plant could produce compared to bulbs left uncooled and forced at temperatures below 21°C (De Hertogh and Wilkins, 1971a, b). Nevertheless, the forcer must remember that the 6 weeks of programming (cold and/or equivalent light treatments) is essential for rapid flowering. Programming allows the forcer to accomplish the two basic goals. Programming treatments accelerate flowering of the crop and reduce the length of time between the first and last plant to flower. Therefore, cool temperature is necessary to time accurately and produce a uniform crop. These are the important and critical factors that must be considered, not loss of the potential number of flowers. An added benefit or effect of the 6 weeks of cold is that plant height, numbers of nodes, and leaves at flower are reduced when compared to nontreated plants (Tables III A and III B).

The programming phase of lily forcing is initiated in mid to late October. Three basic or traditional methods are used for programming the northwest-grown Easter lily bulb for rapid forcing (Wilkins, 1976, 1977). These methods are (a) cooling bulbs in the case prior to potting, (b) natural cooling as a potted

Table IIIA

Overall Effects of 6 Weeks of Cooling Regardless of Programming Method[a]

1. Reduces the total number of flowers and leaves that the lily can produce (see Table IIIB)
2. Reduces number of days required for uniform shoot emergence
3. Reduces total number of days to flower (see Table IIIB)
4. Reduces number of days from first plant to flower to last plant to flower (see Table IIIB)
5. Reduces total plant height at time of flowering
6. Reduces length of lower leaves

[a]From De Hertogh and Wilkins (1971a,b).

Table IIIB

Effect of Increasing Weeks of 4.5°C on Number of Days to Flower, Height (cm), Time Span between First and Last Plants to Flower, and Numbers of Leaves and Flowers on Plants from "8- to 9-Inch U.S.A. Grade" (20- to 22.5-cm) Bulbs Which Were Control Temperature-Forced[a]

Days to flower				$\bar{X}$	Leaf No.	Height (cm)	Flower No.
First flower		Δ	Last flower				
0 168		54	202	194	152	71	18
2 152		43	195	174	103	56	12
4 131		38	169	150	95	38	10
6 120		12	132	126	85	36	8

[a]From De Hertogh and Wilkins (1971a,b).

bulb in the field or cold frame under prevailing temperatures, or (c) controlled temperature forcing (CTF), rooting, and/or cooling the bulb in the pot under controlled conditions (De Hertogh et al., 1969). All of these methods can, and under some conditions probably should be, coupled with a long-day treatment or "insurance policy" at time of emergence to ensure rapid flower induction (Wilkins et al., 1968b). New experimental programming concepts are not considered here in detail but are of interest in programming a crop with superior bud counts (Wilkins and Roh, 1976; Roh and Wilkins, 1977a,b,c,d). Possibilities include combining or interrupting the cold and long-day treatments (apply 3 weeks of cold; allow the plants to emerge; then treat with 3–4 weeks of long days) or interrupt the 6 weeks of cold for a week at higher temperatures or interrupt the 6 weeks of long days with normal days.

Nevertheless, the three basic commercial programming methods fall into two types. In type 1, case-cooled bulbs are left in moist peat moss in the original containers and cooled for 6 weeks. Normally, this is carried out at a commercial cold-storage facility but knowledgeable greenhouse operators are encouraged to do their own cooling. This will reduce the problems of overcooling and shipping of the bulbs in freezing temperatures of early December to mid-December at the end of the 6 weeks of cold storage treatment. In type 2, natural cooling and CTF, bulbs are shipped directly to the greenhouse operator in October and potted immediately. Natural cooling methods use naturally occurring temperature conditions. The CTF method uses a controlled temperature sequence of 16.7°–18.3°C for 2 or 3 weeks prior to the 4.5°C for 6 weeks.

The basic similarity underlying both types of programming is that 'Ace' lilies must receive a total of 6 weeks of temperatures at 1.7°–4.5°C, and 'Nellie White' lilies need 6 weeks at 4.5°–7.4°C. It appears that the least destructive cold treatment, which reduces bud counts least, is higher for 'Nellie White' than for 'Ace.' A 4.5°C temperature has been a compromise for both cultivars. Soil temperatures should be recorded daily at several locations to ensure that temperatures remain at recommended levels. Uniform temperatures and moisture throughout the case or the medium of a potted bulb will ensure a responsive and uniform crop during forcing.

Each of these programming methods has its advantages and disadvantages (Table IV). It is a good practice for greenhouse operators to do their own programming (cooling) either in the case or in the pot as in the CTF or natural cooling methods. If forcers do their own programming, they can be assured that bulbs are properly programmed provided temperatures are monitored daily. Records should be kept and accumulated yearly concerning programming, forcing conditions, and bulb response (Table V).

Table IV

Advantages and Disadvantages of Different Programming Methods[a]

Programming method	Advantages	Disadvantages
Precooling (PC)	1. Takes small amount of refrigeration space 2. Can be performed by supplier or forcer	1. Reduces number of leaves and flowers produced 2. Has short basal leaves 3. Greenhouse time and space overlap with poinsettias
Natural cooling (NC)	1. High leaf and flower numbers 2. Long basal leaves 3. Greenhouse time does not overlap with poinsettias 4. Shorter plants	1. Must be performed by forcer 2. Takes additional time 3. Dependent on prevailing weather conditions
Controlled temperature forcing (CTF)	1. Control of flowering process 2. Standard conditions every year 3. High leaf and flower number 4. Long basal leaves 5. Greenhouse time does not overlap with poinsettias	1. Requires controlled temperature space 2. Must be performed by forcer

[a]From De Hertogh and Wilkins (1971a,b).

Table V

Factors Affecting Timing of Easter Lily[a]

1. Date of Easter
2. Bulb maturity at harvest time
3. Preshipping storage and shipping temperatures
4. Method of programming and length of cold treatment
5. Moisture during programming phase
6. Long-day "insurance policy"
7. Greenhouse temperature
8. Cultivar
9. Bulb size

[a]From De Hertogh and Wilkins (1971a,b).

C. Greenhouse Phase

Stage 1 of the greenhouse phase is the time span between placement of the bulbs in the greenhouse and the initiation of flower primordia which occurs around January 15 to 21 (De Hertogh *et al.,* 1976).

When bulbs are first brought into the greenhouse from cold storage or potted after the end of the cold treatment, soil temperatures should be immediately increased to 15.5°–18°C, since this is the optimal range for both root growth and leaf initiation. Temperatures should not go above 21°C since devernalization and delay of flowering occur. Rapid elongation of the lower internodes may also occur at 21°C, which results in a poorly shaped plant. Future flower-bud counts and potentials may also be reduced. At shoot emergence use of the "insurance policy" is recommended, particularly if it is an early Easter (Wilkins *et al.,* 1968b).

Floral initiation occurs when the apical meristem of the lily ceases producing leaves (vegetative stage of growth) and begins forming floral buds (reproductive stage of growth). Normally, plants are 10 to 15 cm tall when they become reproductive (Pfeiffer, 1935).

If Easter is late or the crop is ahead of schedule, as determined by the leaf counting technique (Wilkins, 1970), night temperature at this time can be lowered to increase bud counts (Wilkins and Roh, 1976). The number of days that temperatures can be lowered is determined by the date of Easter and the stage of growth, as judged by the experienced lily forcer. This means that the length of time for stage 1 will be approximately 7 weeks for case-cooled bulbs and approximately 4 weeks for CTF and natural-cooled lilies.

Stage 2 of the greenhouse phase is the time span from floral initiation to the time when floral buds become visible in the foliage. This time span will vary for each Easter. This forcing stage is the most important phase in timing of the crop for Easter. The leaf-counting technique should be utilized by all forcers to monitor the speed of this specific greenhouse stage. During the early portion of stage 2 the total number of flower buds that finally will develop on the plant is determined. The forcer should be aware that floral bud initiation is a progressive event (De Hertogh et al., 1976).

At the beginning of initiation the meristem first produces a basic number of primary flowers, usually five on an "8- to 9-inch U.S.A. grade" bulb. This number is dependent upon the bulb grade, which influences the ultimate size of the surface area of the meristem at the time of initiation. After the first set of primary floral buds has been initiated on the perimeter of the meristem, additional secondary floral buds may be initiated as a second whorl of buds on a scape that arises from the middle of the meristem. If the potential exists and greenhouse conditions are optimal, not only secondary buds form but also tertiary flowers sometimes are produced in the axil of the bract leaf of the primary and secondary flowers (Roh and Wilkins, 1977b) (Fig. 4).

Because all flowers do not initiate at one time, the time span needed to complete floral initiation in the lily can be approximately 3 to 4 weeks. This partly explains why many factors can affect the ultimate number of salable flowers produced (Table VI). It is believed that the optimal temperature for secondary flowers is 7.2°C for 'Nellie White' and 12.8° for 'Ace.' For tertiary flowers the optimal temperature is 15.6°C for 'Nellie White' and 21°C for 'Ace.' Temperatures may be lowered in mid-January to late January if Easter is late or if timing is adequate to develop secondary flowers, and then may be increased for tertiary flower formation (De Hertogh et al., 1976; Roh and Wilkins, 1977b).

Stage 3 is the time span from visible buds in the foliage until the first floral bud opens. This stage is affected mainly by temperature. Under normal conditions, this stage should take no longer than 30 to 35 days. At an average day/night temperature of 21°C, Roh and Wilkins (1973b) found that plants flowered in 28 days. At a 26.6°C/15.5°C (day/night) temperature regime, plants flowered in 30 days. It was not until the average day/night temperatures fell below 21° or a day/night temperature of 21°C/15.5°C did the days increase, i.e., 40 days for flowers to open.

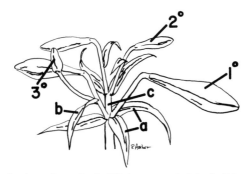

Fig. 4 Lily plant showing two primary buds (1°), two secondary buds (2°), and one tertiary (3°) with whorl-arranged bracts from the main stem (a), the bract on the pedicel (b), and the elevated flower stalk (c) for 2° buds (Roh and Wilkins, 1977b).

Table VI

Factors Influencing Total Number of Flowers Produced[a]

---

1. Bulb size
2. Meristem diameter
3. Method of programming and length of cold treatment
4. Cultivar
5. Greenhouse forcing temperature
6. Rate and number of roots developed
7. Root rot
8. Light intensity

---

[a]From De Hertogh and Wilkins (1971a,b).

Thus, during stages 2 and 3 of the greenhouse phase, it is not only a question of floral initiation but also of development. Therefore, the entire development period from floral bud initiation in late January to flowering is approximately 8 to 10 weeks depending on the date of Easter. Deviations from optimal conditions will adversely affect the number of buds that are initiated as well as those that ultimately will mature and flower. Although flower number is a vital consideration, timing is still the most critical and important aspect of lily forcing. To assist the forcer, the leaf counting technique has been developed.

D. Leaf Counting

Blaney *et al.* (1967) were responsible for Wilkins and Roberts (1969) appreciating the fact that there is a stable number of leaves formed annually and that one can determine this early in the forcing period. Thus, this technique for timing the rate of growth or speed of leaf unfolding is based on the formation of a basic number of leaves and control of their developmental rate by temperature (Smith and Langhans, 1962). Leaf counting commences when leaves unfold and small flower buds are visible. The number does vary from year to year (Table VII), but with knowledge of the leaf numbers unfolded and the number yet to unfold in order to expose the flower buds, informed forcers should not encounter any problems if proper temperatures are maintained to control the rate of leaf unfolding.

The steps in shoot dissecting, leaf counting, and timing of an Easter lily crop are given below:

1. Record the average date of shoot emergence.

2. When plants are 10 to 15 cm tall, flower buds should be initiating and the total leaf complement should be present. At this time, cut off 10 random shoots at soil level for every 2000 bulbs from each cultivar and bulb source. Do not select shoots from double-nosed bulb plants.

3. Take these shoots to a well-lighted area, count, record, and average the total number of leaves per cultivar and source. A large needle and magnifying lens (reading glass) will help one remove the small, scalelike leaves near the apical growing point. The embryolike flower buds should be present (Fig. 5). An estimate of the future bud count can be made at this time and no further plants are sacrificed. After plants have flowered, it is interesting to compare the actual leaf number to the estimated leaf counts. These data should be recorded for future reference and for comparison (Table VII).

4. Randomly select and tag ten average plants in the greenhouse that correspond to plants just sacrificed, and individually count, record, and average the number of leaves that have unfolded to a 45° angle on these plants. A bamboo stake with a paper label wired to it can be used to tag or mark plants used to record the weekly individual leaf data.

5. Subtract the average total number of leaves that have unfolded from the estimated or predicted average leaf total from step 3. This will tell how many leaves are yet to unfold.

6. Divide the number of leaves already unfolded by the number of days from emergence to date. This will tell how many leaves have been unfolding each day at present greenhouse temperatures.

7. Determine the desired visible bud date. This is 30 to 35 days before Palm Sunday. It takes at least 30 days to develop an open flower at an average temperature of 21°C from the time buds are first seen.

8. Divide the number of estimated leaves left to be unfolded by the number of days left from the date of counting to 30 days before Palm Sunday (estimated visible bud date). This figure tells how many leaves must be unfolded each day in order to make the estimated visible bud date.

Table VII

Yearly Average Number of Leaves on Plants from 'Ace' and 'Nellie White' "8- to 9-Inch U.S.A. Grade" (20- to 22.5-cm) Bulb

	Cooled in case		Cooled by CTF method	
Year	'Ace'	'Nellie White'	'Ace'	'Nellie White'
1969	—	—	105	89
1970	92	90	104	91
1971	95	70	104	90
1972	96	70	106	90
1973	85	68	95	83
1974	90	80	98	87
1975	83	74	80	77
1976	83	72	87	82
1977	67	56	67	65
1978	71	75	92	75
Average	85	72	92	83

Fig. 5 Reproductive meristem: five primary buds and two secondary buds. Stage of development that is found in late January.

9. On a weekly basis, count and record the number of leaves unfolded to a 45° angle from the stem. The last individual leaf counted can be marked weekly with a paper punch hole or paint to avoid repetitious leaf counting. Only the newly unfolded leaves above the most recently marked leaf will have to be counted each week.

10. After the weekly count has been recorded and determined, compare data from the previous week and determine if the leaf number was greater or smaller than the number required to keep the crop on time. Increase forcing temperatures if leaf number is less, decrease temperature if more.

Over the last 10 years, the average numbers of leaves to form on plants have varied from 67 to 91 for 'Ace' and 56 to 80 for 'Nellie White.' This 10-year average has been for 'Ace' and 'Nellie White' bulbs that were given the CTF treatment.

VI. CULTURAL CONSIDERATIONS

A. Temperature

Proper forcing temperature is considered by the author to be the single most important environmental, cultural, or growth factor in forcing a healthy bulb into flower. Many forcers maintain optimal forcing temperatures from 0730 to

1630 hours or only when the labor force is present, and not from dawn to dusk. Many valuable forcing hours are lost during forcing unless temperatures are maintained from dawn to dusk (Wilkins and Roh, 1972). Thermostats for correct temperatures should also be placed at plant height. Day temperatures above 21°C also can result in tall plants (Roh and Wilkins, 1973b).

Soil temperature should be monitored in the bulb case or medium during the programming period and the early part of stage 1, as the optimal temperatures for root growth is 18.3°C, and 4.5°C for cooling. The possible cause for high flower bud numbers for the CTF programming method is the presence of roots on bulbs prior to and during cooling (Hartley, 1968; De Hertogh et al., 1969).

B. Light

During forcing it is believed maximum sunlight is desired for high quality plants. Glass should be kept clean. Short days (black shadecloth from 1600 to 0800) will produce shorter plants. Many experienced forcers claim that light is important. Roberts (unpublished data) has forced and flowered lily plants from programmed bulbs in total darkness in the same time span as plants in light. The author (unpublished data) has recently observed little differences in rate of leaf unfolding as well as rate of flower bud development under different reduced light intensities and high energy discharge lamps.

C. Medium and Nutrition

A well-drained and aerated open medium is a prerequisite for top-quality plants with good root growth. The medium should be pasteurized and analyzed to determine nutrient content and pH before bulbs are potted. Bulbs are placed deep in the pots to allow for stem root development during greenhouse forcing.

Proper fertilization is essential to produce quality plants. Soil pH should be slightly acid to neutral. Studies (Widmer et al., 1976) with 'Ace' and 'Nellie White' have shown that excessively alkaline conditions resulted in shorter, narrower plants ('Ace' especially), a slightly lower flower count ('Ace' only,), paler foliage color, significant and undesirable quantities of leaf tip burn (most severe on 'Nellie White'), and some increase in root discoloration. The leaf scorch problem commonly observed with 'Ace' was not completely eliminated (Tizio and Seeley, 1976).

Growers frequently avoid or limit phosphorus applications because phosphorus has been associated with leaf scorch (Tizio and Seeley, 1976). However, phosphorus is one of the essential nutrients. Lack of phosphorus will lower bud counts; thus the potting medium should contain adequate available phosphorus. Either (a) make two applications of a soluble fertilizer with a significant phosphorus content early in the forcing period, or (b) mix 347 to 521 gm of superphosphate or 174 to 260 gm of treble superphosphate per cubic meter of potting soil (Widmer et al., 1976).

Nitrogen and potassium levels in the starting soil should be at a medium or low level. Fertilizer applications should continue until 10 days before Easter. Usually unfertilized plants will make taller, less full, and less attractive plants.

The University of Minnesota (Widmer et al., 1976) has consistently produced quality plants with applications of a neutral nutrient mix of 1 part ammonium sulfate and 4 parts sodium or calcium nitrate made at 374 gm/100 liters of water every 2 weeks starting 1 to 2 weeks after shoot emergence. In addition, an application of muriate of potash at 250 gm in 100 liters of water is made in alternate weeks until flower buds are 1 to 2 cm long.

Alternate fertilizer programs include the following:

1. Calcium nitrate at 187 gm/100 liters of water and postasium nitrate at 94 gm/100 liters applied weekly until flower buds are 1 to 2 cm long; then calcium nitrate only at 250 gm/100 liters weekly. This program is preferable if the soil pH is low, the water supply is not alkaline, or the presence of fluorine is a problem.

2. A 25–0–25 fertilizer at 250 gm/100 liters of water applied at the first watering and a 200 ppm nitrogen solution from 25–0–25 at every watering thereafter.

3. A 25–0–25 fertilizer at 250 gm/100 liters of water applied every week.

The presence of fluorine (fluoride) in water and fertilizer source has not prevented the production of good quality plants in Minnesota (Widmer et al., 1976). We recommend the use of a phosphate fertilizer as previously mentioned. An alternate nonfluorine water supply should be used if available. Because of possible fluoride contamination, we do not suggest the use of perlite; excess boron that may come from some limestone sources should also be avoided (Marousky and Woltz, 1977; Widmer et al., 1976). Furthermore, proper pH and nutrient levels should be maintained, soil should be tested at a competent soil testing laboratory prior to potting the bulbs, and routine soil analysis should occur at least every 2 weeks.

D. Watering

The medium should be kept moist at all times. If pots are stacked during the low-temperature period for CTF programming, plants at the bottom may receive more water. Too much water in early stages and during periods of low light should be avoided. An open medium lessens the risk of restricting soil oxygen and root growth.

E. Gases

Oxygen is essential for a healthy and actively functioning root system. Thus, an open and well drained (aerated) medium is desired.

If bulbs are properly vernalized, carbon dioxide injections into the atmosphere result in increased plant height with no difference in date of flower (Wilkins et al., 1968a). Thus, carbon dioxide is never recommended for lily forcing.

Ethylene will cause many and assorted problems and damage depending on concentration, length of exposure, temperature, and the developmental stage of the lily bulb or plant (Wilkins, unpublished observations). Emergence may be prevented or delayed with leaf abnormalities caused by exposure to ethylene. If the shoot is exposed to ethylene at flower bud formation, malformations and reductions in numbers result, and if at or near flower bud opening, ethylene will actually hasten anthesis of the older, and abortion of the younger buds.

VII. PROBLEMS

A. Possible Causes of Premature Leaf Senescence

There are many reasons for dried lower leaves. A few are root injury, root loss (heavy soil, overwatering, and root rot), inadequate or excessive fertilizer, moisture stress (insufficient water), plant crowding (insufficient light and air circulation at base of plants), or excessive fluorine levels in the plants (Widmer *et al.,* 1976).

B. Insect Control

Aphids and symphilids on Easter lilies can be controlled through the appropriate use of chemicals. Because excessive doses can cause some phytotoxicity, always use an appropriate applicator for correct dosage rate. Cultivar phytotoxicity has been noted; therefore, treat only a few plants and observe for sensitivity before treating the entire crop.

C. Mites

Bulb mites are ubiquitous, feeding on dead tissue, but can apparently enter into stem tissue and cause extensive damage. Plants appear to be weak, stunted, and frequently have injured leaves. Preliminary experimentation indicates that a bulb soak of an appropriate chemical for lily bulb mite control (Wilkins, unpublished observations) is of value. This treatment in conjunction with root rot control drenches can be predicted to greatly reduce any possible mite damage.

D. Disease Control

Virus is often present; however, constant discarding of infected plants by the bulb grower must be practiced and is an effective control method.

Root rot control is started at time of potting when the bulb is first watered with a fungicidal drench. Follow-up drenches should occur every 4 weeks through-out the forcing season with the correct concentrations and combinations to control *Rhizoctonia solani, Fusarium* species, and *Pythium* species. Control of root rot cannot be overemphasized (Pfleger, 1977).

E. Height

Height control can be accomplished by A-Rest (ancymidol) (Wilkins *et al.,* 1972). It is, however, expensive, and its effectiveness can be reduced by high temperatures, low levels of night lighting, and absorption of the chemical by the growing medium. A-Rest may also cause hollow stems in some cultivars and such plants must be staked (Roh and Wilkins, 1977e). Environmental restraints (Table VIII) are best, as for example, 18.3°C maximum temperatures at the early forcing stages, temperatures never over 21°C during the entire forcing period (Roh and Wilkins, 1973b), no low level lighting at night, or excessive watering. Short days (blackcloth from 1600 to 0800 hours) reduces internodal stretch (Kohl and Nelson, 1963).

F. Storage

Storing plants in the dark at 1.7°–7.2°C when buds are white and puffy will keep plants in good condition for 20 days (Wilkins, unpublished observations). Soil should be moist during storage. A soil fungicidal drench should be added 10 days before storage. White (1940) stored cut stems in water at 3°–4°C for 8 weeks and kept the stems 4 days at room temperature, but the tight buds failed to open.

Table VIII

Factors Affecting Final Plant Height[a]

1. Method of programming and length of cold treatment
2. Light intensity and photoperiod
3. Temperature
4. Cultivar
5. Bulb size
6. Time of root development
7. Root rot
8. Fertilizer practices
9. Watering practices
10. Carbon dioxide
11. Chemicals

[a]From De Hertogh and Wilkins (1971a,b).

REFERENCES

Bailey, L. H. (1916). *Lilium.* "The Standard Encyclopedia of Horticulture," Vol. IV, p. 1862. Macmillan, London.

Blaney, L. T., and Roberts, A. N. (1967). Bulb production. *In* "Easter Lilies: The Culture, Diseases, Insects and Economics of Easter Lilies" (D. C. Kiplinger and R. W. Langhans, eds.), pp. 23–36. Cornell Univ. Press, Ithaca, New York.

Blaney, L. T., Roberts, A. N., and Lin, P. (1967). Timing Easter lilies. *Florists' Rev.* **140**(3624), 19.

De Hertogh, A. A., and Blakely, N. (1972). Influence of gibberellins A$_3$ and A$_4$ + $_7$ on the development of forced *Lilium longiflorum* Thunb. *J. Am. Soc. Hortic. Sci.* **97**, 320–323.

De Hertogh, A. A., and Wilkins, H. F. (1971a). The forcing of northwest-grown 'Ace' and 'Nellie White' lilies. Part 1. *Florists' Rev.* **149**(3857), 29–31.

De Hertogh, A. A., and Wilkins, H. F. (1971b). The forcing of northwest-grown 'Ace' and 'Nellie White' lilies. Part 2. *Florists' Rev.* **149**(3858), 57, 104–111.

De Hertogh, A. A., Carlson, W. H., and Kays, S. (1969). Controlled temperature forcing of planted lily bulbs. *J. Am. Soc. Hortic. Sci.* **94**, 433–436.

De Hertogh, A. A., Roberts, A. N., Stuart, N. W., Langhans, R. W., Linderman, R. G., Lawson, R. H., Kiplinger D. C., and Wilkins, H. F. (1971). A guide to terminology of Easter lilies (*Lilium longiflorum* Thunb.). *HortScience* **6**, 121–123.

De Hertogh, A. A., Rasmussen, H. P., and Blakely, N. (1976). Morphological changes and factors influencing shoot apex development of *Lilium longiflorum* Thunb. during forcing. *J. Am. Soc. Hortic. Sci.* **101**, 463–471.

Hartley, D. E. (1968). Growth and flowering responses of Easter lily, *Lilium longiflorum* Thunb., to bulb storage. Ph.D. Thesis, Oregon State Univ., Corvallis.

Kays, S., Carlson, W., Blakely, N., and DeHertogh, A. A. (1971). Effects of exogenous gibberellin on the development of *Lilium longiflorum* Thunb. 'Ace'. *J. Am. Soc. Hortic. Sci.* **96**, 222–225.

Kohl, H. C., Jr., and Nelson, R. L. (1963). Daylength and light intensity as independent factors in determining height of Easter lily. *Proc. Am. Soc. Hortic. Sci.* **83**, 808–810.

Laiche, A. J., and Box, C. O. (1970). Response of Easter lily to bulb treatments of precooling, packing media, moisture and gibberellin. *HortScience* **5**, 396–397.

Lin, P. C., and Roberts, A. N. (1970). Scale function in growth and flowering of *Lilium longiflorum* Thunb. 'Nellie White'. *J. Am. Soc. Hortic. Sci.* **95**, 559–561.

Lin, W. C., and Wilkins, H. F. (1973). The interaction of temperature on photoperiodic responses of *Lilium longiflorum* Thunb. cv. Nellie White. *Florists' Rev.* **153**(3965), 24–26.

Lin, W. C., and Wilkin, H. F. (1975a). Influence of bulb harvest dates and temperature on the growth and flowering of *Lilium longiflorum* Thunb. 'Nellie White'. *J. Am. Soc. Hortic. Sci.* **100**, 6–9.

Lin. W. C., and Wilkins, H. F. (1975b). Exogenous gibberellins and abscisic acid effects on the growth and development of *Lilium longiflorum* Thunb. 'Ace'. *J. Am. Soc. Hortic. Sci.* **100**, 9–16.

Lin, W. C., Wilkins, H. F., and Brenner, M. L. (1975). Endogenous promoter and inhibitor levels in bulbs of *Lilium longiflorum* Thunb. 'Nellie White'. *J. Am. Soc. Hortic. Sci.* **100**, 106–109.

Marousky, F. J., and Woltz, S. S. (1977). Influence of lime, nitrogen and phosphorus sources on the availability and relationship of soil fluoride to leaf scorch in *Lilium longiflorum* Thunb. *J. Am. Soc. Hortic. Sci.* **102**, 799–804.

Miller, R. O., and Kiplinger, D. C. (1966). Reversal of vernalization in northwest Easter lilies. *Proc. Am. Soc. Hortic. Sci.* **88**, 646–650.

Oglivie, L. (1957). Notes on the history of the Easter lily (*Lilium longiflorum*). *In* "Royal Horticultural Society, Lily Yearbook" (P. M. Synge and G. E. Petersons, eds.), No. 20, pp. 45–49. Royal Hortic. Soc., London.

Pfeiffer, N. E. (1935). Development of the floral axis and new bud in imported Easter lilies. *Contrib. Boyce Thompson Inst.* **7**, 311–321.

Pfeiffer, N. E. (1966). Great names in lilies: II. Early explorers in Japan. *In* "North American Lily Society, Lily Year Book." (G. L. Slate, ed.), pp. 51–57. North Am. Lily Soc., Geneva, New York.

Pfleger, F. L. (1977). Lily disease management program. *Minn. State Florists' Bull.* Oct., p. 8.

Roh, S. M., and Wilkins, H. F. (1973a). The influence and substitution of long days for cold treatments on growth and flowering of Easter lilies (*Lilium longiflorum* Thunb. 'Georgia' and 'Nellie White'). *Florists' Rev.* **153**(3960), 19–21, 60–63.

Roh, S. M., and Wilkins, H. F. (1973b). The influence of day and night temperature from visible buds to antheses of the Easter lily (*Lilium longiflorum* Thunb, cv Ace). *HortScience* **8,** 129–130.

Roh, S. M., and Wilkins, H. F. (1974a). Decay and dark reversion of phytochrome in *Lilium longiflorum* Thunb. cv. Nellie White. *HortScience* **9,** 38–39.

Roh, S. M., and Wilkins, H. F. (1974b). Red and far-red treatments accelerate shoot emergence from bulbs of *Lilium longiflorum* Thunb. cv. Nellie White. *HortScience* **9,** 37–38.

Roh, S. M., and Wilkins, H. F. (1977a). Influence of interrupting the long day inductive treatments on growth and flower numbers of *Lilium longiflorum* Thunb. *J. Am. Soc. Hortic. Sci.* **102,** 253–255.

Roh, S. M., and Wilkins, H. F. (1977b). Temperature and photoperiod effect on flower numbers in *Lilium longiflorum* Thunb. *J. Am. Soc. Hortic. Sci.* **102,** 235–242.

Roh, S. M., and Wilkins, H. F. (1977c). The control of flowering in *Lilium longiflorum* Thunb, cv. Nellie White by cyclic or continuous light treatments. *J. Am. Soc. Hortic. Sci.* **102,** 247–253.

Roh, S. M., and Wilkins, H. F. (1977d). The effects of bulb vernalization and shoot photoperiod treatments on growth and flowering of *Lilium longiflorum* Thunb. cv. Nellie White. *J. Am. Soc. Hortic. Sci.* **102,** 229–235.

Roh, S. M., and Wilkins, H. F. (1977e). The influence and interaction of ancymidol and photoperiod on growth of *Lilium longiflorum* Thunb. *J. Am. Soc. Hortic. Sci.* **102,** 255–257.

Smith, D. R., and Langhans, R. W. (1962). The influence of photoperiod on the growth and flowering of the Easter lily (*Lilium longiflorum* Thunb. var. Croft). *Proc. Am. Soc. Hortic. Sci.* **80,** 599–604.

Stearn, W. T. (1947). The name *Lilium japonicum* as used by Houttuyn and Thunberg. *In* "Royal Horticultural Society, Lily Yearbook" (P. M. Synge, ed.), No. 11, pp. 101–108. Royal Hortic. Soc., London.

Stuart, N. W. (1954). Mositure content of packing medium, temperature and duration of storage as factors in forcing lily bulbs. *Proc. Am. Soc. Hortic. Sci.* **63,** 488–494.

Tizio, M., and Seeley, J. G. (1976). Nitrogen source, fluoride applications and leaf scorch of 'Ace' lilies. *Florists' Rev.* **159**(4115), 43–85.

Tsukamoto, Y. (1971). Change in endogenous growth substances in Easter lily as affected by cooling. *Acta Hortic.* **23,** 75–81.

Wang, S. Y., and Roberts, A. N. (1970). Physiology of dormancy on *Lilium longiflorum* Thunb. 'Ace.' *J. Am. Soc. Hortic. Sci.* **95,** 554–558.

Waters, W. E., and Wilkins, H. F. (1967). Influence of intensity, duration and date of light on growth and flowering of uncooled Easter lily, (*Lilium longiflorum* Thunb. 'Georgia'). *Proc. Am. Soc. Hortic. Sci.* **90,** 433–439.

White, H. E. (1940). The culture and forcing of Easter lilies. *Mass. Agric. Exp. Stn., Bull.* No. 376, pp. 1–20.

Widmer, R. E., Mugaas, R., and Wilkins, H. F. (1976). Lime and phosphate effects on Easter lilies, *Lilium longiflorum* Thunb. *Minn. State Florists' Bull.* Dec., pp. 1–7.

Wilkins, H. F. (1970). University of Minnesota's Easter Lily Research Report: Paper No. VIII. Leaf counting. *Minn. State Florists' Bull.* Dec., pp. 4–10.

Wilkins, H. F. (1973). Our Easter lily: Where did it come from, why does it flower at Easter time, chasing the wild lily. *Minn. Hortic.* **101,** 36–38.

Wilkins, H. F. (1976). Methods and schedules for forcing Easter lilies—1977, a late Easter. *Minn. State Florists' Bull.* Oct., pp. 3–5.

Wilkins, H. F. (1977). Methods and schedules for forcing Easter lilies—1978, an early Easter. *Minn. State Florists' Bull.* Oct., pp. 2–4.

Wilkins, H. F., and Roberts, A. N. (1969). University of Minnesota's Easter Lily Research Report: Paper No. IV. Leaf counting—a new concept in timing Easter lilies. *Minn. State Florists' Bull.* Dec., pp. 10–13.

Wilkins, H. F., and Roh, S. M. (1970). University of Minnesota's Easter Lily Research Report: Paper No. IX. Lighting lilies at shoot emergence. Night interruption shown to be most effective. *Minn. State Florists' Bull.* Dec., pp. 10–12.

Wilkins, H. F., and Roh, S. M. (1972). The importance of day/night temperature control. *Minn. State Florists' Bull.* Dec., pp. 4–5.

Wilkins, H. F., and Roh, S. M. (1976). Even higher flower bud numbers are now possible in Easter lilies by dipping your greenhouse temperatures. *Florists' Rev.* **159**(4127), 33, 76–79.

Wilkins, H. F., Waters, W. E., and Widmer, R. E. (1968a). The effect of carbon dioxide, photoperiod and vernalization on flowering of Easter lilies, (*Lilium longiflorum* Thunb. 'Ace' and 'Nellie White'). *Proc. Am. Soc. Hortic. Sci.* **96,** 650–654.

Wilkins, H. F., Waters, W. E., and Widmer, R. E. (1968b). University of Minnesota's Easter Lily Research Report: Paper No. II. An insurance policy: Lighting lilies at shoot emergence will overcome inadequate bulb precooling. *Minn. State Florists' Bull.* Aug., pp. 6–11.

Wilkins, H. F., Rosacker, D., and Kise, H. (1972). University of Minnesota's Easter Lily Research Report: Paper No. XIII. Bulb temperature treatments and soil applications of Quel during forcing effectively reduced the height of *Lilium longiflorum,* 'Ace', 'Arai' and 'Nellie White'. *Minn. State Florists' Bull.* Feb., pp. 6–10.

Wilson, E. H. (1925). Subgenera, sections, and species (Lilium longiflorum). *In* "Enumeration of the Lilies of Eastern Asia" (E. H. Wilson, ed.), pp. 23–28. Dunlan and Co., London.

14
Hydrangeas

T. C. Weiler

I. INTRODUCTION

Hydrangeas [*Hydrangea macrophylla* (Thunb.) Ser., Saxifragaceae] are potted florists' plants and deciduous landscape shrubs, winter hardy to USDA Zone 6. As potted plants, their inflorescences are spectacular spheres of pink, blue, or white. They are produced primarily for the Easter (March–April) and Mother's Day (May) holidays.

Although known in the United States as "hydrangea," the plant is better known internationally as "hortensia." Officially *Hydrangea macrophylla* subsp. *macrophylla* var. *macrophylla* (Thunb.) Ser., the species is native to Honshu, the large Japanese island (Bailey and Bailey, 1976) at latitude 35°N.

Florists' hydrangeas are easily hybridized among themselves, but other species and interspecific hybrids may be incompatible with them. The florets are sterile or fertile; fertile florets can be hybridized by standard emasculation and pollination procedures. A successful cross yields over 100 seeds that can be germinated as soon as the seed capsule ripens (Haworth-Booth, 1950).

Only a few cultivars dominate the United States market (Table I). For example, Kenyon (1972) reported that 'Rose Supreme,' 'Merveille,' 'Strafford,' and 'Todi' represented 80% of his sales. In Europe, some of those cultivars as well as many others are grown (Aldrichem *et al.,* 1978; Dersch, 1973; Fritzsche, 1977; Hargreaves, 1973; Haworth-Booth, 1950; Litlere, 1974; Loeser, 1974; Schulte-Scherlebeck, 1977).

Fewer hydrangeas are grown in the United States as a florists' crop than in the past (Table II), apparently because of long cropping time, difficulty in transporting when in bloom, and the large postgreenhouse demand for water.

II. GROWTH

Water deficiency severely slows crop growth and damages tissues. Therefore, well-aerated media with high water-holding capacity such as peat moss mixes are used (Ray, 1946; Shanks, 1975). Matric tension is kept more positive than −0.1 bar and soluble salts less than 1.25 mmhos/cm (5 water : 1 medium dilution by volume).

Sepals, the conspicuous parts of the florets, are white in a few cultivars, but for most cultivars are pink or blue, depending on the pH of the growing medium. Sepal color is determined by availability of heavy metals from the medium rather than by changes in plant sap pH (Kikkawa *et al.,* 1955). The heavy metals, once in the sepals, form salt complexes with anthocyanin. These complexes, plus anthocyanin's relationship to tannin and flavonol copigments, determine sepal color (pink or blue) (Asen *et al.,* 1957; Robinson, 1939). The color-changing pigment is a glycoside of delphinidin (Asen *et al.,* 1957; Robin-

Table I

United States-Grown Cultivars Listed by Sepal Color and Response Group[a]

Cultivar	Sepal color	Response group (total weeks forcing at 15°C night plus last 2 weeks at 12°C night)	Introduction		
			Hybridizer	Year	Country
Kuhnert	Blue pink	13	Matthes	Unknown	Germany
Improved Merveille	Pink red	13	—[b]	1966	United States
Merritt Supreme	Blue, pink	13	Draps [c]	ca. 1950	Belgium
Merveille	Pink red	13	Cayeux	1927	France
Regula	White	12	Moll	1934	Switzerland
Rose Supreme	Blue, pink	14	Swanson	1950	United States
Soeur Thérese	White	12	Gaigne	1947	France
Triomphe (Strafford)	Pink red	14	Cayeux	1920	France

[a]Modified from Haworth-Booth (1950), Jung (1964), Koths *et al.* (1973), LeMattre (1963), and Merritt (1978).
[b]Selected for disease and insect resistance from 'Merveille' by Merritt of the United States.
[c]Selected from Draps' seedlings by Merritt of the United States.

Table II

United States Crop Production Statistics, 1950 to 1977[a]

Wholesale	1950	1959	1970	1977
Plants sold (million)	3.3	3.2	2.0	2.5
Average value (U.S. $/plant)	1.26	1.31	1.86	2.22

[a]Modified from Anonymous (1952, 1959, 1973b, 1978).

son, 1939) and contains an orthodihydroxyl system to form colored pigment–metal complexes (Asen, 1967).

Aluminum is the implicated heavy metal ion (Allen, 1931). Tissue of blue-flowered plants at pH 5.5 contains above 950 ppm aluminum, mauve-flowered plants at pH 5.8 to 6.0 contain 200 to 950 ppm aluminum, and pink-flowered plants at pH 6.0 to 6.2 contain below 200 ppm aluminum (Allen, 1943; Okada and Funaki, 1967; Okada and Okawa, 1974). Molybdenum (Asen et al., 1959; Kikkawa et al., 1955) and potassium (Asen et al., 1960) may also be essential for maximum blue color.

Hydrangea foliage is chlorotic from iron deficiency at media pH above 6.0 to 6.2 (Münch and Fritzsche, 1975). Any pH between 5.5 and 6.0 is acceptable during plant growth, but when forcing begins, pH for a crop with pink sepals must be 6.0, and for a crop with blue sepals must be 5.5. White can be obtained at either pH. Media pH should be adjusted, based on mix analysis, before potting. Since acid peat moss is often used in mixes, pH is adjusted upward with limestone; if necessary, pH can be lowered by adding sulfur. To maintain optimum pH in regions with alkaline irrigation water, acid residue fertilizers may be used (e.g., ammonium sulfate, potassium chloride) or the water can be acidified with citric acid (Yock, 1978). Sulfuric or nitric acid can be used to substitute for citric acid. Phosphoric acid, which contains phosphate and affects sepal color, should not be used. As an alternative, slow-acting sulfur supplements can be added to the medium before potting. In addition, periodic applications of aluminum sulfate or ferrous sulfate are usually required. These salts are applied as solutions with an agitating sprayer that has its nozzle detached. Aluminum sulfate at 3.4 to 12 gm/liter is applied to a blue-flowered crop, ferrous sulfate at 3.4 gm/liter to pink (Allen, 1934a; Laurie et al., 1968; Poesch, 1935; Post, 1949). Higher rates will elevate soluble salts to toxic levels, so several weekly applications may be needed. In regions with irrigation water that is too acid, optimum pH is maintained with alkaline residue liquid fertilizers (e.g., calcium nitrate), bases such as potassium hydroxide added to the water, or a slow-acting limestone addition to the medium before potting.

Growing plants have a high demand for fertilizer, especially nitrogen (Link and Shanks, 1952), and the potting soil must be adjusted to optimum levels before potting; the nutrient effects on sepal color must also be considered. Low potassium best promotes pink sepals (Asen et al., 1959), whereas high potassium best promotes blue (Asen et al., 1960; Link and Shanks, 1952). High phosphorus (Asen et al., 1959; Okada and Okawa, 1974) or high ammonium relative to nitrate (Asen et al., 1963) reduces sepal aluminum and promotes pink sepals, probably by antagonizing aluminum uptake. No superphosphate should be incorporated into the medium for a blue-flowered crop. Optimum modified Spurway soil nutrient levels for blue sepals are 20 to 30 ppm nitrate, 1 to 3 ppm phosphorus, 25 to 45 ppm potassium, and over 100 ppm calcium. The levels for pink sepals are 30 to 50 ppm nitrate, 6 to 8 ppm phosphorus, 15 to 25 ppm potassium, and over 100 ppm calcium (Bing et al., 1974). Either level can be used for plants with white sepals. To maintain these levels during growth, a 25-5-30 (nitrogen-phosphorus-potassium) fertilizer ratio is desirable for blue sepals (Koths et al., 1973), and a 25-10-10 ratio is desirable for pink (Shanks, 1975).

Supplemental carbon dioxide at 1500 ppm (by volume) will promote growth at warm temperature and high light. Below 15°C, cool temperature rather than carbon dioxide is probably the factor limiting growth, so no supplemental carbon dioxide should be used.

Growth in June through August is greatest under 22 to 50% shade at southern latitudes (32-41°N) (Furuta, 1960; Ray, 1946; Shanks, 1975), although almost full irradiation is optimum at northern latitudes (42-59°N) (Litlere and Strømme, 1975; Post, 1949). Shade optimizes growth by reducing plant temperature as well as by raising relative humidity to reduce water stress (Shanks, 1975). In hot, bright weather occasional syringing of the crop may be beneficial (Jung, 1964). Some cultivars such as 'Strafford' branch poorly at high temperatures and are grown only at northern latitudes (Jung, 1964; Shanks, 1975).

III. FLOWERING

Formation of the terminal cymes has been well described (Kosugi and Arai, 1960; LeMattre, 1963; Litlere and Strømme, 1975; Peters, 1975; Struckmeyer, 1950). Six to 9 weeks of late summer–early autumn conditions are required for complete inflorescence formation (Anonymous, 1971; Post, 1949) (Fig. 1). Both the cool temperatures and short photoperiods of that time of year are involved.

Inflorescences initiate rapidly at 13°–18°C under both long and short photoperiods (LeMattre, 1975; Litlere, 1975b; Litlere and Strømme, 1975; Peters, 1975) (Fig. 2). Thus at northern latitudes the plants need to be grown in greenhouses maintained above 18°C during the summer to prevent inflorescences from forming "prematurely" (Post, 1949). At 19°–22°C the critical photoperiod is 14 to 16 hours (Fig. 2); short photoperiods especially promote inflorescence initiation (Fig. 2) (Hunter, 1950; Smeal, 1964). Few inflorescences initiate above 22°C (Fig. 2), so at southern latitudes the plants are

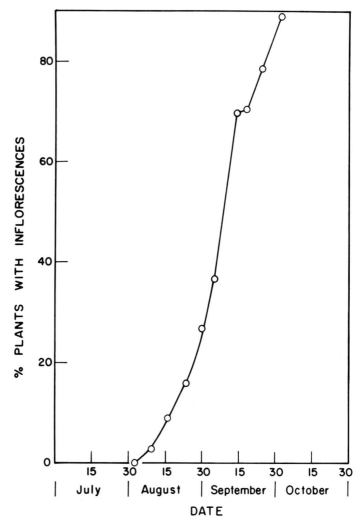

Fig. 1. Percentage of plants with inflorescences on several late summer and fall dates for 'Merveille' plants pinched June 10 to 17 and grown near Paris. (Modified from Anonymous, 1971.)

placed outdoors in summer not only for moderate growing temperatures, but also to maximize exposure to late summer and early autumn temperatures below 22°C which promote inflorescence initiation. In addition, reduced fertilization in late summer promotes flowering (Jung, 1964). However, the effect of these environmental factors on inflorescence initiation varies with cultivar (Peters, 1975; Piringer and Stuart, 1958).

Weak stems, particularly those in the understory, do not form inflorescences and are called "blind" stems. They may be weakened by interplant or intraplant

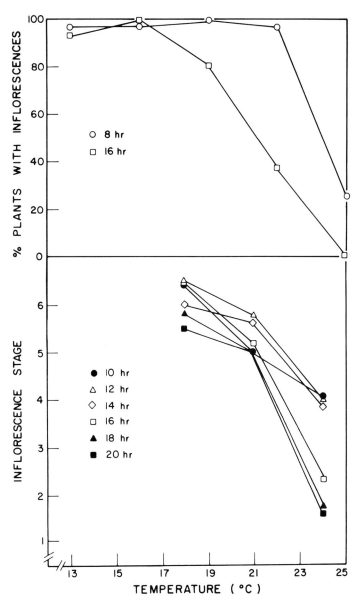

Fig. 2. Inflorescence formation at various photoperiods and temperatures for 'King George' hydrangeas after 50 days of treatment (modified from Peters, 1975) (upper) or 'Eldorado' hydrangeas after 56 days (modified from Litlere and Strømme, 1975) (lower). Stages for 'Eldorado' were 1–3 = vegetative; 4 = primary inflorescence formed; 5 = secondary inflorescence formed; 6 = sepals and petal primordia formed; 7 = pistil primordia formed. Numbers denote photoperiod (hours).

competition for light, or may arise either under conditions not conducive to inflorescence initiation or from dormant vegetative buds during forcing.

Although short photoperiods in late summer through autumn promote inflorescence differentiation to the G stage [i.e., when the gynoecia (pistils) have completely formed], the continued short photoperiods of winter and early spring inhibit inflorescence expansion and the inflorescences are then called "dormant." Dormancy under naturally short photoperiods is broken commercially by cold storage (Allen, 1934b; Stuart, 1951). This is applied to plants from which the leaves have been removed to prevent *Botrytis* storage rot of the inflorescences. Storage at 2°–9°C for at least 6 weeks is sufficient to promote rapid expansion of the inflorescences. Temperatures of 10°C or above are much less effective (Link and Shanks, 1951; Litlere, 1975a; Stuart, 1951).

Light during cold storage aids in breaking dormancy (Litlere, 1975a), and experimentally, fully developed inflorescences enlarge quickly at long photoperiods without cold storage (LeMattre, 1975). Research has shown that gibberellic acid can replace the requirement for cold storage or long photoperiods. For example, at short photoperiods, inflorescences of plants not cold treated will expand and flower, if sprayed twice weekly at 1 ml per plant using 1 ppm gibberellic acid ten times or 10 ppm gibberellic acid five times. The best plants develop, however, if partial cold treatment is followed by twice-weekly gibberellic acid sprays at 1 ml per plant, e.g., 4 weeks of cold followed by four sprays at 10 ppm or 2 weeks of cold followed by four sprays at 50 ppm (Stuart and Cathey, 1962). Even fully cold-treated plants bloom 1 to 2 weeks earlier when sprayed once or twice with 10 ppm gibberellic acid. The optimum inflorescence diameter for treatment is 1.5 to 2 cm (Adriansen, 1976; Dörr, 1960; Jansen, 1960; Jongkind and Sytsema, 1966; Loeser, 1962, 1963; Möhring, 1961; Wasscher, 1958). Earlier treatment hastens flowering only slightly, whereas later treatment causes stems and pedicels to stretch. Because timing of application is so critical, the crop may have to be partitioned into five to six groups for treatment on different dates because of plant-to-plant variability. Even at the optimum stage, two applications may cause excessive elongation with tall-growing or white-flowered cultivars.

IV. GROWTH RETARDANTS

Because hydrangeas are shrubs, dwarf cultivars are used for potted plant production. Even so, finished plants are often too tall without chemical retardation (Adriansen, 1976).

Summer growth is regulated by a 5000 to 7500 ppm daminozide spray. Treatment is made when shoots are 3 to 5 cm long and a second application may be made 2 to 3 weeks later (Jung, 1964), but if applied after early August the effect will carry over to finished plant forcing (Lavsen, 1968; Shanks, 1969;

Shanks and Link, 1964). For example, one application of 2000 ppm daminozide just before leaf removal and cold storage will reduce the height of subsequent flowering plants 22 to 32%. A 2000 ppm chlormequat spray is ineffective (Kohl and Nelson, 1966). A 4800 to 19,200 ppm ethephon spray in late October, after inflorescences have formed and just before cold storage, also retards growth during spring forcing (Shanks, 1969), but such high rates may cause abnormal plants and inflorescences (Tjia and Buxton, 1976). If applied earlier, ethephon inhibits inflorescence formation (Shanks, 1969). An early September chlormequat drench at 0.4 gm/13-cm pot increases the number of inflorescences per plant (Gugenhan, 1969), but also has a carry-over effect.

During spring forcing plant height is also excessive, particularly at cool forcing temperatures (12°–17°C) (LeMattre, 1975) and the longer photoperiods of late spring (Piringer and Stuart, 1955; Stuart et al., 1955). Plants from storage have no leaves to absorb a spray application of growth retardant but chemical height reduction may begin immediately if a retardant drench is applied to the medium. Chlormequat at 0.3 to 1.6 gm/15-cm pot (Anonymous, 1973a; Cathey and Stuart, 1961; Gugenhan, 1969; Loeser, 1968) or ancymidol at 2 to 4 mg/15-cm pot (Tjia et al., 1976) can be used. Two milligrams of ancymidol reduces height 30 to 38%. Daminozide spray applications, however, are more commonly applied, and treatment is made as soon as sufficient leaf area develops to absorb the chemical. This stage is described as two to five visible leaf pairs (Lavsen, 1968), when the first leaves are 3 to 5 cm long (Paquet, 1966), 2 to 4 weeks after forcing begins (Anonymous, 1973a; Münch and Fritzsche, 1970; Shanks, 1975). One to several sprays of 2500 to 5000 ppm daminozide are applied at 10- to 14-day intervals (Adriansen, 1976; Andersen, 1967; Anonymous, 1973a, 1977; Lavsen, 1968; Loeser, 1968; Münch and Fritzsche, 1970; Paquet, 1966; Shanks and Link, 1964). Exact application procedures vary with cultivar and season. For example, 'Merveille' for Easter may require two spray applications at 2500 to 3500 ppm whereas 'Rose Supreme' for Mother's Day may require three to four applications at 3500 to 5000 ppm (Anonymous, 1977; Shanks, 1975). Treatment ends at least 6 weeks before sales to avoid excessive reduction of inflorescence size. Chlormequat sprays are ineffective at 2000 to 4000 ppm (Loeser, 1968; Münch and Fritzsche, 1970), whereas one 50 ppm ancymidol spray 3 weeks after forcing begins reduces height 25 to 37% (Tjia et al., 1976).

V. SCHEDULING

Typical production simulates nature: the crop is grown in the spring and summer, allowed to form buds in the fall, overwintered, and forced to bloom in late spring (Fig. 3 and 4).

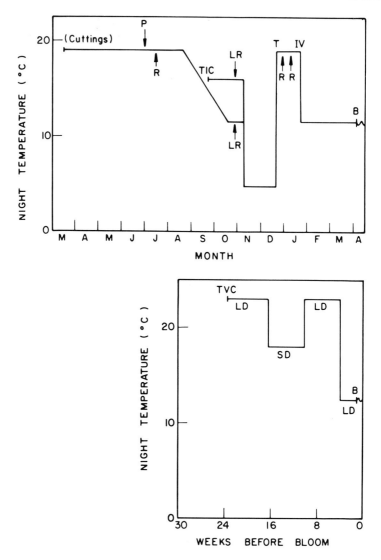

Fig. 3. April 15 Easter schedule for typical production [modified from Koths *et al.,* (1973) and Shanks (1975)] and quick crops [modified from Furuta and Martin (1963)] in 15-cm pots (above) as well as for hypothetical year-round production in 10-cm pots [modified from Weiler and Lopes (1973)] (below). The cultivar response group is 13 weeks. B = bloom, IV = inflorescence visible, LD = long photoperiod, LR = leaf removal, P = final pinch, R = growth retardant, SD = short photoperiod, T = transplant to 15-cm pot, TIC = terminal cutting with inflorescence, TVC = terminal vegetative cutting.

Fig. 4. Plants during outdoor summer growth (upper left), in storage (upper right), when the inflorescence is 4 cm in diameter (lower left), and in bloom (lower right).

A. Stock Plants

Hydrangeas are propagated vegetatively. Selection for good cultivar characteristics, freedom from pests, and vigor is essential to success. Historically, cuttings were made by each finished plant grower from nonflowering ("blind") shoots of the Easter and Mother's Day finished crops since such shoots will grow and flower normally (Kiplinger, 1945a,b; Ray, 1946), but the best cuttings are taken from stock plants. Today specialists propagate the crop. The cuttings are selected for vigor and large stem diameter. Stock plants are saved for several years or selected each year. The shoots are cut back to remove inflorescences before they are allowed to start growing in March for late April to June cuttings (Jung, 1964). Flushes of terminal cuttings develop every 5 to 7 weeks at 15°–18°C. Although most northern stock plants are grown in greenhouses as described above, Pacific Northwestern stock is grown outdoors; hardwood cuttings are available from outdoors January to March but are rarely used, whereas softwood cuttings are available from outdoors in late spring and early summer (Jung, 1964; Laurie et al., 1968; Yock, 1978).

B. Propagation

A few specialists propagate and produce dormant plants. Terminal cuttings 9 cm long, or, on older stems, a terminal cutting plus a one-node ("butterfly") stem cutting, are commonly used (Yock, 1978). Whereas leaf-bud cuttings will root, they are vulnerable to disease and slow to grow. Only cuttings with large stem diameter (0.75–1.25 cm) should be selected.

Cuttings are taken with a sharp blade sterilized frequently to avoid spread of systemic pests. To minimize water stress while avoiding disease, intermittent mist is applied sparingly at southern latitudes until roots are established; at northern latitudes the crop is propagated on greenhouse benches covered with white plastic "tents" to retain moisture and reduce irradiance. The basal end of the cutting is dipped in indolebutyric acid (IBA) or naphthaleneacetic acid (NAA) in talc (1000 ppm IBA or NAA) or dilute alcohol solution (500 to 2400 ppm IBA or NAA for 5 seconds) to promote rooting (Bunge and Weiler, 1977; Shanks, 1975).

Cuttings can be lined out in the propagation medium or stuck into 5- to 7-cm pots and transplanted to 10-cm pots after rooting. They also can be stuck directly into 10- to 12-cm pots equidistantly arranged pot-to-pot. Direct sticking requires greater propagation space, but eliminates transplanting. The foliage is sometimes trimmed to conserve propagation space, but this loss of photo-synthetic area reduces the potential of the cutting. With 21°C bottom heat, terminal cuttings root in 3 to 4 weeks (Koths et al., 1973), node cuttings take about 1 week longer to root and reach a comparable size.

C. Production of Dormant Plants

During summer, established cuttings are grown one per 10-cm pot or two per 12-cm pot (Ulery, 1969). Although the plants grow more without root restric-tion (Jung, 1964), they are not moved to larger-sized containers. This proce-dure minimizes shipping weight and reduces finished plant size. At southern latitudes after the spring frost-free date, the plants are either moved outdoors under partial shade, or if in polyethylene-covered greenhouses, the covering is removed (Ulery, 1978) and shading fabric is installed. At northern latitudes the plants remain in covered, heated greenhouses. Cuttings propagated in May to early June are pinched once while cuttings propagated in April are pinched twice (Table IV). Pinching promotes branching, and once-pinched plants finish with about three shoots, whereas twice-pinched have about five shoots. At pinching, at least two nodes are left on the plant since remaining leaf area is directly related to the number of branches after the pinch, stem diameter, and inflorescence size (Dunham and Roberts, 1948). Because the plant is opposite-leaved, after a second pinching the axils of the remaining top leaves should not point inward (toward the shaded plant canopy) since low light will prevent the shoots from developing and only one shoot will form per pinch (Dunham and Roberts, 1948). The last pinch is made June 20 to July 5 (Merritt, 1976), so shoots are of ideal size by late summer for inflorescence bud set and finishing in 15-cm pots.

Propagation can be delayed to as late as early August and pinching to mid-September if the autumn climate is mild (Miller, 1976), but buds quickly form. Thus earlier propagation, earlier pinching, and a longer growth period lead to larger plants and inflorescences (Jung, 1964).

A quick crop schedule for dormant plant production (Fig. 3) utilizes July-pinched plants as stock. After inflorescences have initiated in September, terminal cuttings are made, rooted, and potted to one to three uniform single-stem plants per 10- to 15-cm pot. This method is appealing because space is used for less time.

D. Storage

Completion of inflorescence formation can be determined by dissecting a few buds and examining the buds with a hand lens. All flower parts must be present by early November, at least 6 weeks before forcing begins. After leaf removal, dormant plants in the north are stored in dark sheds kept above freezing by a heating system. In the South refrigeration may be required.

E. Production of Flowering Plants

Finished plant grade is based on size of pot and number of blooms per pot (Table III). The most popular grades are two to five bloom plants in a 15- to 18-cm pot.

Table III

Production Specifications for Various Hydrangea Grades [a]

			Finishing	
Blooms/pot	Number of pinches	Propagation date	Pot size (cm) [b]	Final spacing (cm²/plant)
1	0	June	14	645
2	1, 0 for butterfly cutting	Mid-May, June	15–16	1086
3	1	Mid-May	16–17	1267
5	2	Mid-April	18	1750

[a]Modified from Shanks (1975).
[b]Use pots 1 cm larger for 'Rose Supreme.'

Finished plants are grown from dormant plants received after cold storage. Dormant plants are bought with 10-cm root balls and transplanted to ¾ (azalea) pots. The intertwined roots must be loosened during transplanting either by pressing the root mass or by slicing vertically with a knife or trowel. The soil level in the new pot should remain the same relative to the plant as it was in the previous pot to prevent either rotting of the buried stem or drying of the uncovered upper roots. Purchased plants can be grown the first 2 to 3 weeks in 10-cm pots before shifting to the finishing pots (Jung, 1964).

Production time varies with cultivar (Table I) and temperature (Table IV). Commonly, the 12- to 13-week response groups are forced for an early Easter, whereas the 13- to 14-week response groups are used for a late Easter and Mother's Day.

Hydrangeas have traditionally been forced at 15°C night temperature with day temperatures 5°–6°C warmer, but cooler nights promote robust stems, long internodes (LeMattre, 1975), maximum inflorescence expansion (Shanks 1975), and hardened finished plants, so a preferred sequence is 18°C nights until the inflorescences are 0.5 cm in diameter followed by 12°C nights (Fig. 4). The crop is grown warmer or cooler if the inflorescences are tighter or more open than desirable (Table IV). Regardless of how the crop is produced, it must be finished at cool temperatures. Cool finishing intensifies sepal color and acclimates the plant to market and interior conditions. Although the crop is grown at or close to full spring irradiance, as the inflorescences expand some shade is applied to prevent "sunburning."

When the inflorescences are visible, plants are pruned to remove stems with inflorescences that will bloom too early or too late as well as blind shoots (Shanks, 1975). Before the inflorescences fully expand, stems are frequently tied to green stakes inserted into the soil. This procedure prevents flowering stems from bend-

Table IV

Forcing Times for Various Intervals of Growth and Development at Three Temperatures for a 13-Week Response Group[a]

Interval	Night temperature (°C)		
	12	15	19
Planting to bloom (weeks)	16	12	10
Plant to inflorescence visibility and 0.5 cm in diameter (weeks)	6	4	3
Inflorescence diameter (cm) to bloom (weeks)			
0.5 (pea-sized)	10	8	7
2 (U.S. nickel-sized)	7.5	6	5
4 (U.S. silver dollar-sized)	5	4	3

[a]Flowers after 13 weeks when grown at 15°C night plus last 2 weeks at 12°C night. Modified from Anonymous (1977), Jung (1964), Koths et al. (1973), Shanks (1975), and Yates (1970).

ing or breaking from the weight of opened inflorescences. For small plants one stake in the center of the pot is satisfactory but for larger plants one stake per stem is required.

New warm-temperature flowering schedules may be feasible (Fig. 3) that avoid pinching, leaf abscission, and cold storage since these procedures prolong production time. Production at warm temperatures, however, will be possible only when disease-free clones are available (Weiler and Lopes, 1974). Such commercial stock is currently being developed using tissue culture and indicator plants (Jones, 1977).

Table V

Pests of Hydrangea[a]

Insects
  Aphid (*Neomyzus, Aphis*)
  Leaf tier (*Exartema*)
  Rose chafer (*Macrodactylus*)
  Scale (*Pulvinaria*)
  Tarnished plant bug (*Lygus*)
  Thrips (*Hercinothrips*)
Mites
  Two-spotted mite (*Tetranychus*)
Nematodes
  Leaf nematode (*Aphelenchoides*)
  Root nematode (*Meloidogyne, Pratylenchus*)
  Stem nematode (*Ditylenchus*)
Other pests
  Slugs (*Limax*)
Fungi
  Inflorescence blight (*Botrytis*)
  Leaf spot (*Ascochyta, Cercospora, Colletotrichum, Corynespora, Phyllosticta, Septoria*)
  Powdery mildew (*Erysiphe*)
  Root rot (*Puccineastrum, Armillaria*)
  Southern blight (*Sclerotium*)
  Stem rot (*Rhizoctonia, Polysporus*)
Bacteria
  Bacterial wilt (*Pseudomonas*)
Mycoplasma [b]
Viruses
  Cucumber mosaic
  Hydrangea ring spot
  Tobacco ring spot
  Tomato ring spot

---

[a]Modified from Beauchesne (1974), Brierley (1954), Hartleb (1974), Hearon *et al.* (1976), Müller (1971), Paludan and Christensen (1973), Welvaert and Samyn (1973), Welvaert *et al.* (1975), Westcott (1964, 1971), and Zeyen and Stienstra (1973).
[b]Data from Hearon *et al.* (1976), Müller (1971), and Welvaert *et al.* (1975).

VI. PESTS

There are many injurious components of the hydrangea biotic environment (Table V). Severity and control vary with location and pesticide regulations. Among the most serious and difficult to control is *Botrytis* blight of inflorescences. Most resistant to most susceptible cultivars are 'Kuhnert,' 'Strafford,' 'Soeur Thérese,' 'Merritt Supreme,' 'Regula,' 'Improved Merveille,' 'Todi,' and 'Merveille' (Powell, 1973). Reduced relative humidity will control *Botrytis* as well as powdery mildew, but supplemental fungicide applications also are often required. Although the crop thrives in moist situations, such as on capillary watering benches, these conditions may lead to increased *Botrytis* and powdery mildew infections.

To reduce *Botrytis* rot of the inflorescence buds in storage, leaves are removed, since they would drop in dark storage and harbor the fungus. Abscission can be chemically induced in 7 to 8 days at 21°C by either vapors or sprays. Vapors are suitable for relatively air-tight enclosures with good air circulation. Either ethylene or sodium methyl dithiocarbamate vapors can be used. Ethylene is supplied from either ripe apples (1.3 kg/m^3; Post, 1947) or a canister (Ulery, 1978). Sodium methyl dithiocarbamate is applied to the floor at 1.77 ml/m^3 in enough water for even application (Kofranek and Leiser, 1957; Shanks, 1975). Poorly sealed enclosures may require higher rates.

Spray of an abscission-causing chemical onto the plants does not require special enclosures and can be applied in the dormant plant production area so plants can be cleaned of abscising leaves as they are moved to storage (Tjia and Buxton, 1976). Concentrations of 10,000 ppm 2-butyn-1,4-diol (Shanks, 1975), 10,000 to 15,000 ppm tributyl phosphorotrithoate (Kofranek and Leiser, 1957), or 1000 to 3000 ppm ethephon (Shanks, 1969; Tjia and Buxton, 1976) are effective. Ethephon, however, will reduce height at bloom compared to no treatment (8–31% reduction with a 1000 ppm spray), which should be considered during subsequent height control treatments.

Mycoplasmas in hydrangeas have recently been observed by electron microscopy (Table V). They are systemic and cause abnormal inflorescences with phyllody (sepals reverted to leaves) and may be the cause of distorted growth, observed particularly at production temperatures above 19°C (Weiler and Lopes, 1974).

Viruses are ubiquitous, systemic components of hydrangeas. Ninety-one to 98% of the cultivars surveyed contain hydrangea ring spot virus (Paludan and Christensen, 1973; Welvaert and Samyn, 1973). Foliage symptoms include stunting and chlorotic spots and rings, but vary with environment and season. Hydrangeas freed of virus by heat therapy have been established from terminal cuttings (Brierley, 1957) or cultured meristems (Beauchesne, 1974; Paludan and Christensen, 1973), but are not widely available at present.

VII. POSTGREENHOUSE CARE

Postgreenhouse life is prolonged by maintenance of a moist medium, placement in a cool, well-lighted site, and periodic fertilization. Lack of watering by merchandisers or consumers is probably the most frequent cause of short postgreenhouse life. When flowering is finished, consumers can rebloom hydrangeas by cutting the plants back and following basic production procedures.

REFERENCES

Adriansen, E. (1976). Kemisk vaekstregulering af potteplanter. *Tidsskr. Planteavl* **48,** 725–841.

Aldrichem, P. V., Boonstra, J. J., and Jansen, H. (1978). Opbloei teelt Hydrangea (hortensia). *Vakbl. Bloemisterij* **33**(27), 18–19, 21; (29), 18–19, 21.

Allen, R. C. (1931). Factors influencing the flower color of hydrangeas. *Proc. Am. Soc. Hortic. Sci.* **28,** 410–412.

Allen, R. C. (1934a). Controlling the color of greenhouse hydrangeas (*Hydrangea macrophylla*) by soil treatments with aluminum sulfate and other materials. *Proc. Am. Soc. Hortic. Sci.* **32,** 632–634.

Allen, R. C. (1934b). The effect of storage temperature on flowering of the greenhouse hydrangea (*Hydrangea macrophylla*). *Proc. Am. Soc. Hortic. Sci.* **32,** 638.

Allen, R. C. (1943). Influence of aluminum on the flower color of *Hydrangea macrophylla. Contrib. Boyce Thompson Inst.* **13,** 221–242.

Andersen, G. P. (1967). Potteplante-sektionens forsøg. *Gartner Tidende.* **83,** 69–70.

Anonymous (1952). "1950 Census of Agriculture," **5**(1). U.S. Bur. Census, Washington, D.C.

Anonymous (1959). "1959 Census of Agriculture," **5**(1). U.S. Bur. Census, Washington, D.C.

Anonymous (1971). Observations sur la mise á fleur de l'hortensia de forsage et essai d'un silo adapté au climat de la région parisienne. *Hortic. Fr.* **10,** 1–6.

Anonymous (1973a). Good results achieved with growth regulators on hydrangeas. *Grower* **80**(4), 647.

Anonymous (1973b). "1969 Census of Agriculture," **10**(5). U.S. Bur. Census, Washington, D.C.

Anonymous (1977). Sand Point gives secret to good Easter hydrangeas. *Florists' Rev.* **159**(4119), 86.

Anonymous (1978). "Flowers and Foliage Plants, Production and Sales, 1975 and 1976, Intentions for 1977." USDA Stat. Rep. Serv., Washington, D.C.

Asen, S. (1967). How anthocyanins relate to color. *Florist Nursery Exch.* **147**(6), 18–19, 30.

Asen, S., Siegelman, H. W., and Stuart, N. W. (1957). Anthocyanin and other phenolic compounds in red and blue sepals of *Hydrangea macrophylla* var. Merveille. *Proc. Am. Soc. Hortic. Sci.* **69,** 561–569.

Asen, S., Stuart, N. W., and Siegelman, H. W. (1959). Effect of various concentrations of nitrogen, phosphorus, and potassium on sepal color of *Hydrangea macrophylla. Proc. Am. Soc. Hortic. Sci.* **73,** 495–502.

Asen, S., Stuart, N. W., and Specht, A. W. (1960). Color of *Hydrangea macrophylla* sepals as influenced by the carry-over effects from summer applications of nitrogen, phosphorus, and potassium. *Proc. Am. Soc. Hortic. Sci.* **76,** 631–636.

Asen, S., Stuart, N. W., and Cox, E. L. (1963). Sepal color of *Hydrangea macrophylla* as influenced by the source of nitrogen available to the plants. *Proc. Am. Soc. Hortic. Sci.* **82,** 504–507.

Bailey, L. H., and Bailey, E. Z. (1976). "Hortus Third." Macmillan, New York.

Beauchesne, C. (1974). Kultur von Hortensien "in vitro," ausgehend von meristemen. *Landwirtsch. Zentralbl.* **19,** 2881–2882.

Bing, A., Boodley, J. W., Gortzig, C. F., Helgesen, R. G., Horst, R. K., Johnson, G., Langhans, R. W., Price, D. R., Seeley, J. G., and Williamson, C. E. (1974). "Cornell Recommendations for Commercial Floriculture Crops." *Cornell Univ. Agric. Bull.,* Ithaca, New York.

Brierley, P. (1954). Symptoms in the florists' hydrangea caused by tomato ringspot virus and an unidentified sap-transmissible virus. *Phytopathology* **44,** 696–699.

Brierley, P. (1957). Virus-free hydrangeas from tip cuttings of heat-treated ringspot-affected stock plants. *Plant Dis. Rep.* **41,** 1005.

Bunge, B., and Weiler, T. C. (1977). Unpublished data. Purdue Univ., West Lafayette, Indiana.

Cathey, H. M., and Stuart, N. W. (1961). Comparative plant growth-retarding activity of AMO-1618, Phosfon, and CCC. *Bot. Gaz.* **123,** 51–57.

Dersch, H. (1973). Hortensien Sortenvergleichsanbau 1972/73. *Gartenwelt* **73,** 432–434.

Dörr, G. (1960). Gibberellin Spritzversuche an Zierpflangen. *Gartenwelt* **60,** 403–404.

Dunham, C. W., and Roberts, R. H. (1948). Notes on growth habits and pinching of hydrangeas. *Proc. Am. Soc. Hortic. Sci.* **52,** 525–527.

Fritzsche, G. (1977). Treiberei von Hortensien. *Dtsch. Gartenbau* **31,** 1337–1338.

Furuta, T. (1960). Alabama study evalutes production methods, polyethylene packing. *Florist Nursery Exch.* **135**(1), 22–24, 26–27, 29–30, 32.

Furuta, T., and Martin, W. C., Jr. (1963). Propagation of hydrangeas for spring flowering. *Florist Nursery Exch.* **139**(16), 12, 50.

Gugenhan, E. (1969). Einsatz-moglichkeiten von Stauchemitteln. *Zierpflanzenbau* **9,** 274–277.

Hargreaves, G. (1973). Charting a blueprint for the forcing of hydrangeas. *Gard. Chron.* **174**(19), 24–25, 27.

Hartleb, H. (1974). Ein kombinierter Routinetest bei der Grossproduktion von Hortensien zum Nachweis des Hydrangearingfleckenvirus. *Arch. Gartenbau* **22,** 411–417.

Haworth-Booth, M. (1950). "The Hydrangea." Constable, London.

Hearon, S. S., Lawson, R. H., Smith, F. F., McKenzie, J. T., and Rosen, J. (1976). Morphology of filiamentous forms of a mycoplasmalike organism associated with hydrangea virescence. *Phytopathology* **66,** 608–616.

Hunter, F. (1950). Hydrangea tests. *Ohio Florists' Assoc. Bull.* **248,** 2–3.

Jansen, H. (1960). Gibberellin—Anwendung bei Hortensien. *Gartenwelt* **60,** 482–483.

Jones, J. B. (1977). Commercial use of tissue culture for the production of disease-free plants. Presented to Ohio State Univ., Columbus, by Paul Ecke Poinsettias, Encinitas, California.

Jongkind, M., and Sytsema, W. (1966). Bespruiting van Hortensia mit gibberellazuur. *Jversl. Proefstn. Bloem. Ned. Aalsmeer* p. 82.

Jung, R. (1964). The status of hydrangea growing today. *Florists' Rev.* **135**(3486), 13–14, 35–37, 40.

Kenyon, O. (1972). Short term production of long lasting hydrangeas. *Minn. State Florists' Bull.* Oct. pp. 5–9.

Kikkawa, H., Ogita, Z., and Fujito, S. (1955). Relation of plant pigments and metals. *Kagaku* **25,** 139.

Kiplinger, D. C. (1945a). Well grown hydrangeas are valuable for the spring holidays. I. *Florists' Rev.* **95**(2464), 23–25.

Kiplinger, D. C. (1945b). Well grown hydrangeas are valuable for the spring holidays. II. *Florists' Rev.* **95**(2465), 29–30.

Kofranek, A. M., and Leiser, A. T. (1958). Chemical defoliation of *Hydrangea macrophylla* Ser. *Proc. Am. Soc. Hortic. Sci.* **71,** 555–562.

Kohl, H. C., Jr., and Nelson, R. C. (1966). Controlling height of hydrangeas with growth retardants. *Calif. Agric.* **20**(2), 5.

Kosugi, K., and Arai, H. (1960). Studies on flower bud differentiation and development in some ornamental trees and shrubs. VII. On the date of flower bud differentiation and flower bud development in *Hydrangea macrophylla*. *Kagawa Daigaku Nogakubu Gakujutsu Hokoku* **12,** 78–83.

Koths, J. S., Judd, R. W., Jr., and Maisano, J. J., Jr. (1973). "Commercial Hydrangea Culture." *Univ. of Connecticut Agric. Ext. Bull.,* 73–63.

Laurie, A., Kiplinger, D. C., and Nelson, K. S. (1968). "Commercial Flower Forcing." McGraw-Hill, New York.

Lavsen, E. R. (1968). Retarderingsmidler. *Gartner Tidende* **84,** 235–238.

LeMattre, P. (1963). Mise au point sur la mise á fleur de l'hortensia. *J. Etvd. Hortic. Pepin (Versailles)* pp. 75–80.

LeMattre, P. (1975). Influence du facteur température sur la mise á fleur de l'Hortensia (*Hydrangea macrophylla*). *In* "Phytotronics in Agricultural and Horticultural Research III" (P. Chouard and N. de Bilderling, eds.), pp. 338–344. Gauthier-Villars, Paris.

Link, C. B., and Shanks, J. B. (1952). Experiments on fertilizer levels for greenhouse hydrangeas. *Proc. Am. Soc. Hortic. Sci.* **60,** 449–458.

Link, C. B., and Shanks, J. B. (1954). Studies of the factors involved in terminating the rest period of hydrangeas. *Proc. Am. Soc. Hortic. Sci.* **64,** 519–525.

Litlere, B. (1974). Hortensiasorter. *Gartneryrket* **20/21,** 476–478.

Litlere, B. (1975a). Factors affecting growth and flowering in hydrangea (*Hydrangea macrophylla* (Thunb.) Ser.). Lic. Agric. Thesis, Agricultural Univ., Ås Norway.

Litlere, B. (1975b). Virkning av temperatur på knoppdanning hos Stuehortensia *(Hydrangea macrophylla)*. *Gartneryrket* **65,** 240–242, 256.

Litlere, B., and Strømme, E. (1975). The influence of temperature, daylength, and light intensity on flowering in *Hydrangea macrophylla* (Thunb.) Ser. *Acta Hortic.* **51,** 285–298.

Loeser, H. (1962). Gibboe—Versuche bei der Hortensiensorte 'Bodensee.' *Gartenwelt* **62,** 224–225.

Loeser, H. (1963). Versuche mit Gibboe bei Hydrangea. *Gartenwelt* **63,** 280–281.

Loeser, H. (1968). Versuche mit Wuchshemmitteln. *Dtsch. Gaertnerboerse* **68,** 51–59.

Loeser, H. (1974). Hortensien-sortenvergleich 1972/73. *Dtsch. Gaertnerboerse* **74,** 195–198.

Merritt, J. S., Jr. (1976). "Hydrangea Culture in Brief." Joseph S. Merritt, Baltimore, Maryland.

Merritt, J. S., Jr. (1978). Personal communication. Joseph S. Merritt, Baltimore, Maryland.

Miller, D. (1976). Blueprint for quick-growing hydrangeas. *Nursery Gard. Cent.* **162**(9), 18–19, 21.

Möhring, H. K. (1961). Tätigkeitsberich 1960. *Gaert. Versuchsanst. Friesdorf/Bad Godesberg* **32,** 1–40.

Müller, H. M. (1971). Elektronenmikroskopischer Nachweis von mycoplasmaähnlichen Organismen im Phloem von *Hydrangea macrophylla. Zentralbl. Bakteriol. Parasitenkd., Infektionskr, Hyg., Abt. 2* **126,** 564–565.

Münch, J., and Fritzsche, G. (1970). Versuche mit Cycocel und B-Nine bei Topfpflanzen. *Erwerbsgaertner* **24,** 797–801.

Münch, J., and Fritzsche, G. (1975). Substratversuche mit Hortensien. *Dtsch. Gartenbau* **29**(6), 189–192.

Okada, M., and Funaki, S. (1967). Influence of variations in soil acidity on sepal color of *Hydrangea macrophylla. Engei Gakkai Zasshi* **36,** 122–130.

Okada, M., and Okawa, K. (1974). The quantity of aluminum and phosphorus in plants and its influence on sepal color of *Hydrangea macrophylla. Engei Gakkai Zasshi* **42,** 361–370.

Paludan, N., and Christensen, M. (1973). Hortensie—ringmosaik—virus i hortensie (*Hydrangea macrophylla* Ser.). Diagnostik, kortlaegning, termoterapi og meristemkultuur. *Tidsskr. Planteavl* **77**(1), 1–12.

Paquet, L. (1966). Growth retardants—their application and results. *Ohio Florists' Assoc. Bull.* **438,** 3.

Peters, J. (1975). Über die Blütenbildung einiger Sorten von *Hydrangea macrophylla. Gartenbauwissenschaft* **40**(2), 63–66.

Piringer, A. A., and Stuart, N. W. (1955). Responses of hydrangea to photoperiod. *Proc. Am. Soc. Hortic. Sci.* **65,** 446–454.

Piringer, A. A., and Stuart, N. W. (1958). Effects of supplemental light source and length of photo-period on growth and flowering of hydrangeas in the greenhouse. *Proc. Am. Soc. Hortic. Sci.* **71**, 579–584.

Poesch, G. H. (1935). Coloring and fertilizing hydrangeas. *Bimon. Bull. (Ohio)* **20**, 92–93.

Post, K. (1947). Removing hydrangea leaves and hydrangea fundamentals. *N. Y. Flower Growers Bull.* **25**, 1–3.

Post, K. (1949). "Florist Crop Production and Marketing." Orange Judd Publ., New York.

Powell, C. C. (1973). Botrytis blight of hydrangea. *Ohio Florists' Assoc. Bull.* **528**, 3.

Ray, S. (1946). Reduction of blindness in hydrangeas. *Proc. Am. Soc. Hortic. Sci.* **47**, 501–502.

Robinson, H. M. (1939). Notes on variable colors of flower petals. *J. Am. Chem. Soc.* **61**, 1606–1607.

Schulte-Scherlebeck, H. (1977). Produktionsprogram Hortensien. *Zierpflanzenbau* **17**, 354–361, 403–406.

Shanks, J. B. (1969). Some effects and potential uses of Ethrel on ornamental crops. *HortScience* **4**, 56–58.

Shanks, J. B. (1975). Hydrangeas. *In* "The Ball Red Book" (V. Ball, ed.), pp. 352–368. Geo. J. Ball, Inc., West Chicago, Illinois.

Shanks, J. B., and Link, C. B. (1951). Some studies on the effects of temperature and photoperiod on growth and flower formation in hydrangea. *Proc. Am. Soc. Hortic. Sci.* **58**, 357–366.

Shanks, J. B., and Link, C. B. (1964). The chemical regulation of plant growth for florists. *M. Florist* **108**, 1–16.

Smeal, P. L. (1961). "Factors Influencing the Induction, Formation and Development of the Inflorescence of *Hydrangea macrophylla* (Thunb.)." Ph.D. thesis. Univ. of Maryland, College Park.

Struckmeyer, B. E. (1950). Blossom bud induction and differentiation in hydrangea. *Proc. Am. Soc. Hortic. Sci.* **56**, 410–414.

Stuart, N. W. (1951). Greenhouse hydrangeas. *Florists' Rev.* **109**(2813), 37–40.

Stuart, N. W., and Cathey, H. M. (1962). Control of growth and flowering of *Chrysanthemum morifolium* and *Hydrangea macrophylla* by gibberellin. *Proc. Int. Hortic. Congr.* **15**(2), 391–399.

Stuart, N. W., Piringer, A. A., and Borthwick, H. A. (1955). Photoperiodic responses of hydrangeas. *Proc. Int. Hortic. Cong.* **14**, 337–341.

Tjia, B., and Buxton, J. (1976). Influence of ethephon spray on defoliation and subsequent growth on *Hydrangea macrophylla* Thunb. *HortScience* **11**, 487–488.

Tjia, B., Stoltz, L., Sandhu, M. S., and Buxton, J. (1976). Surface active agent to increase effectiveness of surface penetration of ancymidol on hydrangea and Easter lily. *HortScience* **11**, 371–372.

Ulery, C. J. (1978). Quality hydrangea production. *Ohio Florists' Assoc. Bull.* **582**, 3–4, 9.

Ulery, P. (1969). Hydrangeas. *Ohio Florists' Assoc. Bull.* **475**, 5.

Wasscher, J. (1958). Gibberellienen. *Jversl. Proefstn. Bloem. Ned. Aalsmeer* pp. 102–103.

Weiler, T. C., and Lopes, L. C. (1973). New hydrangea production technique. *Focus Flori (Purdue)* **1**(1), 2–3.

Weiler, T. C., and Lopes, L. C. (1974). Hydrangea distortion. *Focus Flori (Purdue)* **2**(2), 9.

Welvaert, W., and Samyn, G. (1973). De verspreiding van het hydrangea ringspot virus ij de *Hydrangea macrophylaa* (Thunb.) Dc. *Meded. Fac. Landbouwwet., Rijksuniv. Gent* **38**, 1647–1654.

Welvaert, W., Samyn, G., and Lagasse, A. (1975). Recherches sur les symptomes de la virescence chez l'*Hydrangea macrophylla* Thunb. *Phytopathol. Z.* **83**(2), 152–158.

Westcott, C. (1964). "The Gardener's Bug Book." Doubleday, Garden City, New York.

Westcott, C. (1971). "Plant Disease Handbook." Van Nostrand-Reinhold, New York.

Yates, H. O. (1970). Hydrangea timing schedule. *Greenhouse Notes (PA)* Dec., p. 2.

Yock, N. (1978). Personal communication. Oregon Propagating Co., Brookings.

Zeyen, R. J., and Stienstra, W. C. (1973). Phyllody of florists' hydrangea caused by hydrangea ringspot virus. *Plant Dis. Rep.* **57**, 300–304.

15
Cyclamen

Richard E. Widmer

I. INTRODUCTION

K yklos" is Greek for circle, apparently referring to the leaf shape. The original species, *Cyclamen persicum,* is native to Palestine, Asia Minor, and islands of the Aegean and eastern Mediterranean seas, but has not been found as far east as Iran (Blasdale, 1949). In their native habitat, cyclamen are dormant during the hot dry summers and new foliage develops in response to fall rains and cooler temperatures. Flowering follows and continues until terminated by dry summer heat. Seedlings may require 2 to 3 years to bloom under such conditions.

II. HISTORY AND TAXONOMY

Earliest mention of the species was probably in fifteenth century transcripts (Blasdale, 1949, 1951; Doorenbos, 1950a and b). It was introduced into Western Europe as a collector's item in the early seventeenth century. Breeding was begun in the middle of the nineteenth century when the plant started to achieve economic significance. Taxonomy of the genus remains partially unresolved, largely because of genetical heterogeneity. As many as 24 species have been described, but deHaan and Doorenbos (1951) list 15 species. The herbaceous plants consist of a cluster of bluish green, heart-shaped to ovate leaves with

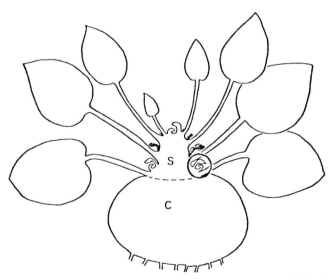

Fig. 1. Diagrammatic longitudinal section of cyclamen. The primary shoot(s) is shown atop the well-developed corm (C). Axillary branch shoots are present at the lowest nodes (one such branch is circled on the right) and flower primordia are present in the axils of the upper leaves. The youngest leaf primordia exhibit hyponastic curvature and are folded over the shoot apex. (Courtesy of Marshall Sundberg, Department of Biology, University of Wisconsin-Eau Claire.)

silvery markings and crenate dentate margins, on long petioles arising from flattened tubers (Fig. 1). Attractive sympetalous five-parted, strongly reflexed flowers are borne above the leaf canopy on scapes also arising from the corm. The cyclamen is a pseudomonocot in that only one cotyledon is found in the embryo (Hagemann, 1959). The first true leaf develops directly opposite the cotyledon. Cotyledons closely resemble true leaves.

The cyclamen has been a leading year-round pot plant crop in northern Europe for many years. It is less popular in America, where sales have been limited primarily to late fall and winter, but production and demand are now overlapping to other seasons. Production and sales have been centered in northern areas and areas with a cool coastal climate. American interest in cyclamen is increasing with the development of improved cultivars and improved, accelerated production techniques. Research studies have centered in Europe, but some Japanese (Niizu, 1967), Canadian (Molnar and Williams, 1977), and U. S. (Stephens and Widmer, 1976) studies been noted in recent years.

III. CULTIVARS

Early forms had small flowers of relatively pale color. British breeders first developed more intense petal color and broader, flatter corolla lobes. Double-sized flowers were noted in England and Germany by 1870 (Doorenbos, 1950b). Both diploid and polyploid cultivars are currently on the market. Large, intermediate and small, as well as common, fringed, crested, frilled and double-flowered forms, are now available in many colors (Wellensiek, 1952). Uniformity of cultivars is less than desired. Recently introduced F_1 hybrids are much more uniform, although not as much so as F_1 hybrids of many other plant species.

Cultivar	Flower size	Comments
Dark salmon red TAS	Large	—
Pure white TAS	Large	—
Rosa von Zehlendorf TAS	Large	Salmon-pink with dark eye
Cardinal	Large	Red
Hallo	Large	Red
F_1 Merry Widow	Intermediate	White-purple eye, fragrant
F_1 Gypsy	Intermediate	Salmon-red
F_1 Swan Lake	Small intermediate	White
F_1 Rosamunde	Intermediate	Rose
Beautiful Helena	Small	Slowed by limited light; numerous colors
Puppet	Small	Numerous colors

Primary objectives sought in today's cultivars include good germination; early, uniform flowering; floriferousness; attractive foliage; fast growth; compact, uniform plants; above average life in the home and office. Selection within cultivars often results in greater differences in flowering time than found between cultivars. Some of the best cultivars available are listed on p. 376.

New cultivars should be considered as they are released. Almost all seed is from European sources. Frequently, different cultivar names are used in the United States than in Europe, although the cultivars are identical.

IV. PRODUCTION

Until the 1800s cyclamen was considered difficult to propagate and produce. Corms were split to start new plants that were rested in the summer and production time was 2 years. By 1825, the Englishman John Wilmott started plants from seed and grew them in 15 months with no summer rest period (Doorenbos, 1950b). Some florists still grow cyclamen at temperatures around 10°C over a period of 15 months or more, but modern techniques make 8-month production schedules a reality (Widmer *et al.*, 1976). Figure 2 illustrates well-grown, fast-crop cyclamen.

V. PROPAGATION

Today propagation is primarily from seed that is sold by count rather than by weight. Propagation by corm splitting is laborious and not practical, except to

Fig. 2. Well-grown, fast crop specimens in 12.5-cm pots. Rosa von Zehlendorf TAS (left) illustrates large flowers and Rosamunde (right) has intermediate-sized flowers. These plants are large enough for transfer to 15-cm pots for better aesthetic balance and for easier home care.

Table I

Nutrient Additions to the Sphagnum Moss Peat Medium Used in Cyclamen Production

Materials	Grams/bushel	Cubic meter	
Ground dolomitic limestone, CaCO $_3$—45%, MgCO $_3$—36%	200	3.4 kg	
Magnesium sulfate, 10% Mg	20	345	gm
Potassium nitrate, 13-0-44	7	120	gm
Superphosphate, 0-20-0	12	215	gm
Slow-release fertilizer, 14-14-14	16	270	gm
Fritted microelements [a]	1	16	gm

[a]Mn, 7.5%; Fe, 18.0%; Cu, 3.0%; Zn, 7.0%; B, 3.0%; Mo, 0.2%.

maintain specific clones for breeding purposes. Cotyledons cut from corms will root and form new plants, but true leaves will not root.

Pollination of flowers is simple. Pollen is merely applied to the pistil with a label, pipe cleaner, or similar object. Once the ovule is fertilized, the peduncle continues to elongate and may bend or curve. Usually the seed pod is not lowered close to the ground, as is the case with many of the *Cyclamen* species. Seed ripens in 2 to 3 months. Menzel (1972b) found that small seed is not desirable, but this trait can vary with cultivar and numerous other factors. Many larger-flowered cultivars are tetraploids and have larger seeds. Diploids usually have smaller seed, may germinate more quickly, flower faster, and thrive better under home conditions (Wellensiek, 1961). Individual mother plants (seed-bearing parents) significantly influence seed qulaity, germination, and subsequent growth (Noordegraf, 1977). Cyclamen average approximately 10,500 seeds/100 gm.

Most seedsmen store seed at room temperatures of 15°–20°C and at relatively low humidity (Maatsch and Runger, 1954; Noordengraaf, 1977). Massante (1964) stored cyclamen seed for 52 months at 2° and 10°C with no serious loss in germination. Cultivar and quality of the seed produced significantly influence the viable life of the seed. Fresh seed is preferable. No afterripening period is required. No specific seed treatment consistently improves germination. Soaking the seed at room temperature for 12 hours is sometimes beneficial, but not essential (Anderson and Widmer, 1975; Lyons, 1978). Widmer et al. (1976) suggested that seed be sown at 7 × 7-cm spacing ⅓ cm deep in flats filled with moist, nutrient-enriched sphagnum moss peat (Table I). A similar mix recommended for seed germination and growth of some plants is commercially available. Fine or powdery peat should not be used. The peat should be compressed to two-thirds of its fluffed up volume prior to sowing. This growth medium and spacing method has proved superior to others, although some growers may prefer to broadcast the seed or plant in rows, or to sow seed in peat disks or individual pots. Other light-weight, organic-type mixes can also be used.

Cyclamen seed germinates best at 19°–20°C in the dark (Massante, 1964), whereas temperatures of 22°C and above may be inhibitory. Such conditions are best maintained in a temperature-controlled room with good air circulation, rather than in the greenhouse, where solar radiation elevates the germination medium temperature excessively. Flats should be watered after seed sowing, but allowed to dry for several hours prior to placement in the germination area. This practice lessens the probability of fungal growth on the medium or the container. Moss peat should be kept moist during germination. Cyclamen are sensitive to growth medium pH levels below 5.5; above 6.0 is preferable (Maatsch and Isensee, 1959). Lime should be added before sphagnum moss peat is used for germination. Seeds will germinate poorly and fail to develop after germination because roots do not develop in the acidic, noncalcified medium (Fig. 3). Cyclamen seed will germinate if only lime is mixed in the moss, but the seedlings must then be fertilized a few weeks after they are visible above the surface (Fig. 4).

Visible evidence of germination of inbibed seed starts below ground within 5 days (Anderson and Widmer, 1975). First the primary root penetrates the soil, then the hypocotyl begins to swell to form the corm, and at 28 days the thin hypocotyls are usually evident. The cotyledon blade is the last organ to emerge from the seed coat. Seedlings should be moved to a humid, shaded (February to November) greenhouse when the cotyledon petioles are stretching, to prevent excessive elongation. After the cotyledon blade has unfolded and a true leaf is evident, the plants can be transferred to a less humid area, but the 20°C night temperature should be continued for optimum growth (Menzel, 1972a).

Germination percentages up to 95% may be expected, but 80 to 85% is more common. Seedlings that take more than 45 days to germinate are usually

Fig. 3. Cyclamen seedlings at 45 days. The two plants on the right were sown in moss peat to which lime and nutrients were added—note roots over 2 cm long. The three plants on the left were sown in moss peat with no additions—note that only root stubs are present.

Fig. 4. Germination 90 days after seeding of four cyclamen cultivars sown in unaltered moss peat, moss peat to which pulverized limestone was added, and in moss peat enriched with pulverized limestone and nutrients as listed in Table I.

weak or crippled specimens and should be discarded. Up to 5% of the remaining plants may need discarding if growth is not normal. A maximum of 75 to 85% of the seeds can be expected to produce good plants. Usually hybrids produce fewer off-types for disposal. This factor is probably best attributed to the greater degree of genetical homogeneity of the hybrids.

Storage of seedlings for up to 5 weeks is possible if desired. Maatsch (1958) placed seedlings with roots bedded in moist peat in polyethylene bags and stored them up to 5 weeks in a 3°C refrigerator with no negative effects. The seedlings required shielding from direct sunlight and drafts when first removed from storage. A 6°C storage temperature was not satisfactory.

VI. VEGETATIVE GROWTH

Growth is slow in early stages and an optimum environment should be provided to maximize growth. After seed has germinated, both the corm and the cotyledon gradually increase in size. The first true leaves do not unfold simultaneously on all plants but are usually clearly evident within 80 to 90 days after sowing. After two true leaves have unfolded and five leaves have initiated, the rate of leaf initiation accelerates to about 1.3 per week and remains fairly constant through Leaf No. 17 (Sundberg, 1978).

A. Potting

At 17 weeks after sowing, plants should average approximately 6 to 7 un-folded leaves or 13 to 15 leaf units in age (Stephens and Widmer, 1976). They are then ready for potting. If the seeds were spaced out at 7 × 7 cm in flats or benches when sown, no transplanting is needed prior to this stage. Plants grown in moss peat can be transplanted with a minimum of root disturbance. The corm top is kept flush with the surface of the growth medium. The nutrient-enriched moss peat used for germination (Table I) is also recommended for potting. Some pea rock can be placed in the pot bottom for ballast, if desired. Plunging the corm encourages development of wider-spreading plants. Corms should not be plunged in heavier soils, which are not recommended. Light soil mixes consisting of a maximum of one-third loam plus moss peat, vermiculite, perlite, leaf compost, or similar materials are usually satisfactory.

Quality specimens can be grown in 10-, 12.5-, 15-cm, and larger pots. Plastic pots with drainage openings are preferable to clay pots because they facilitate maintenance of uniform moisture levels in the soil. Smaller flowered cultivars are preferable for 10-cm pots and may also be grown in 12.5-cm pots. Inter-mediate and large-flowered cultivars are preferable for 12.5-cm and larger pots. Plants may be placed pot to pot until the foliage reaches the pot rim, but should be spaced promptly thereafter. Crowding of cyclamen plants results in elongated petioles and peduncles, leggy, weak plants and a significantly in-creased possibility of disease. Well-grown, 10-cm pot plants will ultimately require up to 600 cm²; 12.5-cm pot plants, 900 cm²; 15-cm pot plants, 1400 cm² of bench space. Production costs follow a similar ratio. Should a plant become too large for its pot, it can be repotted in a larger container, even when in full bloom, with no noticeable setback.

B. Fertilization

Cyclamen are slow to exhibit conspicuous symptoms in response to low or high nutrient or salt levels in the growth medium. The first response is usually a decrease in the growth rate. Without control plants for comparison, the de-crease may go unnoticed or be attributed to weather or other factors. Cycla-men require a constant, moderate supply of nutrients applied in proportion to plant size to maintain optimum growth. Usually, if the suggested nutrient-enriched moss peat mix is employed, no supplemental fertilizer is needed for 2 months after seed sowing. Analyzing the growth medium at intervals thereafter helps determine when fertilizer is required.

Platteter and Widmer (1978) noted that vegetative characteristics of cycla-men are affected by rate of application of nitrogen and potassium. Effects are similar at all growth stages beyond the seedling stage. The following sugges-tions are averages and may require modification for various cultural and en-vironmental conditions. Before young plants are potted, they usually benefit when 100 ppm nitrogen from a balanced fertilizer such as soluble 20-20-20 is applied every 3 weeks. Regular applications should begin 4 weeks after potting. For plants grown in moss peat and fertilized with every watering, 100 ppm nitrogen (balanced for nitrate and ammonium nitrogen) is advisable until the plants are potbound. Then, 150 and eventually 200 ppm nitrogen may be necessary (Fig. 5). Lower concentrations result in fewer, smaller leaves and smaller plants (Fig. 6). Slightly more (25–50 ppm) potassium than nitrogen is required to obtain optimum leaf and plant size. European growers claim that failure to apply adequate potassium fertilizer increases plant susceptibility to plant pathogens. Chloride and sulfate sources of potassium are equally satisfactory.

Phosphorus is neither fixed nor held in a moss peat medium and is subject to leaching (Puustjarvi, 1976–1977). Thus, incorporation of phosphate fertilizer in the growth medium prior to planting is not adequate for the duration of the crop. Applications of 35 to 50 ppm phosphorus are recommended when plants are fertilized with every watering, or higher concentrations if applied less frequently.

Foliage becomes pale green or chlorotic with excessive calcium levels, insufficient iron, or a high pH. An application of chelated iron is then recommended. Cyclamen grow best at a minimum soil pH of 6.0 for loam mixtures but established plants grow well in moss peat with a pH as low as 5.0. Cyclamen

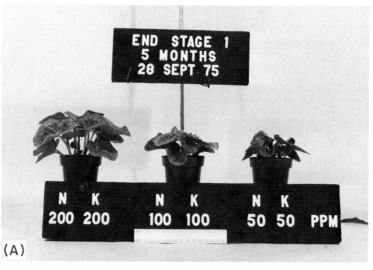

Fig. 5. Effect of the quantities of nitrogen and potassium applied with every watering at three stages of plant development. Plants of cultivar Rosa von Zehlendorf TAS were grown in a moss peat medium in 7.5-cm plastic pots for stage 1 and in 12.5-cm plastic pots thereafter. (A) End of Stage 1. (B) End of stage 2. (C) End of stage 3.

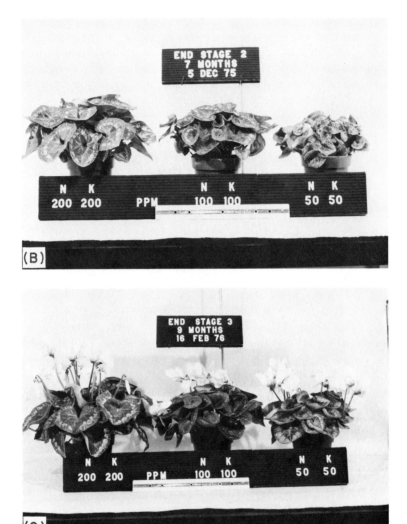

Fig. 5. *Continued*

respond favorably to levels of 1000 ppm carbon dioxide during the season when ventilators are kept closed. Plant growth and flowering are accelerated with the carbon dioxide injection.

C. Watering

Once the cyclamen wilts, especially in hot weather, some of the leaves will turn yellow within 24 to 36 hours. Moss peat should not be allowed to appear dry or to get as dry as a loam soil. (If the peat is so dry that one cannot wring water out of it when squeezing the moss in one's hand, it is too dry.) Watering should be done in the morning whenever possible, to minimize *Botrytis* development. Overhead or subirrigation may be used, but the latter may cause excessive plant stretch in short days. An occasional leaching may be beneficial if salts accumulate in the medium and if subirrigation is used. A daytime relative humidity of 50 to 70% is considered desirable.

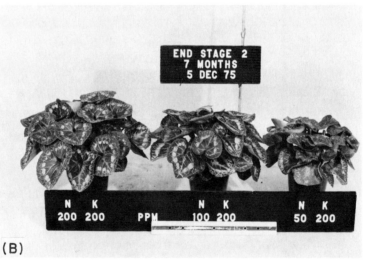

Fig. 6. Effect of three different concentrations of nitrogen accompanied by a constant potassium concentration applied with every watering. Plants of cultivar Rosa von Zehlendorf TAS were grown in a moss peat medium in 7.5-cm plastic pots for stage 1 and in 12.5-cm plastic pots thereafter. (A) End of stage 1. (B) End of stage 2. (C) End of stage 3.

Fig. 6. *Continued*

D. Temperature

A night temperature of 20°C is preferable until six to seven unfolded leaves per plant are present. A drop to 17°–18°C is then recommended. Day temperatures should be 20°C (cloudy) and 23°–24°C (sunny). Pad and fan cooling are definitely recommended for most areas of the United States. Lack of cooling during a hot summer may delay the plants 1 to 2 months and decrease plant quality significantly. Some growers may be successful growing plants outdoors under lath shade during the summer, provided they can maintain adequate humidity levels and pest control.

E. Light

Plants should be shaded from April to October to provide a maximum of 4.3 klx. Full radiant energy the remainder of the year should not be excessive in most areas of the country. Symptoms of excessive radiant energy include hardened plants, pale, chlorotic foliage, and necrotic areas on the leaves. Inadequate radiant energy slows growth and causes weak, spindly petioles and weak plants. Supplementing radiant energy with high-intensity electric lighting of young plants in winter has accelerated plant development, but results have not been consistent or significant enough to warrant the cost when considering energy costs and supplies.

Good air circulation is desired to minimize diseases. Open mesh bench bottoms, low bench sides, proper spacing, and tube or pad and fan ventilation in season are all helpful. When old, bruised, yellow, and decomposing leaves need to be removed from the plant, they should be twisted or snapped off to avoid leaving undesirable stubs.

VII. FLOWERING

Cyclamen will not flower until a certain vegetative condition is attained (Sundberg, 1978; Hagemann, 1959). Anything that encourages accelerated early plant development should hasten flowering. Flower buds initiate in the axils of the sixth and successive true leaves (Stephens and Widmer, 1976). Thus, floral initiation in the axil of the sixth leaf occurs between the initiation of the tenth and thirteenth leaf units. Initial growth of flower buds is extremely slow and actual flowering often does not occur until the plants have 35 or more leaves unfolded, although this figure may vary with cultivar, pot size, and plant treatment. Axillary branch shoots or growing points usually develop in the axils of the first five leaves (Fig. 1).

A. Fertilization

Time of cyclamen flowering is affected by rates of application of nitrogen and potassium (Platteter and Widmer, 1978). High (200 ppm) potassium accompanied by lower (50–100 ppm) nitrogen applied with every watering to plants in a moss-peat medium prior to the development of 15 unfolded leaves per plant can delay flowering at least a week. Application of 200 ppm nitrogen versus 50 ppm, and/or 200 ppm potassium versus 50 or 100 ppm with every watering when the plants had 15 to 35 unfolded leaves delayed flowering up to 2 weeks. Nutrient applications at any of these concentrations after the plants had 40 unfolded leaves did not influence flowering time. Nutrition within normal ranges does not alter total flower production. Excessively high nutrient levels can inhibit plant development at any stage.

Neuray and Henrard (1966) and Niizu (1967) noted that a competition existed between leaves and buds. Thus, factors such as above-average but not excessive applications of nitrogen fertilizer and high growing temperatures that encourage vegetative growth inhibit or delay flowering.

B. Temperature

Soil temperatures of 13°–18.5°C for 6 weeks at sometime during the plant stage from 6 to 40 unfolded leaves accelerated flowering up to 2 weeks and more over soil temperatures of 24 and 29.5° (Stephens and Widmer, 1976; Gembis, 1978). Final plant size was smallest at the lowest temperature and largest at the two highest temperatures. Preliminary trials indicated that lower air temperatures are similar in effect to soil temperatures (Gembis, 1978). In a European cyclamen study, Menzel (1972a) reported that plants were smaller and flowered earlier at 15°C than at 20°C ambient temperature. Vegetative and reproductive plant responses form the basis for temperature recommendations presented in the vegetative growth section. About 45 days before the scheduled flowering date when plants of most cultivars grown in 12.5- or 15-cm pots have about 35 leaves, night temperature can be lowered to 16°C and the day temperature to 21°–23°C, especially during short days. A night temperature of 20°C at this time will result in bud abortion, small flowers, and poor plant quality.

C. Light

Neuray (1973) reported that cyclamen do not exhibit a clear photoperiodic response but daylength and light intensity play a part in flower bud formation and flowering. Apparently, the greater the total light unit accumulation, if other environmental factors are proper, the more leaves and flowers develop and the earlier the flowering.

D. Gibberellic Acid

Application of gibberellic acid (GA_3) to adequately sized plants (Fig. 7) 45 to 60 days prior to desired date of bloom will hasten the start of flowering of many cultivars by as much as a month (Widmer et al., 1974). In addition, flowering is more uniform. A spray of 25 ppm GA_3 plus a safe wetting agent is directed on the crown of the plant of most cultivars. The F_1 hybrids are more responsive

Fig. 7. A closeup of the crown of a cyclamen showing young flower buds (white with swollen tips) and ready for an application of Ga_3.

and should be treated with a 10 ppm GA_3. Quantity of spray applied per plant is a key point. Excesses should be avoided. Eight milliliters per plant (60 plants per pint of spray) is adequate. Growers who have not treated cyclamen with GA_3 previously should treat a limited portion of the crop the first time to adjust to the system and to determine cultivar response. Excessive applications can cause weakening of the peduncles.

VIII. KEEPING QUALITY

A. Plants

Well-grown specimens of modern-day cultivars have excellent keeping quality if properly watered and kept in a bright, cool (18°–20°C nights) location. Individual flowers last about 4 weeks on plants in the greenhouse, office, or home. Plants should remain attractive for a minimum of 6 weeks in the home. Plants in plastic pots are preferable as the medium in them remains moist longer. Small specimens (10-cm pots) may not last quite as long unless given close attention.

Lack of fertilizer in the medium can shorten home life of the cyclamen. A slow-release fertilizer should be applied to the plants before they leave the greenhouse. Use of care cards is especially helpful as the care details for this plant are less well known than they are for chrysanthemums, poinsettias, and similar plants. The well-aerated moss peat medium decreases the probability of overwatering.

B. Cut Flowers

Cut cyclamen flowers are commonly used in some parts of Europe (Maatsch and Isensee, 1960). Cultivars with peduncles are grown for this purpose. Flowers are removed from the corm with a snap or twist so that no stub remains to decay and encourage disease. Old, undesired leaves are removed in the same manner. If the peduncle is cut, flowers will last up to 14 days (depending on cultivar) in plain water. Without the cut, flowers may last only 2 days. Kohl (1975) reported that flower life varied by cultivar, and that a solution of 5% sucrose and 25% silver ions in deionized water substantially increased flower life.

IX. SCHEDULES

Temperatures and methods suggested herein are for fast culture production. Lower temperatures may be employed, as they have been for many years. Low temperatures slow plant growth to such an extent, however, that more total fuel

Fig. 8. Plants of F_1 Swan Lake cultivars in 10-cm (two on the left), 12.5-cm (middle), and 15-cm pots (on the right). All plants are 32 weeks old and were grown in nutrient-enriched moss peat. Note that the larger the pot, the more time required for flowering.

is required to produce a plant and the total production cost is excessive, especially in northern climates.

Average fast culture production time for cyclamen is shown in the following tabulation.

Final pot size (cm)	Time required (months)
7.5	6½
10.0	7½
12.5	8–8½
15.0	9–9½

Plants in small pots usually flower earlier than do plants in larger pots (Fig. 8). Flowering can be scheduled for any month of the year. Quickest production is from seed sown in February through April. Appropriate flower colors should be selected for individual seasons. In most areas, sales are most limited in June through August.

Small growers may find it more practical to purchase young plants from a specialist.

X. PROBLEMS

A. Diseases

Diseases can be troublesome. Growers should disinfest everything from potting bench to growing bench and pots to minimize difficulty. Some of the more common and important disease problems follow.

1. Fungi

a. Mold on Seed Flats.   Excess moisture should be avoided and an appropriate fungicide such as Benlate drench applied at 1 tablespoon/7.5 liters (0.25 kg/388 liters). Captan inhibits cyclamen seed germination.

b. Crown Rot or Botrytis Blight (Botrytis cinerea).   Crown rot is a soft decay of flowers and leaves, often in the crown. Affected parts are often covered with a downy gray mold. Botrytis development is encouraged by high humidity, poor air circulation, crowded plants, under-fertilization, and a night temperature below 16°C. For disease control, environmental conditions should be improved and an appropriate chemical spray or drench should be applied in the crown of the plant.

c. Fusarium Wilt (Fusarium oxysporum, F. cyclaminis).   This disease usually begins with yellowing at the base of the leaf blade or elsewhere on the leaf. The spots enlarge and discoloration may occur in roots and corms, but outward symptoms are limited until the flowering stage when plants wilt quickly. Everything including soil should be pasteurized to control this organism.

d. Stunt (Ramularia cyclaminicola).   Stunt is less common than the aforementioned diseases. Symptoms include flowering below the leaves and reddish-brown discolored areas in the corm. The growing medium should be pasteurized and infected plants should be discarded. Young plants can be sprayed with an appropriate fungicide if brown areas are evident on the foliage.

e. Root Rots (Pythium, Rhizoctonia, etc.).   Appropriate drench material should be applied for control of root rots.

2. Bacteria

Soft Rot (Erwinia carotovora).   A sudden wilting and plant collapse characterize this disease, and part of the corm may become soft and slimy while the roots are intact. Petioles and flower scapes may also become soft and slimy. Hot weather encourages rapid progress of the rot. Proper spacing, avoiding splashing water, discarding diseased plants, and applying an appropriate control chemical will reduce the severity of this disease problem.

B. Insects and Mites

Approved insecticides only should be applied to control insect and mite infestations. Some of the more common pests include the following.

1. Cyclamen Mites (Steneotarsonemus pallidus Banks)

These mites cause curling and distortion, some discoloration, and stiffening of young leaves and flowers. Mites are tiny, not visible to the naked eye and semitransparent with a brownish twinge.

2. Spider Mites, Red Spiders (Tetranychus urticae)

After infestation, a stippled yellow or brownish pattern develops on the foliage and in advanced cases forms webs of silky strands. When present, spider mites are usually found on leaf undersides and on the flowers.

3. Aphids

The most common is the green peach aphid (*Myzus persicae* Sulzer). Symptoms include crinkling and distortion of foliage, usually accompanied by shiny specks of honeydew, a sugary excretion. Aphids are visible to the naked eye.

4. Thrips

White, silvery or brownish streaks develop in a somewhat stippled pattern. Thrips are small, narrow, elongated insects of various colors and are visible but often overlooked. They are often hidden in buds and flowers.

5. Fungus Gnats (Bradysia species and Sciara species)

Fungus gnats resemble fruit flies and reside primarily in and on the soil. Heavy infestations attack roots and lower the plants vigor. Chemical soil drenches are helpful.

C. Physiological Disorders

There are a variety of physiological disorders known to reduce the quality of cyclamen plants:

1. *Blasting of flower buds* may be caused by high temperatures, insufficient light, insufficient water, or excessive soil fertilizer levels.

2. *Delayed flowering* may be caused by growing the wrong cultivars, high or low temperatures, faulty nutrition, oversized pots, or insufficient light.

3. *Small flowers* may be caused by high temperatures, excessive soil fertilizer levels or growing the wrong cultivar.

4. *Stretched plants* (too tall) may be caused by insufficient space per plant, excessive soil moisture, insufficient light, or high temperatures.

5. *Stunted plants* may be caused by stunt disease or excess soluble salt levels in the soil.

6. *Weak growth* may be caused by high temperatures, disease, genetic variability, faulty nutrition, crowding, or insufficient light.

7. *Wilting and soft plants* may be caused by dry soil, excess soluble salt levels in soil, extreme temperatures, poor light, or disease.

8. *Yellow or chlorotic foliage* may be caused by lack of nutrients, high pH, excessive light intensity, dry soil, or disease.

Symptoms of nutrient deficiency (Bussler, 1969) are varied:

1. Nitrogen—small, pale (chlorotic) foliage and, with extreme deficiency, weak growth.

2. Phosphorus—dark-green, stiff leaves rich in anthocyanins, especially in petioles and lower leaf surfaces.

3. Potassium—smaller leaves with necrotic dotted margins on older foliage; necrotic areas increase with deficiency severity, flower scapes are shorter than normal.

4. Calcium—flexing down of leaf and flower stalks and development of macroscopic brown streaks on edges of young leaves; roots remain short; corms internally glassy with vessels partially brown.

5. Magnesium—as little as half the normal flower production with no visible foliar symptoms.

6. Boron—young leaves thickened and irregularly curled, flower buds remain small and dry on short peduncles thickened near the base.

A summary of suggestions for successful fast crop production is presented in Table II.

Table II

Summary of Key Suggestions for Successful Fast Crop Production

1. Select proper cultivars.
2. Germinate seed in proper medium and environment.
3. Maintain appropriate growing temperatures.
4. Maintain appropriate humidity levels.
5. Transplant on schedule and only once.
6. Minimize root disturbance during transplanting.
7. Use a light, well-aerated growth medium with good water retention capacity.
8. Maintain uniform, adequate moisture levels in the growth medium.
9. Fertilize regularly in proportion to plant size.
10. Avoid excessive growth medium soluble salt levels.
11. Keep plants actively growing at all times.
12. Maintain appropriate solar radiation energy levels.
13. Use evaporative pad cooling in summer (in most areas).
14. Space plants properly.
15. Provide for good air circulation.
16. Apply GA_3 when appropriate.
17. Utilize good sanitation practices at all times.
18. Control insects and diseases promptly.

REFERENCES

Anderson, R. G., and Widmer, R. E. (1975). Improving vigor expression of cyclamen seed germination with surface disinfestation and gibberellin treatments. *J. Am. Soc. Hort. Sci.* **100**(6), 597–601.

Blasdale, W. C. (1949). Early history of the Persian cyclamen. *Nat. Hortic. Mag.* **28**, 156–161.

Blasdale, W. C. (1951). Additional notes on the history of Persian cyclamen. *Nat. Hortic. Mag.* **30**, 192–197.

Bussler, W. (1969). Dungungsversuche zu Cyclamen. *Gartenbauwissenschaft* **34**, 495–510.

deHaan, I., and Doorenbos, J. (1951). The cytology of the genus Cyclamen. *Meded. Landbouwhogesch. Wageningen* **51**, 151–166.

Dorrenbos, J. (1950a). Taxonomy and nomenclature of cyclamen. *Meded. Landbouwhogesch. Wageningen* **50**(3), 17–29.

Doorenbos, J. (1950b). The history of the Persian cyclamen. *Meded. Landbouwhogesch. Wageningen* **50**(3), 31–59.

Gembis, J. (1978). M.S. thesis study. Dep Hortic. Sci. Land. Archit., Univ. of Minnesota, St. Paul.

Hagemann, W. (1959). Vergleichende Marphologische, Anatomische und Entwecklungsgeschichtliche Studien on *Cyclamen persicum* Mill. sourie einigen Cyclamen-Arten. *Bot. Stud.* **9**, 1–88.

Kohl, H. C. (1975). Cyclamen as cut flowers. *Calif. Agric. Ext. Flower Nursery Rep.* March, p. 6.

Lyons, R. (1978). M.S. thesis study. Dep. Hortic. Sci. Land. Archit., Univ. of Minnesota, St. Paul.

Maatsch, R. (1958). Kuhllagerung von Cyclamen-Jungpflanzen. *Gartenwelt* **58**, 51–52.

Maatsch, R., and Isensee, H. (1959). Keimung von Cyclamen in Substraten mit verschiedengen p H-Werten. *Gartenwelt* **59**, 363–364.

Maatsch, R., and Isensee, H. (1960). Schnittblumenertrage bei Cyclamen V. *Gartenwelt* **60**, 46–47.

Maatsch, R., and Runger, W. (1954). Ein weiterer Beitrag zur Keimung von Cyclamen. *Gartenwelt* **54**, 88.

Massante, H. (1964). Unterschungen uber den Einfluss der Temperatur auf Lagerung und Kermung von Aierpflanzensamen. *Gartenwelt* **64**, 291–293.

Menzel, K. (1972a). Vorteilhafte Cyclamen-Entwicklunstemperaturen. *Dtsch. Gaertnerböerse* **72**(19), 424–425.

Menzel, K. (1972b). Vererbund der Fruh- und Spatbluhigkeit bei Cyclamen. *Dtsch. Gaertnerböerse* **72**(30), 653–654.

Molnar, J. M., and Williams, C. J. (1977). Response of *Cyclamen persicum* cultivars to different growing and holding temperatures. *Can. J. Plant Sci.* **57**, 93–100.

Neuray, G. (1973). Bud formation in *Cyclamen persicum. Acta Hortic.* **31**, 77–79.

Neuray, G., and Henrard, G. (1966). L'influence de la lumiere sur la corissance du cyclamen. *Bull. Rech. Agron. Gembloux* **2**(3), 536–550.

Niizu, Y. (1967). Flower bud differentiation in cyclamen. *Agric. Hortic.* **42**(8), 1269–1270.

Noordegraf, C. V. (1977). Personal communication. Res. Stn. Floric., Aalsmeer.

Platteter, R. J., and Widmer, R. E. (1978). Cyclamen responses to nitrogen and potassium regimes *Annu. Meet. Am. Soc. Hortic. Sci., 75th* Abstr. No. 235, p. 368.

Puustjarvi, V. (1976–1977). Phosphorus fertilization of sphagnum moss peat. *Peat Plant Yearb.* pp. 24–30.

Stephens, L. C., and Widmer, R. E. (1976). Soil temperature effects on cyclamen flowering. *J. Am. Soc. Hortic. Sci.* **101**(2), 107–111.

Sundberg, M. (1978). Ph.D. thesis study. Dep. Bot., Univ. of Minnesota, St. Paul.

Wellensiek, S. J. (1952). The breeding of cyclamen. *Int. Hortic. Congr. Rep.* No. 130, pp. 771–777.

Wellensiek, S. J. (1961). The breeding of diploid cultivars of *Cyclamen persicum. Euphytica* **10**(3), 259–268.

Wellensiek, S. J., Doorenbos, J., van Bragt, J., and Legro, R. A. H. (1961). Cyclamen, a description of cultivars. *Lab. Tuinbouwplantenteelt Landbouwhogesch. Wageningen,* Public. No. 200.

Widmer, R. E., Stephens, L. C., and Angell, M. V. (1974). Gibberellin accelerates flowering of *Cyclamen persicum* Mill. *HortScience* **9**(5), 476–477.

Widmer, R. E., Platteter, R. J., and Gembis, J. (1976). Minnesota fast crop cyclamen-1976. *Minn. State Florists' Bull.* April 1, pp. 3–9.

16
Begonias

Roy A. Larson

Introduction to Floriculture
Copyright © 1980 by Academic Press, Inc.
All rights of reproduction in any form reserved.
ISBN 0-12-437650-9

I. INTRODUCTION

Begonias, named in honor of Michael Begon, a patron of botany and superintendent of Santa Domingo, could justifiably be considered as one of the most versatile of all potted plants grown commercially in many parts of the world. They are grown as flowering potted plants with tremendous variability in flower size, form, color, and texture. Some species are grown as foliage plants, with many different markings on the foliage. Begonias also are among the most popular bedding plants, thriving in sunny or shaded locations. The plants can provide long-lasting masses of color in a flower bed, or be outstanding specimen plants in window boxes or hanging baskets.

Begonias also are classified according to their root systems, such as rhizomatous, tuberous, or fibrous rooted.

There are over 1000 species of begonias distributed originally from diverse areas such as Africa, Central and South America, and Asia. Approximately 200 species are grown commercially to some extent but only a few are prominent. The genus began to emerge as an important cultivated crop in the middle of the nineteenth century but the English were improving begonia culture as early as 1777.

This chapter will not be concerned with most of the species, which would be more appropriate for a botanical monograph, but will concentrate on the species that are of value in commercial floriculture. Undoubtedly there are some species which are not important now but could be very popular in a few years.

II. BEGONIA SPECIES

A. *Begonia semperflorens*

Plants in this species are the fibrous-rooted bedding plants that have been consistently increasing in importance and popularity as newer and better cultivars are developed. The most prominent cultivars are the dwarf types, seldom exceeding 20 cm in height, with glossy green or bronze foliage. Flower colors range from white to bright scarlet. Intermediate types range from 10 to 25 cm in height.

Begonia semperflorens is propagated from seed, although additional plants can be obtained by taking stem cuttings from stock plants. The seeds are extremely small, as indicated by the fact that there are approximately two million seeds in a 28-gm packet (about one-tenth the size of petunia seed). The minuteness of the seed necessitates caution when seed are sown, as an untimely sneeze or trembling hand could result in a massive loss of seed. The propagation medium must be very fine, and the seed should be sown thinly on the surface. Propagation with fine mist is helpful, because the seed will remain in place and water will not be limiting. Seed should germinate in 2 to 3 weeks if the night temperature is at least 18°C.

Seedlings are transplanted to peat pots, packs, or similar containers as soon as the seedlings can be conveniently handled. Often a second transplanting, to the final container, is necessary. This is particularly true if the plants are to be sold as flowering pot plants or in hanging baskets. Crop time from sowing to anthesis is 13 to 14 weeks but not much greenhouse space is required for the first 8 to 10 weeks.

Batson (1973a) suggested putting two plants in a 12-cm pot, if the crop was to be grown as flowering pot plants. Crowding in the pot could be avoided if the plants were placed at the edges of the pot, rather than toward the center. Plants should be pinched about 5 weeks after potting, and proper placement of the plants would allow room for the lateral shoots to develop. Batson recommended a final spacing of 25 × 27 cm.

The plants grow well in media with a pH range of 5.5 to 7, although good growth also can be realized in a more acid medium because some of the native habitats of the begonia have acidic soils. Many growers use a soluble complete fertilizer such as 20-20-20, with infrequent applications of iron chelate to avoid chlorosis.

The photoperiodic response of *B. semperflorens* is not as definite as for some crops such as chrysanthemums and poinsettias. According to Post (1950), the plants will remain vegetative under short days if the night temperature is 21°C or higher but no photoperiodic response is evident if the night temperature is less than 21°C. The optimum night temperature has been considered to be 16°C. Begonias that are sold as bedding plants would stand a better chance of survival or adjustment to outdoor conditions if the plants are finished at a cool night temperature prior to sale.

In recent years air pollution has become a serious problem, particularly in urban areas. Leone and Brennan (1969) studied the effects of ozone and sulfur dioxide on *B. semperflorens,* after they had observed light-colored spotting and necrosis on leaves of begonias grown in trial grounds at Rutgers University. They used levels of the pollutants that are attained in the atmosphere in New Brunswick, New Jersey, evaluated over a dozen prominent cultivars, and noted large cultural differences. Some cultivars were particularly susceptible to injury at high relative humidities. In some instances such pollution injury probably has been diagnosed as a disease symptom or nutritional disorder.

Diseases and insect pests will be discussed at the end of the chapter, as most are common to all begonia species grown commercially. A physiological disorder of *B. semperflorens,* however, is the tendency of some cultivars to drop leaves and flowers in abundance. This is especially apparent on the popular and attractive variegated cultivar Charm, often used in hanging baskets. The abscised plant parts are not as conspicuous when the plants are grown en masse as bedding plants.

B. Christmas Begonias

The nomenclature and cultivar listings of Christmas begonias are confusing. Some authors classify cultivars such as 'Lady Mac,' 'Melior,' and 'Marjorie Gibbs,' simply as *Begonia socotrana* whereas others refer to them as results of crosses between *B. socotrana* × *B. dregei*. Cultivars of the species *B. cheimathas,* such as 'Gloire de Lorraine,' and the cultivars known as the Scandinavian or Norwegian begonias are also categorized as Christmas begonias. This chapter is more concerned with proper cultural practices than with restoring order to begonia taxonomy, and the cultural requirements of the Christmas begonias are very similar, whatever their true classification. Goldschmidt (1974) has tabulated many of these cultivars and the reader who wishes to learn more about begonia classification is referred to his excellent publication (published in German).

The Christmas begonias were assessed by Post (1950) to be the most prominent of the commercially grown begonias, but he made that assessment prior to the introduction of the Elatior begonias. Christmas begonias are grown in much of the world, however, and still are very popular. One might expect that the major season of sale would be Christmas but manipulation of photoperiod could make it possible for flowering plants to be available throughout the year.

This group of begonias also is classified as "semituberous," because the basal portion of the stem does increase in size as the plant matures. It is not a tuber, however, and does not become dormant, as does the true tuberous begonia.

Propagation can be achieved with leaf petiole cuttings or with terminal cuttings. A larger number of plants can be started if leaf petiole cuttings are used, but these cuttings have to be started several weeks before terminal cuttings have to be made for the same flowering period. Handling of the rooted cuttings is very similar to the procedures followed for other plants. Plants that are to be finished in 15-cm pots often will be transplanted one more time than plants that are to be sold in 10-cm pots.

The Christmas begonia once required 11 months from time of propagation to flowering at Christmas but studies by Post (1942) and Horton (1948) did much to reduce crop time to a more economical duration, and a 6-month crop time was developed. The crop also was not confined to the Christmas season, although that was when the plants were in greatest demand. This scheduling could be achieved because of the response of the plants to photoperiod.

Early studies at Cornell (Post, 1942) almost failed to show the photoperiodic response of *B. socotrana* because of the low light intensities that were used during the interrupted dark period. Later work showed that the flower buds were initiated between October 10 and 20 under natural daylength at 42° north latitude. Plants could be maintained in a vegetative state by supplying artificial long days, or flowering could be promoted by supplying artificial short days by pulling blackcloth. Kiplinger (1955) listed such a schedule and allowed 7 to 8 weeks from the start of short days to the date of anthesis. Plants given short days on August 1 flowered on September 20 whereas plants exposed to short days on October 1 were in flower on December 1. Post (1950) recommended night temperatures of 16°–18°C but Kiplinger (1955) advocated 15°–16°C in the fall and early winter months, with a drop to 13°C 2 weeks before the time of sale. Heide (1962) reported that abundant flowers would result if plants were grown under a 9-hour daylength for 2 weeks at a night temperature above 20°C but that treatments would have to be prolonged 1 week at cooler temperatures. He recommended finishing plants at 18°C to reduce the elongation that occurs if the plants are finished at a higher temperature.

Light intensity, particularly during the summer months, is very important in the culture of Christmas begonias. Light-colored foliage frequently results at excessively high light intensities, while unattractive plants are produced if the light intensity has been too drastically reduced. Horton (1952) found 410 lx to be perhaps the optimum light intensity, as the leaves would not be chlorotic or burned and the plants would have small flowers and a compact growth habit.

A potting medium similar to that described for *B. semperflorens* is satisfactory, and the fertilization program could be the same. Kiplinger (1955) warned against inadequate nitrogen, which causes foliage to be light green. Foliar analysis and soil tests would help avoid nutritional disorders.

C. Tuberous Begonias (*Begonia tuberhybrida*)

Tuberous begonias can be attractive flowering pot plants, garden specimens, or window box plants, or the large, spectacular flowers can be used for corsages. The rather demanding environmental requirements limit the importance of tuberous begonias in commercial floriculture, however. Post (1950) stated that these beautiful plants grow best when the night temperature does not exceed 16°C, thus confining them to areas with cool night temperatures, but some of the newer hybrids do grow satisfactorily at higher temperatures.

Tuberous begonias can be propagated by seed but sexually propagated plants must be started in November to be in flower in the spring. They can be started from tubers in February and be in flower in May. Begonia seed will remain viable for 9 years but most seeds that are sown are only 1 year old. The seeds do require an afterripening period of 1 month.

Begonia tubers are produced in California, in a climate where, it is hoped, the early arrival of short days in late summer will promote early tuber formation. This early tuberization enables the California producer to compete with growers in Belgium. In California tubers are dug in mid-December but are not sold until at least January 10. Belgian growers usually can dig tubers earlier and sell them in mid-December.

Tubers purchased by the forcer can be started in boxes, flats, or pots and then transplanted to the final container when the first two leaves have developed equally. Some plants are sold in 10-cm pots although many are sold in

15-cm pots. A potting medium high in organic matter, particularly of a fibrous nature, is preferred.

Excessive light reduction in winter in the greenhouse can result in poorly formed, unattractive plants, or a complete cessation of growth. Supplementary light for 4 to 5 hours each night until March has been suggested as a countermeasure (Anonymous, 1975). Low light intensity during the flowering period when the plants are outdoors in the summer will curtail leaf and flower production, increase susceptibility to disease, and cause the plants to grow too tall. Selection of a site where the plants will receive a few hours of sunlight daily will help avoid these handicaps.

Tuberous begonias are grown primarily for their flowers and there is great variation in flower color, form, size, and texture. There are staminate and pistillate flowers on each plant; it is the double flowers that are desired, and fortunately the most abundant.

Flowering is promoted by long days, and the begonias become dormant under short days. The plants can be dug and allowed to dry up in September, and the tubers can be stored at 10°C until the following spring when they are planted. (This information is primarily for the customer rather than for the commercial grower, as the grower will purchase new seed or tubers each year.)

D. Rhizomatous Begonias

There was a time when this section could have been entitled 'Rex' begonias, as *B. rex* was the truly dominant rhizomatous begonia in commercial floriculture. Now there are other rhizomatous begonias that would challenge 'Rex' begonias in beauty and perhaps eventually in popularity. The 'Iron Cross' begonia (*B. mansoniana*) is a very attractive pot plant (Fig. 1), that is regarded as 'Rex' begonia in some references. *Begonia imperialis* also is attractive with its very dark foliage. Brilmayer (1960) has an extensive list of rhizomatous begonias, and since her book was published many improvements have been made in the choices of cultivars that are available.

Cultural requirements are quite similar for the different species. A potting medium that contains as much as 60% peat moss is frequently used. Environmental requirements of these begonias are similar to the requirements already discussed for other begonias. Effects of environment on flowering are not directly important, as these begonias primarily are grown for their foliage characteristics, but often the factors that favor flowering inhibit vegetative growth, which is important. Light intensity of approximately 200 to 230 lx is the maximum to avoid leaf burn. Watering can be crucial, as the species such as *B. mansoniana* is adversely affected by overwatering.

Plants are propagated by leaf vein sections, as described by Batson (1973b). Approximately 7 weeks are required for rooting, at which time the plants are potted in 10- or 15-cm pots, or in hanging baskets. More than one cutting is placed in the container, to obtain a full appearance.

Fig. 1. 'Iron Cross' begonia.

Batson (1973b) has developed a year-round production schedule that should be of interest to the commercial begonia grower.

E. Elatior Begonias (*Begonia* × *hiemalis*)

Very few flowering potted plants have gained popularity as quickly or dramatically as the elatior begonias (Fig. 2). These begonias were the results of crosses between *B. socotrana* and hybrid tuberous begonias. The history of these crosses has been reported by Doorenbos (1973) and White (1973). Two prominent dates in this history are 1883 when the original cross between *B. socotrana* and *B. tuberhybrida* was made and 1954 when Otto Rieger of Germany introduced the Rieger elatior begonia. These revolutionary introductions had attractive flowers, were easy to propagate, and reportedly quite free from flower bud abscission. The "Aphrodite" series had a growth habit that made the plants ideally suited for hanging baskets whereas the other introductions were more upright in growth habit and made excellent potted plants. In the United States Jim Mikkelsen and his associates of Mikkelsen's, Inc., of Ashtabula, Ohio, must be credited for introducing and promoting the Rieger begonias (1978).

Research by Sandved (1969), White *et al.* (1973), and others revealed much about the response of Rieger begonias to the environment, while Nelson *et al.* (1977) thoroughly examined the nutritional requirements but Mikkelsen (1973;

Fig. 2. Rieger elatior begonia.

Anonymous, 1973) reported on all facets of Rieger begonia production in a manner readily followed by growers.

Rieger elatior begonias are short-day plants with a critical daylength slightly less than 13 hours. Four hours of light in the middle of the night are recommended for the winter months when vegetative growth is needed whereas a 1-hour interruption is adequate in early September and early April. The photoperiodic response of elatior begonias is not as pronounced as for chrysanthemums and poinsettias, as some flowers will be produced even under long days. More uniform flowering on shorter plants will be produced if definite short days are provided in the summer months. For precise flowering schedules, such as those shown in the following tabulation, blackcloth should be pulled after March 1.

Pot	Prune	Lights on	Lights off	Crop time	Bloom
September 24	October 15	September 24	November 5	14 weeks	January 1
December 3	January 7	December 3	January 28	16 weeks	March 25
April 8	April 22	—	—	10 weeks	June 17
July 15	July 29	—	—	10 weeks	September 23

Flowering generally occurs 9 weeks after the start of short days. White (1973) reported that only four photoinductive cycles were needed for flowering, which means that blackcloth would not have to be pulled for much of the 9-week period. Molnar (1974), working with the cultivars Schwabenland Red and Aphrodite Cherry Red, found that 3 weeks of 10-hour days resulted in the earliest and most prolific flowering, and that plants treated in this manner flowered 6 weeks after the start of short days.

Temperature has a striking effect on growth and flowering and the photoperiodic response. Sandved (1971) reported that high night temperatures after flower buds of 'Schwabenland Red' were initiated hastened flowering but that the flowers were small and the plants were too tall. The cultivar Liebesfeuer was not affected adversely by the high temperatures. Mikkelsen (1973) recommended night temperatures of 20°–21°C during the early stages of production, 18°C 3 weeks prior to the start of short days, and 16°–17°C after flower buds were initiated.

Foliage and flower burn at high light intensities are often reported but White and Holcomb (1973) found that the best plants in their studies were those grown in full sun if evaporative cooling was provided in the summer. This research was done in western Pennsylvania and different results might be expected in some other areas. Some reduction in light intensity is needed if cooling is not provided, because the higher the temperature, the lower the light intensity, to avoid plant injury.

As seen in the sample schedule, pruning is an essential cultural practice if abundant lateral shoots and flowers are to be attained. White et al. (1973) believed that four to six branches were needed on a well-developed plant grown in a 15-cm pot. Chemical pruning has been tried but manual pruning still seems to be the best treatment. Pruning out one or two of the largest shoots 2 to 4 weeks after potting is a recommended procedure.

Though a large number of shoots per plant perhaps is desirable it also can be a handicap, particularly if the plants are crowded on the bench. Poorly formed, excessively succulent, and tall plants will be produced under such conditions, and will be more subject to injury from Botrytis and powdery mildew, two of the most serious diseases of Rieger begonia.

Watering of Rieger begonias also has received attention. Hammer (1973) had good results with capillary watering because no water got on the foliage, reducing the incidence of foliar diseases. Guttation on Rieger begonias is a problem, however, particularly under very moist conditions, so mat watering is not totally advantageous. Watering in the morning will reduce the guttation problem, compared to watering in late afternoon.

Plant quality is influenced by the fertilization program to which the plants are subjected. White et al. (1973) recommended 50 ppm of nitrogen at each irrigation during the early stages of growth and 100 ppm during the later stages. A top-dressing of the slow-release fertilizer 14-14-14 Osmocote has been used as a supplement to the constant application of dilute soluble fertilizer. The nitrogen rate can be reduced to 50 to 70 ppm at each watering if Osmocote is used. Nelson et al. (1977) described the symptoms of deficiencies of seven nutrients and the color photographs in the article are very helpful.

Rieger begonia plants, even those of the highest quality, will have a tendency to break off unless some support is provided. String attached to two to three stakes and holding up the largest shoots in each pot will usually be adequate.

Disease problems are more severe on Rieger begonias than on the other types of begonias discussed in this chapter, and many of the cultural practices are related to disease control. These practices will be discussed at the conclusion of the chapter.

Very few flowering potted plants will remain in flower for so long a period of time as the Rieger elatior begonia, after the plants are in the customer's home. Florists should be informed about the proper care of these plants, to enable the customer to realize this asset. Applying water that is approximately 20°C has proved beneficial. Perhaps the greatest mistake that can be made in the home is overwatering, even at the proper temperature. The plants seem to do well in most areas of the home as long as the light intensity is sufficient. Customers could also be informed about the color and beauty these plants can provide in the garden, patio, and window boxes.

III. INSECT AND DISEASE PROBLEMS

All greenhouse crops are subject to insect and disease problems, and begonias are no exception. Insects usually are not too troublesome, when compared to many floricultural crops, although two or three of the disease problems are severe enough to warrant considerable discussion.

Perhaps a major insect problem would be mealybugs, with the conspicuous white cottony mass that reveals the presence of this pest. There are many insecticides available to control mealybugs, ranging from granular systemic materials to fog applications. The reader should refer to recent insect control charts for the most effective and approved methods of control. Mealybugs and the cottony masses should be eliminated prior to sale.

Aphids frequently can be found on begonias. The insects and the damage they cause can be very conspicuous on the glossy begonia foliage. Again, there are many insecticides that will control this insect problem, and large, damaging populations should never be permitted to develop.

Whitefly is troublesome and repeated applications of effective chemicals are necessary, as the adults are very mobile and the eggs might escape destruction.

Trial applications of the insecticides should be made prior to full-scale treatment as the fine-textured foliage of some begonias could be damaged. This is particularly true for some of the rhizomatous types.

Cyclamen and spider mites can be problems because the minute pests often are not observed until the foliage has been injured. The resistance to miticides that are applied too regularly also make control difficult. Plants should be closely scrutinized to detect the presence of mites. Often the webbing and accumulation of dust on the underside of the foliage are the first obvious signs of mites.

Other insect pests such as thrips occasionally infest begonias but usually are not as damaging as the pests already listed.

There are several important diseases affecting all begonias but most attention in recent years has been directed to the elatior begonias (Strider and Jones, 1973).

Powdery mildew is a major disease affecting begonias, and it has discouraged some growers from continuing the production of elatior begonias. The powdery growth on the foliage is very conspicuous and severe infection can cause distorted growth and eventual death of the plant. The symptoms seem to intensify in the home, as reported by Powell and Quinn (1978), alienating the customers who were pleased at the time of purchase.

The disease organism (*Oidium begoniae*) is favored by high relative humidity, a condition that frequently occurs in the greenhouse, particularly if growers do not ventilate and heat greenhouses properly. Close spacing, watering late in the day, guttation, and cultivar susceptibility also influence the severity of powdery mildew.

There are fungicides available that will control this serious disease problem but growers should combine environmental control with the use of chemicals, rather than relying just on the fungicides. Some fungicides that do not injure foliage might damage the flowers. Some of the fungicides, if applied too frequently, will leave a residue that is as conspicuous as the powdery mildew signs. Confining production to resistant cultivars perhaps is not a practical solution, as Powell and Quinn (1978) reported that a new strain of powdery mildew might now be affecting Rieger begonia cultivars that had been considered to be resistant. Earlier Strider (1974) had found that 'Schwabenland Red' elatior begonia and similar cultivars were susceptible whereas the "Aphrodite" series, 'Charm,' and 'Lady Mac' begonias were immune but later (Strider, 1978) found that some cultivars previously listed as immune did become infected.

Vaporization of sulfur has long been practiced in greenhouse management and is still very effective.

Bacterial leaf spot and blight (*Xanthomonas begoniae*) also must be controlled. Symptoms of this disease are translucent spots on the foliage, which become blisterlike dead areas. Leaf drop will occur. Harri *et al.* (1977) have described this disease and suggested methods of control, as has Forsberg (1975). Strider (1975, 1978) has categorized cultivars based on resistance or susceptibility.

The same environmental conditions favoring powdery mildew also favor this disease. Correcting poor greenhouse management practices will be as necessary for bacterial leaf spot as for powdery mildew. Effective bactericides have been listed by Strider (1975), but some were injurious to the plants.

Botrytis blight and stem rot (*Botrytis cinerea*) affects elatior begonias at all stages of growth and portions of the plant. Leaves will have a brownish-gray mold and eventually turn black. Stems will have water-soaked lesions and might shrivel up and mummify.

Clean cultural practices, such as removing old leaves and flowers, will reduce the incidence of *Botrytis*. Spores are readily spread by splashing water, fan ventilation, and by many other means, so eliminating the spore-infested plant parts will be beneficial. Reduction in relative humidity, good air circulation, and proper temperature control are other sound practices to observe.

There are fungicides in several different forms that will aid in control. Spray application of an ineffective fungicide might spread more spores than it eliminates. There are no reports of cultivars resistant to *Botrytis*.

A disease affecting the basal portion of begonias is *Pythium* crown and stem rot (*Pythium species*). The water-soaked, discolored stem base is indicative of this problem. *Pythium* can be found in most greenhouses, as it is a very common organism, so growers should follow practices that prevent the organism from infesting the soil. Pasteurization of the potting medium, preferably with aerated steam, ensures the grower of a clean start as far as the medium is concerned but sanitary practices must be observed to avoid recontamination.

Rieger elatior begonias are particularly subject to foliar nematodes (*Aphelenchoides fragariae*), although the problem seems to be less serious now than it was a couple of years ago. Clean propagation stock is necessary, though this does not ensure the grower of nematode-free plants for tte remainder of the production period. Nematodes can be spread by splashing water, so the use of tube or mat watering could reduce foliar nematode infestations.

Several pesticides have been used successfully in the control of foliar nematodes, as reported by Strider (1973). Some of the most prominent pesticides are frequently used for insect control. Strider also found that the "Aphrodite" types of elatior begonias were less affected by nematodes than the "Schwabenland" types.

It is readily apparent that the major begonia disease problems are most severe when the relative humidity is high, when the foliage is allowed to become and remain wet, when the plants are crowded together, and when temperature control and ventilation are inadequate. Since all the begonias are vegetatively propagated, with the exception of *B. semperflorens,* which is most generally started from seed, it is very important that only disease-free plants be used as stock, and that the propagation area be extremely clean. The propagator has a major commitment to produce healthy cuttings, and the grower has an equal commitment to follow sound greenhouse sanitation practices and effective pesticide programs.

REFERENCES

Anonymous (1973). "Rieger Begonias." Mikkelsens, Inc., Ashtabula, Ohio.
Anonymous (1975). "The Ball Red Book." Geo. J. Ball, Inc., West Chicago, Illinois.

Anonymous (1978). "Production Procedures for Hiemalis Begonias." Mikkelsens, Inc., Ashtabula, Ohio.

Batson, F. (1973a). A guide to year-round production of minor potted crop. 9. Rex begonia. Beautiful. *Florists' Rev.* **152**(3945), 17–18.

Batson, F. (1973b). Fibrous begonia, neat. *Florists' Rev.* **152**(3939), 22, 23.

Brilmayer, B. (1960). "All About Begonias." Doubleday, New York.

Doorenbos, J. (1973). Breeding 'Elatior' begonias (*B.* X *Hiemalis* Fotsch). *Acta Hortic.* **31,** 127–131.

Forsberg, J. L. (1975). "Diseases of Ornamental Plants," Spec. Publ. No. 3 (Rev.), pp. 28–29. Univ. of Illinois Press, Urbana.

Goldschmidt, H. (1974). "Marktwichtige Blütenbegonien. Gärtnerische Berufspraxis," No. 41. Parey, Berlin.

Hammer, A. (1973). Capillary watering of Rieger begonias. *Focus Floric., Purdue Univ.* **1**(2), 14–15.

Harri, J. A., Larsen, P. O., and Powell, C. C., Jr. (1977). Bacterial leaf spot and blight of Rieger elatior begonia: systemic movement of the pathogen, host range, and chemical control trials (*Xanthomonas begoniae*). *Plant Dis. Rep.* **61**(8), 649–653.

Heide, O. M. (1962). Interaction of night temperature and daylength in flowering of *Begonia* × *Cheimantha* Everett. *Physiol. Plant.* **15,** 729–735.

Horton, F. F. (1948). Christmas begonias in six months. *N.Y. State Flower Growers' Bull.* **29,** 7.

Horton, F. F. (1952). What light intensity for begonias during summer. *N.Y. State Flower Growers' Bull.* **85,** 4.

Kiplinger, D. C. (1955). "Greenhouse Potted Plants," Book Ser. B-2. Ohio Agric. Exp. Stn., Wooster, Ohio.

Leone, I. A., and Brennan, E. (1969). Sensitivity of begonias to air pollution. (*Begonia semperflorens*). *Hortic. Res.* **9**(2), 112–116.

Mikkelsen, J. (1973). Simplified growing instructions for Rieger elatior begonias. *Pa. Flower Growers' Bull.* **263,** 3–5.

Molnar, J. M. (1974). Photoperiodic response of *Begonia* × *hiemalis* cv. Rieger. *Can. J. Plant Sci.* **54,** 277–280.

Nelson, P. V., Krauskopf, D. M., and Mingis, N. C. (1977). Visual symptoms of nutrient deficiencies in Rieger elatior begonia (× Hiemalis). *J. Am. Soc. Hortic. Sci.* **102**(1), 65–68.

Post, K. (1942). Effects of daylength and temperature on growth and flowering of some florist crops. *Cornell Univ. Agric. Exp. Stn. Bull.* No. 787, 1–70.

Post, K. (1950). "Florist Crop Production and Marketing." Orange Judd Publ., New York.

Powell, C. C., and Quinn, J. A. (1978). Preventing mildew on Rieger begonias. *Florists' Rev.* **163**(4225), 64–65.

Sandved, G. (1969). Flowering in *Begonia* × *Hiemalis* Fotsch as affected by daylength and temperature. *Acta Hortic.* **14,** 61–63.

Sandved, G. (1971). Effekt av daglengde og temperatur på vekst og blomstring hos Begonia × hiemalis 'Schwabenland' og 'Liebesfeuer.' (The effect of daylength and temperature on growth and flowering in Begonia × hiemalis 'Schwabenland' and "Liebesfeuer.') *Gartneryrket* **19**(61), 378–379.

Strider, D. L. (1973). Control of *Aphelenchoides fragariae* of Rieger begonias. *Plant Dis. Rep.* **57,** 1015–1019.

Strider, D. L. (1974). Resistance of Rieger elatior begonias to powdery mildew, and efficacy of fungicides for control of the disease. *Plant Dis. Rep.* **58,** 875–878.

Strider, D. L. (1975). Susceptibility of Rieger elatior begonia cultivars to bacterial blight caused by *Xanthomonas begoniae*. *Plant Dis. Rep.* **59**(1), 70–73.

Strider, D. L. (1978). Reaction of recently released Rieger elatior begonia cultivars to powdery mildew and bacterial blight. *Plant Dis. Rep.* **62,** 22–23.

Strider, D. L., and Jones, R. K. (1973). Common diseases of Rieger begonia and their control. *N.C. Commer. Flower Growers' Bull.* **17**(1), 1–2.

White, J. W. (1973). Rieger elatior begonias: history and European research. *Pa. Flower Growers' Bull.* **263,** 1–2, 5.

White, J. W., and Holcomb, E. J. (1973). Rieger elatior begonias research at Penn State. Progress Report III. *Pa. Flower Growers' Bull.* **264,** 6–8.

White, J. W., Guthrie, H., and Watt, B. (1973). Rieger elatior begonias research at Penn State. Progress IV. *Pa. Flower Growers' Bull.* **264,** 8–10.

17
Kalanchoe

Joseph W. Love

Introduction to Floriculture
Copyright © 1980 by Academic Press, Inc.
All rights of reproduction in any form reserved.
ISBN 0-12-437650-9

I. HISTORY

The kalanchoe, long considered a minor crop, was introduced in Potsdam, Germany, in 1932 by Robert Blossfeld (Broertjes and Leffring, 1972). Many mutations and hybrids were developed for florists' use from the original *Kalanchoe blossfeldiana*. Some of the earlier Swiss hybrids were not true from seed and had to be propagated by vegetative methods. Adolph Grob of Switzerland was able to produce several hybrids that could be grown true from seed. Many of these hybrids were not acceptable in the United States since they lacked uniformity in color, form, and growth; most were too tall, and, more important, were heat sensitive (Irwin, 1972a,b). The impetus to start kalanchoes from terminal cuttings was started in the early 1970s.

Most U.S. growers still consider the kalanchoe a minor crop, but in Oklahoma and Texas it is considered as the second most important flowering pot plant. With its variation in leaf shape, flower colors, and good keeping quality in the home, the kalanchoe has good potential as a flowering potted plant for many growers. An interesting review of present-day kalanchoes was recently compiled (Manzitti, 1978a,b).

II. BOTANICAL INFORMATION

Kalanchoe blossfeldiana Poelln. (family, Crassulaceae) is a native of Madagascar. Other related species originated from arid regions of tropical Africa. The kalanchoe is a succulent with fleshy leaves. The leaves are arranged along the stems in pairs, each pair at right angles to the pair above or below. The small, star-shaped florets are produced under short-day conditions. The inflorescence is a dichasial cyme that terminates in cincinni (Schwabe, 1969). A dichasium is called a cyme by some since the term applies to any inflorescence that is flat-topped (Porter, 1967).

Since Blossfeld's introduction of the kalanchoe, numerous reports have been published on the species. Unfortunately, during the early years after its introduction, there were few hybrid selections that could be used as potted plants. Major interest was focused on several seedlings developed by hybridizers.

Until recently the only kalanchoe cultivars produced were grown from seed. Few seed-grown cultivars have been produced since the introduction of cultivars propagated by cuttings. Both Swiss and U.S. breeders have been instrumental in developing new types of kalanchoe cultivars.

III. PROPAGATION

A. Vegetative Propagation

1. Stock Plant Culture

Any commercial grower who considers propagation of his own cuttings should make every effort to provide the best conditions possible for success.

There are several major specialist-propagators who provide disease-free rooted plants. A source of stock should always be obtained from one of the reliable propagators.

There are numerous kalanchoe cultivars available for a successful flowering program. Many of these cultivars are patented and a license must be obtained from the licensor in order to propagate them. A royalty is charged for each cutting produced and sold.

Growers who intend to propagate their own cuttings should realize that propagation constitutes another phase of their business and that the various costs associated with propagation and stock plant care must be attributed to the final expense of growing flowering plants.

Stock plants should be grown in isolated areas where the environment can be controlled at optimum conditions: Established 6-cm plants are purchased from a specialist-propagator and potted, one plant to a 15-cm clay or plastic container. Some growers prefer 3.8-liter nursery containers. The growing medium should be well drained and aerated to ensure good root development.

Two weeks after planting the plants are adequately established so that the shoot tip can be removed with a soft pinch (approximately 1 cm) to encourage branching. The rate of plant growth dictates when additional pinches are made.

Stock plants are grown pot tight for several weeks and then spaced 28 × 28 cm. It is important to provide good air circulation around the plants to minimize potential foliar diseases. As the plants mature more space is provided.

Long days are provided constantly to ensure that the stock plants remain vegetative. Plants are lighted during the middle of the dark period at 161 lx for 2 hours, May through August; 3 hours, September–October, March–April; and 4 hours, November–February. Mace cultivar (cv.) stock plants require only 2 hours of light in the middle of the night (Carlson, 1975). Interruption of the dark period is more effective in keeping kalanchoe plants vegetative than long days of continuous light of 16 or more hours.

The air temperature should be accurately regulated to ensure good growth. During the heating period the night temperature should be maintained at 18°C. Under no circumstances should the night temperature exceed 24°C. Daytime temperatures should be adjusted 8°C higher.

Full light is provided for the stock plants during autumn, winter, and early spring. In late spring and summer, light intensity is regulated to a maximum of 38 to 54 klx.

Stock plants should receive adequate water and at no time should experience a water stress. Frequency of watering depends on the growing medium, nature of the plant container, plant size, and rate of water loss from the plant tissue due to increased temperature. Sufficient water is applied to the medium's surface to affect some water loss from the bottom of the plant container. It is important to keep water off foliage to lessen the possibility of disease.

Stock plants should be fertilized at each watering or every 7 to 10 days. A complete fertilizer such as 20–20–20 is adequate. (See Section IV, B, 4.)

Cutting potential for each stock plant depends on the cultivar, plant size, frequency of pinching or removal of cuttings, temperature, watering, fertilization, and light intensity. Two-year-old Mace cv. stock plants provide from 20 to 30 cuttings every 3 weeks (Carlson, 1975; Rathmell, 1970).

It is important to renew stock plants periodically, at least two to three times per year to avoid the occurrence of premature bud setting (Masson, 1973). Mace cv. stock plants provided with continuous long days were kept vegetative for a number of years (Carlson, 1975). The development of premature buds occurs when stock plants are not pinched or cuttings removed regularly, and when long days are not provided continuously throughout the year. Growers should check their stock plant growing area at night to determine that all lights are functioning.

2. Cutting Production

Cuttings are routinely removed from stock plants for rooting, depending on the number of plants required for flowering. Unrooted cuttings may be purchased from a specialist-propagator, eliminating the necessity for maintaining stock plants (Mikkelsen, 1977).

Terminal cuttings, 5 to 7.5 cm in length, are adequate for rooting. Only two sets of leaves are necessary (Carlson, 1975). Kalanchoe cuttings root easily, eliminating the need for a rooting hormone.

The rooting medium selected should be loose, well drained, and aerated. A combination of 2 parts peat moss and 1 part coarse perlite (v/v) is satisfactory (Love, 1976a,b). Other rooting media include sand, peat and sand, and soil, peat moss, and coarse aggregates (Carlson, 1975).

Cuttings can be rooted in wooden or plastic flats or in propagation benches. The spacing required depends on the cultivars since some have large fleshy leaves. Leaves of such cultivars are trimmed in half to facilitate spacing them closer in the rooting bed or flat (Fig. 1). Cuttings are lined in rows with adequate space within and between rows so that leaves just touch. Lower leaves are removed before the cutting is inserted in the medium to a depth of 2.5 to 4 cm.

Excellent rooting is accomplished with an intermittent misting system. A reliable time clock is necessary to ensure the frequency of misting. A film of moisture should always be on the foliage and stems. During the winter, misting is provided initially during the daylight hours, 6 seconds, each 6 to 10 minutes. The mist cycle is increased during the warm, high-light months to 6 seconds each 3 to 5 minutes. After the cuttings begin to callus (about 7 days), the frequency of misting is every 6 to 10 minutes. Most cultivars develop an adequate root system within 3 weeks. Cuttings rooted in a peat moss and perlite medium develop a root ball about 2.5 cm in diameter.

Successful rooting depends on accurate regulation of air and medium temperatures. Air temperature at night should be 16.5°–18°C; the day temperature

Fig. 1. Kalanchoes rooted in a medium of peat moss and perlite. Cuttings in upper part of photo were trimmed to facilitate closer spacing.

should be 21°–24°C. Temperature of the rooting medium should be adjusted to 21°C for optimum rooting. This control is provided with thermostatically regulated heating cables placed under the rooting medium, or steam or hot water pipes situated beneath the propagation bench. Temperature control of the growing medium is especially important during the winter months, when the mist water is cold. Some greenhouse firms heat their irrigation water to at least 21°C.

A primary advantage of intermittent mist is that it allows cuttings to root in strong light. Full light should be provided during autumn, winter, and early spring. Summer light needs to be reduced approximately 25 to 30%.

While being rooted, cuttings receive long days to prevent premature flower bud formation. Lighting is provided during the middle of the dark period, as described previously for stock plants.

In recent years some growers have circumvented the propagation bed entirely and have relied on rooting kalanchoe cuttings directly in the final container (Masson, 1973; Mikkelsen, 1977). This practice requires that the medium is loose and well drained. During the rooting period the containers are placed pot tight. A larger area is needed than for conventional rooting beds and this requirement may be considered a disadvantage. An alternate method to intermittent mist is to syringe the unrooted cuttings during the first week often enough to keep a film of moisture on the foliage. It is necessary to reduce the light intensity to prevent drying and burning of the cuttings.

B. Seed Propagation

Seed propagation once was the major method of propagating kalanchoes. *Kalanchoe blossfeldiana* has long been produced in Europe by sexual methods. From its introduction in Germany in 1932, numerous kalanchoe hybrids have been developed and introduced to the commercial trade. The cultivar, Tom Thumb, was introduced in the United States by the Dauernheim Corp., Wantagh, Long Island, New York (Post, 1950a). Since the introduction of Tom Thumb, other European seed cultivars have been added to an increasing list of cultivars. Several U.S. plant breeders have made significant contributions (Manzitti, 1978a; Anonymous, 1968).

Kalanchoe seed are extremely small with as many as 2.5 million seeds per 28 gm. Seed are sown from January to July. Some growers sow seed regularly in order to have seedlings available for planting on a year-round basis.

The medium used for sowing seed should be well drained and aerated (Anonymous, 1968; Post, 1950a). Several excellent peatlite mixtures are commercially available for seed germination. A mixture of 1 part peat moss and 1 part No. 4 grade vermiculite is satisfactory (Batson, 1973). The selected medium should be pasteurized since germinating kalanchoe seedlings are susceptible to damping-off diseases.

Commercial firms sell kalanchoe seeds in small lots or packs that make it easier for the grower to estimate the number of seed to sow. Standard wooden or plastic flats are popular containers for starting seed in large numbers. Growers who start seed regularly throughout the year find it advantageous to use clean, 17.5-cm diameter clay pots.

The tiny seed are carefully broadcast or sown in rows. One unique method of sowing kalanchoe seed was recently described (Batson, 1973). The prescribed number of seed are placed in a 30-ml beaker. Fifteen milliliters of water and 3 to 5 drops of a nonionic spreader are added to the seed. The spreader is necessary to prevent the seed from floating. The mixture should be stirred vigorously and placed in a standard eye dropper. One-centimeter furrows are pressed in the moistened medium's surface, and the furrows are spaced 2.5 cm apart. The water and seed suspension is discharged into the furrows by rapidly moving the dropper along the furrow at a height of 2.5 to 5 cm. To prevent the seed from settling to the bottom in the dropper the grower should position the dropper at an angle. The seed pot is then placed in a plastic bag, sealed, and placed away from direct sun.

The medium temperature should be maintained at 21°C for optimum germination. It is not necessary to cover kalanchoe seed since light is necessary for germination. Most cultivars germinate after 7 to 10 days (White, 1974; Batson,

1973). After the seedlings commence growing, the plastic cover must be removed from the seed pot. The seed pots are moved to a cooler area and placed under a fluorescent light.

Kalanchoe seedlings grow very slowly in seed pots or flats. Generally, at least 7 weeks are required before the developing seedlings are large enough for transplanting. Seedlings should be fertilized every 7 to 10 days with 30 ml of 20–20–20 fertilizer/3.8 liters of water (Batson, 1973).

Seedlings are transferred from the seed pots 6 to 7 weeks after sowing. One method of culture is to transplant seedlings in a wooden or plastic flat on 5-cm centers. They are allowed to develop until the plants become crowded (Post, 1950a).

An alternate method of culture is to plant individual seedlings in 6-cm peat pots (Anonymous, 1975). The growing medium should be well drained and aerated. An excellent growing medium is 1 part soil, 1 part peat moss, and 1 part vermiculite (v/v/v) (Batson, 1973). The small seedlings should be planted shallow to prevent crown rot.

One commercial firm provides the floriculture industry with super seedlings that are prestarted and ready for transplanting. Growers may request shipment of super seedlings at regular intervals.

IV. PLANT CULTURE

A. Vegetative Stage

1. Media

Commercial growers should be concerned about the growing medium selected for kalanchoe culture. It is well known that most firms have their own recipes for pot plant culture.

Kalanchoes do not grow well with "wet feet" and must be grown in a medium that is well drained and aerated (Mikkelsen, 1977). Various media are recommended for kalanchoe culture. These include ⅓ peat, ⅓ perlite, ⅓ soil (Mikkelsen, 1977); 5 parts soil, 4 parts peat, and 4 parts terra green (Irwin, 1972a, b); 45% coarse peat moss, 45% coarse vermiculite, and 10% ground limestone (20 mesh) (Anonymous, 1976a); 3 parts milled pine bark, 1 part sand, and 1 part peat moss (Love, 1976a,b).

The pH of the growing medium must be adjusted to be between 6.0 and 7.0. Plants produced in a medium with a pH of 5.5 have a browning of the upper leaves whereas a pH above 7.0 causes a yellowing of the upper leaves (Carlson, 1975). Dolomitic limestone is recommended since it contains a source of both calcium and magnesium. Only the fine-grade dolomitic limestone should be used since coarse or medium grades are too slow acting and have little effect on the ultimate pH of the medium. A sample of the growing medium should be sent to a soil testing laboratory for lime requirements to adjust the pH.

There are numerous soil-less mixes on the commercial market. Most have large proportions of organic matter such as ground pine bark and/or peat moss. Other additives include vermiculite, perlite, sand, and calcined clay. A mixture should be tested prior to its acceptance as part of the cultural program. Any medium should possess good drainage and aeration.

Good management includes some form of pasteurization of the growing medium. Steam is the most popular way of pasteurizing a growing medium. Maintenance of the medium at 82°C for 30 minutes is adequate. Special carts are available for pasteurization and they may also serve as portable potting benches.

Most of the soil-less mixtures are advertised as ready-to-use from the bag without pasteurization. The reliability of such a claim by the manufacturer must be assessed by the firm's manager.

2. Potting

Most kalanchoe growers start kalanchoes on a regular schedule, as compared to an earlier program of flowering plants only for Christmas and the following 2 to 3 months. The source of plant material is a specialist-propagator (rooted or unrooted cuttings) or the production of one's own rooted or unrooted cuttings.

The use of either clay or plastic pots is still a managerial decision. In earlier days when most growing media were of the heavy clay types, watering was a precise art and clay pots were preferred. In recent years the loose, well-drained media have gained acceptance. These media make it possible to produce quality potted plants without danger of constant overwatering.

Many kalanchoe cultivars have been introduced that possess various sizes of foliage and growth rates. The wide assortment of cultivars enables the plant manager to select growth types for container size and potential market. The most popular size containers are the 7.5-, 10-, 12.5-, and 15.25-cm pots (Post, 1950a), (Mikkelsen, 1977). Small containers are used for the small foliage cultivars while large containers are reserved for the large, fleshy-leafed types (Carbonneau, 1975).

The number of plants potted per container varies with the cultivar, pot size, and potential market. Small, 7.5- and 10-cm containers require only one plant. Since the growing period is lengthy from planting to flowering for some small, slow-growing cultivars, multiple plants are used in a container (Batson, 1973; Love, 1976a,b; Masson, 1973). This practice is expensive and should be weighed against the bench time conserved by producing the finished plant in a shorter period.

The kalanchoe rooted cutting should be planted carefully. (Fig. 2). The soil ball of a 5.7-cm plant, the stem of a rooted cutting, or the stem of a seedling from a seed flat should never be "buried." At least 1.5- to 2-cm depth should be

Fig. 2. Kalanchoe cuttings with well-developed roots should be planted shallow in the medium.

left above the medium's surface to allow for proper watering. Uneven planting produces an uneven crop response. Plants or cuttings are carefully graded when more than one plant is potted in a container (Carbonneau, 1975).

Several companies furnish cultivars that make large plants. One rooted cutting is recommended for a 15.25- or 16.5-cm pot (Anonymous, 1976a,b; Manzitti, 1978a). Research conducted with the cultivar Mace indicates that excellent plants are produced when a rooted cutting is planted in such containers.

3. Spacing

The spiraling increase in costs of producing potted plants has made commercial flower growers cognizant of efficient utilization of greenhouse space. The period required to produce flowering kalanchoe plants depends on the cultivar response (start of short days to flower), size of container used, and size of plant required for a specific market (White, 1974).

An elaborate method of producing plants at the final spacing with "no-move," "one-move," and "two moves" has been outlined by a commercial specialist-propagator for both the large, foliage-type kalanchoes and for small-leaved European and U. S. cultivars (Tables I and II).

Production of plants in various zoned areas of the greenhouse range facilitates the photoperiod control necessary for kalanchoe growth and flowering.

The "two-move" program allows for development of a long-day area, a short-day area, and a natural season area for finishing the crop.

4. Pinching

Pinching, or removal of the terminal vegetative growing point, is necessary for some kalanchoe cultivars. (Fig. 3). It increases the number of axillary shoots and thus ensures a larger plant and more flowers. Pinching offers some height control, and tends to make a more even inflorescence distribution on some cultivars.

Slow-growing kalanchoe cultivars require pinching (Mikkelsen, 1977). Like the potted chrysanthemum, some kalanchoe cultivars require a certain number of long days to produce vegetative growth before a pinch is made. The amount of growth desired usually depends on the size of container in which the particular kalanchoe cultivar is grown. For instance, cultivars grown in 10-cm pots require no long-day treatment before pinching. They are potted, pinched, and placed directly under short-day treatment. By contrast, cultivars produced in 15.25-cm pots require at least 4 weeks of long-day treatment after planting and

Table I

Spacing of Large-Leaved Kalanchoe Cultivars[a]

Move	Spacing (cm)	Weeks	m²	Total m² weeks
No	31 × 31	14	1.35	1.35
OR				
No	28 × 28	14	1.1	1.1
One	20 × 23	6	0.28	—
	31 × 31	8	0.77	1.05
OR				
One	20 × 20	6	0.24	—
	28 × 28	8	0.63	0.87
Two	15 × 20	3	0.09	—
	20 × 23	3	0.14	—
	31 × 31	8	0.77	1.00
OR				
Two	15 × 15	3	0.07	—
	20 × 20	3	0.12	—
	28 × 28	8	0.63	0.82

[a]The following spacing systems compare square meter week requirements, based on a maximum 14-week crop time. Plants were grown in 16.25-cm containers.

Table II

Spacing of Small-Leaved European and U.S. Cultivars[a]

Container size (cm)	Daylength	Spacing (cm)	Weeks	m²	m² weeks
10	Long	10 × 10	0.5	0.01	—
	Short	11.5 × 11.5	6	0.08	—
	Natural	13 × 15	6	0.12	0.21
12.7	Long	13 × 13	2.5	0.04	—
	Short	15 × 15	6	0.14	—
	Natural	20 × 23	6	0.28	0.46
15.25	Long	18 × 18	4.5	0.15	—
	Short	20 × 20	6	0.24	—
	Natural	31 × 31	6	0.58	0.97
OR					
15.25	Long	18 × 18	4.5	0.15	—
	Short	20 × 20	6	0.24	—
	Natural	28 × 28	6	0.47	0.86
OR					
15.25	Long	18 × 18	4.5	0.15	—
	Short	20 × 20	6	0.24	—
	Natural	26 × 26	6	0.41	0.8

[a]Total area requirement based on a two-move system of plants grown in 10, 12.7-, and 16.25-cm containers.

Fig. 3.   Kalanchoe plants pinched soft. Three cuttings planted in a 15.25-cm container.

before they are pinched. Extremely slow-growing cultivars should receive 1 to 2 weeks of additional long days after the pinch. This requirement usually occurs in the low light months of winter. Rapidly growing types should receive a "delayed pinch," i.e., the shoot tip is removed 1 week after short days are started.

A soft pinch is preferred for kalanchoes. This involves removal of 1.0 to 1.5 cm of the growing shoot tip. A hard pinch or the removal of 2.5 to 5 cm growth should be avoided, as such a pinch delays flowering and extends cropping time (Anonymous, 1976b).

Several specialist-propagators sell kalanchoe plants prepinched with all the long-day requirements satisfied. The commercial grower pots the plant upon arrival and places them directly under short-day inductive cycles for flowering (Anonymous, 1977).

One commercial grower in North Carolina makes hard pinches on his kalanchoe plants and uses the removed shoot tips as cuttings. This technique eliminates the need for stock plants.

B. Environmental Control

1. Light Intensity

Although a succulent, kalanchoes should not be grown under limited light. Most reports indicate that cultivars produced from seed require less light than the newer hybrids. A range of 16.1 to 54 klx is recommended for the cultivars propagated from seed (Batson, 1973; Post, 1950a). One seed broker suggests full light for the seedling Tetra Vulcan (Anonymous, 1975).

Kalanchoe cultivars produced from cuttings are grown under various light intensities. One commercial guideline indicates that European hybrids should be grown under 27 klx from May to August. Moderate shade is required in March, April, September, and October. No shade is necessary from November through February (Anonymous, 1976a). Most recommendations suggest full light during fall, winter, and spring, and reduced light during the summer months (Love, 1976a, b; Irwin, 1972a, b). Low winter light reduces the number of basal shoots developed and limits the plant's fullness and spread (Anonymous, 1976a).

2. Water

The kalanchoe is a succulent and withstands long periods without water. *Kalanchoe blossfeldiana* plants produced under short days require less water than plants produced under long days. This is possible because of considerable water storage and small leaf surface (Harder, 1948). The new hybrid cultivars require frequent watering to maintain quality foliage and flowers. Good-quality water must be provided that is low in total soluble salts.

An early worker who experimented with *Kalanchoe blossfeldiana* and other seed-type cultivars indicated that high soil moisture is conducive to crown rot.

The growing medium should be kept on the dry side and watered only when needed (Post, 1950a). Open, well-drained media have been instrumental in changing the watering practices of kalanchoes. The very nature of the large, fleshy leaves that cover the lower part of the kalanchoe plant and container makes it extremely difficult to water properly by overhead methods except in the early stages of growth. Growers who hand-water their plants are cautioned to water early in the morning and to keep the water off the foliage (Love, 1976a, b; Mikkelsen, 1977). Some cultivars are extremely susceptible to powdery mildew and crown rot.

The spaghetti-tube method of watering is suited for kalanchoe culture. (Fig. 4). The small end of the tube is placed on the surface of the medium. This system avoids splashing water on the foliage or crown. Enough water should be added to ensure some dripping through the bottom of the container. A good rule of thumb to follow is to allow 10 to 15% of the water applied to leach from the bottom of the container to prevent high soluble salts.

Tube-watered plants should be examined periodically to determine if the water is distributed evenly over the surface. Many of the new media are so well drained that water penetrates only where the water is applied. Such media may be treated with a "water-wetter" to permit uniform wetting of the whole profile of medium in the container. Growth is uneven and flowering erratic if dry areas persist (Carbonneau, 1975).

Fig. 4. Kalanchoes are ideally suited for spaghetti-tube watering. Plants are produced on wire bench for good air circulation.

Capillary mat watering is suited for kalanchoe culture and facilitates rapid movement of plants when spaced once or twice (Gillette, 1978). Water is applied to the mat surface and the water is drawn into the pot by capillarity. The mats are constructed of many materials, such as reprocessed cloth, virgin synthetic fiber, or even three or four layers of newspaper (Nelson, 1978). Mats should be placed only on benches that are level. The potting medium should be uniform, water quality excellent, and the fertilization practices modified for overhead fertilization (Hanan *et al.,* 1978).

There appears to be some controversy in the literature regarding watering practices. One firm suggests that the kalanchoe should be subject to water stress as the peduncle begins to elongate. Such treatment results in shorter plants and earlier flowering (Anonymous, 1976a,b). They do caution against excessive drying since it results in red-pigmented stems and foliage. Other workers caution against allowing any water stress for kalanchoes (Carlson, 1975; Anonymous, 1977).

3. Temperature

Temperature control is important for vegetative plants. Most cultivars grow at accelerated rates when the night temperature is adjusted to 21°C. This is usually impractical since other stages of plant development are represented in the same house. The ideal temperature for root development is 21°C and bottom heating is highly recommended.

Day temperatures are adjusted 6°–8°C higher than night temperatures. High summer daytime temperatures are reduced with an evaporative cooling system, roof shading, or medium pressure mist.

4. Fertilization

Very little nutritional research has been conducted on kalanchoes but many popular articles do suggest fertilizer programs.

Seedling kalanchoe cultivars, such as Tetra Vulcan and Tom Thumb, require less fertilizer than the newer hybrids. A nitrogen fertilizer should be applied about the time flower buds show (Post, 1950a; Anonymous, 1968). A complete fertilizer is recommended for the cultivar Tom Thumb every 3 to 4 weeks (Laurie *et al.,* 1968). One grower advocates that the cultivars Vulcan and Gelber Liebling should receive fertilizer 3 to 4 weeks after potting. The recommendation includes application of a dilute fertilizer, 20–20–20, every 2 weeks at the rate of 368 gm/380 liters (Batson, 1973).

For the new hybrids good-quality plants are produced when a regular fertilization program is practiced. Constant or injection fertilization is popular with many growers. Recommendations range from 200 or 300 ppm nitrogen; 50 to 200 ppm phosphorus; 150 to 250 ppm potassium (Mikkelsen, 1975; Masson, 1973; Carlson, 1975). Several kalanchoe growers include the application of additional fertilizer that is applied with the constant fertilization program. One such schedule includes 600 ppm nitrogen and 200 ppm potassium plus minor elements each week (Mason, 1973). Additional calcium is guaranteed with a monthly supplemental fertilization of calcium nitrate (Mikkelsen, 1977).

Fertilization rates should be reduced 1 week prior to and 2 weeks after short days start. Plants checked in growth are more receptive to the short-day treatment for flower bud initiation (Carbonneau, 1975). Winter fertilization rates are increased 25 to 50% since plants receive fewer waterings (Anonymous, 1976a).

Fertilizer concentrations should be reduced several weeks prior to flowering (Mikkelsen, 1977; Carbonneau, 1975). One method of reducing the amount of nutrients applied is to alternate clear water with fertilizer applications (Anonymous, 1976a).

Soluble salt injury occurs when insufficient water is applied, the medium is allowed to become excessively dry between waterings, too strong concentrations of fertilizer are applied, or combinations of any of these factors. Plants injured from high salts have damaged roots, burned foliage, and stunted growth.

Excellent kalanchoe plants are produced when fertilized every 7 to 10 days. A rate of 540 to 720 ppm nitrogen–phosphorus–potassium may be applied to kalanchoes weekly (Carlson, 1975; Link, 1978).

A slow-release fertilizer, Osmocote, is suggested as a supplemental source of fertilizer. It permits reducing nitrogen and potassium applications several weeks before flowering (Mikkelsen, 1977). The material is usually applied as a top-dressing on the medium's surface. One-half teaspoon is recommended for 10-cm containers and 1 level teaspoon for a 15.25-cm container (Love, 1976a, b).

Zinc deficiency is a serious nutrient disorder of some kalanchoe cultivars (Nelson, 1978). Research conducted with the cultivar Segantini revealed that soil phosphorus either inhibited the absorption of zinc by kalanchoe roots, or inactivated zinc in plant tissue. Recommendations to prevent zinc deficiency include: (1) avoid using soil high in phosphorus; (2) avoid fertilizing crops with high concentrations of phosphorus; (3) use minor elements that include zinc; (4) adjust soil pH from 5.5 to 6.5; and (5) maintain soil temperature at 20°–25°C (Asif, 1974).

The essential micronutrients iron, manganese, zinc, copper, boron, and molybdenum are required by kalanchoe plants in very small quantities. Some manufactured fertilizers include micronutrients. Fritted trace elements are incorporated into the medium during preparation and will last for 12 months. Several formulations of soluble micronutrients are available. They may be used once and will last for 3 or 4 months or they may be incorporated into the irrigation water in small quantities and applied at each watering.

V. FLOWERING

The kalanchoe is a classical short-day plant. The first recorded photoperiod study conducted with *Kalanchoe blossfeldiana* was by the Dutch investigator,

Roodenburg. Since that beginning numerous workers have investigated the species. An excellent review of *Kalanchoe blossfeldiana Poellniz* flowering is available (Schwabe, 1969).

A. Effect of Daylength

There are several conflicting reports concerning the critical daylength of the kalanchoe. Some early studies indicated that the critical daylength of *Kalanchoe blossfeldiana* was 12 hours (Schwabe, 1969; van der Veen and Meijer, 1959). The critical daylength of the seedling, Tom Thumb, is 12¾ hours (Post, 1950a). A later investigation of nine cultivars revealed that the critical daylength ranged from 10¾ to 12½ hours (Runger, 1967a).

B. Flower Bud Initiation

Flower initiation is prevented when kalanchoes are exposed to daylengths longer than the critical daylength. The most effective time to light kalanchoes to prevent flower initiation is during the middle of the dark period with 161 lx light intensity. Plants are lighted from early September to late March (Love, 1976a, b; Carlson, 1975; Carbonneau, 1975).

The number of long days required varies with the cultivar, plant size desired, and time of year. During the high-light period long days are applied to plants prior to the pinch date. This treatment varies from 2 to 4 weeks. During the winter additional weeks of long days are necessary for desired growth, and varies with the cultivar. Adequate long days are provided if the lower foliage touches the container rim just prior to short-day treatment (Anonymous, 1976b).

Since the optimum daylength for most cultivars is 9 to 10 hours (14 to 15 hours of darkness), it is necessary to provide artificial short days most of the year. Most guidelines recommend shading from February 15 to October 15 (Mikkelsen, 1977; Masson, 1973).

Since the development of new hybrid cultivars in the early 1970s there was renewed interest in kalanchoe flowering. The photoperiod or dark period that results in the fastest flower bud initiation is of primary concern to commercial growers. Most growers are aware of photoperiod manipulation necessary for flowering chrysanthemums out of season. Good-quality black sateen cloth or plastic enables a grower to reduce the daylength by covering plants daily for a prescribed period. Recent reports suggest that 14 hours of darkness is the optimum dark period for flower bud initiation of kalanchoes (Mikkelsen, 1977; Masson, 1973). Other workers state that excellent flowering occurs when the dark period is adjusted to 15 hours (Anonymous, 1977).

Change in the apical meristem is detected anatomically after ten short-day inductive cycles. The meristem begins to bulge above the leaf axils and forms a dome. An enlargement of the shoot apex diameter also occurs. Four pairs of leaves develop during the transition from the vegetative to reproductive state.

The last pair are bractlike. From the next-to-last pair of leaves, axillary bud development occurs. These two axillary buds, plus the stem tip above, complete the first dichasium (Stein and Stein, 1960).

The cultivar Mace requires only 12 short-day inductive cycles for initiation and subsequent development under long days. It is postulated that organogenesis and maturation seem to be independent of daylength (Carlson, 1975). Ten or more short-day cycles cause flower and normal inflorescence development of *Kalanchoe blossfeldiana* (Younis, 1955).

Kalanchoe cultivars that receive inadequate short-day stimulus develop abnormal inflorescences. The minute scalelike bracts in the inflorescence enlarge and finally resemble foliage leaves (Harder, 1948; Younis, 1955). This phenomenon, phyllody, is observed on some cultivars and several stages occur. It varies from an inflorescence that exhibits slight phyllody of the bracts to one that has few flowers and bracts that are large and resemble foliage leaves (Harder, 1948). When the cultivar, Feuerball, receives 4 or 5 weeks of short-day treatment phyllody occurs. Normal inflorescence develops when 6 weeks of inductive cycles are given.

The effect of the short-day inductive cycle is accumulative and must be given consecutively. The number of flowers for *Kalanchoe blossfeldiana* increase exponentially over a range of one to several hundred (Fig. 5). After 14 consecutive short days, the rate of flower initiation decreases (Schwabe, 1969). The amount of floral stimulus produced for floral initiation is directly proportional to the number of short days applied and the length of each dark period (Harder, 1948).

Many of the early flowering cultivars require only 3 or 4 weeks of short-day treatment for optimum flower bud initiation (Post, 1950b; Batson, 1973; Pertuit, 1973a). The new hybrids developed by the plant breeders, Grob, Hope and

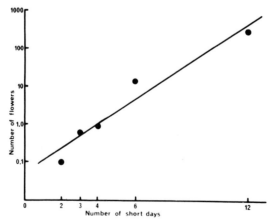

Fig. 5. Effect of number of short days at induction on flower number. (By W. W. Schwabe, *In* "The Induction of Flowering: Some Case Histories," edited by L. T. Evans. Copyright © 1969 by L. T. Evans. Used by permission of the publisher, Cornell University Press.)

Fig. 6. European-type cultivars produced in 15.25-cm clay pots: spaced 28 × 28 cm; automatic blackcloth system; watered and fertilized through spaghetti tubing.

Irwin, require 5 or 6 weeks of consecutive short-day treatments (Mikkelsen, 1977; Irwin, 1972a, b; Anonymous, 1976b).

The multi-move scheme devised by Yoder Bros. is particulary suited for kalanchoe culture (Tables I and II). All short-day treatments are given in the same area of the greenhouse. Sophisticated automated shading systems facilitate the application of short-day treatment (Fig. 6).

It is extremely important that continuous short days are applied during the inductive period (Bachthaler, 1969). Earlier work with *Kalanchoe blossfeldiana* showed that 1 long day is capable of overcoming approximately 2 short days (Schwabe, 1956). For the newer cultivars shading is carried out 7 days a week for the whole 5- or 6-week period. Growers cannot skip 1 night a week with kalanchoes as they do with chrysanthemums because this procedure negates the floral stimulus that occurs during the previous 6 nights (Anonymous, 1976a; Mikkelsen, 1977).

Macroscopic buds are detectable on most cultivars after 5 or 6 weeks of short-day treatment. After the terminal bud is detected, short days are unnecessary (Mikkelsen, 1977; Love, 1976a, b).

C. Flower Development

Once flower buds are initiated, flower development continues under short days, long days, or natural daylength treatments. Perhaps the strongest effect from long-day treatment is with several of the seed-type cultivars. The foliage of the cultivars Vulcan and Gelber Liebling becomes hard and turns bronze if developed under short days (Batson, 1973). Continued short-day treatment results in elongation of the primary inflorescences above the secondary or lateral flower stems. Plants that receive long days after the initial short-day treatment develop no such long primary shoots (Post, 1950b). Studies conducted with the cultivar Tetra Vulcan showed that continuous short days resulted in fewer flowers than 8 weeks of short days followed by long-day treatment. However, faster flowering occurred under continuous short days (Doss et al., 1975).

Kalanchoe cultivars vary in the number of weeks required for flowering under optimum photoperiod conditions. The period of time from start of short days to anthesis varies from 9 to 14 weeks (Mikkelsen, 1977). Growers may wish to consider those cultivars that represent shorter response groups.

There are gradual changes in plant structure when kalanchoe plants are transferred from long days, conducive for vegetative growth, to short days, necessary for reproductive growth. Long-day plants possess large, thin leaves, long petioles, and long internodes. In contrast, short-day plants have few leaves with small surface area, thick leaves, short internodes, and significant anthocyanin development, and terminate development with an inflorescence (Harder, 1948; Post, 1950a; Runger, 1967b; Neyland et al., 1963).

D. Temperature

Temperature control in the greenhouse is most important in developing quality flowering kalanchoe plants. Temperature affects vegetative growth, flower bud initiation, and flower development. As with several other floral crops, there are many different plantings represented in one greenhouse section.

With increased emphasis and importance placed on the energy shortage, it is important to utilize heating fuel judiciously. The zoned spacing system allows for both photoperiod and temperature control (Table I and II). Optimum night temperature for many kalanchoe cultivars varies from 15° to 18°C (Carlson, 1975; Anonymous, 1976a,b). Maintenance of night temperature below the suggested night temperature extends the flowering time about 3 weeks (Carbonneau, 1975; Anonymous, 1976a, b). Several firms suggest that the night temperature should be regulated at 20°C.

The early European seed hybrids were unacceptable for production in southwestern United States because they are sensitive to high temperatures. This "heat delay" of some cultivars extends flowering time as much as 3 to 4 weeks and in some instances prevents flowering altogether. The reason for heat delay is associated with the necessity of pulling blackcloth over the plants for flower induction. If plants are shaded in late afternoon the temperature may reach 35°–40°C beneath the cloth or plastic. Several authorities consider that temperatures above 24°C are excessive and should be avoided (Mikkelsen, 1977; Carlson, 1975; Hammer, 1976; Pertuit, 1977).

It is the opinion of some (Mikkelsen, 1977; Anonymous, 1976b) that high night temperature is most detrimental to flower induction at the beginning of the dark period but Runger (1955, 1968) reported that it is more harmful to maintain high temperatures at the end rather than in the beginning of the short-day treatment.

Kalanchoe growers are advised to pull blackcloth over their plants at 7:00 P.M. and to remove it the following morning at 9:00 A.M. or 10:00 A.M. Thus, much of the heat buildup beneath the cloth is avoided (Mikkelsen, 1977). Some greenhouses are equipped with an automatic shading system for a whole house or section(s) within a house. Forced-air cooling under blackcloth is suggested to help maintain a more optimum temperature.

VI. HEIGHT CONTROL

Some cultivars are considered too tall when grown as a potted plant. Several cultural practices can be used to develop a potted kalanchoe that is proportional to its container. Growth regulators can control plant height but unfortunately none are federally registered for grower use.

B-Nine is the most popular growth regulator used on kalanchoes. It is sprayed on plants 3 to 5 weeks after the start of short days. A second treatment is generally required and should be applied 4 to 5 weeks later. Associated with height reduction is a corresponding decrease in plant spread (Nightingale, 1970). B-Nine is also applied after a pinch when axillary shoots reach 4 to 5 cm in length (Masson, 1973).

Ancymidol (A-Rest) is used as a foliar spray or soil drench. The drench is more effective and may be applied up to 4 weeks after potting (Schnabel and Carlson, 1976; Pertuit, 1973b).

A shorter, more compact plant is obtained if the terminal inflorescence is removed 4 or 5 weeks after the start of short days. This is prior to the elongation of the peduncle or flowering stem. This treatment results in additional inflorescences that normally would not develop if the terminal inflorescence was not removed. Treated plants are 7.5 to 10 cm shorter than untreated plants, and flowering is delayed only several days (Anonymous, 1968; Rathmell, 1970; Love, 1976a, b).

Pinching the vegetative terminal shoot breaks apical dominance and allows development of axillary shoots. The number of potential inflorescences is increased and results in a more desirable plant. A "delayed pinch" is made 1 to 2 weeks after start of the short-day treatment. This type of pinch results in a well-shaped floral display without any delay in flowering. It offers some height control for tall cultivars (Anonymous, 1976b).

Tall-growing cultivars are shorter when water is withheld periodically between irrigations. This "toning" practice is initiated when the flower heads develop but the peduncles have yet not begun to elongate (Anonymous, 1976b).

Flowering kalanchoe plants are shorter when grown under high light intensity. Growers must provide as much light as possible during the dark, short days of winter (Laurie *et al.,* 1968).

VII. HANDLING THE FINISHED PRODUCT

A. Flowering Stage for Sale

It is important to have florets of the inflorescences open before plants are sold. Kalanchoes should be in full color in the greenhouse before they are marketed, and when sold at this stage are very attractive (Anonymous, 1976a). Plants should be fertilized before they are sold so they will hold up better in the home (Carbonneau, 1975); they can be enjoyed for 5 to 7 weeks in the home or office.

B. Storage

If plants develop ahead of schedule they may be stored at 10°C to slow flower bud development. Some growers store plants at 10°C 3 to 4 weeks prior to their normal bloom date. The plants can be handled as azaleas and removed periodically from storage and placed in a warm, 15°C house for 3 or 4 weeks to force into flower.

C. Demand-Time of Year

The kalanchoe is a relatively new potted plant in some areas. Those growers who have developed a market sell the plants year-round. The greatest demand for large 16.25-cm-size containers is from January to May with less demand from September to November 15. The small 10-cm size sold through the mass market has demands similar to those in the large containers.

D. Promotional Pointers

The kalanchoe has been described as an "idiot-proof" plant for the homeowner. It has tremendous life under home conditions: it withstands periods of drought and tolerates low light. The kalanchoe may be promoted as a flowering "green plant" and may be successfully reflowered in the home. The original cluster of dried flowers is removed and the stem is cut back to the first nonflowering pair of leaves. The plant should be placed in strong light.

Various kinds of sales aids are available to the grower for kalanchoe promotion. One propagator supplies miniposters, shelf talkers/counter cards, newspaper ad slicks, free care tag labels, mailing stuffers, and preprinted plant sleeves.

E. Florist and Produce Manager Care

Plastic or paper plant sleeves should be removed immediately upon arrival at the store. Good air circulation for the plant is necessary to help prevent powdery mildew. Although kalanchoes may be stored for short periods at 10°C, best plant quality is maintained at 16°–20°C. Kalanchoes should not be stored in rooms where the ethylene concentration is allowed to accumulate. Unvented heaters should be avoided. Plants exposed to levels at or greater than 0.5 μl of ethylene/liter of air are injured. Ethylene toxicity is expressed as premature flower fading, desiccation, and failure of flower buds to open (Marousky and Harbaugh, 1978).

Kalanchoes should be stored and exhibited in strong light. Prolonged storage in low light causes lower leaves to turn yellow. Plants should be watered thoroughly when needed. Some water should drip from the pot after a thorough watering.

F. Consumer Care

Several specialist-propagator firms supply their customers with care cards that are sold with the plant. The information is brief and factual and easy for the consumer to understand. One card states, "Stand in bright sunny area at temperatures between 18° and 21°C. Keep soil moist. DO NOT OVERWATER!"

VIII. DISEASES

A. Powdery Mildew (*Sphaerotheca humuli* var. *fulgininea*)

Many kalanchoe cultivars are susceptible to powdery mildew. Others exhibit a degree of resistance whereas some are highly resistant. The occurrence of powdery mildew is associated with high humidity and may be controlled or prevented with proper manipulation of heating and ventilation. Plants should be spaced to ensure good air circulation. Water should not be applied to the fleshy, succulent leaves.

The disease is characterized as grayish white powdery growth on the leaves and stems. The infected parts dry out and cause scalelike spots on the foliage. If sufficiently severe, powdery mildew will kill the leaf.

B. Crown Rot, Wilt (*Phytophthora cactorum*)

This disease appears at the basal part of the plant, usually near the soil line. Black lesions are the first symptoms that appear. The rot progresses upward, causing leaves, stem, peduncles, and flowers to wilt.

Crown rot is a particular problem with many of the cultivars started from seed. Plants should be grown in pasteurized soil. Plants should not be overwatered or syringed. Small plants or cuttings should be planted shallowly.

IX. INSECTS

A. Lepidoptera Larvae

Worms are serious pests of kalanchoes during summer and early fall. Moths are attracted to plants that are artifically lighted to provide long days. Each moth may lay from 275 to 350 eggs on the upper side of a leaf. The larvae usually go unnoticed when first hatched from eggs.

One of the most persistent worms found on kalanchoes is the cabbage looper and is conspicuous, with a stripe down its side. The larvae loop over the plants, humping the back high with each leg movement. They inflict serious damage by chewing holes in the leaves.

B. Aphids [*Myzus persicae* (Sulzer)]

Aphids (greenfly, plant louse, or aphis) represent several species that are pests of kalanchoe. They possess piercing and sucking mouthparts and distort the foliage and stunt growth. They produce a sticky honeydew that falls on leaves below.

The greenhouse aphids are all females that give birth to live, wingless, females. One female may produce 1400 progeny at 21°C. If not controlled, one generation follows the other.

C. Common or Citrus Mealybugs (*Pseudococcus citri*)

Mealybugs may be troublesome at times. Both the short- and long-tailed mealybugs develop from eggs that are deposited in a compact, cottony, waxy sack (approximately 200 eggs). They are usually found in the axils of branching stems and leaves. The young larvae hatch in 10 days and feed by inserting their slender mouth parts in the tissue and suck plant sap. The nymphs move about feeding for 6 to 8 weeks, when they become adults.

D. The Greenhouse Whitefly (*Trialeurodes vaporcorium* Westwood)

The greenhouse whitefly is a small, white insect about 1.6 mm long with four wings. The scalelike young larvae hatch from eggs deposited on the underside of leaves. It usually requires 5 to 10 days to hatch. The whole life cycle may take 4 to 5 weeks.

The young feed with piercing and sucking mouthparts. They excrete honeydew, which supports black, sooty mold. Pesticides are required three times per week to kill the adult whitefly. The adults must be controlled and prevented from laying eggs. The scalelike nymphs and eggs are resistant to most pesticides.

REFERENCES

Anonymous (1968). Something new in kalanchoes. *Florist Nursery Exh.* **149**(1), 14–15, 19.

Anonymous (1975). Kalanchoes, *in* "The Ball Red Book" (V. Ball, ed.), pp. 372–373. Geo. J. Ball, Inc., West Chicago, Illinois.

Anonymous (1976a). "Kalanchoes: Background Information and Production Practices for the Varieties, Mace and Telstar." Yoder Brothers, Barberton, Ohio.

Anonymous (1976b). "Kalanchoes: Production Procedures for Year-round Production of the European Kalanchoe Production." Yoder Brothers, Barberton, Ohio.

Anonymous (1977). "Aztec Kalanchoe Culture, Your Formula for Profits." Pan-American Plant Co., West Chicago, Illinois.

Asif, M. I. (1974). Abnormal stem of kalanchoe in relation to phosphorus and zinc nutrition. *Florists' Rev.* **155**(4007), 71, 130–131.

Bachthaler, E. (1969). Möglichkeiten einer Unterbrechung der Kurztagperiode bei *Kalanchoe blossfeldiana*. *Gartenwelt* **69**, 514–516.

Batson, F. (1973). Assembly-line kalanchoes. *Florists' Rev.* **152**(3943), 20–21, 55–56.

Broertjes, C., and Leffring, L. (1972). Mutation breeding of kalanchoe. *Euphytica* **21**, 415–423.

Carbonneau, M. C. (1975). Kalanchoes. *Ill. State Florists' Assoc. Bull.* **359**, 2–4.

Carlson, W. H. (1975). The culture of *Kalanchoe blossfeldiana* cultivar, 'Mace.' *Mich. Florist* **531**, 7, 31, 34.

Doss, R. P., Byrne, T. G., and Kretchum, T. M. (1975). *Kalanchoe blossfeldiana* 'Tetra Vulcan'. Suggestions for growing as a pot plant. *Flower Nursery Rep., Univ. Calif.* Nov./Dec., pp. 7–8.

Gillette, R. (1978). Missouri mum specialist John Lochner mats begonias, calceolarias, gloxinias, kalanchoes and mums. Mechanization is another tool, but space is his forte. *Florists' Rev.* **162**(4204), 26–28, 67–68.

Hammer, P. A. (1976). Kalanchoe trials 1975–76. *Focus Floric., Purdue Univ.* **4**(4), 9–14.

Hanan, J. J., Holley, W. D., and Goldsberry, K. L. (1978). "Greenhouse Management." Springer-Verlag, Berlin and New York.

Harder, R. (1948). Vegetative and reproductive development of *Kalanchoe blossfeldiana,* as influenced by photoperiodism. *Symp. Soc. Exp. Biol.* **2**, 117–140.

Irwin, J. T. (1972a). Kalanchoes—a new crop. *Ohio Florists' Assoc. Bull.* **514**, 1–3.

Irwin, J. T. (1972b). Try a "new" crop—kalanchoes. *Florists' Rev.* **151**(3917), 23, 56–58.

Laurie, A., Kiplinger, D. C., and Nelson, K. S. (1968). Kalanchoe. *In* "Commercial Flower Forcing," pp. 413–414. McGraw-Hill, New York.

Link, C. B. (1978). Kalanchoe—an outstanding flowering pot plant. *Md. Florist* **214**, 3–5.

Love, J. W. (1976a). Kalanchoe production. *N. C. Flower Growers' Bull.* **20**(2), 1–3.

Love, J. W. (1976b). Kalanchoe production. *Hortic. Inf. Leafl. (N. C. State Univ.)* **434**, 1–4.

Manzitti, C. (1978a). New kalanchoe hybrids. Pt. I: A breed that's easier to produce than pronounce. *Florist* **11**(8), 70–74.

Manzitti, C. (1978b). New kalanchoe hybrids: Pt. II: A production cookbook for consistent crop results. *Florist* **11**(9), 61–63.

Marousky, F. J., and Harbaugh, B. K. (1978). Ethylene and temperature interaction. *Hortic. Sci.* **13**(3), 26. (Abstr.)

Masson, A. (1973). Kalanchoes. *Ohio Florists' Assoc. Bull.* **521**, 9.

Mikkelsen, J. C. (1975). ABC of kalanchoe culture. *Ohio Florists' Assoc. Short Course* (mimeo).

Mikkelsen, J. C. (1977). Kalanchoe culture. *Focus Floric., Purdue Univ.* **5**(1), 12–17.

Nelson, P. V. (1978). "Greenhouse Operation and Management." Reston Publ., Reston, Virginia.

Neyland, M., Ng, Y. L., and Thimann, K. V. (1963). Formation of anthocyanin in leaves of *Kalanchoe blossfeldiana*—a photoperiodic response. *Plant. Physiol.* **38**, 447–451.

Nightingale, A. E. (1970). The influence of succinamic acid 2,2-dimethylhydrazide on the growth and flowering of pinched vs. unpinched plants of the kalanchoe hybrid 'Mace.' *J. Am. Soc. Hortic. Sci.* **95**(3), 273–276.

Pertuit, A. J., Jr. (1973a). The effects of temperature during dark exposure and date of exposure to naturally-occurring daylengths on growth and flowering of *Kalanchoe blossfeldiana*, v. Poellnitz. *Univ. Ga. Res. Rep.* No. 170.

Pertuit, A. J., Jr. (1973b). The effects of terminal pinching and chemical growth regulation of *Kalanchoe blossfeldiana,* v. Poellnitz. *Univ. Ga. Res. Bull.* No. 132.

Pertuit, A. J., Jr. (1977). Influence of temperatures during long-night exposures on growth and flowering of 'Mace', 'Thor', and 'Telstar' kalanchoe. *HortScience* **12**(1), 48–49.

Porter, C. L. (1967). "Taxonomy of Flowering Plants." Freeman, San Francisco, California.

Post, K. (1950a). Kalanchoe. In "Florist Crop Production and Marketing," pp. 590–592. Orange Judd Publ., New York.

Post, K. (1950b). Give kalanchoes only twenty short days. *N.Y. State Flower Growers Bull.* **57,** 7.

Rathmell, J. (1970). Rathmell reports: kalanchoes make profits. *Florists' Rev.* **145**(3762), 24.

Runger, W. (1955). Über den Einfluss der Temperatur und der Lichtintensität auf die photoperiodische Reaktion und die Blütenentwicklung von *Kalanchoë blossfeldiana* Poellnitz cv. Tom Thumb. *Gartenbauwiss* **2,** 485–504.

Runger, W. (1967a). Über die Abhängigkeit der Blütenbildung und -entwicklung mehrerer Kalanchoesorten von Tageslänge und Temperatur. *Gartenbauwiss* **32,** 213–225.

Runger, W. (1967b). Über Kurz- und Langtageinflüsse auf noch nicht blühfähige Pflanzen mehrerer Kalanchoesorten. *Gartenbauwiss* **32,** 399–407.

Runger, W. (1968). Interaction of temperature and day length in flower initiation. *Symp. Flower Regul. Florist Crops,* August 12–16, 1968, Vollebekk, pp. 139–147.

Schnabel, S. A., and Carlson, W. H. (1976). Effects of ancymidol on *Kalanchoe blossfeldiana* cv. Mace. *Mich. State Flower Notes* **8**(3), 4.

Schwabe, W. W. (1954). The effects of light intensity on the flowering of *Kalanchoe blossfeldiana* in relation to the critical daylength. *Physiol. Plant.* **7,** 745–752.

Schwabe, W. W. (1969). *Kalanchoe blossfeldiana* Poellniz. In "The Induction of Flowering: Some Case Histories" (L. T. Evans, ed.), pp. 227–246. Cornell Univ. Press, Ithaca, New York.

Stein, D. B., and Stein, O. L. (1960). The growth of the stem tip of kalanchoe cv. 'Brilliant Star'. *Am. J. Bot.* **47,** 132–140.

van der Veen, R. and Meijer, G. (1959). "Light and Plant Growth." Macmillan, New York.

White, J. W. (1974). New and renewed pot plants—kalanchoe. *Pa. Flower Growers Bull.* **275**(7), 1–2.

Younis, A. F. (1955). Studies on the photoperiodism of *Kalanchoe blossfeldiana*. 1. Effect of age on response to short-day treatment. *Physiol. Plant.* **8,** 223–229.

18

Other Flowering Pot Plants

P. Allen Hammer

Introduction to Floriculture

435

I. INTRODUCTION

Many pot crops grown in the greenhouse have been termed "minor" because they are not grown in large numbers across a wide geographic area. In a particular greenhouse or region, however, a "minor" crop becomes a "major" crop when it is grown in large numbers; therefore the term "other" pot crops seems more appropriate. Another very important aspect of these "other" pot crops is the lack of detailed and published research results. In many cases, it appears the reason these crops are not grown in large numbers is the lack of information concerning culture. However, this situation does not diminish the need for a diverse product line to present to the consumer. This should be of prime importance when considering these other pot crops.

Sachs *et al.* (1976) presented criteria for evaluating new pot plant species (Table I). They proposed an interesting scheme to evaluate the suitability of species for pot plant culture, using a rating system. The rating system may not have universal appeal but it would be well to evaluate each greenhouse crop according to the proposed criteria. It can provide insight into the strong and weak points of each crop, particularly when comparisons are made among present and potential pot crops. Research and development expenditures could be aimed at improving these weak areas. A simple example might be deciding between two very similar cultivars except that cultivar A requires growth retardant application whereas cultivar B is naturally of proper dimensions for a pot plant. From a production point of view, cultivar B would be easier and less costly to produce and from a research point of view, why develop a lot of growth retardant response data for cultivar A when cultivar B is available? Very few decisions on crop selection are this simple. However, one should evaluate each potential pot plant carefully before selecting which pot crops to grow.

Table I

Selected Criteria for Evaluating New Pot Plant Species [a]

1. Propagation time and special environment requirements during propagation
2. Greenhouse production (forcing) time
3. Seasonal or year-round production possible
4. Special environmental requirements for production and/or flowering
5. Special medium and fertility requirements
6. Natural growth habits relative to pot size
7. Requirement and response to growth regulating chemicals
8. Freedom from insects and diseases
9. Floral qualities
10. Foliar qualities
11. Market potential

[a]Modified from Sachs *et al.* (1976).

436

A. *CALCEOLARIA HERBEOHYBRIDA*

Calceolaria herbeohybrida Voss (*Scrophulariaceae*) is a group of cultivars generally grown as flowering pot plants in the greenhouse and was probably derived from *Calceolaria crenatiflora* Cav. It is sometimes called the "pocketbook plant" because its flowers are large, inflated pouches of many colors (Bailey Hortorium Staff, 1976).

Moe (1977b) has divided *Calceolaria* cultivars into four groups according to flower and plant size: *Grandiflora,* with 3.8- to 5-cm-wide flowers on 30- to 40-cm plants; *Grandiflora primula compacta,* with 4.5- to 5-cm-wide flowers on 20-cm plants; *Multiflora,* with 3- to 4-cm-wide flowers on 25- to 30-cm plants; and *Multiflora nana,* with 2- to 3-cm-wide flowers on 30-cm plants. Many cultivars are available, with continued improvements being made (Fig. 1). The F_1 hybrids are more uniform in size and color, flower 4 to 5 weeks earlier, and are more widely grown.

Calceolaria are seed propagated. The seed are small, with 17,000 to 40,000 seeds per gram. They germinate in 8 to 10 days in 18°–20°C. Seed are sown on the surface of the germination medium and are not covered. Damping-off can be a serious problem; thus sanitation and watering should be carefully controlled.

It has generally been accepted that *Calceolaria* require a period of cool temperature below 15°C for flower initiation (Post, 1937; Poesch, 1931). Recent studies with the newer cultivars have shown *Calceolaria* to be a long-day plant, particularly at high irradiance (Rünger, 1975; White, 1975b; Johansson, 1976). Rünger (1975) found *Calceolaria* 'Zwerg Meisterstuck' to be a long-day plant with a critical daylength of 14 to 15 hours when grown at high irradiance. At low irradiance (winter), flowering in long days must be preceded by treatment in cool temperatures of 10°C or short days at 15°–20°C. Daylength had little effect during the cool temperature treatment. Johansson (1976) observed flowering during long days but not short days at 15°C. Plant quality (number of flowers and height) shows an interaction between temperature and daylength (Table II).

From this work, several schedules can be proposed to flower *Calceolaria* without the traditional (Table III) long cold production (Tables IV and V). Of particular importance in the schedules are the following: (1) incandescent lighting (12 W/m²) should be used to extend the daylength (Rünger, 1975); (2) plants must have developed four to five pairs of leaves before long-day exposure; and (3) cultivar selection is important. Whatever schedule one uses, long days should be provided during flower development to increase floriferousness.

Chlormequat has been used as an effective height control agent for calceolarias. Two sprays of 400 ppm with the first applied when the flower buds are about 1.5 mm in diameter and the second 2 weeks later reduced the height by 18%. Single sprays at 800 ppm gave the same height reduction but resulted

Fig. 1. Two cultivars (A,B) of *Calceolaria* grown in 13-cm pots. Note the differences in finished plant size.

Table II

Effect of Temperature and Daylength on Flowering of *Calceolaria* 'Harting's Red' [a]

Temperature (°C)	Daylength (hours)	Days [b]	Number of flowers	Height at anthesis (cm)
9	9	111	75	8
	12	73	104	10
	16	67	177	11
	24	46	113	12
12	9	150	55	9
	12	74	81	10
	16	46	93	11
	24	35	95	10
15	9	—	—	—
	12	94	64	12
	16	34	68	13
	24	31	63	14

[a] Cultivar was grown in a growth chamber with 6000 lx Cool White fluorescent light for 9 hours per day. Daylength extension was with 60 lx of incandescent light. 'Portia' responded similarly except it is earlier flowering. Modified from Johansson (1976).
[b] From start of treatment to visible flower buds.

in some foliar phytotoxicity (Johansson, 1976). White (1975b) reported a chlormequat drench at 3000 ppm at the time of visible flower buds reduced plant height by 50% without injury. Chloremequat does not affect flowering time.

The major insect pests of calceolarias are whiteflies, aphids, and mites. Chemical control is a necessity. Good sanitation should be practiced to avoid

Table III

Traditional Schedule for the Production of Flowering *Calceolaria* in 13-cm Pots [a]

Operation [c]	Time of year	Night temperature [b] (°C)	Daylength
Sow seed	Early September	18	Natural
Transplant to flats	Late September	15–18	Natural
Transplant to 9-cm pot	Early November	13	Natural
Transplant to 13-cm pot	Early December	13	Natural
Begin cool temperature treatment	Early December	7–10	Natural
End cool temperature treatment	Mid-January	13	Natural
Flowering	Late March		

[a] Modified from Reiss (1974) and White (1975b).
[b] Day temperature should be below 18°C.
[c] The time from seeding to flower is 25 to 29 weeks.

Table IV

Schedule as Proposed by Wikesjö (1976) for 'Hartings' and 'Portia' *Calceolaria* [a]

Operation	Time of year	Temperature (°C)
Sow seed	Late July	18
Transplant to flats	Mid-August	15
Transplant to 13-cm pots	Late September	15
Begin long days (18 hours) [b]	Late October	13
Flowering	Mid-late January	

[a]'Portia' is earlier; thus seeding can be delayed 2 weeks if the two cultivars are flowered together.

[b]Plants must have developed four to five leaf pairs before long days are given.

Table V

Proposed Schedule for Fast Crop Production of 10-cm Pot Flowering *Calceolaria* **Cultivars 'Portia OE,' 'Hartings,' 'Lenz,' 'Zwerg Meisterstuck,' and 'Yellow with Red Spots'** [a]

Operation	Time of year	Night temperature (°C)	Daylength (hours)
Winter flowering [b]			
Sow seed	Late September	18	18
Transplant to flats	Mid-October	18–21	18
Transplant to 10-cm pot and begin short days [c]	Mid-November	15–18	8
Begin long days	Late December	13	18
Flowering	Late January		
Summer flowering [d]			
Sow seed	Early April	18	18
Transplant to flats	Mid-April	18–21	18
Transplant to 10-cm pot and begin short days	Mid-May	15–18	8
Begin long days	Early July	15–18	18
Flowering	Late July		

[a]From White (1975b) and Rünger (1975).
[b]Time from seeding to flowering, 17 to 19 weeks.
[c]Plants should have at least four to five pairs of leaves before short days begin.
[d]Greenhouse should be shaded to provide 54 klx. Evaporative cooling is essential. Summer flowering should be on a trial basis and will probably work only in cooler regions.

stem rot and *Botrytis* infections. The plants should not be planted too deeply and a well-drained growing medium is essential.

III. *CAMPANULA ISOPHYLLA*

Campanula isophylla Moretti (*Campanulaceae*), sometimes known as "Italian bell," "star-of-bethlehem," or "falling stars," is grown as a flowering pot plant or hanging basket for its many flowers that are borne erect in short, corymbose panicles. Cultivars are 'Alba' with white flowers, 'Caerulea' with blue flowers, and 'Mayi' with large grayish-pubescent flowers (Bailey Hortorium Staff, 1976). A cultivar, Blao, with blue flowers has been reported from Norway (Fig. 2).

Campanula isophylla is a long-day plant with a critical daylength of 16, 15, and 14 hours at night temperatures of 12°–15°, 18°, and 21°C, respectively. Plants, once flowering, must be maintained under long days for continued development of flowers (Heide, 1965). Propagation is by cuttings from stock plants maintained vegetatively under short days (12 hours). Root formation and growth are greatly inhibited on cuttings in flower, even when the cuttings are treated with a rooting hormone (indole butyric acid, IBA) (Moe, 1977b).

Fig. 2. *Campanula isophylla* in flower. (Photograph courtesy of Tom Weiler, Department of Horticulture, Purdue University, West Lafayette, Indiana.)

In a growth chamber study, Moe (1977a) showed that stock plants produced more cuttings with increased fresh and dry weight when grown at an irradiance of 10 klx and 900 ppm carbon dioxide than when grown at lower irradiance and carbon dioxide levels. The cuttings rooted better and produced more vigorous plants when taken from stock plants grown at increased irradiance and carbon dioxide. He recommended that stock plants to be grown at 15°–18°C with a 12-hour daylength using cool white fluorescent lamps (1–5 klx) as supplemental light and 900 ppm carbon dioxide. The supplemental fluorescent light would not be required in much of the United States because natural light levels reach 10 klx.

Cuttings are about 4 cm long with five to six visible leaves after the lowest two to three leaves are removed. The cuttings are dipped for 5 seconds in 1000 to 1500 ppm IBA solution and rooted in a 18°C air and 21°C medium temperature. They are ready for potting in 2 to 3 weeks. Plants are generally produced in 10-cm pots with one cutting per pot. After potting they are grown for 6 to 9 weeks at 18°C under short days (12 hours). Plants should then be exposed to long days (16–18 hours) to initiate flowering. Hildrum (1968) reported the addition of fluorescent lighting produced more vigorous plants than incandescent lighting and that shoots were shorter on the blue-flowered cultivar but not on the white-flowerd cultivar when grown under fluorescent lamps. Fluorescent lighting was recommended to extend the daylength.

Daminozide is a more effective height control chemical for *Campanula isophylla* than is chlormequat (Brundert and Stratmann, 1973; Lavsen, 1967). A spray application of 2500 to 5000 ppm daminozide is recommended whereas 10,000 ppm is phytotoxic. Shoots on the cultivar Bla tended to grow upright rather than pendant when treated with daminozide (Hildrum, 1968). The cultivar Alba (white) is more vigorous than 'Bla' (blue), so it has a greater requirement for height control. The spray application of daminozide is recommended 1 week after the start of long days (Moe, 1977b).

During long days, the best-quality plants are produced when grown at a constant 18°C day/night temperature. Plants flower 10 to 12 weeks from the start of long days.

A leaf spot on *Campanula isophylla* caused by *Ascochyta bohemica* has been reported (Garibaldi and Gullino, 1973). *Fusariuim culmorum*-infected plants have also been reported (von Wachenfelt, 1968) and great care should be taken to avoid propagating plants suspected of infection.

IV. *CAPSICUM* SPECIES AND *SOLANUM PSEUDOCAPSICUM*

Capsicum species L. (Solanaceae), commonly known as Christmas peppers, and *Solanum pseudocapsicum* L. (Solanaceae), commonly known as Jerusalem or Christmas cherry, are grown as Christmas potted plants for their attractive fruit. Christmas pepper fruit is yellow, purple, orange, or red and of various sizes and shapes. Jerusalem cherry has scarlet or yellow globose, persistent fruit (Fig. 3). It is of Old World origin, but has naturalized in the tropics, subtropics, and USDA Zone 9 in the United States (Bailey Hortorium Staff, 1976).

Christmas peppers have 320 seeds per gram. They are generally sown from late April to early May and germinate in 12 to 21 days at 21°–27°C. They are grown in 6-cm pots until large enough to be transplanted into the final pot. One plant per 10-cm pot, three plants per 13-cm pot, and four plants per 15-cm pot make a nice display (Rigdon and Wolfram, 1976). The plants are pinched beginning at two to three nodes of growth and again when the new growth is 5 to 8 cm long, but not after early July. They should be well fruited by early December. Since fruit set is important, the plants should be grown where they are exposed to wind and/or bees for pollination. Although no work has been published on optimum temperature for growth, a temperature of 16°–18°C night is commonly used.

Christmas cherries have 425 seeds/gm. They germinate in 15 days at 21°C, but will germinate at temperatures of 13°–30°C and do not require light for germination (Table VI). They are sown in mid-February for a well-fruited plant in early December. They are transplanted to 6-cm pots until they are large enough to transplant to the final pot. They are seldom grown in pots smaller than 14 cm because of plant size. Plants are pinched beginning at two to three nodes of growth and again when the new growth is 5 to 8 cm long. They cannot be pinched after July 17 for a Christmas crop.

Davis (1978) suggested the following schedule to produce a Christmas cherry tree for Christmas. Seed are sown in mid-February and transplanted to 6-cm cell packs when large enough to handle. When roots fill that container, they are transplanted to 15-cm pots. When the plant is 10 to 15 cm tall, two applications, 10 days apart, of 250 ppm solution of gibberellic acid are sprayed on the plant until runoff. A wooden stake should be placed in the pot to support rapid growth. Large applications of nitrogen are made during this rapid growth period. When the rapid growth and elongation stop, all the bottom foliage is removed so only six leaves remain at the top of the plant. It is pinched at this time, and again whenever the new growth is 5 to 8 cm long. The last pinch should not be made after July 17 for Christmas sales. To split the timing on the finishing of a crop, half of the plants can be pinched on July 1 and half on July 17.

Christmas cherries are generally grown at a 10°–13°C night temperature. They are commonly grown outdoors in cold frames in the summer to aid in pollination for fruit set. It is important not to allow the roots to grow into the soil on which plants are placed, as root injury can cause loss of leaves and fruit when they are moved back into the greenhouse in the fall. Growers should be careful not to over- or underwater the plants during this reduced growth period in the fall to avoid loss of leaves and fruit.

Before the plant is shipped, tips of shoots without fruit are pruned off to

Fig. 3. *Capsicum* species (A) and *Solanum pseudocapsicum* (B) in fruit.

Table VI

Percentage Germination of Several Seed-Propagated Pot Plants at Eight Temperatures with and without Light[a]

Genus (cultivar)	Light treatment	Percentage germination at temperature (°C)							
		10	13	16	18	21	24	27	30
Solanum pseudocapsicum	Dark	0	92	84	84	88	96	88	84
(Masterpiece)	Light	0	96	80	92	96	76	92	96
Exacum	Dark	0	0	1	0	1	1	3	0
(Tiddly Winks)	Light	0	0	100	100	100	100	100	98
Primula malacoides	Dark	0	0	0	0	0	2	0	0
(White Giant)	Light	0	0	8	12	26	10	0	0
Primula obconia	Dark	0	0	0	0	8	2	0	0
(Fasbender's Red)	Light	0	0	42	48	48	42	2	0
Streptocarpus	Dark	0	0	0	0	0	0	0	0
	Light	0	0	80	80	80	85	0	0

[a]Modified from Cathey (1969a,b).

improve the appearance of the plant. Fruits hold well but long or rough shipping will cause some fruit loss.

Jerusalem cherry has a long-established reputation for human toxicity, but there are no clear recorded cases of such toxicity. Solanaceous alkaloids have been isolated from it, and it would be wise to caution against eating the berries (Kingsbury, 1967).

V. *CLERODENDRUM THOMSONIAE*

Clerodendrum Thomsoniae Blaf. (*Verbenaceae*), known as bleeding-heart vine, is grown for its attractive red and white flowers (large, white persistent, calyx and crimson corolla) (Fig. 4). It is a woody twining evergreen shrub native to West Tropical Africa (Bailey Hortorium Staff, 1976).

No known commercial cultivars of *Clerodendrum* are available. Hildrum (1973) showed that plants from commercial greenhouses varied considerably in growth and flowering characteristics. He selected a clone that flowered profusely on short shoots. Beck (1975) reported a Wisconsin clone which shows very little flower abscission, a problem with the European clone. It would be advisable to carefully select a superior clone for pot plant production since much variability does exist.

Initiation of flower buds in *Clerodendrum* seems not to be affected by daylength, but development of flowers is delayed under long days. When long days were established by low-intensity irradiance from incandescent lamps,

Fig. 4. A 10-cm pot of *Clerodendrum Thomsoniae* in flower. (Photograph courtesy of G. E. Beck, Department of Horticulture, University of Wisconsin, Madison, Wisconsin.)

few flowers developed and the stems elongated considerably even at a 16-hour daylength. However, daylength extension with fluorescent (20 W/m²) lamps produced plants with short shoots with many flowers, even at a 24-hour daylength. Gibberellic acid delayed flower development (Hildrum, 1973).

Clerodendrum Thomsoniae is propagated from stock plants with good vegetative growth. The stock plants should be grown in full light at 21°C night temperature under long days (16–20 hours). Iron chlorosis develops at a pH above 6.3; therefore, soil pH should be maintained at 5.0 to 5.5 for best growth. Use of an acid fertilizer is recommended. Iron sulfate additions have also given good results. (Beck, 1975; Wendzonka, 1978).

Stock plants should be renewed every 6 to 8 months. Plants grown from cuttings from older stock are taller, more juvenile, and viny (Beck, 1975).

Single node cuttings will root under mist at an air temperature of 21°C and medium temperature of 22°–23°C in 10 to 14 days (Hildrum, 1972; Beck, 1975). Long days during propagation are recommended. Rooting hormone will speed rooting, but is not essential. Beck (1975) suggested defoliation of the cutting before sticking to enhance uniformity of axillary bud break. Wendzonka (1978) suggests a small "hard wood" single node cutting 3 cm long as best for more rapid flowering.

Once rooted, cuttings are potted one to three cuttings per 10-cm or larger pot and grown under long days at a night temperature of 21°C. If a single cutting is used per pot, pinching is required when the shoots are 3 to 5 cm long. Hildrum (1972) has recommended a soft pinch whereas Vereecke (1974) has recommended a pinch just above the first pair of leaves.

Short days (10 hours) should start at the time pinching is begun. Temperatures under blackcloth in summer should not be higher than 21°C because high temperature enhances shoot growth and inhibits flowering. Night temperatures below 21°C result in very slow growth. Ancymidol reduces internode length and enhances flowering. Artificial short days are not essential when the plants are treated with ancymidol (Hildrum, 1972). A drench application of ancymidol at 0.15 mg/10-cm pot (Beck, 1975) or 0.3 mg/14-cm pot (Sanderson and Martin, 1975) when the new shoots are 5 to 8 cm long gave the best results. Vereecke (1974) and Noordegraff et al. (1975) showed that two sprays of ancymidol (100–200 ppm) applied 10 days apart gave satisfactory results. Daminozide and chlormequat gave poor results.

The production time from cuttings to flowering plants is 12 to 14 weeks during summer months and 16 to 18 weeks during winter months.

Tobacco ringspot virus-infected plants have been reported (Khan and Maxwell, 1975). Since C. Thomsoniae is asexually propagated, plants suspected of infection with this virus should be discarded. There appear to be few other disease problems with C. Thomsoniae. Botrytis has been observed on older leaves and flowers but it is easily controlled. Whitefly is the major insect pest on C. Thomsoniae and chemical controls are necessary.

Exposure of flowering plants to high temperature and low light levels can cause flower-bud and flower abscission. Fumigation with insecticides also promotes abscission. Shipping of flowering plants in darkness at high temperatures for more than 1 day will also cause flower abscission. High light or low temperature (below 16°C) will prevent flower abscission (Hildrum, 1972).

VI. EXACUM AFFINE

Exacum affine Balf. f. (Gentianaceae) is the annual species of Exacum grown in the greenhouse as a flowering pot plant (Fig. 5). It is commonly known as the German or Persian violet and has bluish flowers up to 1.3 cm across. "Hortus Third" lists Exacum macranthum as the best of the genus with large

Fig. 5. Exacum 'Midget' in flower. (Photograph courtesy of Tom Weiler, Department of Horticulture, Purdue University, West Lafayette, Indiana.)

rich blue flowers, but it is probably not grown in the greenhouse because it is a biennial (Bailey Hortorium Staff, 1976). *Exacum affine* also has a mild fragrance when in flower.

Jim Irwin, of Canyon, Texas, has been the leader in growing and promoting *Exacum* as a flowering pot plant. He grows one plant per 15-cm pot year-round (Ball, 1975b). Presently, production in smaller pots (8–10 cm) for spring sales appears to be the most marketable (Ball, 1978).

Exacum affine is seed propagated. There are approximately 35,000 seeds per gram. The major cultivars are 'Tiddly Winks,' 'Elfin,' and 'Midget.' 'Midget' is generally preferred because it is naturally dwarf. *Exacum* can be germinated over a wide range of temperatures (16°–27°C) but requires light for germination (Table VI) (Cathey, 1969b). Seedlings grow slowly in the early stages but do not require much space (Ball, 1975b; Kamp and Nightingale, 1977). Night temperatures of 16°–18°C and 21°C or higher during the day are desirable during the production period.

Recommendations from Texas A & M suggest seed be sown January 1 and transplanted to 5-cm pots. After approximately 5 weeks they are shifted to 15-cm pots and placed pot-to-pot for 3 weeks. They are then spaced on 30-cm centers and are of salable size in 6 weeks (Kamp and Nightingale, 1977). Other schedules suggest a late fall seeding for spring sales in small pots (8–10 cm) or a December–January seeding for summer sales. Three plants per 13-cm pot have also been suggested to reduce production time (Ball, 1978). The difference in winter temperature and irradiance between Texas and the northern areas probably accounts for the difference in scheduling.

Exacum does not require pinching or chemical growth retardants to produce a plant of good proportions. It has few reported insect or disease problems. It can be used as an outdoor bedding plant and will tolerate full Texas sun until mid-July, but will flower until frost in partial shade (Kamp and Nightingale, 1977).

VII. *PACHYSTACHYS LUTEA*

Pachystachys lutea Nees. (Acanthaceae), sometimes erroneously called the "golden shrimp plant," has much potential as a small flowering pot plant. Its flower has a white corolla about 5 cm long, subtended by golden yellow bracts, cordate to 2.5 cm long, borne on large, terminal upright spikes usually to 10 cm in length. The plant is fast growing with dark green glossy, narrowly ovate, opposite leaves. It is a small shrub from Peru (Bailey Hortorium Staff, 1976).

Pachystachys is easily rooted from single node cuttings. Mist and bottom heat probably speed propagation but are not essential (Holland, 1975).

Earliest flowering and best growth have been obtained at a night temperature of 23°C minimum (Pedersen *et al.,* 1973; Pedersen, 1975). With bench heating, Moes (1976) recommends a bench temperature of 20°–22°C and ambient temperatures of 16°–19°C during the day and 13°C at night. Joiner *et al.,* (1977) showed that shade (light reduction) increased the time to flower and decreased the number of flowers per plant (Table VII). More inflorescences and darker leaves were obtained with 200 ppm nitrogen and potassium at each watering as compared to half that rate (Pedersen, 1975). These results suggest that flowering *Pachystachys* can be produced from a cutting in approximately 100 days if it is grown in a 10-cm pot, pinched, receives high light, 20°–23°C night temperatures, and adequate fertilizer.

Table VII

Response of *Pachystachys lutea* to Reduced Light Levels[a]

Light treatment	Shoot length (cm)	Number of nodes	Number of flower spikes/plant	Number of days to flower
Control (Florida greenhouse)	30	5.6	7.7	83
40% shade	34	6.3	2.7	100
60% shade	31	6.6	2.2	115

[a]Modified from Joiner *et al.* (1977).

As most of the plants are grown in a small pot size (10 cm), chemical growth retardants are required for a proper plant and pot balance. Phosfon is not effective (Holland, 1975). Ethephon reduced the number of lateral branches and plants remained vegetative (Adriansen, 1974; Holland, 1975). A single spray of daminozide at 1000 ppm at 8 to 9 cm of plant growth has been shown to increase the number of inflorescences and reduce plant height (Adriansen, 1974) whereas the same treatment was not effective in another study (Joiner *et al.,* 1977). Ancymidol sprays were not effective (Holland, 1975; Joiner *et al.,* 1977). Pedersen *et al.* (1973) reported a 25 to 50 ppm spray of ancymidol to be more effective than chlormequat. Chlormequat reportedly has been the most effective growth retardant (Adriansen, 1974; Holland, 1975; Hermann, 1975; Joiner *et al.,* 1977). Generally, a 1500 to 3000 ppm drench was most effective but several 800 to 1500 ppm spray applications were also effective but caused some chlorotic leaf blotches. Applications of growth retardants were made when new growth was 8 to 10 cm long.

Postharvest care of *Pachystachys* has not been studied in great detail. The high light requirement for growth suggests postharvest life would be extended under high light conditions. *Pachystachys* has been criticized as being brittle for packing and transport but Holland (1975) states that this is not a problem.

VIII. *PELARGONIUM*

Pelargonium ×*hortorum* L. H. Bailey (Geraniaceae), the bedding geranium of complex hybrid origin largely derived from *P. inquinans* and *P. zonale,* and *P.* ×*domesticum* L. H. Bailey, the 'Lady' or 'Martha Washington' geranium, are the most important for greenhouse pot culture. The present summary of geranium culture will in no way be a complete summary of research on the florists' geranium. The reader is referred to "Geraniums," edited by Mastalerz (1971), for a detailed account of research and suggestions for growers.

In 1977, 46 million potted geraniums were sold in the 28 states surveyed in the United States, with major production in the Midwest and Northeast (Anonymous, 1977b). Most are grown and sold in 10-cm pots as a spring bedding plant and nearly all are the *P.* ×*hortorum* type (Fig. 6).

Pelargonium ×*hortorum* can be propagated from cuttings or seed. The large differences in production techniques justify separate discussions.

A. Vegetatively Propagated Plants

Many cultivars of geraniums are available with various characteristics. Cultivar selection is generally based on flower color (red is the most popular), and performance in the greenhouse and garden. Cultivars, therefore, vary in different regions of production.

Growers may propagate their own cuttings or purchase them from a specialist. Cuttings can be purchased unrooted, calloused, or rooted.

Fig. 6. Cutting in 7.5-cm pots (A), 10-cm pots, eight per flat for ease of handling (B), and greenhouse of 10-cm flower plants ready for market (C).

Fig. 6. *Continued*

To avoid major systemic geranium diseases (Table VIII) culture-indexed plants should be purchased each year from a specialist-propagator. The plants should also be virus indexed (Thorn-Horst *et al.,* 1977). All geraniums from the previous year should be discarded before arrival of clean stock. If stock is to be selected from one's own production, the best plants should be selected from the 10-cm production program in early April. Selection should be made from disease-free plants for early bloom with the most desirable horticultural characteristics, such as form, flower color, prolific branching, and flowering. The carryover of one's own stock is not recommended, however.

There are several methods of cutting production, a few of which are listed below.

1. Conventional Method

Rooted cuttings in 6-cm pots are planted from June to August, either in a bench at a spacing of 30 × 30 cm or in individual 11- to 19-liter containers. Plants are soft-pinched as the shoots reach 5 to 8 cm long until the first cuttings are taken. It is necessary to go over the plants every 2 weeks to pinch any shoots that are of proper size. One could take cuttings for additional stock instead of soft-pinching the plants. Generally, 30 to 50 terminal cuttings are produced per stock plant from December to mid-March.

Table VIII

Major Disease Problems Encountered in Geranium Production[a]

Fungi
    Alternaria leaf spot (*Alternaria tenuis*)
    Black root rot (*Thielaviopsis basicola*)
    Botrytis blight (*Botrytis cinerea*)
    Cercospora leaf spot (*Cercospora brunkii*)
    Pythium blackleg (*Pythium*)
    Rust (*Puccinia pelargonii-zonalis*)
    Verticillium wilt (*Verticillium albo-atrum*)
Bacteria
    Bacterial blight (*Xanthomonas pelargonii*)
    Bacterial fasciation (*Corynebacterium fascians*)
Virus
    Chlorosis
    Crinkle or leaf curl
    Leaf breaking and mosaic
    Leaf cupping
    Yellow-net vein
Others
    Edema

---

[a]From Dickey (1971), Linderman (1971), Nichols *et al.* (1971), Nelson *et al.* (1971), Kiplinger (1973), and Forsberg (1975).

2. Single Stem Method

Much the same schedule is followed as with the conventional method except the terminal growing point is not pinched. The plant is staked for support. All side shoots are soft-pinched as they become large enough. The advantage of this system is the production of more cuttings per stock plant (80–100) because of better light and air movement through the utilization of more vertical greenhouse space.

3. Cuttings from Cuttings Method

Many variations of this method exist, depending on when the original cuttings are planted. A 2 : 1 schedule may consist of planting rooted cuttings in mid-February and taking terminal cuttings from those plants in mid-March. Both original plants and the cuttings are finished as flowering 10-cm pot plants. Schedules for 12 : 1 and 40 : 1 have been proposed (Skou, 1971).

4. Stock Plant Culture

Stock should be grown in a well-drained medium with good water-holding capacity and at a pH of 6.0 to 6.5. For maximum growth, plants should not be allowed to wilt. Geraniums require moderately heavy applications of fertilizers and have a particularly high requirement for phosphorus and potassium. If adequate levels of superphosphate are added to the medium, a constant application of 200 ppm nitrogen and potassium is often used. The plants should be grown at a night temperature of 15°–18°C with a 3°–5°C increase in day temperature. Older foliage turns red if the plants are grown too cool or too dry. Increased growth results when carbon dioxide levels are 1000 to 2000 ppm. Geraniums, although responsive to additional artificial light, do not respond to photoperiod.

Botrytis blight can be a serious problem in stock plants. Regular applications of a fungicide are necessary. Major insect problems are whiteflies, mites, caterpillars, aphids, and geranium plume moth (*Platyptilia pica*). Applications of proper insecticides and miticides will control these pests.

All flower heads should be removed from stock plants as they develop. The pedicel should be broken in half so it will abscise naturally without opening a wound on the plant stem. Stock plants tend to produce very large leaves, which should also be removed to allow better air circulation and more light to the new growth.

Today, most producers sell stock plants as large patio plants in the spring. It probably would be unprofitable to grow such large plants for the market, but they are often sold at a price sufficiently high to recover most of the overhead costs.

5. Cuttings

Cuttings can be taken and rooted any time of year. Cuttings 5 to 8 cm long should be snapped from the plant. If a knife is used it should be sterilized in 95% alcohol between stock plants. Bottom leaves are removed from the cuttings. Rooting hormone is not necessary. Cuttings root faster with bottom heat (21°–24°C) and an air temperature of 18°C. Intermittent mist should be used in the early stages of rooting. Cuttings can be rooted in 6-cm containers and later transplanted to 10-cm pots. Many are now rooted directly in the final pot (10 cm), which saves the labor of transplanting but requires more space. At a 15°C night temperature, it takes approximately 5 weeks before a cutting can be taken from the breaks resulting from a soft or hard pinch (cutting) (Tayama *et al.*, 1972). *Pythium* blackleg and *Botrytis* can be serious diseases during propagation. Sanitation and chemical applications are required.

6. Production of Flowering 10-cm Pot Plants

General cultural conditions given for stock plants apply to 10-cm pot plant production with the addition of scheduling and height control. Geranium production in 10-cm pots follows a multitude of schedules depending on when cuttings are taken (not all cuttings on a stock plant are available at one time), type and time of year cuttings are purchased, whether plants are soft-pinched, hard-pinched (terminal cutting), or unpinched, and when plants are to be sold.

When grown at a minimum 16°C night temperature, production time for un-pinched plants is approximately 17 to 18 weeks for unrooted cuttings, 15 weeks for calloused cuttings, 11 weeks for 8-cm plants, and 7 to 9 weeks for culture-indexed 8-cm plants (Randolph, 1966; Mastalerz, 1967). Tayama and Poole (1976) prepared schedules for pinched plant production in Ohio (Table IX). They suggested only growing pinched plants, but many self-branching cul-tivars are grown unpinched because of reduced production time. For late May flowering, a hard pinch (leaving at least three nodes on the plant) should not be made after February 15 at a night temperature of 13°C and March 1 at 16°C. A soft pinch should not be made after March 1 at 13°C and March 15 at 16°C (Tayama et al., 1972).

Chlormequat has been successfully used to control height, slightly increase breaks on unpinched plants, reduce pedicel length, and allow closer spacing. A 1500 ppm solution is sprayed 2 to 3 weeks after potting unpinched plants or when new shoots are 3 to 4 cm long on pinched plants (Tayama et al., 1972; White and Mastalerz, 1972). Chlormequat causes a slight yellowing of leaf margins but this disappears after several weeks.

The final spacing should be 15 × 15 cm, which gives 43 pots/m². Wider spacing produces a better-quality plant but it is difficult to justify the additional cost of production (Rogers, 1961).

B. Seed-Propagated Plants

A major change occurred in geranium production with the release in 1963 of 'Nittany Lion Red,' the first of the seed-propagated geraniums. However, it was not until the mid-1970s that large-scale production started, mainly because the initial seedling cultivars required a long production time from sowing to an-thesis, plants were not very floriferous, and germination was poor. Newer cul-tivars are easy to germinate and can be produced in 14 to 16 weeks from seed to flower in 10-cm pots (Holden et al., 1977) (Table IX). The major faults today are single flowers and shattering of flower heads. In general, seed geraniums perform better in the garden than most of the vegetatively propagated cul-tivars. The trend will probably be toward more seedling geranium production in

Table IX

Production of 10-cm Flower Geranium for Mother's Day as Suggested for Ohio[a]

Operation	Dates			
Take cuttings	December 1	December 15	December 22	January 5
Plant in 10-cm pot	December 22	January 5	January 12	January 26
Pinch	January 12	January 26	February 2	February 16
Flower	April 24–30	May 1–9	May 9–19	May 20–30

[a]From Tayama and Poole (1976). The plants are grown at a minimum 16°C night temperature.

flats as bedding plants instead of in pots. Only pot production will be presented here, however.

There are 200 seeds/gm. Germination requires a 24°C soil temperature. Intermittent mist is highly recommended as germination is improved. Pasteurized medium should be used because damping-off can be a serious problem.

Cumulative solar energy is a major environmental factor controlling flowering in seed geraniums (Craig and Walker, 1963). Time from sowing to flowering decreases as the sowing date moves from December to February (Konjoian and Tayama, 1978). Lighting the seedlings with Wide Spectrum Gro-Lux fluorescent lamps (1.3 lamp W/m²) for 6 to 10 weeks produced earlier flowering (24–55 days) with two to six fewer nodes at flowering (Carpenter and Rodriguez, 1971). Norton (1973) has shown the same effect when using high-intensity lighting. Chlormequat as a drench reduces plant height and causes earlier flowering (Holcomb and White, 1968; Ball and Randolph, 1968; White, 1970; Carpenter and Carlson, 1970). Chlormequat as a spray also reduces height, slightly reduces the time to flower, slightly increases the number of flowers, and is much easier to apply than a drench (Konjoian and Tayama, 1978). Generally, two sprays of chlormequat at 1500 ppm are applied, the first 40 days after seeding and the second 1 to 2 weeks later (Ball, 1977). Ancymidol as a 200 ppm spray also reduced plant height and caused earlier flowering (Ball, 1975c). Daminozide as a 2500 ppm spray was not effective on seedling geraniums (Carpenter and Carlson, 1970).

A growing temperature of 16°–17°C is recommended as the most reasonable given cost of production. Plants flower 9 days earlier at 18°C and 10 days later at 13°C when compared to 16°C (Konjoian and Tayama, 1978). A typical schedule for the northern latitudes in the United States is shown in Table X.

Seedling geraniums should be grown in a pasteurized, well-drained medium because damping-off and root rot diseases can cause serious losses. Regular fungicide drenches are recommended. Constant fertilizer applications of 200 ppm nitrogen and potassium produce maximum growth. High soluble salts caused by improper watering and fertilizing can be a problem in the early stages of growth.

Seedling geraniums can be attacked by the same insect and disease problems, as was mentioned for vegetatively propagated plants. Sanitation and chemical controls are required.

C. *P.* × *domesticum*

Pelargonium × *domesticum* plants are vegetatively propagated with culture similar to *P.* × *hortorum* except for flower initiation. The cultivars Lavender Grand Slam, Grand Slam, Aztec, and Frühlingzauber require a night temperature below 15.5°C for flowering (Crossley, 1968; Hackett and Kister, 1974; Nilsen, 1975). Hackett and Kister (1974) also suggest that flowering does not occur when day temperatures are greater than 15.5°C. The cultivars Applause,

Table X

General Production Schedule for Seedling Geranium Production in 10-cm Pots[a]

Operation	Time of year	Night temperature (°C)	Comments
Sow seed [b]	Mid-December	22-24	Soil temperature of 24°C critical, intermittent mist recommended
Transplant to 8-cm container	Early January	16-17	Fungicide application should be made to avoid damping-off
Apply growth retardant [c]			
First application	Late January	16-17	Chlormequat at 1500 ppm, spray to run off
Second application	One week later	16-17	
Transplant to 10-cm pot	Early March	16-17	Apply drenches for root rot diseases every 4 weeks
Flowering	Mid-April		

[a]Modified from Ball (1977).

[b]This schedule would be for northern latitudes in the United States. Later sowing or more Southern growing areas would require 1 to 2 weeks less production time.

[c]One spray application of ancymidol at 200 ppm can also be used.

Sunrise, Parisienne, and Rapture will flower at a night temperature of 15.5°C (Crossley, 1968; Hackett and Kister, 1974). However, the numbers of flowers were increased on 'Sunrise' when plants were grown at a 13°C night temperature. Long days interact with low temperature to promote earlier flowering in 'Lavender Grand Slam,' so long days are recommended. Low light flux is detrimental to flowering and can cause problems in dark greenhouses during the winter (Hackett and Kister, 1974; Nilsen, 1975). Hackett *et al.,* (1974) showed exposure of rooted cuttings of 'Lavender Grand Slam' in 6-cm pots for 6 weeks at a constant 7°C and 540 lx incandescent light would produce excellent flowering 10-cm pot plants. They suggested a schedule of 3 to 4 weeks for rooting (15.5°C night, 21°–25°C day), and 6 weeks of low temperature and 6 to 8 weeks of growth (15.5°C night, 21°–25°C day) for producing flowering plants. Other cultivars requiring low temperatures for flowering could probably be produced with the same schedule.

IX. *PRIMULA*

Several species of *Primula* (Primulaceae) have been grown as flowering pot plants. *Primula malacoides* Franch; the annual primrose; *Primula veris* L., the hardy perennial primrose with several subspecies; and *Primula vulgaris* Huds.

and *Primula* ×*polyantha* Hort., called polyanthus, which is a hybrid group with parentage of *P. veris, P. elatior,* and *P. vulgaris,* are the most widely grown. *Primula sinensis sab.* ex. Lindl. and *Primula* ×*kewensis* W. Wats have been grown in the past as pot plants. *Primula obconica* Hance. is still grown but is not recommended as it has hairs that cause a skin rash on some people (Bailey Hortorium Staff, 1976).

Of the species listed, many selections, cultivars, and hybrids are available (Fig. 7). Several seed sources should be consulted before making the decision on which species to grow. *Primula vulgaris* is the most popular in Sweden although some *P.* ×*polyantha* is also grown (Wikesjö, 1975). The comments

Fig. 7. *Primula malacoides* 'Rhinespearl White' (A) and *Primula* species 'Laser Formula Mixture' (B). (Photograph courtesy Geo. J. Ball, Inc., West Chicago, Illinois.)

(B)

Fig. 7. Continued

here will be for *Primula,* in general, with the understanding that small differences exist among species.

Primula is seed-propagated. It germinates best at temperatures of 15°–21°C and is generally said to require light for germination (Thompson, 1967, 1969; Cathey, 1969b). The light requirement is questionable from other work (Anonymous, 1977a), particularly for *P.* ×*polyantha*. The seed do germinate best when sown on the surface and left uncovered (Turner and Heydecker, 1974). Germination does not take place above 21°C and presents a problem when seed are sown during the summer (Table VI). For 8- to 10-cm pot production, seeds are generally sown in either June or August and transplanted to 6-cm pots after 6 to 8 weeks. Some growers will transplant directly to the finishing pot while others transplant to the finishing pot when forcing starts. *Primula* require low light (probably 32 klx maximum) and should be shaded most of the year. They are grown at 5°–7°C until three to four flower buds are clearly visible. During this period it is best to keep plants on the dry side. When flower buds are visible, plants can be forced (January–March) at a temperature of 13°C. Forcing time is usually 2 to 4 weeks. Forcing before the flower buds are visible will result in poor flowering and excessive leafiness. Forcing at temperatures above 13°C will result in elongated, weak flower stalks. *Primula malacoides* should be given short days during the low-temperature, flower initiation period for best flowering (Smith, 1969; Zimmer, 1969).

Overwatering (poorly drained soil) can result in disease problems. Leaf spots from *Rumularia* fungus have been reported. Aphids, red spider mites, and caterpillars are major insect pests.

The plants provide an interesting change for the consumer. They should be maintained in a cool place out of direct sunlight for best postharvest life. Some selections are fragrant and the perennial types can be planted in the garden, adding consumer value to the plant.

X. *ROSA*

Several *Rosa* species L. (Rosaceae) are grown as flowering potted plants for the Easter and Mother's Day holiday market or as spring-flowering pot plants. Even with the very large number of different roses available, few are suitable for pot culture. The major groups used are polyantha, floribunda, and miniature roses (Table XI).

The polyantha group is by far the best for pot culture relative to plant size, shape, and flower display (Fig. 8). The miniature types have not received much attention, but are certainly well suited for the smaller pot sizes (10 cm) and should play an increasing role in the market.

Production of potted roses in the northern United States would begin with the arrival and potting of dormant 2-year-old budded plants (miniatures are not budded) in early January for the Easter market and late January for the Mother's Day market. Plants are available in three grades: "X," at least one strong cane; "XX," at least three strong canes; and "XXX," at least four strong canes. Most producers force "XXX" plants because they make a more uniform, attractive potted plant. The plants should not be delivered to the grower until the time of potting unless they can be stored at $-0.6°C$ with very high relative humidity. When received the plants should be unpacked, immersed in water for several hours or wet thoroughly, and covered with moist burlap for a day (Ball, 1975a). This will aid in new root growth and bud break when potted. The plants are usually grown in 18-cm pots because of the finished plant size.

Before or right after potting, plants are pruned to remove dead branches and to reduce the length of good canes to 17 to 20 cm. The canes should be pruned to an "eye" (bud) that is toward the outside of the pot. This will direct the new top growth to the outside of the pot. Plants are pinched when new growth is 8 to 10 cm long, with the last pinch 6 to 7 weeks before Easter and 5 to 6 weeks before Mother's Day. Previous recommendations suggested a cold start at $7°-9°C$ for pot roses (Laurie *et al.,* 1969). Work by Moe (1970) and grower experience (Clark, 1978) recommend $17°-18°C$ for a more uniform and well-proportioned plant even though the numbers of flowers per shoot were reduced at the higher forcing temperatures. Finished plants are also shorter at

Table XI

Rose Cultivars Commonly Forced as Flowering Potted Plants

Cultivar	Commercial synonyms	Date of origination or introduction	Flower color	Remarks
Polyantha				
Dick Koster		1929	Deep pink	Sport of 'Anneke Koster'
Margo Koster	'Sunbeam'	1931	Salmon	Slightly fragrant, sport of 'Dick Koster'
Mothersday [a]	'Fêtes des Mères' 'Morsdag' 'Muttertag'	1949	Deep red	Sport of 'Dick Koster'
Triomphe Orléanais		1912	Cherry-red	Slightly fragrant
Tammy [b]			Clear pink	Sport of 'Mothersday'
Floribunda				
Carol Amling		1953	Deep rose-pink, edged lighter	Sport of 'Garnette'
Garnette		1951	Garnet-red, base light lemon-yellow	
Marimba		1965	Pink	Sport of 'Garnette,' slightly fragrant
Roswytha		1968	Pink	Sport of 'Carol'
Thunderbird		1958	Rose red	Sport of 'Skyland,' vigorous spreading
Bright Pink Garnette [b]			Bright deep pink	Sport of 'Garnette'
Miniature				
Chipper		1966	Salmon-pink	Slightly fragrant
Cinderella		1953	Satiny white, tinged pale flesh	Fragrant (spicy)
Pixie	'Little Princess' 'Princesita'	1940	White, center faint Hermosa pink	Slightly fragrant
Red Imp	'Maid Marion' 'Mon Tresor'	1951	Deep crimson	Slightly fragrant
Scarlet Gem	'Scarlet Pimpernel'	1961	Orange scarlet	Slightly fragrant
Starina		1965	Orange, scarlet	
Sweet Fairy		1946	Apple-blossom pink	Fragrant

[a] Correct spelling according to Modern Roses (1969).
[b] Not listed in Modern Roses (1969).

Fig. 8.   Potted rose of the polyantha group growing in 17.8-cm pot, two weeks before Mother's Day.

this higher forcing temperature. Moe (1970) showed Phosfon was not effective for height control of 'Margo Koster' and 'Morsdag'; daminozide gave a pale color to the flowers, while the best control was obtained with two sprays of chlormequat. The first application was made when the shoots were 6 cm long (15–20 days after cutback) and the second 10 days later. The spray concentration should be less than 2000 ppm to avoid foliar injury.

Moe (1970) found that 'Morsdag' grew more vigorously when budded on *Rosa multiflora* Thunb. than on *Rosa multiflora* 'Japonica,' which suggests some interesting possibilities in using root stock to control growth.

Moe (1973) proposed a scheme of growing potted roses from cuttings. Single node cuttings with one attached five-leaflet leaf were taken from stems with flower buds in color or in bloom. The upper position cuttings showed higher percentage rooting and bud break than lower position cuttings. A reduction in leaf area decreased root formation and growth. Dips in 500 to 2000 ppm IBA solution for 5 seconds increased rooting but decreased the percentage of bud break. Indoleacetic acid (IAA) and naphthalene acetic acid (NAA) were not effective in promoting rooting. An attractive potted plant was produced with three to five cuttings per 11- to 12-cm pot, following the schedule presented in Fig. 9.

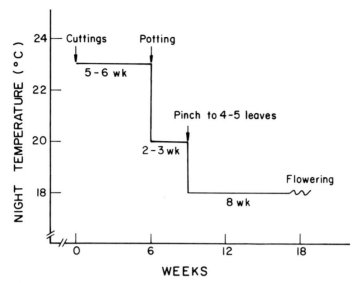

Fig. 9.   Proposed schedule for producing potted roses from cuttings. (From Moe, 1973.)

Powdery mildew is the most serious disease in the production of potted roses. Chemical applications and humidity regulation by temperature are necessary to control this disease. Mites and aphids are major insect pests and must be controlled with appropriate pesticides.

Temperature during postharvest handling is important, as shown by Maxie *et al.* (1974). When potted "Mothersday' plants in flower were boxed and placed in the sun for 4 hours, unopened buds failed to open and subsequently abscised from the plant. There were no adverse effects on open flowers. Air temperature inside the box was recorded within the range of 22°–40°C. They observed the same response in the field to several days of high temperature. 'Margo Koster' did not show this response of bud abscission from high temperature in the field.

XI. *SCHLUMBERGERA*

Schlumbergera bridgesii Lofgr. (*Cactaceae*), commonly known as the Christmas cactus, and *Schlumbergera truncata* Moran, the Thanksgiving cactus, are epiphytic cacti with flat-jointed stem segments (phylloclades) and are native to Brazil. They are both similar except *S. truncata* has margins of joints sharply two to four serrate (Fig. 10). The natural flowering periods also differ, with *S. truncata* flowering in November and *S. bridgesii* flowering in December (Bailey Hortorium Staff, 1976).

Fig. 10. Stem segements of *S. truncata,* Thanksgiving cactus (right) and *S. Bridgesii,* Christmas cactus (left).

Much confusion exists over the identity of the species used in research. *Schlumbergera truncata* was formerly named *Epiphyllum truncatum* and *Zygocactus truncatus.* These names are used in the literature with the common name Christmas cactus, but it would appear from photographs and descriptions that most of the work was done with Thanksgiving cactus. Most of the new hybrids that are called Christmas cactus in the trade also appear to be Thanksgiving cactus, *S. truncata.*

Probably one of the largest producers of Christmas cactus (Thanksgiving cactus) in the United States is B. L. Cobia Co. Inc., Winter Garden, Florida. They shipped more than one million pots (8–11 cm) in flower during November and December, 1977. They also have an extensive research and breeding program and hold nine patents on their original selections. In their breeding program they are able to grow these cacti from seedling to flowering size in 17 months (Patch, 1977).

Roberts and Struckmeyer (1939) reported that Christmas cactus (*Zygocactus truncatus*—probably *S. truncata*) flowered under short days (9.5–10 hours) but not long days (16–18 hours), at a night temperature of 17°–18°C. At 13°C plants flowered under both short and long days, whereas at 21°–24°C the plants did not flower under either short or long days. Rünger (1961) reported similar findings with *Zygocactus* 'Weihnachtsfreude' ('Christmas Cheer') (probably *S. truncata,* particularly from photograph shown) except at the higher temperature. At 30°C, flowering required daylengths of less than 12 hours, whereas at 15°C flowering occurred regardless of daylength. He found the critical daylength to change gradually between 15° and 30°C, and 10°C prevented flower initiation. He reported vegetative growth takes place only at temperatures above 20°C and under long days. Later, Rünger (1968) found under short days that a 15°C night temperature was optimum for flowering and when combined with a higher day temperature more flower buds were formed. Under long days, flower initiation was similar to short days when the day temperature was 10° or 15°C, but day temperatures of 25° and 30°C almost completely supressed flower initiation even when combined with low night temperature. Long days inhibited bud development until the buds became visible. Rünger (1970) also reported that the rate of development of the buds increased with increasing temperatures (treatments went to 25°C). From 15 days after the start of short days until buds were 2 to 3 mm long 15°C inhibited development. At 10°C buds aborted. When the flower buds were 5 mm long or longer, high temperature (25°C) was shown to cause the abortion of buds.

Poole (1973) also reported Christmas cactus (*Zygocactus truncatus* 'Christmas Cheer'—probably *S. truncata*) flowered at temperatures as high as 32°C when given short days for 6 or more weeks. Flower buds were visible 3 to 4 weeks after the start of short days and flowering time was not affected whether the plants received 6, 9, or 12 weeks of short-day treatment. Temperatures above 32°C probably caused flower abscission and increased the time to flower by 3 to 4 weeks.

From these studies, it would appear that optimum conditions for flowering would be 6 weeks of short days (8 hours) at a 15°C night temperature and 20°–21°C day temperature. The night temperature could be raised to 18°C after the initiation period to hasten flower development. High day or night temperatures (≥25°C) during the development period should be avoided to prevent bud abortion. Pruning the plants 6 to 8 weeks before short days start improves uniformity of flowering by increasing uniformity of maturity of shoots when flower initiation begins. Some growers suggest running plants dry at the beginning of short days to increase the number of flower buds. If this practice is followed, it should be discontinued during the development and flowering period as it will delay flowering and reduce flower size. A schedule for flowering Thanksgiving cactus, *S. truncata,* for Christmas in 10-cm pots is presented in Table XII.

Although these plants are cacti, they should be kept moist if growth is to be maximized. A well-drained soil high in organic matter is recommended.

Knauss (1975) reported that several pathogens are capable of causing severe basal stem and root rot of Christmas cactus (*S. truncata*). He studied *Phytophthora parasitica* and *Pythium aphanidermatum* and reported that either can produce a root and basal stem rot. Disease development was more rapid with *Pythium* and phylloclade abscission more prevalent with *Phytophthora*. Soil pasteurization and fungicides control the pathogens.

Table XII

Proposed Schedule for Flowering *Schlumbergera truncata* for Late November to Mid-December [a]

Operation	Time of year
Stick cuttings [b]	January–February (18°–20°C night temperature, long day)
Prune terminals	Late June
Begin short days (8 hours)	Early to mid-September (15°C night, 20°–21°C day)
Begin natural day	Mid-October to late October (18°C night, 20°–21°C day)
Flower	Late November to mid-December

[a]*Schlumbergera bridgesii* would probably follow a similar schedule.
[b]Propagation can be delayed until May on some of the faster-growing free-branching hybrids, particularly for 10-cm pot production.

Schlumbergera bridgesii and *S. truncata* are bothered by few insects. Mealybugs and scales are the two most important pests. Both are difficult to control when populations are large, so early detection is essential.

Schlumbergera truncata plants remain in flower 4 to 6 weeks (Poole, 1973), with a bloom life of 6 to 9 days (Patch, 1977). The main post-greenhouse problem perhaps is flower abscission from exposure of flowering plants to high temperatures (>25°C). Plants are usually not shipped great distances with many open flowers because the blooms are fragile.

XII. *SENECIO* ×*HYBRIDUS*

Senecio ×*hybridus* Regel (Compositae) is a member of one of the largest genera of flowering plants, estimated at 2000 to 3000 species. The florists' cineraria is a perennial but is often grown as an annual. It appears to have originated in England as hybrids between *S. cruentus* and *S. heritieri* and possibly other species from the section Pericalli in the Canary Islands. It is a very showy flowering pot plant and has many daisylike flowers available in a wide range of colors and flower patterns (Bailey Hortorium Staff, 1976). Plants are sometimes divided into grandiflora and multiflora cultivars. The grandiflora group has fewer, larger flowers and blooms earlier than the multiflora group (Moe, 1977b). Finished plant size (width and height) also vary tremendously among cultivars (Fig. 11). Careful cultivar selection should be made, based on final pot size.

Cineraria plants are seed-propagated. The seeds are small, with 5300 seed/gm, and are easily germinated at 18°–20°C. Seeds are usually sown in September, October, and November. They are transplanted to cell packs in flats or 6-cm pots as soon as they are large enough to handle. They should be grown at 18°C at this stage. When they become crowded they should be

Fig. 11.   Two cultivars (A, B) of *Senecio* ×*hybridus* grown in 13-cm pots. Note the differences in finished plant size.

transplanted to 10- to 15-cm pots for finishing. Most in the United States are finished in 15-cm pots at present, but smaller pots should be considered for mass market production.

Low temperature treatment (below 15°C) is required for flowering of cineraria (Post, 1942; Hildrum, 1969), thus most production is for the late winter to early spring market. January flowing can be achieved by selecting early-flowering cultivars and sowing seed in early August (Moe, 1977b). Although various cultivars have different critical temperatures and length of exposure time for flower initiation, 9°–12°C for 6 weeks appears to be optimum (Hildrum, 1969). Plants should be grown at 18°C for 8 to 10 weeks before the cold treatment is given to have adequate leaf area for optimal response to low temperature (Moe, 1977).

Daylength is reported to have no effect on flower initiation (Hildrum, 1969), but Hammer (1975) observed 90% flowering in 'Starlet' and 'Early Dwarf Erfurt' when grown under long days at 18°C minimum temperature. Plant quality is poor, however. Additional photoperiod research with all cultivars is needed and may suggest that long-day plants can be selected.

Gibberellic acid can replace part of the cold requirement; however, flower stems were elongated and plant quality was very poor (Moe, 1977b).

Chemical height control is generally not recommended for cineraria. Chlormequat is not effective although daminozide spray of 5000 to 10,000 ppm applied when buds are first visible will limit plant stretch. It will delay flowering if applied during flower initiation (Moe, 1977b).

After the cold treatment, an additional 9 weeks are required until flowering. During this period, long days and a temperature of 12°–13°C accelerate flower development. Temperatures above 13°C reduce plant quality. Flowering can be delayed by forcing at a cooler temperature. Some producers use this technique to expand the time of flowering. When flowering cineraria during spring months, shade may be required to reduce irradiance.

High fertility levels, particularly nitrogen, should be avoided as the leaves may become too large for the finished plant. A constant fertilizer program of 100 ppm nitrogen and potassium is probably adequate. A high nitrate nitrogen fertilizer is recommended because of the cool growing temperature. Cinerarias are affected by overwatering but frequent watering is necessary because of the large leaf area. Plants may wilt on bright, sunny days even if the medium is moist (Wilkins, 1974).

Mosaic and streak viruses can cause losses in cineraria production (Jones, 1944; Singh *et al.*, 1975). Both can be seed transmitted and great care must be taken in seed production, so seed should be purchased from reliable sources. Mosaic can also be transmitted by aphids and streak by thrips. Diseased plants should be discarded as soon as they are noticed (Forsberg, 1975). *Phytophthora erythroseptica* has been identified as causing wilt of the laminae of larger basal leaves and epinasty of the petioles (Lucas, 1977). If these symptoms are observed a pathologist should be consulted as little information is available on control.

Major insect problems with cineraria are mites, aphids, whiteflies, and caterpillars. Chemical applications are necessary to control these pests.

Cineraria plants generally have a short post-greenhouse life because of the dry, warm conditions found in most homes. They do well when held at temperatures below 13°C and at high humidity. They require frequent watering because of their large leaf area. Drying of the growing medium is probably the most severe post-greenhouse problem.

XIII. *STREPTOCARPUS*

Streptocarpus ×*hybridus* Voss. and *Streptocarpus Rexii* Lindl. (Gesneriaceae), commonly known as Cape primrose, make excellent flowering 10-cm pot plants (Fig. 12). Most plants grown today are complex hybrids derived from several species. The name comes from the spirally twisted two-valved calyptra fruit. Seeds are minute (Bailey Hortorium Staff, 1976).

'Constant Nymph,' derived from Merton Blue ♀ × *S. Johannis* LL Britten ♂ (Marston, 1964; Zeven, 1972) in the 1940s by W. J. Lawrence, is responsible for the present interest in *Streptocarpus*. Several studies have been reported on the genetics of *Streptocarpus* (Crane and Lawrence, 1956; Lawrence and Sturgess, 1957; Lawrence, 1957). In 1969, 'Purple Nymph,' 'Mini Nymph,' 'Blue Nymph,' 'Netta Nymph,' and 'Cobalt Nymph' (a tetraploid) were released. They were obtained by irradiation of 'Constant Nymph' with X rays (Broertjes, 1969). A Dutch grower found a white sport of 'Constant Nymph' that has become known as 'Maassen's White' (Krause, 1974). Recently, a renewed interest in *Streptocarpus* has produced many new hybrids (Davies, 1974; Hammer, 1976; Pride, 1977; Widmer and Platteter, 1975). Some of the hybrids are given in Table XIII.

Plants are usually propagated from seed or leaf cuttings. Seed propagation results in a mixture of flower forms and colors because true breeding lines have not been developed. Seed germination requires light and a temperature of 16°–24°C (Table VI). Seed-propagated plants grow slowly at first and require little space. They should not be transplanted until they are large enough to be easily handled (2 to 3 months). A flowering plant in a 10-cm pot can be produced from seed to flower in 5 to 6 months.

Vegetative propagation is quick and relatively easy with *Streptocarpus*. The best method is to remove the midvein of a newly matured healthy leaf and to insert remaining lamina parts (lengthwise) into the rooting medium with the cut surface down. Mist is not required for rooting (Marston, 1964; Appelgren and Heide, 1972). Leaves root in 3 to 4 weeks with three to four dozen plantlets forming along the cut surface. The plantlets should not be transplanted until

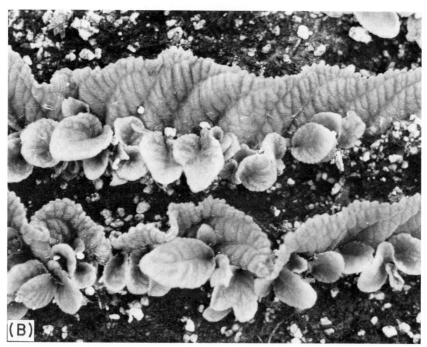

Fig. 12. *Streptocarpus* ×*hybridus* flowering in 10-cm pot (A) and leaf cuttings with small plantlets (B).

Table XIII

Some *Streptocarpus* Cultivars Commonly Grown as Flowering Pot Plants Propagated from Cuttings

Cultivar	Flower color
Constant Nymph	Blue
Blue Nymph	Light blue
Cobalt Nymph	Deep intense blue (tetraploid)
Mini Nymph	Blue
Netta Nymph	Deep blue, dark blue venation
Purple Nymph	Deep purple
Maassen's White	White, yellow throat
Albatross	White (tetraploid)
Snow White	White
Tina	Pink
Paula	Blue
Louise	Dark blue
Helen	Blue
Sonia	Cerise
Margaret	Blue violet
Conny	Blue
Diana	Deep cerise, white throat
Fiona	Pink
Karen	Magenta pink
Marie	Dusty purple
Olga	Bold cerise
Wiesmoor cultivars	White to blue to pink to rose to crimson (very large flowers)

they are of sufficient size to easily handle (2 to 3 months). Leaves can be used again to produce a second batch of plantlets. A flowering plant in a 10-cm pot can be produced in 5 to 6 months.

Once *Streptocarpus* is germinated or rooted, the requirements for its growth are the same. Night temperature should be 16°–18°C for growth and flowering. Day temperatures should be below 30°C as higher temperatures slow growth and flowering. Plants should be grown at 15 to 20 klx light intensity so heavy shade is needed during much of the year. Some work has suggested greater flowering under long days (15 hours) as compared to short days (8 hours) (White, 1975a) whereas other research has shown that long days and increased photosynthetic radiation hasten flowering and increase the numbers of flowers. Plants naturally flower more prolifically in the early spring in the northern United States with increased daylength and photosynthetic radiation.

Streptocarpus plants do not require high fertility levels. With a constant fertilization program, 100 to 125 ppm of nitrogen and potassium is recommended.

Few insect or disease problems have been observed with *Streptocarpus*. Mealybugs are probably the most serious pest.

Streptocarpus plants have a prolonged post-greenhouse life when sold with sufficient numbers of flower buds. The plant can be easily grown in most homes and will flower periodically if it receives sufficient light. It should have much appeal, particularly as a spring-flowering pot plant.

REFERENCES

Adriansen, E. (1974). Retardering af *Pachystachys lutea* med AR.-85, Ethrel og CCC. *Tisskr. Planteavl* **78**(3), 331–341.

Anonymous (1977a). Strong future seen for primrose sales. *Grower* **87**(14), 794–795.

Anonymous (1977b) "Flower and Foliage Plant." Crop Reporting Board, SRS, USDA, Washington, D.C.

Appelgren, M., and Heide, O. M. (1972). Regeneration in streptocarpus discs and its regulation by temperature and growth substances. *Physiol. Plant.* **27**(3), 417–423.

Bailey Hortorium Staff (1976). "Hortus Third." Macmillan, New York.

Ball, V. ed. (1975a). "The Ball Red Book," 13th Ed. Geo. J. Ball, Inc., West Chicago, Illinois.

Ball, V. (1975b). Ohio—'75. *Grower Talks* **38**(11), 17.

Ball, V. (1975c). Why seed geranium culture is growing. *Grower Talks* **39**(8), 1–5.

Ball, V. (1977). Seed geraniums—sowing dates of '78. *Grower Talks* **41**(5), 1–5.

Ball, V. (1978). Six other pot plants—Exacum—interesting. *Grower Talks* **41**(10), 17–18.

Ball, V., and Randolph, P. (1968). Carefree geraniums—spring flowering. *Grower Talks* **32**(4), 1–10.

Beck, G. E. (1975). Preliminary suggestions for the culture and production of clerodendrum. *Ohio Florists' Assoc. Bull.* **547**, 6–7.

Broertjes, C. (1969). Mutation breeding of streptocarpus. *Euphytica* **18**, 333–339.

Brundert, W., and Stratmann, S. (1973). Einsatz von Zusatzlicht und Wuchshemmitteln als Kulturhilfe bei *Campanula isophylla,* Moretti. *Dtsch. Gaertnerboerse* **73**(1), 4–6.

Carpenter, W. J., and Carlson, W. H. (1970). The influence of growth regulators and temperature on flowering of seed propagated geraniums. *HortScience* **5**(3), 183–184.

Carpenter, W. J., and Rodriquez, R. C. (1971). Earlier flowering of geranium cv. Carefree Scarlet by high intensity supplemental light treatment. *HortScience* **6**(3), 206–207.

Cathey, H. M. (1969a). Guidelines for the germination of annual, pot plants and ornamental herb seeds—I. *Florists' Rev.* **144**(3742), 21–23, 58–60.

Cathey, H. M. (1969b). Guidelines for the germination of annual, pot plant and ornamental herb seeds—2. *Florists' Rev.* **144**(3743), 18–20, 52–53.

Clark, S. (1978). Personal communications. Andrews Greenhouses, Andrews, Indiana.

Craig, R., and Walker, D. E. (1963). The flowering of *Pelargonium hortorum* Bailey seedlings as affected by cumulative solar energy. *J. Am. Soc. Hortic. Sci.* **83**, 772–776.

Crane, M. B., and Lawrence, W. J. C. (1956). "The Genetics of Garden Plants." Macmillan, New York.

Crossley, J. H. (1968). Warm vs cool short days as preconditions for flowering of *Pelargonium domesticum* cultivars. *Can. J. Plant Sci.* **48**, 211–212.

Davies, D. R. (1974). New AYR cape primrose able to cope with low light and power economies. *Grower* **81**(12), 563.

Davis, W. E. (1978). Personal communications. Sandpoint Greenhouse, Fort Wayne, Indiana.

Dickey, R. S. (1971). Root rots; bacterial fasciation; *In* "Geraniums" (J. W. Mastalerz, ed.), pp. 228–231. Pennsylvania Flower Growers, University Park.

Forsberg, J. L. (1975). "Diseases of Ornamental Plants," Spec. Publ. No. 3 (Rev.). Univ. of Illinois, Urbana.

Garibaldi, A., and Gullino, G. (1973). Malattie nuove o poco note delle piante da fiore e ornamentali in Italia. *Not. Mal. Piante* **88/89**, 53–71.

Hackett, W. P., and Kister, J. (1974). Environmental factors affecting flowering in *Pelargonium domesticum* cultivars. *J. Am. Soc. Hortic. Sci.* **99**(1), 15–17.

Hackett, W. P., Kister, J., and Tse, A. T. Y. (1974). Flower induction of *Pelargonium domesticum* Bailey cv. Lavender Grand Slam with exposure to low temperature and low light intensity. *HortScience* **9**(1), 63–65.

Hammer, P. A. (1975). Unpublished data. Purdue Univ., West Lafayette, Indiana.

Hammer, P. A. (1976). Breeding *Streptocarpus* for pot plant use. *Acta Hortic.* **63**, 99–100.

Heide, O. M. (1965). *Campanula isophylla* som langdagsplante. *Gartneryrket* **55**, 210–212.

Hermann, P. (1975). Optimale Nährstoffversorgung und Gartenbau-Cycocel ergänzen sich. Ergebnisse aus Versuchen zu *Pachystachys* und *Pelargonium* F_1 - Hybriden. *Gartenwelt* **75**(24), 507–508.

Hildrum, H. (1968). Virkning av lyskvalitet og B-nine på vekst og Glomstring hos *Campanula isophylla,* Moretti. *Gartner Tidende* **84**, 491–493.

Hildrum, H. (1969). Factors affecting flowering in *Senecio cruentus* D. C. *Acta Hortic.* **14**, 117–123.

Hildrum, H. (1972). New pot plant—*Clerodendrum thomsonae* Balf. *N.Y. State Flower Ind. Bull.* Nov./Dec., p. 3.

Hildrum, H. (1973). The effect of day length, source of light and growth regulators on growth and flowering of *Clerodendrum thomsonae* Balf. *Sci. Hortic.* **1**(1), 1–11.

Holcomb, J., and White, J. W. (1968). Cycocel for height control of fast-crop seedling geraniums. *Pa. Flower Growers Bull.* **203**, 4–5.

Holden, J., Umstead, J., Heldman, D., and Ball, V. (1977). Best of the new seed geraniums—4″ pots. *Grower Talks* **41**(4), 8–9.

Holland, R. (1975). Lee Valley EHS Trials reveal the right qualities for a good future in pachystachys. *Grower* **83**(14), 709.

Johansson, J. (1976). The regulation of growth and flowering in *Calceolaria xspeciosa* Lilja. *Acta Hortic.* **64**, 239–244.

Joiner, J. N., Gruenbeck, E. R., and Conover, C. A. (1977). Effects of shade and dwarfing compounds on growth and quality of *Pachystachys lutea*. *Fl. Flower Grower* **14**(5), 1–4.

Jones, L. K. (1944). Streak and mosaic of cineraria. *Phytopathology* **34**, 941–953.

Kamp, M., and Nightingale, A. E. (1977). Exacum a durable, low-maintenance crop. *Florists' Rev.* **161**(4171), 98–99.

Khan, M. A., and Maxwell, D. P. (1975). Identification of tobacco ringspot virus in *Clerodendrum thomsoniae*. *Phytopathology* **65**, 1150–1153.

Kingsbury, J. M. (1967). "Poisonous Plants of the United States and Canada." Prentice-Hall, Englewood Cliffs, New Jersey.

Kiplinger, D. C. (1973). Oedema on geraniums—a review. *Ohio Florists' Assoc. Bull.* **519**, 6–7.

Knauss, J. F. (1975). Control of basal stem and root rot of Christmas cactus. *Florida Flower Grower* **12**(12), 3.

Konjoian, P. S., and Tayama, H. K. (1978). Production schedules for seed geraniums. *Ohio Florists' Assoc. Bull.* **579**, 1–2.

Krause, W. (1974). Constant Nymph may have opened door for the easy launching of other varieties. *Grower* **81**(22), 1049.

Laurie, A., Kiplinger, D. C., and Nelson, K. S. (1969). "Commercial Flower Forcing," 7th Ed. McGraw-Hill, New York.

Lavsen, E. R. (1967). Vaekstretarderende stoffer til *Campanula isophylla*. *Gartner Tidende* **83**, 71.

Lawrence, W. J. C. (1957). Studies on streptocarpus. IV. Genetics of flower colour patterns. *Heredity* **11**(3), 337–357.

Lawrence, W. J. C., and Sturgess, V. C. (1957). Studies on streptocarpus. III. Genetics and chemistry of flower colour in the garden forms, species and hybrids. *Heredity* **11**(3), 303–336.

Linderman, R. G. (1971). Root rots; Thielaviopsis, In "Geraniums" (J. W. Mastalerz, ed.), pp. 221–227. Pennsylvania Flower Growers, University Park.

Lucas, R. (1977). New plant disease record. N.Z. J. Agric. Res. **20**, 253–254.

Marston, M. E. (1964). The morphology of a streptocarpus hybrid and its regeneration from leaf cuttings. Sci. Hortic. **17**, 114–120.

Mastalerz, J. W. (1967). Geraniums in six weeks. Pa. Flower Growers Bull. **193**, 1–2.

Mastalerz, J. W., ed. (1971) "Geraniums." Pennsylvania Flower Growers, University Park.

Maxie, E. C., Hasek, R. F., and Sciaroni, R. H. (1974). Keep potted roses cool. Flower Nursery Rep., Univ. Calif. March, pp. 9–10.

"Modern Roses" (1969). No. 7. Compiled by Int. Regist. Auth. Roses, Am. Rose Soc., McFarlane Co., Harrisburg, Pennsylvania.

Moe, R. (1970). Growth and flowering of potted roses as affected by temperature and growth retardants. Meld. Nor. landbrukshoegsk. **49**, 1–16.

Moe, R. (1973). Propagation, growth and flowering of potted roses. Acta Hortic. **31**, 35–50.

Moe, R. (1977a) Effect of light, temperature and CO_2 on the growth of Campanula isophylla stock plants and on the subsequent growth and development of their cuttings. Sci. Hortic. **6**, 129–141.

Moe, R. (1977b). Campanula isophylla Moretti culture—Cineraria—Calceolaria herbeohybrida Voss. Minn. State Florists' Bull. April, pp. 1–6.

Moes, E. (1976). Temperature til Pachystachys lutea. Gartner Tidende **92**(18), 269–270.

Nelson, P. E., Nichols, L. P., and Tammen, J. (1971). Vascular wilts, In "Geraniums" (J. W. Mastalerz, ed.), pp. 232–240. Pennsylvania Flower Growers, University Park.

Nichols, L. P., and Nelson, P. E. (1971). Root rots; pythium black leg, In "Geraniums" (J. W. Mastalerz, ed.), pp. 218–220. Pennsylvania Flower Growers, University Park.

Nilsen, J. H. (1975). Factors affecting flowering in regal pelargonium (Pelargonium xdomesticum Bail.). Acta Hortic. **51**, 299–309.

Noordegraaf, C. V., Kuip, J., and Sytsema, W. (1975). Gaat de Clerodendron een interessante potplant worden? Vakbl. Bloemisterij **30**(50), 14–15.

Norton, R. A. (1973). Stimulating earlier blooming of seed geraniums with high intensity lighting. Florists' Rev. **153**(3959), 25, 67–68.

Patch, F. W. (1977). It's Christmas every day for Cobia cacti. Florists' Rev. **161**(4177), 28.

Pedersen, A. M. (1975). Standarddyrkning af Pachystachys lutea Nees. Tidsskr. Planteavl **79**(4), 474–480.

Pedersen, A. M., Adriansen, E., and Moes, E. (1973). Forsög på Søhus med Pachystachys. Gartner Tidende **89**(45), 638–639.

Poesch, G. H. (1931). Forcing plants with artificial light. Proc. Am. Soc. Hortic. Sci. **28**, 402–406.

Poole, R. T. (1973). Flowering of Christmas cactus during the summer. HortScience **8**(3), 186.

Post, K. (1937). Further responses of miscellaneous plants to temperature. Proc. Am. Soc. Hortic. Sci. **34**, 627–629.

Post, K. (1942). Effects of daylength and temperature on growth and flowering of some florist crops. Cornell Agric. Exp. Stn., Bull. **787**, 1–10.

Pride, G. (1977). The Streptocarpus are coming. Horticulture **55**(1), 70–73.

Randolph, P. (1966). Geraniums - total crop time. Grower Talks **30**(1), 6–11.

Reiss, W. (1974). Calceolarias and cinerarias. Ohio Florists' Assoc. Bull. **537**, 2.

Rigdon, K., and Wolfram, N. (1976). May sowings. Grower Talks **39**(12), 27.

Roberts, R. H., and Struckmeyer, B. E. (1939). Further studies of the effects of temperature and other environmental factors upon the photoperiodic responses of plants. J. Agric. Res. **59**(9), 699–709.

Rogers, M. N. (1961). Increasing geranium yield. Florists' Rev. **128**(3325), 21–22, 78–79.

Rünger, W. (1961). Über den Einflub der temperatur und der tageslänge auf die blütenbildung von Zygocactus 'Weihnachtsfreude'. Gartenbauwissenschaft **26**, 529–536.

Rünger, W. (1968). Über den Einflub diurnal und einmal weckselnder temperatur während kurztag—und langtagperioden auf die blütenbildung von *Zygocactus* 'Weihnachtsfreude'. *Gartnerbauwissenschaft* **33**, 149–165.

Rünger, W. (1970). Einflub von temperatur und tageslänge auf die blütenentwicklung von *Zygocactus* 'Weihnachtsfreude'. *Gartenbauwissenschaft* **35**(17), 379–386.

Rünger, W. (1975). Flower formation in *Calceolaria* × *herbeohybrida* Voss. *Sci. Hortic.* **3**, 45–64.

Sachs, R. M., Kofranek, A. M., and Hackett, W. P. (1976). Evaluating new pot plant species. *Florists' Rev.* **159**(4116), 35–36, 80–84.

Sanderson, K. C., and Martin, W. C. (1975). Cultural concepts for growing *Clerodendrum Thomoniae* Balf. as a pot plant. *Proc. Fla. State Hortic. Soc.* **88**, 439–441.

Singh, S., Verma, V. S., and Padma, R. (1975). Studies on a mosaic disease of *Senecio cruentus* L. *Gartenbauwissenschaft* **40**(2), 67–68.

Skou, W. J. (1971). Scheduling, *In* "Geraniums" (J. W. Mastalerz, ed.), pp. 179–186. Pennsylvania Flower Growers, University Park.

Smith, D. R. (1969). Controlled flowering of *Primula malacoides*. *Exp. Hortic.* **20**, 22–34.

Tayama, H. K., and Poole, H. A. (1976). Extension slants—geranium production—the Mother's Day connection. *Ohio Florists' Assoc. Bull.* **555**, 9.

Tayama, H. K., Staby, G. L., Powell, C. C., and Lindquist, R. K. (1972). Extension slants—Pointers on geranium production. *Ohio Florists' Assoc. Bull.* **508**, 6.

Thompson, P. A. (1967). Germination of the seeds of natural species. *J. R. Hortic. Soc.* **92**, 400–406.

Thompson, P. A. (1969). Some effects of light and temperature on the germination of some *Primula* species. *J. Hortic. Sci.* **44**, 1–12.

Thorn-Horst, H., Horst, R. K., Smith, S. H., and Oglevee, W. A. (1977). A virus-indexing tissue culture system for geraniums. *Florists' Rev.* **160**(4148), 28–29, 72–74.

Turner, Y. J., and Heydecker, W. (1974). The germination of polyanthus seeds. *Seed Sci. Technol.* **2**, 293–303.

Vereecke, M. (1974). Chemical control of growth and flowering in *Clerodendrom thomsonae*, Balf. *Rijksuniversiteit, Gent* **39**(4), 1597–1602.

von Wachenfelt, M. A. (1968). Fusarium-rôta på *Campanula isophylla*. *Vaextskyddsnotiser* **32**, 45–49.

Wendzonka, P. (1978). Clerodendrum hanging baskets. *Focus Floric., Purdue Univ.* **6**(2), 6–7.

White, J. W. (1970). Effects of cycocel, moisture stress and pinching on growth and flowering of F_1 hybrid geraniums (*Pelargonium* × *hortorum* Bailey). *J. Am. Soc. Hortic. Sci.* **95**(5), 546–550.

White, J. W. (1975a). New and renewed pot plants—*Streptocarpus*. *Pa. Flower Growers Bull.* **279**, 3.

White, J. W. (1975b). Calceolarias—a year-round crop. *Pa. Flower Growers Bull.* **283**, 1, 6–9.

White, J. W., and Mastalerz, J. W. (1972). Geranium height control. *Pa. Flower Growers Bull.* **249**, 2–5.

Widmer, R. E., and Platteter, R. J. (1975). *Streptocarpus* (cape primrose) culture. *Minn. State Florists' Bull.* August, pp. 3–5.

Wikesjö, K. (1975). "Production Programs for Potplants and Cutflowers in Sweden," Hortic. Advis. Bull. No. 89. Agric. Coll., Alnarp, Sweden.

Wikesjö, K. (1976). Calceolarias for winter blooming. *Focus Floric., Purdue Univ.* **4**(3), 1–8.

Wilkins, H. F. (1974). Cineraria (*Senecio cruentus*). *Minn. State Florists Bull.* December, pp. 13–14.

Zeven, A. C. (1972). Inheritance of functional male sterility in streptocarpus Constant Nymph and its mutants. *Euphytica* **21**, 265–270.

Zimmer, K. (1969). Zur blütenbildung bei *Primula malacoides*. *Gartenwelt* **69**, 137–138.

19
Bedding Plants

William H. Carlson
and Edward M. Rowley

Introduction to Floriculture
Copyright © 1980 by Academic Press, Inc.
All rights of reproduction in any form reserved.
ISBN 0-12-437650-9

I. INTRODUCTION

The bedding plant industry has grown steadily for the last 35 years. A major factor in that growth has been the increased population and its expanding use of bedding plants. No other flower commodity has been as stable in its growth rate or in its demand by the consumer.

II. BEDDING PLANTS—A DEFINITION

The term, bedding plants, no longer applies only to those plants grown for planting into outdoor flower beds. Over the years it has been broadened to include any herbaceous plant that is primarily used in the home landscape. Flowering plants, herbs, ground covers, perennials, and small fruits—even some woody ornamentals—can be found in such a listing.

Today, the home landscape includes, in addition to garden beds, planters for porches, patios, and window boxes—both indoors and out. It even includes special artificially lighted indoor planters. The bedding plant grower supplies plants for all of these plantings.

Perhaps the best definition of a bedding plant would be, Any plant (usually herbaceous) that is started under controlled conditions and then purchased and grown by a home dweller. This definition includes widely different types such as tomatoes, strawberries, and garden chrysanthemums. It also differentiates between started plants and finished ones, such as fully flowered pot mums, poinsettias, or cut flowers.

III. HISTORY

A. Bedding Plants

There is no recorded history of the bedding plant industry and available information is scattered. Early bedding plant growers were probably vegetable growers or market gardeners who grew extra plants for consumer sale before field planting.

We do know that bedding plant growers have been in the United States for some time. Dutch gardeners were reported in 1655 to be growing lily flowers, pinks, wallflowers, stocks, sweet William, crown imperial (fritillaria), violets, marigolds, other flowers, and many kinds of vegetables. It is not known whether there was actually a bedding plant trade at this time, or if the colonists sowed their own seed for the many garden flowers they used.

According to Ball (1976) bedding plants were definitely part of early American horticulture. Many lovely gardens, such as the Williamsburg Palace Gardens in Virginia, attested to this. In 1789, Peter Crouwels of Philadelphia was advertising such obvious bedding plants as geranium, myrtle, sensitive plant, Jerusalem cherries, and passion flowers in pots.

Ball also stated Richard Morris (1825), a great early American gardener, suggested that tender plants, especially annuals, be raised in greenhouses and set outside when weather permitted. Plants suggested were ageratum, fuchsias, lobelia, calceolaria, heliotropes, zonal geraniums, *Phlox drummondi,* alyssum, begonias, and verbena.

A large market was provided by carpet bedding both before and after the Civil War. Patterns were created by mass areas of flowers or brightly colored foliage plants. To help create colorful effects, alternantheras, ageratum, and fibrous begonias were used, along with cacti, coleus, and feverfews. To these were added geraniums, iresine, and lobelias. Petunias were being used, as were scarlet salvias and heliotropes. Fuchsias, cannas, and ornamental grasses also made their contributions. To this varied list were added subtropical plants such as bananas, crotons, caladiums, castor beans, dracaenas, ferns, and palms.

Before 1870, the American florist business dealt mostly with outdoor bedding plants. By 1923, bedding plants were in great demand and a major source of income for flower growers. Pansies, forget-me-nots, and English daisies were among the types of hardy annuals recommended for early spring sales.

Kalamazoo County, Michigan, is today a leading bedding-plant-producing county in the United States. This leadership began in the early 1930s when vegetable growers started producing extra vegetable plants and some flowering annuals for sale. Marigolds and petunias were some of the first such flowering annuals. This type of experience was repeated in many areas near large population centers.

The use of evergreens and flowering shrubs apparently caused a decline in the demand for bedding plants in the 1920s and 1930s. However, this was offset by increased use of porch planters, window boxes, hanging baskets, and other containers. The trend away from flower beds was short-lived and by 1941 many people were looking for garden colors other than green.

Tremendous growth of the bedding plant industry occurred after World War II. The wholesale value of bedding plants increased 94%, from $16.9 million to $32.8 million, between 1949 and 1959. From 1959 to 1970 there was another 88% increase, to $61 million.

In 1970, the wholesale value for flowering bedding plants was $44,824,000 'and for vegetable plants was $16,803,000, a ratio of approximately 2.7 : 1. In 1970, bedding plants ranked second in value only to chrysanthemums ($119,621,000) in the nation's total commercial floriculture industry.

In 1976 the USDA Crop Reporting Board began to include bedding plants in its survey of 28 states. The report indicated that $94,094,000 worth of flower and vegetable plants were produced in 1976. This figure increased to $113,093,000 in 1977 (Table I). Other items often grown with bedding plants,

Table I

1977 Wholesale Values of Flowering, Foliar, and Vegetable Bedding Plants for the Ten States Leading in Production

State	Number of vegetable producers	Vegetable wholesale ($)	Number of flower and foliage producers	Flower and foliage wholesale ($)	Total wholesale
California	36	5,787,000	47	14,462,000	20,249,000
Michigan	303	3,881,000	336	10,928,000	14,809,000
Ohio	298	3,457,000	316	9,623,000	13,080,000
New York	333	2,116,000	353	4,742,000	6,858,000
Florida	9	843,000	16	4,075,000	4,918,000
Texas	32	2,134,000	38	2,480,000	4,614,000
Illinois	65	996,000	81	3,381,000	4,377,000
Minnesota	127	1,108,000	132	2,876,000	3,984,000
Pennsylvania	131	1,250,000	161	2,661,000	3,911,000
Massachusetts	174	959,000	201	2,793,000	3,752,000

such as strawberries, perennials, ground covers, and hanging baskets, were not included. The following statistics were given for the ten leading states (Voigt, 1976): impatiens, 20%; begonias, 13%; vegetables, 11%; geraniums, 11%; petunias, 11%; marigolds, 8%; and all others, less than 5%.

Table II gives a typical breakdown of species raised in 1973 and 1978 by wholesale growers in Michigan. The trends indicate a tremendous increase in impatiens, begonias, and coleus, dramatic decreases in petunia, and minor changes in other items. It must be stressed, however, that species mixes vary greatly from area to area.

B. Seeds

Flowering plants as we now know them did not exist three decades ago. Bedding plant history closely parallels that of the growth of the seed industry. The grower used seeds of new cultivars as they were developed. The most important of these, and the one that undoubtedly revolutionized the bedding plant industry, was the petunia.

Petunias were known as bedding plants as early as 1880. About this time Mrs. Theodosia Shepherd bred California Giant or Superbissima types which, because of large flower size, were the leading petunia types until the 1930s.

E. Benary of Erfurt, Germany, and T. Sakata of Yokahama, Japan, began introducing large-flowered, fringed types in 1930. As late as 1940, these petunias were still being grown from cuttings, as they did not come true from seed.

Seedsmen and plant breeders are to be commended for their relentless efforts to improve cultivars. Those such as 'Rosy Morn' and 'Elk's Pride' had

Table II

**The Percentage of Major Bedding Plant Species
Grown by Michigan Wholesale Growers**

Bedding plant species	1973	1978
Flowers		
Petunia	39.4	17
Begonia	3.7	10
Impatiens	1.6	10
Coleus	2.5	10
Marigolds	10.7	9
Salvia	6.0	5
Celosia	1.2	3
Ageratum	2.7	2
Portulaca	2.9	2
Alyssum	2.8	2
Verbena	1.4	2
Vinca	<1	2
Snapdragon	2.7	1
Zinnia	2.4	1
Pansy	<1	1
Aster	1.5	0.5
Vegetables		
Tomatoes	8.1	9
Cole crops	1.9	3.5
Peppers	3.5	6.5
Total	97.0 [a]	96.5 [b]

[a] In 1973 the remaining 3% was composed of balsam, dahlia, dianthus, lobelia, stock, dusty miller, and phlox.

[b] In 1978 the remaining 3.5% was composed of balsam, dahlia, lobelia, and several other flower items.

small flowers and poor growth habit, but the breeders persisted until they finally developed 'Fire Chief,' the first open-pollinated, light red, multiflora petunia. It was the All-America Selection (AAS) in 1950 and probably gave the bedding plant industry its greatest boost.

'Ballerina,' the first hybrid grandiflora, was an AAS in 1952. It was followed by 'Comanche' in 1953, as the first red multiflora hybrid. Both of these cultivars still enjoy popularity in many areas. It is interesting to note that Charles L. Weddle, Claude Hope, and other breeders were told that petunias would never make it. The seeds were considered much too expensive.

The development of petite, dwarf marigolds in 1958 gave the bedding plant industry another big push. 'First-Lady,' a semitall marigold, was another landmark in 1968. Since that time, the selection of all types of outstanding marigolds has proliferated. Seed-propagated geraniums have promoted the growth of the bedding plant industry during the 1970s. They are typified by the 'Sprinter' series, started in 1973. As new developments continue, these hybrid geraniums are beginning to challenge the domination of cutting–grown geranium production and many new hybrid cultivars are on the horizon.

Much skill and ingenuity have recently been invested in the improvement of begonias, impatiens, and zinnias. Garden mums can also be added to the list, as well as pansies and snapdragons. Not to be overlooked are the many new developments in tomatoes, melons, and other vegetables.

All these improved varieties would not be available commercially, however, without the ability of seedsmen to produce quality seed at a reasonable cost. Again, it is a situation where the seed and bedding plant industries have worked together.

Perhaps as important as the history of growing plants is the history of the evolution of containers and growing media. Both are closely linked to modern technology. Although the variety of growing containers still ranges from a plot of ground to plastic cell packs, modern methods can be credited for much of the growth in the bedding plant industry. Plastic containers have brought us into a new era.

IV. BEDDING PLANT FAMILIES

For purposes of identification, plants are designated as cultivars. For example, a red petunia would have a cultivar name, such as 'Comanche,' whereas a white one has another cultivar name, such as 'La Paloma.' All the different cultivars of petunia would compose a species. The common garden petunia comes from the species known as *hybrida,* which is what might be designated as a hybrid species, obtained from crossing two original species. *Hybrida*, along with other species, comprise a genus. One who deals with bedding plants seldom encounters a need for classifications more general than family. In fact, genus is usually sufficient.

The meaning of the word "cultivar" varies. With tomatoes, for example, the term is used to designate various types in the species *esculentum.* These include the varieties *cerasiforme* (cherry tomato), *commune* (common garden tomato), *grandifolium* (potato-leaved), and *pyriforme* (pear tomato). Then, with disregard for strict use of terms, the cultivar *commune* is divided into different garden cultivars, such as 'Marglobe,' 'Bonny Best,' and 'Pritchard.' The foregoing discussion is simply intended to remind the reader of inconsistencies sometimes encountered in horticultural naming.

Named cultivars are sometimes further divided into strains. For example, an improved strain that has shorter stems and is more disease resistant has been selected from plantings of the tomato cultivar, Marglobe. An improved strain of a cultivar may have larger or more intensely colored flowers, less conspicuous seed pods, more uniform fruit, or any number of other characteristics which may be considered desirable.

Seventy species represent the bulk of bedding plants sold, but 250 species contribute overall. The 70 species represent 25 plant families. Those 25 families follow in alphabetical order, with a representative plant from that family indicated first.

1. Celosia—Anyone who has observed seed from the common pigweed will see a close resemblance in celosia seed. Both belong to the family Amaranthaceae, which also includes gomphrena and amaranthus.

2. Carrot—This family is most important for its herbs, condiments, and vegetables. Designated as Apiaceae (Umbelliferae by earlier classifications), it contains bedding plants such as celery, dill, and parsley.

3. Vinca (periwinkle)—The Apocynaceae includes the creeping myrtle (*Vinca minor*) and the *Vinca rosea* cultivars that are actually perennial but are grown mostly as tender annuals where freezing temperatures occur. Also included in this family are tropical plants such as oleander and *Plumeria.*

4. Aster—The family Asteraceae (Compositae by earlier designation) includes so many bedding plant types that it is difficult to select a single representative. However, the members of this second-largest plant family have a common characteristic—flower heads usually composed of many smaller flowers. The heads contain one or both of two types of flowers. The disk flowers are like those found in the eye of the black-eyed Susan and the ray flowers are like those in the yellow fringe on the same flower head. Asteraceae heads can have disk flowers only, such as ageratum; ray flowers only, such as chicory; or both disk and ray flowers, such as the daisy. Bedding plants in the Asteraceae include African daisy, ageratum, aster, chrysanthemum, cornflower, cosmos, dahlia, dusty miller, gaillardia, lettuce, marigold, calendula, strawflower, zinnia, and cineraria.

5. Impatiens—This is the only significant bedding plant in the family Balsaminaceae. There is, however, one species called balsam. *Impatiens* is a genus name. The common balsam is called *Impatiens balsamina.* Today's hybrid impatiens have come from *Impatiens holstii* and *sultani* and their hybrids—thus, the common name, "Sultana."

6. Begonias—Begonias have the same name as their genus, the only genus of horticultural use in the family Begoniaceae. Both tuberous and fibrous-rooted types are included. Although those with showy flowers are preferred, when begonias are used as bedding plants, some types are grown mainly for their attractive foliage.

7. Forget-me-not—This is in the family Boraginaceae. Mostly herbs, including borage, are found in this family.

8. Cabbage—This is in the family Brassicaceae (Cruciferae by an earlier classification). It is economically important because of the many food plants, condiments, ornamentals, and weeds found therein. Bedding plant members

of this family include alyssum, broccoli, brussels sprouts, cabbage, candytuft, cauliflower, collard, and stocks. The so-called flowering cabbage and kale also fit into this family.

9. Cleome—Cleome is probably the only bedding plant member of the family Capparidaceae—Most members are trees, shrubs, or climbing plants.

10. Carnation—Also included in the family Caryophyllaceae are garden pinks, various other forms of dianthus and baby's breath (Gypsophila).

11. Morning glory—Convolvulaceae is the name of this family. Most important is the genus *Ipomea,* which includes morning glory, sweet potato, and wood rose. The genus *Dichondra* is also in this family.

12. Cucumber—The Cucurbitaceae is economically important as a source of many food and ornamental plants. Melons, gourds, and squash are also in this family.

13. Sweet peas—A large family with but few bedding plant members is Fabaceae (Leguminosae). It includes many trees, shrubs, herbs, and vines. Besides sweet pea, possible candidates for bedding plants include garden peas, crown vetch, peanuts, beans, shamrock, and lupines.

14. Geraniums—Geranaceae is this family name. It includes the genus *Pelargonium,* to which belong all forms of geranium, ivy geranium, and Martha Washington geranium.

15. Coleus—The family Lamiaceae (Labiatae) includes many useful herbs such as basil, marjoram, mints, sage, and thyme. An important flowering member is salvia. Bells of Ireland, lavender, the popular "Swedish ivy" or "Creeping Charlie" (*Plectranthus australis*), and other *Plectranthus* species used for foliage belong to this family.

16. Lilies—The many forms of lilies, tulips, and hyacinths are in the family Liliaceae. It also includes chives, garlic, and onions in the subfamily Alliodeae, genus *Allium.*

17. Lobelia—Lobeliaceae is the name of this family.

18. Fuchsias—These belong to the family Onagraceae, as do clarkia and godetia.

19. Phlox—This is included in the Polemoniaceae, which also includes *phlox subulata* or moss pink.

20. Portulaca—Portulacaceae is this family's name, with moss rose probably the only important bedding plant.

21. Snapdragon—Foxgloves are also in this family, which is called Scrophulariaceae.

22. Petunia and tomato—The family Solanaceae is of great economic importance and includes potatoes, tobacco, tomatoes, petunias, browallia, eggplant, nicotiana, peppers, and salpiglossis.

23. Nasturtium—This is in the small family Tropaeolaceae.

24. Verbena—The family Verbenaceae also includes lantana.

25. Pansy—The relatively small family of the Violaceae includes pansies, violas, and sweet violets.

The families listed on p. 485 are only the major ones from which bedding plants are grown. Many plants from other families are either being grown, experimented with or should be experimented with to be used as bedding plants. Remember also that bedding plants in California and Florida have a wider scope than they do in northern areas.

V. PLANNING FOR FUTURE CROPS

The plan for next year should begin with the current year's production. Beginning growers will depend upon the experience of others until sufficient personal experience is accumulated. Since personal experience is best, a good record should be kept of planting dates, quantities, germination times, special problems, and observations. Notebooks should also be kept in locations where important information can be recorded by employees. From all this information a complete, permanent record should be established to plan for future crops. Future planning includes the ordering of seed and supplies, such as containers, labels, and growing mix or its ingredients.

A seed-ordering chart could have a wide column down one side for listing cultivars. Small columns could include (1) number of containers (flats, packs, or pots) grown; (2) number dumped; (3) number planned; (4) quantity of seed needed; (5) seed on hand (properly stored and tested); (6) quantity to order; (7) source of seed; (8) amount of seed actually ordered; and (9) date ordered. Special conditions will determine the number of columns and their headings for each grower. Information on number of flats grown should come from daily transplanting records.

Study quantities per ounce of seed to determine needs. Many wholesale catalogs indicate average seeds per ounce for each type of plant. Determine how many plants can be expected from a given quantity. For example, at 80% yield of usable seedlings, 1/64 ounce of petunia seed at 256,000 seeds per ounce, would yield $256,000 \times 1/64 \times 0.80 = 3200$ plants. Thirty two hundred plants at 72 plants per flat would yield $3200 \div 72 = 44$ flats plus 32 plants. Similar calculations can be made for other types. For petunias it would be wise to obtain a chart of seeds per ounce (available from seed companies) since there is considerable variation. Depending on cultivar, at 80% usable seedlings, 1/64 ounce of petunia seed could yield from 32 to 72 flats, each containing 72 plants.

Growing space will determine the number of seed to order. Apportion the space to various types of plants according to the market. Some plants must be kept inside during freezing weather. Others can tolerate some frost. Therefore, petunias, pansies, onions, snapdragons, asters, cabbage, and many perennials can be moved into cold frames after they are started. This makes space inside greenhouses for starting more plants. Knowledge of the number of flats that can be moved out by certain dates will aid in planning both the seed order and planting schedule.

For planning purposes, 1 yard of growing medium can be considered to fill approximately 1000 10-cm standard round pots; 260 standard round 15-cm pots; 160 25-cm round hanging baskets; 140 flats of 4–8 cell packs (28 cm × 56 cm flats); 160 flats of 6–12 cell packs; 170 flats of 12–8 cell packs and 160 28 cm × 56 cm plastic germination flats.

A planning calendar with large spaces can be used to plan the work of the season. Expected arrival dates of all cuttings, plants, bulbs, etc., should be recorded. Seed sowing dates and quantities should be on this schedule. Each week for the entire year should be scheduled. This procedure will ensure better preparation when materials arrive and planting must be done.

The person responsible for ordering should be aware that most things must be ordered far in advance, even up to 1 year for some supplies.

VI. PROPAGATION

With few exceptions, most bedding plants are now started from seed. The most notable exceptions are geraniums (however, seed-grown geraniums are on the increase), chrysanthemums, some perennials, ground covers, and small fruits. This discussion will be confined to seed propagation.

It is important that fresh, high-quality seed be used for a high-quality crop. Lower-cost seed should be tried on a small scale. Cost of seed is often determined by the extent to which they are cleaned, selected, and stored for best quality. Naturally, this extra care will bring up the cost.

Seed should be the best that can be purchased. The best cultivars of flowers come from hybrid seed. This is also generally true for vegetables. While these are higher priced than nonhybrids, the results obtained by the consumer will warrant the expense. Market demand will determine the advisability of growing favored old cultivars. Many people order old cultivars mainly because they are not familiar with newer ones. The best cultivars should be chosen based on personal observations of their performance at field trials and in local gardens.

A. Seed Storage

Ideally, a grower will calculate the exact amount of seed needed for a season with none left to be stored for the following year. However, this is not always practical. Unexpected germination percentages, disease, and market conditions will alter seed requirements.

When seed must be stored from one year to the next, most will be usable if stored at proper temperature and humidity. Harrington (1968) recommends that the temperature in degrees Fahrenheit plus the relative humidity in percent should not exceed 100. Thus, at 50°F storage, relative humidity should not exceed 50%; at 60°F, relative humidity should be no more than 40%, etc. Store seed in a cool location—about 50°F—and in glass containers that are airtight and rodent proof.

Some seed can be kept viable for many months or years (Table III). Other seed can lose viability in a year and should not be saved. Among these are columbine, aster, cornflower, cleome, delphinium, kochia, larkspur, linum, lunaria, *phlox*, salvia, torenia, verbena, periwinkle, and viola.

A germination test will indicate the viability of stored seed. One such method is given below:

1. Count out an exact number of seed . . . 50, 100, etc.
2. Place seed between two pieces of blotting paper, paper towel, or soft muslin. A plastic container makes a good growth chamber.
3. Moisten the seed and maintain temperature at 18°–24°C.
4. When the seed germinates, count the seedlings to determine percentage of germination. Do this by dividing the number of seed sown into the number of seeds germinated.
5. If germination is poor, below 60%, it will probably not be worth the time and effort to germinate the seed.
6. If germination is fairly good, sow more seed than is needed to make up for the poorer percentage.

When using stored seed, plan well in advance to determine its worth. Counting on seed that will have a poor percentage of germination, or will not germinate at all, can be disastrous. Many customers will not understand this lack of planning and profits could be lost. Quality seed is basic to a quality crop.

B. Scheduling

Sowing dates depend upon market dates, as well as location. Because of great variations in plant growth and bloom dates due to environment, sowing schedules cannot be determined on a national scale. Conditions vary from year to year even in one location. Early springs and rainy spells can upset schedules. At best, a schedule cannot ensure complete correlations between sowing and marketing, but it can significantly reduce the uncertainty.

The sowing schedule also depends upon whether plants are to be sold green or in bloom. If the market will stand it, considerable greenhouse time can be saved by marketing a crop green. It may be worthwhile to educate customers on the desirability of using green plants, a major advantage being more extensive branching without pinching. There is also less transplant shock on account of overgrown or interlaced roots which must be broken for transplanting. Smaller plants with better air circulation also reduce disease problems in the greenhouse. Although there are significant advantages in marketing a

Table III

Seed Information and Production Schedule for Selected Annuals[a]

Common name	Scientific name	Approximate seeds per 28 gm	Germination light requirement	Germination soil temperature (°C)	Germination time (days)
Flowers					
African daisy	Dimorphotheca aurantiaca	10,000	D	16–21	7–15
Ageratum	Ageratum houstonianum	210,000	L	21–27	5
Alyssum	Lobularia maritima	80,000	D or L	21	5–14
Amaranthus	Amaranthus tricolor	45,000	D or L	21–24	8–10
Aster	Callistephus chinensis	12,000	D or L	21–27	8–12
Baby's breath	Gypsophila elegans	25,000	D or L	21–27	10–14
Begonia (fiberous)	Begonia × semperflorens-cultorum	2,000,000	L	21–24	14–21
Begonia (tuberous)	Begonia × tuberhybrida	2,000,000	L	18	15–20
Browallia	Browallia speciosa	125,000	L	21–24	7–10
Candytuft	Iberis coronaria	9,500	D or L	21	7–14
Celosia (crested)	Celosia cristata (crested group)	28,000	D or L	21–27	8–10
Celosia (feathered)	Celosia cristata (plumosa group)	28,000	D or L	21–27	6–10
Chinese forget-me-not	Cynoglossum amabile	5,000	D	16–21	5–10
Clarkia	Clarkia elegans	90,000	L	18–21	5–14
Cleome	Cleome spinosa	12,500	D or L	16°N–29°D	7–21
Coleus	Coleus blumei	112,000	L	18–24	10–15
Cornflower	Centaurea cyanus	7,000	D	18–21	10–15
Cosmos	Cosmos bipinnatus	5,000	L	21–24	5–14
Dahlia	Dahlia pinnata	3,000	D or L	18–24	5–10
Dusty miller	Centaurea candidissima	10,000	D	16–18	10–15
Dusty miller	Cineraria maritima	90,000	L	24	10–15
Forget-me-not	Myosotis aplestris	44,000	D	13	10–14
Gaillardia	Gaillardia pulchella	15,000	L	21–27	15–20

(Continued)

Table III (*Continued*)

Common name	Scientific name	Approximate seeds per 28 gm	Germination light requirement	Germination soil temperature (°C)	Germination time (days)
Garden pinks	*Dianthus chinensis*	25,000	D or L	21	5–7
Geranium	*Pelargonium hortorum*	6,200	L	21–24	5–12
Gomphrena	*Gomphrena globosa*	5,000	D	21–27	14–20
Impatiens	*Impatiens holstii and I. sultana*	52,000	L	21–24	15–18
Lobelia	*Lobelia erinus*	725,000	D or L	21–24	14–20
Marigold (African)	*Tagetes erecta*	10,000	D or L	21–27	5–8
Marigold (French)	*Tagetes patula*	10,000	D or L	21–27	5–8
Morning Glory	*Ipomoea purpurea*	1,000	D or L	27	7–14
Moss rose	*Portulaca grandiflora*	280,000	D or L	27	7–14
Nasturtium	*Tropaeolum major*	175	D	18	10–15
Nicotiana	*Nicotiana alata*	200,000	L	21	7–14
Pansy	*Viola tricolor*	20,000	D	18	10–20
Periwinkle	*Catharanthus roseus*	21,000	D	21–24	14–21
Petunia	*Petunia hybrida*	280,000	L	21–27	4–10
Phlox	*Phlox drummondii*	14,000	D	18	10–15
Pot marigold	*Calendula officinalis*	3,000	D	21–27	5–10
Salpiglossis	*Salpiglossis sinuata*	125,000	D	21–24	14–21
Salvia	*Salvia splendens*	7,500	L	21	14–21
Satinflower	*Godetia grandiflora*	100,000	L	16	15
Snapdragon	*Antirrhinum majus*	180,000	L	18–21	7–14

Stock	*Mathiola incana*	18,500	21	L	7-10
Strawflower	*Helichrysum bracteatum*	45,000	21-27	D or L	5-14
Sweet Peas	*Lathyrus odoratus*	400	13-16	D	14-35
Verbena	*Verbena hybrida*	10,000	18	D	14-20
Zinnia	*Zinnia elegans*	2,500 [b]	21-27	D or L	5-10
Vegetables					
Broccoli	*Brassica oleracea italica*	9,000	20-30	D or L	3-10
Brussels sprouts	*Brassica oleracea gemmifera*	9,000	20-30	D or L	3-10
Cabbage	*Brassica oleracea capitata*	9,000	20-30	D or L	3-10
Cantaloupe	*Cucumis melo reticulatus*	1,200	20-30	D or L	4-10
Cauliflower	*Brassica oleracea botrytis*	9,000	20-30	D or L	3-10
Celery	*Apium graveolens*	72,000	18-21	L	10-21
Collard	*Brassica oleracea acephala*	4,500	20-30	D or L	3-10
Cucumbers	*Cucumis sativus*	1,000	20-30	D or L	3-7
Eggplant	*Solanum melongena esculentum*	6,000	20-30	D or L	10-14
Lettuce (head)	*Lactuca sativa*	25,000	20-21	L	5-7
Lettuce (leaf)	*Lactuca sativa*	25,000	20-21	L	5-7
Onions	*Allium cepa*	9,000	20	D or L	6-10
Peppers	*Capsicum frutescens*	4,500	20-30	D or L	6-14
Squash (summer)	*Cucurbita pepo melopepo*	400	20-30	D or L	4-7
Tomatoes	*Lycopersicum esculentum*	9,500	20-30	D or L	5-14
Watermelon	*Citrullus vulgaris*	300	20-30	D or L	4-14

[a] The information in this table was compiled from "Bedding Plant Information Chart" (1977) and Dietz (1976).
[b] Seed count varies greatly.

green crop, most bedding plants are marketed in flower and it is the instant color that sells the crop.

Temperature is one factor that can be controlled in working with a schedule. Table III indicates ideal soil temperatures for germination and growing of some of the most widely grown flowering annuals and vegetables. Variations in temperature will cause variations in times. Note that by temperature, we mean temperature in the soil, not the air in the greenhouse. A thermostat placed at eye level will not be an accurate indicator of temperature in the flat. Soil thermometers are needed to keep proper temperatures and to maximize germination percentages.

The desired selling date can be used to establish a general sowing date by counting back the number of days to flower or to sale time. Caution must be exercised in taking these guidelines as absolute. Any number of environmental factors can alter this timing. Actual growing experience and good record keeping of dates and time for growing will bring the guidelines down to specifics for a specific geographic area.

C. Germination Media

A good germination medium can be made by mixing field soil with other ingredients, such as peat moss, vermiculite, or perlite. One can also mix ingredients to prepare a completely artificial mix containing no soil. A number of commercially prepared soilless mixes are available. The medium should be well aerated and well drained and should also hold some water and be loose enough to prevent excess damage to roots when seedlings are removed. Either the medium should contain sufficient nutrients to feed the developing seedlings or they be given regular applications of a dilute fertilizer after germination. However, do not use germination media high in fertility. This procedure may result in soluble salts damage and poor seedling growth.

The following soil mixtures can be used in germinating all bedding plants: (1) 1 part loamy soil, 1 part peat, 1 part sand, perlite, or vermiculite; (2) 1 part loamy soil, 1 part peat, 2 parts sand; (3) 1 part soil, 2 parts humus, 1 part sand or perlite; (4) 1 part soil, 2 parts peat, 1 part perlite; (5) 2 parts soil, 2 parts peat, 1 part perlite; (6) 2 parts soil, 1 part peat, 1 part perlite; (7) Straight sand— dilute fertilizer is necessary immediately after germination.

Some soilless mixtures which have been successfully used are (1) straight vermiculite; (2) straight perlite; (3) 50% peat, 50% perlite, or vermiculite; (4) commercially prepared mixes; (5) Cornell mix: (a) shredded German or Canadian sphagnum peat (0.035 m³); (b) Vermiculite No. 4 particle size 0.035 m³; (c) ammonium nitrate (42.6 gm); (d) 20% powdered superphosphate (85 gm); (e) dolomitic limestone (105 gm). If ammonium nitrate is not used in this mix, soak containers after sowing in a solution made of 226.8 gm ammonium nitrate/ 378.5 liters of water. Allow the mix to drain and use plain water for all other waterings. This mix is for germination only. Mixes used for transplants will be discussed later in this section.

A good germination medium should be free of weeds, insects, and diseases. It should be thoroughly mixed to provide a proper balance of moisture and air. If it holds too much water, the seeds will rot. If it does not hold enough water, the seeds may dry out and fail to germinate. The pH of the medium should be between 5.5 and 7.0 and the K value of soluble salts, when mixed 1 : 2 with distilled water, should be less than 80.

Selecting the medium that is best for an operation depends upon economic factors, availability, specific cultural practices, and experimentation. Never forget the importance of trying procedures on a small scale before investing money and time in them for full-scale use.

D. Soil and Seed Flat Sterilization

The importance of sterile growing mix and containers cannot be overemphasized. Sterilization can prevent many weed and disease problems. Good sanitation practices before sowing the seed can save time and money as the season progresses.

Steaming is the most satisfactory method of sterilizing. The media should be steamed at 82°C in the coldest spot for 30 minutes. Some growers are using aerated steam at 71°C for 30 minutes. Steaming on a large scale usually is done in specialized dump trucks or steam wagons. There are several commercial models available.

Various methods of steam sterilization are used by smaller growers. One method is to mount a cabinet above a 75.7- or 113.6-liter drum. The cabinet is about 1.05 m² (inside measurements) and is lined with sheet metal. The drum, filled with water is mounted over a gas burner from a discarded water heater. Wooden flats filled with the soil mix are stacked on a rack over the water. A thermometer is inserted through a hole in the top of the cabinet and into the soil mix in one of the top flats. A metal-lined door is secured on the front of the cabinet and the gas burner is lighted. After the thermometer reads 82°C the temperature is maintained for 30 minutes before the heat is turned off and the door is opened. Remember, however, plastic flats cannot be steamed.

Electric sterilizers are also available. Consult greenhouse supply catalogs for sterilizing equipment.

Several chemicals are also employed for sterilizing soil; however, methyl bromide is the most commonly used in the bedding plant business. Salvia and carnations should not be grown in soil treated with methyl bromide, as damage will occur. The germination of seed of ageratum, alyssum, antirrhinum, aster, calendula, celosia, chrysanthemum, cleome, coleus, coreopsis, datura, dianthus, digitalis, godetia, helichrysum, iberis, lobelia, matricaria, myosotis, nemesia, nierembergia, portulaca, salpiglossis, verbena, viola, and vinca has also been reduced when planted in methyl bromide-treated soil. Therefore, it is best to use steaming methods whenever possible.

Tools and flats used in germination should be disinfested. The disinfestant LF-10 (available through supply catalogs) can be used when mixed with water

1:50, soaking flats and tools for 10 minutes. Clorox or a similar product can also be used, diluted 1:10, soaking for 30 minutes.

Before used flats are dipped in the disinfesting solution, they should be washed with water from a pressure nozzle to remove soil particles. New flats, taken from their original packages, may be clean enough without disinfesting.

Warm, humid conditions in the greenhouse are ideal for disease to thrive. Problems can be prevented through sanitation practices. If diseases occur despite precautions, immediate corrective measures should be taken, such as treating infested areas with fungicides.

E. Soil Testing

When soil is used in a mix, it should be free of herbicides. Before deciding to use soil from a field where herbicides may have been used, conduct a sample test. If the soil still contains weed killers, it should not be used.

It is a good practice to send a soil sample to a local testing laboratory long before seed are to be sown. The main tests to be concerned with are those for pH and soluble salts. High salt content may require leaching of the soil in flats before sowing. If it is extremely high, perhaps a new source should be sought. Use of proper amendments can alter pH to a desirable level. Limestone can be used to raise pH and acids or acid-producing substances can lower it.

While the soil is being tested, analyses should also be made for nitrogen, potassium, phosphorus, calcium, and magnesium.

It is easier to change soils or to take corrective measures before the medium is in the flat. Most problems discovered after seed have germinated result in malformed plants that cannot be salvaged.

It is also wise to test soil with a seed germination test, especially if one is unfamiliar with the source. Take samples from five or six different locations in the soil pile. Make two portions from each sample, moistening the soil before placing it in the containers. Sow beans approximately 2.5 cm deep in one set of containers and tomato seeds about 0.5 cm inch deep in the second set. Now there will be two kinds of seed planted in each soil sample. All samples should be numbered. Germinate the seeds at 16°–21°C, keeping the soil moist. Within 1 week seeds should have germinated. They should be kept until the second set of true leaves appear. If there are malformed seedlings, further testing might be warranted.

Remember, it is important to test the soil *before* the crop is affected.

F. Seed Sowing

Before being sown, seeds can be treated with a light covering of fungicide. Thiram, captan, chloranil, or dichlone are most often used. Three millimeters of powder on the tip of a knife will coat an entire packet of seeds. Put the fungicide into the packet, close the packet, and shake it vigorously. Some seed is already treated when purchased and should not be treated again.

Another practice is to drench the flat with an appropriate fungicide either before or after the seeds are sown and covered. If the effects of fungicides on germinating seeds are unknown, prior testing should be done.

Flats should be thoroughly watered after they have been filled level with the top and before seeds are sown. It may be desirable to mark rows for sowing before watering. If rows are marked first, watering should be done carefully to avoid washing away the row marks. The marks can also be made after the soil is wet, if it is allowed to set for a while.

Seeds can be sown in rows, by broadcasting, or directly with mechanical seeders. When sowing in rows, make a crease down one flat side of the seed packet to form a trough for lining up the seeds in a single row. Seed can be sown by tapping the edge of the packet with a finger while the packet is moved along the row. Vibrating seeders can also be used. Some homemade types have been created from electric razors.

Avoid sowing too thickly, as thinning is very time-consuming and most seeds are very expensive. Do not put more seeds into the sowing container than are intended to be sown in one flat. A general rule followed by many growers is to plant no more than enough seed to produce 1000 seedlings in each 28 × 56-cm flat. Experience will help determine the best methods and amounts.

When growing geraniums from seed, it is best to space the seed so there are no more than 200 in one flat. On the other hand, some growers sow seeds of tomato and other nonspreading type plants much thicker. Up to 4000 tomatoes or peppers can be germinated in one flat, but they must be transplanted soon after emerging, or kept cool. Fertilizer should not be used in the sowing medium.

Before seeds are sown for each cultivar, the flats for that cultivar should be isolated so other flats will not be contaminated with these seeds. The smaller seeds can fly into an adjacent flat without one being aware of it.

The main advantage to sowing in rows is to help avoid damping off or its spread. Space between rows allows better air circulation. If disease does occur, it will usually spread lengthwise down the row. It can be controlled by treating the diseased section with a small amount of fungicide mixed with water in a plastic squeeze bottle. Always shake the mixture before applying it and overlap the treatment into the healthy plants. They may have already been infested.

All that is needed for row sowing is a depression distinct enough to use as a guide. A shallow depression will avoid caving in of the medium on the seeds, thus covering them too deeply. In fact, it is possible to sow in rows with no marks. A ruler or marked stick can be placed across each end of a flat and used as a guide.

Planting in rows also makes digging easier for transplanting. Another advantage is prevention of crowding and, if some areas have been overplanted, seedlings can crowd into spaces between rows, minimizing loss due to unusable seedlings.

If seeds are to be broadcast, divide those for each flat into equal parts. Use the first half to sow the entire flat. Then spread the second half over the entire flat, but at right angles to the first. This procedure ensures the best distribution. Broadcasting can be done by hand, but many growers use salt and pepper shakers. Depending upon seed size, some of the holes can be covered with masking tape to control the flow of seeds.

When using a vibrator, shaker, or any common container for different cultivars of seed, always clean out all seed before using the container for another cultivar to avoid mixed cultivars.

Direct sowing is gaining acceptance by many growers. It is used mainly with inexpensive seed and with types that can stand several plants in one clump. Types commonly sowed this way are alyssum, portulaca, ageratum, and lobelia.

Mechanical or vacuum seeders are also available for the highly mechanized grower. Seeders have different size plates for various seed sizes. This is a direct sowing method and eliminates transplanting. However, thinning may be needed after germination with some types of plants.

After the seeds are sown, they should be covered with some unfertilized medium. Even those requiring light for germination can be covered, if the particles used for covering are coarse enough to form spaces for light passage. This way the seeds can be kept more uniformly moist. Vermiculite, with particles no larger than 0.3 cm in diameter, is good to use for the light-requiring species. Some growers use it to cover all seeds, covering the darkness-demanding ones a little deeper. Coverings should never be deeper than twice the thickness of the seed when fine material is used. Coarse vermiculite will naturally make the covering thicker in some spots, but seedlings can usually move to the side and emerge through spaces between the particles.

Geranium seeds should be covered deeply enough to hold them down as they germinate. This depth might be 0.6 cm or more, depending upon the weight of the coverings. If seeds are not held down, root growth may push the seedlings above the surface with the seed leaves, resulting in poor-quality seedlings.

Another advantage of covering with vermiculite is that it absorbs water readily. Therefore, it can be watered more heavily than other materials without washing seed around.

Many growers cover their seed flats with glass or polyethylene to retain moisture and to create small growth chambers. These are raised above the surface of the flat. Burlap and newspaper are also sometimes used, but these coverings do inhibit light to seed that require light for germination. One caution is that the temperature under the coverings should be monitored closely,

especially on hot days. Reduced air circulation in combination with sun re-
flected through the glass or polyethylene can raise temperatures and literally
cook the seeds and seedlings.

Coverings can be removed when the first seedlings appear. With glass
coverings, lift them gradually so seedlings are conditioned to air and sun.

G. Conditions for Germination

After the seeds are sown, ideal conditions should be maintained as nearly as
possible. Remember that seeds need heat, air, and water to germinate. Some
also require light.

It is desirable to place seeded flats in a slightly shaded location, free from
drafts. Maintain adequate soil temperatures constantly. This is best accomplished with some form of bottom heat.

Although optimum germination temperatures vary from one crop to another,
an average of 21°–24°C soil temperature is sufficient for most seed. It is often
impractical to attempt to provide many temperatures. However, to allow for
some extreme cases, warmer temperatures can be attained by locating flats
closer to the heat source or by enclosing them in a plastic tent with supplemental heat. Cooler temperatures can be achieved by isolating flats behind plastic
curtains next to an outside wall and raising or lowering the curtain to adjust the
temperature. There are probably just about as many methods as there are
growers.

More and more, growers are beginning to use controlled growth chambers.
These are enclosed cabinets where the entire environment from light to water
and temperature is automatically controlled. They do have advantages in that
the environment is ideal, regardless of outside conditions. Germination tends to
be more uniform and faster. Initial costs and operating costs, however, prevent
many growers from converting to these systems.

Seeds must not dry out during germination. A light watering every 6 hours will
prevent drying out, if a vermiculite covering is used. It may not be necessary to
water that often, depending upon the heating system used. Fan-forced air
heating systems cause drying to occur faster than steam or hot water heat. The
mist system should not be so saturated that air cannot enter the growing
medium. Hand watering with a hose must be done very carefully. Too strong a
spray may wash out, cover too deeply, or uncover seeds, and may throw seeds
into a neighboring flat that is sown with a different cultivar or species.

After seedlings emerge, it is desirable to allow the surface of the medium to
dry out occasionally, provided roots are sufficiently well established to draw
water from below. This drying helps discourage diseases, but the medium
must not remain dry too long. Seedlings must be watched carefully at this
stage. If they dry out to the wilting point, they may not recover.

Efforts to produce begonia seedlings may be more successful if exceptions are made to some of the previous suggestions. Begonias develop roots slowly and the seedlings are extremely small. Hand watering, unless a mist nozzle is used, can move them easily and may cover them. If the surface dries at all, seedlings may perish. Extra watering encourages disease.

Prepare the planting medium for begonias in a flat that is deep enough to allow about 2.5 cm of space between the surface and the top of the flat. It is advantageous to put a unit of six plastic packs in the flat first. The divisions can be used to support a plastic cover. After leveling the soil in each pack, saturate it with water. When excess water has drained away, drench the soil with a fungicide to prevent damping off. Each pack can be seeded with the same or different cultivars. Use extra care in sowing to avoid clumping of the seed.

After sowing, cover the flat with a sheet of plastic wrap. It may be necessary to insert identifying labels on a slant so they will not protrude above the top. Place the flat in a location where temperature will not go below 21°C. Temperatures no lower or higher than 18°C will produce the best results for tuberous begonias.

Watch for first seedlings of fibrous begonias about 6 days after sowing. Tuberous begonias will take 9 to 10 days. When seedlings are first observed, they should be fertilized. Use a flat or other container that will hold water and into which the seed flat will fit. Pour in a solution of complete fertilizer that has been mixed at half the strength of the recommended foliage application rate. Set the seed flat into this solution and leave it until the surface of the medium appears wet. After this first fertilizer treatment, place the flat under a special plant-growing fluorescent light. Although not essential, this step hastens growth considerably, especially that of tuberous begonias. The light can be left on constantly.

Each time the surface of the medium begins to dry out, repeat the fertilizer treatment. If this treatment were applied over an extended period, soluble salts might reach undesirable levels, but begonia seedlings will be transplanted before that occurs.

About the time the third leaf shows on some of the seedlings, remove the plastic cover. Lay clean wooden pot labels or other clean small sticks across the packs so they protrude past the edges of the flat. Cover the flat again with a new piece of plastic wrap. Fasten the plastic only at the ends and the cross pieces will hold it up enough to provide ventilation. Leave the new cover on until seedlings are large enough to handle—the largest leaf should be 0.6 to 1 cm in diameter.

When transplanting begonias, remember that the leaves are very crisp. They will break easily if held edgewise between thumb and forefinger. Try to hold them flat between the fingers and transplant them only as deep as they grew in the seed flat. This will not be very deep, as they still will have relatively underdeveloped roots. Drench the transplants with a fungicide again at the same rate as before.

H. Fertilization

Fertilization requirements are determined by type of plants and the time seedlings will remain in the flat. Germination media are often low in nutrients. This is especially true in media without soil. They have no natural fertilizer and are sometimes low in nutrient holding capacity.

Fertilizer solutions of 20–20–20, or the equivalent, should be applied at the rate of 254 gm/378.5 liters of water immediately after seedlings emerge and weekly thereafter. For a small number of flats, a fertilizer solution is best applied with a sprinkling can which has been fitted with a fan-shaped flaring nozzle. A fertilizer proportioner in the water line is a good system for a larger number of flats.

VII. PREPARATION FOR TRANSPLANTING

The two main considerations here are the medium and the containers. Ideally, the medium used for germination will be of a type that can be used for all phases of growing. This will eliminate mixups and reduce preparation procedures. However, if fertilizer is to be incorporated into the mix, this will be an added task. Even this difference can be eliminated by using a nutrient-containing medium for a germination medium. An exception to fertilizing before seeding would be tomato seedlings and others grown by the thick-broadcast, early transplant method.

Clean packs in which plants are to be marketed should be inserted into clean flats and filled with the sterilized medium. They may be stacked, as long as they are kept clean, but never set a flat that has been on an unclean surface on another one. Unclean surfaces include the floor, ground, wheelbarrow, or any other surface which is not regularly disinfested.

Selection of the marketing container will necessitate consideration of the potential market. It will be necessary to get as much money as possible from each square meter of growing space. The pricing–packaging combination will determine how much the space yields.

Some examples will show that there can be many combinations. Suppose 8 packs of 6 plants are grown in a flat and sold for $1.00 each, bringing $8.00 per flat. One needs to ask, Could I get the same amount for the same number of plants in a smaller pack? or Could I get the same amount for fewer plants, each grown in the same size space, but with more packs per flat?

Basically, four types of growing containers are used in bedding plant flats. They are the following: (1) open packs, most commonly made from pressed wood fiber or plastic, in which a given number of plants are grown; (2) divided, or cell-containing, plastic packs, which can be obtained with various numbers of packs per flat and cells per pack (a widely used one contains 6 cells per pack and 12 packs per flat); (3) a pellet composed of compressed peat moss that expands upon wetting and becomes an individual container for one plant; and (4) pressed fiber or peat moss plantable pots.

The market determines, to a great extent, the type of growing container used. The following tabulation shows some of the advantages and disadvantages of each type. The list is not intended to be all-inclusive.

Type	Advantages	Disadvantages
Open packs	1. Hold more soil, therefore require less watering	1. Plant roots intermingle and must be broken to remove plants 2. Soil cost per flat is higher
Cell packs	1. Less soil needed to fill 2. Plants can be pushed out with roots intact 3. Plants have a head start in the garden 4. Cell divisions act as barriers to spread of disease organisms 5. Easier to transplant in uniform rows	1. Need watering more often 2. Leaves of wilted transplanted seedlings, if large, can stick to container cell division
Peat pellets	1. No other growing medium required 2. Plant and containers are one plantable unit	1. Exposed sides can dry out easily 2. Much of the water runs off when watering 3. Roots can merge with those of adjacent plants 4. Fertilizer cannot be incorporated, limiting them to liquid or no fertilizers
Plantable pots	1. Plant and container in one plantable unit 2. Many sizes available	1. Pots break easily if handled when wet 2. Roots can merge with those in adjacent pots

Whether or not the medium in the growing flats is watered before transplanting occurs depends upon preferences of managers and transplanters. However, the medium should be moist before the seedlings are transplanted for best results.

A. Transplanting

The process of transplanting seedlings from the seed flat to the growing and sales container is one of the most time-consuming jobs in the bedding plant business. Attempts are constantly being made to reduce the time needed for transplanting. Time reduction may be achieved by a more efficient physical arrangement, by improving transplanting techniques, or by adapting mechanical systems such as direct seeding or automatic transplanting.

Although much recent research has been devoted to mechanical transplanting equipment, hand transplanting is still the most commonly used method (Fig. 1).

There are basically two systems for hand transplanting. One is to transplant in the greenhouse where the finished plants are to be produced. For the other system, the transplanting is done in a central location, after which the flats are moved to the growing area.

In some operations, the transplanter is responsible for all steps from dibbling, to transplanting, then moving the flat to the greenhouse, and watering. In other operations the transplanter only plants the seedlings. Other personnel carry out the remaining steps.

To speed transplanting, some greenhouse managers have established assembly line processes, where many transplanters work on the same flat. The flats move constantly and each worker places an assigned number of seedlings in each. In other assembly line types of operations, the transplanter is responsible for an entire flat.

Whatever the overall procedure may be, certain basic requirements must be met. These are (1) removing seedlings from their growing medium with minimum damage; (2) inserting them in their new location without damage; and (3) getting plant roots into contact with moisture and nutrient-containing particles of the soil or other growing medium.

It is difficult to separate seedlings from a saturated growing medium. Therefore, flats should be thoroughly watered no later than noon of the day before

Fig. 1.   Hand transplanting of seedlings

seedlings are to be removed. It is best to have the medium on the dry side, as long as seedlings are turgid. Transplanters should be instructed to avoid squeezing stems tightly or pulling on leaves too hard. Seedlings should be removed by scooping under the medium with the fingers, rather than pulling on them from the top. They can then be easily separated from the side if the medium is not too wet.

Various methods are used to insert seedlings into the growing flat. In some cases, holes are made with a dibble board, single dibble, a wooden pot label, a finger, or some other instrument. The seedling is inserted and medium is pushed in against it with fingers or a dibbling instrument. In other cases the seedling is pushed into the medium with a finger, and no dibbling instrument is used. The opening is made as the seedling is pushed down. Whenever this method is used, care must be exercised in positioning the seedling against the finger to avoid breaking stems or roots. Plants with broken stems or main roots often fail to recover and, when they do recover, they are behind others in growth. With this method there is also the possibility of scraping stems, thus exposing tender tissue to disease organisms.

For plants to replace rapidly destroyed or damaged roots and to establish themselves in the transplant flat, the roots should be in contact not only with water in the medium but also with the particles. This means that the medium should be pressed against the root and not merely pushed together to close the top of the hole, leaving the root suspended in a hollow cavity. There are important exchanges which occur between root hairs and soil particles. Also, unless the medium is saturated, the suspended roots will not be in contact with nutrient-bearing water. Plants left in this condition will fall behind in their development. Root hairs in contact with soil particles will receive moisture as well as nutrients from the particle surfaces. One should not keep the medium saturated to keep the cavities full, as plant roots also need air.

If careful attention is paid to fulfilling the three mentioned basic requirements, flats of transplanted seedlings will develop more uniformly. There will be fewer stunted plants and recovery time will be minimal. It will take less time to develop salable plants.

Another practice to help ensure more uniform growth is grading plants by size before transplanting. Some growers will have transplanters using as many as three flats at one time, putting seedlings with those nearest their size. Two sizes are usually adequate.

It has been a general rule to transplant seedlings as soon as they show their first true leaves (Fig. 2). This practice continues with most growers in regard to spreading types, such as petunias. It is sometimes an advantage for handling to allow them to even grow another set of leaves.

However, the first-true-leaf tradition is being challenged, and successfully so, by an increasing number of growers. As previously mentioned, up to 4000 tomato seedlings can be produced in one 28 × 56-cm flat at one time. If this is done, the flats should be moved from the warm greenhouse to a cooler one as

Fig. 2. Seedlings ready for transplanting.

soon as the seedlings emerge. By the time the seedlings are standing erect, they can be transplanted. There is no need to await the arrival of the true leaves. When this method is used, the sowing medium should contain no fertilizer and none should be added. Fertilizer will cause undesirable lengthening of stems and roots.

Marigolds are especially adaptable to this method since they develop long roots so rapidly. Transplanting them earlier will avoid root entanglements. Others for which this method works well include peppers, zinnias, and asters.

If seedlings are transplanted well and given sufficient water immediately afterward, they do not even appear to slow down.

B. Posttransplanting Considerations

Flats of transplanted seedlings should be watered thoroughly. Again, use a method that will avoid washing out soil or pelting the plants.

When flats are placed in their final location, keep all of one type together. That way, each type can receive the care most suited to it. Also, tall types will not be growing up and overcrowding or shading lower-growing types.

When placing flats of a new planting, leave a space between them and more advanced plantings. The older plants will cover the smaller ones on the edge and interfere with proper development. Different watering needs also make this separation important (Fig. 3).

Plant types that are most susceptible to damping off should be placed where

Fig. 3.   Transplanted flats placed on plastic risers for finishing.

they can be watched and treated if necessary. Some growers treat the most susceptible ones, such as begonia, coleus, impatiens, celosia, alyssum, portulaca, and vinca, with a fungicidal drench a few days after transplanting. Others treat all plants with fungicide. Close observation will help determine a specific grower's needs.

C. Mechanical Direct Seeding

Perhaps, at some future time, much of the labor of transplanting will be widely eliminated as more efficient and reliable machines are developed. There are problems with this type of machinery, but if man can create new cultivars on such a grand scale, he will undoubtedly perfect machines to simplify production.

One limiting factor in the use of mechanical seeders is the variability of seed size, both within a species and among different species. Work has been done and is being done to develop methods of sorting seed within a species. Methods are also being developed for improved handling of different types of seed through pelletization.

Another obstacle to mechanized seeding is the need to develop and meet precise standards for maximum germination. Information has been accumulated and efforts are being made to put it to use.

Another need is for seed from a source that can guarantee 95 to 100% germination. This would require methods not yet developed and may also increase the cost of seed.

A fourth limiting factor is germination time. Since one seed flat usually transplants ten finished flats, the area used for germination would need to be ten times as large.

VIII. GREENHOUSE SOILS AND MIXES

The basics of soil science and container soil science must be followed. The unique situation of the bedding plant grower is that of producing plants in very shallow containers usually 5 to 7.5 cm deep. Therefore, it is essential that any mix used have good aeration. Many of the production problems associated with bedding plants can be traced to poor or improperly mixed soils.

Historically, most bedding plants were grown in soil-based mixes. Mixes varied with the geographic area of the country, depending on native soils and water supplies. The biggest problem was the variability in native soils and the extreme difficulty in obtaining a similar mix time after time. This variability, as well as increased cost of labor, caused many growers to switch to soilless mixes. One of the first was the U.C. mix developed by the University of California. This mix worked well in the western United States; however, one of the ingredients is a sharp, coarse, white sand not found in other parts of the United States. This is the primary reason for a lack of wide acceptance of this mix.

The Cornell peat-lite mix has received a much wider acceptance. Its materials, sphagnum peat and horticultural vermiculite, are readily available and very competitively priced. More and more growers are successful with this type of mix and its use has been growing steadily.

Most recently, mixes containing bark have been introduced to the trade. These mixes have found greatest use in the southern and western United States. As more information and research is conducted, these mixes will become very important in bedding plant production.

Since soilless mixes are relatively insect, disease, and weed free, they afford

Table IV

A Typical Soilless Mix Used in Bedding Plant Production

Ingredients	For seeding	For transplants
Sphagnum peat	0.46 m³	0.46 m³
Horticultural vermiculite	0.46 m³	0.46 m³
Ground limestone	2.30 kg	2.30 kg
Treble superphosphate (0-46-0)	0.50 kg	0.50 kg
Potassium nitrate	0.50 kg	0.50 kg
Trace elements	57.00 gm	57.00 gm
Osmocote 14-14-14	—	0.90 to 1.8 kg
Wetting agent	90.00 ml	90.00 ml

the grower fast and easy media for germination. Most growers do not steam sterilize this mix; they merely open the bagged mix and fill their flats.

Table IV outlines a typical mix used in bedding plant production. A number of commercial mixes similar to this type of Cornell peat-lite mix are now available. Many greenhouse firms buy trailer-load lots of either bagged or bulk mix and fill directly into their flat fillers, thus eliminating equipment and storage areas that are necessary when mixing is done on the premises.

IX. THE GROWING ENVIRONMENT

A. Temperature

Temperature is the most controllable factor in the greenhouse. Thus, the grower uses temperature to control growth and to produce the type of plant desired.

Growing temperature recommendations are based on air temperature although plant and air temperatures may not be the same. Raising the temperature increases growth rates but above 30°C there are detrimental effects.

High temperatures stimulate soft growth, resulting in taller, thin-stemmed plants. The build-up of proteins and amino acids predominates. Low temperatures cause slow plant growth, with a build-up of carbohydrates. This results in plants with thick stems and shorter, stockier growth.

Night temperature is used to classify greenhouse crops, as it is easier to control than daytime temperature. There is no one optimum temperature for a given bedding plant crop. The optimum temperature depends on the species to be grown. For example, pansies grow better at a lower temperature than celosia or impatiens. The amount of light available also dictates the best temperature. The lower the amount of light energy available, the lower the temperature should be maintained to produce a quality plant.

The stage of growth is also an important factor to consider. Germination will usually require the highest temperature. Seedlings and young plants have a higher optimum temperature requirement for optimum growth than older plants. When all the plants in a greenhouse are the same age, adjusting temperature in relation to plant age might improve quality and yield of the crop.

In some bedding plants, flower bud initiation may depend on temperature with the plants initiating buds more rapidly when given the optimum temperature for the plant.

The optimum temperature for flower initiation may be different from the optimum temperature for flower development, which may also change as flower development progresses. Some plants must be kept below a certain temperature for flowering to occur. For example, 'Martha Washington' geraniums form inflorescences only at temperatures below 16°C. Many ivy geranium varieties require temperatures below 13°C to initiate flower buds. Stocks must have ten or more fully developed leaves and be exposed to at least 21 days of 13°–16°C to initiate flower buds. Other plants must have the temperature above a critical level for flowering to start. Below this temperature, only succulent vegetative growth occurs.

Leaf and flower color can also be influenced by temperature. At low temperatures, starch is converted to sugar. An accumulation of carbohydrates results with increased anthocyanin. Thus, a reddish color on the edges of the leaves of geraniums may be a symptom of low temperatures. The lower leaves of the plant and even the stem can turn red or bronze. Flower color is also usually more intense. Some white flowers, however, may turn a pinkish color under low temperatures. At high temperatures, the plants may have faded flower color and lighter green leaves.

Nutrition of the crop and fertilizer practices will also be dictated by the temperature regime used. The higher the temperature, the more frequent the need for watering and fertilization. Cooler temperatures require less water and fertilizer. Temperatures below 10°C should be considered as holding temperatures and little fertilizer or water will be needed.

It has long been established that many crops grow optimally when greenhouse night temperatures are maintained at a lower level than the day temperature. In general, the day temperature is set 4°–6°C higher than the night temperature on bright days, and 0°–2°C higher on cloudy days.

Most bedding plant seedlings, after germination, are grown at 18°–21°C and the temperature is reduced after transplanting.

Quality bedding plants can be produced at a temperature range between 10° and 16°C. Bedding plants grown at 10°C from transplanting to sale are short, compact, and well branched, but they require 2 to 3 additional weeks, are excessively hard, and start slowly in the garden. Nights of 16°C from transplanting to sale cause more rapid stem elongation, hasten flowering, and produce a fine plant without reducing plant quality of many species. Night temperatures of 21°C cause excessive stem elongation, weak stems, and poorer quality, and are not recommended.

Nights of 7°–10°C during the last 2 to 3 weeks before flowering harden plant growth. Lower temperatures for hardening generally delay bedding plant flowering about 1 week. However, reduced night temperatures before flowering allow better control of flowering. Shorter, stronger-stemmed plants are produced and the plant is acclimatized to garden conditions.

It must be stressed that it is not enough to think that one temperature will cause adequate growth at all times. Sophisticated computer programs can be developed to predict results in flowering time or any other factor related to plant growth. However, an astute grower, one with experience and who is observant, intelligent, and conscientious, will be best able to provide the optimum temperature at each stage of plant growth for the quality desired.

Smaller growers with small amounts of many types of plants may have to divide greenhouses with plastic curtains to provide the variety of temperatures needed.

B. Watering

One of the most critical, cultural practices in producing bedding plants is watering. If watering is not done properly, it can lead to inferior quality or completely destroyed plants. If a grower applies too much water, the plants will become excessively soft and tall. These will have poor shelf life and will be difficult to ship or to transplant to the garden. On the other hand, if water is restricted, plants will be short, have visible damage on foliage, or be completely dried out.

The water source should have a pH between 5.5 and 7.0 and a soluble salt level of K value 1:2 = to 120 or less. There are many areas of the country where this quality of water does not exist. In these areas, the water must be treated to conform to these standards. Some growers have installed systems to remove dissolved solids from their water supply. Others find that the water pH is very high and resort to additives such as phosphoric acid or sulfuric acid to reduce the pH. In the Michigan area, there are many growers who inject 1 part phosphoric acid to 10,000 parts water to bring the pH of the water supply in the optimum range.

Growers must be cautious about their water supplies. Many problems can be encountered by using water directly from ponds or streams that is not checked or treated. The best source usually is from wells or municipal water supplies.

1. Watering Seedlings

Seed is usually germinated under a mist system. Alternatively, flats are completely saturated and allowed to drain, seed is sown, and then the entire flat is covered with polyethylene or glass to prevent evaporation and to keep humidity very high. If watering of flat is done immediately after the seed is sown, finer seeds may be washed away and germination will be reduced. A very fine nozzle must be used to ensure that the force of the water will not uproot young seedlings or wash any seed. It is important to remember that moisture is necessary for germination. If the flat is allowed to dry out during this critical germination period, germination will be greatly reduced or completely eliminated. Once seed has completely germinated, the moisture level can be reduced to allow the seedlings to become more sturdy for easier transplanting. However, a day before transplanting, the seedling should be watered properly so the seedling soil is moist but not soaking wet for transplanting.

2. After Transplanting

Transplanted seedlings should not be allowed to dry out enough to wilt. They should be kept well watered for several days until new top growth indicates that roots are developing adequately. Thereafter the soil surface can be allowed to dry out each day to discourage diseases and to allow adequate aeration in the soil.

For the watering of new transplants by hand, a nozzle should be used that will not knock them down, wash them out, or cover them with soil. A flaring fan-shaped Rose nozzle on the hose end with a shut-off valve between is good. Mechanized watering systems have been developed and are used primarily in the southern and western United States or in the northern areas when light is abundant and quick drying occurs. They are usually not used in the northern areas during the winter months under low light conditions.

3. Watering Established Bedding Plants

For the fastest growth of bedding plants, water stress must be minimal. Plants should receive water frequently enough to prevent wilting. Watering must be thorough, both in quanitity and distribution. However, thorough does not necessarily mean frequent.

It is possible to apply water to a flat much faster than it can be absorbed. Therefore, much of the water from a heavy watering may run over the top of the flat and soak into the ground. The soil in the flat may be left only partially watered. If water is not absorbed as fast as it is applied, it is best to water until the flats are filled and then water again a half hour later. This would be especially desirable with hand watering.

4. Finishing the Crop

Some growers claim that water is the best growth retardant. Just as adequate amounts are needed for unchecked growth, lack of water can hold back a crop that threatens to reach maturity before marketing time. Since excessive water loss may cause injury or death to plants, such practices should be handled with care.

Depending upon general growing conditions in producing the crop, it may be desirable to water-stress plants prior to sending them to market. If this is not done, plant tissues may be too succulent. A test can be made by setting a well-watered flat of plants outside for an hour on a clear day. If the plants wilt, they would be better prepared for market by withholding some water for a few days. Care should be taken to avoid letting them wilt beyond recovery (Fig. 4).

C. Fertilization

Historically, early bedding plant growers obtained rich field soils with good fertility because of previous farming practices or composting. They used this soil along with organic fertilizers to produce a crop. Many times the fertility level was not high enough, thus producing plants that were excessively stunted and hardened. On the other extreme, fertility levels could even be so high that high soluble salts caused plant damage or death.

Fig. 4.   Mature crop ready for sale.

As fertilizers became available, many growers mixed dry-type, farm fertilizers into their soil mix. They were usually low analyses types. This method is still used by some growers and works well if the soil is thoroughly mixed and the fertilizer is applied after steaming.

Today, most growers use a high analyses, liquid-type fertilizer that is applied after transplanting. If this system is used, the soil is mixed and tested, and the pH is adjusted to the range of 5.5 to 7.0. Optimum pH would be 6.2 throughout the entire growing period for most bedding plants. Many growers will incorporate superphosphate into the soil at mixing time. Nitrogen and potassium are applied at a rate of 150 to 200 ppm N and K as needed.

D. Daylength

Most bedding plant growers do nothing to manipulate daylength, but depend on natural daylength to produce the various bedding plants they grow. With certain species, daylength plays an important part in the time needed to flower.

Alyssum, balsam, begonia, gomphrena, impatiens, French marigold, pansy, vinca, carnation, lobelia, tomatoes, pepper, and cabbage are reported to have no photoperiodic preferences. Therefore, they will flower in about the same number of days whether under long- or short-day regimes.

African marigolds, zinnia, salvia, basil, coleus, celosia, cleome, cosmos, dahlia, morning glory, perilla, and rudbeckia are plants that will flower faster under short-day conditions. Therefore, early winter sowings will flower in fewer days than if the plants were sown later in the spring.

Phlox, verbena, snapdragons, centaurea, feverfew, gaillardia, gypsophila, hollyhocks, nicotiana, scabiosa, salpiglossis, ageratum, and lobelia are plants that require long days to flower quicker. Petunia, grown between 13° and 21°C, also responds as a long-day plant. There are several perennials on this list. This is why it is impossible to flower many perennials in the short winter months in bedding plant containers under natural conditions.

Although general statements about the photoperiodic effects on a species have been made and documented on a specific cultivar, many times the effect depends on a specific variety. For example, a photoperiodic study was conducted at Michigan State University on 74 cultivars of marigolds in 1976. The plants were grown under a 9- or 16-hour photoperiod. It was evident that not all African types are short-day types; some are very much affected by daylength, whereas others are not greatly affected. Likewise, some French types are not affected by daylength while others do show a tendency to flower sooner under short daylength.

Another example of the cultivar response can be seen with salvia. It is generally stated that this is a short-day plant, although, in fact, certain cultivars are short day and others flower sooner under long days. Other cultivars flower in the same amount of time regardless of daylength.

A grower who has no facilities for controlling daylength can choose some cultivars that are not greatly affected by it. For example, 'Honeycomb' marigold and 'Caribiniere' salvia both perform admirably when flowered in pots or packs without light control. Variations in height are insignificant.

Remember, only generalizations have been made about photoperiodic effects. On some species they are valid while on other species, especially marigold and salvia, the effects are varied and one must be very specific in order to time the crop properly.

There is increased awareness by the bedding plant grower of the effect of daylength on certain species. Manipulation of photoperiod on marigolds is now being used to flower certain cultivars year-round. More of this type of production will occur as species timing becomes more important for profitable production of marigolds and salvia.

E. Growth Retardants

Growers are interested in producing short, compact plants and, therefore, use cultural manipulations as well as growth-retarding chemicals to accomplish their goal. Cultural methods have long been used to keep plants compact. For example, lack of water may be the best growth regardant. Many growers use this technique to keep their plants short. Another technique is to reduce or eliminate phosphorus from the soil mix and to add it only as a liquid and at low levels. Until the introduction of growth-retarding chemicals, these cultural methods were the only ways possible to produce short plants.

Today, however, there are three chemicals most used by growers. B-Nine SP or Alar is the most widely used and is effective on a wide range of bedding plants. A-Rest, the newest of the chemicals, is also used. It has the widest species range, but it is the most expensive. The third chemical, Cycocel, has become important since the seed geranium crop has become a leading bedding plant item. This chemical is very effective in reducing plant height as well as hastening flowering.

One must remember there are advantages and disadvantages in using growth retardants. The advantages are (1) reduction in plant height (shorter internodes), (2) improved plant shape, (3) darker green foliage, (4) thicker leaves, and (5) more uniform flowering. Shelf life is usually greater on account

Table V

Effect of Growth Retardants on Specific Annuals[a]

Annual	B-Nine SP Alar[b]	A-Rest[b]
Ageratum	+	+
Anthirrhinum (snapdragon)	+	+
Browallia	+	+
Celosia	+	+
Centaurea (cornflower)	+	+
Chrysanthemum	+	+
Cleome	−	+
Coleus	+	+
Convolvulus (morning glory)	−	+
Cucumis (cucumber)	+	+
Dahlia	+	+
Dianthus (carnation)	−	+
Gomphrena	−	−
Hedera (English ivy)	+	+
Impatiens	+	+
Lactuca (lettuce)	+	+
Lycopersicom (tomato)	+	+
Pelargonium (geranium)	−	+
Petunia	+	+
Salvia	+	+
Tagetes (marigold)	+	+
Verbena	+	+
Viola (pansy)	−	−
Zinnia	+	+

[a]For most crops, spray 2 to 4 weeks after transplanting. Remember the retardant will only retard future growth; it will not make plants that are already tall shorter.
[b]+, Effective; −, not effective.

of the plants' ability to withstand stress better. The plant is more resistant to water stress and to heat, cold, or smog injury. There also seems to be less transplant shock. Use of growth retardants allows the grower more flexibility in growing, since retardants keep plants short over a wide range of temperatures, fertilizer, and light levels. Usually they are safe and easy to apply.

One disadvantage is that not all annuals are responsive to growth retardants. Another is that if retardants are applied late, flowering may be delayed. Furthermore, some cultivars are more responsive than others and duration of effectiveness varies. It is extremely important that the grower use proper concentrations, or injury may occur on certain species. Lastly, the use of retardants costs money, which, of course, means an increased cost in production.

It should be apparent that the advantages of using a growth retardant on bedding plants, when needed, far outweigh the disadvantages.

Table V indicates the effect of B-Nine SP and A-Rest on specific annuals. Check the label for registered uses, and use only according to the label.

Cycocel is the primary retardant used on seed geraniums. A-Rest is also very effective, but the cost is greater and, therefore, its use is limited. For bedding plants, B-Nine SP has the greatest use, whereas A-Rest is used primarily on items not affected by B-Nine SP.

It is important to remember that application of growth retardants is only another useful tool to produce a quality crop. They are not substitutes for a good grower and will not make a poor grower or poor crops better.

X. PROBLEMS

A. Diseases

Bedding plants are meant to provide beauty. Diseases can turn that beauty into an eyesore. They can turn a homeowner against bedding plants and lose money for the grower. Diseases should not only be controlled in the greenhouse, but also every effort should be expended to see that the customer is not taking problems home.

Parasitic diseases of bedding plants are usually caused by bacteria or fungi. The following outline gives basic information on parasitic disease most commonly encountered by the bedding plant grower.

I. Damping off
  A. Usually caused by *Rhizoctonia* fungi and two water mold fungi, *Pythium* and *Phytophthora*
  B. Symptoms to consider:
    1. Usually first detected in germination flats
    2. Weeds in flat may indicate unsterilized soil
    3. Poor stands of seedlings

    4. Plants fall over at the soil line
    5. Circles of dead and dying plants enlarge daily
    6. Threads of fungus can be seen on dead plants

II. Sclerotinia crown rot
  A. Caused by *Sclerotinia sclerotiorium*
  B. Symptoms to consider:
    1. Cottony mold on soil or crown of the plant
    2. May be found on older flowering plants
    3. Causes rapid rot of plant tissue
    4. Its resistant, spreading structure (sclerotia) looks like large rodent droppings. They may be in rotted stems or on the soil near plants
    5. Spreads rapidly in warm, damp weather
    6. May also attack seedlings, causing damping off symptoms

III. Botrytis crown rot
  A. Caused by *Botryis cinerea.*
  B. Symptoms to consider:
    1. Soft decay of seedlings
    2. Fuzzy, gray growth
    3. Spores puff off like dust when disturbed
    4. Works from top of seedling downward
    5. Starts on injured or dead parts of plants
    6. Restricted to cool, moist conditions

IV. Rust diseases
  A. Caused by various species of *Puccinia.*
  B. Symptoms to consider:
    1. Red leaf spots—caused by fungus spores
    2. Red dust on hands
    3. May begin on lower leaves and on undersides of leaves
    4. Zones or rings of spores form as older leaf spots enlarge
    5. Most commonly seen on geranium, hollyhock, fuchsia, and snapdragons

V. Powdery mildews
  A. Caused by species of *Oldium.*
  B. Symptoms to consider:
    1. White, fluffy growth on leaf surfaces—may be in spots
    2. White spores may fly into the air when leaf is flicked
    3. Usually seen on older zinnias and snapdragons
    4. Rarely seen on seedling plants

The greenhouse environment and cultural practices can aid in the spread of parasitic diseases. Threadlike parts of fungi can be found clinging to soil particles and decayed plant parts. Some of these can be transferred unknowingly to other flats, tools, and clothing. They can be carried through the air on dust particles. Some spores are capable of swimming through water in pore spaces between soil particles and on soil and plant surfaces. Some can get their start on a dead leaf or other part which falls onto a healthy plant. Injured plants make good starting places for diseases.

There are three basic considerations in controlling parasitic diseases. They are (1) prevention, (2) avoidance of physiological diseases, which is really another form of prevention, and (3) use of fungicides to eradicate or prevent the spread of infections.

Prevention was listed first because of its prime importance. By following strict preventive guidelines, one may never have the task of diagnosing these diseases in greenhouses under his/her supervision. The long list that follows can help to minimize disease organisms. Every greenhouse manager should take this list, revise it to fit local conditions, and see that every employee is aware of its contents and importance.

1. See that all growing media are made sterile by steaming or other acceptable method.
2. Hose down the interior walls and roofs of greenhouses when they are empty, before a new crop is put in, to remove accumulated dust.
3. Keep hose nozzles off the ground.
4. Keep the rest of the water system clean.
5. Do not water late in the day.
6. Do not splash water onto plants from the ground, walks, or other plants.
7. Do not drag hoses over flats.
8. Try to keep hoses off the ground.
9. Wash hands after handling infected plants.
10. Have transplanters wash hands regularly.
11. Treat seed flats with fungicide.
12. Disinfest used flats, tools, benches, etc.
13. Do not stack flats of soil that may have unclean bottoms.
14. Avoid holding a flat that has been sitting on the ground over another flat of plants or clean soil.
15. Use care in removing diseased plants to avoid contaminating others.
16. Avoid raising dust by sweeping or other activity.
17. Consider using cell-pack-divided containers to help prevent spread of disease across the soil surface.
18. Devise a means to keep flats of plants off the ground.
19. Keep loose clothing from brushing across plants or flats of clean soil.
20. Spot treat with fungicide or remove flats with diseased plants in them.
21. Try to keep out dust when the wind blows.
22. Keep animals out of greenhouses.
23. Do not use a tool that has been dropped onto the floor without cleaning it.
24. Ventilate properly to control humidity.
25. Use disease-resistant cultivars as much as possible.

Physiological diseases must also be avoided. Throughout all forms of life it has been observed that the strongest individuals have better chances of survival. Predators, whether in the form of food-hunting carnivores or root-rotting bacteria, prey upon the weak members of a population. Thus, the importance of maintaining vigor in the bedding plant crop cannot be overstressed. A plant that is properly nourished will not be as likely to have dead leaves or leaf margins where spores can lodge and await the arrival of a few drops of water to start them on their destructive course.

Plants that have received nutrients in proper balance will have exterior tissues which are less susceptible to infection than those which are succulent and soft because of excessive nitrogen. Plants grown far enough apart to admit light and air will likewise be better fortified against pathogens. Air circulation will provide fresh oxygen and carbon dioxide to keep photosynthetic and respiratory processes in balance as well as discourage anaerobic disease organisms.

The importance of avoiding build-up of soluble salts bears repeating. Keep plants well watered but not waterlogged. A grower must be watchful and detect any condition that may weaken the crop and render it susceptible to attack.

As previously mentioned, fungicides can be used as part of the preventive program. They can also be used to attack and eradicate the pathogen or render it immobile when even the most strategically sound defenses have been penetrated.

To summarize, fungicides may be needed (1) when warm, moist conditions in germination flats create ideal conditions for disease to proliferate, (2) immediately after transplanting to protect highly susceptible plant types until they get a good start, and (3) to eradicate or immobilize a localized infestation of disease in a seed flat or growing container. Fungicides may be also needed when that uncontrollable factor, weather, creates conditions favorable for diseases over extended periods of time.

B. Insects and Mites

A properly managed bedding plant greenhouse should have little or no major insect problems. In the North, insects are usually not a problem at the time seed is sown or seedlings transplanted. Only in late spring when ventilators are open and insects are active outside can they become a real problem.

Prevention is the best approach in both insect and disease control. Start with a clean greenhouse, free of weeds, with benches disinfested and the structure painted and in good condition. Know the vegetation outside in close proximity to the greenhouse. Soil should be pasteurized and the container new or properly cleaned.

Manipulation of environment can also be used to limit the pest population. For example, if fungus gnats are a problem, reduction of watering, to dry surfaces of soil and greenhouse floors, will greatly help to limit their numbers. If red spider mite is a problem, syringing the plants will aid in controlling their numbers.

An observant grower is the best key to insect control. By keeping a close watch on the crops, there should never be a large insect population developing.

The trend today is toward integrated pest management, which is using a combination of factors to control pest populations. Therefore, the good grower will understand the effects of cultivar, environment, life cycles of the insect, and proper use of pesticides in a complete program.

When using pesticides, read the label directions and follow them exactly. Proper safety precautions must also be considered. Many of the compounds used today are highly toxic to humans. The chances of injury to employees or to the applicators are considerably greater than when other, less toxic materials are used.

There are only eight to ten pests that are often problems in producing bedding plants.

Aphids (Aphididae) commonly called plant lice or greenfly, usually attack tender annuals in the spring of the year. They usually are found on the young, immature terminal areas and feed with piercing and sucking mouthparts. They vary from green to pink to black. A by-product of their feeding is a sticky, honeydew substance that coats the foliage of infested plants. This honeydew will turn black under high-humidity conditions. Aphids overwinter outside the greenhouse as eggs. In the spring, they hatch and develop into winged females that fly into the greenhouse, where they produce live, wingless female progeny. Occasionally, a winged female is produced and flies to another plant, thus spreading the infestation. The higher the temperature, the greater the number of aphids produced. One female produces 1400 young at 21°C in 2 weeks.

Ants (Formicidae) can be a problem. They may live on the greenhouse floor, especially if a sandy fill is used. They have been known to carry aphids from one plant to another and can carry spores of botrytis from one plant to another. Ants can be easily controlled by preventive spraying before flats are set on the greenhouse floor.

Whitefly [*Trialeurodes vaporarionim* (Westwood)] infests many common bedding plants such as ageratum, heliotrope, asters, begonias, coleus, fuchsias, geraniums, morning glories, salvia, eggplant, squash, tomatoes, cucumbers, lettuce, muskmelons, peppers, watermelons, and strawberries.

The life cycle starts with oval eggs 0.25 mm long deposited on the underside of leaves. They hatch in 4 to 12 days into pale yellow, six-legged crawlers. These larvae or nymphs move about for a short time, avoiding direct light. They insert their heads and start sucking sap. In the next phase, they lose their legs and antennae and look like very small, flat, oval scales, often with a marginal fringe of white, waxy filaments, sometimes covered with plates or rolls of wax. They secrete large amounts of honeydew. After a second molt, the insect becomes a pupa and then the four-winged adult leaves the pupal skin and the cycle starts over. The grower can usually see all stages of development on the underside of leaves of host plants. Chemical control on a regular application basis can eliminate this insect problem.

Larvae of several moths (Lepidoptera larvae, caterpillars) that invade the greenhouse can cause considerable damage to various bedding plants. They are usually noticed in the "worm" stage. Most go unnoticed when the eggs have been laid or just hatched. They are usually ferocious eaters and can do great damage. Biological control with *Bacillus thuringiensis* preparations (dipel, thircide, biotrol) or chemical sprays are used. Make certain the foliage is thoroughly covered, since these worms are "chewers"; when they eat the treated foliage, they ingest the material and die.

The two-spotted mite [*Tetranychus telarius* (linnalus)] is the common spider mite or red spider mite found in greenhouses. It is commonly associated with damage to marigolds, lantana, alyssum, phlox, and geraniums. They often go unnoticed for several weeks because of their small size and feeding habits of infesting the undersides of leaves. The female is less than 0.5 mm whereas the male is even smaller. They are greenish or reddish with two black spots on either side of their body. The female lays several hundred tiny, sphere-shaped eggs on the underside of leaves in 3 to 4 weeks. Eggs from unmated females only develop into males. The mites make mealy cobwebs on the underside of leaves and from one leaf to another, sometimes entirely covering a new shoot and flower buds.

The number of generations increases with temperature. At 24°C, the adult stage is reached in 5 days; at 13°C it takes 40 days. At 27°C one female spider mite could theoretically give rise to over 13 million progeny in 4 to 6 weeks. There are many common pesticides used to control outbreaks of this pest. Kelthane (dicofoe) and malathion are the most common. Environmental control can be obtained by reducing temperatures and washing mites from leaves.

There are other mites that can cause problems, such as the broad mite, *Heimtarsonemus latus* (Banks), the false spider, *Brevipalpus,* and the "French fly" mites, *Tyrophagus*. These can be problems in popular annuals such as fuchsias, begonias, and petunias. Kelthane and malathion again control these pests.

Thrips (Thysanoptera) cause damage to foliage as well as to flowers by rasping surface cells and sucking up the content. Silver or white streaks, some turning brown, indicate thrips activity. This usually occurs in the shoot tip and young thrips develop, usually in the flower buds. Systemic insecticides are the best method of controlling this pest.

Presently there are certified pest application exams and information available in every state. One should obtain appropriate application licenses and know the safety precautions and methods of application for any insecticide required.

C. Weeds

Weeds, growing under benches, along walls, and outside the greenhouse, are a common problem. They are not only unsightly but also ideal places to harbor insects and disease organisms. It is very difficult to control insects and diseases on a crop if weeds are present.

Many growers still use the hand method of hoeing weeds to eliminate them from the greenhouse. This method is not only costly but also time-consuming.

Newer greenhouse structures are being built with complete ground coverings of materials such as porous concrete, to eliminate the soil where weeds can germinate and grow. Porous concrete is a new way to utilize a concrete surface so that water will pass through it and not puddle or pond. Large amounts of water can easily pass through this type of concrete almost instantaneously. The mix is basically the same as standard concrete except that *no sand* is used. Sand acts as a binder that prevents water from flowing through the slab. Depending on the thickness of the slab, various amounts of weight can be supported, e.g., a 7.5-cm slab should support a fork-lift truck pulling about 907-kg weight. The breaking strength appears to be about 272 kg/6.45 cm²/2.54 cm per thickness. It does not require a tamped sand base, but a 10- to 15-cm subbase of compact gravel is recommended to facilitiate drainage. The subsurface grade does not allow drainage; a 10-cm diameter underdrain system is recommended.

The proportions of the mix are critical. The mix is essentially a "dry mix" with a negative slump . . . in other words, the mix will not flow as does regular concrete, will stick to the mixing containers, and will have to be manually shaped or moved. For 0.76 m³ use 1270 kg of 0.95-cm stone (uniform and graded), 5½ bags of cement, 13.25 liters of water per bag of cement (this is *critical*). (If concrete is poured in temperatures above 21°C, the mix may also require a retardant agent.) Use forms to direct the shape. Work the concrete as little as possible—the more floating or troweling that is done, the more the cement will come to the surface and seal it so water will not penetrate. A proper surface will be slightly rough, but level, with many pore spaces visible. It can be colored in the mix or painted after drying, but this will be more difficult than on smooth concrete.

Another technique is to cover the floor of the greenhouse with a straw mulch or with a material such as black plastic.

Some growers use flame throwers to burn the weeds physically from under the greenhouse benches and aisles. In some cases, growers have used high concentrations of salt or a similar material sprinkled on weeds to kill them. This practice is not usually recommended because of problems with the runoff of water that would contain high amounts of this material.

There are no herbicides legally registered for use within the greenhouse. When the covering is off the polyethylene houses, many growers use materials such as paraquat to control weed problems. Paraquat is a contact herbicide and will kill any plant with which it comes in contact.

Herbicides that have been used around greenhouses for weed control include the following. Paraquat, one of the best herbicides on the market, kills by contact and does not leave a residue. The weeds must be present to achieve control. Do not spray steam pipes or desirable plants. Amitrol-T should only be used in cold frames or plastic houses that have the plastic removed. It is effective against all weeds, but does have a 4 to 6 week residual effect. Under greenhouse conditions, it may not leach away and cause problems. This material could also be used in a noncrop area outside the greenhouse. Monuron (Telvar), Diuron (Karmex), and Simazine (Princep) kill most weeds. Acting through the roots, they are most effective against young weeds and less effective against older weeds. Because they are long-lasting herbicides, they must not be applied on soil that will be used for crops in the next 2 to 3 years. Do not spray on heating pipes and do not place pots or flats on soil treated with one of these herbicides. Round-Up is an effective herbicide for grasses in noncrop areas. This material would be effective in controlling quackgrass around the outside of the greenhouses. None of these materials have a label for use in greenhouses. They can be legally used for weed control around the outside of greenhouses.

If improper herbicides are used and fumes are released in the greenhouse, severe crop losses can occur. To minimize this problem, a slurry of activated charcoal must be spread on the entire affected area of the greenhouse. Usually 1 pint of charcoal is used per 100 square feet of surface area. This material will absorb the herbicide and reduce or eliminate the fumes.

Be careful with any herbicide in or around the greenhouse and follow label instructions and safety rules.

XI. FINDING A MARKET

Many bedding plant growers think that finding a market is the last step in a bedding plant operation; however, the opposite is more logical. Finding a market should be the first step in a successful operation. A study by Ernest Dicter (1968) indicated people buy bedding plants for three reasons: creativity, excitement, and therapy. With the rise in food prices, perhaps necessity could be added as a fourth factor for producing vegetable transplants. When the product is promoted or sold, it is important to establish a need. This need can be established by appealing to one of these four reasons why people buy bedding plants.

With the tremendous increase in gardening, because almost everyone loves flowers, and the avid ecological movement, bedding plants have enjoyed an ever-widening rate of growth.

Surveys have been conducted to determine consumer purchasing patterns. For example, one survey in Michigan (Zehner, 1969) showed 78% of the families interviewed bought bedding plants within the last year. Generally, women made the actual purchase.

An independent garden center was the most often mentioned as the retail outlet where plants were purchased. Expenditures for bedding plants increased as the average size of the family increased. Homemakers 30 to 44 years of age were the biggest buyers of bedding plants.

The reasons plants were not bought by the people interviewed were as follows: (1) they were not interested in gardening; (2) they preferred to grow plants from seed; (3) they were unfamiliar with growing plants; and (4) bedding plants were too expensive.

Not every grower can grow all things for all people. Not every grower can meet his competition in all respects, but one can specialize. Instead of trying to grow all things for all people, the grower can become a specialist in one area and earn a good return on the investment and an adequate gross profit on the merchandise. Perhaps one can grow hanging baskets better than the competition, or grow different cultivars in different containers than what the competition will grow. Some producers have made a profitable venture out of growing potted annuals in 7 or 10-cm material for late spring or early summer sales. If one is a small retail grower, it would be very unprofitable to attempt to compete with large mass producers on the same item they produce. There are many profitable areas to be filled, if one is aware of what is needed in the marketplace.

REFERENCES

Anonymous (1968). Seedling machine decimates nursery's labor requirements. *Growers* Jan. 6.
Anonymous (1974). Cornell Staff. Cornell recommendations for commercial floriculture crops, Part I. "Cultural Practices and Production Programs," p. 56. Cornell Univ. Press, Ithaca, New York.
Anonymous (1978). "Floriculture Crops Production Area and Sales, 1976 and 1977, Intentions for 1978," March SpCr6-1(78). Crop Reporting Board, U.S. Dep. Agric., Washington, D.C.
Baker, K. F., ed. (1957). The U. C. system for producing healthy container grown plants. *Calif. Agic. Exp. Stn., Man.* **23,** 332.
Ball, V. (1970a). Eight ways you can mechanize bedding plants. *Grower Talks* **26**(8), 14–22.
Ball, V. (1970b). Meet the new Fricke machine seeder. *Grower Talks* **26**(8), 1–6.
Ball, V. (1976). Early American horticulture. *Grower Talks* **40**(3), 50.
Boodley, J. W. (1976). Production . . . Back to basics—soils. *Proc. Int. Bedding Plant Conf., 9th* pp. 175–182. Bedding Plants, Inc., Okemos, Michigan.
Boodley, J. W., and Sheldrake, R. S. (1972). Cornell peat-lite mixes for commercial plant growing. *Cornell Univ. Plant Sci. Inf. Bull.* **43,** 148.
Carlson, R. H. (1973). How to market your product. *Proc. Nat. Bedding Plant Conf., 6th* pp. 90–102. Bedding Plants, Inc., Okemos, Michigan.
Carlson, W. H. (1976). Production . . . back to basics—temperature and daylength. *Proc. Int. Bedding Plant Conf., 9th* pp. 205–215. Bedding Plants, Inc., Okemos, Michigan.
Carlson, W. H. (1978a). Daylength and Salvia varieties. *Am. Veg. Grower* **26**(3), 20–21.
Carlson, W. H. (1978b). "Bedding Plant Information Chart," Bedding Plants, Inc., Okemos, Michigan.
Carlson, W. H., and Carpenter, W. J. (1972). Optimum soil and plant nutrient levels for petunias. *Mich. Florist* **496,** 16–18.
Carlson, W. H., and Havey, C. R. (1973). A survey on mechanization in the bedding plant industry. *Flower Notes Mich. State Univ., Hortic. Dep.* **5**(4), 2–5.

Cathey, H. M. (1969a). Guidelines for the germination of annual pot plant and ornamental herb seeds-1. *Florists' Rev.* **144**(3742), 21–23, 58–60.

Cathey, H. M. (1969b). Guidelines for the germination of annual pot plant and ornamental herb seeds-2. *Florists' Rev.* **144**(3743), 18–20, 52–53.

Cathey, H. M. (1969c). Guidelines for the germination of annual pot plant and ornamental herb seeds-3. *Florists' Rev.* **144**(3744), 26–29, 75–77.

Cathey, H. M. (1976). Growth regulators in bedding plants. *In* "A Penn State Manual" (John W. Mastalerz, ed.), pp. 177–189. Pennsylvania Flower Growers, University Park.

Christianson, L. (1974). Germination by trial and error—The best way to learn how. *Florists' Rev.* **154**(3981), 52, 95, 96.

Colegrave, D. (1973). First find your market. *In* "Colegrave Bedding Plants Grower Manual," pp. 103–114. Grower Books, London.

Dichter, E. (1968). "To Buy or Not to Buy," p. 48. Geo. J. Ball, Inc., West Chicago, Illinois.

Dietz, C. (1974). "Garden Seed Product Information Manual," p. 54. Vaughan's Seed Co., Downers Grove, Illinois.

Dietz, C. (1976). Sowing schedules for bedding plants. *In* "A Penn State Manual" (John W. Mastalerz, ed), pp. 55–65. Pennsylvania Flower Growers, University Park.

Harrington, J. E. (1968). Factors affecting seed environment. *Veg. Crop Manage.* January, pp. 6–11.

Holden, J. (1976). Production . . . back to basics—seed & scheduling *Proc. Int. Bedding Plant Conf., 9th* pp. 183–196. Bedding Plants, Inc., Okemos, Michigan.

Karser, R. (1973). Marketing bedding plants to the garden centers. *Proc. Nat. Bedding Plant Conf., 6th* pp. 103–114. Bedding Plants, Inc., Okemos, Michigan.

Miller, W. F., and Sooter, C. (1967). Improving emergence of pelleted vegetable seed. *Trans. ASAE* **10**(5), 658–666.

Nichols, L. P., and Nelson, P. E. (1976). Diseases in bedding plants. "A Penn State Manual" (John W. Mastalerz, ed.), pp. 406–422. Pennsylvania Flower Growers, University Park.

Pederson, C. A., and Wright, M. (1961). "Salesmanship, Principles and Methods," p. 710. Richard D. Irwin, Inc. Homewood, Illinois.

Streu, H. T. (1976). Insects in bedding plants. "A Penn State Manual," pp. 423–436. Pennsylvania Flower Growers, University Park.

Tayama, H. K., Kiplinger, D. C., Brooks, W. M., Staby, G. L., Powell, C. C., Lindquist, R. K., Poole, H. A., Farley, J. D., and Robertson, J. L. (1975). "Tips on Growing Ornamental and Vegetable Bedding Plants." Coop. Ext. Serv., Ohio State Univ., Columbus.

White, J. W. (1970). Growing media for geraniums. *In* "A Penn State Manual" (John W. Mastalerz, ed.), pp. 56–71. Pennsylvania Flower Growers, University Park.

White, J. W. (1976). Growing media for bedding plants. *In* "A Penn State Manual," pp. 113–133. Pennsylvania Flower Growers, University Park.

Zehner, M. (1969). Consumer purchase patterns for bedding plants. *Mich. Florist* **455,** 5, 21, 25, 29.

20
Hanging
Baskets

James K. Rathmell, Jr.

I. INTRODUCTION

Hanging baskets are grown by many flower growers all over the United States. Forerunners of the hanging baskets in use today were wire frames lined with sheet moss. In the late 1960s, the use of plastic containers helped to expand the hanging basket production and sales.

Holiday pot plant growers, bedding plant producers, carnation growers, rose growers—to name a few—all have hanging baskets in their production houses. A wide range of plant material is being grown. Hanging baskets in some parts of the United States are tiered five or six plants high in production houses. This type of growing is satisfactory in high light areas and is used mainly for foliage plants.

Many growers regard hanging baskets as an excellent way to supplement their income. The reasoning is that the air space above the bench crop is free space. Since growers must heat the greenhouse for other crops, a hanging basket is considered a bonus crop. One carnation grower realizes $30,000 from the sale of hanging baskets grown over his carnation crop.

A Lancaster County, Pennsylvania, grower produces 5000 hanging baskets in a wooded area. This crop is grown during the summer months and is sold before danger of frost.

Hanging baskets have given flower growers and nurserymen another dimension to their production. Many growers have discovered that the range of plant material they can grow is limited only by their imaginations.

All kinds of bedding plants and foliage plants are grown in hanging baskets. Hanging baskets started out as a spring sales item, but the production has become a year-round enterprise.

II. CONTAINERS

Plastic containers are used by the majority of growers for their hanging basket crop. These containers have attached wires and attached or removable saucers. Conventional colors for most plastic hanging basket containers are white, green, or brown, although various shades of yellow, blue, or red are also used. Some growers spray a dull black paint on plastic containers in an effort to hide the plastic pot. Plastic containers come in a range of sizes, the most popular being 20 and 25 cm. Other sizes frequently used are 10, 15, 17, and 22 cm.

Overwatering can be a problem in plastic containers, especially if the plants used are small. Problems are avoided, however, if excess water is allowed to drain. Attached saucers do not allow the soil to dry out, since water may be confined to the saucer.

Fig. 1. (A and B) Established poinsettia plants placed in lower half of plastic pot.

(C) Top plastic rim is put in place.

(D) Hanging basket of poinsettias are ready for sale.

Clay pots with attached saucers and chains are also used as hanging baskets. In some areas of the United States, a wire clip hanger (orchid hanger) is used for a hanging basket.

Cedar and redwood containers come in several shapes and sizes. Cedar slabs nailed into various shapes make attractive containers. Wood containers are very durable and have more appeal than plastic ones.

Ceramic pots, Mexican-type pottery, and fiberglass containers are also available. Generally, these containers are offered for sale to the homeowner at garden centers, flower shops, and similar outlets. The customer uses these containers for planting at home. The disadvantages of this type of container are higher cost and lack of drainage holes.

Wire baskets are available with a liner insert, or can be lined with sheet sphagnum moss. The sides of the wire basket lined with moss can be planted to give the appearance of a large ball of growing plants. This container will dry out rapidly and should not be placed in a windy location. A plastic-netted basket is available in some stores.

A new plastic basket is now available. This basket separates into three parts (see Fig. 1). The bottom has side holes or windows. Full-grown plants can be laid into place, but are not pushed through. The lid covers the side hole openings and snaps into place, thus giving the basket additional height. The saucer has a snap-on feature and can be added prior to final sale.

Other types of containers include pressed fiber shells, fern roots cut into various shapes, coconut husks, clear plastic bowls, and glass bowls.

The following guidelines may help in the selection of a hanging basket container: (1) Does the pot have drainage holes? (2) Is the container easy to hang? (3) Will the container last for a reasonable time? (4) Is there ample root space? (5) Could a saucer be attached? (6) Is the filled basket and container too heavy for the hanger support? (A watered container becomes very heavy.) (7) Is the container more conspicuous than the plant? (Plants should be more prominent than containers.)

III. SOIL MIXTURES

A prime rule for soil mixtures used in hanging baskets, as well as other containers, is to keep the medium loose. A standard potting mixture such as 1:1:1 or 2:1:1 (soil, sphagnum moss, and perlite) can be used. The medium should be free of weed seeds, insects, disease organisms, and harmful chemicals.

Soilless mixtures (peat–perlite or peat–vermiculite) are satisfactory because they are lightweight. These mixtures, however, will dry out very rapidly. A mixture that is primarily soil will become very heavy when wet.

IV. WATERING

Watering hanging baskets in a greenhouse can be a time-consuming operation. Baskets are generally hung high enough above eye level in the greenhouse so that people do not bump into the pots. Therefore, care must be taken that all pots are watered.

Growers producing large numbers of hanging baskets use plastic watering tubes to water each container (Fig. 2). The "spaghetti" system can be used to good advantage when pots are grown over walk areas or alongside walls. Where possible, containers should be hung over the walk area and not above other growing plants. Plants growing below, therefore, are not splashed with dripping water from plants above. This practice prevents the spread of disease from one plant to another. Hanging baskets tend to dry out quickly because of air circulation. Plants with large leaf areas or plants grown in wire or open-sided containers should be checked frequently and watered when necessary.

Use of a wetting agent will help moisten the peat in the potting medium. The medium should be watered thoroughly each time, so plant growth is uniform.

A new material, Hydrogel soil amendment, can be incorporated into the potting medium. Use of this material will increase available water in the container, thus reducing time between waterings.

Plants should never be allowed to wilt, nor should they be overwatered.

Fig. 2. Individual plastic water tubes are added to each pot to help prevent disease problems.

Watering, although a time-consuming operation, is critical if plants are to develop normally.

Plants grown in wire and sphagnum moss baskets can be plunged into a container filled with water. This type of basket is very hard to resoak once the peat is allowed to dry.

V. FERTILIZATION

Plants in hanging baskets require proper nutrient balance. One should use standard greenhouse fertilization practices, based on the type of plant grown in the container.

Liquid or water-soluble fertilizer can be used. Slow-release fertilizers are excellent choices for hanging baskets. If a soilless mixture is used, slow-release fertilizer can be applied and will provide an adequate fertilizer reserve. The manufacturer's recommendations on slow-release fertilizers should be followed, since excessive amounts can burn plant roots and are hard to leach.

VI. PLANTING IN THE CONTAINER

The best results are obtained with seedlings or cuttings that have been started in cell paks or separate pots. Plant material should be well established before it is transplanted into the hanging basket. Plant material grown in 5 to 15-cm pots can be used to plant up hanging baskets.

Seeds or cuttings can be started in the basket, but the grower must wait for the containers to look "filled out" before adding more plants to the pot. Crowding the container is not recommended. Ample room should be allowed for the seedlings or cuttings to grow.

A 1- to 5-cm space from growing medium to container rim is necessary for proper watering. Filling the hanging basket even with the rim makes it very difficult to water the plants adequately, whereas overwatering can occur if too much space is available.

Most hanging baskets sold in the United States are planted with one cultivar or plant species, such as 'Pink Cascade' petunias or impatiens. Combination baskets are very popular in Europe and some parts of the United States, especially in California. The outer rim of the container has trailing plants, such as lobelia or campanula. The center of the container is planted with upright or half-erect plants, such as dusty miller, geraniums (but not the ivy type), and heliotrope.

An unusual hanging basket can be created by using a wire basket lined with sphagnum moss. This container is filled with potting mix, a board is then placed on top of the basket, and it is inverted. The result is a hemisphere of sphagnum moss ready for planting. Cuttings or young seedlings are inserted into the wire frame. Plants must be spaced to allow for growth. After plants have become established the container is inverted so the basket is hanging normally. The top of the container is then planted with the same type of plant material. It is suggested that a swivel attachment be used so the basket turns freely. This will permit all the plants to receive ample sunlight.

A globe effect can be created using two wire baskets planted upside down. The two containers are then wired together to form a ball of plants. Supporting the container is important, and a strong wire can be run through the center of both baskets. A swivel will ensure that the globe spins freely. This type of container (wire frame and sphagum moss) will dry out very rapidly when placed in a windy location.

VII. GROWING PROCEDURE

Growers who specialize in hanging baskets generally provide a special support framework to hang the baskets. This type of support is very useful. Frequently, however, growers hang containers on every available pipe or nail in the greenhouse, causing an extra weight load on the roof structure: some plastic greenhouses have collapsed because of the added weight (see Fig. 3).

The use of A or T frames eliminates the stress of weight on the roof structure. In addition, it is possible to pull a thermal curtain over the top of the frame. It is, however, impossible to use a thermal curtain where hanging baskets are hung from every roof rafter.

Fig. 3. Hanging baskets on greenhouse rafters

In high light areas, growers frequently hang baskets creating a "curtain effect" (Fig. 4). One pot is placed over the top of another pot, and these may be hanging at a height of 2 m or more.

Side walls or space under gutters are frequently used for hanging baskets. Plants hanging over walks should be high enough so they do not present a safety hazard. Hanging baskets can also be grown on greenhouse benches or floors. Generally, the grower places the hanging basket on individual inverted pots. Top-quality plants can be grown using this method.

Outdoor production of hanging baskets is another possibility. The use of a shadecloth or snow fence is recommended to reduce light intensity and to prevent plants from drying out too rapidly. In areas where frost occurs, outdoor growing must be limited to summer production.

One Lancaster County, Pennsyivania florist produces hanging baskets in a wooded area that had been cleared. Barbed wire was strung between the trees to hang the pots. The barbs prevented the pots from sliding together. A special water line was laid and the pots were hand watered.

Hanging baskets are frequently considered as being grown in the "free" air space of the greenhouse. Growers sometimes try to put too many pots in this space, because it is heated. This practice results in poor-quality plants, since the crop below suffers from lack of light. Furthermore, splashing water and falling flower petals or leaves can intensify disease problems (*Botrytis*) on crops located under hanging baskets.

Fig. 4. Ferns growing in "curtain effect."

VIII. PINCHING

Uniform plants in a hanging basket can be best achieved through a regular schedule of pinching and shaping of the plants. Cuttings and/or seedlings can be pinched on a regular schedule prior to planting in the final container. Pinched plants generally will be larger, more floriferous, and better shaped than plants that have one or two dominant shoots.

IX. SHIPPING AND HANDLING

Shipping and handling of the finished product are the biggest problems encountered by the producer of hanging baskets. The majority of growers

Fig. 5. Hanging basket dropped in container used for sleeving in plastic.

sleeve the finished basket (Fig. 5). Another approach is to place the finished product into a large supermarket paper shopping bag.

Plants are sometimes shipped in flats or cardboard boxes, but care is needed when plants are handled in this way. Hanging baskets cannot be trucked by hanging them from supports inside the van. The motion of the truck will cause the baskets to sway back and forth, resulting in damaged flowers and foliage.

X. MARKETING

The following suggestions may help to increase retail sales.

1. Hang plants at eye level, to make it easy for customers to see the plants.
2. Display hanging baskets effectively. Mass displays are quite effective.
3. Keep plants watered.
4. Maintain the appearance of the plants while in the sales area. Old flowers and dead or dying leaves should be removed.
5. Do not crowd containers. Allow ample room for the basket to be removed by the customer. This practice will prevent broken branches or flowers on adjoining plants.

XI. SELECTION OF PLANT MATERIAL

The following list has been compiled from various sources which are given in the references at end of chapter.

A. Flowering Plants

Abutilon (flowering maple)—Several species of this plant make attractive hanging basket plants. One of the best species is *Abutilon megapotamicum variegatum* (weeping Chinese lantern).
Other successful varieties include *A. pictum* and *A. striatum*. Propagate by cuttings. Pinch back to make a bushy plant.
Achimenes (nut orchid, cupid's-bower, magic flower)—Plant six to eight rhizomes in a 15-cm pot. Pinch to induce branching. New European cultivars offer larger blooms. Beautiful pastel shades in blooms. Member of gesneriad family.
Ageratum houstonianum (floss flower, paint brush)—Sunny location. Mix two colors in one pot. Upright, bushy growth.
Antirrhinum majus (snapdragon)—Sunny location. Use dwarf types.
Begonia (*Begonia* species)—Many *Begonia semperflorens* hybrids as well as other cultivars can be used. Many of the tuberous cultivars and florist-type

pot plants can be readily adapted for hanging baskets. Sun or partial shade is needed, depending on the cultivar.

Browallia speciosa, variety major (browallia)—Sunny location. At temperatures below 16°C, foliage becomes chlorotic and growth ceases. Browallia blooms for an extended period of time and grows from seed or cuttings. Seed sown in September–October will result in plants ready for sale in May. Use four to six plants in a 25-cm container. Take cuttings up to March. Do not overwater, as Browallia roots will be readily damaged by excessive watering.

Campanula isophylla (star of Bethlehem, Italian bellflower)—Sunny location. Use three plants in 20-cm pot or four to six plants in a 25-cm pot.

Chrysanthemum morifolium (chrysanthemum)—Sunny location. Cascading cultivars will give best results.

Clerodendrum Thomsoniae (glory bower, bleeding heart vine, tubeflower)— Propagated by tip cuttings. A shrub with twining vinelike properties. Use three plants per 20-cm basket and four plants per 25-cm basket. These plants grow best in a growing medium that is acid, which helps to prevent chlorosis. Plants are salable in 8 to 10 weeks. Requirements include full sun in winter and partial shade in summer. Do not overwater.

Coleus blumei (coleus)—New cultivars used for bedding plants make excellent hanging basket material. Pinch frequently to ensure bushy growth. Remove flower buds as they form.

Coleus rehneltianus cv. 'Trailing Queen'—Generally used in hanging baskets.

Columnea—A wide assortment of Columnea make excellent basket plants, including: *C. arguta; C. gloriosa; C. hirta; C. microphylla; C. rulae; Columnea* X 'Chocolate Soldier'; and *Columnea* X 'Maarsen's Flame.' To set flowers, grow 13°–16°C in December to January. Start to dry out plant in October. Give no water in December.

Convolvulus tricolor (morning glory, dwarf glorybind)—Sunny location. Use dwarf cultivars. Provides abundant flowers in a dry, sunny location.

Cuphaea platycentra (firecracker plant, Mexican cigar plant)—Sunny location. Plants bloom 4 to 5 months after seed is sown. Uniform flowering.

Dianthus latifolius; Dianthus deltoides; Dianthus plumarius (garden pinks; carnations)—Sunny location. Use new cultivars. Plants are free blooming and have intense colors.

Dimorphotheca auranticus (Cape marigold)—Sunny location. Plants have sprawling growth. Flowers are yellow and white.

Felicia ammeloides (blue daisy, blue Marguerite)—Sunny location. Pinch to induce branching. Old flowers do not drop off and must be removed by hand.

Fuchsia hybrids (lady's ear-drops)—Partial shade. One of the most popular hanging basket items for spring sales. Use three plants in 20- or 22-cm pot and four to six plants in a 25-cm pot. Pinch plants to develop shape. Constant pinching is necessary to achieve good branching. Last pinch for

Mother's Day sale is April 1 and for Memorial Day sale is April 12. Remind customers that fuchsias need shade. Foliage will burn if placed in direct sun.

Gamolepis tagetes (sunshine daisy)—Sunny location. Plants grow 10 to 25 cm high. Flowers are daisylike, bright yellow to orange, and 1 to 2 cm in diameter. Profuse flowering. Seedlings are difficult to transplant, except when very small.

Gilia capitata (blue thimble flower)—Sunny location. Long-lasting flower. Blooms are 2 cm across and globe-shaped. The cultivar, Stardust, is 15 to 22 cm tall. Flower colors are golden yellow, bright rose, cream, orange, red, and sky blue.

Heliotropium peruvianum or *H. arborescens* (heliotrope)—Sunny location. Fragrant blooms. Pinch to shape plant and to provide flowering shoots. Long lateral shoots that abscise when flowering will occur after pinching unless dwarf selections are used.

Impatiens sultani (sultanas, snapweed, busy Lizzie, and patience)—Shady location. New Guinea cultivars will tolerate full sun. Pinch to induce branching and compactness. An excellent plant for a shady location. New hybrids are very colorful and everblooming. Use four to six plants in a 25-cm basket. This plant is considered a problem while it is growing in the greenhouse, as the blooms drop readily on the crop underneath and disease problems can start during cloudy, wet weather.

Ipomoea (morning glory)—Sunny location. This is a vine, so plants may grow uncontrollably. The vines will climb the wires supporting the basket. Colorful blooms.

Lantana delicatissima (trailing lantana)—Sunny location. Pinch plant frequently to shape. Good for hot, windy location. Long-flowering. Excellent plant for combination pots.

Lathyrus odoratus (sweet pea)—Sunny location. Use dwarf and bush cultivars that are heat resistant. Start seedlings in pots, and then transplant. Do not plant seedlings sparsely in basket. A cool-climate plant.

Layia campestris or *L. elegans* (tidy tips)—Sunny location. Plants grow 30 to 45 cm tall. Daisylike flowers.

Lobelia erinus (fairy wings)—In hot locations keep plants in partial shade. Plants grow best during cool summers. Use cascade cultivars. Flowers are blue. Sow seed January 1 and transplant clumps in 7.5-cm pots. Use three or four pots in a 25-cm basket. Pinch plants to shape. Do not allow soil to dry out. Makes an excellent edging plant in combination baskets.

Myosotis (forget-me-not)—Semishade–sunny location. Blue flowers.

Nasturtium tropaeolum majus (nasturtium)—Sunny location. Use annual cultivars that are dwarf.

Nemesia strumosa (nemesia)—Sunny location. A cool-climate plant. Use dwarf cultivars.

Nierembergia hippomanica caerulea (cup flower)—Sunny location. Use dwarf cultivars. Shear back to 7 to 10 cm after heavy flowering.

Oxalis oregano (Irish shamrock, redwood sorrel)—Propagation by division and bulblets. Plant will bloom any time. Other species include *Oxalis Deppei* and *Oxalis braziliensis.*

Pelargonium peltatum (ivy geranium)—Sunny location. Considered one of the most popular hanging basket plants for spring sales. Pinch plants to make them fuller. The main problem is a foliage disorder called edema. This physiological disorder develops on the underside of the leaves and can detract from the plant. It can be prevented by maintaining the pH of the medium at 4.5 to 5.5, by keeping nitrogen and iron levels high, by watering in the morning with container saucers removed, by maintaining the light intensity between 21 and 37 klx, by growing plants in a well-ventilated greenhouse, and by keeping plants away from the upper part of the greenhouse because of excessive heat. Use three plants in a 20- to 25-cm basket. The following schedule was developed by Carlson (1973) and is based on an 18°C night temperature.

Time planted	No. cuttings	Pinching
December 1	1	When ready, until mid-March
February	3	Two to three times
March 1	5	No pinching

Cultivar selection is very important, as some plants lose flowers too readily.

Petunia hybrida (petunia)—Full sun. Use six plants in a 25-cm basket or three to four plants in a 20-cm container. Hanging baskets can be started from seed sown in mid-January. Seedlings can be grown about 6 weeks in packs, and then can be shifted to the final containers. A cascading series makes excellent basket plants. Some growers rely extensively on multiflora cultivars.

Portulaca grandiflora (portulaca, rose-moss)—Sunny location. Excellent for hot sun and drought conditions. Free-blooming annual. Plants start flowering in 8 weeks.

Sanvitalia (creeping zinnia)—Sunny location. A good trailer with double golden flowers.

Schlumbergera truncata (Christmas cactus)—New cultivars have added to the popularity of this plant. It normally blooms from Thanksgiving through Christmas. Propagate with stem cuttings that have at least two segments. Flowering can be initiated by giving plants a 12-hour period of darkness.

Streptocarpus (Cape primrose)—New hybrids from the United States and Europe have resulted in attractive foliage and flower colors. Member of gesneriad family. Propagate by seed, division of plant, or leaf cuttings.

New hybrids flower over long period of time. Several species make good hanging basket plants, including *S. saxorum* (false African violet) and *S. Holstii.*

Thunbergia alata and *Thunbergia gibsonii* (Black-eyed Susan vine)—Sunny location. Grow from seed or cuttings. Vine blooms over a long period of time. Do not allow plants to dry out completely.

Torenia fournieri (wishbone flower or torenia)—Shady location. Grows 20 to 30 cm tall. Blue purple flowers.

Verbena elegans var. asperata (verbena)—Sunny location. An excellent hanging basket plant. Pink flowers, constant bloomer. Use six cuttings in a 25-cm pot. Pinch to shape. When this plant is grown at cool temperatures (13°C), flower color is intense and growth is compact. Plants can wilt but will recover rapidly when watered.

Vinca rosea (periwinkle)—Shady location. Sow seed in January for June bloom. Use creeping periwinkle or border-type for baskets. Cultivar Little Blanche has white flowers and makes attractive basket plants.

Viola tricolor (pansy)—Sunny location. Makes attractive hanging basket plant.

B. Foliage Plants

Asparagus densiflorus cv. *Sprengeri* (asparagus fern, Spengeri fern)—Grow from seed or division. An excellent hanging basket plant. Can tolerate 2°C without damage. Pinch tips to induce bushiness.

Cactus—Another group of plants that has many species excellent for hanging baskets, including *Aporocactus flagelliformis* (rattail cactus), *Chamaecereus Sylvestri* (peanut cactus), and *Hylocereus undatus* (night-blooming cereus).

Ceropegia Woodii (rosary vine, string of hearts)—Small, gray tubers dangle from the thin, purple stems. This plant is a succulent and has a low humidity requirement. Can be grown on a small trellis. Grow from tip cuttings or bulblets. Cut back old stems to induce new growth.

Chlorophytum comosum 'Variegatum' (foliage light green and white) (spider plant, airplane plant)—One cultivar is *C. comosum picturatum,* white-green leaves with white or yellow stripe. *C. comosum* has a solid green leaf. Wide, deep pots are suggested. Fleshy roots tend to push entire plant out of pot. Propagate by aerial plantlets, or division of plant. Can withstand temperatures of 2°C without damage. Tip burn is associated with fluoride damage. Keep calcium levels high.

Cissus rhombifolia (grape ivy)—Excellent basket plant because of its growth habit. It will cascade as well as climb. Propagate by tip cuttings or leaf-bud cuttings. Pinch back when 30 to 40 cm tall to encourage new growth. Makes excellent houseplant because of low light requirement.

Cissus discolor (trailing begonia, tapestry vine)—Attractive foliage. Do not overwater. Propagate by tip cuttings. Pinch often to make bushy.

Cissus antartica (kangaroo vine)—Has large foliage. Does well in low light. Propagate by tip cuttings.

Crassula perforata (weeping jade or necklace vine)—Attractive plant because side shoots develop continually. Propagate by top cuttings.

Epipremnum aureum (marble queen ivy)—Use three small plants in a 20-cm pot. Can be trained to climb as well as to cascade in a hanging basket. Propagate by tip cuttings.

Ficus pumila (creeping fig)—A difficult plant to grow, but makes a good basket plant. Will grow as a vine. Propagate by tip cuttings.

Fittonia Verschaffeltii argyroneura (fittonia silver-nerve, silver-threads, mosaic plant)—Foliage and shoots cascade over edge of container. Low-growing plant. Do not overwater. Propagate by division or tip cuttings.

Ferns—A wide range of ferns do well in hanging baskets. Some of them are *Adiantum tenerum* (fan maidenhair fern), *Asplenuim* daucifolium (mother fern), *Davallia fejeensis* (rabbit's foot fern), *Nephrolepis exaltata 'Bostoniensis'* (Boston sword fern), *N. exaltata* 'Florida Ruffles' (Florida ruffles sword fern), *N. exaltata* 'Compacta' (dwarf Boston sword fern), *Platycerium bifurcatum* (staghorn fern), *Polypodium aureum* (hare's-foot fern), and *Pteris cretica* (table fern). Staghorn ferns are generally grown on a piece of *Osmunda* fern that is attached to wood. Some growers cut a hole in a plastic hanging basket and place the staghorn fern so it grows out of the hole.

Gynura aurantiaca (purple-passion vine)—A vine with foliage of a different color. Propagate by tip cuttings. Prune frequently to encourage side shoots. Yellow or orange daisylike flowers. Remove flower buds as they appear.

Hedera helix (English ivy)—A number of cultivars of this plant make excellent hanging basket material. Prune frequently to stimulate bushy growth. Train some runners on basket supports.

Helixine soleirolii (baby's tears)—High moisture requirements. Excellent in small hanging pots. Can be trained to grow over mossed wire baskets.

Hemigraphis alternata 'Exotica' (purple waffle plant)—Propagate by tip cuttings. It has purple foliage that is deeply puckered (resembling a waffle). Cut back to stimulate bushiness.

Hoya carnosa 'Compacta' (compact wax plant)—This is one of several cultivars that make attractive basket plants. Propagate by tip cuttings or stem segments. Vine trails and climbs its support. Flowers are attractive and have pleasant odor. Avoid direct sun because the foliage burns.

Oplismenus hirtellus variegatus (basket grass)—White stripes in leaves add to interest. Propagate by cuttings or division.

Othonna crassifolia (little pickles)—This succulent has fleshy and cylindrical leaves, hence its common name. Propagate with cuttings or division. Small, daisylike flowers. Pinch to induce bushiness.

Pellionia daveauana (watermelon begonia)—Another species is *Pellionia pulchra* (satin pellionia), which is creeping plant that has good hanging tendencies. Stems trail and follow the container. Propagate by cutting or division. Prune to shape plant.

Peperomia—An assortment of these plants make good hanging basket plants. Some species are *Peperomia caperata* 'Emerald Ripple' (emerald ripple peperomia), *Peperomia obtusifolia variegata* (variegated peperomia), *Peperomia sandersii* (watermelon peperomia), and *Peperomia peperomia* (prostrate peperomia). Propagate by tip cuttings. Prune to shape plant. Do not overwater.

Pilea—Several species make excellent hanging baskets, including, *P. depressa* (creeping pilea), *P. involucrata* (friendship plant), *P. nummulariifolia* (creeping charlie), and, *P. repens* and *P. microphylla* (artillery plant or artillery fern). A rapid grower. Propagate by cuttings or seed. Can stand several prunings if it grows too vigorously.

Pereskia aculeata (leafy cactus, Barbados gooseberry, lemon vine)—Member of cactus family. Propagate from tip cuttings.

Plectrantus australis (Swedish ivy) called creeping charlie by West Coast growers—several other species are *P. oertendahlii, P. minima,* and *P. coleoides* 'Marginatus' (candle plant or Australian ice plant). A fast grower. Member of mint family (has square stems). Propagate by tip cuttings. Pinch back to shape plant.

Rhipsalis—Member of the cactus family. One species, *R. capilliformis* (old man's head), resembles a bunch of green sticks of various sizes on branches. Propagate by cutting. A slow grower.

Saxifraga stolonifera (mother-of-thousands, strawberry geranium)—The small plantlets develop on long runners. Propagate with these runners. Can be overwatered.

Sedum—A wide range of sedums make excellent basket plants. Many of the hardy outdoor varieties can be used. One popular plant is *S. morganianum* (burro's tail)—Tails on this plant can be as long as 2 m. Grow dry: water only from April through September. The tails are brittle and break off easily. This plant is difficult to ship. Propagate by tip cuttings or leaf cuttings. Other plants include *Sedum caeruleum* (can be planted on a mossed basket), *S. divergens* (old man's bones), *S. × rubrotinctum* (Christmas cheers), *S. sieboldii* (October plant), *S. brevifolium, S. dasyphyllum,* and S. pachyphyllum (jelly beans).

Senecio—Another large family that has many species adapted for hanging baskets. Some popular ones are *S. macroglossus c.v. Variegatus'* (Cape ivy, orange glow vine; rubber ivy plant, Natal ivy, wax vine), *S. mikanioides* (German ivy, parlor ivy, water ivy), *S. Rowleyanus* (string of pearls), and *S. confusus* (orange glow vine, Mexican flame vine)—Propagate all species by tip cuttings. Pinch to induce bushiness.

Tolmiea Menziesii (piggyback plant, pickaback plant, thousand-mothers, youth-on-age)—Never let soil dry out. Propagate by young plantlets that develop on the leaves.

Tradescantia species—The wandering Jews have many species that make attractive hanging basket plants. Some of these are *T. multiflora* (Tahitian bridal veil, wedding bell vine), *T. navicularis* (chain plant), *T. sillamontana* (white velvet, white gossamer), *Zebrina pendula* (wandering Jew, inch plant), and *Z. pendula* 'Quadricolor' (has green, red, and white stripes in leaves). The majority of these plants are very fast growers. Propagate by tip cuttings. Pinch to induce bushiness.

C. Herbs, Vegetables, and Fruit

A wide range of herbs, vegetables, and fruits will grow in hanging baskets and provide an unusual marketable item.

1. Herbs

Chives—Use clumps, or seed heavily.
Mint—Excellent trailing plant.
Parsley — Use six plants in a 20-cm basket.
Thyme—Use creeping thyme.
Rosemary—Use prostrate cultivars.

2. Vegetables

Tomatoes—Use small-fruited cultivars
Cucumbers—Use dwarf nonvining types.
Squash—Use dwarf nonvining types.
Sweet potatoes—Attractive foliage: use 25-cm pot, and slips, and do not fill container full of growing medium.
New Zealand spinach—Good for summer greens.
Lettuce—Cool-temperature crop.

3. Fruit

Dwarf pomegranate—Interesting plant and unique fruit.
Strawberries—Use alpine or conventional cultivars, and use bare root plants.

The suggestions developed by Dr. Peter A. Ferretti at The Pennsylvania State University for hanging baskets are shown in Table I. Dr. Ferretti had a number of suggestions for strawberry crops: 'Earlibelle' ripened earliest; 'Pocahontas' had the greatest number of fruit ripening in a 6-week period (an average of 45 per basket) and 'Apollo' plants had the largest, most uniform fruit.

All strawberry cultivars grown at 17°–18°C had some ripe fruit by the first

Table I

Suggestions for Hanging Baskets [a]

Crop	Cultivar	Estimated days to salability [a]	Plants per pot
Lettuce	Oak leaf	23	10–15
Lettuce	Ruby	29	10–15
Lettuce	Salad bowl	29	4–6
Lettuce	Slobolt	34	4–6
Lettuce	Buttercrunch	35	6–8
Spinach	Winter bloomsdale	25–30	8–10
Summer greens	New Zealand spinach (not a true spinach)	60	8–10
Swiss chard	Rhubarb (red)	45	12–15
Chives	—	40–50	40–50
Parsley	Extra triple curled	60	8–12
Parsley	Dark green curled	60	8–12
Parsley	Moss curled	60	8–12
Parsley	Plain or Italian	64	12–15
Strawberries	Earlibelle	50–60	6–7
(Plants)	Pocahontas	50–60	6–7
	Apollo	50–60	6–7

[a]For a 20-cm pot.

[b]Days to salability of January–February grown crops will probably be about 15 to 20 days shorter than the maturity dates given for crops growing under optimum conditions in the home garden (Pennsylvania).

week in May and were salable at that time. Plants were planted in pots on March 15.

For heavier fruit production and sturdier, salable strawberry plants it has been suggested that plants be started in January and held at 2°–4°C until they bloom. At this time, they should be given 4°C. night temperature and 10°–13°C day temperatures.

D. Standard or Tree-Form Plants

Standard is a term used by horticulturists to describe a plant that stands upright with a single stalk. An example is a standard or tree rose. Many greenhouse plants with woody stems can be trained to grow upright and trained into tree shapes.

A plant grown as a standard is featured as a single specimen in a container. Frequently such plants are seen in outdoor parks or inside conservatories at botanical gardens. They are not generally grown by commercial florists because of the high cost of production. Retail sales are therefore limited because of the cost factor. Many wholesale growers cannot determine sale price because of the longer production time.

Plants which can be trained as standards include abutilon, angel-winged begonia, chrysanthemum, coleus, daisy, English ivy on Fatshedera, fuchsia, geranium, heliotrope, *Streptosolen Jamesoni,* impatiens, lantana, and some herbs. Any plant that is a fast grower and lends itself to branching when pinched might be considered for standard training.

Some basic guidelines should be considered in the selection of plant material for standards. The young plant should have strong tip growth. A seedling or rooted cutting that has one strong stem should be used. Training can start at any time.

The main shoot is staked to prevent it from breaking off or growing crooked. This procedure also encourages the plant to grow in an upright position. Leaves on the main stem should be left on the plant to help it grow, which is essential to keep the plant alive and growing while it is being trained. Side shoots should be removed as soon as possible. As the plant assumes the desired shape and is able to produce active growth at the top or head of the plant, lower leaves on the main stem may fall off, on account of old age or other causes. The plant is then shifted to a larger pot. A plant 30 cm tall can be grown in a 20-cm pot. Wooden tubs are used for older standards.

A regular potting mix is used, depending on the plant being grown. Use of an artificial soil mix, such as peat–vermiculite, is not recommended. This light mix may not support the plant if the plant becomes top-heavy. The potting mix should include some soil or clay particles.

The stem should be as straight as possible. A bamboo stake of sufficient height and diameter is used to support the plant while it is being trained. After the stem has matured the stake may be removed. If the bamboo stake is placed in a pot filled with artificial soil, it tends to fall over easily. The stake must be securely anchored in the pot. Wire ties ("Twist-ems") or string can be used to hold the stem against the stake, but the fastener must not cut into the stem.

When a grower repots a plant into a large container, some ballast such as crushed stone might be placed in the bottom, which would prevent the pot from tipping over, particularly if the plant is top-heavy.

After the plant grows to a predetermined height, the main growing tip is given a soft pinch. Side branches are pinched as needed to form a ball, pyramid, cone, or umbrella effect of flowers and leaves.

Topiary art can be practiced on some plants, which results in two or three "heads" on a single stem. By allowing one stem to go unpinched, one can form a new head from a single stem. Pinching is done as described previously. Twelve to 14 months are often required to develop a topiary.

1. Azaleas

The azalea is an attractive plant when grown in a standard shape. European growers have offered tree azaleas for many years. Many azalea trees are grafted.

It is possible to grow tree azaleas from strong, well-rooted cuttings that are single stemmed and straight. Side branches are pruned as they develop, and the main stem is staked to keep it straight. Plants can be headed at 100 to 120 cm. The top is pinched out and side branches are allowed to develop. Pinching must be continued to encourage more branching and bushiness.

2. Geranium Trees

Pelargonium cultivars that grow upright are easily trained into trees or standards. Basic rules for growing a standard plant should be followed. It is possible for a tree geranium to grow for 5 years or longer.

Gibberellic acid sprays at 250 ppm will hasten standard plant growth. It is possible to have a standard tree geranium in 4 to 6 months by using this growth regulator. For comparison, an untreated plant may take 12 to 16 months to attain the same results.

3. Fuchsia Trees

Fuschia trees are very popular items in Europe. Most garden centers, especially in England, offer fuchsia trees for retail sale. Fuchsia standards are planted in many outdoor flower beds in public parks. They are usually 1 to 2 m tall.

A straight-stemmed, vigorous plant is used, and the stem is supported by a stake. All side branches are removed as they develop, but leaves on the stem are not removed. After the plant has reached its desired height, the growing tip is pinched. To develop a bushy tree top, the new shoots resulting from the pinch are also pinched, leaving four leaves on each shoot. Pinching is repeated until the desired shape and size are achieved.

A wire frame can be placed on top of a 2-cm² redwood stake. A circular wire frame that has two horizontal cross-braces or spokes is used. The frame is hidden by shoots and foliage as the plant matures.

Some retail florists have fuchsia trees over 20 years old that are used for display.

4. Heliotrope Trees

Seedlings or cuttings can be used to start the standard, but seedlings make better standards than do cuttings, according to Craig (1906). Heliotrope is a long-term crop when grown as a standard. March or April plants that are trained into standards will produce large heads the following summer. Plants are generally over 1 m tall.

Four crops of flowers can be bloomed between May and October. Sometimes a heliotrope plant that is being trained into a tree form will start blooming. These flowers are removed and one of the growing tips is selected to continue training.

5. Ornamental Pepper Trees

Capsicum annuum plants can be trained into standards. They are generally grown to a 45-cm height from seedlings or cuttings. The top of the plant can be shaped into various forms, such as balls, squares, or cones.

A fruit crop develops in about 6 months. This plant is considered a novelty item and production is very time-consuming. Production costs are hard to realize when the plants are finally sold.

XII. WINDOW BOXES

The Hanging Gardens of Babylon could be considered the forerunner of today's window or balcony boxes. The king of Babylon, Nebuchadnezzer II (605–562 B.C.), had his workers construct a 64-ha square, 15-m high, stone platform. Platforms, in decreasing size, were built on top, creating a terraced pyramid that was 105 m high. Each flower bed was lined with lead to prevent leakage. Flowers, vines, and fruit trees were planted, resulting in a fabulous floral tribute to the new queen.

Smaller versions of these hanging gardens can be seen in many European countries. Use of window boxes or balcony boxes is very widespread in Europe. Tourists from the United States are amazed to see these colorful displays. In West Germany, it has been estimated that there are over 40,000 km of window or balcony boxes. Boxes of flowers are seen on cottages, high-rise apartments, bank buildings, and even at airports. A wide assortment of plant material is used in these containers. A national competition is held so that several European countries can select the city or town with the most colorful window boxes. Each year a selection committee chooses one town in Austria as having the best window or balcony box display in that country. The British Tourist Authority sponsors a national competition called "Britain in Bloom." Each year since 1963, approximately 300 cities, towns, and villages have entered this contest. York, in England, has even published a "how-to-do-it" leaflet for business firms.

Window boxes or balcony boxes are used on a very limited scale in most parts of the United States. Despite a statement made in 1907 by the National Council of Horticulture ("The use of window boxes is not to be recommended extensively except for crowded down-town districts, apartment houses and hotels."), window boxes or balcony boxes offer another market for bedding plant producers.

Harsh building lines can be softened with window and balcony boxes filled with flowers. A small bit of nature can be provided for people who lack gardening space. Regardless of the type of building or its use, window boxes will help beautify everyone's environment.

A. Types of Containers

Custom-made window boxes, generally made out of redwood or cedar, are available in various sizes and shapes. Other types of wood, such as pine, can be used but must be treated with a recommended wood preservative, such as copper naphthanate. Wooden window boxes can be constructed easily by many "do-it-yourself" builders. Custom-made boxes may be required on some buildings. There are metal inserts that can be used with some wooden boxes. Plastic-molded window boxes are generally shallower than wooden boxes and do not hold much growing medium. All boxes must contain drainage holes, so that soil does not become waterlogged, with the consequent damage to roots.

B. Potting Mixture

The planting medium for window boxes should be light and well aerated. Supports holding the filled window box must be sturdy enough to hold the box when the medium is wet. (See Section III on potting mixtures.)

C. Watering

Plastic pipe permanently attached to the building and trickle tubes to each window box will help make the watering job much easier. Watering with a garden hose can be laborious and difficult.

Table II

Window Box Plants[a]

Full sun
   Ageratum houstonianum (floss flower, paintbrush)
   Antirrhinum majus (snapdragon)
   Dimorphotheca aurantiaca (African daisy)
   Lobularia maritima (sweet alyssum)
   Pelargonium hortorum cultivars (geranium)
   Pelargonium peltatum cultivars (ivy geranium)
   Petunia hybrida (petunia, especially cascade cultivars)
   Phlox drummondi (annual phlox)
   Tagetes cultivars (marigold)
   Tropaeolum majus (nasturtium)
Light shade
   Begonia semperflorens (fibrous-rooted begonia)
   Campanula isophylla (Italian bellflower)
   Nierembergia species (cupflower)
   Oplismenus compositus (basket grass)
   Phacelia campanularia (desert bluebell)
   Torenia fournieri compacta (torenia)
Northern exposures (little sun, but not too dense shade)
   Begonia semperflorens (fibrous-rooted begonia)
   Begonia × *tuberhybrida* (tuberous begonia)
   Coleus blumei (coleus)
   Cymbalaria muralis (Kenilworth-ivy)
   Fuchsia × *hybrida* (lady's eardrops, ladies'-eardrops)
   Vinca minor (periwinkle)

---

[a]From Teuschev (1958).

Table III

Groupings for Window Box Plants[a]

Trailers (hang down 60 to 80 cm)
  Cymbalaria muralis (Kenilworth ivy)—dainty flowers
  Senecio mikanioides (German ivy)—best green and easiest to grow
  Vinca major cv. *variegata* (periwinkle)—best variegated
Edgers (hang down 8 to 25 cm)
  Mesembryanthemum cordifolium (ice plant)
  Saxifraga sarmentosa (strawberry geranium)
  Tradescantia species (wandering Jew)—easiest to grow
Centers
  Aloysia triphylla (lemon verbena)—best for fragrant leaves
  Nephrolepis exaltata 'Bostoniensis' (Boston sword fern)—best for shade
Climbers or trailers used for floral effect (climb or hang down 60 to 80 cm)
  Asarina erubescens (creeping gloxinia)
  Coboea scanelens (Mexican ivy, monastery bells, cup-and-saucer vine)—unique purplish
    flower
  Convolvulus mauritanicus (morning glory)
  Ipomoea acuminata (blue moonflower, blue dawn flower)
  Ipomoea alba (white moonflower)
  Manettia inflata (firecracker vine, Brazilian firecracker)
  Nasturtium tropaeolum majus (nasturtium)—the most popular trailers only (hang down 60
    to 80 cm)
  Pelargonium peltatum (ivy geranium)—the best edgers (hang down 15 to 20 cm)
  Alyssum maritimum (alyssum)—best white, fragrant
  Browallia speciosa cv. *major* (browallia)—best large blue
  Cuphea platycentra (cigar plant)
  Gazania splendens (treasure flower)—flowers close at night
  Lantana montevidensis (weeping lantana, trailing lantana)—best changeable
  Lobelia erinus (lobelia)—hangs down less
  Lobelia gracilis (lobelia)—best small blue
  Mimulus cupreus (monkey flower)—best yellow spotted
  Verbena × *hybrida* (verbena)—many colors
Centers
  Ageratum houstonianum (floss flower, paintbrush)—purplish blue
  Antirrhinum majus (snapdragon)—mixed colors
  Heliotropium peruvianum (heliotrope)—fragrant, violet
  Impatiens sultani (busy Lizzie, sultanas)
  Pelargonium × *hortorum* (geranium)
  Petunia hybrida (petunia)
Shade-demanding centers
  Begonia semperflorens (fibrous-rooted begonia)
  Begonia × *tuberhybrida* (tuberous begonia)
  Fuchsia hybrids (lady's ear-drops)

---

[a]From Miller (1907).

D. Plant Material and Planting

The choice of ornamental plants suitable for growing in window boxes or balcony boxes is enormous. Both upright and trailing plants can be used to advantage. The majority of window boxes are planted for display. A well-planted window box will look as good from behind as from the sidewalk.

Plant material should be chosen that will thrive in the light available to the window box. Window boxes can be planted for either seasonal or permanent effects.

A list of window box plants developed by Henry Teuscher, Curator of the Montreal Bontanical Garden (Teuscher, 1958) is presented in Table II. Another grouping for window box plants presented by Miller (1907) is provided in Table III.

Another list has also been prepared by Hieke (1976). Many of the same plant species are included in Hieke's list.

The choice of plant material ranges from annuals, biennials, houseplants, bulbous and tuberous plants, perennials, broadleaf trees, shrubs, and conifers. Any pendulous plant material planted on the outside edge can be attractive.

XIII. COMBINATION BOXES OR POTS

Combination boxes or pots are frequently sold in some parts of the United States for spring sales. This type of container is used to decorate graves in some cemeteries on Memorial Day (May 30).

One container used is made from cedar wood slabs. The bark helps give a rustic appearance to the container. Large clay pots (25- or 30-cm pans) are also used.

An assortment of annual flowering plants is used in the combination container. Generally, established plants growing in 5-, 7.5-, or 10-cm pots are used. The florist usually plants the container shortly before time of sale. Flowering plants are usually in full bloom or buds are showing color at the time of sale.

XIV. VERTICAL GARDENS

"Bluhende torfwande" or "flowering peat walls" have been featured at European flower shows for a number of years. The idea of vertical gardens is reported to have originated in 1944 by a seed firm in Switzerland. The popularity of growing plants in this dimension has spread in Europe, where it is used in public parks, garden centers, and other locations. This technique provides an attractive method of displaying plants, and creates a conversation piece.

There are a number of possibilities for growing plants vertically. The homeowner can use it to screen out an unwanted view. It can serve as a colorful back drop for an outdoor area. Garden centers use them to display bedding plants. Vertical gardens can be constructed and planted to any shape. A frame can be constructed in a square or rectangular shape and can be planted on one or both sides, depending upon placement. The ends can be planted, if desired. A barber pole design can be created. A square pillar offers another possibility for design. A modular design can be made to give a patchwork effect. A half-round design could be used as a wall hanger.

Commercial greenhouse owners in Guernsey, the Channel islands, and in England have adapted vertical gardens for strawberry production. They have used 10-cm polyethylene tubes filled with a soilless mix. The tubes vary in length from 4.8 to 7.2 m and are hung over a bar. Plants are spaced 22 cm apart in the tube.

The following information on vertical gardens can serve as a guide for construction, planting, maintenance, and plant material.

A. Construction Details

The frame is built out of metal or wood. If the garden is to be planted on both sides, the box should be 25 to 30 cm wide. A wall planted on both sides needs to be only 15 or 20 cm. (*Note:* Treat wood with copper naphthanate.) Attach wire to the inside or outside of the framework. A plastic-coated wire will not rust. The wire can be chicken wire mesh or a type of wire fencing. A plastic liner is placed inside the wire. Polypropylene screening will last much longer than polyethylene. Using horizontal wire cross-bracing at various places in the container will prevent bulges in the vertical garden (Fig. 6). The bottom of the box should be closed and made out of wood or asbestos to support the weight of the soil and plants. Casters can be attached to facilitate moving the vertical garden, if so desired. Do not use aluminum materials in the box, since fertilizers cause corrosion.

B. Planting Details

Use a light soil mix. A commercial peat-lite mixture is excellent. Moisten the medium prior to planting. Cut holes in the plastic at the desired spacing. Allow ample growing room for the plants. Plants should be close enough to create the look of a solid wall. Use small plants or cuttings. They should be slanted slightly upward when placed in the wall. The plants will bend up within a few days. The wall is best overplanted since gaps become noticeable and the sideways spreading of most plants is limited. Some examples of spacing include the following: *Begonia semperflorens* planted on a 1-m² wall at 12 × 15 cm requires 50 plants; at 10 × 10 centimeters, 80 plants are needed.

Fig. 6.   Wires attached at various points to prevent wire mesh from bulging out in the center.

C. Maintenance

Watering can be a problem. The top of the planter will tend to dry out, while the bottom of the planter is still moist. A plastic pipe with holes in it can be inserted in a horizontal position at the center of the wall. A pipe can be inserted in a vertical position in the barber pole design. A soil-soaker or ooze hose is very effective. It is possible to tie in an automatic watering device to the watering system. A fine spray of water can be used on the sides of the garden to help keep plants moist.

The vertical wall is very heavy after it is watered. It should be in its final location before it is filled, planted, and watered.

Slow-release fertilizer can be added to the growing medium before it is placed in the container. Regular application of a water-soluble fertilizer is also suggested. Follow the manufacturer's directions for all fertilizers.

D. Choice of Plant Material

A wide assortment of flowering plants, foliage plants, ground covers, bulbs, herbs, and vegetables can be planted in vertical gardens. Care must be taken to use appropriate plants in shady and sunny sites. *Begonia semperflorens,* impatiens, and petunia are excellent choices for vertical gardens (Fig. 7).

The following is a partial list of plants suitable for a vertical garden: Ageratum, Alternanthera (excellent), Alyssum, Arabis, Asparagus sprengeri, Begonia semperflorens (excellent), Begonia, tuberous (shade), Browallia, Calceolaria (small flowering types), Calendula, Campanula, Coleus, Dianthus, Exacum affine midget, ferns, Fuchsia (shade), Gazania, geranium, ivy-leaf, grass (ornamental), herbs (basil, chives, parsley, marjoram, rosemary), impatiens (shade), Lantana, Lobelia, marigold (dwarf types), Mesembryanthemum, pansy, petunia, Pilea, Portulaca, Primula, Sedum, snapdragon (dwarf cultivars), strawberries (nonrunning type, such as Alexandria), succulents, vegetables (lettuce, spinach), Verbena, Vinca rosea, and zinnia (dwarf varieties). The top of the vertical garden area can be planted with an assortment of plant material.

Fig. 7. Vertical garden of red and white fibrous rooted begonias planted as "barber pole." Wire frame is bent into circular shape, then plastic is inserted. Soilless mixture is added and begonia plants are inserted.

REFERENCES

HANGING BASKETS

Anonymous (1974). "Sunset Ideas for Hanging Garden." Lane Publ., Menlo Park, California.
Anonymous (1975a). "Container and Hanging Gardens," Ortho Book Series, pp. 40–47. Chevron Chem. Co., San Francisco, California.
Anonymous (1975b). Hang'em high summer baskets. *Plants Alive* **3**(7), 14–15.
Anonymous (1975c). 'Living With Hanging Plants." John Henry Co., Lansing, Michigan.
Anonymous (1977). "Gardening In Containers" (by editors of Sunset Books and Sunset Magazine). Lane Publ., Menlo Park, California.
Anonymous (1978). The Hanging Gardens of Babylon. *Can. Florist* **73**(2), 32–33.
Baumgardt, J. P. (1972). "Hanging Plants for Home, Terrace and Garden," Simon & Schuster, New York.
Buxton, B. R. (1954). Plants for hanging pots. *Plants Gard.* **10**(3), 182–185.
Carlson, W. (1973). Ivy geranium baskets—A growing demand. *Grow Mag.* 1, 6–7.
Coleman, M. J. (1975). "Hanging Plants for Modern Living." Merchants Publ. Co., Kalamazoo, Michigan.
Courter, J. A. (1977). Strawberries, promising, colorful bedding plants. *Ill. State Florists' Assoc. Bull.* **369,** 18–20.
Crane, W. D. (1968). Plants in hanging containers. *Plants Gard.* **24**(1), 81–83.
D'Eliscu, J. (1975). Hanging baskets, how to make and sell them—western style. *Proc. Int. Bedding Plant Conf, 8th* p. 135–140.
Graf, A. B. (1978). "Vines and Basket Plants Tropica," p. 13. Roehrs Co., East Rutherford, New Jersey.
Hull, O. S. (1962). Plants for hanging baskets. *Plants Gard.* **18**(3), 27–30.
Judd, R. W., Jr. (1975). Hanging-pots. *Conn. Greenhouse Newsl.* **68,** 6–10.
Kramer J. (1971). "Hanging Gardens," Scribner's, New York.
Maddux, R. (1978). Foliage hanging baskets–8-inch. *Ohio Florists' Assoc. Bull.* **583,** 9.
Maisono, J. (1973). Keeping hanging baskets healthy. *Conn. Greenhouse Newsl.* **52,** 9–11.
Peters, R. M. (1963). Plants that climb and hang. *Plants Gard.* **19**(2), 50–53.
Rathmell, J. K., Jr. (1974). Swingers. *Plants Alive* **2**(6), 10–13; **2**(8), 24–27.
Rathmell, J. K., Jr. (1975a). Hanging baskets. *Bedding Plant News* January, p. 3–4.
Rathmell, J. K., Jr. (1975b). Filling the basket. *Can. Florist* Mar. 15, p. 46.
Rathmell, J. K. (1975c). Hanging baskets, how to make and sell them—eastern style. *Proc. Int. Bedding Plant Conf, 8th* p. 141–145.
Rathmell, J. K., Jr. (1976). Speciality items, bedding plants. *In* "A Manual on the Culture of Bedding Plants as a Greenhouse Crop" (J. W. Mastalerz, ed.), pp. 325–343. Pennsylvania Farm Growers, University Park, Pennsylvania.
Rathmell, J. K., Jr. (1977). A view of the changing U.S. floriculture scene. *Florists' Rev.* **161**(4174) 29, 71–74.
Thompson, M. & E. (1976). Suspend your best begonias. *Plants Alive* **4**(4), 18–21
Wendzonka, P. (1978). Cleodendrum hanging baskets. *Focus Floric. Purdue Univ.* **6**(2), 6–7.
Wott, J. A. (1976). Swing'em high, swing'em low. *Plants Alive* **4**(6), 14–17.

CONTAINERS

Cathey, H. M. (1977). Planting in containers. *Am. Hortic.* **56**(3), 3–5, 33.
Graf, A. B. (1978). "Container Plants Outdoors Tropica," p. 11. Roehrs Co., East Ratherford, New Jersey.
Taloumis, G. (1974). Annuals in containers, a handbook on annuals. *Plants Gard.* **30**(2), 51–56.

BASKET AND WINDOW BOX PLANTS

Bahr, F. (1922). Basket and window box plants. *In* "Commercial Floriculture," pp. 188–193. A. T. DeLaMare Co., New York.

WINDOW BOXES

Anonymous (1973). "York in Bloom Advisory Service." City of York, Dep. Tourism, York, England.

Anonymous (1978). "Balcony Gardens," pp. 18–19. Longwood Gardens, Kennett Square, Pennsylvania.

Berrisford, J. (1974). "Window Box and Container Gardening." Faber & Faber, London.

Hieke, I. K. (1976). "Window-Box, Balcony and Patio Gardening." Hamlyn, New York.

Miller, W. (1907). Summer window boxes. *Gard. Mag.* **5**(5), 286–288.

Stat, R. (1978). Building a window box. *House Plants Porch Gard.* **3**(5), p. 78–82.

Taloumis, G. (1962). "Outdoor Gardening in Pots and Boxes." Van Nostrand, Princeton, New Jersey.

Teuscher, H. (1958). Gardening in window boxes. *Plants Gard.* **14**(1), 13–19.

VERTICAL GARDENS

Anonymous (1972). Exit tomatoes—enter strawberries under glass. *Nurseryman Gard. Cent.* June 27, p. 96.

Anonymous (1973). Bluhende torfwande Torfstreuverban GMBH. Leaflet.

Anonymous (1975a). Strawberries: Wall to wall. *Commer. Grower* June 6, p. 1093–1094.

Anonymous (1975b). "Container and Hanging Gardens," Ortho Book Series, pp. 88–91. Chevron Chem. Co., San Francisco, California.

Anonymous (1976). Vertical garden. *Univ. Mass. Suburban Exp. Stn., Waltham* 1 page.

Anonymous (1978). Small space? Go vertical. *In* "Ortho Lawn & Garden Book," Northeast Ed., p. 1. Chevron Chemical Co., San Francisco, California.

Rathmell, J. K., Jr. (1974). Vertical gardens—A new angle on increasing sales. *Florists' Rev.* **154**(3990), 10.

Rathmell, J. K., Jr. (1978). Versatile vertical garden. *Woman's Day* **41**(12), 81, 120.

Shepherd, S. (1975). A 'vertical garden' for the city grower. *New York Times* June 1, p. 37.

STANDARDS

Anonymous (1969). Bedding plants, Michigan's blooming industry. *Mich. Sci. Action* September, p. 12–13.

Carstens, J. (1971). How Longwood Gardens develops coleus for topiary. *Grounds Maint.* April, p. 15.

Craig, W. N. (1906). A bedding plant grown as a tree. *Gard. Mag.* **3**(3), 142.

Edwards, J. E. (1961). Azaleas-Standard or tree-form plants. *Plants Gard.* **17**(2), 57.

McDonald, E. (1973). Greenhouse plant to tree form. *Under Glass* **27**(5), 9–15.

21
Foliage Plants

Charles A. Conover

Introduction to Floriculture
Copyright © 1980 by Academic Press, Inc.
All rights of reproduction in any form reserved.
ISBN 0-12-437650-9

I. HISTORY AND BACKGROUND

The wide diversity of foliage plants and relatively recent placement of many genera, species, and cultivars into the loose grouping adapted to interior environments make any discussion of the foliage plant history difficult.

A. Origin and Development of the Industry

The origin of the foliage plant industry is obscure in that initially most plants used indoors were collected and no organized commercial industry existed. During the late Victorian era foliage plants, including ferns, palms, *Aspidistra* and *Sansevieria,* were grown in greenhouses in Europe and the United States and sold for interior use in local areas. In the United States, Swanson (1975) traced the present foliage industry to Florida as early as 1906 when a northern Boston fern grower recognized the potential for growing foliage plants in Florida. However, greenhouse producers in northern states had already been growing limited numbers of ferns and other foliage plants for over 25 years.

Since the early 1900s the foliage plant industry developed dramatically in the United States as well as in Europe, and the advent of central heating systems in homes undoubtedly contributed tremendously to this growth. In southern parts of Florida, Texas, and California the industry developed initially outdoors and under slat sheds, whereas more recently it has moved into fiberglass and glass greenhouses. In northern areas, production in glass greenhouses has been centered in Ohio, Pennsylvania, New York, and nearby states. More recently (mainly since 1968), a number of companies have developed stock production units in the Caribbean region for shipment of propagative units to the United States and Europe. In 1977 it was estimated by Scarborough (1978) that at least 16 million dollars worth of propagative material was shipped into Florida for finishing.

B. Production Areas

Major U.S. production areas are shown in Table I. The concentration of the foliage industry in Florida, Texas, and California is primarily due to reduced production costs associated with moderate winter temperatures and high light intensity throughout the year. Production in northern areas is made feasible by access to local markets and a product mix that stresses easy-to-grow, rapid turnover of smaller pot size foliage crops. Production of foliage crops is also increasing rapidly in Europe and in the Caribbean.

C. Economic Importance

Foliage crops were not of major economic significance in relation to other floriculture crops until the late 1960s. As late as 1970 foliage plants accounted

Table I

Major United States Foliage Plant Production Areas and Estimated Acreage and Sales in 1977[a]

Area	Hectares	Wholesale value (millions of dollars)
Florida	769	120
California	186	70
Texas	62	18
Ohio	16	11
United States—16 states total	1033	271

[a]Anonymous (1978).

for only 15 million dollars wholesale value in Florida. The most recent data from USDA (Anonymous, 1978) indicate that the total U. S. foliage plant wholesale value was nearly 271 million dollars in 1977 (Table I). Foliage crops have become of major economic importance in a relatively short span of time.

II. BOTANICAL INFORMATION

The best general sources of botanical information on foliage plants include those by Bailey and Bailey (1976) and Graf (1970).

Many definitions exist for foliage plants but the plants are so diverse in habit and use that it is difficult to develop one definition that is inclusive. One definition by Conover *et. al.* (1971) that addresses itself to both form and use and is commonly used is, Any plant grown primarily for its foliage and utilized for interior decoration or interior landscape purposes. While it may have flowers, these will be secondary compared to foliage features.

A. Taxonomy

Anyone examining a representative group of foliage plants soon realizes that diversity among plants is enormous. In addition to monocotyledon and dicotyledon members of the Angiospermae, foliage plants also contain representatives of the Gymnosperme—*Araucaria* (cone-bearing trees)—and Pteridophyta (ferns). Another problem with taxonomy of foliage plants is that the origin of many plants is confused since many have been collected in the tropics and introduced into the industry without being identified taxonomically. The fact that many foliage plant cultivars are sports of the same species, although very different in appearance, confuses the matter further.

B. Native Habitats

Most foliage plants are native to tropical and subtropical areas of the world, although a few such as *Aucuba* and *Pittosporum* are also found in temperate zones. Within tropical and subtropical zones, however, vast differences in climate may occur within relatively short distances because of rainfall amount or distribution, changes in temperature because of elevation, and variation in light intensity because of cloud cover. For these reasons, foliage plants are able to tolerate a wider range of soil moistures, light intensities, and temperatures than most people realize. However, the largest volume of foliage plants sold are adapted to areas where temperatures range between 13° and 38°C and where rainfall is somewhat evenly distributed throughout the year. Even where dry periods occur foliage plants often grow in the understory of forest trees or other vegetation and thus their water requirements are reduced.

C. Flower Types

As described in the definition of a foliage plant, most foliage plants are valued for their attractive foliage rather than their flowers. There are some exceptions, including *Aphelandra, Spathiphyllum,* bromeliads, Christmas cactus, and several others. However, flowers of most foliage plants are small or inconspicuous and not very colorful, and are hidden within the foliage. Some genera such as *Epipremnum* or *Syngonium* normally remain in the juvenile form when used indoors and thus never flower. Others such as *Aglaonema, Dieffenbachia,* and *Philodendron,* all within the Araceae, produce flowers indoors when grown under good conditions. However, the flowers serve as a novelty rather than enhance the beauty of the plant.

D. Prominent Cultivars

Well over 1000 different foliage plant types are commonly sold in the foliage plant industry and thus any discussion of a limited group is subject to inaccuracies. One of the best sources of information on numbers of any specific plant type produced is the list of Bellinger and Griffith (1978).

Detailed information on the national foliage plant product mix is unavailable, but it has been compiled recently by Smith and Strain (1976) for Florida, which accounts for 44% of national production. Data in Table II are not listed by genera throughout, since many diverse genera may be included in plants sold as hanging baskets. On a national basis, these statistics are probably low for hanging baskets and terrarium plants, which are often grown for local markets in northern areas of the United States. Also, larger foliage types are listed at percentages higher than the actual national percentage, because Florida is responsible for well over 75% of plants grown in 25-cm or larger containers.

Table II

Foliage Plant Product Mix in Florida, 1975[a]

Produce	Percentage
Philodendron spp.	20
Dracaena spp.	11
Palms	7
Ficus spp.	6
Dieffenbachia spp.	5
Brassaia actinophylla	5
Maranta spp.	3
Epipremnum spp.	3
Totem pole plants	3
Ferns	3
Peperomia spp.	3
Sansevieria spp.	3
Syngonium spp.	2
Combinations	2
Hanging baskets	2
Aphelandra spp.	2
Aglaonema spp.	2
Aralias	2
Hoya spp.	2
Terrarium plants	1
Crotons	1
Cacti	1
Ardisia spp.	1
Spathiphyllum spp.	1
Others	9

[a]From Smith and Strain (1976).

For the most part, plant form is predicated by pot size, since it strongly influences actual plant size. Plants in 5-cm or smaller pots are generally considered terrarium plants while those in 7.5- to 10-cm sizes are for sale or growing-on. Small specimen plants are sold in 12.5- to 20-cm sizes and plants in pots over 20 cm in diameter are considered large specimens. Divisions within pot size include hanging baskets, totem poles, trees, standards, and normal upright forms. Normal plant forms are sold by pot size with number of stems and/or height (from the bottom of the pot to the top of the plant) often mentioned. Specialty plants such as those trained on totem poles or in hanging baskets will be listed by pot size as well as by their specialty form. More detailed information on forms can be found in a recently published specification guide by Gaines (1978).

III. PROPAGATION

A. Stock Plant Culture

Foliage stock plants are grown under various cultural regimes. In tropical areas they are often grown under natural shade from trees, or in full sun, but more commonly under polypropylene shade structures. In areas where frost occurs, stock is most often grown in greenhouses but also may be grown in shade houses covered with plastic in winter and heated or in nonheated structures where overhead irrigation water is applied on frosty nights for temperature control.

B. Field Cultural Systems

Growth of foliage stock plants in the field (outdoors) is restricted to southern Florida and California and the tropics. Only a few stock plant species can be grown in full sun. Conover and Poole (1972, 1974) have shown that selection of the correct shade level is very important as too little shade reduces the salability of propagative units because of yellowing or burning of edges of foliage whereas too much shade may greatly reduce yield. For the most part, stock plants are grown under polypropylene shadecloth that provides the desired light levels (Table III).

Land selected for stock production should have good internal drainage as well as sufficient slope to allow surface water to drain off rapidly when excessive rainfall occurs. Temperature ranges should preferably be between 18°C minimum at night and 35°C maximum day for best quality and yield. Infrequent low temperatures of 10°C and high temperatures still below 41°C will not damage plants but will reduce yields. Location of a farm should also take wind speed, direction, and frequency into consideration because they may affect the types of structures that can be built, as well as crop growth. Wind-induced problems include foliar mechanical damage from abrasion, tipburn due to wind, and drought caused by low humidity. Consideration should also be given to competition within the area for labor, willingness of individuals for "stoop-labor" employment, and ability of individuals to learn cultural aspects of production.

Many foliage types will grow in ground beds which should have a north–south orientation with a width of about 1.2 m and elevated about 15 cm above the aisles to facilitate drainage. Some plants well adapted to this type of culture are listed in Table III.

Structures used to support shadecloth are generally constructed of treated lumber with 10- × 10-cm posts 3 to 4 m on center and connected by 2.5- × 15-, 5- × 10-, or 5- × 15-cm stringers. Where wind is a problem, internal or external braces are often added between posts and stringers. More recently, some

Table III

Light and Fertilizer Requirements of Foliage Plants Adapted to Stock Production in Full Sun or Under Shadecloth

Botanical name	Suggested light level (klx)	Average fertilizer requirement (kg/m ^{2}/year)		
		N	P_2O_5	K_2O
Aglaonema spp.	21–26	0.14	0.04	0.09
Codiaeum variegatum cvs.	74–85	0.17	0.05	0.11
Cordyline terminalis cvs.	37–48	0.17	0.05	0.11
Dracaena deremensis cvs.	32–37	0.14	0.04	0.09
Dracaena fragrans cvs.	37–106	0.17	0.05	0.11
Dracaena marginata	37–106	0.20	0.07	0.13
Dracaena spp. (not above)	32–48	0.17	0.05	0.11
Epipremnum aureum cvs.	37–48	0.17	0.05	0.11
Ficus elastica cvs.	37–106	0.20	0.07	0.13
Ficus lyrata	37–106	0.20	0.07	0.13
Monstera spp.	37–48	0.17	0.05	0.11
Philodendron spp.	32–48	0.17	0.05	0.11
Sansevieria spp.	37–106	0.10	0.03	0.06

shade structures have been constructed with concrete or steel posts having cable stringers running at 90° and 45° angles to posts. Height and size of the structure are important because they influence temperature at plant height. Because heat rises and air movement is slow through shadecloth, it is wise to provide a minimum of 2.5 m and preferably 3 m of clearance. Erection of several smaller 0.4- to 2-ha units with empty spaces between or elevated strips with open spaces as shown in Fig. 1 will help prevent excessive temperature buildup.

Foliage stock plants grown outdoors or under shadecloth are usually watered with impulse or spinning sprinklers and these systems are also commonly used for fertilization. Therefore, it is very important to have a properly engineered system so that good coverage will be obtained. Use of low-angle trajectory sprinklers will be necessary to prevent contact of water with shadecloth. Normally, foliage plants grown under shadecloth require 2.5 to 5 cm of water a week.

Unamended soils in tropical and subtropical areas are rarely satisfactory for foliage stock production. Sandy soils usually require organic components such as peat moss to improve water and nutrient-holding capacities whereas heavy tropical soils require peat moss, bark, coarse sawdust, or rice hulls to improve internal aeration.

Harvesting propagative units from stock plants requires an understanding of sizes and forms required by the industry as well as how harvesting influences future production. It is imperative that sufficient viable foliage always remain on

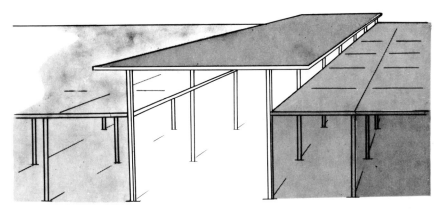

Fig. 1. Elevated sections in shade structures aid in cooling and provide the additional height required for vehicle movement.

the stock plant after cutting harvest to allow for extensive bud break. Constant removal of all cuttings of marketable size will reduce yields to the point that stock becomes unprofitable.

C. Greenhouse Cultural Systems

Although most foliage stock plants grown for cuttings or divisions may be grown in greenhouses, the economics of production limit the final selection. Size of plants in relation to yield of cuttings per square meter and need for specific types to be grown under cover for pest protection govern selection. Some of the most common greenhouse-grown foliage plant genera with their light and fertilizer requirements are shown in Table IV.

Foliage stock plants can be grown in any type of greenhouse that provides sufficient light and required temperatures. However, in greenhouses where condensate drips on plants during the winter, there is the possibility of cold water damage on *Dieffenbachia, Philodendron,* and *Syngonium.*

Greenhouse-grown stock plants should be in raised benches that provide sufficient medium volume for good root growth, drainage, and adequate aeration. Benches with 15-cm sides and wire bottoms serve this purpose best, but some smaller plants will grow well where 10-cm sides are used. Wood, cement, or transite benches can be used, but spaces for aeration should exist every 30 to 45 cm in bench bottoms, and an open, well-aerated medium should be used for growing. Major advantages to bench growing versus utilization of ground beds include elimination of stoop labor, increased growth because of higher soil and plant temperatures, and elimination of or reduced problems with soil-borne insects, nematodes, and disease organisms.

Selection of specific growing media will depend on local availability, cost, and personal preference. Some excellent media for foliage stock plant

Table IV

Light and Fertilizer Requirements of Selected Foliage Plants Adapted to Stock Production in the Greenhouse

Botanical name	Suggested light level (klx)	Average fertilizer requirement (kg/m ^{2}/year)		
		N	P_2O_5	K_2O
Aglaonema spp.	16–21	0.14	0.04	0.09
Aphelandra squarrosa cvs.	7–10	0.17	0.05	0.11
Calathea spp.	16–21	0.14	0.04	0.09
Dieffenbachia spp.	26–42	0.17	0.05	0.11
Epipremnum aureum cvs.	32–42	0.17	0.05	0.11
Hoya carnosa cvs.	21–32	0.14	0.04	0.09
Maranta spp.	16–21	0.10	0.03	0.06
Nephrolepis spp.	21–32	0.14	0.04	0.09
Peperomia spp.	26–37	0.10	0.03	0.06
Philodendron spp.	26–37	0.17	0.05	0.11
Pilea spp.	26–32	0.10	0.03	0.06
Schlumbergera truncata cvs.	32–42	0.10	0.03	0.06
Syngonium podophyllum cvs.	32–42	0.14	0.04	0.09

benches include (1) 50% peat moss–50% pine bark, (2) 75% peat moss–25% pine bark, (3) 75% peat moss–25% sharp mason sand, and (4) 75% peat moss–25% perlite. Because stock plants remain in benches for many years, it is important to select components that will not decompose rapidly.

Knauss (1971) has shown that selection of watering systems for stock plants grown in greenhouses is very important, since foliar disease control is much less or no problem where the foliage is kept dry. Another advantage to keeping foliage dry and reducing pesticide usage is the reduction in foliar residues. The best method of irrigation that keeps foliage dry is irrigation tubing that seeps through the entire surface wall or is emitted at specific intervals. Spacing at 30-cm intervals across the bench will provide excellent coverage and will help prevent soluble salts buildup between lines. Overhead sprinklers or spray stakes can also be used for stock plant production where foliar diseases are not a problem or can be easily controlled.

Temperatures needed for maximum yield from stock plants are 18°C minimum and 35°C maximum. Maintenance of the minimum temperature is expensive during winter months and if heat conservation is a problem, it is better to keep soil temperatures at 18°C minimum and allow air temperatures to drop slightly lower.

Light intensities listed in Table IV will maximize cutting yield, but may be exceeded by as much as 25% if air temperatures are 27°C or less. Where excessive temperatures occur (38°–43°C), the lowest suggested intensity should be used to improve plant appearance of *Aglaonema, Calathea, Maranta, Peperomia, Pilea,* and other low-light intensity requiring plants.

Fertilizer levels suggested are for listed light intensities; any change in light level above or below those shown in Table IV will require a change in the fertilizer level. Higher light levels require use of more fertilizer to maintain similar quality, whereas lower levels require less because of reduced total demand.

D. Economic Aspects of Stock Plant Culture

Growth of foliage stock plants in greenhouses is limited only by economics; valuable and costly space devoted to stock plant production may be better used for production of potted plants and propagation of purchased cuttings. It is generally conceded that bench space in northern greenhouses costs $90.00 to $130.00 a year per square meter, whereas in warmer areas the cost may range between $26.00 and $103.00. Only a few groups of foliage plants yield sufficient cuttings to make them profitable where heating costs are high. Therefore, before establishment of a stock production area, it is wise to compare costs of purchased cuttings versus those expected for a stock production area.

E. Propagation Methods

Most foliage plants are relatively easy to propagate, and producers are most interested in practices which control quality, percentage, and speed of rooting.

Propagation methods used for foliage plants include cuttings, seed, air layers, spores, division, and tissue culture. Conover and Poole (1970) have previously discussed propagation of specific foliage genera in some detail.

Propagation by cuttings is one of the most popular methods and can be tip, single- and double-eye leaf bud, leaf, or cane cuttings. Selection of a specific method depends on plant form (upright, vining) and availability of propagative material.

Seed propagation is increasing in popularity because costs are lower than for vegetative propagation and there is no need for stock production areas; however, seeds of many foliage plants are not available, or the plant type is not stable from seed. Some of the more popular foliage plants grown from seed include *Araucaria, Brassaia, Coffea, Dizygotheca, Podocarpus,* and nearly all of the palms. Mikorski and White (1977) have conducted research on propagation requirements of some tropical seeds, but detailed information is lacking on many genera. Seed of tropical genera should be planted soon after harvest because germination percentage decreases rapidly with increased time between harvest and planting.

Air layering is decreasing in importance as a propagation method because of high costs and need for large stock plant areas. Plants that are most commonly air layered include *Codiaeum, Ficus,* and *Monstera.* One of the problems with air layers is that their large size makes them difficult to ship without mechanical damage occurring.

Division is the only method of propagation of *Calathea, Ctenanthe,* and *Sansevieria.* This is a high-labor-requiring method and presents problems of carrying disease, insect, or nematode pests to new plantings.

Spores are commonly used to propagate a number of fern genera, although many ferns are grown from divisions or offsets. Fern production from spores can take 1 to 2 years before marketable plants are produced.

Tissue culture is becoming an important method of propagation for foliage plant producers. Rapid multiplication of new cultivars is an important advantage of tissue culture but some old cultivars such as Boston fern are commonly propagated by this system.

F. Propagation Systems

The usual propagation system is a mist bed where cuttings are misted for 15 to 30 seconds each 30 to 60 minutes. Cuttings are stuck in the bed and, when rooted, pulled and potted. During the last 10 years many producers have shifted to direct-stick propagation, where cuttings are placed directly in the growing pot, rooted, and finished without being moved. This system is especially adapted to plants such as *Philodendron,* where three to five single-eye cuttings may be placed in each pot.

Light requirements are the same as required for plant production of the species to be rooted. The frequency of misting depends on light intensity and temperature, and it should be set to keep some moisture on foliage at most times. In cooler climates growers often use tents over the propagation bench to provide 100% humidity and to eliminate misting.

G. Propagation Media, Fertilization, and Temperature

Numerous media have been used for foliage plant propagation. Sphagnum peat moss is most commonly used either singly or when amended with perlite, styrofoam, pine bark, or other organic components. Research has shown that dolomitic limestone and slow-release fertilizer are useful during propagation, since as soon as roots are initiated, nutrients are available to the plant. Nutrient mist has also been used on foliage plant cuttings, but owing to high temperatures algae have been a serious problem on leaves and have reduced overall quality.

Mist application is very useful in lowering temperatures in summer months, but can prolong rooting during periods when the propagation medium temperature drops below 18°C (Poole and Waters, 1971). For this reason, propagation beds or benches should be maintained at 21°–24°C at all times within the medium. This can be accomplished by under bench heating or use of heating cables.

H. Breeding Programs

Only limited breeding work has been conducted on foliage plants. Some of the foliage plants receiving the most breeding attention to date include *Aglaonema,* bromeliads as a group, *Dieffenbachia, Hoya, Philodendron,* and *Schlumbergera.* Breeding has been concentrated primarily on cosmetics, such an objective being to produce a different-looking plant that will be bought in quantity by the consumer. However, with *Philodendron,* another aim has been to produce a plant that is better adapted to interior environments: to increase tolerance to low light intensity and low humidity.

IV. CULTURE

A. Vegetative Stage

Systems for growing foliage plants vary between producers, which indicates that high-quality foliage plants can be grown using different cultural systems. The key to any system depends on knowing how the various cultural factors interrelate, so that logical decisions can be made if it becomes necessary to change one portion of the system.

B. Planting

Cultural variability among foliage plant species prevents development of a detailed crop production guide, but factors influencing most foliage crops are discussed, so that logical decisions can be made.

The potting medium used to grow foliage plants can range from 100% organic matter to approximately 50% organic and 50% inorganic matter. Waters *et al.* (1970) reported that key factors to consider in selection of potting media include aeration (measured as capillary and noncapillary pore space), moisture retention (water-holding capacity), and nutrient retention (cation exchange capacity). Table V provides an indication of the properties provided by some popular media components. Several other factors that must be considered when selecting potting media include consistency, availability, weight, and cost.

Examples of potting media utilized by commercial foliage growers are shown in the lower portion of Table V. The objective of foliage producers is to provide a potting medium with excellent aeration that has good water and nutrient holding capacities, but is not excessively heavy.

Normally, pH is adjusted at the time potting mixtures are developed. The best range for most foliage plants is between 5.5 and 6.5, but several genera, including *Maranta* and most ferns, prefer a pH between 5.0 and 6.0. Dolomitic limestone is suggested for pH correction, but any calcium-containing material

Table V

Physical and Chemical Characteristics of Potting Medium Components Commonly Used, and Selected Commercial Combinations [a]

Medium	Aeration	Water-holding capacity	Cation exchange capacity	Weight
Sphagnum peat moss	M (V)	H	H	L
Composted pine bark	H	M	M	M
Perlite	H	L	L	L
Sand	M	L	L	H
Shavings	H	M	M	L
Peat : perlite (2 : 1)	H	M	M	L
Peat : bark (1 : 1)	H	H	H	L
Peat : sand (3 : 1)	M	H	H	M
Peat : bark : shavings (2 : 1 : 1)	H	H	H	L

[a] Abbreviations used: H, high; M, average; L, low; and V, variable.

can also be used. Superphosphate should not be incorporated into potting media unless foliage plants not sensitive to fluorides are being grown. Micronutrients are normally included in the fertilizer program, although they may also be included in the potting medium.

Potting methods and systems fall into two main categories—hand potting and pot fillers. Hand potting is still used by the majority of producers with small- or medium-sized operations. Systems vary, but the potting medium is usually delivered to a central site where potting occurs, and potted plants are then moved to growing areas. Pot fillers are used by many larger producers. Most pot filling machines are stationary; potting takes place in a central location. However, smaller portable pot fillers are being incorporated into the foliage industry.

Spacing of foliage plants directly controls final plant quality. Plants that will be finished within 3 months are usually placed at their final spacing when placed on the bench with spacing distance varying from 0 (pot to pot) to 3 times pot diameter. Cavity trays are frequently used by growers to provide automatic spacing and pot support.

Plants grown in container sizes of 15 cm or larger may take 6 months to 2 years to reach maturity. Such plants are often placed pot to pot until they become crowded and are then spaced to their final spacing. Depending on type of growth, spacing varies from one to six times the container diameter.

Spacing is important to producers (Christensen, 1976). Crowding of plants reduces light reaching lower foliage and may cause it to abscise, or may cause plants to grow tall without proportionate spread, which reduces value. Crowding also increases disease problems because plants are more difficult to spray, remain wet longer when watered, and have higher humidity around the foliage. Crowding also influences the ability to control insect pests.

Fertilization directly influences growth rate, and thus profitability, but because fertilizer levels provided also influence longevity indoors, it is important to be sure excessive levels are not used.

Maximum growth rate of acclimatized foliage plants can be obtained with moderate levels of soluble, organic, or slow-release fertilizer applied constantly or periodically. Research by Conover and Poole (1974) has shown that fertilizer requirement is related to light intensity. Suggested levels of fertilizer in Table VI are for plants grown under light intensities that will produce acclimatized, high-quality plants.

Poole and Conover (1977, 1978) found that fertilizer ratios for foliage plants need to be approximately 3 : 1 : 2 when potting mixtures listed in Table V are utilized. A ratio of 1 : 1 : 1 is also acceptable, but because nitrogen is the key element in growth of foliage plants, this ratio will result in higher fertilizer costs to obtain the desired nitrogen level. Rates listed in Table VI can be easily calculated on a periodic basis and applied weekly, or every other week. Periodic fertilization less than every 2 weeks often results in decreased growth. If a constant fertilization program is desired, the suggested level of nutrients at each application is 150 to 200 ppm nitrogen, 50 to 75 ppm phosphorus, and 100 to 150 ppm potassium. To aid producers in refining fertilizer programs,

Table VI

Suggested Light and Fertilizer Levels for Production of Potted Foliage Plants for Indoor Use

Botanical name	Light intensity (klx)	Average fertilizer requirement (kg/m²/year)		
		N	P_2O_5	K_2O
Aphelandra squarrosa cvs.	10–16	0.17	0.05	0.11
Brassaia spp.	53–64	0.20	0.07	0.13
Chamaedorea spp. (palms)	26–37	0.14	0.04	0.09
Cordyline terminalis cvs.	32–42	0.14	0.04	0.09
Dieffenbachia spp.	26–42	0.14	0.04	0.09
Ficus spp.	53–64	0.20	0.07	0.13
Dracaena marginata cvs.	53–64	0.20	0.07	0.13
Dracaena spp.	32–37	0.14	0.04	0.09
Maranta spp.	16–21	0.10	0.03	0.06
Peperomia spp.	26–37	0.07	0.02	0.04
Philodendron spp.	26–37	0.17	0.05	0.11
Pilea spp.	26–32	0.07	0.02	0.04
Spathiphyllum spp.	16–26	0.17	0.05	0.11

Poole and Conover (1976) reported levels of macro- and micronutrients found in leaf tissue of 26 species of good-quality foliage plants.

Potting media used for foliage plant production are normally very low in micronutrients, and thus most fertilizers used should contain at least the minimal micronutrient levels suggested in Table VII. However, levels only slightly higher than desired have been reported to be phytotoxic on *Aphelandra* and *Brassaia* (Conover et al., 1975).

Acclimatization of foliage plants utilized for interior use is necessary to ensure they perform well indoors. Acclimatization is the adaptation of a plant to a new environment—in this instance, preparation for growth in building interiors under low light and humidity conditions. The most important aspect of acclimatization is development of shade foliage that is characterized by large, thin leaves with high chlorophyll levels. A second important factor is nutritional level, which should be as low as possible while still producing a quality plant. Extensive research by Conover and Poole (1977), Collard et al. (1977), Fonteno and McWilliams (1978), and Vlahos and Boodley (1974) has shown the importance of acclimatization.

Foliage plants such as *Brassaia actinophylla, Chrysalidocarpus lutescens,* and *Ficus benjamina* are often grown in full sun and then acclimatized by placing them under suggested shade conditions and by lowering fertilizer levels for 3 to 9 months. Although chloroplasts and grana are capable of reorientation within sun-grown foliage, the leaf anatomy—small size and thick cross section—prevents them from being as efficient after acclimatization as shade leaves. Therefore, such plants are less tolerant of low or medium light levels indoors than plants acclimatized during production.

Table VII

Average Levels of Several Micronutrients Required for Foliage Crops

Element [a]	Spray application (gm/liter)	Soil drench (gm/m²)	Soil incorporated (gm/m³)
B	0.01	0.009	0.37
Cu	0.12	0.092	3.71
Fe	1.20	0.915	37.08
Mn	0.60	0.458	18.54
Mo	0.01	0.003	0.04
Zn	0.36	0.305	11.12

[a] One application is often sufficient for short-term crops, whereas reapplications are usually necessary for crops grown 6 months or more.

C. Environmental Control

Proper control of environmental factors is necessary for production of high-quality foliage plants. All too often producers fail to regulate the environment properly, with resultant loss of quality or plants.

Temperature is very important, since most foliage plants are tropical and require high night temperatures in the range of 18°C minimum. Soil temperatures are also important, and, if they can be maintained at 18°–21°C, the air temperature may drop as low as 16°C at night without significant crop response. The best temperature range for a wide number of foliage genera is 18°C minimum night and 24°C minimum day. Night temperatures of as high as 27°C and day temperatures as high as 35°C will not be damaging; however, it is often uneconomical to maintain these in temperate climates.

Some foilage crops such as *Aphelandra, Aglaonema, Dieffenbachia, Epipremnum, Fittonia, Maranta,* and *Pilea* may be damaged by chilling temperatures of 10°C or below (McWilliams and Smith, 1978), whereas others such as *Ardisia, Brassaia, Hedera,* and *Pittosporum* tolerate temperatures as low as freezing without injury.

Information on light intensity levels has been included in Tables III, IV, and VI for many foliage crops. Light intensity is one of the most important factors to consider in culture because it directly controls quality factors such as internode length, foliage color, carbohydrate level, growth rate, and acclimatization. Light green foliage or faded colors, such as in the case of *Codiaeum,* are indicative of excessive light and reduced chlorophyll levels. This problem can be corrected in most cases by increasing fertilization (Rodriguez and Cibes, 1977) or reducing light intensity. Because increases in fertilizer often cause excessive soluble salts levels, the proper corrective method is to reduce light intensity. In addition to color, many foliage plants change their leaf size, or shape, and orientation in response to light intensity. For example, leaves of *Aglaonema* and *Dieffenbachia* will assume a nearly vertical position under excessive light, whereas leaf orientation will be nearer 60° under proper light. *Ficus benjamina* leaves will be folded along the midrib under high light conditions.

Watering levels should be established which ensure that foliage plants receive sufficient water to remain turgid at all times. The water requirement during winter, when temperatures are low and growth is slowed, may be less than once a week; in spring or summer, daily application may be necessary.

Use of watering systems that water the potting medium without wetting foliage is desirable because this reduces foliar disease and residue problems. Leader tubes provide best watering control and provision for leaching. Mat irrigation can also be used to produce foliage plants but fertilizer should be incorporated into the potting medium for best results. Conover and Poole (1977) found that application of fertilizer to mats may cause excessive soluble salts at the surface of the container and may also contribute to excessive algae growth on mats. Overhead application of water is strongly influenced by plant canopy, which may cause much of the applied water to be deflected, thus it is an inexact way to apply water or fertilizers.

Application of carbon dioxide to foliage plants is uncommon, although growth increases of up to 25% have occurred with several foliage plants. However, it appears that temperature is the key to increased growth during periods when greenhouses are closed, and unless a range of 18°–24°C minimum is maintained, the injection of carbon dioxide will not be beneficial.

Humidity requirements of foliage plants during production are not verified by research, but maintenance of 50% or higher relative humidity appears to be desirable. In areas where humidity falls below 25%, many growers install mist lines or raise humidity in some other way. Plant damage from low humidity has been observed on *Calathea, Ctenanthe,* and *Maranta.*

The effect of humidity on condensation within greenhouses can be detrimental to foliage production if the temperature of the condensate is in the range of 0°–4°C and falls on warmer foliage. In addition to *Episcia* and *Saintpaulia,* cold water from condensate or greenhouse leaks can also injure *Aglaonema, Dieffenbachia, Philodendron,* and *Syngonium* and often causes brown or greasy gray spots where it falls (Fig. 2). The best controls for this problem are to use structures where condensate does not drip or to ventilate to reduce the problem.

Wind can be a severe environmental problem if it causes physical damage to foliage, knocks over containerized plants, or increases the severity of cold damage to plants grown in outdoor shade structures. The best solution to

Fig. 2. Cold water damage on *Philodendron scandens oxycardium* caused by 2°–5°C water on 16°C foliage.

excessive wind is to enclose structures, but use of windbreaks can also be beneficial. Many foliage plants will tolerate temperatures as low as 2°-7°C if protected from winds of 8 km/hour or more.

D. Chemical Control

Regulation of vine length or plant height of foliage plants has been achieved by Henley and Poole (1974) and McConnell and Poole (1974) with ancymidol, chlormequat, and Alar. However, except for use of ancymidol (Florida label only) to control vine length of *Gynura procumbens,* growth regulators have not received wide producer acceptance. This is primarily because they increase production time without a significant increase in quality or sales price.

Breaking bud dormancy of foliage plants by use of chemicals has been reported by Joiner *et al.* (1978) but is not of significance at this time. It could be very advantageous to producers if a way to induce bud break of leafless *Dracaena* or *Yucca* canes could be found.

V. FLOWERING STAGE

For the most part, foliage plants are not grown for their flowers, and thus the flowering of most genera is not desirable. There are, however, a few important factors which should be considered.

A. Environmental Control

A temperature near 7°C has been shown to be involved in flowering of *Aphelandra* (Christensen, 1969). Cool temperatures have also been used to aid in the induction of flowering in *Schlumbergera,* but temperatures higher than 27°C after flower initiation often cause bud drop. Influence of temperature on flowering of most foliage plants is unknown, but observations indicate it is often a factor.

Photoperiod, as shown by Poole I(1971), controls flowering of *Schlumbergera,* but has not been demonstrated to influence flowering of other foliage plants. This might be expected, since most foliage plants are of tropical origin, where photoperiod is relatively constant year-round. With *Schlumbergera*, 4 to 6 weeks of short day will initiate buds which will develop on either short or long days.

Light intensity and duration have been shown to influence flowering of *Aphelandra.* This plant appears to be photoaccumulative and flowers when intensity is high or when lower intensity is received over longer periods (Kerbo and Payne, 1976). Light intensities of less than 11 klx for 8 to 10 hours a day will keep plants vegetative, whereas 16 to 21 klx will result in flowering.

B. Chemical Control

Flower initiation in many bromeliads (including pineapple) is by chemical control in commercial operations. Research has shown that ethephon sprayed or poured into the vase, acetylene gas bubbled through water in the vase, or use of ethylene in an enclosed chamber will initiate flowering of many bromeliads (Adriansen, 1976). The plants must be of sufficient size to support a flower or fruit and usually take 2 or more years to grow to this size when started from seed.

C. Cultural Control

Influence of fertilization on flowering of foliage plants is mainly unknown at present. Observations on *Dracaena, Cordyline,* and many other foliage plants indicate that excessive nitrogen reduces flowering, but since commercial growers are mainly interested in vegetative growth, this area of research receives little attention.

Influence of soil moisture on flowering of *Schlumbergera* has been reported, but seems to be of little importance provided photoperiod is controlled. Where precise photoperiodic control is lacking, but the correct photoperiod is partly received, drying plants down for 1 to 2 weeks is sometimes beneficial. However, regulation of soil moisture for flowering of foliage plants is not a common commercial practice.

VI. CONTROL OF INSECTS, DISEASES, NEMATODES, AND PHYSIOLOGICAL DISORDERS

A. Insects and Mites

Although most producers recognize the importance of producing high-quality plants, they often fail to recognize the importance of pest control. It only takes a few insects or mites to increase populations rapidly to the point that they can severely damage plants.

Factors that affect pest populations include temperature, humidity, irrigation method, potting medium, and access to the structure. Temperatures above 27°C can cause rapid increases in mite populations, especially if humidity is low. Under such conditions, heavy dependence on chemical control is necessary to produce mite-free plants. Cold or cool temperatures reduce pest problems in unheated production areas, whereas in greenhouses they present year-round problems. Fungus gnats are much more of a problem in greenhouses than outdoors, especially where organic potting media are kept too wet. When a particular pest such as scale becomes a problem, cultural procedures must be checked carefully to see if stock plants are infested and if crawlers or adults have been carried through propagation to potted plant production areas (Hamlen, 1975). It is imperative that stock be kept as free of pests as possible to reduce the need for spraying of potted materials for sale. Frequent and continued spraying is undesirable because it increases potential for phytotoxicity and leaves persistent residues on foliage.

In areas open to pest movement, spraying or drenching with pesticides are primary methods of control at present. Mites present most problems in spring, summer, and fall when temperatures are high, whereas caterpillars and thrips are heaviest in spring and fall. Use of high-pressure sprayers and careful application to both sides of foliage provides the best assurrance of control. Air-blast sprayers, while providing high pressure and wide dispersal, often do not properly coat both sides of foliage with pesticides. Major pests of foliage plants and some of the hosts they are most commonly found feeding upon, as described by Hamlen et al. (1975), are shown in Table VIII. Chemicals registered for control of specific pests are currently undergoing EPA review, and thus their future availability is in question. For current recommendations on chemical pest control procedures on foliage plants, cooperative extension agricultural agents should be contacted.

Producers growing foliage plants in greenhouses have some chemicals used outdoors or under shade structures available with label clearance, as well as smoke bombs or thermal fogs. However, smoke bombs or thermal fogs only work where greenhouses can be entirely closed for several hours or more. Because many greenhouses in warm climates are open on the pad side of the greenhouse for 6 months or more each year, this system is best used in cooler climates. Another problem in hot climates is the problem of phytotoxicity, which may occur if fogs or smoke bombs are applied when temperatures are above 29°C.

Table VIII

Major Foliage Plant Insect and Mite Pests and Crops Commonly Serving as Hosts

Pest	Hosts
Aphids	Aphelandra, Brassaia, Gynura, Hoya, Dieffenbachia
Caterpillars	Philodendron, Dracaena, Brassaia, Maranta, Aglaonema
Fungus gnats	Schlumbergera, palms, Peperomia
Mealybugs	Aphelandra, Ardisia, Dieffenbachia, Gynura, Asparagus, Maranta, Dracaena, Dizygotheca
Spider mites	Brassaia, Codiaeum, palms, Cordyline, Calathea, Dieffenbachia, Maranta
Broad mites	Hedera, Aphelandra, Pilea
Scales	Aphelandra, bromeliads, Ficus, palms
Thrips	Brassaia, Ficus, Philodendron, Ctenanthe, Syngonium

B. Diseases (Fungi, Bacteria, and Viruses)

These diseases are severe pests of foliage plants if proper cultural procedures are not followed. In some cases where diseases are systemic within tissue (*Erwinia, Xanthomonas*), they can not be fully controlled until indexed (disease-free) stock becomes available.

Fungal and bacterial diseases are more troublesome where wet foliage is combined with high temperatures and humidity. Therefore, these diseases are most prevalent in tropical and subtropical areas with high rainfall. Even in these areas, however, growing plants under cover and irrigating without wetting foliage will nearly prevent their occurrence (Fig. 3). Soilborne fungal diseases become more severe where poor-quality growing media without good aeration and drainage exist, or where plants are constantly overwatered. Several bacterial diseases become more severe where plants are grown with excessive nitrogen fertilization or are stressed through high soluble salts, excessive temperatures, or high light intensity. Virus diseases are disseminated by insects in nonenclosed areas, but Zettler *et al.* (1970) have found that many foliage plants already contain at least one known virus, and thus insect exclusion may not be beneficial.

Since outdoor production is usually in subtropical and tropical areas with high rainfall, disease control is difficult except with preventative spray programs. Depending on disease pressure and during periods of frequent rainfall, it may be necessary to spray weekly or more often; however, during dry seasons little, if any, pesticide application may be necessary. Irrigation application to the soil or overhead application during the middle of the day when rapid drying can occur and proper plant spacing to reduce humidity will aid in reducing disease pressure. Directed high-pressure sprays rather than air-blast sprayers provide the best control of disease pests and are usually worth the extra cost of application.

A listing of some of the major disease pests and primary hosts has been compiled by Knauss (1973, 1974) and is shown in Table IX. As with insecticides and miticides, current control information can be obtained from local cooperative extension agents.

Foliar fungal and bacterial diseases can easily be controlled in greenhouses by keeping foliage dry. Where this is not possible, fairly good control can be obtained with chemical sprays to the foliage. Soil drenches for control of most of the soilborne diseases are fairly successful in raised benches and in containers off the ground. No control procedures are presently recommended for plants with virus except to rogue infected plants.

C. Nematodes

These soilborne pests are often found on foliage plants grown in the soil and propagated by division, or when foliage plants are planted in contaminated potting mixtures.

Fig. 3. Both groups of *Dracaena sanderiana* inoculated with *Pseudomonas* species, but plants on left were watered with seep irrigation and plants on right were irrigated with overhead sprinklers.

Table IX

Major Foliage Plant Disease Organisms and Crops Commonly Serving as Hosts[a]

Organism	Plant parts affected	Common hosts
Fungal diseases		
Alternaria	Leaves, stems	*Brassaia*
Cephalosporium	Leaves	*Syngonium*
Cercospora	Leaves	*Brassaia, Cordyline, Ficus,* palms, *Peperomia, Pilea*
Fusarium	Leaves	*Dracaena*
Leptosphaeria	Leaves	*Dieffenbachia*
Rhizoctonia	Leaves, stems, roots	*Aglaonema, Dieffenbachia,* ferns, *Gynura,* palms, *Philodendron*
Pythium	Stems, roots	*Aglaonema, Dieffenbachia,* ferns, *Gynura,* palms, *Philodendron*
Phytophthora	Leaves, stems, roots	*Aglaonema, Dieffenbachia, Peperomia, Philodendron*
Sclerotium	Stems, roots	*Brassaia, Dieffenbachia, Epipremnum, Peperomia, Philodendron, Syngonium*
Bacterial diseases		
Erwinia	Leaves, stems, roots	*Aglaonema, Dieffenbachia, Philodendron, Syngonium*
Xanthomonas	Leaves	*Aglaonema, Dieffenbachia, Philodendron*
Pseudomonas	Leaves	*Aglaonema, Dracaena, Epipremnum, Philodendron*

[a] From Knauss (1973a,b, 1974).

Use of clean planting stock, raised benches, and pasteurized growing media is the best way to prevent nematode infestations. Once nematodes are present, they usually cannot be eradicated and thus partial control measures must be initiated on a continuing basis.

Once foliage plants are infested with nematodes, chemical control is the only way of preventing economic losses. Both granular and liquid nematicides are available that can be applied to the medium surface or as drenches. Hamlen (1976) has found that application to ground beds is beneficial, but will require more frequent reapplication than those made to raised benches.

Root-knot nematodes are most prevalent on many foliage plant hosts, but the burrowing nematode is also a serious pest.

D. Physiological Disorders

A wide number of problems occur on foliage plants that are due to excessive or insufficient amounts of chemicals applied to plants or potting media and may cause serious economic losses if not recognized.

1. Nutrient Deficiencies

Within the macronutrient group, limited nitrogen availability results in light green foliage (which should not be confused with excessive light intensity) and loss of lower foliage. Potassium deficiency occurs on lower foliage as a general marginal chlorosis, which may develop into necrosis, whereas magnesium deficiency occurs as chlorotic bands on each edge of older foliage. Deficiencies of phosphorus, calcium, and sulfur have not been described for any of the popular foliage plants, probably because of the use of complete fertilizer programs rather than of limited requirements.

Within the micronutrient group, iron, manganese, and copper deficiencies on foliage plants have been described, whereas zinc, boron, and molybdenum have not. Iron deficiencies exhibit the general chlorosis to terminal foliage

Fig. 4. Copper deficiency of *Aglaonema commutatum* 'Fransher.'

listed for most crops, as does manganese. Copper deficiency appears as cupped and dwarfed terminal foliage with some associated chlorosis (Fig. 4). Quite a number of disorders that appear on foliage plants are commonly corrected with application of a complete fertilizer or a micronutrient application.

2. Nutrient Toxicities

Excessive application of macronutrients commonly causes soluble salts toxicities. Symptoms of excess soluble salts include dwarfed plants, marginal necrosis of foliage, and poor-quality roots. All of these symptoms may not appear together, and if all plants are treated the same, it may not be possible to determine that growth reductions are occurring. High soluble salts levels can be even more serious for the consumer, because plants received from producers will decline rapidly indoors if sold with levels exceeding 1000 to 1500 ppm total salts (Conover and Poole, 1977). In production areas, salts levels ranging between 1000 and 3000 ppm total salts [as measured with a 2:1 (v/v) water:dry potting mix] should provide excellent growth.

Excessive applications of micronutrients to foliage plants have been reported to cause damage, such as dwarfing, chlorosis, and necrosis. In time, specific micronutrient levels that cause problems will be published, but in the meantime, as long as levels listed in Table VII are not exceeded, toxicities should not occur.

3. Spray Material Toxicities

Unfortunately, large numbers of foliage plants are injured by careless or indiscriminate use of pesticides. Because of the vast number of foliage plant genera, species, and cultivars, most pesticides have been tested only on a relatively few. Even though a specific pesticide lists foliage plants on the label does not mean that it is entirely safe (Hamlen and Knauss, 1977). Symptoms of pesticide toxicity include dwarfed plants, chlorosis, and/or necrosis of foliage, ring-spots on foliage, leaf drop, and dull-appearing foliage. Once damaged, the entire crop may be unsalable, since attractive foliage is the selling point of a foliage plant. Some of the most important factors that influence the potential for spray material toxicities include (1) use of an excessive rate, (2) application at high temperatures, (3) too frequent application, (4) application to wilted plants, and (5) application when pesticide may remain for many hours on foliage before drying.

4. Other Problems

In recent years it has been found that severe damage may occur on a number of foliage plant genera from fluoride toxicity (Poole and Conover, 1973; Conover and Poole, 1974). Fluorine may exist as a contaminant in water, air, potting media, and fertilizer. Some potting media identified as being high in fluoride include German peat moss, perlite, and vermiculite. The most common source in fertilizers is superphosphate, which may contain from 1 to 2% fluorine.

Foliage genera developing foliar tip or marginal chlorosis or necrosis from fluorine include *Calathea, Chlorophytum, Cordyline, Ctenanthe, Dracaena, Maranta, Spathiphyllum,* and *Yucca.* When growing sensitive genera, the producer will benefit from using potting media and fertilizers that do not contain fluorides.

Methods that will limit uptake of fluoride present in water or potting media include shading or cooling to reduce transpiration and water usage, and raising the pH to 6.0 to 6.5 to tie up fluoride in the potting medium.

VIII. HANDLING OF FINISHED PLANTS

A. Grading

At present there is no industry-wide grading system for foliage plants. However, all producers grade their crops and thus only the most desirable plants should reach the market.

The most generally used initial grading is based on plant size in relation to pot size. Essentially, this selection requires that in general appearance the overall symmetry is correct, i.e., the plant is not too small or large in relation to pot size. Some producers list minimum plant height for specific plants but this is the exception rather than the rule. If the overall size is acceptable, then other factors are considered: (1) Is the plant free from defects due to insect feeding, disease attack, nutrient deficiency, and any physical or chemical damage and (2) is it well rooted, but not pot-bound with large roots growing out of container holes?

Because foliage plants are sold primarily for the beauty of their leaves and stems, any physical or chemical damage to foliage seriously affects marketability. In Europe, even one damaged leaf on a plant is cause for rejection by a consumer, but in the United States the damage must be fairly obvious before rejection occurs.

Residues on foliage, such as calcium, magnesium, or iron from use of impure water sources or as residues from sprays or fertilizer, can reduce marketability. With increased labor costs constantly occurring, retailers cannot afford to remove residues by hand, which is the best method. Because consumer resistance takes place upon viewing dirty foliage, it is unknown how seriously this factor affects the market. This problem can be controlled to a great extent by producers in selection of water sources, method of application and spray, and fertilizer materials.

The Florida Foliage Association has developed a grading system for 30 species that they recommend be followed by their members (Gaines, 1978).

Grading criteria include height, width, number of stems or plants per pot, leaf color, freedom from pests, physical damage, and others. It is hoped the system will be accepted and will become part of the foliage plant industry.

B. Packaging

Packaging systems in the foliage industry are very variable and still in need of development.

Nearly all foliage plants are shipped in the containers in which they were grown (usually plastic). Generally, they are placed in corrugated boxes, with larger specimens (15 cm and above) often enclosed with a plastic, fiberglass, or paper sleeve.

The two main packaging systems are boxing and shipping loose in specially constructed racks and trucks. When one uses the boxing system, the boxes must meet interstate shipping regulations for weight of corrugated cardboard and must be either waxed or moisture resistant. This latter requirement is necessary to prevent deterioration of boxes in transit because of moisture in containers.

Plants in containers up to 15 cm in size are usually placed in a waxed tray and the tray is slid into a box of the proper height. Such boxes usually do not contain dividers or other restraints. Some progressive producers have designed boxes with dividers and other restraints that hold the pot in position and the potting medium in the container. However, there is usually an additional boxing charge when such boxes are used. Plants in 15-cm or larger pots are usually sleeved and placed directly in containers of the proper height.

Several large producers with their own truck fleets have built adjustable racks to accommodate variously sized plants, which they load directly into trucks. Usually, no dividers or restraints are necessary with this system and physical damage is minimal.

Although several companies have developed special see-through packages of several materials, none are presently of any significance in the market. Several problems have occurred with these packages, including increased disease problems, ethylene buildup, and inability of plants to adapt back to a low-humidity interior environment (Harbaugh et al., 1976).

This packaging system has merit and could be an excellent system for direct sales of plants in 5- to 10-cm pots. However, use of the system must await additional research.

C. Storage

Storage of foliage plants is not a normal practice, but with increased sales in mass market outlets that use central distribution points there has been a need for information on how long plants can be held without significant decrease in quality.

Because several species of foliage plants experience chilling injury at 10°–13°C, storage temperatures between 16° and 18°C are safest for mixed lots.

Observation and limited research on dark storage of foliage plants indicate that light exclusion for up to 7 days is not detrimental to quality. Between 7 and 14 days, leaf drop and chlorophyll destruction increase to the point that even if plants are salable, they will be of poor quality. Beyond 14 days, most foliage plants are not salable, and if they are, their chance of providing consumer satisfaction is limited.

If light can be provided in storage, average levels should be at least 1 klx and preferably 1.6 klx. However, as light must be received on all portions of plants, they must be removed from boxes and spaced. This practice is unlikely unless they are being held in a wholesaler's holding or display area. Light duration should be at least 12 hours daily, but not more than 18 hours.

Boxes used for plant storage should have air vents present for air exchange. It is possible that plants in nonvented boxes may experience 100% relative humidity, which may severely increase disease problems. Relative humidity should be maintained between 50 and 90%, if possible, for maintenance of best quality.

Foliage plants are not extremely sensitive to ethylene and other aerial contaminants but can be injured if placed in storage areas with fruits and vegetables. Generally, 1 ppm or more ethylene for several days will injure many foliage plants.

D. Shipping

More than 75% of foliage plants sold in the United States are grown in Florida, California, and Texas, so shipping is an important part of the foliage industry. Most plants are shipped by truck, but small amounts also move by air and ship.

A small number of finished plants are shipped to the United States mainland from Hawaii and Puerto Rico, and some move within the United States. However, it is estimated that this accounts for less than 2% of total sales. Although air shipments are fast, they are expensive for potted plants.

Refrigerated trucks are used to ship approximately 90% of foliage plants within the United States. Truck transportation is reliable, relatively low in cost, and reaches almost all parts of the United States within 5 days. Foliage plants shipped in this manner are handled by specialty truckers rather than by those who haul general cargo. Trucks used for this purpose should have refrigeration and heating equipment that maintain a temperature between 16° and 18°C in all weather. In addition, trucks with air suspension are of value in limiting physical damage to foliage plants.

Since finished plants can enter the United States from Hawaii and Puerto Rico, and the cost of air containerization is so high, ship containerization is being utilized. Although the containers are the same as those used for trucks, the long shipping time is a definite disadvantage. From either Puerto Rico or Hawaii the average period plants are in containers is 10 to 12 days. Plant quality is greatly reduced when plants are moved by this method.

E. Consumer Care of Products

A large number of books, bulletins, and other articles have been made available to consumers during the last 5 years on foliage plant care indoors. All too often there is conflicting information on care of specific plants, but all provide general information that can be valuable. Some of the main factors are mentioned here to aid in obtaining greatest satisfaction from foliage plants.

Light, or lack of it, is probably the main reason many foliage plants decline when used indoors. The three important factors to consider are intensity, quality, and duration.

Light intensity that is required for growth indoors varies among species. Foliage plants are generally listed as low, medium, or high light intensity-requiring plants. Low light intensity plants are usually listed as requiring 0.5 to 0.8 klx of light, medium from 0.8 to 1.6 klx, and high from 1.6 to 3.2 or more klx. Although these are somewhat inexact, since they fail to take into consideration quality and duration, they are still useful (Table X).

Light quality relates to the wavelength of light plants receive. As natural light provides both red and blue wavelengths, and plants are responsive in both these bands, it was concluded that if artificial light was provided it must provide both red and blue light. Recently this has been proven untrue by Cathey and Campbell (1978), because foliage plants grow under blue light alone as well as under a combination. For this reason, cool or warm white fluorescent lamps have proven to be one of the best light sources indoors.

Light duration is important, since suggested intensities allow for light being received for at least 8 hours a day. Even better responses will be obtained when 12 or 16 hours light is received daily if the intensity is above the light compensation point.

Table X

Light Requirements of Some Popular Foliage Plants

Low light (0.5–0.8 klx)	Medium light (0.8–1.6 klx)	High light (1.6–3.2 klx)
Aglaonema commutatum	Brassaia actinophylla	Aphelandra squarrosa
Chamaedorea elegans	Calathea Makoyana	Codieum variegatum
Dracaena deremensis 'Warneckii'	Chrysalidocarpus lutscens	Ficus benjamina
Maranta erythroneura	Dieffenbachia maculata	Ficus lyrata
Peperomia obtusifolia	Dracaena marginata	Hoya carnosa
Philodendron scandens oxycardium	Syngonium podophyllum	Saintpaulia ionantha
Sansevieria trifasciata	Epipremnum aureum	Nephrolepis exaltata

There is no secret to watering indoors. Most foliage plant potting media should be moist, but not wet, and not allowed to dry out to the point that wilting occurs. When watering, water thoroughly so some leaching occurs, and then allow the medium to become fairly dry before watering again. Amount of water and frequency will depend on pot size, plant size, ability of the potting medium to hold water, light intensity, humidity, and rate of plant growth. A small plant in a large container under low light and high humidity might only need water once a week, whereas a large plant in a small container under high light and low humidity might have to be watered every day.

Relative humidity indoors during the winter heating season often falls below 25% but will be about 50% when air conditioning is on. Most foliage plants do best at a humidity of 50% or higher. Foliage plants requiring high humidity can be maintained on a bed of wet pebbles, placed in a bathroom or kitchen where humidity is higher, or a humidifier can be installed into the heating system.

Normal interior temperatures between 18° and 27°C are satisfactory for most foliage plants. Basically, temperatures comfortable to people will be satisfactory for foliage plants.

Foliage plants need very little fertilizer when grown indoors under low or medium light intensities. Under such conditions, fertilizer applications three or four times a year will be adequate. When grown under high light, fertilizer application may have to be made six or more times a year for best growth.

F. Acclimatization

Acclimatization is the process of adapting a plant grown under a different environment to that of the home. Some of the ways to aid a plant to acclimatize include the following: (1) Leach the potting medium to remove excess fertilizer and wait 2 to 3 months before beginning indoor fertilization; (2) keep the plant in a higher humidity area indoors for the first 1 to 2 weeks; (3) give the plant, no matter what the light requirement, at least 1.6 klx for the first 1 to 2 weeks; and (4) be sure the plant is not allowed to completely dry out as root damage may occur from high soluble salts remaining in the potting medium.

REFERENCES

Adriansen, E. (1976). Induction of flowering in bromeliads with ethephon. *Tidsskr. Planteavl* **80,** 857–868.

Anonymous (1978). "Floriculture Crops Production Area and Sales, 1976 and 1977, Intentions for 1978," Crop Reporting Board, SpCr6–1(78). U.S. Dep. Agric., Washington, D.C.

Bailey, L. H., and Bailey, E. Z. (1976). "Hortus Third." Macmillan, New York.

Bellinger, P., and Griffith, S. (1978). "Florida Foliage Buyers Guide." Florida Foliage Buyers Guide, Inc., Apoplka.

Cathey, H. M., and Campbell, L. E. (1978). Zero-base budgeting for lighting plants. *Foliage Dig.* **1,** 10–13.

Christensen, O. V. (1969). The influence of low temperature on flowering of *Aphelandra squarrosa*. *Tidsskr. Planteavl* **73**, 351–366.

Christensen, O. V. (1976). Planning of production—timing and spacing for year-round production of pot plants. *Acta Hortic.* **64**, 217–221.

Collard, R. C., Joiner, J. A., Conover, C. A., and McConnell, D. B. (1977). Influence of shade and fertilizer on light compensation point of *Ficus benjamina* L. *J. Am. Soc. Hortic. Sci.* **102**, 447–449.

Conover, C. A., and Poole, R. T. (1970). Foliage plant propagation. *Grounds Maint.* **5**, 27–29.

Conover, C. A., and Poole, R. T. (1972). Influence of shade and nutritional levels on growth and yield of *Scindapsus aureus, Cordyline terminalis* 'Baby Doll' and *Dieffenbachia exotica. Proc. Am. Soc. Hortic. Sci., Trop. Reg.* **16**, 277–281.

Conover, C. A., and Poole, R. T. (1974a). Influence of shade, nutrition and season on growth of *Aglaonema, Maranta,* and *Peperomia* stock plants. *Proc. Am. Soc. Hortic. Sci., Trop. Reg.* **18**, 283–287.

Conover, C. A., and Poole, R. T. (1974b). Influence of shade and fertilizer source and level on growth, quality and foliar content of *Philodendron oxycardium* Schott. *J. Am. Soc. Hortic. Sci.* **99**, 150–152.

Conover, C. A., and Poole, R. T. (1974c). Fluoride toxicity of tropical foliage plants. *Florists' Rev.* **154**, 23, 59.

Conover, C. A., and Poole, R. T. (1977a). Effects of cultural practices on acclimatization of *Ficus benjamina* L. *J. Am. Soc. Hortic. Sci.* **102**, 529–531.

Conover, C. A., and Poole, R. T. (1977b). Influence of potting media and fertilizer source and level on growth of four foliage plants on capillary mats. *Proc. Fla. State Hortic. Soc.* **90**, 316–317.

Conover, C. A., and Poole, R. T. (1977c). Influence of fertilization and watering on acclimatization of *Aphelandra squarrosa* Nees cv. Dania. *HortScience* **12**, 569–570.

Conover, C. A., Sheehan, T. J., and McConnell, D. B. (1971). Using Florida grown foliage plants. *Fla. Agric. Exp. Stn., Bull.* No. 746.

Conover, C. A., Simpson, D. W., and Joiner, J. N. (1975). Influence of micronutrient sources and levels on response and tissue content of *Aphelandra, Brassaia* and *Philodendron. Proc. Fla. State Hortic. Soc.* **88**, 599–602.

Fonteno, W. C., and McWilliams, E. L. (1978). Light compensation points and acclimatization of four tropical foliage plants. *J. Am. Soc. Hortic. Sci.* **103**, 52–56.

Gaines, R. L. (1978). "Guidelines for Foliage Plant Specifications for Interior Use." Florida Foliage Assoc., Apopka.

Graf, A. B. (1970). "Exotica 3." Roehrs Co., Rutherford, New Jersey.

Hamlen, R. A. (1975). Hemispherical scale control on greenhouse grown *Aphelandra. Fla. Entomol.* **58**, 187–192.

Hamlen, R. A. (1976). Efficacy of nematicides for control of *Meloidogyne javanica* on Maranta in ground bed and container production. *J. Nematol.* **8**, 287.

Hamlen, R. A., and Knauss, J. F. (1977). Pesticides and tropical foliage plants. *Florists' Rev.* **161**, 35, 75–82.

Hamlen, R. A., Short, D. E., and Henley, R. W. (1975). Detect and control insects and pests on tropical foliage plants. *Florist* **9**, 72–79.

Harbaugh, B. K., Wilfret, G. J., Engelhard, A. W., Waters, W. E., and Marousky, F. J. (1976). Evaluation of 40 ornamental plants for a mass marketing system utilizing sealed polyethylene packages. *Proc. Fla. State Hortic. Soc.* **89**, 320–323.

Henley, R. W., and Poole, R. T. (1974). Influence of growth regulators on tropical foliage plants. *Proc. Fla. State Hortic. Soc.* **87**, 435–438.

Joiner, J. N., Poole, R. T., Johnson, C. R., and Ramcharam, C. (1978). Effects of ancymidol and N, P, K on growth and appearance of *Dieffenbachia maculata* 'Baraquiniana'. *HortScience* **13**, 182–184.

Kerbo, R., and Payne, R. N. (1976). Reducing flowering time in *Aphelandra squarrosa* Nees with high pressure sodium lighting. *HortScience* **11**, 368–370.

Knauss, J. F. (1971). Nature, cause and control of diseases of tropical foliage plants. *Ann. Res. Rep. Fla. Agric. Exp. Stn.,* p. 206.

Knauss, J. F. (1973a). Common diseases of tropical foliage plants. *Florists' Rev.* **152,** 26, 27, 55–58.

Knauss, J. F. (1973b). Common diseases of tropical foliage plants: II—Bacterial diseases. *Florists' Rev.* **153,** 27, 28, 73–80.

Knauss, J. F. (1974) Common diseases of tropical foliage plants: III—Soilborne fungal diseases. *Florists' Rev.* **154,** 66, 67, 114–121.

McConnell, D. B., and Poole, R. T. (1974). Influence of ancymidol on *Scindapsus aureus. SNA Nursery Res. Jr.* **1,** 13–18.

McWilliams, E. L., and Smith, C. W. (1978). Chilling injury in *Scindapsus pictus, Aphelandra squarrosa* and *Maranta leuconeura. HortScience* **13,** 179–180.

Mikorski, D. J., and White, J. (1977). Foliage plants—seed propagation and transplant research. *Florists' Rev.* **160,** 55, 99–102.

Poole, R. T. (1971). Flowering of Christmas cactus as influenced by nyctoperiod regimes. *Proc. Fla. State Hortic. Soc.* **84,** 410–413.

Poole, R. T., and Conover, C. A. (1973). Fluoride induced necrosis of *Cordyline terminalis* Kunth 'Baby Doll' as influenced by medium and pH. *J. Am. Soc. Hortic. Sci.* **98,** 447–448.

Poole, R. T., and Conover, C. A. (1976). Chemical composition of good quality tropical foliage plants. *Proc. Fla. State Hortic. Soc.* **89,** 307–308.

Poole, R. T., and Conover, C. A. (1977). Nitrogen, phosphorus, and potassium fertilization of the bromeliad, *Aechmea fasciata* Baker. *HortScience* **11,** 585–586.

Poole, R. T., and Conover, C. A. (1978). Nitrogen and potassium fertilization of *Aglaonema commutatum* Schott cvs Fransher and Pseudobracteatum. *HortScience* **12,** 570–571.

Poole, R. T., and Waters, W. E. (1971). The influence of elevated medium temperature upon development of cuttings and seedlings of tropical foliage plants. *HortScience* **6,** 463–464.

Rodriguez, S. J., and Cibes, H. (1977). Effect of five levels of nitrogen at six shade intensities on growth and leaf-nutrient composition of *Dracaena deremensis* 'Warneckii' Engler. *J. Agric. Univ. P. R.* **61,** 305–313.

Scarborough, E. F. (1978). "Fresh Foliage Plants Summary 1977." Fed. State Mark. News Serv., Orlando, Florida.

Smith, C. N., and Strain, R. (1976). Market outlets and product mix for Florida foliage plants. *Proc. Fla. State Hortic. Soc.* **89,** 274–278.

Swanson, H. F. (1975). "Countdown for Agriculture in Orange County Florida." Designers Press of Orlando, Orlando, Florida.

Vlahos, J., and Boodley, J. W. (1974). Acclimatization of *Brassaia actinophylla* and *Ficus nitida* to interior environmental conditions. *Florists' Rev.* **154,** 18, 19, 56–60.

Waters, W. E., Llewellyn, W., and NeSmith, J. (1970). The chemical, physical and salinity characteristics of twenty-seven soil media. *Proc: Fla. State Hortic. Soc.* **83,** 482–488.

Zettler, F. W., Foxe, M. J., Hartman, R. D., Edwardson, J. R., and Christie, R. G. (1970). Filamentous viruses infecting dasheen and other araceous plants. *Phytopathology* **60,** 983–987.

Glossary

Abscission Dropping of leaves, flowers or fruit, usually following formation of a layer of separate cells.

After-ripening Physiological changes that must take place in a primary dormant seed before it can germinate.

Aldicarb (Temik) Systemic insecticide.

Ancymidol-α-cyclopropyl-α-(p-methoxyphenyl)-5-pyrimidine methanol The active ingredient in the commercial growth regulator A-Rest or Reducimol.

Annual A plant that completes its life cycle in 1 year.

Antagonism Situation in which the presence of one kind of nutrient ion interferes with the uptake of another.

Anthesis Full flower; the period of pollination.

Apical meristem The growing point of the shoot or root.

Artificial long days Interruption of dark period or extension of natural daylength to prevent flower bud initiation of short day plants such as chrysanthemums and poinsettias.

Asexual propagation Reproduction by vegetative means, such as cuttings, division.

Atrinal (Dikegulac) Chemical pinching agent used to promote lateral shoot development on azaleas.

B-Nine (SADH) [(N-dimethylamino)-succinamic acid] Growth retardant used to control height of several floricultural crops and to promote flower initiation in others, such as azaleas.

Basal plate Perennial, shortened, modified stem that has a growing point and to which bulb scales and roots are interjoined.

Benlate (Benomyl) Systemic fungicide.

Biennial A plant that lives through two growing seasons. It bears fruit and dies the second year.

Blackout system A means of covering plants to shorten the photoperiod, to promote flowering in a short-day plant such as *Chrysanthemum morifolium*. Black sateen cloth or black polyethylene film generally used.

Blasting (flower) The failure of a bulb to produce a marketable flower after the floral initiation has taken place.

Blindness (flower), The failure of a bulb to produce any floral parts.

Blind shoots Shoots that remain vegetative under conditions which normally stimulate formation of inflorescences.

Bract Modified leaf, frequently associated with flowers.

Break   New lateral shoot, often developed following removal of apical dominance by pinching.

Breaker   A device on the end of a hose to permit application of water at low velocity.

Bud opening   Development of mature flowers in the wholesale or retail outlets; flowers cut prior to opening.

Bud scales   Leaflike structures that surround some flower buds, such as on azaleas.

Bulb   A specialized underground plant organ consisting of a greatly reduced stem (basal plate) surrounded by fleshy, modified leaves called scales.

Bulb dealer (jobber)   An individual or firm who stores, ships, and distributes bulbs.

Bulb forcer   A greenhouse operator who produces pot plants and cut flowers from bulbous species using artificial growing conditions.

Bulb grower (producer)   An individual or firm who propagates bulbs for wholesale purposes.

Bulb maturity   Measure of capacity of a healthy daughter stem axis to sprout without delay and to respond to flower-inducing treatments.

Bulb production phase   All aspects of bulb production which lead to the sale of forcing sized bulbs. The production phase may take 1–3 years depending on the species.

Bulb programming phase   All temperature treatments given to the bulbs from the time they are harvested until they are placed under greenhouse conditions.

Bulk density of soil   Weight per unit volume, such as grams per cubic centimeter.

Bullhead   Spherically shaped flower bud, usually resulting in a malformed flower.

Bullnose   A physiological disorder of *Narcissus* characterized by failure of the flower to open properly after it reaches the gooseneck stage of development.

Bypassing shoot   Vegetative shoot that develops immediately below the flower bud, often occurring on azaleas.

Case-cooled bulbs   Bulbs that are given low temperature treatment while still in the shipping container.

Caudicle   The stalk of the orchid pollinia.

Chimera   Plant part consisting of tissues of diverse genetic constitution, often observed in flowers.

Chlormequat-(2-chloroethyl)trimethylammonium chloride   The active ingredient in the commercial product Cycocel.

Chlorosis   The yellowing of foliage due to loss or breakdown of chlorophyll.

Cold treatment   A cold-moist treatment prior to bulb planting which induces rapid shoot elongation and flowering.

Conidia   Asexual fungus spores.

Controlled temperature forcing (CTF)   Procedure for treating Easter lilies in which non-precooled bulbs are potted, placed in a controlled temperature area at approximately 16°C for 2 – 4 weeks and, subsequently, cooled at 2° – 7°C for 6 – 7 weeks prior to being placed in the greenhouse.

Corm   A specialized underground organ consisting of an enlarged stem axis with distinct nodes and internodes and enclosed by dry, scalelike leaves.

Cormels   Small corms arising on stolons which develop between the mother and daughter corms.

Corolla   Inner perianth (petals) of a flower.

Critical day length   The day length above or below which a plant will flower, depending on whether the plant is a short- or long-day plant.

Crown bud   Chrysanthemum inflorescence formed under adverse conditions, such as improper daylength. The bud may abort.

Cultivar   Horticultural or "cultivated" variety.

Cutting   Vegetative portion of a plant stem which is rooted to produce a new plant.

Cyathium   Inflorescence of plants such as poinsettia. Relatively inconspicuous but bears pistils, stamens, and nectary glands.

Cyclic lighting   Intermittent illumination during the dark period, to simulate a long day and prevent flowering of short-day plants.

Cyme   A relatively flat-topped determinate flower cluster (spray) with the central flowers or inflorescences first to open.

Daminozide (succinic acid 2,2-dimethylhydrazide)   The active ingredient in the commercial products B-Nine and Alar (SADH).

Damping off   Disease of seedlings caused by several organisms, such as *Pythium, Rhizoctonia,* and *Botrytis.*

Dark storage   A term used to describe the time foliage plants remain in darkness within shipping containers during transit or storage.

Daughter bulb   Scales and leaves initiated by, and developing below and around the new daughter apex. This apex arises from a bud in the axil of a scale subtending the old or mother axis.

Determinant inflorescence   One in which the apical flower blooms first.

Devernalization   Negation of a vernalizing stimulus by termperatures above a critical level.

Dieback   Death of shoots, originating at the shoot tips.

Disbudding   The removal of lateral flower buds on stems of plant such as the carnation and chrysanthemum.

Disc florets   Florets in center of chrysanthemum inflorescence, conspicuous in daisy or anemone-flowered types.

Disorders (physiological)   Abnormal growth and development patterns brought about by suboptimal environmental conditions.

Division   Separation of roots system of parent plant into several units; a method of asexual propagation.

Dormancy   The period of inactivity in buds, bulbs, and seeds when growth stops. Some change in environment usually required before growth will be resumed.

Dry-pack storage   The storage of cut flowers in vapor-proof containers with the stems not in water, usually at 0°C.

EC$_e$, Electrical conductivity of the saturated soil paste extract measured in millimhos per centimeter.

Endosperm   The seed tissue that contains stored food.

EPA   Environmental Protection Agency, authorized to regulate, among other duties, labeling of pesticides.

Epiphyte   An organism growing upon a plant for support, without establishment of a parasite-host relationship.

Erwinia   Genus of bacterium that causes disease of succulent tissue, often called soft rot.

Ethylene   Colorless, odorless gas that hastens senescence of flowers. Often emitted by fruit, foliage, and incomplete combustion of oil and gas in heaters.

Ethylene scrubbers   Chemicals used to remove ethylene from the atmosphere.

Ethephon (2-chloroethylphosphonic acid)   The active ingredient in the commercial products Ethrel and Florel which is metabolized to ethylene in the plant.

Eye   A lateral bud, as on a rose stem.

Flaccid   Wilted.

Floral bud   Immature flower that consists of petals, stamens, and pistal.

Floral preservative   Chemical added to water to extend vase life of cut flowers.

Floral primordium   Very early stage of flower bud.

Flower blasting   Phase of flower bud abortion occurring after flower differentiation is completed. When blasting has occurred visible signs of the floral organs are evident.

Flower bud abortion   Cessation of floral bud development at any stage of development.

Flower bud development   Progressive change in flower bud, from transition to flowering.

Flower bud initiation   Formation of floral primordium.

Flower differentiation   Complete morphological development of the floral organs following initiation.

Flower induction   An unobservable, preparatory step that occurs prior to visible flower bud initiation.

Flower initiation   Visible organization of flower primodia (buds) at the stem apex.

Foliage plant   Any plant grown primarily for its foliage and utilized for interior decoration or interior landscape purposes. While it may have flowers, these will be secondary compared to foliage features.

Forcing   Acceleration of flowering by manipulation of environmental conditions.

Fumigun   A large "hypodermic needle" device for hand-injection of fumigant chemicals into soil.

Fungicide   Chemical used to control diseases caused by fungi.

Fungus gnats   Small black flies, damaging to plants when the maggots feed on plant roots and stems.

Fusarium   Genus of fungi that causes several plant diseases; can affect several portions of the plant.

Geotropic bending   Upward curvature of tips of spike flowers such as snapdragons and gladiolus when held horizontally, due to negative response to gravity.

Gibberellic acid   Chemical compound used to break flower bud dormancy or stimulate shoot elongation.

Grading   Classification of plants and flowers for market, based on size and quality.

Grassy growth   Excessive and noticeable production of axillary branches, e.g., on snapdragon stems.

Greenhouse phase   That portion of forcing which encompasses the time from placing the plants in the greenhouse until flowering.

Green pruning   Pruning of actively growing rose plants without benefit of a dormancy period.

Gooseneck   Term describing the proper stage of flower development to cut daffodils.

Gynandrium   The structure in the orchid flower which results from the fusion of the male and female portions of the flower.

Gypsum   Calcium sulfate, used to alter pH of the medium.

Hamper   Container used for shipping gladiolus.

Hanging basket   Container, usually plastic, used for bedding plants, foliage plants, poinsettias, and other plant material, Usually suspended from supports in greenhouse, and used to suspend plants in the home or garden.

Heat delay   A delay in the initiation of a flower bud due to an abnormally high temperature.

Herbicide   Weed killer, used to control weeds chemically.

Hypobaric storage   Storage at less than atmospheric pressure for long-term holding of plant material.

IBA [α(indole-3)-n-butyric acid]   An auxin commonly used to promote rooting of cuttings.

Indexed plants   Plants that have been tested by pathological methods and found to be free of known pathogens. Plants may also be indexed for one specific pathogen.

Inflorescence   A flower cluster.

Interveinal   Area between the veins of a leaf.

Interveinal chlorosis   Yellowing of leaf tissue between the veins.

Latex   Milky white fluid found in stems, foliage, and bracts of poinsettias.

Leaching   Applications of water to media to reduce soluble salts level.

Leaf counting   Procedure used to time Easter lily flowering.

Leaf scorch   Crescent-shaped necrotic areas that develop along the margin and tips of leaves as a result of physiological imbalances (also referred to as tip burn).

Light compensation point   That light intensity at which respiration and photosynthesis of the entire plant are balanced.

Light flux   The light intensity times the duration of light.

Long-day plant   Plant that flowers when the day length is longer than the critical.

Marketing phase   The movement of the plants and/or flowers from the forcing facilities to the wholesaler and/or retailer at the proper stage of development so that the consumer receives the maximum possible enjoyment.

Mat watering (capillary watering)   Irrigation of potted plants by capillarity. Mats are composed of fabric, cellulose, or other water-absorbing materials.

Mealy bugs   Small, sucking insects that feed on plants. Females, often wingless, are usually covered with a white mealy layer of wax.

Media   Substrates in which plants are grown. Can include soil, sand, peat moss, vermiculite, pine bark humus.

Meristem   Growing point where cell divisions occur. The undifferentiated plant tissue from which new cells arise by division.

Mesophyll   Large parenchyma cells located within the epidermis layers of a leaf.

Methyl bromide   Chemical sterilant used to eliminate pests in growing media. Often contains chloropicrin (tear gas) for detection.

Mhos   Measurement of conductivity; denotes amount of soluble salts in a medium. Measured with a Solubridge instrument.

Micronutrients   Elements required in small amounts for plant growth and flowering.

Milliequivalent per liter (mEq/liter)   One thousandth of an equivalent of an ion in a liter of solution.

Millimhos per cm (mmhos/cm)   Unit used to express electrical conductivity of water or the soil solution. One millimhos equals 0.1 mhos.

Miticide   Pesticide that is used to control mites.

Monopodial   Having a strong terminal bud and forming a single upright stem, e.g., coconut palms. A plant with a primary upright stem that continues growth year after year, i.e., Vanda orchids.

Mother block (nucleus block)   A group of selected, tested, and disease-free plants, used as basic stock for propagation of several species.

Mother bulb   That portion of the bulb that is currently flowering and producing a daughter bulb in the axil of a scale subtending the mother axis. The old mother scales encompass the new daughter axis.

Multibranched plant   One plant with several shoots and flowers. Achieved by pinching.

Multiflowering   More than one flower or inflorescence produced by the branching of a single plant.

Mutation   Change in genetic potential in a cell and subsequent change in growth of all other cells derived from the mutated cell.

Naphthaleneacetic acid (NAA)   Component of rooting hormone used to accelerate rooting.

Natural cooling   Technique in which nonprecooled commercial bulbs are planted immediately on arrival and grown under cool natural conditions, but with frost protection, prior to being placed in the greenhouse.

Necrosis   Symptom of plant injury, caused by spray damage, insect or disease injury, or other causes, which is characterized by dead, discolored cells and tissue.

Nematicide   Chemical used to control nematodes.

Nematodes   Wormlike organisms that can affect roots, stem, and foliage.

Node   The point on the stem where the leaf is attached.

Noncooled bulb   Bulb that is delivered direct to the forcer and has not received a cold treatment.

Nymph   An immature stage of an insect.

Off-Shoot-O,   Methyl ester of a fatty acid that is used to kill shoot apices and promote lateral branching. Primarily used on azaleas.

Osmocote   Slow-release, encapsulated fertilizer.

Osmunda fiber   Potting medium for orchids; obtained from Osmunda fern.

Panning   Transplanting or potting of rooted cuttings or bulbs.

Parts per million (ppm)   equivalent to milligrams per liter.

Pasteurization   Process used to eliminate harmful pathogens. Temperature usually does not exceed 82°C, to distinguish pasteurization from sterilization at 100°C. Terms are often incorrectly used as synonyms.

Pathogen   Infectious agent that causes disease.

Peat moss (moss peat)   Partially decayed plant material often used as an ingredient in a growing medium. Usually acidic.

Pedicel   Flower stalk.

Peduncle   Stalk on which an inflorescence is borne.

Perched water table   Concentration of soil moisture at the bottom of a plant growing container.

Perennial   Plant that lives more than 2 years.

Perlite   Volcanic rock heated to 980°C. Expanded, porous aggregates are used in growing media to facilitate drainage and improve aeration.

Pesticide   Chemical used to control undesirable organism. Growth regulators also are classified as pesticides, subject to EPA regulations and labeling.

Phosfon (2,4-dichlorobenzyltributylphosphonium chloride)   Growth retardant applied as a soil drench to control plant height. Often used in Europe on potted chrysanthemums.

Photoperiod   The length of the day used in reference to its effect on growth and flowering.

Photoperiodic response   Behavior of an organism to the length of day.

Phyllotaxy   Arrangement of leaves on a stem.

Physiological disorders   Undesirable effects caused by a nonpathogenic agent or factor.

Phytophthora   Genus of fungi that causes plant diseases, such as root and crown rots. A water mold.

Pinch   The removal of the shoot apex to overcome apical dominance and promote lateral shoot development.

Pine bark   Ingredient in potting mix, usually used as pine bark humus. Obtained primarily from southern pine trees, and very popular in the Southeast.

Plant tissue culture   Term applied to methods that allow growth and development *in vitro* of plant cells, tissues, or organs, in or on nutrient media, usually under aseptic conditions.

Plant vase   A nontechnical term that describes the rosette of leaves that ascent forming a cup at the base of the plant. It is common to many genera within the Bromeliaceae family.

Plastochron   The time interval between two successive and similar occurrences, for example, the rhythmic initiation of leaves by the apical meristem.

Ploidy (diploid, tetraploid, etc.)   Refers to number of complete sets of chromosomes.

Precooling   The dry storage of bulbs at temperatures between 2° and 9°C (35° and 48°F) after floral initiation and development is completed but prior to planting.

Prepared (PR) hyacinths   Hyacinths that have been harvested earlier than normal and given special temperature treatments by the bulb grower so that plants may be forced very early in the season.

Product mix   A term common to the foliage plant industry which describes the ratio of different plants produced by individual producers or by the industry annually.

Propagation   Any method used to increase plant populations, either sexually or asexually.

Pruning   Removal of lateral vegetative shoots, or the shaping of plants such as azaleas by trimming with shears.

Pythium   Genus of fungi which can cause root rot of plants and damping-off of seedlings. A soil-borne water mold.

Quantitative long-day plant   Plant that is not completely inhibited from flowering by short-day treatment, but hastened by long-day treatment.

Ray florets   The long, conspicuous florets that radiate from the center of an inflorescence; conspicuous on the standard or double chrysanthemum flowers.

Receptacle   Portion of the flower stalk or axis that bears the floral organs.

Regular hyacinths   Hyacinths that have been harvested at normal times and given temperature treatments for medium and late forcing periods.

Response group   Classification of cultivars, based on response to environment; for chrysanthemums, indicates number of response group. Weeks required to flower after the start of short days. For snapdragons, indicates time of year cultivar should be in flower.

Retarded iris   Dutch iris that has been stored at 30°C to prevent flower development.

Rhizoctonia   Genus of fungi that can cause root rots and damping-off.

Rhizome   A horizontal stem either on the ground or just below the surface of the soil

Rogueing The elimination of undesirable plants, which might be diseased, inferior, or nontypical.

Rooting hormone Compound such as IBA or NAA which stimulates rooting.

Rooting room A controlled temperature facility used to root and satisfy the cold requirement of bulbs.

Rostellum A gland, literally a small beak, on the orchid stigma.

Saran cloth, Material installed in greenhouse or field to reduce light intensity and radiant heat.

Scaling Technique used to propagate foundation stock, wherein the scales of a bulb are removed and planted. This produces numerous scale bulblets from a single mother scale.

Scape Peduncle originating at the base of the plant and bearing one or more flowers at the apex.

Self-branching Axillary buds may initiate growth without pinching.

Senescence Aging of plant parts, such as the flower. Usually the stage from full maturity to death.

Sepal A unit of the calyx, the first formed series of floral parts which are often green but may be other colors.

Shattering Abscission of snapdragon florets, caused by ethylene or pollination.

Shoot Upright stem, often arising from axillary position following a pinch.

Short-day plant Plant that flowers when the day length is shorter than the critical.

Single-stemmed plant Plant confined to one stem, in contrast to a multistemmed, pinched plant.

Slab-side A carnation flower where the petals elongate and expand first on one side of the calyx; a lopsided flower.

Slipping of bark Period of extreme cambial activity in spring when the bark–phloem section of a stem separates readily from the xylem at the cambial layer.

Slipping stage The time when the inflorescence emerges from the leaf sheaths.

Slow-release fertilizer Fertilizer not immediately soluble or readily available to plant roots because of coating of the granule, relative insolubility, or need for bacterial breakdown.

Sodium hypochlorite (Clorox) Common household bleach, used for surface sterilization of greenhouse benches and tools.

Sodium methyl dithiocarbamate The active ingredient in the commercial product Vapam, used in soil fumigation.

Solubridge An instrument used to measure the electrical conductivity of the soil solution. When used with a saturated paste extract (EC_e), the units are in millimhos/e_{cm}; with a 1:2 or 1:5, soil:water extract, the units are mhos $\times$ 10^{-5}.

Spadix A succulent stalk bearing an inflorescence, as on plants in the Aroid family.

Special cooling of tulips A special technique used to program tulips for cut flower forcing. When used, the entire cold requirement is given as a dry cold treatment and rooting takes place during the greenhouse phase of forcing. Also known as "5°C (41°F) forcing" and "direct forcing."

Spider mites Various species of mites, often parasitic on plants.

Spike An elongated inflorescence, exemplified by gladiolus, stock, and snapdragon.

Spitting In hyacinths, the abscission or release of the entire floral stalk and inflorescence from the basal plate during forcing.

Spores Reproductive units of fungi, equivalent to seeds of higher plants.

Sport A mutant that is inherited and transmitted to progeny.

Spray treatment (chrysanthemums) Removal of apical flower bud to stimulate development of lateral flowers.

Spring-flowering bulbs The broad classification given to those bulbous plants that are planted outside in the fall, overwintered under low temperatures, and which flower in the spring months.

Stage "G" The term used to indicate that the gynoecium (pistil) has formed in the flower of the tulip. The same stage occurs in other Liliaceae species.

Standard forcing A technique used to program spring-flowering bulbs in which all or most of the cold requirement is given after planting of the bulbs. Rooting takes place during the programming phases of forcing. Also, known as container forcing, normal forcing, or conventional forcing.

Stem topple   In tulips, the physiological disorder that is characterized by the collapse of a small portion of the internode of the floral stalk located just underneath the flower. It can occur either just before or during flowering.

Stock plants   Plants from which cuttings are taken for propagation.

Sun scald   Injury caused by excessively high light intensity and radiant heat; often associated with standard chrysanthemum flowers in summer.

Supplementary illumination (lighting)   A means of supplying additional light (usually in the middle of the dark period) to lengthen the photoperiod; used to keep chrysanthemums, poinsettias, and other short-day plants vegetative.

Sympodial   Plants with a main stem or axis that ceases growth each year, and new growth arises from the base, i.e., Cattleya orchid.

Syringing   Application of water, sprayed on the foliage. Used to reduce transpiration, control some insect pests, reduce leaf temperature, or as a means of watering.

Systemic   Usually used to indicate that a pesticide can be translocated throughout the plant. Generally longer lasting than a spray application.

Taxonomy   The science of classification of plants and animals.

Tensiometer   Instrument used to measure tension with which water is held in the growing medium.

Tuber   A thickened, often short, subterranean stem, enabling the plant to be asexually propagated.

Tunic   The dry, papery scales that surround the fleshy organs of a bulb or corm.

Understock   The lower portion of a budded or grafted plant which develops into the root system.

Vase life   Longevity of cut flowers.

Vermiculite   Mica platelets, formed by heating to about 738°C, and used as an ingredient in growing media.

Vernalization   Cold-moist treatment applied to a seed, plant, or bulb to induce or hasten the development of the capacity for flowering.

Verticillium   Genus of fungi which causes vascular disorders of plants.

Viaflo (twin-wall tubes)   Commercial designations for irrigation systems composed of tubes through which water is applied to media at very slow rates.

Wardian case   A glass-topped enclosure usually supplied with bottom heat and used for propagation of plants.

Xanthomonas   Genus of bacterium which can cause leaf spots on plants.

Year-round flowering   Control of day length and temperature to produce flowering plants throughout the year. Often used to describe azalea and chrysanthemum programs.

Zygomorphic   An irregular flower capable of being divided in half, but in only one plane. Used to describe some orchid flowers.

Index